CARVED FROM GRANITE

Sir,

Thank you for your continued support and contribution to SCUSA. We appreciate you taking time to speak to us about our theme of Disruptive Technology and American Influence in the Coming Decade.

SCUSA 72 XO
CDT Daylon Williams
2023

SCUSA 72 Commander
CDT Lillian Brown
2022

SCUSA 72 CSM
CDT Benjamin A. Mayo
2023

This book's publication is supported by the Rudder-Hatfield Fund
established by Robert A. Lacey '60 and Linda F. Lacey
in memory of James Earl Rudder '32
and in honor of Thomas M. Hatfield.

Number 138
Williams-Ford Texas A&M Military History Series

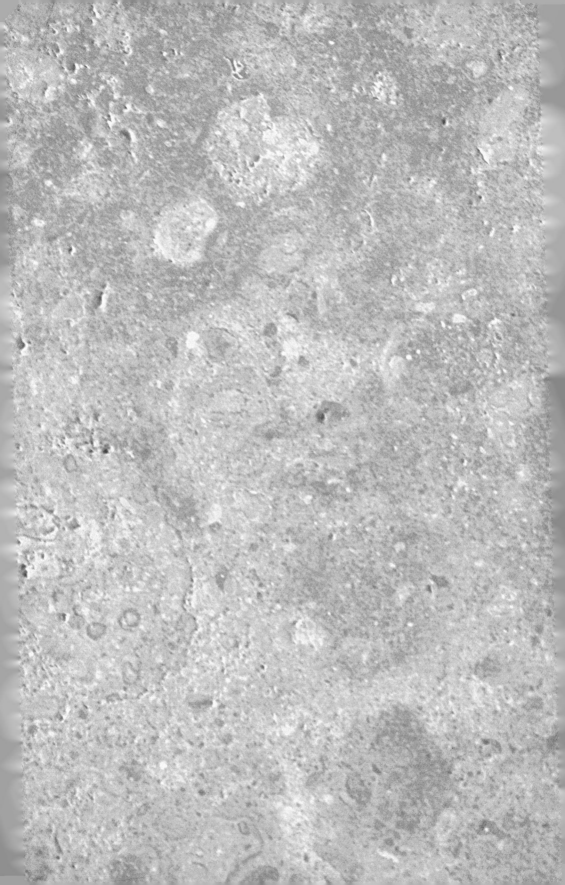

CARVED

from

GRANITE

★ ★ ★

WEST POINT SINCE 1902

LANCE BETROS

TEXAS A&M UNIVERSITY PRESS

College Station

Library of Congress Cataloging-in-Publication Data

Betros, Lance, 1955–
Carved from granite : West Point since 1902 / Lance Betros. — 1st ed.
    p.   cm. — (Williams-Ford Texas A&M University military history series ; no. 138)
Includes bibliographical references and index.
ISBN-13: 978-1-60344-771-3 (cloth : alk. paper)
ISBN-13: 978-1-62349-427-8 (paper)
ISBN-13: 978-1-60344-787-4 (e-book)
    1. United States Military Academy — History — 20th century. 2. United States
Military Academy — History — 21st century. 3. Military education — United States —
History — 20th century. 4. Military education — United States — History — 21st
century. 5. Leadership — Study and teaching (Higher) — United States. I. Title.
II. Series: Williams-Ford Texas A&M University military history series ; no. 138.
U410.L1B48 2012
355.0071'173 — dc23   2011042868

Front endpaper: Painting of West Point in 1870
Back endpaper: Aerial photograph of West Point looking south, circa 2008

*To the men and women entrusted with the leadership
of the United States Military Academy at West Point:*

*Theirs is the solemn task of developing
leaders of character for service to the nation.*

They must never fail.

Contents

Illustrations

Acknowledgments

I COULD NOT have completed this multiyear project without the steadfast support of many people. While I am indebted to all of them for their help, I am solely responsible for any errors that may reside in these pages.

During the course of my research and writing, I consulted many experts on topics relating to West Point. Col. Deborah McDonald, the current director of admissions, and Brig. Gen. Dave Allbee, the long-serving chair of the West Point admissions committee, both gave generously of their time to help me understand the complexities of the admissions system. Cols. Kelly Kruger, Dave Gray, and Gus Stafford—all of whom served as senior staff officers at West Point—provided insights that infiltrated the book in various ways. Maj. Jason Daugherty, the Special Assistant to the Commandant for Honor, assisted me in understanding the trends in the modern honor system. Dr. Stephen Grove, the command historian at West Point from 1978 to 2008, was an invaluable authority on virtually every aspect of the Academy, and especially the events of the last three decades. Several of my colleagues within the West Point department of history offered sage advice, but two deserve special mention. Cols. Ty Seidule and Matthew Moten (both experts on military and West Point history) devoted countless hours discussing with me the fine points of each chapter and offering helpful suggestions.

In addition to those listed above, I am indebted to my students in LD720—a graduate-level course on the history of West Point. LD720 is part of the Eisenhower Leader Development Program (ELDP), a one-year course of study for future tactical officers that leads to a master's degree in organizational psychology. (See chapter 7 for more on the ELDP.) In 2009 and 2010, the student-officers in LD720 read selections from the partially completed *Carved from Granite* manuscript. Their spirited debate on many points of the book helped me improve the manuscript considerably.

My analysis and conclusions in several chapters relied heavily on quantifiable data derived from a variety of sources. Shirley Sabel, a talented statistician in West Point's Institutional Research and Analysis Branch, generated much useful and well-organized information that appears in several tables in the book. Similarly, Elaine Shipman, the senior budget analyst in the Office of the Dean, provided historical data and analysis on budgetary issues. Dr. James

Dalton, the West Point registrar, helped gather historical data on class absences and explain their significance. Madeline Salvani, a senior public affairs specialist in the Army Sports Information Office, helped me compile the win-loss records for each intercollegiate varsity team since 1890 (a surprisingly daunting task). Maj. Jason Daugherty provided valuable statistical data from the Center for the Professional Military Ethic on trends in the honor system since 1977.

While I did work at several research facilities, I spent the most time by far in the Special Collections and Archives Division of the West Point library. Indeed, I was there so often that the staff set up a permanent and well-appointed work space for me. I am very grateful to the director of Special Collections and Archives, Suzanne Christoff, and her talented staff: Alicia Mauldin-Ware, Susan Lintelmann, Casey Madrick, and Deborah McKeon-Pogue. They are a hardworking and committed group who were always helpful, friendly, and responsive to my many requests for assistance.

As the manuscript took shape, several people were kind enough to read all or part of it and to provide constructive criticism. They included Lt. Gen. Dave Palmer, Dr. Lewis Sorley, Dr. Stephen Grove, Professor Clifford Rogers, Brig. Gen. Howard Prince, Professor Robert Citino, Col. Manley Rogers, Brig. Gen. Jack Pollin, Col. Casey Haskins, Bill McWilliams, Brig. Gen. Peter Stromberg, Col. Stephen Hammond, Lt. Col. Dean Batchelder, Lt. Col. Joseph Doty, Professor Robert McDonald, Dr. Bruce Keith, Col. Gregory Daniels, Col. Ray Nelson, Professor Theodore Crackel, Col. Matthew Moten, Col. Ty Seidule, Maj. Jason Daugherty, Maj. Matthew Dawson, Robert Ryan, Holly Betros, and Heather Betros.

Publication of *Carved from Granite* culminates a seven-year effort during which I focused my energy in a narrow direction, often at the expense of those who deserved much better. I owe my wife, Laurel, and our daughters, Holly, Heather, and Rosemary, an enormous debt for their unflagging love and support. While they had every right to demand more of my time and attention, they chose instead to be unselfish enablers who lifted me up and helped me forward. I will always be grateful to them.

—Lance Betros
West Point
1 November 2011

Notes on West Point Terminology

WHILE THE TERMS "West Point" and "Academy" are used interchangeably in most places in the book, there is actually a subtle distinction between them. West Point is the army base established in 1778 — during the Revolutionary War — and today consisting of about sixteen thousand acres; it is the oldest continuously serving military base in the nation. The principal organization residing at West Point is the United States Military Academy — that is, the institution founded by Congress in 1802 to produce officers for the army. Hence, West Point is the place, while the Academy is the school. Because West Point has had no other purpose since 1802 but to house the Academy, the place name has become synonymous with the institution.

Cadets use distinctive and sometimes confusing terms to designate each of the four classes at West Point. Listed in the following table are the most commonly used designations. To prevent confusion, I avoid the slang when referring to cadets of various classes, but visitors to West Point will hear the slang more often than not.

Year	Cadet Class	Cadets Known As	Slang	Civilian Equivalent
1st	Fourth	Fourth classmen	Plebes	Freshmen
2nd	Third	Third classmen	Yearlings	Sophomores
3rd	Second	Second classmen	Cows	Juniors
4th	First	First classmen	Firsties	Seniors

West Point is commanded by an active-duty army officer known as the "superintendent." Since 1977, the superintendent has held the rank of lieutenant general — that is, three stars. In terms of command authority, the superintendent is the equivalent of any other three-star commander in the military.

AT WEST POINT
MUCH OF THE HISTORY WE TEACH
WAS MADE BY THE PEOPLE WE TAUGHT

Preface

HIGH ABOVE a bend in the Hudson River, about fifty miles north of New York City, lies the United States Military Academy at West Point. From the river, West Point's granite walls resemble a medieval fortress — massive rock foundations, high crenellated walls, even a portcullis or two. These features were hardly coincidental. The architectural style was meant to evoke a sense of strength and constancy, values well-suited to the professional focus of this military institution.

Founded in 1802, West Point's first and only mission is to prepare young men — and, since 1976, young women — to be leaders of character for service as commissioned officers in the United States Army. West Point's success in accomplishing that mission has secured its reputation as one of the foremost leader development institutions in the world. An Academy promotional poster leverages these points: "At West Point, much of the history we teach was made by the people we taught."

Carved from Granite: West Point since 1902 is a critical history of the modern Military Academy. It describes how, and assesses how well, West Point has accomplished its mission of developing leaders of character.

West Point is an impressive institution in many ways, and the book gives credit where credit is due. But not all is well behind the parapets. Portions of *Carved from Granite* will stir controversy by exposing the problems and challenging long-held but tenuous assumptions.

An opening chapter on the Academy's early (nineteenth-century) history provides context for the topic of each subsequent chapter. The primary focus of the book, however, is on the period since 1902 — the year of the Academy's centennial — because of the fundamental changes at West Point beginning around that time. While West Point's nineteenth-century history is interesting and colorful, its subsequent history is far more relevant to the issues that face the Academy today.

Except for the introductory chapter, the book is organized thematically. There is one chapter each on governance, admissions, academics, military training, the physical program (including intercollegiate athletics), leader development, and character building. Within each chapter the narrative is chronological; as a result, the most important aspects of West Point's history receive overlapping coverage from different thematic perspectives. A concluding chapter, subjective and interpretive, suggests ways of improving the institution.

Inspiration for this project came from my work as the editor of *West Point: Two Centuries and Beyond* (McWhiney Foundation Press, 2004). The twenty-four essays in that volume examined many aspects of West Point's history that hitherto had received little attention. Still, there remained considerable gaps in the historical coverage. For example, there had never been a serious account of the military training program at West Point, despite its centrality to cadet development and officer professionalism. Likewise, no one had ever examined closely the history of the admissions system, which reflects societal attitudes toward equal opportunity and civilian control of the military. Other neglected topics included governance of a dual academic-military institution, methods of character building, the influence of intercollegiate athletics on institutional priorities, and the evolution of leader development techniques.

In *West Point: Two Centuries and Beyond*, I asserted that continuity trumped change as the defining feature of the Academy's history: "Steeped in military tradition and proud of its long legacy of service, West Point stands like granite against the tide of shifting social currents. . . . Continuity — not change — is what most characterizes West Point and the Corps of Cadets." Seven years of further research have led me to a decidedly different opinion. Continuity certainly dominated West Point's first century, as Academy leaders resisted changes to their proven method of leader development. During the second century, however, the pace of change was at times frenetic. As *Carved from Granite* focuses on the period since 1902, it amply demonstrates that change, not continuity, best describes the history of West Point since the centennial.

The thesis of this book concerns the two qualities — character and intellect — that have distinguished West Pointers, as a group, since the founding of the Academy. Throughout its history, West Point has been most successful when its leaders focused on character and intellect as the preeminent developmental goals for cadets; conversely, the institution experienced the greatest difficulties when its leaders gave unwarranted priority to other, less important goals. The focus on character and intellect was sharp during the nineteenth century, but it blurred from time to time during the twentieth. On those occasions the Academy was thrown into turmoil until far-sighted leaders restored the proper focus. Unfortunately, the Academy may once again be headed for trouble, as internal and external forces have conspired in recent decades to weaken the emphasis on character and intellect relative to other developmental and institutional goals.

The aforementioned discussion suggests an important motive for writing this book — namely, to prod the institution to confront issues that have gone unresolved for too long. These issues undermine the ability of West Point to provide the best possible military officers for the nation, but West Point leaders have been slow to respond. Unless those in authority have the wisdom and courage to address the problems, the institution will gradually lose its standing as the preeminent source of officer talent for the military. Moreover, failure to act voluntarily increases the likelihood that change will come as the result of crisis rather than through calm deliberation. These outcomes would be a hard blow to West Point, the Army, and the nation.

Readers will surely note the heavy emphasis I have placed on the superintendents. The emphasis is appropriate since, in the military, the commander is responsible for everything a unit does or fails to do. That said, I do not wish to imply that they are the only ones responsible for what goes on. The superintendents have many influential subordinates who often determine the course of events at West Point. The commandant, dean, department heads, chief of staff, and many others play active roles in governance. They usually operate in the background, supporting (and occasionally resisting) the superintendents; hence, they play secondary roles in the story except when their influence or contributions merit a higher billing.

Readers will also surely note that a small group of superintendents gets a disproportionate share of attention. The reason for the emphasis on these men is their vision and energy in bringing positive and lasting change to West Point. Because the book is organized thematically, the spotlight may sometimes seem excessive as the same names appear repetitively in different chapters. I do not apologize for this emphasis, which is based on my research into the tenures of every superintendent since 1902. These superintendents loom large in the text because their reforms and initiatives loom equally large in the history of West Point.

Much of the information I gathered during several years of research appears in the charts and tables throughout the book. While some readers may find the detail excessive, I chose to include it as a means of preserving valuable information that could be useful to Academy leaders now and in the future. The same principle applies to the extensive endnotes, which provide background on many topics and identify pertinent sources of information. Readers who do not need that level of detail can skim the tables, charts, and endnotes without doing harm to their understanding of the key points of the book.

West Point is a strong institution, but the carved-from-granite exterior belies the growing problems within. The majority of this book is an attempt to address these problems by examining the cause-and-effect relationships that produced them; hence the thematic approach in most chapters. A concluding chapter offers subjective analysis and recommendations on how the Academy might address its problems. With deep commitment to the ideals of West Point, I dedicate these pages to future Academy leaders. They have the difficult task of making the Academy better able to achieve its essential leader development mission.

Carved from Granite

CHAPTER ONE

Old West Point

1802–1902

T HE MORNING air was electric as the crowd watched the train roll to
a stop at West Point's riverside station on 11 June 1902. After a short
pause, a lively bespectacled man debarked, and the throng of spectators threw
up a cheer. It was Theodore Roosevelt, the war-hero president, on hand for
the United States Military Academy's centennial celebration and graduation
exercises. A cavalry detachment escorted the president's carriage up the hill to
the main campus, past the crowds and the neat rows of cadets lining the path
to the superintendent's quarters. A twenty-one gun salute followed, and then
a presidential review of the battalion of cadets on parade. In the stands were
military, civilian, and foreign dignitaries whose uniforms and regalia rivaled
even the resplendent cadets in their full-dress uniforms.

There had been thousands of cadet parades at West Point, but none had
ever ended like this one. After marching the battalion of cadets to within a few
feet of the president, the adjutant cried out, "Private Titus!" Cadet Calvin P.
Titus, a "plebe" completing his first year at the Academy, strode from his place
in the formation to a position directly in front of Roosevelt. As he approached,
the announcer explained that Congress had awarded Titus the Medal of Honor
for conspicuous bravery during the China expedition in 1900, when Titus was
a soldier in the 14th Infantry Regiment. Roosevelt and Titus chatted for a moment before the president pinned the decoration on the cadet's tunic. As Titus
returned to the formation, the crowd cheered with delight. Titus was the first
and so far the only cadet to receive the nation's highest military honor.

The Medal of Honor ceremony lent poignancy to Roosevelt's keynote speech in Memorial Hall that afternoon. In his remarks, the president lavished praise on West Point and its "Long Gray Line" of graduates:

> This institution has completed its first hundred years of life. During that century no other educational institution in the land has contributed as many names as West Point has contributed to the honor roll of the nation's greatest citizens. . . . And more than that, . . . the average graduate of West Point during this hundred years has given a greater sum of service to the country through his life than has the average graduate of any other institution.[1]

The presidential tribute filled every graduate's heart with pride. A century earlier, however, no one could have foreseen the outcome Roosevelt described at the centennial celebration. The little school on the Hudson had a rocky start and almost miscarried through mismanagement, war, official neglect, and the petty bickering of administrators. In the earliest years there was no established curriculum, the Academy's buildings and facilities were primitive, cadets came and went as they pleased, and admission standards were minimal. Even after overcoming these early challenges, the Academy faced powerful opponents who viewed the school as a bastion of elitism and special privilege and tried to abolish it.

The Academy's footing steadied soon after the War of 1812. With new leadership, both at West Point and in the War Department, the Academy evolved into an efficient and focused institution designed to produce officers of high character and intellect. It was the first engineering school in the country and the finest until the Civil War; moreover, it provided the leadership and faculty for many other technical schools. Its graduates did the work of the expanding the nation by building roads, laying rails, erecting bridges, improving harbors, and surveying the vast western expanses.

The most conspicuous contributions, however, came during times of war. West Pointers proved themselves mainly as engineers in the War of 1812 and as staff officers and junior leaders during the war with Mexico. A few years later, they commanded most of the major formations in blue and gray during the American Civil War. Their successes brought acclaim to the Military Academy and silenced the voices of those who would disestablish it.

Following the Civil War, the exalted status of the Academy had a powerful influence on its leaders. The wartime performance of West Pointers, they concluded, validated the design of the Academy's technical curriculum and militated against change. Judging the educational system to be near perfect, they made a virtue of complacency and resisted changes that might have upended the carefully constructed curriculum. Consequently, West Point was badly behind the times by the end of the nineteenth century as it clung to outmoded

assumptions about education, military training, leadership, and other developmental activities. The Spanish-American War and the nation's inheritance of a
global empire began to shake the Academy out of its lethargy. A few years later,
the First World War caused changes that signaled the end of the old West Point
and give rise to a new and far different institution.

By the end of the twentieth century, the Academy would be hardly rec-
ognizable to a cadet of the nineteenth century. The bewilderment would go
beyond the obvious manifestations of change, such as a larger Corps, more
buildings, and modern technology. Of far greater import would be the differences in aspects of the Academy that define its character. The cadet would
confront, for example, an academic curriculum more diverse in content and less
rigid in pedagogy than that of an earlier day. His assumptions about leadership
and the treatment of subordinates would run him quickly afoul of his tactical
officers. His conception of honor and character development would be out of
step with that of his classmates. He might fumble in the presence of cadets in
skirts and fume at the racial diversity of the Corps. He would applaud the increased responsibilities and privileges of modern cadets while disdaining their
loosened standards of appearance and behavior. He would marvel at the talents
and credentials of most of his classmates, yet wonder why so many of them
lacked the commitment to make the army a career.

The contrast between the Academy then and now is so striking that the
centennial marks a fitting place to start this history of the modern Academy,
following an introductory chapter on the first hundred years. While other histories describe the Academy's two-century evolution in the context of continuity, this one argues the reverse — that change, not continuity, best characterizes
the modern Academy in relation to its nineteenth-century forebear. This might
seem surprising to those who rightly view military institutions as inherently
conservative. In the case of twentieth-century West Point, however, Academy
leaders overcame the forces of inertia in many important areas despite the institution's unchanging mission of producing leaders of character for the army. In
each developmental area — moral, mental, military, and physical — the assumptions and methods that undergirded the Academy's developmental system of
the nineteenth century had changed dramatically by the end of the twentieth.[2]

I. FOUNDING THE MILITARY ACADEMY

Creating a military academy was the vision of Continental Army officers who
recognized the importance of professional training to the nation's security. First
among the visionaries was George Washington, who, at the conclusion of the
Revolutionary War, recommended "one or more" academies for "instruction

of the Art Military; particularly those Branches of it which respect Engineering and Artillery."[3] Throughout his presidency, he urged an unresponsive Congress to implement his recommendation. He continued his advocacy in retirement, noting that "establishment of an Institution of this kind, upon a respectable and extensive Basis, has ever been considered by me as an object of primary importance to this country."[4]

During the 1790s, Congress moved slowly but inexorably toward founding a military academy. In 1794, it established a corps of artillerists and engineers at West Point, with each of the sixteen companies authorized two cadets.[5] There was no formal course of study for the cadets, but that hardly mattered since none were appointed for several years. In 1798, Congress authorized the appointment of four "teachers of the arts and sciences"; a year later it doubled the authorized number of cadets to sixty-four.[6] Meanwhile, it considered several proposals for a military school system but did not approve any of them.[7]

Like Washington, President John Adams favored the creation of a military academy. When Congress would not act, he resolved to take executive action under the authority granted by previous legislation. He directed Secretary of War Samuel Dexter to fill the cadetships, appoint the teachers, and begin regular classes. The process went slowly. By the time Adams left office in early 1801, only a handful of cadets had been appointed and most of the faculty positions remained unfilled.[8]

Adams' successor, Thomas Jefferson, was the leader of the new Republican Party, devoted to small government and a strict interpretation of the Constitution. Given his well-known opposition to a peacetime standing army, the proponents of professional military education had reason to believe that he would quickly dismantle the nascent academy on the Hudson. They were wrong. Almost immediately upon taking office, Jefferson lent his support to the founding of a military academy. He continued the informal arrangements that Adams had begun while Congress considered a bill to establish the school on a permanent basis. On 16 March 1802, Jefferson approved legislation creating a separate Corps of Engineers, which "shall be stationed at West Point, in the State of New York, and shall constitute a military academy."[9] This was the official beginning of the United States Military Academy, and the date is now celebrated every year as "Founders Day" by Academy graduates around the world.

As conceived by Jefferson, the Academy would serve several purposes. First, it would create a professional officer corps to lead the nation's citizen-soldiers in time of war; this was the need Washington cited in his correspondence to friends, associates, and political officials. Just as important, the Academy would help immunize the officer corps from meddling in politics and threatening the civil order in time of peace. During the 1790s, Jefferson had accused his Federalist opponents of filling the officer corps with political loyalists and using the army for partisan purposes. The Military Academy gave Jefferson the means of breaking the Federalist grip on the officer corps and, in the long term, ensuring that merit, not party affiliation, would determine who received a commission.[10] Finally, the Academy would teach subjects of practical value rather than the arcane disciplines of a classical education. In particular, West Point officers would learn military engineering, a field easily adapted to the needs of a physically expanding nation.[11]

Whether or not he realized it at the time, Jefferson's preference for a scientific education would have a lasting impact on West Point and the officer corps. In European armies, the most prestigious branches were the infantry and cavalry — the combat arms of decision and the sources of battlefield glory. The officers to lead such units came primarily from the nobility, whose social status and claim to superior character supposedly justified the arrangement without the need for professional military education. Technological advances of the seventeenth and eighteenth centuries, however, prompted the need for technically trained officers to employ artillery and engineer assets and to serve on the commander's staff. Sometimes the sons of lesser nobles filled these positions, but more often, these officers came from the middle class. Advancement for the latter group thus depended more on ability than bloodline. Schools like the Royal Military Academy at Woolwich, England, and the École de Génie at Mezières, France, educated such officers and contributed to professionalism in the technical branches of service.[12] Jefferson's West Point would be unique in producing officers competent in both types of leadership. It would prepare cadets for command in the combat branches while giving them the technical skills to succeed as engineers, artillerists, and other military specialists.[13]

The appointment of Maj. Jonathan Williams as the first superintendent was consistent with Jefferson's vision for a technical school. Williams was a moderate Federalist who had received his officer commission in the waning days of the Adams administration to teach at West Point; he was the senior instructor present there at the time of Jefferson's inauguration. The new president would have preferred a fellow Republican as the superintendent, but he liked Williams enough to forgive the party affiliation. Williams was a man of many talents, not the least of which was science. Following his graduation from Harvard, he spent much of his early adulthood in France working for his uncle, Benjamin Franklin, and collaborating with him in scientific experiments that garnered the attention of the scholarly community. He had high regard for the educational methods of French engineering schools and was an officer of the American Philosophical Society. Jefferson admired Williams's disciplined mind and scientific bent, just as he admired those qualities in Franklin.

As the new superintendent, Williams's goal was to imbue in cadets a lifelong desire for learning and public service, particularly in the fields of science. Accordingly, he admonished the faculty to "never lose sight of our leading *star*, which is not a little mathematical school, but a great national establishment to turn out characters which, in the course of time, shall equal any in Europe." West Pointers, he continued, were to be "men of science" whose accomplishments would bring them the "notice of learned societies."[14] Toward these ends, Williams established a curriculum that focused principally on mathematics and military engineering. He added drawing, which cadets needed for their engineering classes, and French, the language of the textbooks used at the Academy.[15] Additionally, he founded the United States Military Philosophical Society to make West Point a center of scientific discovery and invention. The Society included all members of the Corps of Engineers, cadets included, as well as interested civilians. Over the next decade, the Society assumed national prominence as it provided the forum for disseminating scientific knowledge in diverse fields.[16]

Despite his successes, Williams was deeply frustrated during much of his tenure. Part of the problem stemmed from his dual role as West Point's superintendent and the army's chief engineer. The latter job imposed heavy responsibilities that included frequent absences from West Point to inspect harbor defenses around the country.[17] Even when he was not away, however, the aggravations mounted as Washington officials often seemed to ignore the interests of the fledgling school. One of Williams's most recurrent recommendations was to relocate the Academy to Washington and thus bring it closer to the seat of government. The administration lent support, but Congress refused to act. Another issue was the peculiar command structure at West Point that gave Williams authority over the Corps of Engineers (i.e., the faculty and cadets) but not the other army units resident there. This time it was Jefferson who refused to make the desired changes.[18] The frustrations continued to mount during the Madison administration as Secretary of War William Eustis often ignored the superintendent's requests and in some cases took actions that seemed overtly hostile toward the Academy. As the nation drifted toward war with England, Eustis ordered cadets home and reassigned the military faculty and staff officers to other duty locations. When the war started in 1812, hardly anyone remained at West Point, educational activities had ceased, and the Academy existed in name only.[19]

Notwithstanding his apparent antagonism toward the Academy, Eustis worked with Congress to address many of the issues raised by Williams. An act of 29 April 1812 increased the size of the student body to 260,[20] set an entry age limit of fourteen to twenty-one (inclusive), and reaffirmed the minimal entrance requirement, first established in 1810, of being "well versed in reading, writing, and arithmetic." It bolstered the faculty by creating three professorships — one each in mathematics, engineering, and natural and experimental philosophy — to join the teachers of drawing and French.[21] It required cadets to complete their course of study — that is, to receive a "regular degree from an academical staff" — to be eligible for commissioning in any of the branches of the army. The law directed the superintendent to establish regulations for cadets at the Academy. The cadets were to be organized into companies and receive annually three months of military training during which they would learn the duties of soldiers, noncommissioned officers, and officers. Finally, the law appropriated $25,000 for much needed construction that would lend an air of permanency to the fledgling Academy. Conspicuously absent from the legislation was any mention of moving the Academy to Washington or giving the superintendent command of all army units at West Point. These and other frustrations induced Williams to resign in July 1812.[22]

Replacing Williams as superintendent was Joseph Gardner Swift, formerly Williams's deputy and, in 1802, the Academy's first graduate. The scion of an established New England family, Swift had benefited from a solid education prior to his appointment as a cadet. His background and subsequent army experiences convinced him that military officers should be more than narrowly trained technicians. They needed a broad education to enable them to interact easily with the political, social, and business elites of the nation. Consequently, Swift took measures to expand the curriculum beyond mathematics and engineering. He introduced geography, history, and ethics into the curriculum and hired a "swordmaster" to provide military and physical training.[23] Other important changes included implementation of a four-year curriculum, use of the Socratic (question-and-answer) method for classroom instruction, and semiannual examinations of cadets. Finally, Swift secured authority to convene a board of visitors to review the curriculum, oversee examinations, and constitute a network of influential patrons in support of Academy interests.[24]

Unfortunately, the War of 1812 undermined Swift's initiatives. In need of every available officer, the War Department curtailed the cadets' education and ordered them commissioned as soon as possible. This policy delayed implementation of the four-year curriculum and Swift's pedagogical innovations.[25] Wartime conditions allowed only one meeting of the Board of Visitors, as Swift spent much time away from the Academy performing his engineering duties. Had he been able to focus solely on the needs of the Academy, his efforts to broaden the curriculum might have taken root. As it happened, however, the curriculum became increasingly narrow following his departure.

The wartime emergency dramatized the need to separate the duties of the superintendent from those of the chief of engineers. In 1814, the War Department made the change; henceforth, it filled the positions with two different officers, with the former reporting to the latter. This arrangement kept Swift as the chief of engineers and elevated Capt. Alden Partridge, the professor of engineering and the most senior engineer officer at West Point, to the super-intendency in February 1815. Partridge had graduated in 1806 and spent his entire military career at the Academy. Just thirty years old, he was smart and en-ergetic, but also jealous, vain, high strung, and dogmatic. While he excelled at military drill, physical training, and discipline, he had no strategic vision for the school. Like Swift, he believed that cadets should learn more than mathematics and science, but his preference was for military training. That and his prickly temperament put him at constant odds with the faculty, who accused Partridge of meddling in their affairs and undermining the academic curriculum. These frictions ultimately cost him the support of Swift and led to his court martial in 1817. By then, however, a new superintendent had been selected who would bring much needed order and discipline to West Point, as well as a narrow fo-cus on mathematics, science, and engineering.[26]

II. SYLVANUS THAYER'S ACADEMY

The poor showing of the American army in the War of 1812 dramatized the need to improve the professional military education of American officers.[27] As part of the solution, Swift suggested sending "two of our best officers," Maj. Sylvanus Thayer and Lt. Col. William McRee, to Europe "to examine the works of France . . . and to form a library for the Academy."[28] President Madi-son agreed, and the two officers set sail in June 1815 with the necessary letters of introduction from the president and a generous line of credit. Over the next two years, Thayer and McRee inspected French fortifications and studied the methods of the École Polytechnique in Paris and the Engineering and Artillery School in Metz. They spent $5,000 for educational materials, including about 1,200 books, virtually all in French, on a variety of subjects — mathematics, military and civil engineering, natural philosophy, military history, chemistry, geography, and military art and science.[29] Upon his return in May 1817, Thayer learned that President James Monroe had selected him to be West Point's next superintendent. He assumed his new duties on 28 July.

From the standpoint of institutional stability and curricular excellence, the president's choice was inspired. Thayer brought order out of chaos with com-mon sense and uncommon vision. During his sixteen-year tenure as superinten-dent, he implemented sweeping reforms that transformed the Academy from an educational backwater into the nation's foremost school of engineering. He instituted a holistic developmental program, much of it borrowed from the ideas of his predecessors and the methods of the École Polytechnique, to pro-duce officers of high intellect, character, and discipline. In contrast to Partridge, he worked harmoniously with the professors and established a framework of governance that lasted for over a century and a half.[30]

Thayer's program for officer development rested on two pillars. The first was a four-year education focused on mathematics, science, and engineering. As shown in table 1.1, cadets devoted their freshman (fourth-class) and sophomore (third-class) years to mathematics and French. In the junior (second-class) year, they studied chemistry, drawing, and natural and experimental philosophy (the nineteenth-century term for mechanics and physics). The senior (first-class) year consisted primarily of military engineering, with a smattering of chemistry, mineralogy, and geology. Also in the senior year, in the two afternoon hours, came the cadet's only exposure to nontechnical subjects — history, geography, ethics, and natural law. Despite objections from those who questioned the value of a technical education for all cadets, this curriculum endured with only minor modifications for the remainder of the century.[31]

Thayer augmented the technical curriculum with a comprehensive assessment system. Every cadet received a grade in every subject every day; even nonacademic developmental activities were weighted, albeit much less than academics. Thayer collected the grades weekly to determine the progress of cadets. He used the information to segregate cadets by ability level, thus allowing each section to progress at an appropriate pace. The grades allowed Thayer to compute each cadet's order of merit at the end of the year and cumulatively upon graduation. Since overall class standing influenced a cadet's branch selection and future promotion as an officer, Thayer's system was a powerful motivational tool. Daily grading and order of merit were conspicuous trappings of the painstakingly fair environment Thayer nurtured at West Point. They became permanent fixtures of the West Point experience and represented one of Thayer's most enduring legacies.[32]

Congress further solidified the technical curriculum at West Point in conjunction with its national program for internal improvements. Legislation of 1824 authorized the president to plan for the construction "of such roads and canals as he may deem of national importance." In carrying out his authority, the president was "authorized to employ . . . officers of the corps of engineers."[33] The implied task for Academy leaders was clear: they would have to broaden the curriculum to include civil as well as military engineering. Thayer and the professor of engineering, David B. Douglass, did not welcome the change, which they viewed as an unwarranted intrusion into Academy business. "Those who are not satisfied with the existing course of studies," Thayer complained, "have not considered that this is a special school designed solely for the purpose of a *military* education."[34] Regardless, the Academy responded quickly to the will of Congress. Douglass experimented with a civil engineering course in the spring and taught it to the entire senior class starting in the

TABLE 1.1   Academic Year Schedule, 1821

Time	Activity by Class			
Dawn to sunrise	Reveille, roll call, police of rooms, cleaning of arms, accouterments, etc.; inspection of rooms thirty minutes after roll call			
	Fourth Class	*Third Class*	*Second Class*	*First Class*
Sunrise to 7 a.m.	Study of Mathematics	Study of Mathematics	Study of Natural and Experimental Philosophy	Study of Engineering and the Military Art
7–8 a.m.	Breakfast; guard mount at 7:30 a.m.; class parade at 8 a.m.			
8–11 a.m.	Recitations in Mathematics	Recitations in Mathematics	Recitations in Natural and Experimental Philosophy	Recitations/ drawing relative to Engineering and the Military Art
11 a.m.–12 noon	Study of Mathematics	Study of Mathematics	Lectures on Natural Philosophy	Lectures on Engineering and the Military Art
12–1 p.m.	Study/ recitations of French	Study/ recitations of French	Tue, Thu, & Sat: Chemistry lectures. Mon, Wed, & Fri: Chemistry study.	Study/lectures of Chemistry, Geology, and Mineralogy
1–2 p.m.	Dinner; recreation from dinner to 2 p.m.			
2–4 p.m.	Study/ recitations of French	Study/ recitations of French	Drawing	Study/ recitations of Geography, History, Ethics, and Natural Law
4 p.m. to sunset	Military exercises; dress parade, roll call at sunset.			
Sunset to ½ hour past sunset	Supper immediately after parade; retire to quarters immediately after supper.			
½ hour past sunset to 9:30 p.m.	Study of Mathematics	Study of Mathematics	Study of Natural and Experimental Philosophy	Study of Engineering and the Military Art
9:30–10 p.m.	Tattoo at 9:30 p.m.; roll call immediately after tattoo. Signal to extinguish lights and inspection of rooms at 10 p.m.			

Notes: US War Department, *General Regulations for the Army* (Philadelphia: M. Carey and Sons, 1821), Article 78, Appendix A. The curriculum at the end of Thayer's tenure in 1833 was remarkably similar to what it had been at the beginning. The only differences were: (1) redesignation of "military art" to the "science of war"; (2) Migration of chemistry entirely to the second-class year; (3) elimination of history from the first-class year; (4) addition of rhetoric and moral and political science to the first-class year.

fall. In 1827, Douglass's talented assistant from the class of 1824, Dennis Hart Mahan, traveled to Europe to prepare a customized textbook, in English, for use in the civil engineering course. In short order, West Point became the nation's premier civil engineering school and retained that distinction until the Civil War.

The second of Thayer's developmental pillars was character, a concept that encompassed moral rectitude and the personal discipline required of army officers. West Point was similar to other colleges in the early nineteenth century in considering character development as part of its educational mission. Unlike its peers, however, the Academy under Thayer approached the task with fanatical devotion because of the unique demands of the military profession and the influence of moral forces in war. Whereas most laymen aspired to integrity, loyalty, courage, and commitment, these virtues were indispensable attributes of an officer's character. Without them, he could not hope to command the respect of his soldiers or muster their courage in the face of the enemy.[35]

In pursuit of building character, Thayer demanded proper behavior, strict obedience, and self-discipline in every facet of cadet life. Cadets could not fight, participate in duels, slander others, use profanity, drink alcohol, play cards, gamble, or engage in any other "vicious, immoral, or irregular" behavior. They could not leave West Point without permission (rare) or absent themselves from their rooms during study hours. Cooking, entertaining, keeping a dog or horse, or hiring a waiter also was forbidden. They were to keep their uniforms and rooms in "perfect order," attend religious services on Sunday, and at all times comport themselves "with the propriety and decorum of gentlemen."[36] These strictures were unpopular with cadets, who found many ways of resisting the tightening noose of discipline. The methods ranged from passive defiance to wanton destruction and were a constant source of aggravation for Thayer.[37]

Thayer never succeeded in raising the level of cadet discipline to the desired standard, but it was not for lack of effort or personal example. He consistently modeled the character and conduct that he expected of others. Cadets may not have liked Thayer's discipline, but they respected him for his constancy and fairness. This was especially true once they had graduated and could reflect on the importance of character in their personal and professional lives. Several decades after his 1826 graduation, George Woodbridge recalled:

> Thayer was one of the most remarkable men in the Army. His comprehensive mind embraced principles and details more strongly than any man I ever knew. The students seemed to feel that his eye was ever on them, both in their rooms and abroad, both in their studies and on parade. His object was to make them gentlemen and soldiers. And he illustrated in his own person the great object he sought to accomplish.[38]

To assist in developing cadet character, Thayer appointed an "instructor of infantry tactics and soldierly discipline" in September 1817. The Academy regulations of 1825 changed the title to "commandant of cadets," a designation that has remained unchanged to the present. The commandant was the legal commander of the battalion of cadets and in charge of discipline and military training.[39] He had a handful of assistant instructors for rudimentary training in infantry, artillery, and, after 1837, cavalry. Some of the training occurred during the school year, but the large majority took place during the three-month summer encampment adjacent to the parade field.[40] The commandant and his staff supervised the cadets in every endeavor and dispensed punishment when necessary. Their most important function, however, was to act as role models for the cadets by demonstrating the character and discipline that Thayer expected of them all.[41]

Outside the realm of cadet development, Thayer's greatest achievement was to create an effective and enduring system of Academy governance. In particular, he established a collegial body known as the Academic Board that consisted of him (as president of the board) and the most senior faculty member in each discipline. Thayer was eager to create a cooperative relationship with the faculty, not only because it suited his temperament, but also to heal the rifts caused by Partridge. Upon his arrival in 1817, he invited each professor to provide recommendations for the academic program. His intent, he told them, was to initiate a discussion on the curriculum and "elicit your opinion thereon. This business is new to me and I rely with pleasure on the superior judgment of the learned professors."[42] Thus flattered, the faculty members responded as Thayer hoped, in the spirit of collegiality. From then on, their relationship was solid and productive.

The Academic Board controlled every aspect of the curriculum. It designed the courses, allocated time, selected and obtained all instructional materials, conducted semiannual examinations, determined cadet proficiency in academics and military training, awarded diplomas, and assessed the overall program.[43] Board members spent so much energy on these tasks that they were reluctant to tamper with the curriculum once established. Change therefore came incrementally, if at all. Even Thayer could not force change since he, like every other member of the board, had only one vote. This is not to say that Thayer was dissatisfied; on the contrary, he and the rest of the Academic Board recognized their mandate to produce engineers and therefore resisted outside pressures to alter the curriculum.

The Academic Board's influence over curricular matters soon spread to virtually every other area of governance at West Point. For the superintendent, whose staff was very small, it was a matter of necessity. He needed a forum for deliberating on issues of Academy governance and receiving mature counsel.

Col. Sylvanus Thayer (class of 1808), superintendent from 1817 to 1833.

Regardless of the differences of opinion that might arise during discussion on one issue or another, the collective decisions of the Academic Board represented a unified, official voice that shielded individual members from criticism or outside influence. For good or bad, the command arrangement defined by the Academic Board was unlike any other in the army. It was collegial, powerful, autonomous, and enduring. Those qualities frustrated many future superintendents who lamented the power of the Academic Board relative to their own. Thayer, however, had no such concern. He and his colleagues were like-minded, and they revered him.[44]

While the Academic Board provided internal governance, Thayer relied on the Board of Visitors for external oversight. Swift had established the latter body during his tenure as superintendent, but the War of 1812 and Partridge's chaotic administration kept it from meeting but once, in 1815. Thayer revived it in 1819 and had it written into army regulations. Accordingly, the secretary of war would appoint at least five persons, "distinguished for military and other sciences," to constitute the Board of Visitors. Board members visited West Point in June to assess the academic and military development of cadets and the overall management of the Academy. While these assessments had value, the board's greatest contributions were in the form of advocacy in Congress. Board members served as the hub of an influential network of patrons whose support furthered the interests of the Academy and helped it through difficult times.[45]

Another means of securing congressional favor was through the admissions process, which evolved in important ways following Thayer's arrival as the superintendent. As the number of applications increased during the 1820s, the War Department sought to improve the efficiency and fairness of the selection system. Starting in 1828, Secretary of War James Barbour asked members of Congress to recommend cadet candidates from their districts; he then presented the list of names to the president, who always accepted the recommendations. Congress formalized the system in 1843 by authorizing one cadetship for "each congressional and territorial district and District of Columbia." The representatives or delegates from those districts would nominate cadet candidates whenever vacancies occurred. The law also authorized the president to fill ten "at-large" appointments.[46] The political benefit of the nomination system was irresistible to congressmen. Appointments to West Point became a prized currency of patronage, a means of pandering to political favorites. Concurrently, the system benefited West Point by encouraging a supportive relationship with most congressmen and by marginalizing the radical minority who called for the Academy's demise.

These benefits came with a price, however. The political nature of the admissions process, coupled with the low entrance standards set by Congress, allowed the nomination of many young men who lacked the academic credentials to succeed at West Point. The problem was visible both before and after the admission of a new class. In the former case, many of the nominees failed to pass West Point's entrance examination, even after a period of tutoring at the Academy in the days before taking it. In the years from 1840 through 1859, for example, 13 percent of the nominees who reported to West Point failed the examination, thus causing a corresponding percentage of vacancies in the incoming classes.[47] In the latter case, many of the candidates who squeaked by the entrance exam and became cadets could not keep up academically. Of the 4,353 cadets admitted to the Academy through 1860, only 2,051 (47 percent) graduated. Such high attrition left the Corps with far fewer cadets than Congress authorized.[48]

Academy leaders sought to strengthen entry requirements throughout the antebellum period, but Congress did not respond until after the Civil War. An act of 16 June 1866 added English grammar, geography, and history to the list of required competencies for admission. Moreover, it set the allowable entry age from seventeen through twenty-two (twenty-four for veterans), whereas previously it had been fourteen through twenty-one. Finally, it allowed members of Congress to designate alternate nominees in the event the principal failed to gain admission for any reason. These measures helped raise the quality of the Corps of Cadets, but still the standards were low compared to other colleges, and the vacancy problem remained a source of frustration until well into the twentieth century.[49]

For the first half of his tenure, Thayer enjoyed the full support of his civilian leaders, President James Monroe and his secretaries of war, William Harris Crawford and John C. Calhoun. It was during these years that he built the Academy's educational foundation — the four-year engineering curriculum, comprehensive grading system, disciplined military environment, Academic Board, and Board of Visitors. The results were favorable for the Academy, which soon earned a widespread reputation for excellence. The later years of Thayer's tenure, however, were far less satisfying. His strict discipline and uncompromising standards put him in conflict with President Andrew Jackson, whose mercurial temperament contrasted sharply with Thayer's equanimity. Disturbed by the Academy's high attrition, the president arbitrarily reinstated cadets who had been separated by the Academic Board for academic and disciplinary reasons. The reinstated cadets, not surprisingly, scoffed at Academy regulations and motivated other troublemakers to do the same. Thayer sent the commandant, Lt. Col. Ethan Allen Hitchcock, to Washington to discuss the matter with Jackson, but the encounter only confirmed the president's hostility. Jackson berated the superintendent for his harsh discipline; not even the "autocrat of the Russias," he exclaimed, "could exercise more power" than Thayer held over the cadets. Jackson's attitude, coupled with other frustrations after sixteen years on the job, induced Thayer to resign in 1833.[50]

Thayer's legacy endured long after his departure. To be sure, his lasting influence owed largely to the excellence of the curriculum and the developmental environment overall. Just as important, however, was the effectiveness of the Academic Board as a bulwark against change. Thayer recruited a core of likeminded professors whose powerful intellects were matched only by their devotion to the carefully constructed curriculum. Three professors in particular—Dennis H. Mahan (class of 1824, military engineering from 1830 to 1871), William H. C. Bartlett (class of 1826, natural and experimental philosophy from 1834 to 1871), and Albert E. Church (class of 1828, mathematics from 1837 to 1878) formed a powerful triumvirate on the Academic Board whose tenures covered the middle decades of the nineteenth century.[51] They embraced the assumption that West Point was primarily an engineering school, even though most of its graduates would never be engineers. The Academy's undeniable success in producing engineers undermined the challenges to curriculum from outsiders and occasionally from "meddling" superintendents. The curriculum's strongest line of defense, however, was the unrivaled power of the Academic Board. With its authority derived from law, army regulation, and tradition, the Academic Board posed a strong obstacle to change.[52]

The war with Mexico gave West Pointers the opportunity to shine. While many of them had served during the War of 1812 and the Seminole and Black Hawk wars, the Mexican-American War provided graduates the chance to operate as part of large armies against a conventional enemy. They excelled as a group and, even though none were generals, earned plaudits for their discipline, staff skills, and battlefield valor. Of the 523 West Pointers in active service during the war, 452 received brevet promotions for bravery or meritorious service, eighty-nine were wounded in action, and forty-nine—9.4 percent—were killed.[53] Looking back on the conflict, Gen. Winfield Scott opined, "But for our graduated cadets, the war . . . probably would have lasted some four or five years, with, in its first half, more defeats than victories falling to our share; whereas, in less than two campaigns, we conquered a great country and a peace without the loss of a single battle or skirmish."[54] The contributions and sacrifices of West Pointers during the war softened the voices of those who had accused the Academy of being a haven of privilege and elitism.

The war did nothing, however, to silence the calls for curriculum reform. Observers of the Academy had long criticized the neglect of subjects deemed necessary for a liberal education in general and a military education in particular. In 1838, for example, the Board of Visitors noted that the Academy routinely graduated cadets who were proficient in mathematics but had "little knowledge of the relative positions of the nations of the earth; their manners, customs, and institutions"; moreover, many cadets had "little ability to communicate in writing . . . with correctness and propriety."[55] Rhetoric, law, moral and political science, and other nonquantitative subjects also were conspicuous in their neglect. In 1843, an external officer's board headed by Winfield Scott also criticized the heavy emphasis on mathematics and engineering and recommended adding practical military training.[56] Many other observers, both civilian and military, echoed these criticisms in subsequent years, but the Academic Board succeeded in preventing any major curricular changes.

Finally, in 1854, the Academic Board was forced to yield. Joseph Totten, the chief of engineers from 1838 to 1864, had tried many times to induce curricular change at West Point, but to no avail. The Academic Board always resisted, claiming that the curriculum already was filled to capacity with subjects that were carefully coordinated and therefore could not be easily shortened or moved. Additionally, board members touted the technical curriculum as the best vehicle for developing the "mental discipline" cadets would need as officers. The only way to add nontechnical subjects, they argued, would be to lengthen the curriculum to five years, although no one at West Point really wanted that. Totten called their bluff and convinced Secretary of War Jefferson

TABLE 1.2 Curriculum for Academic Year 1867–1868, Segregated into Academic (top) and Professional (bottom) Subjects

	Fourth (1st year)	Third (2nd year)	Second (3rd year)	First (4th year)
Academic Subjects	Mathematics (algebra, geometry, trigonometry)	Mathematics (geometry, surveying, calculus)	Natural and Experimental Philosophy (mechanics, acoustics, optics, astronomy)	Civil and Military Engineering and Science of War (fortifications, structures, military theory, and tactics)
	French	French	Chemistry	Mineralogy and Geology
		Drawing (topography, penmanship)	Drawing (landscape)	Ethics and Law
				Spanish
Professional Subjects	Tactics (infantry, artillery)	Tactics (infantry, artillery, cavalry)	Tactics (infantry, artillery, cavalry)	Tactics (infantry, artillery, cavalry)
	Use of small arms (fencing, bayonet)		Practical Military Engineering (signaling, telegraphy)	Practical Military Engineering (obstacles, siege works, bridges, emplacements)
				Ordnance and Gunnery

Note: US Military Academy, *Official Register of the Officers and Cadets of the U.S. Military Academy, 1868*, 24–26.

Davis (class of 1828) to order the change. The Academic Board grudgingly obeyed. They split the entering class into two groups: one that would take the standard four-year curriculum and the other the five-year version. The latter group took new courses in Spanish, history, geography, and military law and expanded instruction in English and military training.[57]

What seemed at the time like a major blow to the autonomy of the Academic Board ended up demonstrating the power and resiliency of that body. The proponents of the change — principally Totten and Davis — soon had more pressing concerns than cadet education. With the outbreak of the Civil War, the former turned his attention to leading the Union's engineering effort and the latter to leading the Confederacy. Meanwhile, the long-serving members of the Academic Board remained implacable opponents of the new curriculum and eventually prevailed on the War Department to return the curriculum to four years in 1861.[58] The new courses either were eliminated or scaled back, and within a few years the curriculum looked much the same as it had prior to 1854 (see table 1.2). Secretaries of war, chiefs of engineers, and even superintendents came and went, but the tenured Academic Board outlasted them all.

III.   THE HAZARDS OF SUCCESS

The Civil War was the epochal event of the nineteenth century for West Point, as it was for the entire nation. At first the Academy weathered severe criticism, both for the number of cadets and graduates who defected to the South and for the early failures of the West Pointers leading Union forces.[59] The critics, including Secretary of War Simon Cameron and radical wing of the Republican Party in Congress, accused the Academy of being a breeding ground for disloyalty, incompetence, and elitism.[60] These negative sentiments diminished, however, as the momentum of the war shifted in favor of the Union and the most successful military leaders were Academy men. By the end of the war, West Pointers dominated every major command on both sides, as well as the logistical operations that sustained them.[61] More than at any time before or since, Americans esteemed the Academy and its graduates. Now it was up to Academy leaders to assess the lessons of war and make the adjustments necessary to maintain high standards and stay relevant as an institution.

In the glow of victory, it was tempting to discern a causal relationship between the education of cadets at West Point and the performance of West Pointers in the war. One of the war's outcomes was indisputable. As a group, Academy graduates had risen to the top of every major military command, North and South. Moreover, one son of West Point had been president of the Confederacy; another soon became president of the United States. To Acad-

(*Left to right*) Col. Peter Michie (class of 1863), professor of natural and experimental philosophy from 1871 to 1901; Col. Samuel Tillman (class of 1869), professor of chemistry, mineralogy, and geology from 1880 to 1911; and Col. Charles Larned (class of 1870), professor of drawing from 1876 to 1911. These long-serving professors were West Point's most ardent and eloquent defenders of the wisdom of the Academy's educational methods.

emy leaders—all of them graduates—the cause of this outcome also was indisputable: since all West Pointers had in common the technical curriculum of Sylvanus Thayer, their performance during the war was the direct result of that curriculum.

This easy analysis, however, glossed over many inconvenient questions. For example, what accounted for the conspicuous failures of some West Pointers during the war? Were the successes of West Pointers in spite of, rather than because of, the technical education? What made the study of mathematics, science, and engineering better for field commanders than history, geography, ethics, law, politics, and other nontechnical subjects? Why did cadets need an identical education when their experiences as officers would vary widely? Academic leaders pondered these questions, but they rarely challenged the underlying assumptions upon which the technical curriculum rested. Consequently, the answers always justified the status quo. Ironically, Sylvanus Thayer, now in retirement, saw the need for curricular reform, but was no longer in a position to implement it.[62]

After the Civil War, the Academy lost its distinction as the nation's premier civil engineering school. It was inevitable, as the knowledge associated with the discipline grew exponentially and the number and quality of specialized engineering schools increased across the land. It was also irrelevant, since the Academy no longer needed to be the principal source of the nation's civil engineers; besides, the large majority of graduates were not destined to be engineer officers. These considerations notwithstanding, the engineering curriculum endured at West Point, and the Academic Board developed a sophisticated rationale for its continuance despite the informed concerns of many observers.[63] They touted the ability of the technical subjects to impart all the necessary mental attributes needed by officers. As Horace Porter, an 1860 graduate and Medal of Honor recipient, put it, the "mental discipline, powers of investigation, and accurate methods of thought" required of the technical curriculum were the same qualities necessary for "planning campaigns against wily savage tribes or conducting battles against trained armies."[64] Left unexplained was why the nontechnical subjects, rigorously taught, could not provide equal or better preparation.

The notion that mathematics, science, and engineering were the most important tools for developing mental discipline reprised a theory about the study of Greek and Latin. In the eighteenth century, academicians considered these classical languages essential for tempering the minds of students, even though they were of no practical use. This was an extreme application of the theory of "transference"—that the methods of thought developed in one discipline could be used to good effect in another.[65] Charles Larned, the long-serving professor of drawing, was the most accomplished spokesman of this view as it related to the Academy curriculum. He described West Point's educational philosophy and methods as the "genius of West Point." The accomplishments of Academy graduates, he boasted, "show that no military institution . . . has more clearly demonstrated the fitness of its purpose and methods to accomplish proposed ends."[66]

Academy leaders were not oblivious to the changes taking place in higher education across America. As the boundaries of knowledge in every discipline expanded rapidly after the Civil War, college faculties no longer could agree on which fields were most important. The situation led many colleges and universities to experiment with electives, allowing students latitude to craft their academic program free of institutional prescriptions.[67] Additionally, they expanded laboratory work and moved away from classroom recitation. These initiatives ran counter to the tenets of the Thayer system, characterized by a prescribed curriculum, daily recitation, and frequent grading. Academic Board members periodically visited other colleges to observe these developments and recommend changes to the West Point curriculum. After one such visit in 1872, Peter S. Michie (professor of natural and experimental philosophy) reported, "So far as the Military Academy is concerned, the character, scope and method of its instruction considering the end in view, is much superior to that of any institution either technical, special, or general."[68] Almost a quarter of a century later, Michie remained firm: "It does not seem possible to suggest any

TABLE 1.3 Curriculum for Academic Year 1896–1897, Segregated into
Academic (top) and Professional (bottom) Subjects

	Fourth (1st year)	Third (2nd year)	Second (3rd year)	First (4th year)
Academic Subjects	Mathematics (algebra, geometry, trigonometry)	Mathematics (geometry and calculus)	Natural and Experimental Philosophy (mechanics, sound and light waves, astronomy)	Civil and Military Engineering and Science of War (fortifications, structures, military theory, and tactics)
	Modern Languages (English composition, French grammar)	Modern Languages (French and Spanish)	Chemistry, Mineralogy, and Geology	History and Historical Geography
		Drawing (topography, surveying)	Drawing (landscape, mechanical)	Law (military, constitutional, international)
				Astronomy
Professional Subjects	Tactics (infantry, artillery)	Tactics (infantry, artillery, cavalry)	Tactics (infantry, artillery, cavalry)	Tactics (infantry, artillery, cavalry)
	Use of Small Arms (fencing, bayonet)	Practical Military Engineering (bridges)	Practical Military Engineering (obstacles, gun emplacements, bridges, signaling)	Practical Military Engineering (bridges, siege works, signaling, telegraphy)
	Military Gymnastics			Ordnance and Gunnery

Notes: *Official Register of the Officers and Cadets of the U.S. Military Academy, 1868*, 30–32. The Department of Modern Languages, established in 1882, provided instruction in French, Spanish, and English. The Department of Law and History, established in 1896, combined both disciplines under one professor.

material change in the methods of instruction that would prove of substantial benefit."[69]

For the rest of the nineteenth century and well into the twentieth, the Academy hewed to the prescribed technical curriculum. The Academic Board allowed a few small inroads of other academic subjects — mostly leftovers from the experimental five-year curriculum — but the large majority of cadet time remained devoted to mathematics, science, and engineering, as shown in table 1.3. The curriculum thus became more crowded than before, with more subjects competing for the same amount of time. Further crowding the curriculum was the expansion of military training, which reflected a new emphasis on preparing cadets for leadership in all branches of the army.[70] While cadets still took heavy doses of practical military engineering, they also learned about infantry and artillery through all four years and cavalry in the three upper-class years. To be sure, the cadets were very busy; less certain was Professor Michie's boast that the curriculum could not benefit from change.

IV.   POSTWAR DEVELOPMENTS

Immediately following the Civil War, the Corps of Cadets experienced a general breakdown in discipline that had unfortunate long-term consequences. The causes of the breakdown were unclear, but they probably included the reluctance of returning officers to enforce regulations that seemed trivial in light of their wartime experiences.[71] Another likely cause was the incessant grind of academics, which had become increasingly demanding with the addition of new subjects to the curriculum. The cadet schedule was packed with mandatory activities seven days a week, and there were few diversions to relieve the tedium. The intensity of the environment was fertile ground for two emergent evils. The first was hazing, which was, at best, a misguided effort to weed out cadets deemed unfit for the rigors of military life. The second was the imposition of extralegal methods of enforcing honor among cadets, who distrusted normal channels of justice. Both hazing and extralegal honor enforcement had the tacit support of many cadets, alumni, and even faculty, but they were blights on the institution and negative influences on cadet development. Academy leaders would spend enormous effort trying to eliminate these practices and dealing with their consequences.

Hazing was not always a feature of the West Point experience. It started sometime in the 1820s and was relatively benign at first. The newly arriving plebes, at the bottom of the cadet hierarchy, endured the "devilment" of upper classmen during the summer encampment. The treatment was usually harmless and amounted to petty inconveniences and indignities. Hazing rituals became more elaborate during the 1830s, but still they were relatively mild and limited only to the summer months.[72]

Hazing became more severe after the Civil War, coincident with a change in the protocol for receiving new cadets. Rather than immediately joining upper classmen in the summer encampment, as they had done before the war, the plebes now started their cadet careers with three weeks of segregated training in the barracks. An upper-class cadre indoctrinated the plebes in cadet culture and trained them in basic military skills. In practice, however, this three-week interlude, known informally as "Beast Barracks," evolved into a period of intense psychological and physical hazing designed to drive out the weak. There was much shouting, sarcasm, condescension, embarrassment, meaningless physical demands, and many other assaults on the newcomers' dignity. The indecorous treatment continued when the plebes joined the encampment after Beast Barracks, but ended with the start of the academic year. According to a senior Academy official who had experienced hazing as a cadet, the treatment was "for the most part harmless, frequently highly absurd and often amusing to the 'plebe' as well as to his tormentor."[73] Perhaps so, but there were enough abuses to warrant stern measures from successive superintendents and the War Department.[74] Even Congress got involved—in 1884, it banned hazing and stipulated that cadets discharged for violating the law were ineligible for re-appointment.

Despite these measures, the situation grew worse. By the late 1880s, hazing had become a year-round phenomenon and more abusive than ever. Otto Hein, the commandant from 1897 to 1901, found hazing to be at "full blast" upon his arrival. He took strong measures to end the practice, which he believed "was akin to torture."[75] Unfortunately, there were no easy solutions. Hein had to deal with several egregious cases of hazing, including one in particular that brought an avalanche of adverse attention on the Academy. Cadet Oscar Booz entered West Point in July 1898 and immediately became the target of un-remitting harassment, including the forced consumption of large quantities of hot sauce at every meal. He left the Academy in October due to declining health and died of respiratory disease in December 1900. Booz's father, con-vinced that hazing had contributed to his son's death, took the story to the press. Newspapers across the country sensationalized the story with headlines such as, "Victim of Hazing at West Point Dies in Agony."[76] Although neither the War Department nor Congress found a link between Booz's treatment at West Point and his subsequent death, both were deeply critical of the Academy for not preventing hazing. Congress again passed strict antihazing legislation in March 1901, but the problem continued to plague the Academy until well into the twentieth century.[77]

Another reflection of the postwar decline in discipline was the use of extra-legal methods to enforce honor. Cadets had always been expected to uphold the standards of honor required of a commissioned officer, and violations resulted in courts-martial and dismissal. Since the 1830s, however, many cadets found guilty of honor violations had gained reinstatement through congressional or executive action. Cadets resented these intrusions and, following the Civil War, increasingly took matters into their own hands. Starting in the early 1870s, first classmen formed "vigilance committees" to conduct informal honor investiga-tions, determine guilt or innocence, and mete out justice, sometimes roughly, against the accused. These proceedings were popular with cadets, who felt more in control of honor enforcement and savored the satisfaction of a tribal form of justice. Unfortunately, the proceedings were also highly improper. Cadets

accosted by the vigilance committees had no legal protections and little opportunity to prepare a defense; the resulting injustices could be devastating to the
accused.[78] Academy leaders were ambivalent toward vigilantism, condemning
the methods but sympathizing with the underlying motive. Consequently, they
never succeeded in stamping it out during the nineteenth century.

Hazing and vigilantism were exaggerations of activities that had started
prior to the Civil War. In the aftermath of that conflict, cadets walked in the
shadows of living legends — West Pointers turned war heroes — whose presence
must have influenced cadet perceptions of professional development. Hazing
was never more than a sophomoric ritual at best, but its apologists claimed
that it identified the weak and helped purge them from the Corps. Likewise,
the honor vigilantes convinced themselves that they knew best how to judge
a fellow cadet's moral credentials. The pressures of unrelenting study and the
dearth of privileges and recreational outlets made cadet life tedious and oppressive. The added stress of measuring up to the graduates of the Civil War
generation weighed heavily on them.

A more wholesome outlet for cadets was physical training, which had
evolved considerably since becoming a programmed activity early in the nineteenth century.[79] In 1814, Pierre Thomas, a Frenchman, was appointed "Sword
Master"—the first full-time physical education instructor at any American college. He instructed cadets in saber, short sword, broadsword, and foil; two
years later, he added dancing to the training. In 1826, the Board of Visitors
commented on the importance of "a thorough physical education" for cadets
throughout the year and recommended construction of a facility that could
accommodate indoor horsemanship, fencing, military drills, and gymnastics.[80]
Within a few years, the War Department provided an instructor of cavalry and
a detachment of enlisted soldiers to conduct mandatory training in "equita-
tion." It also provided funding for a new indoor riding hall, the nation's largest,
completed in 1855.

Despite these advances, the Academy still did not have a coordinated physical development program. That began to change, however, with the appointment of the first Instructor of the Use of Small Arms and Military Gymnastics,
Lt. John C. Kelton, in 1858. Kelton designed a four-year program consisting
of calisthenics, swimming, bayonet training, target practice, fencing, and gymnastics. He took a leave of absence to test these ideas at the leading European
schools of physical education. Unfortunately, the new program was barely under way when he left West Point for other assignments during the Civil War.
Afterward, inadequate facilities and lack of command emphasis attracted the
attention of the Board of Visitors. In 1881, it reported "great deficiency" in
fencing and gymnastics, and criticized the absence of swimming instruction.
The board recommended that Congress authorize funds for an instructional

swimming pool and a gymnasium; additionally, it called for a more rigorous physical program and consolidation of physical instruction under the comman-dant.[81] These and similar recommendations appeared repeatedly in subsequent board reports.

The Academy's physical development program took a huge step forward with the appointment of Herman J. Koehler as Master of the Sword in 1885.[82] Koehler was a physical education professional, a graduate of the prestigious Milwaukee Normal School of Physical Training. He immediately established a full program of calisthenics, fencing, swimming, and gymnastics and per-sonally gave much of the instruction. His success in raising the level of cadet fitness was immediate, and the effects were magnified once construction of a new gymnasium was complete in 1892. Koehler singlehandedly transformed the Academy's physical fitness program into the finest in the nation. Other colleges studied his methods, and the War Department adapted much of his program for general use in the army.[83] His contributions were so conspicuous that Congress, at the urging of successive superintendents, commissioned him as a first lieutenant and promoted him regularly during his forty-year career at the Academy.

In addition to mandatory physical training, cadets enjoyed a growing array of voluntary athletics. Some activities were informal and impromptu: swim-ming, skating, hiking, rock climbing, and unsupervised games of all types. Others were voluntary extensions of programmed physical training, such as fencing, dancing, riding, and gymnastics. Intramural athletics began in 1847, when Superintendent Henry Brewerton invited cadets to form cricket clubs as a means of "healthful and manly exercise."[84] After the Civil War, cadets com-peted in intramural boxing, riding, gymnastics, and baseball. Rowing became particularly popular once the Academy built a boathouse and outfitted each of the upper classes with a crew shell.[85]

At the high end of physical development was intercollegiate athletics, which grew in popularity throughout the nation after the Civil War. Prolonged peace, growing affluence, and more leisure time fueled Americans' fascination with sports, which spread quickly to college campuses. At West Point, however, Academy leaders moved cautiously, fearful that the spectacle of competitive sports would distract cadets from more important developmental activities. A turning point came in 1890, when midshipmen from the Naval Academy challenged the cadets to a game of football at West Point. The midshipmen had fielded football teams for several years, whereas only three cadets had ever played the game; hence, the outcome was predictable—Navy 24, Army 0.[86]

Despite the loss, the addictive appeal of the sport to cadets and alumni was immediate. The cadets vowed to avenge the loss and did so at Annapo-lis the following year—Army 32, Navy 16. Meanwhile, a booster club, the

In the second Army-Navy football game, 28 November 1891, the
cadets avenged the loss of the previous year. The contest remains one
of the most celebrated sports rivalries in the United States.

Army Officers' Athletic Association (AOAA), formed at West Point in the early
1890s to support the football team and other competitive sports. The AOAA
bought football uniforms and equipment, hired civilian coaches, coordinated
the team's schedule, arranged travel, and helped in many other ways to enable
the cadets to compete. By 1894, nearly all of the officers at West Point were
members.[87]

Still, many Academy leaders were uneasy with the phenomenon of football.
The authority granted to football players to travel away from West Point, eat at
special tables, and miss formations violated the Academy's tradition of equality
among cadets and suggested a reordering of institutional priorities concerning cadet development. The Army-Navy game was particularly problematic.
After watching it for the first time in 1893, Superintendent Oswald H. Ernst
concluded that the excitement generated by the match "exceeds all reasonable
limit."[88] These and other concerns induced the War Department to cancel the
game for the next few years, but the sport's popularity led to a resumption of
the interservice competition in 1899. Since then, the Army-Navy game has
continued annually to the present with few exceptions.[89] The popularity of
football led to the organization of varsity teams in many other sports and began
a long history of intercollegiate athletics at the Military Academy.

V. Guiding Assumptions:
Paternalism and Attritionalism

So far we have surveyed the salient developments of the nineteenth century in each of the major activities at West Point — governance, admissions, academics, physical and military training, character building, and intercollegiate athletics. In every case, the evolution of these activities was shaped by two foundational assumptions, embraced by successive generations of Academy leaders and graduates, concerning the nature of the cadet developmental experience. As we will consider the effects of these assumptions in every subsequent chapter, it is appropriate to introduce them here.

The first assumption was that cadets developed best in a climate of paternalism. Academy officials modulated the cadets' living and working environment to nurture and mold the development of intellect, character, physical fitness, and professional skills. They believed they knew what was best for the young cadets; accordingly, they forced strict compliance with every detail and punished every violation. The stark geography of West Point magnified the effect by insulating cadets from the corrupting influences of society and focusing them on their daily tasks. Charles Larned explained the Academy's paternalism in a popular article that included schedules for a typical cadet day. He described a hyper-supervised environment that must have made cadets eager to find relief in one way or another:

> The schedules given illustrate the principle upon which the institution operates, which is . . . to occupy practically the entire time to the best advantage and without detriment to health. At some seasons there is no leisure except a short period after return from meals. At other seasons — particularly during camp — a cadet may have from two to three hours leisure during the day, but at no period of his cadetship is he free from accountability for every moment of his time — sleeping or waking — and for every conscious word and act. For four years he is surrounded by such a network of obligations — orders and regulations covering every detail of his actions — that there is no possibility of escaping from personal accountability for his entire habits of life. . . . His social relations with officers and civilians are strictly regulated, . . . his official correspondence is criticized and returned for correction; his expenditures are administered through a pass-book system by which alone he is authorized to draw all his supplies; and above all, his conceptions of honor, duty, military bearing and professional *esprit* are developed under the powerful influence of an historic tradition and the scrutiny of his fellows, backed by the administration of the Academy.

This is paternalism in education of the most intensified type. The Academy undertakes to become responsible for the moral, physical and mental development of its charge.[90]

For the traditionalists who believed as Larned did—and that was most living Academy graduates—four years of incubation at West Point, at a formative time in a young man's life, would produce a smart, principled, and self-confident officer ready to assume his place in the army.

The second assumption was a tolerance for attrition—that maintaining high standards was more important than graduating a high percentage of cadets. The attritional outlook was a legacy of Thayer, whose rigorous curriculum and exacting standards contrasted with the minimal entrance requirements set by Congress. The low admission standards allowed entry of many cadets who were weak in one or more of the areas—moral, mental, or physical—needed to succeed at the Academy. The standards to graduate, however, were high, and therefore the annual attrition rates through the early twentieth century hovered around 50 percent. Whereas superintendents routinely lamented the high attrition in their annual reports, they refused to lower graduation standards.[91] The weak cadets had to be weeded out, leaving only those cadets capable of maintaining the standards that had secured the Academy's reputation for excellence.

Paternalism and attritionalism were closely related concepts. Academy leaders designed the curriculum, controlled the environment, and regulated cadet behavior with an eye toward optimizing the cadet experience. Cadets, like children, had little say in these matters but were expected to obey without question. If they studied their lessons, stayed within limits, and adhered to regulations, they would earn a West Point diploma, which, according to Larned, was a "comprehensive guaranty of character, and of all around actual accomplishment . . . having but few parallels on earth."[92] Conversely, if they did not meet the standards set by their paternal guardians, they were cast out for the good of the army and the reputation of the Academy.

★ ★ ★

On 12 June 1902, the day following his keynote address to alumni, Theodore Roosevelt handed out diplomas to the fifty-four cadets in the graduating class. When these cadets first entered the Academy in 1898, they had found an environment not much changed since Sylvanus Thayer's day. The Academic Board ruled with undiminished power and influence. The Academy was still small enough that all cadets could know each other personally. The cadets took a curriculum dominated by mathematics and engineering, even though most of them would be infantrymen, cavalrymen, or artillerists rather than engineers.[93] Virtually all military training took place at West Point and consisted of an updated version of the demonstrations and parade-ground exercises of the past; the summer encampments were as much for relaxing as they were for training. Cadets enjoyed few privileges, could not leave the Academy except on furlough after the second year or for an occasional athletic competition, and had little diversion from the tedium of academics. Attrition remained high due to low entrance standards and the inefficiencies of the congressional nomination system. Academy leaders regulated the cadets' every activity and insulated them from the corrupting influences of the outside world.

Upon their graduation, the class of 1902 joined an army that was changing rapidly in response to America's involvement in war and empire. With diplomas in hand, these newest members of the Long Gray Line believed that the Academy had prepared them as well as it had prepared earlier generations of graduates. That the majority succeeded was a testament to the qualities they brought with them to West Point and refined as cadets. In the wars and other military operations that were soon to test their mettle, however, perceptive leaders recognized that the Academy could do a better job preparing cadets for officership. This recognition animated the forces of change over the next century and transformed the Academy from top to bottom. Whereas the Military Academy's mission of producing leaders of character has not changed in over two hundred years, the methods of accomplishing that mission have changed dramatically. The results, in most cases, were good for cadets, the army, and the nation.

CHAPTER TWO

"A Lion's Mouth"

GOVERNANCE AT WEST POINT

O NE MIGHT think that governance at West Point would be simple and straightforward. After all, West Point, like every other army base, has a commanding general — in this case, a "superintendent"—with legal authority over the soldiers and civilians who live and work there. There are talented staff officers and subordinate commanders to carry out the policies of the superintendent. The workforce, military and civilian, embraces the professional ethos of selfless service and helps the commander accomplish missions big and small.

The reality, however, is that governance at West Point has never been simple or straightforward. The complexities stem primarily from the duality implied by the institution's name. The "United States Military Academy" is both a military organization and an academic institution, and the result is a command with built-in tensions. On the one hand, cadets live in an environment that steeps them in the traditional military virtues of loyalty, obedience, and unity of purpose. On the other, they are encouraged to embrace the academic virtues of intellectual freedom, scholarly skepticism, and diversity of opinion.

During the nineteenth century, the Academic Board arbitrated the competing interests of the institution's academic and military identities. Its members, consisting primarily of the superintendent and the professors from each discipline, ruled on all aspect of the curriculum — academic schedule, course content, examination and grading procedures, and graduation requirements. Given the small size of the superintendent's staff, the Board's authority eventually expanded to encompass policy issues of a general nature. With one vote each, no individual member could dominate, but collectively the will of the

Academic Board was absolute. The Board's influence constituted a powerful counterweight to the prerogatives and initiatives of the superintendent; consequently, many needed reforms or foolish initiatives (depending on one's point of view) were blocked by the inertial forces of the Board. The corporate nature of the body ensured that changes, particularly those relating to the curriculum, were incremental and reflective of the will of the majority.

During the twentieth century, the Academic Board continued to dominate governance until the end of the Second World War. At that point, the balance of power shifted gradually to produce rough parity between the superintendent and the other members of the Academic Board. Thirty years later, following a major cheating incident and searching scrutiny of all aspects of West Point, the locus of power shifted decisively to the superintendent. The command structure became increasingly more characteristic of a standard army installation than a college campus; consequently, the institution operated more nimbly and responsively to the priorities of the superintendent. There were many benefits of the new arrangement, but also pitfalls. Enlightened superintendents made far-reaching, positive changes to strengthen the Academy as a leader development institution. Less enlightened superintendents sometimes had the opposite effect, forcing into place shortsighted policies inconsistent with the Academy's mission.

I. FROM THE CENTENNIAL THROUGH THE FIRST WORLD WAR

As Albert Mills prepared to assume command of West Point in September 1898, he could only marvel at the chain of events that had brought him there. After graduating from the Academy in 1879, he joined the 1st Cavalry Regiment on the western frontier and, over the next decade, took part in Indian pacification missions and campaigns against the Crow and Sioux nations. Interrupting the field duty were jobs as a professor of military science and tactics at South Carolina Military Academy in Charleston and as an instructor of strategy, cavalry, and tactics at the Infantry and Cavalry School at Fort Leavenworth, Kansas.

Mills was at Fort Leavenworth when the United States declared war on Spain in April 1898. Since the 1st Cavalry Regiment had been alerted for deployment, Mills packed his bags and awaited his orders. Instead of joining his fellow troopers, however, he was assigned to Maj. Gen. Joseph Wheeler's cavalry division, one of the principal fighting units being organized for the expedition to Cuba.[1] Mills helped organize the regiments of the Wheeler's second brigade: his own 1st US Cavalry, the all-black 10th US Cavalry, and the 1st US

Brig. Gen. Albert Mills (class of 1879), superintendent
from 1898 to 1906, shown wearing the Medal of Honor.

Volunteer Cavalry—the famed "Rough Riders." Impressed by Mills's work, Wheeler appointed him as the brigade adjutant.[2]

The expeditionary force landed at Daiquirí, Cuba, on 22 June. Just two days later Mills saw action during the Battle of Las Guasimas, a Spanish position on the way to Santiago. He was in combat again a week later at Kettle Hill, where he assisted Lt. Col. Theodore Roosevelt, deputy commander of the Rough Riders, in leading the troopers in the final assault. Roosevelt would earn glory and fame that day, but Mills was less fortunate. A Spanish bullet smashed through the side of his skull, permanently blinding him in one eye and nearly killing him.[3]

At West Point, the acting superintendent was Lt. Col. Otto Hein, class of 1870 and, like Mills, a member of the 1st Cavalry Regiment.[4] When Hein

TABLE 2.1   Governance Structure, 1902

Superintendent*

Military Staff	**Academic Staff**
Adjutant*	Commandant of Cadets*
Quartermaster	Professor of Civil and Military Engineering*
Commissary Officer	Professor of Natural and Experimental Philosophy*
Treasurer	Professor of Mathematics*
Surgeon	Professor of Chemistry, Mineralogy, and Geology*
Assistant Surgeon	Professor of Drawing*
Assistant Surgeon	Professor of Modern Languages*
	Professor of Law and History*
	Instructor of Practical Military Engineering*
	Instructor of Ordnance and Gunnery*
	Librarian
	Chaplain
	Teacher of Music

Notes: An asterisk (*) denotes membership on the Academic Board; the adjutant served as the nonvoting secretary. US Military Academy, *Official Register of the Officers and Cadets of the U.S. Military Academy, West Point, New York* (West Point: USMA, 1818–1966), 5–7.

learned of Mills's injury, he wrote to express sympathy and to offer help in getting Mills assigned to West Point as the adjutant. In the meantime, Mills traveled to Washington seeking the War Department's authority to have his wounds treated by a civilian surgeon. President William McKinley took personal interest in Mills and granted his request for medical treatment. Additionally, and quite unexpectedly, he appointed Mills as the West Point superintendent, which came with a local promotion to colonel—an exalted status compared to his regular army rank of first lieutenant.[5] At forty-four years old—

nine years younger than Hein—he became one of West Point's youngest superintendents.[6]

Mills's assignment may have been a reward for battlefield heroism, but it was also a harbinger of new directions at the Academy. The United States was entering an age that would require its military leaders to think beyond the physical and intellectual confines of a constabulary army. The recent war, though successful, had shown the army to be unprepared for the challenges of defending an empire; rapid and drastic changes were necessary to improve its organization, equipment, training, and doctrine. West Point was the seedbed of the officer corps, but its educational methods had changed little since before the Civil War, despite calls for reform from many quarters. Mills may have been blind in one eye, but he had a clear vision of how the Academy should adapt to the new conditions. He was young, intelligent, and energetic, had recent combat experience, and was well connected to the power brokers in Washington and the army. He was the sort of person who seemed capable of bringing West Point into the modern age.

Mills's success would depend on the cooperation of the Academic Board, the powerful governing body at West Point. It consisted principally of a small group of officer-professors who led their respective departments (see table 2.1). Three of them were particularly influential—Peter Smith Michie (USMA 1863), Charles W. Larned (USMA 1870), and Samuel E. Tillman (USMA 1869).[7] Michie, the professor of natural and experimental philosophy, had been at West Point since 1867 and a professor since 1871. Larned had been on the faculty since 1874 and became the professor of drawing in 1876. Tillman joined the faculty in 1879—the year Mills graduated—and became the professor of chemistry, mineralogy, and geology in 1880. Michie, Larned, and Tillman each held the permanent rank of colonel and, collectively, had a total of seventy-four years on the faculty; Michie and Larned had taught Mills as a cadet. The four remaining professors—Edward E. Wood (modern languages), Wright P. Edgerton (mathematics), George B. Davis (law and history), and Gustav J. Fieberger (civil and military engineering)—were lieutenant colonels; regardless, all had more years of service than the new superintendent except for Fieberger, Mills's classmate. Rounding out the Academic Board were Commandant Hein, the instructor of practical military engineering, and the instructor of ordnance and gunnery; the last two were captains who also had more years of service than the new superintendent.

Mills stayed at West Point for the next eight years, the longest tenure of any twentieth-century superintendent. On most issues, he worked effectively with the Academic Board and accomplished much. He led a conspicuously successful effort preparing for the centennial celebration of 1902, which generated goodwill from Congress and the public. He began a decade-long construction effort to accommodate the growth of the Corps of Cadets. Conscious of the historical legacy and natural splendor of West Point, he hired landscape architects to beautify the grounds and a naturalist to manage forestlands.[8] He convinced Congress to increase cadet pay and provide money for hiring civilian foreign language instructors. To raise admission standards, he implemented a policy of accepting high school and college certificates from candidates in lieu of making them take entrance examinations.

Despite these successes, the superintendent and the Academic Board fought bitterly on some issues. One of them concerned Mills's proposal to build quarters for him and his military staff on Trophy Point, the most scenic plot of ground at the Academy. The proposal was only a small part of a multimillion dollar construction program approved by Congress in 1902; the legislation included money for a new headquarters building, cathedral, riding hall, cadet barracks, academic buildings, and many other projects.[9] Mills had appointed an advisory board of professors to help with the overall plan, but he did not consult them on his proposal for Trophy Point. Once they learned of it, they strenuously objected because of the scope of the project at so sensitive a location.[10] They drafted a letter of complaint to the secretary of war, but Mills refused to forward it; consequently, they made their grievances public in the *Army and Navy Journal*, a widely read service newspaper. The article accused Mills of settling important questions "by authority" rather than by opening the matter to "free discussion by those to whom the interest of the Military Academy are subjects of vital concern."[11] Stung by this criticism, Mills forwarded the professors' letter to the War Department as an attachment to his own letter, in which he refuted their points and accused them of obstructionism.[12] The tug of war over the Trophy Point housing continued for the remainder of Mills's tenure and for several years thereafter.

Another confrontation involved Mills's efforts to broaden the curriculum beyond mathematics, science, and engineering. In 1902, the Academic Board had approved a new curriculum that expanded instruction in Spanish, English, chemistry, and electricity and initiated instruction in military hygiene; the curriculum went into effect during academic year 1903–1904.[13] The room for this instruction came from modest reductions in mathematics and natural philosophy and a 25 percent reduction in French. Mills was pleased with the new curriculum but wanted more. In 1904, he proposed further reducing the technical curriculum in favor of nontechnical subjects; moreover, he uttered heresy by dismissing the notion that every cadet should take the same prescribed curriculum.[14] Resenting Mills's intrusion into academic affairs, the professors responded by once again airing their grievances publicly. An editorial in the *Army and Navy Journal* scolded the superintendent for trying to force curricular changes without giving "utmost weight" to the opinions of the academic staff.

They reminded their readers that superintendents spend only a few years at West Point, but the professors "remain as the inheritors and exponents of the ideas which have made the Academy what it is."[15] Unmoved, Mills ordered the Academic Board to consider expanding French and Spanish instruction and moving it to the second- and first-class years; he also wanted physical education all four years. The Academic Board made the changes, but only after cutting the English course rather than mathematics or science.

The continued resistance prompted Mills to ask the War Department for three votes on the Academic Board instead of only one. Secretary of War William H. Taft consulted President Roosevelt, who gave the approval in March 1905. In making the case for the extra votes, Mills argued that the superintendent, by virtue of his elevated position, was more capable than the professors of taking "an absolutely impartial view" of proposals for curricular change. The superintendent had in mind "the good of the Academy as a whole," whereas each professor had an exaggerated opinion of the importance of his discipline relative to the others.[16] Professor Tillman scoffed at such a notion in an editorial appearing to the *Army and Navy Journal.*

> It should be remembered that the reputation of the Academy was well established and universally recognized long before the advent of the present Superintendent. The Academic Board and its Assistants, not the Superintendent alone, has made this reputation; the Board has been the directing and guiding force at the Academy and the admitted success which has followed its guidance emphasize the inadvisability of the change now made.[17]

Tillman's tirade did nothing to convince the superintendent, who continued to press the Academic Board for the curricular changes he favored. By 1906, in the final weeks of Mills's tenure, the Academic Board reached a compromise solution: the instruction Mills desired would be added, but only by starting the plebe year three months early! Like the five-year curriculum of the 1850s, no one liked this solution; regardless, Congress approved the change, and it went into effect starting with the class that entered in 1908. The new schedule soon proved unworkable, as it required new cadets to report to West Point in March rather than in June. Just three years later, the War Department ordered a return to the standard four-year curriculum.[18] The professors, of course, had counted on this outcome. They knew that Mills's days at the Academy were numbered and that, once gone, his successors would have other hobbyhorses to ride. Also in 1911, the War Department revoked the superintendent's three-vote privilege. It had taken several years, but by 1911 the Academic Board had succeeded in sweeping away the objectionable features of the Mills administration.

The professors were delighted to learn that Mills's replacement would be the avuncular Hugh L. Scott. Unlike his predecessor, Scott modeled himself as an enlightened caretaker who "brought to West Point no arrogant project of drastic reform such as we sometimes hear about away from there." He had faith, bordering on mysticism, in the ability of the Academic Board to make wise decisions. West Point, he opined, was not "a subject for reform . . . It goes forward on its majestic course from year to year toward the fulfillment of its destiny, moving serenely under its traditions." A superintendent who tampered with the system was subject to being replaced early. The lesson for Scott was to "keep your powder dry or walk the plank."[19] He would "carry forward and improve where possible" the initiatives of his predecessors while maintaining appropriate discipline within the Corps of Cadets.[20]

With no major reform agenda during his four-year tenure, Scott busied himself with issues that indirectly supported the core mission of the Academy. For example, he oversaw the refurbishment of Revolutionary War fortifications, the enlargement of the enlisted service detachment, and the construction of extra seating in the football stadium. He initiated a quarrying operation on the rocky heights immediately behind his quarters to provide inexpensive stone for the new cadet chapel, administration building, and riding hall. He even developed a new design for cadet shoes, which were notoriously uncomfortable and blamed for a host of foot problems.[21]

Already popular with the professors for his hands-off attitude, he further delighted them by not supporting his predecessor's proposal for Trophy Point housing. He noted that the present quarters had adequately served every superintendent and many visiting dignitaries for nearly a century; hence, it did not seem necessary "that this historic building should be put to other uses or destroyed." Besides, the building project would have removed the superintendent's quarters from the cadet area, necessitated changes to the location of parades, and required the hiring of additional laborers.[22] In short, the project would have created a "less simple life" for the denizens of West Point.[23] If West Point was perfect the way Scott found it, then it would remain that way while he was there.

While Scott relied heavily on the Academic Board for internal governance, he was actively involved in all external matters. The issue that caused the most trouble was hazing, and it resulted in tense audiences with a host of national leaders, including the secretary of war, members of Congress, and even the president. Early in his tenure, Scott disciplined several cadets found guilty of hazing by expelling them, just as the law required.[24] The cadets were well connected, however, and their patrons tried every tactic, including pressuring the secretary of war and the president, to seek reinstatement. Scott was summoned to a Senate hearing during which he was "subjected like a criminal to a severe grilling." He also had to explain himself to Roosevelt at the president's Oyster

As superintendent from 1906 to 1910, Hugh L. Scott (class
of 1876), displayed the moral courage and common sense that
led to his appointment as the army chief of staff in 1914.

Bay, Long Island, home. Despite the pressure, Scott stood his ground by point-
ing out that he was simply enforcing the law. "I am not the Supreme Court to
pass on these laws," he told Roosevelt. "I have taken an oath to obey them and
so have you, and if you and the secretary do what you are now contemplating,
you will do the greatest damage to the discipline of the Military Academy."
Scott's courage and consistency were rewarded when neither the president nor
Congress would force him to reinstate the cadets. Moreover, he provided an
enduring example of a superintendent standing his ground against enormous
external pressure. Instead of being banished "to the Mexican border, Alaska or
any old place away from West Point," Scott kept his job and his dignity.[25]
    More than any previous superintendent, Scott cultivated good relations

with the press. In part, the effort was to soothe public outrage over the recent hazing cases that had grabbed headlines across the nation. More important, however, was his understanding of the long-term benefits of positive press coverage. No matter how well a superintendent might manage internal affairs or the relations with his superiors in Washington, "if he fails in preventing West Point from being continually cried down by the press, he is a failure."[26] Scott conducted press conferences in New York City, paid personal visits to newspaper editors, invited journalists to West Point, and announced the cadet parade schedule to the public. He ordered the construction of restrooms, drinking fountains, and benches to make the Academy more hospitable to the media and the public.[27] West Point, he explained, "can never have too many friends, and how can it have any friends at all if the public does not know about it?"[28]

After a long career that included three years as chief of staff of the army, Scott put his time at West Point in perspective. The job of superintendent, he opined, was "the most difficult in the service, more difficult even than the command of the army itself; for there are many dangerous elements connected with it . . . as many superintendents have discovered to their grief." Would he ever consider returning to West Point for a second tour as the superintendent? "No, indeed! Never again! When a man has once had his head in a lion's mouth and is fortunate enough to get it out safely again, he is a fool to put it in jeopardy a second time."[29]

Maj. Gen. Thomas H. Barry replaced Scott in 1910. Except for John Schofield, also a major general when appointed as superintendent, Barry was the most senior officer to command the Military Academy so far. He believed that the elevated rank was necessary to manage the "lion's mouth" of challenges associated with an environment like West Point. Barry distinguished between a true general officer — like himself — and a more junior officer who was brevetted to higher rank to fill the position. No doubt he was thinking of the young Albert Mills, who vaulted overnight from first lieutenant to colonel and, later, to brigadier general. Barry noted that the eight superintendents from 1864 to 1889 all had been general officers during the Civil War. Even though some of them reverted to lower ranks after the war, they "brought to the superintendent's chair the prestige that went with that rank and command."[30] Assigning a relatively junior officer as superintendent, even if brevetted as a general officer, "always will be humiliating to his superiors on the Academic Board, some of whom are older in years and length of service and his senior in actual rank."[31] Col. Clarence Townsley, Barry's replacement in 1912, agreed wholeheartedly, and recommended making the superintendent a brigadier general rather than a colonel. The "dignity of the position of the Superintendent of this Academy" merited the change, he argued.[32]

Barry's short tour of two years prevented him from effecting major change had he been inclined to do so. Like his predecessor, he was content to allow the Academic Board great latitude in managing the curriculum. The professors seemed confident and capable in this capacity, and the laissez-faire attitude promised to keep the peace with them. Townsley was likewise a caretaker who deferred to the collective wisdom of the Academic Board in all curricular matters. Still, Barry's and Townsley's advocacy of higher rank for the superintendent, coupled with a doubling of the size of the Corps of Cadets in 1916, had an effect. Starting in 1919, the superintendency came with the rank of brigadier general; within a decade, it was not uncommon for a major general to hold the job.[33] As we will see, however, even the higher rank did not guarantee that the superintendent would get his way with the Academic Board.

Col. John Biddle, descendant of prominent military and naval officers, became the superintendent in July 1916, but had little time to have an impact. The United States entered the European war less than a year later, and every effort was directed toward preparing the senior class. As had happened during the Spanish-American War, West Point received orders to graduate the senior class early — on 20 April 1917. Not long after, the War Department directed the next class also to graduate early — in August 1917. In May Biddle left West Point to command the 6th Engineer Regiment being organized for duty in France.

Biddle's replacement was Samuel Tillman, the same man who had decried the alleged usurpations of Mills. Tillman had retired as a colonel in 1911. Five years later as the nation was drifting toward war in Europe, he offered his services as an instructor at West Point to help fill the place of younger officers leaving for war-related duties. The War Department declined, but Tillman renewed the offer following the declaration of war against Germany. Much to his surprise, Chief of Staff Tasker Bliss invited him to Washington as a candidate for the job of superintendent. Tillman was well known to Bliss and his predecessor, Hugh Scott (the former superintendent), and they recommended him highly to the secretary of war, Newton D. Baker. During his interview with Tillman, Baker fretted, "You are the most highly recommended by all these gentlemen, my only uncertainty is as to your age." Tillman, who was sixty-nine years old, responded coolly that he had been born on the same day as Gen. Paul von Hindenburg, commander of German forces, "and he seems to be doing very well."[34] Reassured, Baker made the appointment and the two men became good friends.

As the only professor ever to serve as superintendent, Tillman forged an exceptionally close relationship with the Academic Board. That was fortunate, for they soon underwent a wrenching experience caused by the urgency of the war. In June, the Academy began the final phase of training for the class that was to graduate in August 1917. Tillman anticipated that this would be the first of several three-year classes that would go through the Academy while the war was in progress. Sure enough, the second three-year class graduated in June 1918 and a third was scheduled for June 1919.

Military professionals know that war is the domain of chance and uncertainty. Tillman was reminded of this truism on 3 October 1918, when the War Department ordered him to graduate the two upper classes—the ones that had entered in 1916 and 1917—on 1 November. That would leave only the plebe class—the cadets who entered less than five months earlier. Additionally, West Point was to begin admitting a new class immediately and begin academic instruction out of cycle. Another shock: for the remainder of the war, classes would graduate after only one year rather than three!

These orders seemed surreal to Tillman and the rest of the Academic Board. Allied armies were advancing on all fronts and Germany was nearing collapse. The cadets who graduated in November 1918 would constitute only the tiniest fraction of officers available to American combat forces, and they would need several weeks to be ready for the front lines. By turning West Point into a glorified training camp for officers, army leaders were destroying the carefully crafted program that had proven highly successful in producing combat leaders. Not even during the Civil War had the War Department shortened the course of studies to less than four years. This decision, reached precipitously in the climactic days of the war, threatened to destroy the traditions handed down from class to class since there would be no upperclassmen to provide leadership and stability.

Rarely had there been more need for the superintendent and Academic Board to work closely together. It was therefore fortunate that Tillman and the professors were cut from the same cloth. As an academic, he believed fervently in the wisdom of the four-year program and the primacy of mathematics, science, and engineering in the curriculum. Knowing they could have no better friend as superintendent, the professors worked closely with Tillman to execute the orders of the War Department. They graduated the two classes on time and admitted a new class under the accelerated procedures. Following the 11 November armistice, they received back the junior of the two classes just graduated and put the officer-students through six more months of academics before graduating them again in June 1919. After the crisis, Tillman praised his colleagues for their "zealous and efficient efforts" in meeting wartime emergencies. The Academic Board, he continued, "has been the continuing, developing and stabilizing factor of the Academy . . . and its influence should not be diminished or its conclusions disregarded. Service with this body will convince anyone of the ability and high purpose of the Board collectively and individually."[35] Tillman and his associates had shown how effectively the Academic Board could operate when the superintendent and professors shared a common vision.[36]

II. INTERWAR YEARS

If the Academic Board's relationship with Tillman represented one pole on the spectrum of cooperation, then its relationship with the next superintendent, Douglas MacArthur, represented the other. Tillman had been the most senior Board member, served for many years as a professor, and embraced the assumptions that underpinned the curriculum. MacArthur was everything different. At thirty-nine years old — only sixteen years beyond his graduation in 1903 — he was one of the army's brightest stars. He had shown early promise as the first captain of the Corps of Cadets in his senior year.[37] As an officer, he catapulted to the rank of brigadier general, commanded a brigade and division in the Great War, and returned from France as the army's most decorated officer.[38] He was keenly intelligent, energetic, and irrepressible, as those on Academic Board who had taught him as a cadet well remembered.

Perhaps most troubling to the professors, MacArthur had been sent to West Point as an agent of change. The army's chief of staff, Peyton March, recognized that some of his wartime decisions had caused turmoil at West Point, and he was eager to repair the situation.[39] In the process, he was determined to force changes at an institution that, as he told MacArthur, was "forty years behind the times."[40] March was deeply frustrated with the Academic Board, which he viewed as overly resistant to curricular reform. The recent war seemed to clarify the need for a course of study that did more than immerse cadets in mathematics, science, and engineering; instead, the cadets needed more exposure to history, politics, geography, languages, economics, and other disciplines relevant to an officer's responsibilities in the modern world. Additionally, he wanted an overhaul of the leader development system, particularly an end to hazing. In Douglas MacArthur he had a talented and dashing officer with the determination to make the needed changes.[41]

Upon his arrival at West Point, MacArthur noted that the institution "was in a state of disorder and confusion. . . . Even the proud spirit of the Academy had flagged. In every way, West Point would have to be revitalized, the curriculum reestablished." Some Academic Board members thought the solution was to return to the status quo before the war, but MacArthur saw things differently. Many Americans, he noted, were disillusioned by the futility of the war and the seeming incompetence of the professional military leaders who had overseen the mass slaughter of the fighting. Consequently, some members of Congress sought a drastic reduction in funding for the Academy; others wanted to abolish West Point and rely instead on the Reserve Officers Training Corps for the nation's military leadership. MacArthur was determined to prove that West Point remained relevant to the army and the nation. His task would be difficult, but he could count on the support and confidence of Gen. March.[42]

Subsequent chapters will examine the details of MacArthur's efforts to reform the Academy in a variety of areas—academics, physical fitness, military training, leader development, and character building. For now, the focus is on his relationship with the Academic Board and the methods he used to advance his agenda. There were some unavoidable obstacles, such as his relative youth, the weight of tradition, and the genuine differences of opinion between him and the most senior Academic Board members.[43] Other obstacles stemmed from his personality. He could be abrasive and confrontational when provoked. More characteristic was aloofness, which made him seem arrogant and condescending to those around him.[44] Even his most admiring biographer noted the superintendent's reclusiveness. MacArthur "did not attend the Post parties, hops or informal teas. He did not appear for a drink at the Club or hobnob with any group. . . . Small talk, banalities, front-teeth smiles and vain ritual were particularly harrowing" for him.[45] His avoidance of social contact with the Academic Board members made his differences with them sharper than they might have otherwise been and more difficult to overcome.

Despite these obstacles, MacArthur possessed considerable talents, the greatest of which was intellect. The young superintendent debated the professors on curricular issues and pressed them to justify long-held assumptions in every area of cadet development. Why should cadets not be exposed to subjects of more practical value than calculus and theoretical science? Why not appoint a few non-West Point officers and even civilians to the faculty to give cadets exposure to different ideas and leadership styles? Why not visit other educational institutions for ideas on course content and pedagogy? Why did the Academy persist in treating cadets like children when they would be expected to act like adults after graduation? The old-guard professors had practiced answers that reflected their paternal and attritional assumptions about cadet development. Still, on some points they yielded to the force of the superintendent's arguments.[46]

Patient and persistent, MacArthur won a string of impressive victories. In the area of academics, he shepherded through the Academic Board a new four-year curriculum that included courses in history (modern and military) and economics and government. He moved summer military training for upper classmen from West Point to Camp Dix, New Jersey, where cadets underwent rigorous field training and interacted with the enlisted side of the army.

With the upper classes away for the summer, MacArthur put tactical officers in charge of training the incoming plebes; his intent was to set a high standard for superior-subordinate relationships that cadets could emulate. He established mandatory athletics for cadets of all classes. He liberalized cadet privileges in an effort to exercise cadets in responsible behavior and prepare them for life beyond West Point. He codified the honor system through a cadet-led effort that abolished the vigilance committees but kept the system in cadet hands. These heady accomplishments, any one of which would have stood out by itself, represented a body of reform unprecedented since Thayer.

MacArthur gained legitimacy for his initiatives by soliciting outside support. In 1920, for example, he circulated the newly approved postwar curriculum to senior officers and civilians, including prominent educators, for their review and comments. The result was virtually unanimous approval. Of the ninety-one educators who responded, forty-three gave unqualified praise and forty-eight approved it with constructive comments. MacArthur was thus confident that the curriculum was "set on correct lines."[47] Similarly, he sent a copy of his 1920 annual report to the press and received a favorable review. The *New York Times*, for example, described a "new West Point" that purged many of the evils of the old order. In particular, it hailed the end of Beast Barracks and hazing, the "worst affliction of the old West Point."[48]

While many of MacArthur's reforms endured, others were reversed once his tenure ended in June 1922. For example, the next superintendent, Fred Sladen, returned summer training to West Point, put upper classmen in charge of resurrected Beast Barracks, and withdrew or modified many of the privileges granted by his predecessor. Sladen actions pleased the old-guard professors who had been uncomfortable with many of MacArthur's reforms.[49]

Academy governance became a focal point beginning in 1926, when the War Department ordered a series of curricular reviews that spanned the tenures of several superintendents. There were many advocates of curricular reform in the army, especially among the most senior leaders, and they routinely assailed the resistance of the Academic Board to changes they deemed necessary. One of the most prominent critics was the army's deputy chief of staff, Maj. Gen. Fox Conner, who complained that the long-serving professors were "not sufficiently in touch with other institutions of learning." Their insularity, he believed, was the main reason why theoretical instruction — mathematics in particular — continued to dominate the curriculum even though the number of cadets who would become engineer officers was small. Other perceived problems included academic overload, faulty pedagogy, faculty inbreeding, inadequate practical military training, and ineffective admissions procedures. In November, the War Department therefore ordered Superintendent Merch Stewart to conduct a thorough curriculum review that would include "the whole educational system en masse at the Military Academy . . . and all other matters pertaining to the education of cadets in the broadest and most progressive sense of the word."[50]

Following five months of intensive review, Stewart forwarded the Academic Board's report to the War Department. The report concluded that the curriculum was "substantially sound, balanced, and suited to the special requirements of the Military Academy." The recommended changes were minor and did little to address the points Conner had raised in his critique. Although Stewart signed the report and concurred with its findings, his extended comments revealed dissatisfaction with the nature of the West Point education. In particular, he criticized the failure to arouse in cadets a desire for lifelong learning. The curriculum, while "eminently fair," was inflexible, and the pedagogy was "too aloof, impersonal, and lacking in the human touch." The Academy made little effort to show cadets the practical utility of the education or to stimulate their interest "beyond the menace of discharge" if they failed.[51] These concerns were precisely what Conner had in mind in his critique of the Academy; the modest recommendations in the report seemed to confirm his belief that the Academic Board was incapable of making bold changes.

The frustration in the War Department over Stewart's curriculum review prompted another debate on Academy governance. This time the army's senior operations officer, Brig. Gen. Frank Parker, studied the issue and concluded that the current system was obsolete.[52] Except for the short period during which the superintendent had three votes on the Academic Board, nothing about governance had changed since the time of Thayer. Parker believed that the power-sharing arrangement left the superintendent hamstrung by the conservatism of the older professors who dominated the board. The West Point superintendent, he noted, had less authority than the superintendent at the Naval Academy and the commandants at the army's service schools.[53] To illustrate the governance problem at West Point, Parker quoted an unnamed "recent superintendent" who offered an example of how professors grew stubborn and complacent over time. The superintendent—undoubtedly Douglas MacArthur—had been a student under a professor with whom he later worked on the Academic Board. The professor—undoubtedly Gustav J. Fieberger— had begun teaching the military history course in 1896, but since then

[T]he world had seen the tremendous changes brought about in war by the great struggle between the Central Powers of Europe and the alliance of the Allies. Yet the course as given at West Point had not changed from the one that was taught when I was a Cadet. Upon the retirement of this professor, his course was entirely changed so that not even a vestige of the old one remained. The same situation exists in practically every department where the system is now applied. No matter how brilliant these men may be when first detailed, sooner or later they become provincial. They form a block which almost invariably opposes the Superintendent in any progressive ideas he may bring from the service at large. They are the last word in conservatism and reactionaryism. . . . As a consequence, there always has been and always will be under this system a schism in the Academic Board which invariably results in a stagnating inertia.[54]

The Academic Board's most vexing power, according to Parker, was its authority to apportion time to each department and to dictate the content of instruction therein. This power was the "most absolute and the one which has in the past rendered changes in the curriculum most difficult." Parker therefore recommended relegating the Academic Board to "an advisory capacity only." Except in those cases where the approval of the War Department was required, "final decision on the matters considered will rest with the superintendent whose responsibility will not be affected by any recommendations of the board."[55]

Parker replaced the likeminded Conner as the army's deputy chief of staff in 1927. Not coincidentally, a few months later the new superintendent, Maj. Gen. William Smith, received orders to conduct another curriculum study.[56] Over the next two years, the Academic Board proposed changes that addressed to some extent the issues Conner and Parker had raised. The most significant proposals were for a modest reduction in mathematics and the creation of a physics course for third classmen that would link theory to practice. The War Department approved the proposals under two conditions. First, West Point should avoid reducing the academic time allotted to practical military instruction; second, whatever curtailments were necessary to implement the changes were to come from theoretical courses, not practical courses or physical training.

Whether or not the Academic Board went far enough in satisfying Conner and Parker is unclear, as both men had left the War Department by 1929. For sure, their departure lessened the external focus on West Point, as did implementation of the modest curricular reforms noted earlier. But these outcomes did virtually nothing to change the nature of governance at West Point. As we will see in chapter 4, the curriculum reforms had more to do with developments in higher education than pressure from the superintendent or from Washington. The superintendent could suggest, debate, and cajole, but he was no more able to force changes than any of his predecessors had been. He continued to have only one vote, and his tenure—like that of Conner, Parker, and other senior army leaders—was too short to wait out the professors. Not until the Second World War would the balance of power begin to shift. Even then, the pace of change for the next thirty years was glacial and the best that super-intendents could achieve was parity with the Academic Board.

III.   FROM WORLD WAR II TO THE 1970S—PARITY

Shortly before completing his tour as superintendent in 1940, Maj. Gen. Jay Benedict updated the War Department on a few outstanding issues. One piece of unfinished business was curriculum reform. The Academic Board had re-cently completed another curriculum review, but, as usual, had made only minor changes. Frustrated, Benedict complained that the "pattern of the cur-riculum is still too determined by the Engineer influence of former days." He urged the War Department to appoint outside consultants, military and civil-ian, to study and comment on West Point's curriculum, objectives, and meth-ods. Their analysis would supplement Academic Board deliberations and, as Benedict knew, exert added pressure for curriculum change.[57]

A century of experience had shown that the Academic Board was wary of making major curriculum changes. Under Sylvanus Thayer, the Academic Board had been energetic and innovative in establishing the engineering cur-riculum; subsequently, however, it had made only minor adjustments to the academic program. The core of the curriculum — mathematics, science, and en-gineering — remained intact even as the Academic Board crowded the instruc-tion with a few nontechnical subjects along the way. The long tenures of profes-sors, short tenures of superintendents, and the one-vote rule for all members of the Academic Board created the organizational stasis. Moreover, the success of West Pointers in war and peace seemed to justify the status quo, despite the calls from informed observers (including many West Pointers) for reform. In the few instances when major changes occurred, they were always the result of outside forces — war, congressional intervention, and pressure from the admin-istration. The principal exceptions were the reforms of Douglas MacArthur in military training, athletics, honor, and leadership, as well as academics.

From the perspective of the professors, conservatism was a virtue. It pre-vented the Academy from being whipsawed by every "good idea" proposed by superintendents and political leaders who would not have to live with the consequences of the change. There was, in fact, justification for this view. The resistance of the Academic Board, for example, probably protected West Point from the excesses of curricular decentralization that was fashionable at civilian colleges and universities in the early twentieth century. It certainly prevented the despoiling of Trophy Point by the ill-considered housing complex sought by Superintendent Mills. Historian Theodore Crackel defended the board's conservatism, even though it often left superintendents and outside observers impatient and frustrated. Achieving lasting change in curricular matters, he argued, required "consensus building." The process could take years, but "it seldom permitted poor ideas, for their disadvantages became apparent before sufficient support had been mustered to pass them."[58] This was certainly true. Also true, however, was that the Academic Board was as resistant to good ideas as to poor ones. The professors' conservatism ensured that the curriculum would not adapt as quickly as it might have to the changing world around them.

Benedict's idea of commissioning outside experts proved effective in overcoming the conservatism of the Academic Board once the United States entered World War II. When Secretary of War Henry Stimson ordered the curtailment of the Academy curriculum to three years, he knew the decision would generate opposition from the Academic Board. He therefore directed Superintendent Francis Wilby "to appoint a board of distinguished civilian educators and Army officers" to assist the Academic Board in its task. Stimson offered his full support—money, encouragement, and the promise to replace Academic Board members "who fail to demonstrate the necessary vision, energy, and adaptability."[59] Wilby assembled a distinguished advisory board, including Dr. Karl T. Compton and Dr. James B. Conant, the presidents of the Massachusetts Institute of Technology and Harvard University, respectively. Other board members were senior officers from the army's major commands and the general staff. They worked cooperatively with the Academic Board to devise a three-year curriculum in two versions—one for cadets in pilot training, and one for cadets who would enter the ground forces.[60]

In addition to the use of outside experts, several other forces converged in the years during and after the Second World War to diminish the influence of the Academic Board. Most noticeable was the higher rank of the superintendent and his principal subordinates. Starting with Wilby in 1942, every incoming superintendent was at least a major general, two levels above the rank of the department heads (all colonels). Although the superintendent still had only one vote, and the professors still had tenure, the difference between them in rank made open dissent more difficult than before.

Another boost to the superintendent's influence was the rising status of the commandant. Shortly after becoming superintendent, Wilby asked the secretary of war to increase the rank of the commandant from colonel to brigadier general. As justification, he cited the enlargement of the Corps of Cadets in 1942 and the heightened importance of military training during the war. The commandant, selected from among the army's most promising officers, had always been a strong supporter of the superintendent and a sure ally in Academic Board deliberations; the elevation of his rank magnified the effect.[61] The sec-

TABLE 2.2   Governance Structure, 1947

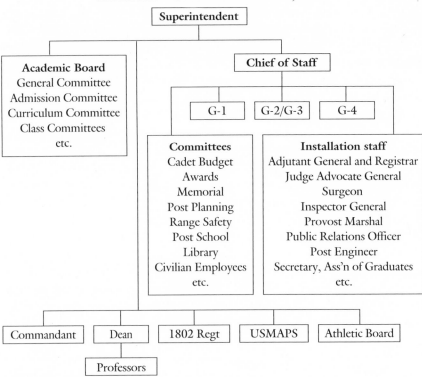

Notes: Annual Report of the Superintendent, 1946, Appendix. Subordinate to the commandant were the
Department of Tactics and the Corps of Cadets. Subordinate to the dean were the academic departments.

retary of war granted Wilby's request and, with only two exceptions, all future
commandants were brigadier generals.[62]

Similarly, the superintendent benefited from the newly created position of
Dean of the Academic Board in 1945. The War Department acted on the recommendation of the faculty committee Wilby had convened a year earlier to
design the postwar curriculum. Committee members responded to what they
viewed as the main weakness in the academic organization at West Point—
namely, that the superintendent "now deals with fourteen heads of departments, either through the Academic Board or directly." In addition to the
span-of-control problem, the Academic Board "cannot remain constantly in
session . . . without taking its members away from their duties in their respective departments."[63] The appointment of the dean, a brigadier general selected
from among the sitting department heads, helped mitigate these problems. He
and his staff relieved department heads of much committee work and administration. Centralizing the effort made all aspects of curriculum management

more efficient. Additionally, it provided the superintendent a single source of counsel on academic affairs and obviated the need for frequent Academic Board meetings. Herein lay the principal consequence for Academy governance. Formerly the superintendent met frequently with the Academic Board on all curricular issues, interpreted broadly; henceforth, they met less frequently and with a more focused agenda. With fewer contacts with the superintendent, department heads had less influence individually and collectively.

Another reason for the gradual decline in the Academic Board's influence was the increase in the size and complexity of West Point as a military reservation. The superintendent commanded an army base that required ever more staff and faculty officers, enlisted soldiers, and civilian employees. In 1902, with the Corps of Cadets numbering around five hundred, the size of the military staff was miniscule — a total of eight officers, of whom three were medical doctors and the highest in rank was a major.[64] The size of the staff grew gradually over the next few years to keep up with the expanding Corps and to supervise the several enlisted detachments that provided training and administrative support.[65] In June 1938, with the authorized strength of the Corps at 1,964, there were twenty officers assigned to staff positions, and the lone colonel on the staff was the surgeon.[66] That was not good enough for Superintendent Benedict, who complained that the size of the staff "had not kept pace with the growth of the Academy."[67] A year later, the War Department increased the staff to forty-four officers, including four colonels; by 1945 there were over fifty staff officers, including eleven colonels.[68] The number of civilian employees likewise grew. In 1938, there were 723 civilians on the payroll; in 1945, there were 1,440.[69] The pattern of growth at West Point continued in subsequent decades, especially after a major expansion of the Corps during the 1960s. The peak came during the mid-1970s, as the combined strength of the military and civilian workforce exceeded 4,200.[70]

The growth in the size of the staff came with organizational changes that further diminished the relative standing of the professoriate. Upon assuming command in September 1945, Superintendent Maxwell Taylor modernized the command structure along the lines of an army division (table 2.2). He created a general staff, complete with a chief of staff and principal subordinates for personnel, security, operations, and logistics.[71] Concurrently, he activated a new command, the 1802nd Special Regiment, to centralize control over the regular army units and detachments assigned at West Point. The new organization brought to West Point yet another colonel, one with the added prestige of commanding soldiers rather than serving on the staff.[72] Taylor also activated the United States Military Academy Preparatory School at Stewart Airfield in nearby Newburgh, New York, to help enlisted soldiers qualify for admission.[73] Under Taylor's scheme of governance, the dean supervised the academic departments, and the professors fell in below him. The relative positions of the superintendent and the professors on the postwar organizational diagram reflected clearly what was happening to the influence of the professors on the Academic Board. The organizational structure continued to evolve under subsequent superintendents, but that did not stop the gradual slippage of the influence of the professoriate.[74]

Taylor challenged the Academic Board in other, more direct ways. He was young, keenly intelligent, and energetic, and he had a sterling record as a combat commander during the war; in these attributes, he closely resembled MacArthur. Taylor was used to giving orders and having them obeyed without question. Hence, when he directed the dean to devote three lessons (20 percent) of the international relations course to atomic fission, he did not worry that his action encroached on the authority of department heads to determine the content of their instruction.[75] Similarly, he expected the Academic Board's cooperation in adding a psychology course to the curriculum, especially since the idea originated with the army chief of staff, Dwight Eisenhower. When the Board demurred, he directed the commandant to provide the instruction through the newly created Office of Psychology and Leadership.[76] Believing that the curriculum was still too heavily weighted toward engineering, Taylor commissioned an external review board to look into the question.[77] The board gave the new postwar curriculum a glowing review, but Taylor continued his keen interest in academic affairs. He was particularly interested in English instruction, as he visited that department's classes and scrutinized the selection of its senior faculty. The professors resented these intrusions, but had little power to stop them. Their only consolation was that the superintendent soon shifted his focus to nonacademic areas of concern — honor, leader development, and military training.[78]

One of Taylor's successors as superintendent, Maj. Gen. Frederick Irving (1951 to 1954), sympathized with Academic Board members troubled by their declining influence. To remedy the situation, he recommended giving professors the pay and allowances of a brigadier general once they reached thirty years' commissioned service; additionally, these officers would receive the retirement pay of a brigadier general upon leaving active duty. Although professors would continue wearing the rank of colonel, the pay increase would enable West Point to continue attracting top-quality officers to the faculty. Furthermore, it would help restore the luster of the professoriate without adding to the number of general officers, which was determined by Congress. Unfortunately for the professors then and now, the army chief of staff disapproved Irving's proposal.[79] Not long after, however, Congress authorized professors to be advanced to the rank of brigadier general upon their retirement. Because the advancement came without the pay of a brigadier, the professors quipped that it was a "gravestone promotion" only.[80]

Perhaps no one managed Academy governance more adeptly in the twentieth century than Garrison Holt Davidson, superintendent from 1956 to 1960. Davidson was every inch a reformer, but he had the wisdom to understand how best to guide change in a conservative institution. As a cadet, he was deeply involved in many of the activities with which he would grapple as superintendent. He was a member of the honor committee, supervised Beast Barracks during his last summer, and was "second captain" of his senior class. Despite his modest build, he lettered twice in football; within three years of his 1927 graduation, he returned to West Point as an instructor and assistant football coach. In 1933, he became head coach and led the team to a 35-11-1 record over the next five years. He had a distinguished combat record in World War II and the Korean War as the combat engineer for George Patton and Douglas MacArthur, respectively. Just prior to his return to West Point, he served as the commandant of the US Army Command and General Staff College at Fort Leavenworth, an assignment particularly well suited to prepare him for his job as superintendent.[81]

Davidson's four years as superintendent were unusually productive. He implemented important reforms in many areas, including academics, admissions, military training, leader development, physical fitness, discipline, and public outreach. Most of these reforms came after his first year, during which he conducted a strategic assessment of the Academy, established goals for reform, and formulated a plan for achieving them. Davidson knew from the start that overcoming the inertia of a conservative institution would be a challenge. "Any academic body is extremely difficult to move," he noted, "but when the group is a military academic body the felony is compounded by tradition."[82]

The most hard-fought reform was in the area of academics, which Davidson believed had lagged behind the rapid advances of knowledge in the postwar era. He therefore set out to accomplish the "most complete survey of our curriculum that has been made in well over half a century."[83] The review was indeed comprehensive, lasting the better part of two years. It started with an analysis of the attributes army officers would need ten to twenty years in the future. To derive the information, Davidson formed a requirements committee and sent questionnaires to all West Point graduates and selected other officers. Next, he formed working groups to consider the issues identified in the requirements study and to provide recommendations for curricular change. For both the requirements committee and the working groups, he hand-picked the officers and ensured broad representation across departments, ranks, and ages. Davidson stayed personally involved in the review process, gently guiding the effort with questions and comments that provided a framework for analysis. In so doing, he co-opted many of his potential opponents and built a broad base of support.

Still, Davidson knew that his personal involvement might not win enough votes on the Academic Board to secure the desired changes. He therefore relied on a proven expedient—an external review board—to comment on the working groups' recommendations. The board consisted of distinguished military officers and civilian educators. He carefully chose the members, including the most senior officer, Gen. Alfred M. Gruenther, his brother-in-law.[84] At their first meeting in December 1958, Davidson complained that the working groups "had not gone far enough in proposing modifications to our curriculum." The board members took the hint and developed recommendations that aligned closely with Davidson's five curricular priorities: (1) establishment of an elective program; (2) accelerated courses for advanced students; (3) expanded instruction in the humanities and social sciences; (4) expanded instruction in nuclear science; (5) decrease in military training to the "minimum essential" during the academic year.[85]

When the time came for the Academic Board to debate the curriculum proposals, Davidson was ready. He already had won the support of a minority of the members, and the recommendations of the external review board weighed in his favor. Another advantage was his rank, now lieutenant general, which gave him a three-grade advantage over his adversaries on the board; even the tenured professors were not immune to the military's culture of deference toward superior officers. Most important, however, was Davidson's handling of the debate. He carefully prepared his case and personally presented it to the Academic Board. He was patient and respectful of the professors' objections but forceful in his responses. The debate, he reported, was "intense to say the least—but friendly. Blood was drawn but the wounded lived."[86] The final vote, by secret ballot, was six in favor of Davidson's proposals and nine in favor of a slightly modified version.[87] Although he did not get everything he wanted at the time, within a few years the Academic Board had adopted all of his recommendations and more. Years later, Davidson commented with sly satisfaction that the enthusiasm of the Board members "mounted with a growing appreciation of the wisdom of 'their' foresight."[88]

A person less adept at organizational leadership might not have been as successful as Davidson in achieving curricular reform. Moreover, even Davidson might have failed to accomplish his reforms in the governance environment of the pre-World War II era. By the 1950s, however, the playing field had leveled to the point of giving a capable superintendent a fair chance of winning approval for his reform agenda. The parity was healthy for the institution, as it challenged the professoriate to avoid complacency while still providing a check

As superintendent, Lt. Gen. Garrison Davidson (class of 1927, far right) hosted a gathering of three of his predecessors. From left to right, they are Gen. Maxwell Taylor (class of 1922), superintendent from 1945 to 1949; General of the Army Douglas MacArthur, superintendent from 1919 to 1922; Lt. Gen. Blackshear Bryan (class of 14 June 1922), superintendent from 1954 to 1956.

on ill-considered initiatives from above. The advantages of the equilibrium are easier to see in retrospect than they were at the time, when both parties complained that their influence was less than it should have been. The mutual complaints were the surest sign that the equilibrium of the postwar years represented a salutary distribution of power in the area of curricular affairs. Good ideas had a reasonable chance of being implemented; poor ones did not.

Before leaving Davidson, it is important to note a far-reaching, but unanticipated, consequence of his curricular changes. The most dramatic reform was to establish a program of elective courses starting in 1960, thus ending the tradition of "every cadet in every subject." The proliferation of electives complicated the task of course design and administration as the curriculum moved far beyond the prescribed courses that had defined the academic program since Thayer. Consequently, the Academy appointed "permanent associate professors"—officers with doctorates in their respective fields who remained at West Point until retirement—to handle the added work. They were bright and committed officers who did more to enrich the intellectual environment of West Point than any other group. As their numbers and contributions grew, the "PAPs" became increasingly desirous of having a voice in governance. Unfortunately the Academic Board was either unaware or unsympathetic. As an example, department heads chaired all seven working groups for the 1969 academic accreditation study even though there were plenty of PAPs available to do the work.[89] Accreditation was (and still is) a major event in the life of American colleges; as a measure of the quality of an institution, it required an intensive self-assessment lasting more than a year. By monopolizing the committee chairs, Academic Board members added to their already heavy burden and thus weakened their ability to stay abreast of the trends ongoing within their departments and across the Academy. Moreover, they denied the PAPs the privilege of serving in meaningful leadership positions.[90]

IV. BIG CHALLENGES, BIG CHANGES IN GOVERNANCE

Starting in the early 1960s, a combination of forces, both internal and external, created a prolonged period of turmoil culminating in the worst cheating incident in the Academy's history. The situation undermined the delicate balance of governance by forcing superintendents to deal with pressing issues far afield from curricular affairs; concurrently, the explosive growth of electives in a variety of disciplinary concentrations made the job of the department heads ever more demanding.

In 1964, Congress authorized the expansion of the Corps from 2,500 to 4,417 cadets—an increase of about 77 percent.[91] The expansion took several years to complete as new barracks and other facilities were made ready. In the meantime, Academy leaders worried about how to maintain the fidelity of the cadet experience as the student body grew to unprecedented size. In normal times, the Academic Board would have patiently studied the question and fashioned appropriate policies; these times, however, were anything but normal.

The most troubling development was the war in Vietnam, which exerted a powerfully negative influence on the Academy during the latter half of the decade. As antiwar sentiment grew, the Academy's ability to attract qualified young men declined precipitously; by 1968 there were fewer qualified candidates than vacancies.[92] The My Lai massacre further tarnished the Academy and, in 1970, led to the removal and demotion of the superintendent, Maj. Gen. Samuel W. Koster, who had commanded the army division involved in the incident. My Lai was emblematic of the moral malaise and careerism that, by some accounts, had infiltrated the officer corps. True or not, the perception of these problems had a chilling effect on junior officers, many of whom left the service out of frustration. Between January 1971 and June 1972, thirty-three of them—about 4 percent of the officers stationed at West Point—resigned their commissions. Among them were some of the brightest officers on the faculty, including several with early promotions and even a Medal of Honor recipient.[93]

In addition to antiwar sentiment, other societal forces — the civil rights movement, feminism, the New Left, and the counterculture — emboldened Americans to challenge the authority of every traditional institution. Many cadets entered West Point with a heightened sense of the individualism and moral relativism characteristic of their society; the Academy's high standards of discipline and honor suffered as a result. Other forces buffeting West Point included legal challenges to the honor system, adverse publicity over the "silencing" of a cadet, a Supreme Court ruling declaring mandatory chapel unconstitutional, and the spectacle of West Point graduates seeking conscientious objector status. In the early 1970s, several sharply critical books about West Point found a receptive audience; the fact that some of the authors were Academy graduates or former faculty members added insult to injury.[94] Even the football team reflected the malaise by going winless in the 1973 season. Also that year, investigations by the General Accounting Office and Defense Department probed the Academy's internal affairs and presaged an increased level of outside scrutiny and control.[95] Finally, Congress directed the service academies to open their doors to women starting in 1976 despite the vehement opposition of Academy and army leaders.

These developments were the backdrop to the discovery of a huge cheating incident involving the junior class in March 1976. The cheating arose when cadets in the EE304 electrical engineering course collaborated on a take-home project, despite instructions to do the work independently. As the number of honor investigations soon overwhelmed the cadet honor committee, Superintendent Sidney Berry commissioned officer boards to conduct the hearings during the remaining weeks of the semester. Eventually 152 cadets from the class of 1977 either resigned or were separated because of the cheating.[96] That was hardly the end of the matter, however. Many of the accused cadets brought legal action to invalidate the honor proceedings, and both houses of Congress initiated investigations. Media sharks circled the Academy and took any bait with the scent of a story.

Since 1802, external pressures — typically from the War Department, Congress, or the press — had occasionally influenced Academy governance. The intrusions were episodic and usually impermanent, such as the War Department order for early graduations during World War I. Following the 1976 cheating incident, however, the interventions were massive and prolonged and the result was to permanently alter the system of governance at West Point.

Because of the magnitude of the cheating crisis, Secretary of the Army Martin Hoffman personally intervened. In September 1976, he formed a special commission headed by astronaut Frank Borman, a 1950 West Point graduate, to investigate the cheating incident and its underlying causes. The commissioners ensconced themselves in the Academy library and conducted hundreds of hours of interviews with the cadets, staff, and faculty; they rendered their final report to Hoffmann in December. Although the commissioners expressed their support of the honor code and acknowledged that the cheaters were culpable for their actions, they believed that "institutional problems were the primary causes of the erosion of respect for the Honor System."[97] Hence, they supported Hoffmann's decision to allow the dismissed cadets to apply for readmission the following year; moreover, they admonished Academy leaders to "acknowledge the causes of the breakdown" and to devote their "full energies to rebuilding an improved and strengthened institution."[98]

In conducting their investigation, the commissioners detected a gap between West Point's official view of its governance structure and the perceptions of the junior faculty. An Academy information paper described the Academic Board as a collegial body with a system of checks and balances that allowed a unique blend of diverse viewpoints:

> The Superintendent and the Commandant, newly assigned approximately every three years, represent the guidance of the Secretary of the Army, the Army Chief of Staff, and a current senior officer view of the Army. The strong influence they have on the board is directly proportional to their experience, prestige, rank, and merited respect. The Department Heads, for their part, are able to maintain a current view of the young Army through their junior officer faculty members and are also influenced by their own and the younger officers' contacts with civilian academic institutions. . . . The resulting consensus reached by the Board, reflecting the operation of a classic check and balance system, is therefore based on a variety of experiences and backgrounds, and changes have traditionally been moderate, gradual, and evolutionary.[99]

Junior faculty, however, had a contrasting view. They characterized the Academic Board as "unduly resistant to change and non-representative of the viewpoints of the 'young Army.'"[100] Swayed by these opinions, the commission recommended strengthening the superintendent by giving him authority over all matters of internal administration and by lengthening his tenure to at least five years. Moreover, they advocated forcing professors to retire once they reached thirty years of active commissioned service.[101] The professors were incensed by the commission's conclusion that they were responsible for the problems leading to the cheating incident. They claimed that the commissioners had drawn hasty conclusions without ever interviewing them. One professor wrote indignantly to Borman, "I have been insulted personally, as has the Corps of Profes-

sors and the Academic Board as corporate bodies."[102] Another wrote directly
to the army chief of staff, Gen. Bernard Rogers, complaining that the Borman
commissioners wanted to "eliminate the educators" from cadet education.[103]

The unprecedented drama at West Point prompted Rogers to take decisive
action. In January 1977, he initiated the most searching external review in the
school's history. Whereas the Borman commission had focused principally on
the honor code and system, Rogers had in mind a comprehensive study of
the Academy that would lead to broad reforms. He formed three investigative
committees, one each for academics, the cadet environment, and professional
development; collectively, these committees were known as the West Point
Study Group (WPSG). The composition of each committee included a one-
or two-star general as chairman and army staff officers, many of whom had
served on the West Point faculty or staff earlier in their careers.[104] Although
they would use the Borman report as a starting point, they would draw their
conclusions and make recommendations based on independent research. Over
the next seven months they interviewed hundreds of Academy leaders, faculty
and staff members, active and retired general officers, civilian educators, and
cadets and midshipmen from all service academies. They visited all five US
service academies, army professional schools, civilian educational institutions,
and foreign military academies. They sent questionnaires to thousands more
officers and cadets and studied the literature relevant to academic and professional education. The WPSG delivered the final report to Rogers in July. As a
blueprint for reform, it was the most significant document since Thayer established the four-year curriculum over 150 years earlier.[105]

Of the 156 recommendations in the WPSG report, none were more controversial than the twenty-one dealing with internal governance.[106] The overall intent was to give the superintendent the same level of authority enjoyed
by commanders at other army bases. The WPSG called for giving the superintendent four to eight years on the job to provide "stability and continuity
of policy" while limiting the Academic Board to "providing policy advice on
academic matters."[107] Displacing the Academic Board as the principal governing body would be the new "policy board," consisting of the superintendent,
commandant, dean, chief of staff, director of intercollegiate athletics, brigade
tactical officer, and four department heads.[108] Even the policy board, however,
would be advisory only. A new deputy superintendent — a one-star general —
would help manage day-to-day operations and implement the recommendations of the WPSG. Finally, a newly reorganized set of standing committees
would provide continuous oversight and counsel on enduring issues, such as
honor education and enforcement, faculty affairs, and intercollegiate athletics.
These changes would refocus the Academic Board solely on academic issues
and allow the professors to "concentrate their efforts on their departments,

their teaching, and their disciplines — in short, on academic excellence."[109] Other faculty members would pick up the slack by becoming more involved in governance on a variety of proposed standing committees.

The WPSG also recommended changes that would bolster the influence of the commandant. It proposed redesignating the Office of Physical Education and the Office of Military Instruction as departments within the Office of the Commandant and giving the new department heads seats on the Academic Board. The rationale was to make the Academic Board the principal deliberative body for all aspects of the curriculum. It was a logical move, but it represented another blow to the prestige of the corps of professors, whose collective voice was fading as the system of governance became more integrated and hierarchical.

While the professors on the Academic Board did not like what was happening, they had no choice but to give ground. They voiced their concerns in committee reports arising from an internal governance study directed by Superintendent Berry in the spring of 1977. The Academic Board, they argued, was "firmly rooted in the history of the Military Academy"; without it, "each Superintendent could redesign the curriculum as he chose." They argued against radical changes that would upend the long tradition of collegial governance and allow superintendents to pursue ill-advised, short-term policies. Still, they sensed the inevitability of change. They knew that army leaders wanted to invest the superintendent with more power and that the WPSG, then in the final stages of its work, would provide the detailed plans to do so. The committee therefore recommended a new governance structure wherein Academic Board decisions "would be clearly advisory and could be overturned at any time by the Superintendent."[110] Berry had little time to act on the committee report prior to his reassignment in June; his successor, however, had not only the time but also the will to take action that went well beyond what the professors had recommended.

In December 1976, just as he was preparing to organize the WPSG, Rogers asked Gen. Andrew J. Goodpaster to come out of retirement to become the new superintendent.[111] Rogers needed someone with sufficient stature to deflect attacks on the Academy and provide steady leadership during the time of crisis. Additionally, he wanted someone who would retire upon leaving the position, thus insulating the superintendent from political and professional pressures while in the job. Goodpaster was an ideal choice. His distinguished military career had culminated with command of NATO forces in Europe, and he was widely respected for his intellect and character. Even his name evoked a sense of benevolence and authority. Although he would wear three stars — the new standard for the superintendency — he retained all of the moral authority of a four-star general; in actual rank, he was more senior than even Rogers.

Gen. Andrew Goodpaster (class of 1939),
superintendent from 1977 to 1981.

An Academic Board member recalled that being in the presence of the august general "was like sitting at the feet of Abraham Lincoln."[112] This was, of course, precisely the effect Rogers intended when he asked Goodpaster to take the job. Both he and Goodpaster were determined to use the crisis to effect sweeping reform, and they would not allow the Academic Board to stand in the way.

In the months leading up to his assumption of command, Goodpaster worked closely with the WPSG and influenced many of the recommendations.[113] The collaborative effort ensured that there were no surprises when he received the final report in July 1977. "From this day forward," Goodpaster announced, "we will make the report our own."[114] He moved aggressively to implement the recommendations of the WPSG. Within two years, 77 percent of them had been executed in original or slightly modified form, 11 percent had been implemented in alternate form or on a trial basis, and 9 percent were still under study for implementation. Only 3 percent were rejected outright.[115]

Goodpaster relied on two key subordinates to assist in the implementation effort. The first was the deputy superintendent, Brig. Gen. Charles Bagnal, who relieved Goodpaster of many routine tasks that had occupied previous superintendents.[116] Thus unburdened, the superintendent could work closely with a second key subordinate, the newly established special assistant for policy and plans. Strategic planning was a major weakness identified by the WPSG. The Academy lacked "accepted common objectives" and an "uncertainty of purpose which repeated recitation of the mission statement cannot disguise." Moreover, there was "a disturbing lack of comprehensive supervision and long-range planning."[117] Determined to resolve the problem, Goodpaster directed all organizations involved in cadet development to compose concept papers that stated their goals and objectives. The special assistant for policy and plans reviewed the papers to ensure they were complementary and fit within the superintendent's strategic plan. The exercise produced no radical changes, but it began the process of systematizing strategic planning within a dedicated staff agency under the superintendent. Despite this precedent, however, future superintendents, with one prominent exception, did not fully exploit the capability for strategic planning, and external review boards continued criticizing the Academy in this area.[118]

In the area of governance, Goodpaster accomplished all of his principal goals. He gained control over an institution that many believed was adrift and, in the process, assumed unchallenged authority in the Academy governance structure. Invested with high rank and the unwavering support of army leaders, he broke the back of the Academic Board by relegating it to an advisory role and limiting its purview primarily to curricular affairs; in this regard, he enacted the changes envisioned by Fox Conner and Frank Parker a half-century earlier. A new staff agency was available to assist the superintendent in long-range and strategic planning. Although the army discontinued the position of deputy superintendent following Goodpaster's departure, and committee structures fluctuated, the foundation of a centralized governance structure was in place (table 2.3). Academy and army regulations reflected the changes, and subsequent superintendents were never timid about exercising their expanded powers.[119]

The superintendent's authority received a further boost when Gen. John A. Wickham became the army chief of staff in 1983. Convinced that tenured professors grew increasingly hidebound and out of touch the longer they stayed at West Point, Wickham ordered them "regreened" at least one summer out of three or one year out of seven. The time would be spent performing duties in the field army or attending army service schools. A related initiative changed the procedures for hiring new professors; henceforth, the selection committees included a representative from army headquarters to ensure that the person

TABLE 2.3   Governance Structure, 1979

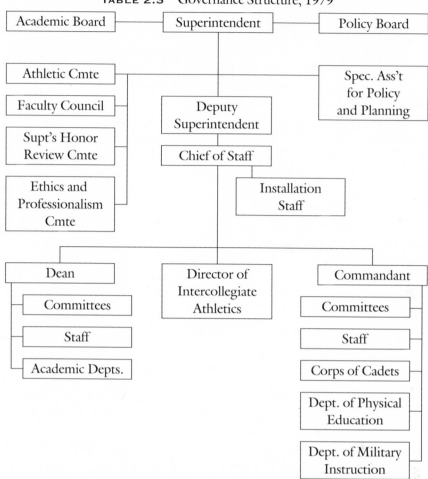

Notes: US Military Academy, *The United States Military Academy in Perspective, 1969–1979: An Institutional Report Prepared for the 1980 Decennial Accreditation.* West Point: USMA, December 1979, 22.

selected had strong professional, as well as academic, credentials.[120] It was hard to argue against these measures, but what came next was galling for the professors. To ensure that the most senior professors remained intellectually and professionally active over the long term, Wickham initiated two-stage program for tenure review.[121] In stage one, the dean and superintendent would evaluate the professor's performance and potential at the thirty-year mark to decide whether or not to extend the professor another five years. In stage two, a panel chaired by the superintendent would assess the professor at the thirty-five and (if necessary) forty-year mark to determined fitness for another five years of service.[122]

The professors viewed the tenure-review process as a vote of no confidence in their service and a reflection of their continuing decline in status.

Perhaps the most telling sign of the new order at West Point was the turn-over on the Academic Board. In the summer of 1977, five professors retired — a record number. Two of them had reached their mandatory retirement age, but the other three could have stayed longer.[123] In subsequent years, the resignation rate from the Academic Board remained high as the professors no longer had the power and influence of an earlier era. Historian Theodore Crackel documented the increased turbulence in the last quarter of the twentieth century. "Those who had experienced the power of the board before 1977, or even those who had been brought up in its shadow, increasingly felt that they had been cut out of the decision-making process. It was a reasoned conclusion that did little to keep them at the helm."[124] Any of them who could remember the collegial governance structure and the elevated role of department heads realized that being a professor at West Point had lost much of its former luster.

V.   CENTRALIZED COMMAND

The six superintendents who followed Goodpaster made ample use of the expanded authority of their position. Lieutenant Generals Willard W. Scott, Dave R. Palmer, Howard D. Graves, Daniel W. Christman, William J. Lennox, and Franklin L. Hagenbeck all adjusted the governance system to suit their individual personality and leadership style.[125] In no case, however, did they gravitate toward the old system of collegial governance with the Academic Board; some of them dispensed even with the policy board.[126] All of them favored more efficient governance methods that centralized power in the hands of a smaller group of people. In most cases the streamlined modes of governance allowed the institution to adapt and respond nimbly to changing conditions. In other cases, the unchecked power of the superintendent allowed shortsighted decisions and developments that would not have been possible under the old governance system.

More than ever before, the centralized command structure empowered superintendents to implement policies they deemed necessary. Dave R. Palmer, superintendent from 1986 to 1991, demonstrated what was possible when strategic vision combined with energy and persistence. Alerted about eighteen months in advance that he would likely be the next superintendent, he immersed himself in the literature of West Point, particularly the studies and reports of the preceding decade. He had a head start by virtue of his experience as a military history instructor in the late 1960s and his detailed knowledge of West Point history.[127] Palmer would assume command during a rare period of tranquility, both externally and internally. The nation was prosperous and at peace, the military enjoyed high public esteem, and the Academy seemed healthy again after a decade of malaise. Even the football team — a barometer of Academy fortunes in the minds of many "old grads"—was having a rare string of successful seasons. Palmer seized the opportunity: "You get that open window about once every fifty years, and it doesn't stay open very long. . . . That gave us the opportunity, indeed the obligation, to go through self-examination. And I went about it with urgency knowing that we didn't have unlimited time."[128]

Palmer's precommand assessment revealed that the Academy lacked "a clearly articulated and understood sense of vision. . . . There was no clear understanding of what our course was, what our azimuth was."[129] Upon assuming command, he therefore asked three simple questions to help develop his strategic guidance: (1) Why does the Military Academy exist? (2) What does the Academy do to fulfill its purpose? (3) How does the Academy accomplish its mission?[130] Over the next year, the faculty and staff conducted a series of studies to answer these questions. The first question led to the creation of a purpose statement: "To provide the nation with leaders of character who serve the common defense." The second question resulted in a revised mission statement: "To educate and train the Corps of Cadets so that each graduate will have the attributes essential to professional growth as an officer of the regular army, and inspire each to a lifetime of service to the nation."[131] The third question was the focus of a series of concept papers on the nature of the cadet experience and the role of the academic, military, physical, and moral-ethical developmental programs. The effort to establish strategic guidance dominated the first year of Palmer's tenure. Not since Garrison Davidson had a superintendent initiated such a thorough internal review and articulated so clearly the strategic direction of the institution.[132]

The strategic review revealed two glaring and related problems at the Academy. The first was the overcrowded schedule. "We were expecting too much of cadets," noted Palmer, "and as a result, we were tending toward mediocrity rather than excellence." The second problem was a lack of effective integration of the various developmental programs. According to Palmer, "We didn't know how our programs fit together. . . . We were not synchronized."[133] He formed a committee headed by Col. Howard Prince, professor of behavioral sciences and leadership, to study the problem and recommend solutions. The committee concluded that no one below the level of the superintendent could accomplish the task of integration since the program directors were too jealous of their activities to integrate them on their own. If the superintendent did not assume the integrator mission, Prince counseled, "it isn't going to get done."[134]

Accordingly, Palmer created a new staff agency, the Office of Leader Development Integration (OLDI), under his immediate supervision.[135] With OLDI's

help, he streamlined the cadet schedule and better integrated the developmental programs. His new "Academy Schedule," written into regulations, imposed
clear lines between the time devoted to academic, military, and other pursuits;
violators of the schedule found themselves explaining to the superintendent
why they were not in conformance with his policy.[136] He reduced the baseline
curriculum to forty courses, trimmed a few minutes from class periods to ease
the daily schedule, and eliminated Saturday instruction. He then protected the
newfound time for approved uses, including weekend trips, passes, and activities that formerly had competed with academics during the weekdays.[137]
Palmer established a two-week "military intersession" between the first and
second semester; during this time, the Academy devoted its full attention to
military and physical training.[138] He created the Cadet Leader Development
System (CLDS) to guide and integrate all developmental activities over the
four-year cadet experience; CLDS represented the most coherent and progressive system of overall leader development ever established at West Point.[139]
These and many other initiatives established Palmer's superintendency as one
of the most productive in the Academy's history; the most important initiatives
have continued to the present.[140]

Palmer tried to be inclusive as he pushed the institution to embrace change.
He consulted the policy board to full extent on broad issues and the Academic
Board on more narrow curricular issues; moreover, he cast a wide net in con-
ducting the many studies and assessments that underpinned his reform agenda.
Still, the breakneck pace of change and Palmer's no-nonsense leadership style
alienated many people. One contemporary recalled that "there was not a soul
at West Point that wasn't unhappy about something."[141] According to another,
"Fair or not, the general perception was that the policy board did whatever
Gen. Palmer wanted. . . . The perception was that he arrived with the agenda
of lowering the profile of the Academic Board."[142] Some of the curricular reforms encountered heavy resistance from the professors, a few of whom acted
unprofessionally to undermine the changes.[143]

Palmer was aware of the discontent and attributed it to the natural resistance
of institutions to change. Still, he was troubled by the disloyalty of some of his
senior subordinates. He accused them of acting "with malice and forethought"
to subvert his policies and "doing a fairly decent job of it."[144] To arrest the
situation, Palmer exploited the tenure-review procedures mandated by Gen.
Wickham. Superintendent Willard Scott had never implemented the tenure-
review process, but Palmer announced that he would do so starting in 1987.
Professors already beyond the thirty-year mark were not exempt. "We will have
a catch up," Palmer told them, and the mere announcement caused a few professors to retire voluntarily. The gambit worked as Palmer had intended: "They
knew that they better leave in good standing rather than wait till they were

boarded and told to leave. So that cleaned house immediately without us ever having to hold a board for a handful that should have gone."[145]

The tranquil external environment that had allowed Palmer to advance his reform agenda ended in late 1989 — three-and-a-half years into his superintendency — mostly because of the sudden end of the Cold War. The new strategic environment brought calls for a "peace dividend" in the form of military manpower reductions that portended reductions in the size of the faculty, staff, and Corps of Cadets at West Point. Another contentious issue stemmed from a Senate bill that would have lengthened graduates' active-duty service obligation from five years to eight; intended as a cost-saving measure, the bill would have made the Academy's recruiting effort more difficult.[146] Finally, the death of former head football coach Earl Blaik prompted his supporters to attempt to have the football stadium renamed in his honor, despite the stadium already bearing the name of a distinguished alumnus who had died in battle. These and other issues "slammed shut" the window of opportunity and diverted Palmer's attention from reform to reaction.[147] Fortunately his early initiatives were complete, or almost so, because the new external environment diverted his focus for the remainder of his tenure.

The Palmer years dramatized the power of centralized governance to enable rapid and significant changes from within. A visionary and strong-willed superintendent, steeped in the history of the institution, achieved a record of success matched only by Douglas MacArthur and Garrison Davidson in the twentieth century. But if enlightened superintendents were able to effect positive change, the reverse was also true under the new system of governance.

The effectiveness of centralized governance depends on the extent to which the commander collects and considers information from all levels to make wise decisions. For the most part, West Point benefited from centralized command as superintendents kept in mind the institution's dual nature as an undergraduate college and a military organization. On occasion, however, they implemented shortsighted policies that compromised the curriculum, lowered admission standards, weakened discipline, over- or underemphasized certain programs, or undermined institutional values. In most of these cases, the superintendents acted without seriously engaging the Academic Board, whose professors, despite their reputation for conservatism, constituted a deep well of professional insight and institutional knowledge. Sometimes the superintendents relied on the policy board, but the composition of that body, except for the dean and the two academic department heads, consisted of short-term officers and civilians who were long on authority but short on their knowledge of institutional history.

Perhaps the most dramatic example of the problems resulting from shortsighted policies can be found in the quest to field winning teams in intercollegiate athletics. West Point has a long and distinguished history of competitive athletics, including two national championships in football in the mid-1940s.[148] Once Coach Blaik left the Academy in 1959, however, the football program began a gradual decline from which it has never recovered. The decline was due mostly to factors beyond the Academy's control — principally, the growing commercialism and professionalism of the sport and the consequent difficulty of recruiting high-quality athletes with the credentials to be successful cadets and officers. Rather than concede to this reality, however, some superintendents succumbed to the pressures of a vocal minority of alumni who saw the football team as a reflection of the Academy; this was despite the absence of any credible evidence to show that the fortunes of the football team affected the number of applicants to the Academy or the quality of West Point graduates.[149] Prior to 1977, the Academic Board tempered the impulse to seek short-term athletic success at the expense of more important institutional goals; additionally it helped superintendents resist the often fanatical entreaties of alumni to "fix" a sport — usually football — that was doing poorly.[150] The diminution of the Academic Board's power after 1977 removed these safeguards and permitted superintendents to elevate intercollegiate athletics to an unprecedented level of importance at the Academy.[151]

Frustrated by a string of losing seasons in the flagship sport of football, Superintendent William Lennox sought the army's help in recruiting better athletes. The resulting policy, known as the "alternate service option," received army approval in 2005. It allowed cadets with "unique talents and abilities" to apply for release from military service after two years instead of the normal five. Approval was granted if there was a "strong expectation" that that the applicant would bring "significant favorable media exposure" to the army and "enhance national recruiting or public affairs efforts." As written, the alternate service option avoided specific mention of athletes to give the impression that it applied to all cadets; in reality, however, it was intended for cadets who played varsity sports.[152] The policy helped coaches recruit talented high school athletes who had dreams of playing their sports professionally. If an athlete succeeded in reaching his or her athletic potential at West Point, the door was open to professional sports after a two-year service obligation; if not, there was guaranteed employment as an army officer.

Conveniently buried in the implementing instructions for the alternate service option was a provision allowing the athletes to work as recruiters to satisfy the two-year active-duty requirement. Lennox and his successor, Franklin Hagenbeck, exploited this provision to enable Academy athletes to play professional sports immediately after graduation. They prevailed upon the army to assign the officer-athletes to recruiting stations in the cities where the professional teams played. The officer-athletes did little actual recruiting, as the intent of the policy was for them to play their sports full time. They were thus able to fulfill the two-year service requirement while drawing both a full army salary and the pay of a professional athlete.

The army was similarly relaxed about what constituted "unique talents and abilities." There was no need to be a once-in-a-generation star like David Robinson or Roger Staubach to qualify for the alternate service option.[153] One needed only to be accepted into the player development system of a professional sports team; a baseball player, for example, could play on a farm team and still qualify.[154] Between 2005 and 2007, six cadets — four in baseball, one in hockey, and one in football — took advantage of the early release program; none achieved much fame or media attention. Still, they inspired hope in talented high school athletes who liked the idea of going to West Point but wanted most of all to be professional athletes rather than professional soldiers.

The alternate service option as practiced by Lennox and Hagenbeck was little noticed outside the Academy for the first few years. That changed, however, when the Detroit Lions football team drafted Cadet Caleb Campbell in 2008. Campbell was a talented defensive back who the Lions selected in the final round of the National Football League draft. His West Point connection intrigued the sports media, which portrayed Campbell as patriot qua football player.[155] As the story wore on, however, the incongruity of a graduating cadet donning the uniform of a professional athlete rather than that of a professional soldier stirred a national debate. The fact that the army was fighting wars in Iraq and Afghanistan and had a serious officer shortage only heightened the irony. Furthermore, the story of Pat Tillman, a professional football player who walked away from a multimillion dollar contract to enlist as an army Ranger, was still fresh in the minds of Americans. Tillman served multiple combat tours before being killed in Afghanistan in 2004; he was universally revered for his patriotism, courage, and sense of duty.[156] Campbell seemed like the anti-Tillman — a soldier who walked away from his military commitment to play professional football. To many, he seemed the epitome of selfish, not selfless, service.

The press had a field day. In a poll conducted by a national newspaper, over half of the respondents thought that Campbell should fulfill his service obligation.[157] The sports journalist, Thomas Hauser, captured the majority view.

Coaches at West Point can now recruit elite high school athletes with the sales pitch, "Come to West Point. If you're good enough to play in the NFL, you can avoid military combat." That's a far cry from World War II and the Korean War, when the United States asked great athletes like Ted Williams to serve in the armed forces alongside everyone else. The most disturbing aspect of all this is the light it sheds on our priorities as a nation. The United States Military Academy is, in effect, saying that it considers entertaining sports fans to be more important than the war in Iraq. How else can one construe giving a young man the choice of (a) living up to his commitment to serve his country or (b) playing in the National Football League?[158]

Academy officials responded that Campbell *was* living up to his commitment. He was serving his two years of active duty as a high-profile recruiter who could encourage young people to consider joining the military. A Philadelphia newspaper deflated the argument by speculating on the dialogue between Campbell and a potential recruit:

> "I'm Caleb Campbell, and I'm here to suggest joining the Army. It's a newly styled dynamic force with exciting opportunities around the world. And the best part is the satisfaction of serving your country in time of war."
> "And what do you do in the Army, Mr. Campbell?"
> "I blitz quarterbacks on national television, make millions of dollars, talk to high school kids once a week and don't have to go to Iraq."
> "Wow! Where do I sign up?"[159]

The negative publicity of the Campbell affair soon earned the army a stern rebuke from the Department of Defense. In April, Undersecretary of Defense David S. Chu directed the army to reassign Campbell and other early-release officers to authentic active-duty assignments for the required two years.[160] The "constructs for 'active-duty' service," Chu emphasized, "should not include arrangements typically unavailable to others in uniform"; this guidance effectively ended the dual compensation of alternate-service officers. The army dithered, however, as Hagenbeck tried unsuccessfully to orchestrate a compromise that would allow the athletes to continue playing professional sports. The army finally issued the reassignment orders in late July, just days ahead of Campbell's report date to the Lion's summer training camp. Consequently, the army took another pounding in the press, this time for reneging on a commitment and waiting too long to issue the reassignment orders.[161]

This vignette is related at length because it so vividly illustrates the potential pitfalls of centralized governance at West Point. Under pressure to "restore the winning tradition" in football, Lennox and Hagenbeck took executive action to improve the prospect of recruiting superior athletes.[162] They did not consult the policy board, which had lapsed into disuse, and they had little interaction with the Academic Board. They limited the dialogue to a small circle of likeminded advisors who were incapable of presenting opposing arguments with the force of conviction. With few dissenting opinions, it was easy to be seduced into thinking that the alternate service option was a sound policy. In fact, there was a deep well of discontent toward the policy among staff and faculty members, but no forum in which to state their opinions. The Academic Board could have provided a countervailing viewpoint if either superintendent had sought its counsel; unfortunately the topic never came up for debate at any of its meetings.

Superintendent Hagenbeck reconstituted the policy board in early 2009. The decision implemented a recommendation made by his transition team in 2006 and studied by an Academy accreditation committee that focused on governance.[163] Without the policy board or an analogous body, West Point would be hard pressed to convince the accrediting agency that its governance structure was appropriate for an institution centered on a four-year undergraduate experience. Collegial governance may be at times slow, inconvenient, and even inefficient, but centralized governance can be equally troublesome. The most successful superintendents understood how to balance the two.

★ ★ ★

The history of governance at West Point is the story of tension between collegial and centralized governance. For the first century of the Academy's existence, and well into the second century, the Academic Board was preeminent. As a collegial body, its strengths were careful deliberation, sense of history, and stability. As a corporate entity, it shielded individual members — particularly the superintendent — from outside pressures and endowed every decision with impersonal authority. The Academic Board's main weaknesses were the reverse of its strengths: ponderous decision making, hyper-reverence for tradition, and excessive conservatism. As the institution expanded and the curriculum grew more complex in the twentieth century, the weaknesses of collegial governance overshadowed the strengths.

By midcentury, the nature of governance at West Point had changed. The heightened rank of the superintendent proved an effective counterweight to the conservatism of the professoriate. There was a healthy give and take between the superintendent and the professors on the Academic Board that produced good policies and salutary changes. The balance achieved during this period between collegial and centralized governance proved highly effective in leading an institution at once military and academic.

Following the 1976 cheating incident, the governance structure at West Point became highly centralized. Three-star superintendents could implement policies as they saw fit, without the need for careful reflection and persuasive arguments that the Academic Board had imposed on their predecessors. On the whole, they used their power wisely. Occasionally, however, they lost strategic focus and pursued short-term objectives that undermined more important institutional objectives. Such abuses were usually the result of self-imposed insularity from dissenting opinions or the unchecked interests of the superintendents themselves.

The most effective superintendents of the twentieth century were those with expansive vision, energy, persistence, and a sense of history. They were men who understood the value of considering the full spectrum of opinions before making their decisions. As subsequent chapters will show, Douglas MacArthur, Garrison Davidson, and Dave Palmer each faced unique circumstances and had widely different leadership styles. But they shared a common commitment to understanding the views on every side of an issue. MacArthur and Davidson had no choice, given the collegial governance structure then in place; both of them received a surfeit of counsel from their colleagues on the Academic Board. Palmer had no obligation to engage in such dialogue; nonetheless, he spent the first year of his tenure conducting a strategic review with participation from every corner of the Academy. That many were dissatisfied with the pace and scope of MacArthur's, Davidson's, and Palmer's changes should not obscure the fact that each had plumbed the depths of opinion before acting. Moreover, these three superintendents shared a sense of historical continuity and an understanding of enduring institutional values. Armed with such insights, they ensured every decision contributed directly to the Academy's mission of producing leaders of character and intellect for the army.

Superintendents no longer need to consult the Academic Board on most issues, and some have dispensed even with the policy board. They do so at their risk, however. Neither a military unit nor an undergraduate college is easy to lead; when the two are combined into a single institution, the leadership challenges are enormous and leaders need all the help they can get.

CHAPTER THREE

"The Corps Starts Here"

ADMISSIONS

T HE PROCESS for admitting cadets to West Point underwent profound change in the twentieth century. In every decade, a large majority of applicants gained entry through a congressional nomination system established in the early nineteenth century to ensure geographic, political, and socioeconomic diversity. While the system met these goals, it was less effective in providing cadet candidates who were academically and physically qualified for the rigors of West Point. The result was a high rate of attrition for both candidates and cadets through most of the century. Academy officials invested much time and effort seeking reforms that would improve the quality of the candidates, lower attrition, and provide better officers for the army.

The greatest changes in the admission system took place after World War II. Academy leaders worked with Congress to improve nomination procedures and thus attract higher-quality candidates than before. Concurrently, they devised better methods to evaluate the character, intellect, physical fitness, and leadership abilities of the candidates. The Academy underwent organizational changes to strengthen recruitment, expand publicity, and improve administrative support. It experienced dramatic demographic changes that included the admission of more racial minorities (starting in the 1960s) and women (in 1976).

Throughout the century, Academy leaders sought to discover the attributes of candidates that were most likely to bring success as a cadet and officer. Pinpointing predictive factors in human subjects is an inexact science; still, repetitive studies revealed the existence of a few reliable indicators of success, which

Academy leaders embedded into the candidate evaluation system of the second half of the century.

Given the century-long effort to raise entry standards, it was ironic that features of the modern admissions system perpetuated earlier weaknesses and allowed entry to a significant minority of applicants less qualified than others who failed to win appointments. Some of the weaker entrants were beneficiaries of the institution's affirmative-action policies, designed to bring the Corps of Cadets more in line with the demography of the army and society; their presence answered the need to provide empathetic leadership for a diverse army. Many others, however, owed their appointments to a growing emphasis on intercollegiate athletics, which assumed an unprecedented level of priority in the last decades of the century.

I. SIZE OF THE CORPS

As noted in chapter 1, the Academy recruited most of its cadets indirectly through a congressional nomination system that began informally early in the nineteenth century and gained de facto legitimacy over time. Congress formalized the system in 1843 when it fixed the size of the Corps to be equal to the number of representatives and delegates in Congress,[1] plus ten cadets from the United States at large. By law the president was the sole appointing authority for cadets, but he delegated the responsibility to the secretary of war. Managing the ten at-large nominations was easy enough; for the others, however, the secretary habitually asked each member of Congress to recommend a principal nominee and an alternate from his district. Since the president always accepted the recommendations presented to him by the secretary of war, the congressional selection process gained acceptance and has been the principal means of nominating young men (and now women) for cadetships ever since.[2]

Congress made two adjustments to the 1843 law around the time of the West Point centennial. First, it added two cadetships per state, thus giving each United States senator the privilege of recommending a nominee to the secretary of war, just as the representatives and delegates had done. Second, it increased the United States-at-large appointments from ten to forty; the intent was to give the sons of army officers better odds of being admitted since their itinerant lifestyles put them at a disadvantage under the congressional nomination system.[3] These two changes, reflected in table 3.1, increased the authorized strength of the Corps of Cadets to 492 at the start of the Academy's second century. This was an increase of about 35 percent over the average authorization of the 1890s.[4]

Over the next few years, the strength of the Corps continued to increase

TABLE 3.1   Allocation of Cadet Nominations, 1902

Source of Nomination	Allocation	Total (492)
Each congressional district (357)	1	357
Each state (45) at large	2	90
Each territory (4)	1	4
District of Columbia	1	1
United States at large	40	40

Notes: John Allan Mallory, *Compiled Statutes of the United States, 1913: Embracing the Statutes of the United States of a General and Permanent Nature in Force December 31, 1913* (St. Paul, MN: West Publishing Co., 1914), 932–33.

steadily. In 1903, a congressional reapportionment added about twenty cadetships. Oklahoma's admission to the Union in 1907 yielded a few more. In 1910, Congress authorized the appointment of a "successor cadet" from each congressional district once the currently appointed cadet reached his senior year; this change boosted the strength of the Corps to 629 cadets.[5]

The next major expansion, to 1,336 cadets, came in 1916 as the European war prompted concern about the state of American military preparedness. As shown in table 3.2, the bulk of the increase came from allocating a second cadetship to each congressional district and ninety cadetships each to the Regular Army and National Guard. Also, the United States-at-large allocation doubled to eighty cadetships, of which sixty were reserved for the president and twenty for "honor schools"—military preparatory schools with an army officer as the professor of military science and a high score on the most recent War Department inspection.[6] With minor exceptions, the authorized strength of the Corps remained stable until the mid-1930s, when the clouds of another world war gathered on the horizon.[7]

In 1935, Congress considered another major expansion of the Corps of Cadets. Most of the increase would come from increasing the number of appointees from each congressional district from two to three. There were many opponents among isolationist legislators who resisted calls for military expansion of any sort. Regardless, army leaders were persuasive. The proposed legislation, they argued, would compensate for the acceleration in age-related retirements among the World War I generation of officers. Additionally, it would increase the proportion of West Pointers in the officer corps, which had expanded sharply to lead American armies during the war with Spain and the First World War. Another argument was that West Point currently had excess capacity and therefore could give more young men the benefit of an excellent education and the opportunity to serve the nation. Finally, there was a question of equity between the services—the Naval Academy was twice the size of West

TABLE 3.2   Allocation of Cadet Nominations, 1916

Source of Nomination	Allocation	Total (1,336)
Each congressional district (435)	2	870
Each state (48) at large	4	192
Each territory (Alaska and Hawaii)	2	4
District of Columbia	4	4
Native Puerto Ricans	2	2
United States at large	80	80
President (60)		
Honor military school s (20)		
Regular Army	90	90
National Guard	90	90
Filipino cadets	4	4

Notes: Mallory, Compiled Statutes, 934; Annual Report of the Superintendent, 1916, 10–11.

TABLE 3.3   Allocation of Cadet Nominations, 1935

Source of Nomination	Allocation	Total (1,964)
Each congressional district (435)	3	1,305
Each state (48) at large	6	288
Each territory (Alaska and Hawaii)	3	6
District of Columbia	5	5
Native Puerto Ricans	3	3
Panama Canal Zone	1	1
United States at large	172	172
President (89)		
Vice President (3)		
Honor military schools (40)		
Sons of WW I veterans (40)		
Regular Army	90	90
National Guard	90	90
Filipino cadets	4	4

Notes: Annual Report of the Superintendent, 1936, 2. Foreign cadets are excluded in the table. Filipino cadets could be commissioned only into the Philippine Scouts.

Point even though the Navy's officer corps was smaller than the army's. Congress was convinced, and the bill became law on 7 June 1935.[8] Table 3.3 shows the new allocations, which expanded the size of the Corps to 1,964 cadets — an increase of about 43 percent.[9]

The entry of the United States into World War II led to another big increase

TABLE 3.4 Allocation of Cadet Nominations, 1942

Source of Nomination	Allocation	Total (2,500)
Each congressional district (435)	4	1,740
Each state (48) at large	8	384
Each territory (Alaska and Hawaii)	4	8
District of Columbia	6	6
Native Puerto Ricans	4	4
Panama Canal Zone	2	2
United States at large	172	172
President (89)		
Vice President (3)		
Honor military schools (40)		
Sons of WW I veterans (40)		
Regular Army	90	90
National Guard	90	90
Filipino cadets	4	4

Notes: Annual Report of the Superintendent, 1943, 1–2. Shortly after both the Second World War and the Korean War, Congress authorized the sons of servicemen killed in those conflicts to seek cadetships in the competitive category formerly reserved for the sons of servicemen killed in the First World War (who by then were too old to enter the Academy).

in the size of the Corps. In June 1942, Congress raised the cap to 2,500 cadets, primarily by adding one cadetship to each state, district, and territory, as shown in table 3.4. With this change in place, the size of the Corps would remain unchanged for the next twenty years.

Before moving on, it would be helpful to review the terminology that West Point admissions officers used to describe the sources of appointment to West Point starting in the early twentieth century. The appointment sources fell under two categories — "competitive" and "noncompetitive." The competitive category consisted of the cadetships reserved for the president, honor schools, sons of deceased World War I veterans, Regular Army, and National Guard. Available vacancies within each of these subcategories were filled by physically qualified candidates with the highest scores on West Point's written entrance exam. There were virtually no exceptions to this testing requirement, which allowed Academy officials to assess the candidates impartially and to admit only the most qualified.[10] Moreover, there was no limit to the number of young men who could seek these appointments.[11] Not surprisingly, Academy officials strongly endorsed this merit-based appointment system, which epitomized the egalitarian principles of West Point. Competitive appointments were virtually nonexistent in the nineteenth century, as Congress controlled all but the ten cadetships allotted to the president. Prior to World War II, they never exceeded

14 percent of the Corps' authorized strength, but they increased in number thereafter.

Noncompetitive appointments consisted of the cadetships reserved for the vice president, members of Congress, District of Columbia, Alaska, Hawaii, Puerto Rico, Panama Canal Zone, and the Philippines. Candidates in these subcategories were handpicked by the appointing official under criteria established by that official; there was no uniform method of qualification as there was for the competitive candidates. The appointing official nominated a principal candidate and several numbered alternates for each cadetship[12] If the principal was fully qualified, as measured by passing the West Point entrance exam or presenting an academic "certificate" (discussed later), then he entered with the next class and filled the vacancy. The principal did not have to score well on the entrance exam — all he had to do was pass it, and he was in. If he failed, then each of the numbered alternates, in descending order, was considered for the appointment; the first one with a passing score on the entrance exam or in possession of a valid certificate gained entry. Virtually all appointments in the nineteenth century and most in the twentieth century were of the noncompetitive type. In both centuries, the overall quality of the Corps of Cadets relied heavily on the appointing officials' commitment to selecting the best candidates.

To summarize, candidates for competitive appointments vied against each other, confident that their test scores would determine their fate objectively and fairly. Candidates for noncompetitive appointments received their nominations through an appointing official; although they still had to meet West Point entry requirements, they could do so with a minimal score, as opposed to the maximum scores required for the competitive candidates. As we will see, for many decades Academy officials tried hard to increase the proportion of competitive appointments and to establish policies that would yield higher quality noncompetitive candidates. Ironically, toward the end of the twentieth century the situation would be turned on its head, with the competitive sources of appointment yielding a preponderance of the lesser-qualified cadets.

II.   ATTRITION IN THE CORPS
THROUGH THE SECOND WORLD WAR

In his annual report of 1902, Superintendent Albert Mills reflected on the Academy's first principles. "The object of the Military Academy," he asserted, "is to make officers of the army, and, of course, to produce as high a type of officer as is possible." Toward this end, the Academic Board designed a curriculum "under the conviction that the development and training, both of character and the mind, in the greatest degree in the cadet should be its object."[13] Mills was advancing the consensus view that character and intellect were the two most important developmental goals at the Academy. They required the greatest investment in time and effort and promised the greatest payoffs for the army of the future.

With a clear understanding of the importance of their work, Academy leaders sought the most talented young men as cadets. They believed that Americans deserved the best possible product in return for their largesse in underwriting the Academy. They took seriously the responsibility of producing competent and loyal guardians of the nation, and they jealously guarded the vaunted reputation that the sons of West Point had established through its history.

Mills and his contemporaries believed that West Point's admission system was poorly designed to meet these priorities. Foremost among the problems was the congressional nomination process, which put a drag on the quality of the Corps of Cadets. While the record of West Pointers since the War with Mexico seemed to belie the concern about the mediocrity of the candidate pool, their success was more indicative of the excellent education they received at the Academy than the overall quality of the nominee cohorts. Attracting better candidates would allow the Academy to improve cadet performance, lower attrition, and provide the army with more and better officers. Virtually every superintendent of the late-nineteenth and early twentieth centuries commented on these issues and recommended solutions in their annual reports to the War Department.[14]

The noncompetitive appointment method, while popular in Congress, undermined the search for quality. Many congressmen used the nominations as a form of patronage and distributed them to the most influential candidates rather than the most deserving. Each one had his own method of selection, with criteria that did not necessarily accord with Academy priorities. The unfortunate results of this system were on display every year, as about half the nominees failed to pass the West Point entrance exam and returned home embarrassed and disappointed.[15] Of those who managed to pass the exam and become cadets, about 50 percent subsequently flunked out.[16]

Another reason for the surfeit of poorly qualified nominees was the Academy's notoriously low standards for admission. In 1812, Congress had required only that cadet candidates be "well versed in reading, writing, and arithmetic." Congress raised the bar in 1866 by adding English grammar, US history, and geography, but still the requirements were minimal.[17] The low entry standards were in keeping with the democratic principles of Americans. Any young man—rich or poor, influential or anonymous, well educated or not—would have an equal chance of attending the prestigious national school on the Hudson. That was the theory, at least. In practice, many well-meaning congressmen, swept up in the democratic Zeitgeist, were unrealistic about the academic capabilities of their nominees. They believed that the minimal statutory requirements, which almost any partially educated young man could meet, were good enough to judge the merits of their nominees.

While the statutory requirements for nominees were low, the entrance exam reflected the high standards that Academy leaders expected of cadets. Until 1870 the exam was oral, which allowed subjectivity in the grading. Afterward, nominees took a written test that faculty members graded anonymously to enhance objectivity.[18] By the late-nineteenth century, the entrance exam had turned into a mental marathon, encompassing a series of subject tests requiring three days to administer. The exam, as unforgiving as it was long, posed a formidable obstacle to admission.[19] The Academic Board refused to make accommodations for the lesser-prepared nominees and cadets. On the contrary, it ruthlessly enforced standards to cull the weak and maintain the institution's hard-earned reputation for excellence.

Predictably, many principal nominees failed the entrance exam. If the alternate nominees from those congressional districts also failed, there would be vacancies in the incoming class since there was no allowance for alternates from one congressional district to fill a vacancy in another.[20] Vacancies also occurred when a cadet flunked out after being admitted or when a congressman chose not to fill an allotted cadetship.[21] The difficulty of the entrance exam and the USMA curriculum kept the vacancy rate high. In the decade from 1904 to 1913, for example, vacancies ranged from 8 percent of authorized strength (1904) to 24 percent (1909); during the 1930s, the average vacancy rate was about 11 percent.[22] The Academy was producing fewer officers than the army needed and far fewer than it was physically capable of educating.

The conundrum of increasing the admission and graduation rates without lowering standards challenged Academy leaders well into the twentieth century. The obvious solution was to attract higher-quality applicants, and virtually every superintendent considered ways of doing this during his time in office. Unfortunately the noncompetitive appointment system presented a formidable obstacle to reform. One superintendent, frustrated by the weak academic credentials of the nominees, lamented that the "class of candidates sent here . . . is in the hands of the appointing powers alone."[23]

Although Congress would not alter the nomination system, it conceded an important point by giving the secretary of war the authority to prescribe the standards for admission starting in 1901. Nominees henceforth had to be proficient in whichever disciplines the secretary "may, from time to time, prescribe."[24] With the approval of Secretary of War Elihu Root, the Academic Board redesigned the entrance exam to cover the subjects of a standard high school curriculum: reading, writing, spelling, English grammar, English composition, English literature, arithmetic, algebra through quadratic equations, plane and descriptive geometry, physical geography (particularly of the United States), United States history, general history, and basic physiology and hygiene.[25] The change underscored the need for nominees to have a solid basic education that was available through a growing number of public high schools across the nation.

Empowered by the 1901 legislation, Root made another important change. He authorized the Academic Board to waive the entrance examination for nominees possessing a valid "certificate" of academic achievement.[26] The certificate movement started among state universities of the Midwest around 1870 and spread quickly across the nation. It was a powerful device in strengthening public high schools, which soon replaced the preparatory programs of individual colleges as the largest source of college-bound students. Under the certificate system, universities accredited high schools that met prescribed standards for college preparatory work. The graduates of these high schools received certificates attesting to their academic achievement. By 1900, almost 200 US colleges accepted certificates from high schools and each other, so West Point was simply keeping pace with developments in higher education when it also began accepting certificates in 1902.[27] Superintendent Mills strongly favored the change. Accepting certificates, he reasoned, would allow well-prepared students to continue their studies rather than making them "review elementary work, with consequent expense, loss of time, and, as usually occurs, attendance at some coaching school."[28]

The certificate experiment at West Point had a rough start. While the program was popular — about 70 percent of the cadets admitted between 1902 and 1907 presented certificates — it did not achieve the desired results. Certificate holders performed poorly relative to their classmates who had taken the entrance exam, precisely the opposite of what the Academic Board had intended. Superintendent Hugh Scott concluded in 1907 that a return to "reasonable and uniform entrance examinations" was the best way to ensure that incoming classes were prepared for the academic work expected of them.[29] He therefore prevailed upon the secretary of war to return to the policy of requiring the written entrance exam of all nominees.

When the vacancy problem still did not improve, the Academic Board decided to give certificates another chance starting in 1914. The War Department gave the necessary permission but set stricter conditions under which they could be accepted.[30] Unfortunately even the tighter standards did not bring the desired results. By the mid-1920s, the attrition rate for cadets who entered with certificates was more than double that of cadets who had passed the written entrance exam. Superintendent Fred Sladen reported that the disappointing performance of certificate holders resulted in "a necessary alteration" of parts of the curriculum to make it "more elementary."[31]

Despite these problems, certificates remained a prominent feature of the West Point admission system for the next two decades. There was really no choice given the widespread acceptance of certificates throughout higher education, but Academy leaders continuously suggested ways of raising the overall quality of the nominee cohort. There were three oft-heard recommendations. The first was to administer a preliminary test for the prospective nominees within their congressional districts — that is, to make noncompetitive appointments more competitive.[32] Members of Congress could still nominate whom they wished, but the test scores would provide a more accurate assessment of the qualifications of each applicant and make it harder to pass over someone with exceptional qualifications. A second recommendation was to seek legislation allowing the secretary of war to keep a list of qualified alternates with which to fill vacancies from any congressional district.[33] The third recommendation was to require a validation exam, shorter in length than the standard entrance exam, for anyone presenting a certificate. West Point was one of the few Eastern colleges not to require such a test, which would disqualify nominees whose certificates masked severe academic shortcomings.[34]

Eventually all three recommendations took hold, but only the last one did so before the Second World War. Starting in 1930, the War Department required nominees with high school certificates to take a short validation exam that assessed mathematical and verbal skills.[35] Nominees with college certificates were exempt under the theory that they already had shown the capacity for college work. The early results of the new policy were heartening. In academic year 1930–1931, the number of plebes separated for academic failure declined by about 30 percent from the previous year, and the trend continued through the decade. The cumulative results for the classes of 1934 through 1937, shown in table 3.5, were unequivocal. Nominees who took a written test — either the standard entrance exam or the validating exam — performed better as cadets than their peers who entered with a college certificate and therefore took no entrance exam.

These results confirmed once and for all that certificates had been a bad idea. While they may have had a salutary effect on the overall quality of American public education, they did not guarantee the quality of individual applicants to West Point. In the future, the Academy would rely increasingly on written tests to admit the best candidates and send the others home.

The predictive value of the written tests led to an expansion of their use. Starting with the class that entered in 1944, the War Department required the holders of all certificates — high school and college — to pass some form of validation exam. High school certificate holders took either the validation exam prepared at West Point or a similar test prepared by the College Entrance Examination Board. College certificate holders took the new West Point Ap-

TABLE 3.5   Comparison of Academic Performance by Method of Entry, Classes of 1934 through 1937

	No. Entered	No. Discharged	% Deficient
College certificate	566	174	30.7
Validation exam	306	59	19.3
Regular entrance exam	635	127	20.0

Note: *Annual Report of the Superintendent*, 1937, 2.

titude Test, one hour in length and composed of equal parts mathematics and English.[36] The West Point Aptitude Test was designed to substantiate basic analytical skills rather than require extensive study; nonetheless, it was an effective check on college students who lacked the credentials necessary to succeed at West Point. Ever since the changes of 1944, West Point has required every nominee to qualify for admission by taking a written test of one form or another.[37]

III.   POSTWAR CHALLENGES AND REFORMS

The outcome of the Second World War lent urgency to the Military Academy's business of developing leaders of character. Graduates could expect to face challenging professional environments in far-flung assignments around the world. The military needed the best that America had to offer, and the service academies were the training ground of the military's future leaders. There had never been a greater need to attract the highest quality candidates to West Point.

Unfortunately, the end of hostilities began a fifteen-year period of declining interest in the Academy. This development was due in part to the understandable desire of Americans to return to a normal way of life, including apathy toward all things military. Adding to the problem were US economic conditions — high wages and accumulated savings, in particular — which lessened the attraction of a free Academy education. For veterans seventeen through twenty-four years old, the GI Bill's educational benefits further diminished the Academy's appeal.[38] For the relatively few who were warm to the idea of a military career, other commissioning sources that were either shorter (Officer Candidate School) or less intense (Reserve Officer Training Corps) drew them away. Finally, the likelihood of extended overseas tours, many in undesirable places, was yet another drag on recruitment.[39]

The decline in interest seemed particularly steep because of a Selective Service Board policy that had swelled the number of young men seeking appoint-

ments during the war. A 1942 board ruling gave deferments to Academy nominees during the application process. Unsuccessful candidates could secure new
nominations for the following year's accession cycle, provided they were within
the age limit. Secretary of the Army Kenneth C. Royall noted in hindsight the
unintended effect of the board's policy. Many young men sought appointments
in a sincere desire to serve the nation as commissioned officers. Many others,
however, took advantage of the deferment opportunity "as a means of avoiding
or postponing induction and possible exposure to hazardous duty." This "painful fact" became evident with the suspension of the draft after the war and the
"complete reversal of the motivating interest in obtaining appointments."[40]

Despite a slight uptick in the strength of the entering classes of the late
1940s, subsequent developments insured a continuation of the recruiting
drought. The start of the Korean War in 1950 was a disincentive, particularly as
the conflict dragged on inconclusively. The founding of the Air Force Academy
a few years later and the spread of Reserve Officer Training Corps programs
across the nation created new competitors for young men with an interest in
the military. As a result, West Point classes routinely entered below their authorized strength. Under admissions procedures then in effect, roughly 3,000 to
4,000 nominees per year could seek qualification by taking the entrance exam,
yet the actual numbers were much smaller. Table 3.6 shows the disparity. From
1947 through 1959, no incoming class ever started with more than 89 percent

TABLE 3.6   Class Entry Data, 1947 through 1958

Class entering in	Authorized class strength	Number examined	Actual class strength (% of authorized)
1947	954	1,757	580 (61)
1948	824	1,884	655 (79)
1949	854	2,093	721 (84)
1950	957	2,299	792 (83)
1951	757	1,977	647 (85)
1952	816	1,942	668 (82)
1953	933	1,894	726 (78)
1954	1,048	2,003	749 (71)
1955	944	2,001	680 (72)
1956	913	2,067	762 (83)
1957	880	2,268	734 (83)
1958	942	2,467	806 (86)
1959	823	2,434	734 (89)

Note: Data compiled from the 1949, 1953, 1954, 1955, 1958, and 1959 editions of the *Annual Report of the Superintendent*.

of its authorized strength.[41] Given the four-year attrition of about 30 percent during this period, the number of officers West Point contributed to the army was considerably less than its legal authorization.

The situation now facing the Academy differed from the recruiting problems prior to World War II. Previously there were plenty of young men interested in West Point relative to the number of cadetships available. The problem then was one of standards — that is, how to adjust the admission system so that the best candidates received the coveted appointments. The problem after the war, however, was one of numbers. West Point was simply not attracting enough qualified candidates to fill each class to authorized strength. Affluence, war, and competition from other educational institutions were the principal forces creating the most challenging recruiting environment in the Academy's history.

The gravity of these problems spurred reform in five broad areas: (1) candidate testing, (2) the congressional appointment process, (3) criteria for assessing cadet candidates, (4) a preparatory school for enlisted soldiers, and (5) organizational structure. Reforms in the first four areas targeted cadet quality and the problem of high attrition. Reforms in the last area streamlined the Academy's admission efforts, strengthened its public outreach, and, most important, increased the number and the quality of young men who applied to the Academy. Collectively, these reforms represented a major break with the prewar system and gave West Point the modern recruiting and admission structures necessary to meet the demands of the postwar environment.

The first area of reform, candidate testing, was a logical extension of previous developments. As noted earlier, by 1944 every candidate had to take a written entrance exam of one type or another, but the multiple tests proved unwieldy to manage. Starting in 1950, the Academic Board substituted achievement tests in mathematics and English for the standard entrance exam and validation exam.[42] Additionally, every candidate now had to take a new West Point Aptitude Test, expanded in length from one hour to two-and-a-half hours. In 1956, the Academic Board jettisoned all of these tests in favor of the College Entry Examination Board's Scholastic Aptitude Test and math and verbal achievement tests. In making this change, the Academy closed a 150-year period during which it prepared and administered its own entrance examinations. The new tests proved to be excellent predictive tools in the admissions process, and the standardized formats allowed useful statistical analysis.[43]

The second area of reform — congressional appointments — actually started during the war. A provision of the 1942 expansion legislation empowered the secretary of war to fill every vacancy that existed on the date of admission of a new class. Two-thirds of the vacancies had to be filled with qualified alternates nominated by Congress; the other one-third would come from the competitive lists. Congress authorized the Academic Board to rank-order the two groups based on merit.[44] The new procedure was immediately effective in reducing vacancies while improving the quality of the Corps. For the class that entered in July 1943, there were 114 entry-day vacancies — roughly 11 percent of the authorized class strength. Those vacancies were subsequently filled with the most qualified alternates, many of whom had better qualifications than the principals who had entered ahead of them.[45]

Academy leaders welcomed these new procedures, but they desired more thoroughgoing reform. The first postwar superintendent, Maxwell Taylor, proposed a system whereby congressmen would nominate four candidates for each vacancy but allow the Academic Board to rank-order the nominees and admit the most qualified as cadets.[46] According to Taylor, both the congressman and the Academy would benefit under this system: "The congressman is assured that one of his boys gets into West Point and he has the assurance that the Military Academy thinks that the best of the lot . . . has been admitted."[47] Unfortunately for Taylor and his immediate successors, very few congressmen agreed to adopt the merit-based nomination system.

A turning point came with the arrival of Garrison H. Davidson, superintendent from 1956 to 1960. Convinced that the quality of the graduate depended largely on the quality of the appointee, Davidson wanted to insure that "no talented applicant for appointment will be turned away in favor of a less promising candidate."[48] Accordingly, he sent a personal letter to each member of Congress proposing a "congressional competitive method of nomination." Under the proposal, the Academic Board would work with congressmen to screen their applicants through competitive examinations in the home districts.[49] The Academic Board would forward the screening results confidentially to the congressmen, who would then make their nominations, presumably selecting the most qualified. Although Davidson had merely repackaged the proposals of his predecessors, his personal intercession had the desired effect. Ninety-three congressmen were using the congressional competitive method of nomination by 1960, and the number continued to rise under subsequent superintendents. By the end of the century, 85 percent of Congress had signed on to Davidson's system.[50]

A third postwar reform effort was to broaden the criteria for assessing cadet candidates to include more than just academic credentials. Superintendent Francis B. Wilby had complained during the war that the admission system gave no weight to other important attributes. "It is generally recognized," he noted, "that the best officers are not necessarily those who receive the highest marks on the entrance examinations or who stood highest in their academic work while at the Academy." To attract applicants better suited to military service, Wilby requested permission to consider athletic ability, leadership, and character development in addition to academic test scores. The War Department turned him down, fearing that such a system would lead to charges that appointments to West Point "were influenced by personal, religious, racial or physical characteristics."[51] Wilby's successor, Taylor, did not seek permission. He simply told the War Department that in borderline academic cases the Academic Board would give special consideration to candidates "whose previous histories showed desirable personal qualities such as capacity for leadership and stalwart character."[52] Although academic preparation would continue to be the most important consideration in evaluating candidates, reliance on non-academic measures soon would become a standard feature of the admission system.

An important example of the broadening of entry requirements was the establishment of physical fitness standards. For many years prospective cadets had undergone cursory physical screenings in conjunction with the written entrance exam, and a surprising number of young men washed out as a result.[53] Academy leaders took aggressive measures to raise the level of cadet fitness, but the situation begged for tighter admissions standards so that entering cadets would be more physically robust.[54] World War II brought the issue into sharp focus. The physical screening of candidates, noted Wilby, "fails to measure physical efficiency, a considerable number of entering cadets being physically weak, uncoordinated, and awkward."[55] These concerns prompted the Academic Board to establish a rigorous fitness test called the Physical Aptitude Examination, or PAE. First administered in 1947, the PAE measured a candidate's strength, coordination, endurance, speed, flexibility, and cardiovascular fitness.[56] The testing events focused on skills related to the demands of military life; hence, the score was a good predictor of a candidate's ability to complete the Academy's physical program. The PAE was immediately successful in raising the fitness level of the Corps by disqualifying physically weak candidates. With occasional modification (and a name change in 2006), it has remained a permanent feature of the West Point admissions system.[57]

The PAE was a straightforward method of assessing physical prowess, but evaluating a candidate's character, leadership potential, and motivation for service was far more subjective. Taylor therefore asked the War Department for help in better focusing the recruiting and selection effort. Specifically, he wanted army social scientists to help identify the personal qualities that would best predict success as a cadet and officer.[58] The War Department had conducted army-wide leadership studies during the war years, but Taylor's interest redirected much of the effort toward West Point. Researchers studied, among many other topics, the correlation between: candidate testing and academic success; cadet performance and officer success; physical fitness and aptitude for military service; and class standing and promotion to general officer. These studies influenced the Academy's methods of evaluating the leadership potential of candidates and complemented the extant evaluations of mental and physical aptitude.[59] They were valuable enough to induce West Point to establish its own centers of personnel research.[60]

Superintendent Davidson was the most influential in broadening entry requirements beyond academics. In 1957 he proposed a system to evaluate candidates' mental, physical, and leadership qualifications and admit those with the highest composite scores. The Academic Board had experimented with this method over the past few years and, according to Davidson, "some of our best all-around cadets" gained entry as a result. Conversely, he noted that many cadets admitted solely on account of their high written test scores "lack motivation or the qualities and attributes necessary for the development of leadership."[61] Davidson argued that the proposal would help West Point reduce attrition and thus achieve the goal of providing 50 percent of army's annual peacetime requirement for new officers.[62] Recognizing that he was tinkering with over one hundred years of tradition, he added, "Refinements will be made as experience is gained."[63] He needn't have worried.

The army approved Davidson's "whole-man" system, effective with the class entering in 1958, and it was an immediate success. The selection procedure assigned percentage weights in three categories — mental ability (60), physical aptitude (10), and leadership potential (30). Under the mental category, the results of a candidate's entry exam were combined with his high school rank to arrive at a composite score. The physical score was derived from the result of the PAE, and the leadership score combined extracurricular activities (sports, clubs, student government, scouts, etc.) and ratings by school officials. The whole-man system for evaluating candidates has remained virtually unchanged in the half-century since its inception.[64] It has withstood the scrutiny of researchers who have tried to pinpoint more accurately the predictors of success, and it continues to reflect the Academic Board's consensus on the relative priorities for cadet time and effort. The whole-man concept applied at first only to the competitive sources of appointment — president, honor schools, sons of deceased veterans, Regular Army, and National Guard. It expanded quickly, however, as Davidson's congressional competitive method of nomination gained acceptance among members of Congress.

Creation of a preparatory school for enlisted soldiers was the fourth major area of admissions reform.[65] The need arose from the 1916 expansion legislation that created eighty cadetships each for the Regular Army and National Guard. Gen. John J. Pershing established the first schools in France during World War I. They were hastily set up, lasted about a month, and succeeded in getting about 10 percent of the graduates into West Point.[66] Following the war, the army established preparatory schools in each corps area within the United

States and also in Hawaii, the Philippines, and the Panama Canal Zone. Up to one hundred soldiers started out at each of the schools, but typically fewer than ten did well enough to compete for the limited number of Regular Army and National Guard appointments to the Academy.

The decentralized preparatory schools operated more or less continuously until 1943, when the demands of war mandated a different approach. The solution was to send the soldier-candidates to civilian colleges, which at the time were begging for students.[67] For the next three years, the army sent soldiers to Lafayette College, Amherst College, and Cornell University for a ten-month program of study. Class sizes started out in the low hundreds, but exams and interviews whittled them down by two-thirds with the successful one-third taking the West Point entrance exam in late spring. Soldier morale on the campuses was high in large part because the male-female ratio was low. According to one survivor of the Amherst program, "the natives were friendly, young men were a scarce commodity and, unlike recent years, soldiers were treated well, and treated often."[68]

In 1946, Superintendent Taylor consolidated the army's schooling effort by establishing the United States Military Academy Preparatory School, or USMAPS, at Stewart Airfield in Newburgh, New York. He did what he could for the fledgling school, but there were many difficult challenges. Students arrived at irregular intervals and at various levels of proficiency.[69] Instructors were overworked as they tried to accommodate the individual needs of students. Facilities were crowded, and there was no athletics program to help release the students' pent-up energies. In 1957, USMAPS moved to Fort Belvoir, Virginia, under the command of the army's chief engineer officer. With more room and better facilities, the school gradually evolved into an effective educational institution. "Prepsters" took a two-semester curriculum consisting of high school English and math in the fall and college-level work in the spring. They benefited from a physical program of intramural and varsity sports throughout the school year.[70] Although USMAPS graduates had above-average attrition at West Point, their maturity and experience leavened the Corps and allowed them to fill a disproportionate number of leadership positions.[71]

The last area of postwar admissions reform was organizational structure. In a variety of ways, Academy leaders strengthened the staff and modernized its operations. Additionally, they bolstered outreach activities to raise public awareness of the Academy and broaden its appeal to prospective cadets. These advances occurred over several decades and the tenures of many superintendents, but once again it was Davidson who made the greatest contributions.

Prior to the Second World War, the Academy adjutant was principally responsible for running the admissions program. He and his small staff maintained candidate records, coordinated testing, kept track of vacancies, met the administrative needs of the Academic Board's admissions committee, and provided information to the War Department as necessary.[72] The job was never easy, and it grew increasingly difficult with increases in the size of the Corps and the number of appointment sources. By the end of the Second World War, it was clear that managing the admissions program needed more specialized attention. In 1946, as part of a major restructuring of the West Point staff, Taylor created the Office of the Registrar to assume primary responsibility for cadet and candidate records.[73] The registrar worked under the adjutant and relieved him of much of the burden of the admissions program, but the workload grew rapidly in the postwar era. He divided his focus between the records-management duties common to college registrars and the myriad responsibilities peculiar to Academy admissions.

Shortly after his arrival as superintendent, Davidson recognized the need for a staff agency dedicated solely to admissions. In 1958 he created a separate admissions office that was technically part of the Office of the Registrar but reported directly to him. Manning the admissions office were seven "carefully selected, very capable officers" whose mission was to advertise the opportunities available at West Point, identify worthy candidates, and assist them in the labyrinthine application process. To lead the new organization, Davidson asked for a senior military officer, assigned on a long-term basis, to provide experience and continuity of effort. Congress obliged the superintendent by establishing the position of director of admissions, which came with the rank and privileges of a permanent professor.[74]

With the establishment of the admissions office and its permanent director, West Point finally had a robust organization for managing the complex admissions process and promoting the Academy to the public. The admissions staff worked closely with high school and college counselors, West Point alumni societies, and the private Association of the United States Army to identify qualified young men. They coordinated with West Point liaison officers in major army commands worldwide to identify enlisted soldiers interested in seeking admission.[75] They worked closely with the Cadet Public Relations Council, through which cadets appeared before student and teacher conferences, Boys State conventions, Boy Scout camporees, and community organizations across the nation.[76] They were often on the road or the telephone communicating with prospective candidates and their parents, teachers, coaches, and ministers.[77] In short, the admissions office leveraged every opportunity to take the message of West Point to the public and stir interest in becoming a cadet. Never before had the Academy been so aggressive in this endeavor, but never before had the need been so great.

The expansion of the public-relations office was another organizational change that bolstered the admissions effort. West Point's first publicity office got its start in the mid-1920s, shortly after Inspiration Pictures filmed the movie *Classmates* at West Point. The film was a hit for Inspiration and a public-relations bonanza for the Academy. Superintendent Fred Sladen crowed, "The picture has put the Military Academy before the public in the best possible way, and has increased interest in it among the young men of the nation"; indeed, on the heels of the movie's release West Point experienced a noticeable increase in correspondence from potential candidates about entrance requirements.[78] The nascent publicity office coordinated media activity at West Point and pushed information to the public. In the years leading up to World War II, varsity sports became popular radio and newspaper fare, but many other activities — cadet interviews, faculty lectures, intercollege debates, glee club concerts, and so forth — also found a receptive audience.

After the Second World War, a newly reorganized Public Information Office went on a media blitz. It expanded its press-release network to three hundred newspapers, magazines, radio networks, and stations throughout the country. It leveraged the hot new medium of television to cover West Point events. In 1947 alone, seven football games were televised, as well as many other sporting and nonathletic events. Radio coverage continued for all football games and the many features of the prewar years. The approach of the sesquicentennial celebration in 1952 provided even more opportunities for media attention of all types.[79]

Academy leaders harnessed the media to help reverse the postwar recruiting slump. Blackshear Bryan, superintendent from 1954 to 1956, promoted public relations events involving cadets in venues around the country and cooperated with major media outlets to film at West Point. In 1955, for example, Hollywood produced *The Long Gray Line*, and a year later CBS premiered the *West Point* television series that ran for thirty-nine episodes and reached a weekly audience of 27,000,000 people.[80] In 1955, Col. Russell "Red" Reeder began publishing a series of novels chronicling the career of Cadet Clint Lane through his four-year West Point experience. The books were popular with young males and went through several printings.[81]

Superintendent Davidson took a personal interest in expanding the publicity effort. His goal was to show Americans the personal side of military life and encourage young men to consider West Point as an option for college and the army for a career. He appeared on several major television programs. On the Ed Murrow show, he brought along his wife and six children to convince skeptical Americans that military officers could lead normal family lives. He reinforced the message in an article entitled, "I Have 2,500 Sons," published in the *Saturday Evening Post*; similarly his wife contributed "My Two Families" for *The American Weekly*.[82] Other media forays included a 1957 Dell Comics series entitled "Cadet Gray," a "Walt Disney-type" cartoon movie about West Point, and an update of the recruiting film, "The Making of a West Pointer."[83]

The postwar reforms in the admissions system were an unqualified success. By 1960, the recruiting crisis was over as the number and quality of young men seeking entry rose sharply. The imminent coming of age of the baby boom generation made the picture even rosier, but the improved situation was not the result of demographic trends. West Point had undergone a quiet revolution in its methods of identifying and qualifying cadet candidates and in the way it interacted with the public. There were many indicators of the improvements. At the low point in 1954, only 92 percent of vacancies had a fully qualified candidate, and of course not all of them chose to matriculate; in 1961, fully qualified candidates represented 171 percent of available vacancies. The class that entered in 1962 amply demonstrated the quality gains of the previous few years. About 78 percent graduated in the top quintile of their high school classes, and 11 percent were valedictorians or salutatorians. Fifteen percent were student body or senior-class presidents, 29 percent were team captains, and 13 percent were Eagle Scouts. Their credentials stood out from those of the previous decade and served as a quality benchmark for subsequent classes.[84] Table 3.7 compares these impressive credentials with the bicentennial class of 2002 (entered 1998), another strong class.

From the standpoint of candidate credentials, the class that entered in 1962 was the best yet. The class benefited from the postwar admissions reforms and

TABLE 3.7   Comparison of Quality Indicators,
Class of 1966 and Class of 2002

Quality Indicator	Class of 1966	Class of 2002
SAT math	653	644
SAT verbal	640	624
Valedictorian	7%	6%
Salutatorian	4%	3%
Top quintile	78%	74%
Athletic team captain	29%	62%
Eagle Scout	13%	11%
Student body/class president	15%	18%
Boys State	20%	18%

Notes: Data compiled from US Military Academy, Institutional Self-Study: Report of the United States Military Academy (1999), 36, and Annual Report of the Superintendent, 1963, 63. The College Board recentered the scores of the SAT Math and SAT Verbal standardized tests in 1995; hence, the scores shown for the class of 1966 have been converted according to the "SAT I Mean Score Equivalents" chart on the College Board website (http://professionals.collegeboard.com/data-reports-research/sat/equivalence-tables/sat-mean). In the early 1960s, high schools normally had one captain per athletic team; in the 1990s, many high schools designated multiple cocaptains for each team. This difference probably accounts for the wide disparity in the category of "Athletic Team Captain" between the class of 1966 and the class of 2002. E-mail comments of Manley Rogers to author, 11 May 2010.

the strengthening of the academic curriculum (discussed in chapter 4). These cadets had heard President John F. Kennedy's stirring call to service. They grew up on the bright side of the world divide, certain that the military was a tool for advancing peace and justice. The war in Vietnam, which eventually would turn a generation of Americans against the military, was still only a faint ripple on an otherwise tranquil sea. One final advantage — the class of 1962 was one of the last to enter before the Corps would experience the largest expansion in its history, thus making the admissions job tougher than ever.

IV. BIG CHANGES IN CADET DEMOGRAPHICS

In 1961, army leaders began the process of seeking congressional approval for an expansion of the Corps to around 4,500 cadets. Superintendent William C. Westmoreland strongly favored the legislation and found an opportunity at the 1962 Army-Navy football game to enlist the support of President John F. Kennedy. The president sat on the Navy side of the field during the first half and then joined Westmoreland on the Army side for the second half. Noticing the difference in the size of the two student bodies, Kennedy asked the superintendent why there were so many more midshipmen than cadets attending the game. Westmoreland explained that the two academies were organized under different statutes, with Navy having an authorized strength double that of Army. He described the situation as "inequitable and certainly unjustified on the basis of differing requirements for officers." Additionally, the disparity gave Navy "2,000 more men to draw from for a football team." Westmoreland added with a smile, "That is one of the reasons we are getting the hell kicked out of us today."[85] Navy won the game 34–14, the fourth victory in a row over Army.

Congress passed the expansion legislation in March 1964, bringing the authorized strength to 4,417 — an increase of roughly 75 percent (table 3.8). The expansion proceeded gradually through 1971 in parallel with the construction of new barracks and the enlargement of the mess hall and academic facilities.[86] Upon reaching full strength, the Academy would equal the size of its sister academies and come closer to meeting the goal of providing 50 percent of the army's annual officer accessions.[87]

The most significant feature of the legislation, besides the raw numbers, was the large increase in competitive appointments. Previously they had numbered only 349, or about 14 percent of the Corps. The 1,700 competitive appointments (excluding foreign cadets) under the new law represented almost 40 percent of the Corps and gave the Academy a long-sought tool to enhance the quality of entering classes. Much of the gain came from the six hundred "con-

TABLE 3.8   Allocation of Cadet Nominations, 1964

Source of Nomination	Allocation	Total (4,417)
Congressional (2,693)		
Each congressional district (435)	5	2,175
Each senator (100)	5	500
Vice president	5	5
District of Columbia	5	5
Panama Canal Zone	1	1
Native Puerto Ricans	6	6
Guam, Virgin Islands, Samoa	1	1
Competitive (1,724)		
President	300	300
Army	680	680
Regular Army (340)		
National Guard (340)		
Sons of deceased veterans	40	40
Honor Schools	80	80
Sons of Medal of Honor recipients	unlimited	unlimited
Congressional qualified alternates	600	600
Foreign cadets	24	24

Note: *Annual Report of the Superintendent, 1964*, 65.

gressional qualified alternates" now authorized under a separate competitive category. Since each member of Congress could nominate up to ten cadets per vacancy, the pool of alternates was deep and the quality high.[88] The whole-man method of selection assured that appointments went only to the best alternates, many of whom were more qualified than the principal nominees of Congress.

Even the congressional appointment process was becoming more competitive. Members of Congress could use one of three methods in nominating young men for the academies. They could designate a principal and numbered (rank-ordered) alternates; a principal and unnumbered alternates; or the entire group as unnumbered nominees. As we have seen, more and more congressmen were choosing the third method, which allowed Academy officials to use whole-man criteria to select the most qualified candidates.[89]

The expansion seemed to come at a good time for the Academy. Recent reforms in the admissions process and the rise of the baby boom generation spread optimism that West Point could attract enough high-quality applicants to fill the new vacancies. For most of the 1960s, the optimism was justified. The admissions director, Robert Day, declared gleefully that West Point "has never been more popular with the young men of the country. For the past several years, we have had an estimated 20,000 young men competing for approximately 800 vacancies."[90]

Unfortunately the good times did not last. As the size of the Corps expanded steadily to its 4,417 end state, the effort required to maintain the quality of incoming classes increased proportionally. Compounding the challenge was the escalation of the war in Vietnam and the firestorm of protest it engendered over the next few years. The antimilitary sentiment on college campuses reflected virulent societal divisions over the nation's national security policies and the assumptions that underlay them. These developments made Superintendent Donald V. Bennett "deeply concerned about the decreasing size of the pool of interested, nominated, and qualified young men from which we can select new cadets."[91] The admissions data of the mid-1960s justified his concerns. In 1965, the year the United States began building up its combat force in Vietnam, West Point had its best recruiting year of the postwar era. There were 2,017 qualified nominees competing for 1,138 appointments—a very favorable quality ratio—and the mean scores on the math and verbal portions of the Scholastic Aptitude Test were the highest ever—660 and 650, respectively. Over the next three years, the most anguishing in Vietnam, the number of qualified applicants dropped by 25 percent despite the Corps' continued expansion toward its authorized strength. The nadir came in 1968, when West Point ran out of qualified nominees to fill the entering class.[92]

There were less obvious reasons, too, for declining interest in the Academy. Talented young men who might have considered applying to West Point increasingly had more college options. Whereas a free education traditionally had been one of the recruiting draws for West Point, many competitor colleges began offering generous scholarships to attract the best students. A survey of the class of 1971 revealed that 55 percent of cadets turned down solid scholarship offers from other institutions to attend West Point. Another issue was the length of the military service commitment, which Congress increased from four to five years in 1964. The extra year by itself would not have made a big difference to Academy recruiters, but it worked in concert with other disincentives to influence the minds of potential applicants and their parents. The Military Academy had traditionally appealed to young men inclined toward the military profession, but in the 1960s the opportunity costs of service were rising relative to other career alternatives.[93]

Bennett took bold steps to reverse the decline in applications. He increased the frequency of educator visits and hosted them for up to three days on each trip. During academic year 1967–1968 alone, 950 educators made the trip, with many "discovering that the 'real' Academy is quite different from the stereotyped image they brought with them."[94] Another initiative was the District Representative Program, which established an admissions field force of alumni volunteers in each congressional district. The representatives identified promising candidates and shepherded them through the admission process; additionally, they established cooperative relationships with local educators and sometimes accompanied them on trips to West Point.

Most significant, Bennett hired a new director of admissions, Manley Rogers, and charged him with developing more effective methods of outreach and recruitment. Rogers, thoughtful and soft-spoken, proved dynamic and innovative in his new job. He found many ways of spreading West Point's recruiting message, which emphasized education, opportunity for service, personal involvement, and moral commitment.[95] In 1969, he began sending promotional literature to National Merit Scholarship semifinalists and other populations of high-potential students. Also that year he began publishing the "Congressional Guide for USMA Admissions," which suggested screening techniques for selecting principal and alternate nominees. Another outreach effort was the nearly tenfold expansion of the Cadet Public Relations Council and its transfer of responsibility from the commandant to the admissions office. With about one-thousand cadets now involved in recruiting, the results were dramatic. By 1970, the number of qualified nominees exceeded that of 1965, and the quality of applicants was comparable.[96]

In 1971, Rogers augmented the District Representative Program with the Military Academy Liaison Officer (MALO) program consisting of eighty reserve officers scattered around the county. Each MALO had geographical responsibility defined by postal zip codes; in exchange for their service, they received retirement points and a week of active-duty training at West Point.[97] Since many of them were Academy graduates or former members of the West Point staff and faculty, the MALOs constituted a potent recruiting cadre that Rogers called the "best trained and managed college admissions force in the country." By the time Rogers retired in 1985, the admissions field force numbered over four hundred, of whom about 120 were MALOs.[98]

Rogers made the admissions process less daunting for applicants. His staff began publishing periodic bulletins that provided clear guidance for applicants and their academic counselors. He convinced the Academic Board to allow candidates to take either the Scholastic Aptitude Test or the newer standardized tests prepared by the American College Testing Program as the principal entrance requirement. Two years later, the Academy dropped the requirement for College Board achievement tests in math and verbal, which until then candidates had to take in conjunction with the Scholastic Aptitude Test.[99] In 1975, Rogers inaugurated the first of his annual summer "workshops" at West Point for 450 of the most promising prospects for the following year's class. A few years later he added an early admission program to encourage more of the very best candidates to accept their offer of admission.[100]

Another of Rogers's initiatives was minority recruitment, particularly for blacks. It was long overdue. Of the twenty-two black cadets admitted prior to US entry in the Second World War, only eight graduated. Between 1889 and 1918, not a single black man wore cadet gray, and none graduated between 1889 and 1936. The situation improved gradually in the 1940s, especially when President Truman ordered the armed forces desegregated in 1948.[101] Starting that year every entering class included blacks, but the numbers were very small; as late as 1968 there was a total of only thirty of them in the Corps. In that year, a black recruitment officer — a West Point graduate — joined the admissions staff and had astounding success in recruiting forty-seven young black men to join the next incoming class. A few years later, Rogers initiated Project Outreach to solidify the gains. The program augmented the admissions staff with eight minority officers (including one woman) whose mission was to travel widely and make contact with promising minority students.[102] An adjunct to Project Outreach was the Summer Enrichment Program, which employed minority cadets for many of the same purposes.[103] Their efforts helped to increase minority enrollments from about 5 percent of the Corps of Cadets in 1971 to about 20 percent by the end of the century.[104]

The most dramatic demographic change in the Academy's history occurred in 1976, when women joined the Corps for the first time. In many ways the event shook the institution to its foundations, but the admissions office was well positioned to respond effectively.[105] Rogers sent letters to high school counselors across the nation, seeking their assistance in identifying qualified women. More letters went out to the nearly 2,000 women who had applied for R.O.T.C. scholarships in the previous two years. Women candidates attended workshops at the Academy in January 1976 and follow-on workshops in February and March.[106] The process went smoothly enough that Academy leaders feared getting too many female applicants and having to make hard decisions about the gender composition of the Corps. As it turned out, the number was not overwhelming — 119 of the 1,479 freshmen in the class of 1980, or about 8 percent, were women.[107] Within a few years, women's representation in the Corps settled at around 15 percent, enough to ensure a "truly coeducational environment."[108]

The presence of a growing number of minorities and women required Academy leaders to think deeply about the optimal composition of the Corps of Cadets. There was no such need prior to the 1970s, as the Corps was entirely male and virtually all white. The focus of admissions officials had been to admit the most qualified applicants using the whole-man score as the yardstick; the lone exceptions were for congressional principal nominees (and numbered alternates) and recruited athletes, who needed only to meet minimal requirements to gain entry. As Congress demanded greater diversity in the Corps of Cadets, and as colleges nationwide adopted affirmative-action programs, questions about the composition of West Point's entering classes became more pressing. What percentage of the Corps should be female? How many minorities should be admitted and in what percentages? What other groups merited special treatment in admissions? To what extent should admission standards be relaxed if not enough qualified women, minorities, and special others applied?

With these questions in mind, Rogers and Jack M. Pollin, chairman of the Academic Board's standing committee on admissions, proposed a new policy for evaluating cadet candidates in late 1977. They consulted many sources for guidance, including academic studies on affirmative action, reports of educational foundations, and pertinent legal cases.[109] Another source was the report of the West Point Study Group, which examined the Military Academy following the cheating incident of 1976 and made many recommendations pertinent to admissions.

Rogers and Pollin's policy proposal reflected these sources. In conformance with latest thinking on affirmative action, it established a two-phased admissions process consisting of (1) determining a candidate's qualification for admission and (2) selecting cadets from among the qualified applicants to shape the incoming class. It established percentage goals for class composition in seven categories: scholars (15–20), leaders (10–20), recruited athletes (10–20), women (6–10), blacks (5–7), Hispanics (2–3), and other minorities (2–3). Under the proposal, once admissions officials identified the qualified candidates for an entering class, they could offer appointments with an eye toward meeting the class-composition goals. Rogers admitted that the staff work involved in establishing the goals had been contentious, particularly since the whole-candidate score already provided a method of assessing mental, physical, and leadership attributes. The debates "brought into sharp focus our inability to gain a consensus within the army as to a single set of criteria for officer candidate selection."[110] Nonetheless, the new policy was approved by Superintendent Andrew J. Goodpaster for implementation in 1978 and, by default, it became the army's policy for admitting cadets to the Military Academy.[111]

Following approval of the new policy on class-composition goals, Goodpaster formed a study group to make further refinements to the admissions system. The biggest changes were procedural, such as improved methods of coordination between the admissions office and other agencies, particularly the office of intercollegiate athletics.[112] There was no change to the underlying philosophy of the system. West Point admissions continued to operate on a two-phased, affirmative-action model designed to shape the Corps of Cadets into a better reflection of the army and society. In general, the system worked effectively to attract an abundance of high-quality applicants every year.[113]

TABLE 3.9 Class-Composition Goals, 1978, 1983, and 2009

	Goals (% of incoming class)		
Category	1978	1983	2010
Scholars	15–20	20–25	30
Leaders	10–20	20–25	30
Recruited athletes	10–20	20–25	18–23
Women	6–10	10–15	16–20
Blacks	5–7	7–8.5	8–12
Hispanics	2–3	3–4	7–9
Other minorities	2–3	2–3	4–6

Notes: Information on class-composition goals is found in various sources. For 1978, see "Academic Board Directive on the Qualification of Candidates," 7 December 1977, file 703–01, USMA admissions files, Prep School, Part II (1979), West Point Archives. For 1983, see Proceedings of the Academic Board 98 (1985), Tab AA, meeting of 27 November 1985. For 2010, see Vincent Lan and Gene Lesinski, "2014 Class Composition Goals," 25 June 2009, Institutional Research and Assessment Branch, Office of the G5, West Point.

Subsequent directors refined administrative processes, automated records, and updated promotional materials, but otherwise they preserved the system inherited from Rogers.

While the admissions system varied little overall, the class-composition goals underwent occasional changes. The three largest categories — scholars, leaders, and recruited athletes — grew to 20 to 25 percent by 1983 and remained at that level through 2009. The following year, the Academic Board increased the goal for scholars and leaders to 30 percent and the goal for women to 16 to 20 percent; concurrently, it reduced the goal for recruited athletes to 18 to 23 percent. Other changes are shown in table 3.9.

As the twentieth century drew to a close, two developments affected West Point admissions, both adversely. The first development stemmed from a 10 percent reduction in the authorized strength of the Corps of Cadets, starting with the 1995 entering class. Congress passed the legislation as part of the post-Cold War downsizing of the military, but then reversed itself a decade later as the military expanded to meet wartime commitments in Iraq and Afghanistan.[114] The downsizing of the Corps led to a parallel shrinkage in the size of the Academy staff, including in the admissions office. Unfortunately, the admissions staff did not recoup its losses when the Corps returned to its original size a few years later.[115] By the early twenty-first century, the admissions staff at West Point had dwindled to roughly half the size of the corresponding staffs at the Naval Academy and Air Force Academy.[116] The number of MALOs likewise declined, from a high of 350 in the early 1990s to just sixty-seven in 2010.[117] The admissions budget saw a similar reduction — 37 percent between

1999 and 2010, greater than that of any other program by far.[118] During those constrained years, the overall numbers of applicants to West Point remained high, but the ability of the admissions office to seek out the best candidates, particularly among hard-to-reach minority populations, declined sharply.[119]

The second development resulted from changes at USMAPS. In 1995, the army transferred command authority of USMAPS to the superintendent, after a break of thirty-eight years.[120] Along with the transfer came a major shift in the purpose of USMAPS. Previously, the school had catered primarily to promising enlisted soldiers, active and reserve, who sought officer commissions through West Point; henceforth, its principal purpose was to graduate candidates "in support of USMA's class composition goals," particularly in the categories of minorities and recruited athletes.[121] Enlisted soldiers still attended USMAPS, but their numbers dwindled gradually to about one-quarter of the total enrollment by the early 2000s. Conversely, the number of "invitational reservists"—that is, civilian students who enlisted in the army for the sole purpose of attending the preparatory school and who owed no service commitment if they dropped out—rose to about three-quarters of the enrollment.[122]

Coincident with these changes, army leaders lowered the entrance criteria for USMAPS. No longer could USMAPS admit soldiers who met minimum Academy standards but needed a year of academic brush-up before joining the Corps of Cadets. Under the new policy, USMAPS would admit only those candidates who were "unqualified for direct entry" into the Academy.[123] The policy was designed to increase the percentage of minorities, particularly African Americans, at West Point and to improve athletic recruiting for varsity teams. The practical effect was to reserve about 15 percent of the spaces in the Corps of Cadets for applicants who otherwise would have had a slim chance of entering the Academy under the whole-person criteria that governed the entry of most other candidates. On the bright side, the new policy succeeded in bringing more minority candidates to West Point.

IV.   RECRUITING ATHLETES

The adoption of class-composition goals diverged in important ways from longstanding priorities concerning cadet qualifications. Academy leaders had always considered intellectual development as one of the two most important goals of the West Point experience. (Character building was the other.) Evidence of this priority was apparent in the entrance requirements that put the greatest weight on academic credentials and test scores. After World War II, when physical fitness and leadership potential were added to the mix of entry criteria, academics continued to be preeminent. The whole-man system emphasized academics with 60 percent of the evaluative weight, and that percentage remained unchanged even in the face of significant demographic changes within the Corps. A body of research spanning several decades confirmed the wisdom of whole-man criteria by showing that intellect was the best predictor of success as a cadet and one of the best predictors (along with military aptitude scores) of success as an officer.[124]

The primacy of intellectual development led Sylvanus Thayer to structure the Military Academy as a four-year undergraduate experience rather than a European-style academy that focused more on military skills. While West Point's leaders and graduates often debated the contents of the curriculum, they never seriously questioned the priority given to intellectual development.[125] That is not to say that leadership and physical fitness were unimportant; as we have seen, Academy leaders eventually found ways of measuring those qualities in candidates. Still, the entrance qualifications and allocation of time and resources at the Academy clearly reflected the emphasis on academic achievement.

Given the importance of intellectual developmental, one might assume that class-composition goals would favor cadet candidates of high academic achievement. As we have seen in table 3.9, however, that was not the case for many years. From 1983 through 2009, the Academy admitted as many candidates categorized as "leaders" and "recruited athletes" as "scholars."[126] Favoring candidates whose salient quality was leadership made sense at a military academy; less justifiable, however, was the admission of up to 300 recruited athletes per year.[127]

Recruited athletes are the raw material for West Point's varsity squads, which could not compete at the national level without them. The cost to the army, however, is considerable. While many recruited athletes are exceptional young men and women who would gain entry without preferment, most of them owe their appointments to the ability to throw a football, dribble a basketball, or hit a home run better than their peers. In 1984, Manley Rogers told an elder graduate concerned about the football team's poor record that West Point "enrolls more low scoring [on entrance exams] athletes than do the Air Force and Naval Academies combined."[128] One hopes that Rogers was explaining rather than boasting, but either way it was clear that class-composition goals allowed many talented athletes to win appointments to West Point despite having relatively poor academic credentials.

For most of the twentieth century, Academy leaders strived to make the appointment system more competitive. Their intent was to improve the quality of incoming classes and thus provide the army with "as high a type of officer as is possible."[129] The biggest obstacle was the congressional nomination process, which allowed candidates to gain entry by meeting minimum standards;

in contrast, candidates vying for appointments under the competitive method confronted a merit-based system that allowed entry to only the most qualified applicants. Academy leaders worked hard to raise competitive standards, and they were largely successful. By the late-twentieth century, most members of Congress accepted the wisdom of competitive nominations and ceded the privilege of naming principal nominees and numbered alternates.

Given the century-long crusade to strengthen admission standards through greater competitiveness, the preferment afforded recruited athletes seemed incongruous. Like all candidates, athletic recruits had to obtain a nomination. But unlike other candidates — except the few remaining congressional principals and numbered alternates — they needed only to meet minimum Academy standards, which have never been high, to gain entry.[130] Moreover, in later decades the selection of recruited athletes was left to the athletics director and his coaches, all civilians.[131] Although they were instructed in the whole-candidate qualities the Academy seeks in cadets, the impulse to field winning teams weighed heavily in the selection process. Accordingly, given the choice between a lesser athlete with a high whole-candidate score and a superior athlete with a marginal whole-candidate score, coaches virtually always selected the latter. This was true even though the former candidate had more of the qualities the institution deemed important for officership, as reflected in the higher whole-candidate score.

Comparative scores on standardized tests illustrated the quality gap between recruited athletes and the rest of the Corps of Cadets.[132] For the classes that entered in 2004, 2005, and 2006, the average SAT scores for recruited athletes trailed the average score of their nonathlete classmates by wide margins, as shown in table 3.10. Similar differences appeared using the whole-candidate score, high school class rank, and virtually every other comparison other than aptitude in the sport of interest. To be fair, other groups — women, blacks, Hispanics, and Native Americans — also received preferential treatment in admissions. The presence of these groups in the Corps, however, reflected the nation's commitment to affirmative action and helped to bring cadet demographics more in line with the composition of the army and society. The admission of recruited athletes satisfied neither concern directly.[133]

In the context of modern American intercollegiate athletics, there was nothing unusual about the data in table 3.10. Many studies have documented the preferential treatment afforded athletes not only at Division 1 schools, but also at lower competitive levels.[134] Collectively, the literature made three main points. First, recruited athletes were far less qualified than other college applicants yet are far more likely to win acceptance. No other group, including minorities and "legacy" students (the sons and daughters of prior graduates), had as great an advantage. Second, recruited athletes, once enrolled, signifi-

TABLE 3.10   Comparison of Average SAT Scores between
Freshmen Recruited Athletes and All Other Freshmen
(combined averages for 2004, 2005, and 2006)

Team	SAT Average	Difference
All freshmen, excluding recruited athletes	1299	—
All freshmen recruited athletes in:		
Men's basketball	1167	−132
Football	1168	−131
Baseball	1173	−126
Men's track and cross country	1243	−56
All other men's teams	1212	−87
Women's track/cross country	1218	−81
Women's basketball	1221	−78
All other women's teams	1208	−91

Notes: Information provided by the Institutional Research and Analysis Branch, Office of Policy, Planning, and Analysis, West Point. Similar information appears in Academy's institutional self-study report for athletic certification. US Military Academy, "2007–2008 Division 1 Athletics Certification Self-Study Report," May 2008, West Point Archives, 47.

cantly underperformed their nonathlete peers academically. Third, while the number of recruited athletes varied from school to school, the role of athletics in the admissions process was huge, and coaches had great influence in gaining admission for favored athletes.[135] The athletic recruiting process at West Point exhibited all three of these trends to varying degrees.

West Point has recruited athletes for a long time. It started in the years after the Academy fielded its first football team in 1890. The sport was a nationwide phenomenon, and college coaches across the land sought the best talent for their teams. The coaches at West Point were no different. They worked hard to get selected players nominated, but the effort ran afoul of the Academy's efforts to raise academic standards. That changed when Douglas MacArthur became the superintendent in 1919. He strongly believed that athletic prowess was an essential element of successful leadership, and he favored football because it included violent bodily contact. He also believed that intercollegiate athletics would develop cadet competitiveness, attract more candidates, and generate positive media attention. According to his adjutant, William Ganoe, MacArthur recognized the potential drawbacks but concluded, "We must be realistic. We must take advantage of things as they are, so long as the end and aim are right."[136]

Athletic recruiting continued after MacArthur left the Academy, although the practice was embedded in the congressional nomination system and therefore obscured from view. Coaches, alumni, and other boosters scouted promising players and then lobbied sympathetic congressmen to give the athletes the nominations.[137] The prevalence of the noncompetitive appointment method was an advantage because it obviated the need for athletes who excelled at academics. Once a recruit received a nomination, he needed only to achieve a passing grade on the entrance exam or present a certificate—just like all other congressional principals and numbered alternates. Not surprisingly, the drop-out rate for athletes was high. For example, in January 1934, only weeks after Army defeated Navy for the fourth straight year, twenty-one plebe football players were separated for academics. Eleven had competed at the collegiate level previously and included a player described by a prominent sportswriter as "one of the best backs who ever entered the Academy." In pondering what might have been, the sportswriter commented impishly, "It would seem that the authorities are still more interested in turning out intelligent officers than in turning out football teams."[138]

The arrival of Earl Blaik as the head football coach in 1941 brought athletic recruiting to a new level. He was effective in bringing top talent to West Point through the help of influential friends who served as intermediaries with Congress.[139] Additionally, he recruited players from other college teams during the war years, and the Selective Service cooperated through its policy of exempting Academy nominees from immediate military service. Many of the recruited players gained entry as qualified alternates to fill entry-day vacancies under the 1942 expansion legislation.[140] The inflow of football talent at West Point (and the outflow at all other colleges) helped Blaik field three undefeated teams from 1944 through 1946 and win two national championships. In the process, he mythologized football at West Point for decades to come.

In most years, Blaik recruited eighteen to twenty-four players for the football team.[141] He realized, however, that the ever increasing competitiveness of collegiate football required a correspondingly greater commitment from the Academy. He struggled constantly with Academy leaders to increase the number of recruits, particularly because the rigors of cadet life took a high toll on the team—only 30 percent of the athletes recruited for football earned a varsity letter.[142]

In 1958, Superintendent Davidson expanded the recruiting effort with the intent of putting all intercollegiate sports on an equal footing and raising their collective competitiveness. He reserved a total of seventy-five vacancies—roughly 9 percent of the incoming class—for recruited athletes. Blaik tried to get thirty-five of the slots for football, but Davidson would allow only twenty-eight. Blaik chafed at the "equality for all sports" policy. He accused the superintendent of basing his thinking "on the days when the Army football schedule did not compare in toughness with what the cadets take on today."[143]

Perhaps he was right. But Blaik's singular focus on football blinded him to Davidson's higher purpose of doing what was best for the Corps of Cadets rather than what was best for the football team. It was this same purpose that led Davidson to implement the whole-man policy to improve candidate quality and optimally balance the strengths of the Corps.

Blaik lost the contest with the superintendent in the near term and retired at the end of the 1958 season. In the long term, however, his views on the importance of athletics in general and football in particular took firm hold at the Academy. Part of the reason for his continuing influence was the contrast between the quality of his teams and those that followed. Once Blaik retired, Army football began a gradual decline from which it has never recovered. The decline was particularly noticeable during four losing seasons ending in 1976 — the same year as a major cheating incident and the start of a series of reviews on every aspect of Academy operations.

The West Point Study Group conducted the most thorough and influential review. In the area of intercollegiate athletics, it called for a much-needed overhaul that would upgrade athletic facilities, remove ineffective coaches, and improve the business side of the operation. Academy leaders moved aggressively to fix the problems, but in the process they unwittingly weakened the Academy's commitment to improving the quality of the Corps in the most important developmental areas. Instead, they invested unprecedented time, money, effort, and, most important, cadet appointments, to the goal of being more competitive in collegiate sports. Whereas recruited athletes represented about 10 percent of the Corps by the late 1950s, they were almost 25 percent by the mid-1980s. By the end of the twentieth century — and especially during the first decade of the twenty-first — intercollegiate athletics had reached a level of priority on par with academics and military training.

The heightened emphasis on intercollegiate athletics was most obvious in the Academy's class-composition goals. Prior to implementation of the goals in 1978 (for the class graduating in 1982), the athletics director had to seek the Academic Board's approval each time he wanted to admit recruited athletes who would not have been able to gain entry on their own merit. The requests irritated the Academic Board members, who resented "our annual conflict between the best young men on the waiting list and the additional special interest athletes."[144] To ease the tension, the athletics director worked hard to find athletes with reasonably strong whole-person scores. Once class-composition goals were established, however, he had less reason to be as scrupulous in the recruitment process. The athletics director now controlled a sizable percentage of the cadetships in each incoming class. Provided his recruits could meet the minimum standards, the Academic Board could not bar them from entry. This was true even when the candidates on the national waiting list had far higher whole-candidate scores, as was usually the case.[145]

An oft-heard reason for the emphasis placed on intercollegiate athletics at West Point was the benefit of free media exposure. Football games, especially between service academies, were big publicity events. Their effectiveness as a recruiting tool for admissions was unclear, however. West Point's own research documented the reasons why applicants considered the Academy as a college choice, and the presence of a Division 1 athletics program hardly registered on the surveys.[146] Admissions trends confirmed the research. The number and quality of applicants to the Academy did not correlate closely to the fortunes of army sports in general or army football in particular. During the first decade of the twenty-first century, for example, the number of applications to West Point remained high despite a long string of losing football seasons. The admissions director from 1995 to 2008 put it bluntly.

> In my opinion — and that's over a lot of years of experience — I have never had a non-football player candidate ask me what the record of the Army football team was. Kids want to come here because of the academics, the leadership training, and the desire to be army officers. . . . They don't come here because it's a great party school or a school that has a winning football tradition. They don't care about that.[147]

The preferment of recruited athletes in the Academy's admissions system was hard to explain objectively. It was not justified by their performance as cadets; although there were many exceptions, athletes generally ranked at or near the bottom of the class.[148] Nor was the preferment justified by athletes' retention on active duty once commissioned; once again there were many exceptions, but overall the attrition of recruited athletes exceeded virtually every other population.[149] Finally, it was not justified by the athletes' contributions as officers, as measured by attainment of high rank; army studies completed in the early 1950s suggested that high academic achievement was far more contributory to becoming a general officer than high athletic achievement.[150]

More recent evidence confirms the deleterious effect of athletic recruiting on the quality of the Corps of Cadets and, by extension, the officer corps. In 2009 and 2010, the Academy's institutional research office compiled a list of graduates from the classes of 1978 through 1989 who had reached or surpassed the rank of colonel.[151] The data revealed that only 13.5 percent of the colonels and generals in those classes were recruited athletes (table 3.11).[152] In none of those years did the percentage of recruited athletes who achieved the rank of colonel or above exceed the percentage of recruited athletes within the class; in most years, the shortfall was significant.[153] While the information in table 3.11

TABLE 3.11   Performance of Recruited Athletes in Achieving the Rank
of Colonel or Above, West Point Classes of 1978 through 1989

Class	Class Size upon Entry	Class-Composition Goal for Recruited Athletes (%)	Class-Composition Achieved for Recruited Athletes (%)	No. of Colonels and Generals	No. of Recruited Athletes among Colonels and Generals	% of Recruited Athletes among Colonels and Generals
1978	1,435	none	—	135	25	18.5
1979	1,435	none	—	131	11	8.4
1980	1,496	none	—	123	17	13.8
1981	1,470	none	—	152	13	8.6
1982	1,404	10–20	19	155	22	14.2
1983	1,405	10–20	18	130	17	13.1
1984	1,452	15–20	24	105	17	16.2
1985	1,527	15–20	24	119	11	9.2
1986	1,420	15–20	23	112	18	16.1
1987	1,428	20–25	20	106	21	19.8
1988	1,400	20–25	21	44	6	13.6
1989	1,425	20–25	20	2	0	0.0
Totals				1,314	178	13.5

Notes: Information in the first, third, and fourth columns is in *Proceedings of the Academic Board 98* (1985),
Tab AA, meeting of 27 November 1985. Class-composition goals were established in late 1977 and first
used to shape the class of 1982; hence, there were no class-composition goals for the classes of 1978
through 1981. Information in the second, fifth, sixth, and seventh columns came from the Institutional
Research and Analysis Branch of the Office of Policy, Plans, and Analysis, West Point. The data on general
officers was provided on 20 November 2009; for colonels, on 12 February 2010. At the time the data was
generated, only the classes of 1978 through 1984 had general officers. The classes of 1988 and 1989 were
in the primary zone of consideration for promotion to colonel; hence, the numbers of colonel and general
officers in those classes are sure to increase in subsequent years. It is possible that the percentages in the fourth
column ("Class-Composition Achieved for Recruited Athletes") are too low. For example, the Academy's
1989 accreditation report lists the following percentages as class-composition achievements: class of 1988:
25 percent; class of 1989: 26 percent; class of 1990: 29 percent; class of 1991: 30 percent; class of 1992:
27 percent. *Institutional Self-Study 1988–1989: Report to the Commission on Higher Education of the Middle States
Association of Colleges and Schools*, 60, West Point Archives. To be consistent and conservative in my analysis,
I chose to use the lower percentages found in the *Proceedings of the Academic Board*, as cited earlier.

does nothing to explain why recruited athletes were poorly represented at the
highest ranks, it suggests that their preferment in the Academy admissions process was unwarranted. The specialized talents that recruited athletes brought to
West Point seemed to be valued less in the army than the whole-person qualifications of their classmates.

There were many recruited athletes who had strong overall credentials,
performed well as cadets, remained on active duty for a long time, and rose to
the highest officer ranks. These facts have often made the discussion of institu-

tional standards subject to emotion, especially given the consensus about the potentially developmental nature of athletics and their historic place at West Point. The object here is not to suggest that West Point should withdraw from varsity sports; rather, it is to expose the high cost of putting the intercollegiate athletics program on par with developmental activities more central to the mission of the Military Academy. Prior to the last years of the twentieth century, Academy leaders affirmed unequivocally the primacy of character and intellect as the most essential developmental goals of the cadet experience. While not dismissing the importance of other developmental activities, they understood that character and intellect were the most difficult human qualities to nurture and had the greatest long-term payoff for the army. The focus on character and intellect set West Point apart from other commissioning sources, enhanced the reputation of its graduates, and provided the most potent answer to those who criticized the high cost of an Academy education.

Intercollegiate athletics have long been an important part of the West Point experience and, for the most part, have had a healthy developmental influence on cadets. At their best, the "fields of friendly strife" provided all the benefits touted by MacArthur during his tenure as the superintendent.[154] Late twentieth-century trends in American sports, however, made the positive benefits more difficult to achieve. College athletics became increasingly professionalized, commercialized, and part of a thriving sports entertainment industry, particularly in popular sports like football and basketball. The results for spectators were all positive — heightened competitiveness, greater consumer choice, and a more exciting show. Athletic professionals — administrators, coaches, trainers, sportscasters, sportswriters, NCAA officials — also reaped handsome rewards. The benefits for athletes and educational institutions, however, were not so clear.[155]

Winning and losing in a hyper-professionalized and hyper-commercialized environment have consequences that can overwhelm the developmental purpose of sports. An athlete serious about competing in such an environment is more likely to specialize in a single sport rather than diversify in several; moreover, the athlete is less likely to excel in academics or participate in extracurricular activities. While specialization is essential for professional athletes, it is contrary to the assumptions undergirding the Academy's whole-candidate assessment methods and the design of its broad-based core curriculum.

During the last decades of the twentieth century, intercollegiate athletics assumed a level of importance that undermined institutional priorities and lessened the overall quality of the Corps of Cadets. Righting the priorities probably would mean competing in some sports at a lower level, one that would allow the Academy to recruit players whose whole-candidate scores are on par with their cadet peers. Doing so would be a logical conclusion to the Academy's century-long campaign to raise standards and graduate the best possible officers for the army.

★ ★ ★

For most of the twentieth century, Academy leaders labored to improve the quality of the Corps of Cadets. While some initiatives proved ill advised, the effort overall was successful. An increasing share of appointments was made on a competitive basis as members of Congress ceded the privilege of rank-ordering their candidates. New testing methods proved reliable in qualifying the best candidates. Adoption of the whole-candidate evaluation system populated the Corps with talented, well-rounded cadets. Toward the end of the century, affirmative-action initiatives helped the Academy honor the nation's commitment to equal opportunity and bring the Corps of Cadets into alignment with demographic trends in the army and society.

The elevation of intercollegiate athletics caused incongruity in the admissions system. This relatively new phenomenon diverged from the Academy's historic and generally successful efforts to improve the quality of the Corps of Cadets. Moreover, it answered to misplaced institutional priorities rather than the needs of the army or the developmental needs of cadets.

CHAPTER FOUR

The Athenian Academy

ACADEMICS

A T THE BEGINNING of the twentieth century, the academic program at West Point looked much the same as it had for the previous eighty years. The success of Academy graduates as leaders in war and peace had convinced the cadets' paternal guardians that the curriculum was as close to perfection as humanly possible. It was the best tool, they believed, for developing character and intellect, the two distinguishing qualities of the West Point graduate. Consequently, cadets in 1900 continued to go to class in small sections, take precisely the same mathematics-based curriculum, recite every day for a grade, and adhere to strict standards of appearance and behavior in the classroom. They had little choice but to succeed, as failure in any subject virtually always resulted in dismissal from the Academy. The result, not surprisingly, was a high rate of attrition throughout the nineteenth century and most of the twentieth.

By the early twenty-first century, small sections were still the norm at West Point. In most other ways, however, the academic program differed markedly from its nineteenth-century forebear. The curriculum balanced mathematics, science, and engineering on the one hand with the humanities and social sciences on the other. Cadets took fewer courses than before, but the material was more challenging and diverse. They no longer were constrained by a totally prescribed curriculum; instead, they could choose from a list of hundreds of electives in dozens of academic majors. Additionally, they benefited from a broad range of academic enrichment activities, including many opportunities for overseas study and travel. Inside the classrooms, instructors departed from the stiff pedagogical methods of the past and embraced Socratic techniques to engage cadets in stimulating intellectual discussions. Their ability to lead such discussions owed largely to their graduate schooling, which became a requirement for employment as a faculty member following World War II.

As the curriculum grew more challenging and complex, the Academic Board became less attritional in its approach to academically weak cadets. New policies following a major cheating incident in 1976 allowed second and even third chances to cadets who failed courses. This trend, which paralleled the waning of attritional attitudes in leader development and character building, peaked in the early 2000s. At that point, a cadet could fail multiple courses and still graduate, provided he or she demonstrated leader potential in other areas and could eventually pass the failed courses. Academy leaders of an earlier era would have condemned such leniency as a weakening of the intellectual standards that had long characterized West Point. They would have to admit, however, that cadets of the modern era received an education the quality of which had never been better.

I. ACADEMICS THROUGH THE FIRST WORLD WAR

In the latter decades of the nineteenth century, West Point transitioned from being a school of civil engineering to an institution for developing highly educated leaders of character schooled in a variety of disciplines. The shift was inevitable given the explosion of knowledge in every technical discipline and, for the practitioners of those disciplines, the need for specialized graduate study. Research universities assumed the principal role of creating, classifying, storing, and transmitting the new knowledge.[1] Meanwhile, educators at the undergraduate level rejected the notion that a collegiate student could master all the knowledge worth knowing; consequently, they discarded prescribed curricula and allowed greater student autonomy in selecting courses for study.

Despite these trends in higher education, the curriculum at West Point during these years continued to be prescribed and highly technical. Academy leaders had designed it under the conviction that the development of "character and mind, in the greatest degree," should be the object of the Academy.[2] The quantitative disciplines, they believed, were the best tools for instilling mental discipline, which cadets developed through individual effort in grappling with theoretical problems. The curriculum therefore emphasized "a thorough study of principles" rather than the application of those principles in practical subjects. Graduates equipped with mental discipline would have the intellectual foundation to advance their learning and "become originators and developers, and not mere craftsmen in their scientific work and profession."[3]

Given West Point's educational philosophy, there were few changes to the academic program at the start of the twentieth century. A "new" curriculum, unveiled in 1902 and implemented in academic year 1903–1904, added a lecture course in military hygiene and expanded existing instruction in English and Spanish (table 4.1). Room for these additions came through modest cuts in mathematics and French. These changes were not enough to satisfy the Academy's many critics, who called for broadening the curriculum beyond its heavily technical base.[4]

Albert Mills, superintendent from 1898 to 1906, was one of the critics. While he welcomed the changes of 1902, he wanted closer coordination among existing courses and better adaptation of those courses "to the present needs

TABLE 4.1 Curriculum for Academic Year 1903–1904 (Approved in 1902), Segregated into Academic (top) and Professional (bottom) Subjects

	Fourth Class (1st year)	Third Class (2nd year)	Second Class (3rd year)	First Class (4th year)
Academic Subjects	Mathematics (algebra, geometry, trigonometry)	Mathematics (geometry, calculus)	Natural and Experimental Philosophy (mechanics, wave motion, astronomy)	Civil and Military Engineering and Science of War (fortifications, structures, military tactics)
	English Composition and French	French and Spanish	Chemistry, Mineralogy, and Geology (chemistry, physiology, hygiene, heat, electricity, magnetism, minerals and rocks)	Law
		Drawing (plane geometry, topographical drawing, sketching)	Drawing (landscape, mechanical, and architectural drawing)	History and Historical Geography
Professional Subjects	Tactics (infantry, siege, and light artillery)	Tactics (infantry, cavalry, light artillery)	Tactics (infantry, cavalry, light, and sea coast artillery)	Tactics (infantry, cavalry, artillery, applied tactics)
	Physical Education (fencing, bayonet)	Practical Military Engineering (surveying)	Practical Military Engineering (bridges, gun platforms, revetments, obstacles)	Practical Military Engineering (siege works, bridges, demolitions, reconnaissance)
	Military Gymnastics		Military Hygiene	Ordnance and Gunnery

Note: Official Register of the Officers and Cadets of the U.S. Military Academy, 1904, 31–32.

of the service"—a reference to the army's new responsibilities as a constabulary force in the territories seized from Spain. Moreover, he believed the curriculum was "overloaded" with theoretical subjects, particularly mathematics, and preferred greater instruction in history, English, and other courses of more practical value. Scaling back the academic curriculum would provide more time for physical training and athletics, which Mills thought should be required of all cadets rather than only fourth classmen. Finally, he sought to move the course in Spanish to the senior year so that graduates would be more proficient in the language prior to their assignments in the territories newly acquired from Spain.[5]

In 1905, Mills pressed the Academic Board to consider his proposed changes. The board members gave ground grudgingly, agreeing to the changes only by starting the plebe year three months early; the expanded schedule lasted only a few years before the War Department directed a return to the 1902 curriculum.[6] Regardless, Mills's constant prodding served as a counterforce to the conservatism of the Academic Board, which gradually accepted the need for greater diversity in the curriculum. In 1908, for example, the Department of English and History was established to consolidate instruction in those two disciplines. This new organization, headed by a civilian scholar from Yale, controlled only a small portion of the curriculum; in time, however, its successor organizations would provide substantial instruction in the humanities and social sciences.[7]

Another of Mills's concerns was pedagogy. The teaching methods then in place dated back to the time of Thayer and reflected the paternalism that guided every aspect of cadet life. The section room was as much a venue for instilling military discipline as mental discipline. Cadets came to class in high-collared tunics, stood at attention until the instructor allowed them to sit, and conformed to rigid classroom protocols. Instructors required cadets "to keep an upright soldierly position of attention" during recitations. They corrected cadets who used "their hands or pointers improperly," acquired "peculiar or nervous habits" while reciting, or demonstrated "any want of neatness in dress or appearance."[8] While these standards succeeded in producing well-ordered cadets and classrooms, their effectiveness in promoting learning was open to question.

Strict classroom discipline went hand in hand with strict methods of teaching. Instructors expected cadets to come to class having mastered the "advance work"—that is, new material presented in the previous night's homework. At the beginning of every class, they graded cadets on the advance work through oral recitations and written quizzes. They devoted the rest of the class to answering questions and exploring the topic of the lesson more fully. Occasionally they might preteach a particularly difficult topic prior to in-class grading, but in general they expected the cadets to work through the material on their own.[9] These pedagogical methods placed a heavy burden on the cadets and contributed to West Point's high attrition rate.

In 1905, the Department of Mathematics experimented with ways to enhance the intellectual environment of the section room. Instructors graded cadets once every few days rather than daily and focused more of their energies on teaching. The point of the experiment was to encourage mastery of the material rather than the superficial understanding necessary for a cadet to receive a good daily grade. After trying the new technique for a year, Mills was pleased with the outcome. Nothing could be more effective in meeting educational goals, he asserted, "than the development of the most cordial and untrammeled intellectual relations between the instructor and cadet."[10] The new pedagogy, he believed, would promote "a reasonable amount of intellectual freedom and frankness" by relaxing the "rigidity of the military atmosphere . . . to an extent compatible with respectful attention and proper subordination."[11]

The grading experiment was the object of much debate because of its potential effect on the mental discipline of cadets. Teaching a difficult concept to cadets before grading them on it may have seemed like a logical way to transmit knowledge; doing so, however, might discourage them from taking responsibility for their learning. In the end, the progressives on the Academic Board prevailed. A majority concluded that "the old method generally employed at the academy . . . is not the best." Cadets should receive "full and clear explanation of all subjects and points which are beyond the power of the student to master by the proper amount of honest effort."[12]

In subsequent years, cadets would be graded less frequently, especially in the nonquantitative subjects, and have more interaction with their instructors. The new pedagogy made headway in every department. In the Department of English and History, for example, Professor Lucius Holt required cadets to take notes during class lectures, but his instructors graded the notes only two or three times during the semester.[13] After written exercises in the English composition course, instructors held one-on-one conferences with cadets to help them improve their writing skills.[14] In the Department of Law, Professor Walter A. Bethel gave short overview lectures to the cadets followed by "explanation of difficult points in the section rooms by the instructors."[15] Ironically, the Thayer system of daily grading lasted longest in the Department of Mathematics, despite that organization's early experimentation with less frequent grading.[16]

The pedagogical reforms of the early twentieth century included academic trips away from West Point. The Department of Civil and Military Engineering started the trend in 1902 by taking the entire senior class on a field trip to the Gettysburg battlefield.[17] The trip was highly successful and became an annual event; moreover, it set a precedent that other departments used to expand

A first-class cadet recites during a lesson on military history. Pedagogical reforms
of the early twentieth century improved the learning environment at West Point,
although strict classroom discipline remained a defining feature of cadet education.

their own instruction beyond the walls of the section room. In 1903, for example, instructors from the Department of Drawing took second-class cadets
to the Metropolitan Museum of Art in New York City. This trip also became
an annual event and, according to the department head, the "returns were well
worth the expenditure of the time and money."[18]

These and other trips, more frequent every year, gradually eroded the Academy's paternalistic culture and broadened cadets' intellectual horizons. They
helped cadets prepare for service in an army that administered distant territories and protected American interests worldwide. Recognizing the need for US
military officers to be cosmopolitan rather than provincial in their intellectual
outlook, Academy leaders adjusted their policies toward cadet travel accordingly.

Yet another improvement in cadet education was the effort to expose cadets
to the ideas of distinguished scholars from other academic institutions. Lucius Holt, for example, invited guest speakers from Yale, Harvard, Columbia,
Princeton, and other prestigious institutions to lecture to the cadets in both

history and English literature. The Department of Law hosted former President William Howard Taft, as well as distinguished law professors from Columbia and Yale. In some cases, the visits reciprocated those made by Academy professors elsewhere. Professor F. G. Highbee of Iowa State University spoke at West Point not long after the professor of drawing, Edwin R. Stuart, had lectured at Highbee's school. Even the surgeon, in his capacity as professor of military hygiene, invited military and civilian scholars from other institutions to address the cadets.[19]

By any measure, the pedagogical reforms of the early twentieth century had a positive effect on cadet education. In December 1910, for example, not a single cadet was discharged for academic deficiency; this was the best first-semester record since the Civil War. By the end of the same academic year, only five cadets had been discharged for academics, one of the lowest rates of attrition ever at West Point. It was an unusual year, to be sure, but the long-term indicators showed a similar trend. From 1892 through 1901, the percentage of cadets graduating from West Point had been about 50 percent. From 1902 through 1911, the figure jumped to about 70 percent.[20] Improved admissions standards may have played a role in the higher graduation rates, as well as the additional instruction now available to cadets during their free time in the late afternoons. According to Maj. Gen. Thomas H. Barry, the superintendent from 1910 to 1912, however, the principal reason was the "conscientious, devoted, and unusual efforts" of the academic departments in improving classroom instruction.[21]

Whereas pedagogical methods were gradually changing, West Point continued to have an entirely prescribed curriculum that reflected the paternal and attritional attitudes of Academy leaders. It did not matter that some cadets might have preferred other disciplines to mathematics, science, and engineering. Academy leaders were convinced that "subordinating inclination to effort" in these difficult subjects was the best method of developing mental discipline.[22] Additionally, they were resolved to weed out the weak cadets as early as possible rather than wasting their time on remediation. Failure in any course normally resulted in discharge, although deficient cadets with otherwise strong records sometimes were "turned back" to the next class and allowed another chance to pass.[23]

Academics did not change much at West Point when the Great War began in 1914. Cadets continued to grind through their mathematics and science courses. Senior cadets continued to visit Gettysburg to study the American Civil War rather than the happenings on European battlefields. Only in Professor Holt's history course did cadets receive programmed instruction on the events in Europe. He used lectures and map studies to deliver the instruction.[24]

Everything changed once the United States entered the war in April 1917.

The War Department ordered the senior class graduated later that month rather than in June; similarly, it ordered the rising senior class to graduate in August and thus completely miss the fourth year of academics. The new superintendent in 1917 was Samuel Tillman, formerly the professor of chemistry, mineralogy, and geology, who had returned to active duty to fill the position.[25] While he criticized the accelerated graduations as a "policy of undue haste," he understood the military exigency and worked with the Academic Board to make the necessary adjustments.[26]

The war brought change to virtually every course taught at West Point. The Department of Modern Languages stopped teaching Spanish and devoted its energies completely to French. In the Department of Law, seniors studied only military law and used the 1917 version of the *Manual for Courts-Martial* as their textbook. The professor of military hygiene instructed cadets on preventive medicine and field sanitation techniques. In the Department of Civil and Military Engineering, the technical portion of the curriculum yielded entirely to the study of military art, an amalgam of military history, theory, and tactics. Superintendent Tillman tried to adapt the curriculum and the totality of the West Point experience to the fluid situation caused by the war. In particular, he sought to direct the cadets "toward an understanding of the standards of conduct and character" they needed to become effective officers.[27]

The wartime conditions put everyone at West Point under heavy stress. Officers on the faculty were impatient to join the units forming for deployment to France. Their restlessness grew worse as the contraction of the curriculum threw their carefully prepared lesson plans into confusion. In some cases, instructors found themselves out of a job as the Academic Board curtailed or eliminated their courses. In other cases, instructors assumed heavier teaching loads as some of their colleagues deployed to war.[28] Cadets were affected, too. Because of the excitement of war, noted Tillman, cadets were "unsettled and had difficulty in making the most . . . of their limited time in the Corps."[29] The professor of modern languages, Wirt Robinson, was blunt in his assessment of the war's effect on the Academy: "The students are overtaxed and overloaded to the verge of breakdown, the instructors are exhausted, and instruction deteriorates correspondingly."[30] These difficulties notwithstanding, Tillman and the Academic Board succeeded in transitioning to a three-year curriculum and reestablishing a tolerable degree of stability and cohesion. Academic year 1917–1918 proceeded unremarkably, with the senior class graduating after three years. Tillman expected the next three-year class to graduate on time in 1919.

In October 1918, however, chaos ensued. The War Department, in response to the military crisis in Europe, ordered the two upper classes graduated on 1 November. Until the Academy could hastily assemble a new class later that month, the Corps of Cadets consisted solely of the plebes who had entered

TABLE 4.2A Timelines of Classes Affected by World War I

1913	1914	1915	1916	1917	1918	1919	1920	1921	1922	1923

Timeline bars numbered 1 through 10:
- 1: 1913–1917
- 2: 1914–1917
- 3: 1915–1918
- 4: 1916–1918
- 5: 1917–1918 (dashed extension to 1919)
- 6: 1918–1920
- 7: 1919–1921
- 8: 1918–1922
- 9: 1919–1922
- 10: 1919–1923

TABLE 4.2B Entry and Graduation Data of Classes Affected by World War I

Note	Principal Date of Entry	Date of Graduation	Number Graduated	Class Designation	Remarks
1	14 June 1913	20 April 1917	139	April 1917	
2	15 June 1914	30 August 1917	151	August 1917	
3	15 June 1915	12 June 1918	137	June 1918	
4	15 June 1916	1 November 1918	227	November 1918	
5	Various dates, June 1917	1 November 1918	284	1919	Returned as student-officers, 1 December 1918 to 11 June 1919
6	14 June 1918	15 June 1920	271	1920	
7	Various dates, Nov–Dec 1918	13 June 1921	17	1921	Opted for three-year curriculum
8	Various dates, Nov–Dec 1918	13 June 1922	102	1922	Opted for four-year curriculum
9	Various dates, Jun–Jul 1919	14 June 1922	30	14 June 1922	Opted for three-year curriculum
10	Various dates, Jun–Jul 1919	12 June 1923	262	1923	Opted for four-year curriculum

Notes: Information in tables 4.2a and 4.2b compiled from *Annual Report of the Superintendent*, 1919, 14–15, and *Official Register of the Officers and Cadets of the U.S. Military Academy*, 1913 through 1923. The members of the class of 1919, after graduating on 1 November 1918, returned to West Point as student-officers immediately after the war. The class graduated a second time on 11 June 1919.

the previous June. The War Department caused further confusion by ordering Tillman to graduate each new class in only one year. As West Point became a glorified officer training camp, the academic curriculum became a casualty of the war. Tables 4.2a and 4.2b show the disruptions to the four-year curriculum caused by the wartime emergency.

Mercifully, the 11 November armistice killed the one-year curriculum before it took effect. To Tillman's great dismay, however, the army chief of staff, Gen. Peyton March, refused to reinstate the four-year curriculum, preferring instead a three-year version. March's decision reflected his frustration with the Academic Board, which clung to a mathematics-based curriculum he viewed as obsolete. If the Academic Board would not make the necessary changes on its own, he would force the issue by cutting a year from the curriculum.[31]

In his last annual report as the superintendent, Tillman wrote passionately about the contributions of West Point graduates to demonstrate the value of the traditional four-year curriculum. The narrative started with a statement of purpose about the importance of character and intellect, the two essential goals for cadet development. West Point, he reminded army officials, existed for the "training and development of the rational faculties to the fullest extent . . . at the same time requiring an engendering obedience and subordination to proper authority, thus molding character." West Point's illustrious history served "to fully justify the great reputation of the Academy as well as strongly to support the theory of education here adopted."[32] Tillman left the Academy in June 1919, but in retirement he continued to work for the restoration of the four-year curriculum.

II. ACADEMICS THROUGH THE SECOND WORLD WAR

Tillman's replacement, Douglas MacArthur, had a rocky relationship with the Academic Board.[33] Despite the tension, however, they saw eye to eye on the issue of reinstating the four-year curriculum. "The opinion of West Point . . . down to the lowest ranking cadet," observed MacArthur, "was in favor of the four-year term."[34] Fortunately for West Point, Congressman John M. Morin, a member of the House Military Affairs Committee and chairman of the subcommittee on Military Academy appropriations, had been the president of the board of visitors in 1919. Morin was a supporter of the standard four-year curriculum and worked hard for its reinstatement. He enlisted Tillman to gather documentary evidence, which included a telegram from General of the Armies John J. Pershing about the importance of the four-year course of study. Pershing warned of "grave injury to the service" if the curriculum were not restored. Not only was the time needed for molding minds, argued Pershing, but "four years is none too great a time for the character forming, which has always been the greatest advantage of West Point."[35] MacArthur traveled to Washington to testify before Morin's military committee and the Senate counterpart. The combined efforts of Morin, Tillman, Pershing, and MacArthur succeeded, as Congress passed the necessary legislation in the spring of 1920.[36]

The legislation was a great relief for the Academic Board, but many of the cadets who had entered during the war years and expected to be commissioned quickly were disappointed. In particular, the cadets admitted in late 1918 and mid-1919 (entries 7 through 10 in table 4.2b) learned that they would be staying far longer than expected. Anticipating a morale problem, Congress empowered the Academy to allow cadets in those classes to choose between a three- or four-year curriculum. A few cadets chose the former (entries 7 and 9), but the large majority opted to stay for four years. The class of 1922 became the first four-year class to graduate since 1917.[37]

Once Congress authorized the reinstatement of a four-year curriculum, the Academic Board took up the business of determining its content. Traditional-ists on the board wanted a return to the status quo before the war. A majority, including MacArthur, however, were determined to adapt the curriculum to the realities of an industrialized, interconnected world. They believed that future wars, like the last one, would involve all of the elements of national power. Cadets needed a broad education that imparted knowledge of the political, social, and economic forces that determined the course of world events. As a starting point, they formulated the institution's first official mission statement, which established the requirement for cadets to be broadly educated.

> The function of the Military Academy is to give, in addition to that character-building for which it has long been famous, and in addition to the necessary military and physical training, such a combination of basic general and techni-cal education as will provide an adequate foundation for a cadet's subsequent professional career.[38]

Next, the board considered for inclusion in the curriculum all of the old courses and several new ones, including economics, government, psychology, sociology, logic, and moral philosophy. Adding a new course required curtailing or eliminating existing courses — painful choices for professors whose disciplines might be affected. In the end, only economics and government, combined into a single course, received approval. In addition to the new course, the Academic Board expanded English instruction to improve the writing skills of cadets.

The curriculum proposal MacArthur forwarded to the War Department for approval in 1920 represented a turning point in the evolution of academics at West Point. To make room for the economics and government course and the expansion of the English course, the Academic Board made substantial reductions in mathematics (25 percent) and drawing (50 percent).[39] As shown in table 4.3a, the Academic Board selected a broad mix of subjects to fill the twenty-four "half-courses" that composed the West Point curriculum.[40] There were seven half-courses in mathematics and science, eight in the humanities and social sciences, five in professional subjects, two in gymnastics, and two in riding. The curriculum still had plenty of quantitative subjects to develop in cadets the "habits of precision and accuracy and rigid reasoning." Nonetheless, it had an unprecedented number of nontechnical courses of "general educational value."[41]

With the War Department's approval of the new curriculum in 1920, West Point had for the first time a truly balanced course of instruction. Cadets spent roughly as much time studying quantitative disciplines as those that were nonquantitative. Henceforth, the Academy's critics would continue to decry the percentage of time cadets spent in particular disciplines (usually mathematics), but no one could seriously argue that the curriculum focused solely on technical subjects in general or on mathematics in particular. The Academic Board, prompted by an able and energetic superintendent, had overcome its characteristic conservatism to achieve substantial curricular reform. There would be many more curricular changes in the years ahead, and the percentage of quantitative courses in the curriculum would wax and wane. Regardless, the rough parity between quantitative and nonquantitative courses would be an enduring legacy of MacArthur and the 1920 Academic Board.

MacArthur pursued other areas of academic reform besides curricular. Based on his frequent classroom visits, he concluded that the instruction needed improvement. Too many of the faculty were poor teachers who owed their West Point assignments to their class rank as cadets and the personal relationships they had nurtured with the department heads. To enhance the quality of teaching and the diversity of the faculty, he encouraged professors to consider hiring non-West Point officers who had college degrees and teaching experience; he even provided them lists of such officers. Several professors scoffed at the idea, arguing that non-West Pointers could not learn the Academy's policies and methods quickly enough to be productive as instructors. The military faculty, they noted, stayed at West Point usually for only three years before moving to other army postings; hence, non-West Point officers would be at a constant disadvantage relative to their West Point peers. These arguments ignored the fact that Professor Lucius Holt was a Yale man and that he already had hired non-West Pointers to serve on the faculty with no evident decrement in efficiency. The same was true in the Department of Modern Languages and in the Office of Physical Education. Regardless, most department heads resisted having non-West Point graduates serve on the faculty.[42]

MacArthur's impatience with the old guard led him to find other ways of breathing new life into academic affairs. One of them was to order the professors to visit civilian colleges to survey new trends in education. Before acting, he secured the War Department's support for the plan, including the money to pay for the month-long absences. As soon as he announced the order, the professors complained that MacArthur was meddling in academic affairs despite his inexperience as an educator. Sending them on forced minisabbaticals during the academic year, they griped, proved his insensitivity to the pressures on the senior faculty. To this he replied, "They seem to be the orders," referring to the War Department's endorsement of his plan. MacArthur wrote letters of introduction to the presidents of the schools that the professors would visit. The replies were all positive, and the visits went well. The progressives on the Academic Board were enthusiastic, and even the old guard had good things to say about the experience.[43]

Other MacArthur initiatives were less successful. He urged Academic Board members to coordinate their offerings better and to invite more guest lecturers to broaden the cadets' perspective. He sought methods to help poorly performing students and to lower the attrition rate. He encouraged professors to allow the officers selected for the faculty to attend graduate school. He had newspapers delivered to cadet rooms so that instructors in English, history, economics, and government could incorporate current events in class discussions.[44] The elder professors were resistant to these initiatives and dug in their heels in hopes of outlasting the irksome superintendent. In the near term, they were successful, as the War Department reassigned MacArthur to the Philippines in June 1922. Still, the liberal forces MacArthur had helped to unleash gained strength over the next two decades, and eventually the Academic Board implemented all of his initiatives.

The decades of the 1920s and 1930s were particularly rich for the academic program at West Point. The curriculum underwent continued refinement, but more important was its acceptance as the centerpiece of an educational system that prepared cadets intellectually for the long-term demands of officership. During World War I, a faction in the officer corps sought to change the curricular emphasis of West Point from academic to military; the imposition of a three-year curriculum in 1919 manifested the trend. These officers argued that West Point should produce lieutenants fully capable of meeting their professional responsibilities upon their arrival at their first unit. Under this idea, academics would be scaled back considerably in favor of more military training.

Historians have likened the tensions between academic and military priorities at West Point as a clash between Athenian (intellectual) and Spartan (military) values.[45] Chapter 6 addresses the Athens-versus-Sparta debate more fully; for now, it is enough to note that the "Athenians" succeeded in maintaining

TABLE 4.3A　Curriculum of Twenty-Four Half-Courses, Academic Year 1920–1921

Area of Concentration	Subject	Number of Half Courses	Remarks
Mathematics and Science (7 half-courses)	Mathematics	3	
	Natural and Experimental Philosophy	2	
	Chemistry and Electricity	2	
Humanities and Social Sciences (8 half-courses)	English	2	Minus 33 lessons for Practical Military Engineering
	French	2	
	Spanish	1	
	History	1	
	Economics and Government	1	
	Law	1	
Professional (5 half-courses)	Military Engineering	1	
	Ordnance and Gunnery	1	
	Military Art and History	1	
	Drawing	1	
	Tactics	1	Minus 45 lessons for Practical Military Engineering
	Practical Military Engineering		78 lessons available from English and Tactics
	Hygiene		30 lessons available from Riding
Physical (4 half-courses)	Gymnastics	2	
	Riding	2	Minus 30 lessons for Hygiene

Note: Adapted from *Official Register of the Officers and Cadets of the U.S. Military Academy*, 1921, 20.

the primacy of the academic curriculum even as the quality of military training improved. In general, army leaders were supportive of keeping the Academy focused on character and intellect as the two most important developmental goals for cadets.

The clash between Athenian and Spartan values was evident in the responses of senior officers to a questionnaire designed to assess the performance of recent West Point graduates in the field. Brig. Gen. Fred Sladen, superintendent from 1922 to 1926 and a "Spartan" by temperament, distributed the questionnaire in late 1925 as a means of validating the emphasis he had put on military train- ing. One of the respondents, Brig. Gen. Robert E. Callan, reported that the

TABLE 4.3B   Courses by Class, Academic Year 1920–1921

Fourth Class (1st year)	Third Class (2nd year)	Second Class (3rd year)	First Class (4th year)
Mathematics	Mathematics	Natural and Experimental Philosophy	Military Engineering
English	English	Chemistry and Electricity	Military Art and History
French	French	Spanish	Economics and Government
	History		Law
Surveying	Drawing	Military Hygiene	Ordnance and Gunnery
Gymnastics	Tactics	Riding	Riding
	Practical Military Engineering		

Notes: Adapted from *Annual Report of the Superintendent*, 1920, 27–28. The Military Art and History course was a blend of military science (e.g., army organization and elements of strategy) and military history (e.g., historical evolution of warfare and study of modern campaigns).

West Point officers under his command were doing well; the reason, however, had little to do with military training. The strength of West Point, he explained, was a rigorous education that formed "not only the basis on which a lieutenant should build, but one deep and modern enough to be the educational foundation of the most accomplished officer throughout his entire service." A similar response came from Maj. Gen. Johnson Hagood, who dismissed the idea that West Point should focus on graduating polished second lieutenants, the lowest officer rank. Far more important, he argued, was to ensure that graduates were "properly equipped to enter upon the duties *of the highest grade to which they may be called in peace or war.*"[46]

The War Department advanced Athenian priorities in a variety of ways. It kept faculty strength at West Point relatively robust, even as the rest of the army was taking deep cuts.[47] Starting in 1925, it allowed officers en route to West Point as foreign language instructors to spend a year in France or Spain. Also that year, it began allowing cadets and officers to compete for the Rhodes scholarship, and immediately three West Pointers — two from the class of 1925 and one from the class of 1924 — were selected for the honor.[48] In 1926, it secured congressional approval for creation of the Department of Economics, Government, and History, which Holt had led provisionally since 1921; concurrently, the former Department of English and History (Holt's previous organization) narrowed its focus to become the Department of English, headed by Chaplain Clayton Wheat.[49] In 1927, the War Department began providing limited funds to help officers pay for graduate schooling; many of these officers were West Point faculty members seeking to better themselves as instructors.[50]

The post-World War I curricular reforms and the army's support of educational priorities helped rejuvenate West Point's reputation as a first-rate educational institution. In 1925, the Association of American Universities, a prestigious body of professional educators, listed West Point as an "approved technological institution."[51] The listing represented the Academy's first external accreditation of its academic program and was important in bringing West Point more in line, philosophically and procedurally, with other institutions of higher learning. Accreditation was important for another, less obvious, reason. Once the Academy submitted itself to routine external review, the priorities of professional educators had more weight in the decisions affecting academic policies and resources. In future years, as decennial accreditation became the norm, the accreditation boards commented on a variety of educational issues, such as governance, faculty credentials, funding levels, library resources, infrastructure, and pedagogy. In so doing, they prodded the army and Academy leaders to safeguard the health of the educational program at West Point.[52]

There were other signs of West Point's gradual adoption of civilian educational standards. One was the appointment of Lucius Holt as the "acting dean" in 1926, the first time the superintendent had had a principal deputy for managing the academic program.[53] Holt's appointment was an experiment that lasted for only two years, after which the position went unfilled. Still, it presaged the governance structure that appeared shortly after World War II and would be necessary to manage an increasingly intricate college curriculum. Another sign of change was the decision to award the Bachelor of Science degree to West Point graduates. Academy and army leaders opposed the proposal when it first surfaced in 1924. They argued that adopting civilian standards for degree conferral might "constitute an impediment to the full independence of the Secretary of War" in tailoring the curriculum to the needs of the army. Their attitudes changed within a few years, however, as graduates discerned the benefits of having the degree. In 1933, Congress authorized graduating cadets to receive the BS degree; four years later, it retroactively conferred the degree on all living graduates.[54]

As noted in chapter 2, the curriculum underwent nearly constant review from the mid-1920s through the 1930s. The scrutiny brought no major changes but many refinements. For example, a new Department of Physics, established in 1931, consolidated the physics-related instruction that had resided in the Department of Chemistry and the Department of Natural and Experimental Philosophy. The new physics course taught third classmen the principles of "elementary mechanics, heat, wave motion, sound, electro physics and light."[55] The Department of Natural and Experimental Philosophy dropped astronomy to make room for additional instruction in hydraulics and thermodynamics; additionally, it assumed responsibility for teaching mechanical engineering.[56]

The greatest curricular changes in the 1930s came in the disciplines of history and social sciences. Military history, taught formerly as an adjunct to the technical studies in the Department of Civil and Military Engineering, expanded in scope and importance. Under Professor William A. Mitchell and his successor, Thomas D. Stamps, the military history course became a capstone experience for cadets in their senior year; moreover, it was the principal academic venue for teaching military leadership prior to the establishment of psychology and leadership courses following World War II.[57] In the Department of Economics, Government, and History, Professor Herman Beukema expanded the coursework to include international relations, comparative governments, and the history of Europe and the Far East.[58]

By the end of the 1930s, the focus on academics had resulted in a curriculum that was more integrated and challenging than ever. It included a broad mix of courses that balanced mathematics, science, and engineering on the one hand with humanities, social sciences, and professional subjects on the other. Moreover, it reflected the commitment of army leaders to the notion that West Point should focus on developing cadets' character and intellect for long-term service rather than expanding the time devoted to military training. Accordingly, the new Academy mission, approved by the army in 1939, was to produce officers having "the qualities and attributes essential to their progressive and continuing development, throughout their careers as officers and leaders."[59]

The outbreak of the Second World War in 1939 prompted many changes at West Point that affected academics. Incoming foreign language instructors stopped going to France and Spain for their year of training and traveled instead to Canada and Mexico.[60] Cadets traveling overseas on furlough similarly altered their travel plans.[61] As the army began to expand and faculty officers left for other assignments, cadets took their places in some courses; by 1942, thirty-six cadets were so employed as an "emergency measure."[62] The War Department eventually put an end to the practice through the activation of reserve, National Guard, retired, limited-service, and temporary officers; by June 1944, these officers comprised 70 percent of the faculty. Many of them had advanced degrees and extensive teaching experience that enabled West Point to maintain high academic standards during the war.[63]

Once the United States entered the war, Maj. Gen. Francis Wilby, the superintendent from 1942 to 1945, tried hard to prevent a recurrence of the disruptions that the First World War had caused at West Point. In particular, he sought to retain the four-year curriculum, which he believed was necessary to produce the high-quality officers for which West Point was known. The War

Department was initially sympathetic, but practical concerns prevailed. Observed one official, "Some clearly evident manifestation of acceleration is necessary to insure for the Military Academy the wholehearted respect and good will of the Service and public."[64] In early September 1942, the War Department ordered Wilby to begin transitioning to a three-year curriculum, and Congress mandated the change with legislation approved on 1 October.[65] Tables 4.4a and 4.4b show the effect of the decision on the wartime classes.

Recognizing the Academic Board's aversion to bold change, Secretary of War Henry Stimson issued firm guidance. He ordered Wilby to shorten class periods, lengthen the academic day, and minimize cadet leaves. He prohibited across-the-board cuts to the existing curriculum; instead, the Academic Board was to prioritize among courses and eliminate those of lesser importance. The first two years of study would provide general coursework for all cadets, while the third (last) year would be devoted to more specialized subjects relating to the branch of service — ground or air forces — selected by the cadets. Finally, he directed Wilby to form an external board of "distinguished civilian educators and Army officers who have no present responsibilities for the curriculum" to oversee the work of the Academic Board.[66]

The Academic Board moved quickly to meet Stimson's guidance. Convinced that the "best mind training is to be had from a study of mathematics and the other sciences," it retained the full course of study in mathematics and added a new segment on statistical analysis.[67] It increased the number of lessons on aerodynamics, thermodynamics, internal-combustion engines, and other topics relevant to industrial warfare. In contrast, the Academic Board cut foreign language instruction from three years to two, but gave cadets the privilege of choosing which language to study; by the end of the war, the choices had expanded to Spanish, French, Portuguese, German, and Russian.[68] Another cut came in civil engineering, considered the "least important subject for officers other than those going into the Corps of Engineers."[69] The reduction left more time for military history, which expanded from eighty-three lessons in 1941 to ninety-two by 1943. Finally, the Academic Board added instruction for first classmen on written and oral communication that went beyond that already given the plebes in writing and public speaking.[70]

The most drastic curricular change resulted from the War Department's decision to allow pilot training for up to 60 percent of each class.[71] Air cadets took a substantially different curriculum than ground cadets, principally because they had to begin full-time air training in mid-April of the second year; the training continued through the summer and intermittently during the third (final) year of academics. In the Department of Mechanics, air cadets received instruction in meteorology rather than thermodynamics, which the ground cadets took. They missed the thirty-one periods of instruction on fluid dynam-

TABLE 4.4A   Timelines of Classes Affected by World War II

1939	1940	1941	1942	1943	1944	1945	1946	1947	1948

TABLE 4.4B   Entry and Graduation Data of Classes Affected by World War II

Note	Principal Date of Entry	Date of Graduation	Number Graduated	Class Designation	Remarks
1	1 July 1939	19 January 1943	409	January 1943	
2	1 July 1940	1 June 1943	515	1943	
3	1 July 1941	6 June 1944	474	1944	
4	Various dates, July 1942	5 June 1945	852	1945	
5	1 July 1943	4 June 1946	875	1946	
6	1 July 1944	3 June 1947	310	1947	Selected for three-year curriculum
7	1 July 1944	8 June 1948	301	1948	Selected for four-year curriculum

Notes: Information in tables 4.4a and 4.4b compiled from the *Official Register of the Officers and Cadets of the U.S. Military Academy*, 1939 through 1948.

ics, but compensated with the instruction taken at pilot school on the theory of flight. Other departments made similar adjustments, even though the course titles were the same for all cadets.[72]

Academy leaders chafed at pilot training on three accounts. First, it diverged from the long-standing practice of requiring every cadet to take the same course of instruction. Second, it weakened morale and cohesion in the Corps, as ground cadets and air cadets identified more closely with the classmates in their subgroup than with their classmates as a whole. Finally, it violated the tradition of producing officers who were generalists rather than specialists. The Academic Board viewed pilot training as a wartime expedient, but they were determined to put an end to it as soon as the war was over.

The same legislation that had shortened the curriculum to three years authorized the War Department to restore the four-year curriculum after the war. After repeated requests from Superintendent Wilby, the War Department finally approved the restoration in May 1945.[73] To ensure no break in the routine of graduating one class per year, half of the class that had entered in 1944 would graduate in 1947; the other half would graduate in 1948 and become the first postwar four-year class.[74]

In anticipation of the War Department's approval, Wilby had already formed a committee to design the postwar curriculum. The committee's report, finished in August 1945, reaffirmed the principles that had long dictated the design of the West Point curriculum. In general, the new curriculum kept character and intellect as the two most important developmental goals of the Academy.[75] In its specifics, the curriculum advanced the reforms achieved during the MacArthur years and the interwar period. As shown in tables 4.5a and 4.5b, mathematics and science comprised roughly half the curriculum, with the other half divided between humanities and social sciences on the one hand and professional subjects on the other.

The curriculum committee report included four recommendations to improve the academic program. It called for an end to pilot training and a restoration of the same prescribed instruction (with the exception of foreign languages) for all cadets. It proposed the establishment of the position of dean, filled by a brigadier general who would advise the superintendent on all aspects of the curriculum and relieve department heads of much of the routine committee work that consumed their time. It also proposed the appointment of additional permanent professors to reduce the workload of the department heads. Finally, to redress the problem of weak faculty credentials, the committee recommended a year of graduate schooling for officers selected for instructor duty.[76]

The appointment of Maj. Gen. Maxwell Taylor as superintendent in September 1945 led to the immediate implementation of the postwar curriculum and the committee's recommendations. The last class with air cadets graduated in June 1946. The professor of topography and graphics, Col. Roger Alexander, became the dean.[77] Congress added nine new permanent professors to the Academy faculty; these "second professors," or "not-heads" as they were known in Academy slang (i.e., not the head of a department), provided depth of intellect and leadership.[78] The War Department began sending inbound faculty officers to graduate school for a year; in the meantime, it retained the temporary officers who had served on the faculty during the war.[79]

Taylor was generally pleased with the new curriculum. The quantitative courses broadened their scope to include new knowledge in the fields of electronics, communication, and atomic energy. More important to Taylor, however, was the strength of the curriculum in the nonquantitative subjects. He favored the "heavy doses" of language instruction, both English and foreign, taken by cadets.[80] He extolled the expanded offerings in the new Department of Social Sciences (formerly Economics, Government, and History). Likewise, he praised the course in military history, which "now occupies a particularly important position in the First Class year where it is an instrument for impressing the principles of leadership" upon the cadets.[81] The breadth and rigor of the academic program accorded with Taylor's belief that West Point was not a "mill for producing second lieutenants for any arm of the service." Instead, the curriculum rightly placed emphasis on "giving a "broad foundation of culture, affording the graduate a base upon which to erect a rich and full life of service."[82]

Despite his overall satisfaction, Taylor wanted the curriculum reviewed by an external board. At his request, the secretary of war gave the job to Dr. Karl Compton, president of the Massachusetts Institute of Technology and a veteran of the committee that had overseen the contraction of the curriculum to three years in 1942.[83] Compton gave the Academy glowing reviews overall, while singling out the quality of instruction, curricular balance, and physical education program. He also praised West Point's "rare insight" in avoiding the academic specialization that was becoming common at other colleges and universities. "The four years of college," he observed, "can best be devoted to education in the general fundamentals, enlargement of social vision and development of cultural appreciation." Given the scope and difficulty of challenges facing army officers, "a foundation of this type of liberal education becomes increasingly the essential mission of the Academy."[84]

Not shown in tables 4.5a and 4.5b are courses in applied psychology and leadership. The army chief of staff, Gen. Dwight Eisenhower, encouraged Taylor to provide such instruction, but the Academic Board could not find a place for it in the crowded curriculum. Refusing to give up, Taylor established a new agency, the Office of Military Psychology and Leadership, to teach the subjects during some of the time normally allotted to tactics training. Instruction began in 1946 for the upper three classes and expanded to all classes by the following year.[85]

Whereas Taylor might have preferred a different mix of academic courses, he was respectful of the collective wisdom of the Academic Board in designing the curriculum. The academic program, he believed, constituted an "optimum combination of undergraduate studies for developing the capacities and aptitudes required for the military profession."[86] Civilian institutions had long

TABLE 4.5A Postwar Curriculum, Academic Year 1945–1946

Area of Concentration	Academic Course	Number of Hours	Percent of Instruction
Mathematics and Science	Mathematics	425	14.8
	Graphics	162	5.6
	Physics	176	6.1
	Chemistry	133	4.6
	Electricity	253	8.9
	Mechanics	300	10.5
	Subtotal	1,449	50.5
Humanities and Social Sciences	English	154	5.4
	Foreign Language	215	7.5
	History and Government	182	6.3
	Economics and International Relations	123	4.3
	Law	70	2.4
	Subtotal	744	25.9
Professional	Military Topography	193	6.7
	Military Instructor Training	37	1.3
	Military Art	141	4.9
	Military Engineering	143	5.0
	Ordnance	118	4.1
	Military Hygiene	28	1.0
	Military Law	20	0.7
	Subtotal	680	23.7
Total		2,873	100.1

Notes: Adapted from U.S. Military Academy, *Post War Curriculum at the U. S. Military Academy*, 55.
Percentages in the final column do not add up to 100 percent because of rounding.

TABLE 4.5B Courses by Class, Academic Year 1945–1946

Fourth Class (1st year)	Third Class (2nd year)	Second Class (3rd year)	First Class (4th year)
Mathematics	Mathematics	Mechanics	Military Engineering
English	English	Electricity	Military Art
Foreign Language	Foreign Languages	History and Government	Economics
	Physics		Law
	Chemistry	Military Correspondence	Ordnance
Military Topography and Graphics	Military Topography and Graphics	Military Instructor Training	Military Hygiene
Physical Training	Tactics	Tactics	Tactics

Note: Adapted from US Military Academy, *Post War Curriculum at the U. S. Military Academy*, 12.

since rejected the notion that a prescribed curriculum could impart the education necessary for success in all occupations, but West Point seemed different. As a vocational school with a narrow professional focus, it could argue that every cadet needed every course as a foundation for professional success.

As the postwar era progressed, Academy leaders found it increasingly difficult to structure a prescribed curriculum that met the needs of all cadets. The boundaries of knowledge in science and engineering expanded rapidly, particularly in fields of importance to the military professional. Moreover, the dominant role of the United States in the world required army officers to have a sophisticated understanding of the disciplines most relevant to the issues of national defense and diplomacy — history, government, politics, economics, international relations, psychology, languages, and the like. In the years ahead, the biggest reform in curricular affairs would result from challenging the assumption that every cadet must take every subject.

III.   FROM PRESCRIPTION TO CHOICE

In 1949, Secretary of Defense James V. Forrestal commissioned a group of distinguished educators and military officers "to recommend the manner in which officer candidates should receive their basic education for a career in the armed services."[87] Known as the Service Academy Board, the group included seven university or college presidents, including the new president of Columbia University, Dwight Eisenhower, and the superintendents of West Point and the Naval Academy. Among the board's many recommendations, most significant was its ringing endorsement of a broad and liberal education for service academy graduates:

> Professional military knowledge alone will not suffice to solve the problems of modern war. In the last war officers of the armed services often became engaged in pursuits other than purely military which required a general education background. Graduates of the Service Academies as they progress to positions of high responsibility in the military establishment will have an increasing range of contacts among leaders in civilian life, both at home and abroad. . . . [Their] field of knowledge, therefore, should include the arts and sciences in addition to professional military subjects.[88]

The postwar curriculum, with its mix of diverse subjects, provided the broad, liberal education envisioned by the Service Academy Board. Although the curriculum was prescribed, there were ample deviations that allowed cadets to learn at their own pace. In most disciplines, for example, the best performing cadets were exempt from many of the reviews and tests required of their classmates and therefore could study advanced topics and spend extra time in laboratory exercises. Third classmen in the top sections in mathematics spent the last part of the course studying statistics while their classmates finished the standard mathematics course. The best students in English had extra debate practice; those in mechanics and engineering completed additional design problems. In the Department of Social Sciences, cadets in the top sections of the international relations course finished the year with "Operation Statesman," a five-lesson seminar in which they grappled with contemporary diplomatic problems and prepared US policy recommendations. There was no way to tell from the West Point transcript whether a cadet had taken the advanced work. Still, it was a good bet that cadets who graduated at or near the top of the class had taken a substantial amount of coursework beyond that which their peers had experienced.[89]

Starting in academic year 1948–1949, the Department of Social Sciences deviated further from the prescribed curriculum. It allowed second-class cadets who could show college-level proficiency in European history (a core requirement) to take instead Russian history in the fall and Latin American history in the spring. Fifty-four cadets — about 8 percent of the class — took advantage of this option. Similarly, cadets with previous college credit in American politics, another core requirement, could opt for a course in US diplomatic history. Thirty-four cadets took that course in the first year.[90] Although these were substitute courses rather than true electives, Social Sciences had set the precedent of teaching courses that were distinctly separate from those in the core curriculum. If some cadets could benefit from taking noncore courses, then others — perhaps *all* others — could benefit as well. The traditionalists argued that the advanced cadets had the privilege of taking substitute courses only because they already had mastered the subjects required by the core curriculum. Still, the conceptual leap from substitute courses to elective courses was getting easier to make.

Academics at West Point improved further as more of the faculty attended graduate school following World War II. Of the sixty-four new instructors at the start of academic year 1948–1949, for example, forty-three had spent one or two semesters at graduate school.[91] With advanced education under their belts, these officers conducted specialized research, wrote books and scholarly articles, and attended professional conferences. As a result, they became better instructors and exemplars of the soldier-scholar ideal that West Point sought to impress upon the cadets.[92]

Sidney Berry was one such soldier-scholar. Following his 1948 graduation from West Point, he served with valor as an infantry officer during the Korean War.[93] Upon his return in 1951, he attended graduate school at Columbia University for two years before joining the Department of Social Sciences to teach European history. Berry relished the time at Columbia because of its intellectually diverse and stimulating environment. As one of the few soldiers on a liberal campus, he reflected on his career choice: "I had to crystallize, articulate, and defend the ethics, the philosophy of life, the purpose, the meaning of a soldier's life in the American Army." Berry found the reflection valuable, as it "advanced . . . the maturity of my thinking as a soldier." Besides preparing instructors for duty at West Point, graduate school allowed officers to return to the field army with broader perspectives on the issues that would affect them as officers. Berry recognized that he would acquire "a greater degree of credibility with civilians" because of his education and would return to the army "dedicated even more strongly to being a soldier." Berry concluded that the army was "extremely wise" in sending many of its officers to graduate school.[94]

Another indicator of the academic program's strength was the continued expansion of the lecture program. Since the early years of the century, the number of lectures had grown considerably and included topics in every academic discipline and in military affairs. During academic year 1950–1951, there were sixty-one lectures by guest speakers and 150 by members of the West Point staff and faculty.[95] Augmenting the lecture program were new extracurricular activities, such as the Student Conference on United States Affairs (SCUSA), sponsored jointly by the Department of Social Sciences and the West Point Debate Council. In 1949, the SCUSA conducted the first of a long series of annual conferences in the field of international relations; the organizing topic that year was "A European Policy for the United States: Problems and Objectives during the 1950s." The SCUSA conferences attracted student representatives from scores of civilian colleges, as well as distinguished guest speakers from academia, government, and the military.[96] Sidney Berry recalled that the SCUSA, Debate Council, and other extracurricular activities allowed West Point to be viewed "not just as a drill ground trainer of soldiers, but as truly a first-rate academic, educational institution."[97]

A validation of the excellence of the West Point education was the performance of cadets on standardized tests. The Graduate Record Examination, administered widely to college seniors by a national testing firm, was given to cadets for the first time in 1948. Superintendent Taylor described the performance of the first classmen as "extremely gratifying," as they outscored the national control group in every tested subject and by wide margins in most of them (table 4.6a).[98] Subsequent classes did equally well, even as the format of the test changed in 1955. Starting in that year, cadets were tested in broad academic areas—humanities, social sciences, and natural sciences. On the humanities portion of the test, cadets in the class of 1955 scored below their civilian peers who had majored in the humanities, but well above the control group of college seniors. In the social sciences and natural sciences, however, they outscored their civilian peers, including the majors in those disciplines, by wide margins (table 4.6b). The stated purpose of standardized testing was to "assess the broad outcomes of education in the liberal arts."[99] Judging from the test results, West Point seemed to be doing well in providing a broad, liberal education to cadets.

When Maj. Gen. Garrison Davidson became the superintendent in 1956, he recognized how far the academic program had improved since he experienced it as a cadet.[100] He cited the "quality of the instruction and the extent of cadet discussion" in the classrooms. He noted with approval the year or more of graduate study for most officers who joined the faculty. He praised the broadening of the science curriculum to include relevant new subjects like electronics and nuclear physics and the social science courses that gave cadets a "comprehensive and realistic appreciation of current national and world problems." He particularly liked the course in military history, which provided a "professional foundation far beyond anything my contemporaries and I ever received."[101]

Still, Davidson believed that West Point could do more to improve the academic program and keep it relevant to the military profession. He considered the faculty weak in academic credentials and far behind other prestigious institutions.[102] He viewed some of the courses to be "as antiquated as . . . strapped leather puttees." Although he favored a strong foundation in mathematics, science, and engineering, he suspected that the "core of subjects necessary to lay the basic foundation was less than the total current technical curriculum." Davidson believed that military art — the "jewel in the Academy's crown"— received too little emphasis. He wanted to place that subject in a new academic department, along with the courses taught by the Office of Military Psychology and Leadership. Another problem, according to Davidson, was pedagogical: despite the reforms of recent years, instructors still graded cadets too frequently; cadets therefore tended to view their education as "a week to week affair" rather than the foundation for a life of learning. Some cadets struggled academically, while others "weren't being challenged mentally" and could get by "without hardly cracking a book."[103] The former group was particularly hard hit because of the encroachments on academic time by the growth of military training and extracurricular activities.[104]

Davidson leveled his harshest criticism at the Academy's prescribed curriculum, which he felt stifled those cadets not predisposed to mathematics, science, and engineering. Their "natural talents," he believed, "were not being developed as they might have been had the demands on them not been overloaded in the wrong direction." Believing that the prescribed curriculum "did not merit the sacred homage paid it," he wanted to eliminate irrelevant and obsolete subjects, such as civil engineering and drawing, and establish a system of elective courses to stimulate cadet learning.[105]

TABLE 4.6A   Graduate Record Examination Scores for the
Class of 1948 and Control Group

Subject	Class of 1948	Control Group
General Mathematics	696	569
Physical Sciences	645	560
Biological Sciences	515	513
Social Studies	568	517
Literature	531	471
Fine Arts	455	444
Effectiveness of Expression	562	473
Vocabulary	522	487
General Educational Index	589	506

Notes: *Annual Report of the Superintendent*, 1949, 4. The scores in table 4.6a are for the eight-part general education portion of the Graduate Record Examination, prepared by the Educational Testing Service, a national testing firm to which many collegiate institutions subscribed. Each part consisted of an hour-long objective test of knowledge. The subjects included in the general education portion of the exam represented the judgment of collegiate educators as to what constituted a general liberal arts education. Students also could take area tests to assess their performance in specialized areas (e.g., humanities and engineering).

TABLE 4.6B   Area Test Scores for the Class of 1955, Compared to
Control Group and Disciplinary Majors

Areas Tested	Group Tested	Number Tested	Average Score
Social Sciences	College seniors (control group)	5,133	463
	Social science majors	4,818	447
	Cadets	468	570
Humanities	College seniors (control group)	5,133	443
	Humanities majors	2,235	506
	Cadets	468	486
Natural Sciences	College seniors (control group)	5,133	471
	Natural science majors	1,864	537
	Cadets	468	582

Notes: *Annual Report of the Superintendent*, 1958, 19. Cadets took the test just before their graduation. The control group consisted of male seniors from twenty-one accredited liberal arts colleges.

Convinced of the need for reform, Davidson resolved to conduct a top-to-bottom review of the curriculum. "If the study can be done the way I plan," he told army leaders, "it will represent the most complete survey of our curriculum that has been made in over half a century."[106] True to his word, Davidson initiated a comprehensive curriculum review in late 1957. The first phase consisted

Superintendent Garrison Davidson (*seated, center*) shown with
other Academic Board members. In 1959, at Davidson's urging, the
Academic Board voted to allow cadets to take elective courses.

of a study of the personal and professional qualities officers would need in the
years ahead; the study relied heavily on responses to a questionnaire Davidson
had sent to thousands of living graduates. In early 1958, the study entered its
second phase, with faculty committees working on the issues identified during
the first phase.[107]

Davidson disliked the limited scope of the curriculum committee's recommendations, which reached him in November. He therefore formed an external panel, composed of like-minded educators and senior officers, to review
the recommendations of the curriculum committee and lend weight to his
arguments. Additionally, he personally prepared the final arguments of his
case to the Academic Board. Despite these efforts, he won only a partial victory when the Academic Board took a final vote. Specifically, he had been unable to break the "unreasonable hold on the curriculum of civil engineering."
Additionally, he failed to achieve the desired departmental realignments — in
particular, the combination of military art and leadership into a single department.[108] "I failed," he told the army chief of staff, "in my efforts to introduce
the degree of flexibility into our curriculum I considered necessary in light of
the probable demands of the foreseeable future."[109]

Davidson was too hard on himself. Although not realizing it at the time, he had accomplished the most significant curricular reform since the time of Thayer. His great achievement was to break the monolithic nature of the core curriculum by convincing the Academic Board to establish an electives program. For the first time in the Academy's history, cadets could take true elective courses in subject areas of their liking. The elective program started in academic year 1960–1961 with first-class cadets allowed one elective; the following year the number increased to two. There were twenty elective offerings initially, but more came on line annually as faculty members with advanced degrees sought to teach specialized subjects.[110] In addition to electives, the Academic Board increased the opportunities for cadets to take accelerated versions of the core courses.[111] It expanded science instruction to nuclear physics, the environment, and the solar system, and gave more weight to the humanities and social sciences, including communication skills. Finally, it decreased military training during the academic year to "the minimum essential."[112]

Table 4.7 shows the details of the new academic curriculum. Mathematics, science, and engineering dominated, with about 60 percent of the contact and credit hours. The humanities and social sciences comprised 37 percent of the curriculum, and the two electives 3 percent. The solid performance of cadets on standardized tests showed that they were at least as proficient as their civilian peers in the humanities and social sciences; still, the heavy weight of mathematics, science, and engineering relative to other types of courses would be a source of debate in the years ahead.

Davidson's scrutiny of the curriculum attracted favorable notice from the Middle States Association of Colleges and Secondary Schools. The decennial accreditation report of 1959 commended West Point for

> [S]etting and revealing . . . standards and procedures for distinguished work, thereby performing a service to the whole community of higher education. Even in an Association devoted to the pursuit and interpretation of educational excellence, there is only so much room at the top; this space is reserved for a few, including, in the Commission's judgment, the United States Military Academy.[113]

IV. OPENING THE FLOODGATES OF CURRICULAR REFORM

With the logjam of prescription broken, cadets took advantage of the opportunity for curricular diversity. Many cadets took the standard program of core courses, augmented with the two electives in the senior year. Many others,

TABLE 4.7   Academic Curriculum, Academic Year 1961–1962

Class	Subject	Contact Hours	Credit Hours
Fourth (1st year)	Mathematics	265	16
	Engineering Fundamentals	180	6
	Environment	90	6
	English	83	5
	Foreign Languages	90	5
	Totals	708	38
Third (2nd year)	Mathematics	141	8
	Chemistry	141	8
	Physics	141	8
	English	45	2.5
	Foreign Languages	141	8
	Social Sciences (European and US History)	90	5
	Psychology	45	2.5
	Totals	744	42
Second (3rd year)	Electricity	283	16
	Mechanics of Fluids	141	8
	Mechanics of Solids	141	8
	Law	90	5
	Social Sciences (Economics, US Government)	90	5
	Totals	745	42
First (4th year)	Civil Engineering	141	8
	Ordnance Engineering	141	8
	English	45	2.5
	History of the Military Art	141	8
	Social Sciences (Economics, International Relations)	141	8
	Military Leadership	45	2.5
	Electives (2)	90	5
	Totals	744	42

Notes: Adapted from *Annual Report of the Superintendent*, 1962, 39–43. Cadets took the equivalent of twelve semester-length courses each year. Morning classes met six days a week and were about one-third longer than afternoon classes, which met only five days a week; hence, the contact hours and credit hours for morning courses were proportionally higher than for afternoon courses. Electricity (283 contact hours) and first-year mathematics (265 credit hours) met virtually every morning (except Sunday) throughout the year. Courses showing 141 contact hours met on alternating mornings (except Sunday) throughout the year; those showing ninety contact hours met on alternating afternoons (except weekends) throughout the year; and those showing forty-five contact hours met on alternating afternoons (except weekends) for one semester only. In the plebe year, the combination of Engineering Fundamentals (180 contact hours) and English (83 contact hours) was the equivalent of four semester courses, since together they comprised daily instruction for an entire year. In the senior year, military leadership (45 hours, 2.5 credit hours) is included as an academic course even though it was technically part of military training under the commandant. The reason for including leadership in table 4.7 is that it was taught as an academic course and would eventually (1977) come under the dean.

however, went further by taking advanced versions of the core courses as well as extra electives. The latter option was available because of the Academic Board's new policy of allowing cadets to "validate" core courses (demonstrate proficiency by examination or transfer credit) and take electives in their place.[114] Cadet Daniel W. Christman benefited from the policy by substituting a course in Russian history for the standard history course, which he had validated. Christman recalled that the instructor, Woodford D. McClellan, held a doctorate in history and "awakened in all of us, because of his . . . incredible knowledge of the then Soviet Union, a real desire" to learn.[115] By the time Christman graduated in 1965, there were sixty-seven electives from which to choose, and 60 percent of his classmates had taken either advanced courses or extra electives.[116]

The Academic Board took measures to ensure cadets were not biting off more than they could chew academically. It required third classmen to consult with academic counselors on the dean's staff prior to choosing electives. It monitored the grades of cadets in overload courses and allowed cadets to withdraw from those courses if the work proved too burdensome. The Academic Board soon discovered that cadets craved more challenging and interesting coursework, as the grades of the cadets who took the overload electives showed no signs of dropping.[117] Maj. Gen. William Westmoreland, superintendent from 1960 to 1963, applauded the new curriculum as a means of developing leaders who could "lead the smallest combat unit or . . . advise the highest government council."[118] The core curriculum would endow cadets with a solid education in a broad range of subjects essential to service as army officers; advanced and elective courses would allow further intellectual development in areas of student interest. The new academic program showed how far and how quickly the Academic Board had moved away from the dictum of "every cadet in every course."

The popularity of the electives program led to its rapid growth. In 1964, the Academic Board authorized second classmen to take two electives, thus doubling the allowable total. Another increase, starting with the class that entered in 1968, raised the number of electives to six. Cadets could either take an eclectic mix of electives or group them in a specific disciplinary field in one of four broad concentrations — basic sciences, applied science and engineering, humanities, or national security and public affairs. The Academic Board added a fifth concentration, management sciences, in 1970.[119] Cadets opting to concentrate in the humanities or in national security and public affairs could take two additional electives (total of eight) in lieu of courses in mathematics and thermodynamics.[120] The concentrations approximated the academic minors offered at civilian colleges, including the practice of recording the concentrations on the transcripts of the cadets who completed them.

The expansion of the electives program brought a new equilibrium to the curriculum. To allow room for the electives, the Academic Board reduced the scope of the electricity, mechanics, and engineering courses. The net result was to balance the core curriculum between twenty-one mathematics, science, and engineering courses on the one hand and twenty-one humanities and social science courses on the other.[121] Depending on the choice of elective courses, a cadet could graduate from West Point having taken a preponderance of non-quantitative courses. This was very different from the situation that existed in the first half of the century, when cadets grappled with a totally prescribed

TABLE 4.8 Comparison of Curricula,
Academic Years 1971–1972, 1978–1979, and 1981–1982

Class	Academic Year 1971–1972		Academic Year 1978–1979		Academic Year 1981–1982	
	1st Semester	2nd Semester	1st Semester	2nd Semester	1st Semester	2nd Semester
Fourth (1st year)	Mathematics	Mathematics	Mathematics	Mathematics	Mathematics	Mathematics
	English	English	English	English	English	English
	Foreign Language	Foreign Language	Foreign Language	Foreign Language	Chemistry	Chemistry
	Planetary Science	World Geography	History	History	History	History
	Engineering Fundamentals	Engineering Fundamentals	Psychology	Computer Programming	Psychology	Computer Programming
Third (2nd year)	Mathematics	Mathematics	Mathematics	Mathematics	Mathematics	Mathematics
	Physics	Physics	Physics	Physics	Physics	Physics
	Chemistry	Chemistry	Chemistry	Philosophy	Foreign Language	Foreign Language
	Foreign Language	Foreign Language	Political Science	Economics	Political Science	Economics
	History	History	Foreign Language	Elective	Philosophy	Elective
	English	Psychology	—	—	—	—
Second (3rd year)	Electrical Engineering	Electrical Engineering	Electrical Engineering	Thermo-fluid Dynamics	Area Course 1	Area Course 2
	Mechanics	Mechanics	Engineering Mechanics	Military History	International Relations	Electrical Engineering
	Mechanics	Physics	Law	International Relations	Literature	Leadership
	Law	Law	English	Elective	Military History	Military History
	Economics	American Government	Elective	Elective	Engineering Mechanics	Thermo-fluid Dynamics
	Elective	Elective	—	—	—	Elective

	Academic Year 1971–1972		Academic Year 1978–1979		Academic Year 1981–1982	
Class	1st Semester	2nd Semester	1st Semester	2nd Semester	1st Semester	2nd Semester
First (4th year)	Engineering	Engineering	Engineering	Engineering	Area Course 3	Area Course 4
	Engineering Sequence	Engineering Sequence	Military Leadership	American Institutions	Engineering	Engineering
	Military Leadership	English	Elective	Elective	Law	Law
	Comparative Polit. Systems	International Relations	Elective	Elective	Elective	Elective
	Military History	Military History	Elective	Elective	Elective	Elective
	Elective	Elective	—	—	Elective	Elective
	Elective	Elective	—	—	—	—
Total	48 courses (42 core, 6 elective)		40 courses (30 core, 10 elective)		43 courses (31 core, 12 area or elective)	

Notes: Adapted from US Military Academy, 1971/1972 Catalog, 18–19, 1978/1979 Catalog, 39, and *Annual Report of the Superintendent*, 1981, 10.

curriculum heavily weighted in the quantitative disciplines. Table 4.8 shows the curriculum of academic year 1971–1972, the senior year of the cadets who entered in 1968.

In parallel with the curricular changes of the late 1950s and the 1960s were improvements in the academic infrastructure at West Point. The army provided money to convert the medieval-looking riding hall into a modern academic building renamed Thayer Hall. Completed in 1958, it housed ninety-six classrooms, eight academic departments, and the West Point museum, whose principal mission was (and still is) to support cadet education.[122] Also housed in Thayer Hall was the new Academic Computing Center, established in December 1962; a month later, cadets began the orientation and programming instruction required to use the computers in their coursework.[123] Across the street from Thayer Hall was the new and spacious library, completed in 1964, that saw an immediate increase of 400 percent in cadet usage compared to the cramped library it replaced. Other improvements included the upgrade of chemistry, ordnance, nuclear engineering, electricity, and mechanics laboratories; addition of new laboratories for rocket engines, ballistic flight, special physics projects, and foreign language instruction; construction of a weather station to support climatology instruction; and installation of a closed-circuit television system for instructional use in the classrooms.[124]

Underscoring the commitment to improving academics at West Point was the army's policy on advanced schooling for graduated cadets. Starting with the class of 1962, the army designated five cadets per year for early graduate schooling in science and engineering. The intent was to provide a "reservoir of highly trained young officers who can be utilized in their specialties either by the Military Academy or by other agencies of the army."[125] Three years later, the army promised graduate schooling leading to a master's degree to the top 5 percent of each graduating class; the schooling could begin anytime within the first five years of service. Of the twenty-seven cadets eligible for the program in 1965, ten chose to begin graduate school immediately. The majority opted to postpone their studies until after they had gained experience in the field army, a trend that continued in future years.[126]

The army likewise promoted faculty scholarship. In 1963, it coded fifteen faculty slots at West Point for extended tours of duty. Officers filling those positions were expected to have (or soon receive) a PhD and serve at the associate professor level. By 1970, there were twenty-eight permanent associate professors assigned to West Point, and the number increased gradually in subsequent years.[127] They received the privilege of taking year-long sabbaticals and serving as fellows at the Army War College; both programs encouraged faculty members to expand the frontiers of knowledge in their respective disciplines. In 1970, the army provided funding for up to twelve faculty members to conduct full-time research. A newly created Science Research Lab provided the venue for the faculty researchers, some of whom achieved national prominence for their work. The researchers received grants from a variety of government agencies, including the Army Research Office, Office of Naval Research, Environmental Protection Agency, and National Aeronautics and Space Administration.[128] Once these agencies discovered the high quality and relatively low expense of research conducted at the Academy, they quickly increased their financial support.[129]

The improvements to the West Point educational experience stemming from the Davidson reforms had been far reaching. Cadets had a voracious appetite for more interesting and challenging courses and responded enthusiastically to the opportunity to pursue their areas of interest.[130] An improved faculty, anchored by the permanent associate professors, had the intellectual talents to teach the new courses; even the junior instructors who rotated through the departments on three-year assignments usually held at least a master's degree. Meanwhile, the added demands of the curriculum brought no apparent drop in student performance. Cadets continued to outperform their civilian peers by wide margins in all areas constituting a liberal education, particularly in mathematics and science.[131] They similarly outperformed their peers from other commissioning sources.[132] The improvements once again earned the plaudits of the accrediting board, which concluded in 1969 that the "Academy is doing — and doing well — what it exists to do."[133]

Still, the rapid changes in the academic program spawned a debate among Academy leaders that was central to the nature of cadet education. On the one hand, many applauded the new developments that brought West Point to the forefront of teaching and scholarship. On the other, there was a gnawing sense that West Point was leaving behind the best features of its educational system, features that had proven successful for generations of officers. Virtually everyone agreed that West Point needed to produce broadly educated generalists in the arts and sciences who had the intellectual foundations to adapt to any situation. The curriculum had long met that need through prescription, yet now it was moving unmistakably in the opposite direction. With every new elective and area of concentration, cadets were able to focus more narrowly in specialized fields. The momentum built with the rising educational level of faculty members who yearned to apply and transmit the knowledge they had acquired in graduate school. Within academic departments, empires of disciplinary specialization were forming, much as they had at civilian institutions. A growing number of permanent associate professors, trained as academic specialists, were enthusiastically leading the way.

The trend toward specialization troubled some members of the Academic Board. The group included Col. Charles H. Schilling (Military Art and Engineering), Col. Elliott C. Cutler (Electricity), and Col. John S. Dick (Mathematics), who voted against the proposal to increase the number of electives to six in 1968. In their dissenting opinion, they warned that the "elementary drive toward optimization" in each area of concentration would accelerate the advance of more electives and greater specialization. The trend would encourage cadets to differentiate themselves according to their areas of concentration and dismiss the benefits of the common curriculum. Those pursuing the humanities concentration, for example, would "increasingly regard their already emasculated engineering component as a useless imposition. . . . The arguments in favor of free cadet choice . . . will then apply with redoubled vigor to the further reduction of the core."[134] The relentless increase in the number of electives from year to year seemed to confirm these fears.

Others were less worried. The faculty authors of the Academy's 1969 accreditation report acknowledged the "continued necessity for retaining traditional educational values." Nonetheless, they asserted that the

[P]ressures on the military profession for diversification and specialization can be expected to increase. With the continually expanding horizons of knowledge, courses at the Academy will have to be redesigned frequently in order to keep abreast of new developments. Increasing specialization in the curriculum will have to be reconciled with the basic requirement of providing a broad general education.[135]

Maj. Gen. Samuel Koster, superintendent from 1968 to 1970, tried to reassure the traditionalists. He explained that the Academy's aim was not "a type of program commonly referred to as a 'major' at other institutions." Rather, it was to acquaint cadets with the "methods and meanings of intellectual specialization" while still providing a "solid foundation for future professional development in any one of a wide variety of disciplines."[136] The preponderance of prescribed courses seemed to confirm Koster's assertion. Of the forty-eight courses required to graduate, forty-two (about 88 percent) were in the core curriculum. For the minority of cadets concentrating their electives in the humanities and in national security and public affairs, the core courses numbered forty (about 83 percent). Still, the pace and scope of the changes during the 1960s portended the continued fracturing of the core curriculum and the potential weakening of the broad education that had been the centerpiece of the cadet experience.

V. ACADEMIC MAJORS

In 1972, the superintendent, Maj. Gen. William Knowlton, appointed a panel of distinguished leaders from academia, business, and the military to conduct an external review of the curriculum. The panel members were generally positive in their assessment, although they recognized that the recent reforms had made an already challenging curriculum more so. Cadets were extremely busy during the minutely scheduled day and had little time for study or reflection. The panel therefore recommended a reduction in the course load overall, and especially in fourth-class mathematics.[137]

Knowlton pressed the Academic Board to address these issues, but there were no easy solutions. Heated resistance came from several departments, particularly those that had taken cuts to accommodate the electives program. They argued that the core curriculum already had shrunk considerably and that no more cuts were possible. In 1973, the Academic Board reached a compromise that pleased no one. Rather than eliminate any existing core courses, it reduced the number of class attendances in all of them by 10 percent. This solution, called the "lesson drop plan," highlighted the difficulty of choosing which courses were more expendable than others.[138]

Knowlton's successor, Maj. Gen. Sidney Berry, initiated another curriculum review in late 1975, and this time the results were different. The review committee proposed cutting the number of courses required to graduate from forty-eight to forty-two. The cuts would come in mathematics, science, and engineering, but they would allow greater depth of study in all disciplines. Early the next year, the Academic Board voted in favor of the course reductions; the decisive twelve-to-three vote was an indicator of how far the board had come in recognizing the need for change. The change never received the army's final approval, however, because of a major cheating incident that unfolded shortly after the vote. The incident, covered in detail in other chapters, involved second-class cadets in an electrical engineering course (EE304). As the scope of the cheating became apparent, the army chief of staff, Gen. Bernard Rogers, decided to defer action on the curriculum until after the Academy underwent thorough scrutiny by external review boards.[139]

The secretary of the army appointed a commission led by Frank Borman to determine the causes of the EE304 incident.[140] Although the commissioners focused principally on the honor code and system, they also scrutinized the academic program for possible connections to the crisis. They found much to criticize. In their December 1976 report, they noted the lack of study time and concluded that overscheduling cadets bred academic mediocrity and created the conditions for cheating.[141] Cadet time had been increasingly sapped by competing activities, particularly military training. The situation convinced the commissioners that "the acquisition of a college education within a military environment must, during the academic year, have first call on the time and energies of each cadet." Military training, they argued, "should be concentrated in the summer months" to allow more study time during the academic year.[142]

A second major study, conducted by the West Point Study Group in the first half of 1977, examined all aspects of the cadet experience and provided many specific recommendations for reform. It endorsed the conclusions of the Borman report in characterizing the academic program as "a fundamental building block of the four-year experience." During the academic year, this program was to have "the highest priority."[143]

The West Point Study Group consisted of officers from the army staff, many of whom were former faculty and staff members at the Academy. They worked closely with internal Academy working groups to speed the reform process. The new superintendent, Gen. Andrew J. Goodpaster, strongly supported the effort, as did the army chief of staff, Gen. Bernard Rogers.[144] With such a powerful combination of forces pushing for change, the Academic Board members had no choice but to act decisively. Over the next few years, they experimented with a variety of changes designed to optimize the balance between a strong core curriculum on the one hand and specialization on the other.

The most jarring reform was the reduction in the total number of courses required for graduation from forty-eight to forty, starting in academic year 1978–1979 (table 4.8). Of the forty total courses, thirty were in the core curriculum and ten were electives. The new curriculum reduced the standard academic load from six courses per semester to five, not counting military science and physical education. Goodpaster approved this change "to emphasize academic excellence and to better focus the use of cadet time."[145] In practice, that meant a reduction in the technical side of the core curriculum. Whereas previously there had been an equal number of quantitative and nonquantitative core courses, now there were thirteen of the former and seventeen of the latter. It was now possible for cadets who concentrated their electives in the humanities and social sciences to graduate from the Academy with two-thirds of their courses in nonquantitative disciplines. For some members of the Academic Board, this was a radical and troubling departure from long-standing academic traditions.

The new curriculum undermined the century-old assumption that mathematics was the best tool for developing mental discipline. The West Point Study Group addressed this point directly in its analysis of the responses to questionnaires it had sent to army field commanders. The questionnaires asked the commanders to evaluate the quality of the West Point officers serving under them. While the commanders rated Academy graduates as "generally superior" to other officers in most professional attributes, they criticized them for lacking skill and confidence "in solving problems that have no set solutions."[146] These responses suggested that the Academy's heavy emphasis on mathematics had fostered mental rigidity and encouraged cadets to search for precise, orderly solutions that rarely existed in the chaotic, messy world beyond the gates of West Point. The West Point Study Group had urged the Academy to give cadets "thorough exposure to theoretical and conceptual problems" that defied precise solutions. The humanities and social sciences already did this, but even engineering and applied sciences, it argued, should "stress problems for which there is no single solution and which include consideration of social values and consequences."[147] This critique of the Academy's curriculum was not new, but rarely before had the forces of change been strong enough to make a difference in this regard.[148]

The Academic Board took several measures to develop cadets into more sophisticated problem solvers. The most important had been to expand the electives program to ten courses, which approximated in size and content the academic majors of civilian colleges.[149] With more allowable electives, cadets could study a subject of interest in far greater depth than was possible in the survey courses of the core curriculum. Here was an opportunity to develop a sophisticated understanding of a particular field and to appreciate the nuances of solving problems therein.

Another way of exposing cadets to problems with "no set solution" was to establish the Department of Behavioral Science and Leadership in September 1977. The new department consolidated under the dean the academic components of the commandant's Office of Military Leadership. According to the West Point Study Group, cadets would benefit by receiving instruction that would prepare them "for the ethical, personal, and leadership problems that confront commissioned officers."[150] In addition to refining the core courses in psychology and military leadership, the new department offered disciplinary fields in psychology and sociology for elective study.[151] For the first time since reluctantly entering the field of theoretical leader development in the mid-1940s, the Academy had a firmly established program comparable to those at other colleges.

Bringing civilian professors to West Point was yet another way of providing cadets new insights in problem solving. The Department of History had experimented with yearlong visiting professors starting in academic year 1971–1972; the results were highly successful, and a few other departments soon followed History's lead. At the urging of both the West Point Study Group and a separate Department of Defense panel convened after the cheating incident, the Academic Board hired visiting professors for all thirteen departments. Individually and collectively, the professors provided valuable service in teaching elective courses, reviewing academic programs, mentoring junior faculty members, advising senior leaders, and linking the Academy to civilian institutions across the nation. Their mature and diverse views on academic and policy issues represented a valuable source of external review.[152]

Other important changes prompted by the West Point Study Group dealt with scheduling and grading. Starting in academic year 1978–1979, virtually all class periods had a standard length of sixty minutes; the change ended the long-standing practice of reserving the mornings for lengthier (eighty-minute) classes, usually in mathematics and other quantitative subjects. Another departure from tradition came the following academic year, with Goodpaster's decision that the first term (and the associated term-end examinations) would end prior to Christmas. Cadets welcomed the change, which allowed them to go home for the holidays with the pressures of first-term academics completely behind them. Goodpaster also changed the traditional grading system—on a 3.0 scale—to the standard letter-grade system used at most colleges. All three changes altered traditions that had been in place for 150 years.[153]

The reforms stemming from the 1976 cheating incident included a variety of methods to remediate poor academic performance. These methods were necessary as the Corps of Cadets became more demographically diverse during the 1970s and the number of academically at-risk students increased correspondingly. Academy leaders compounded the problem by using intercollegiate athletics as a principal means of meeting class-composition goals for minorities. Rather than seeking the most academically qualified minorities, the Academy accepted less qualified candidates who were better athletes and could therefore advance the goal of fielding winning teams. This policy, a derivative of the Academy's affirmative-action program, was justified as a means of building morale during the difficult period since 1976, which Goodpaster described as "grimsville." The result, however, was to increase the number of weak students among the Corps of Cadets in general and the minority populations in particular.[154]

Just before stepping down as the superintendent in 1981, Goodpaster fine-tuned the curriculum he had approved three years earlier. First, he required cadets to select by the end of their plebe year one of two curricular tracks—mathematics, science, and engineering or humanities and public affairs. Cadets in each track could specialize in one of several "fields of study"; additionally, they had to take four common "area courses." Second, Goodpaster increased the number of core courses from thirty to thirty-one by restoring a second semester to military history, law, and chemistry; to make room for the new courses, he deleted a semester of foreign language and the American Institutions course.[155] Finally, he reduced the number of electives from ten to eight, with six electives in the cadet's field of study and two free electives. The net effect of these changes was to increase the number of courses required for graduation from forty to forty-three (table 4.8). Despite these changes, however, the number of nonquantitative courses (seventeen) continued to exceed the number of quantitative courses (fourteen) in the core curriculum.[156]

The back-and-forth changes in the number of courses required for graduation reflected the ongoing divisions within the Academic Board concerning the merits of general versus specialized education. For some members of the Academic Board, the explosion of knowledge in every disciplinary field dramatized the impossibility of specializing in any one of them at the undergraduate level. They preferred the broad education that had a long record of endowing graduates with a foundation for intellectual and professional growth. In this view, cadets were best served by taking an extensive core curriculum and minimizing the number of elective courses; once they were officers and needed specialized training, they could take all the electives they wanted at graduate school. Besides, the core curriculum already comprised a "professional major"—that is, the courses viewed as most essential in preparing cadets for the demands of officership. Any further specialization at the undergraduate level, they believed, was superfluous.[157]

Other Academic Board members thought differently. Citing the "increasing specialization of the Army," they favored the establishment of a study-in-depth component to the curriculum. This was particularly important in the engineering disciplines, which were becoming increasingly specialized at the undergraduate level across the nation. The engineering programs at the Naval Academy and Air Force Academy already had received the endorsement of the Accreditation Board for Engineering and Technology (ABET), the nation's foremost accrediting agency for undergraduate engineering. The ABET's

Lt. Gen. Willard Scott (class of 1948),
superintendent from 1981 to 1986, oversaw the
implementation of the academic majors.

strict requirements for the quantity and quality of technical courses conflicted with the Academy's traditional reliance on general studies. Unless the Academy adopted ABET standards, however, it would put itself at a recruiting disadvantaged compared to the other service academies. Moreover, it would compromise the ability of West Point graduates to gain entry into the most prestigious graduate schools of engineering. These considerations were behind Goodpaster's curriculum decisions of 1981.[158] Dividing the curriculum into two tracks, and adding three more courses to the cadet academic load, permitted the grouping of core and elective courses necessary to meet ABET requirements. In the process, these decisions set precedents that made the adoption of majors inevitable.

Shortly after his arrival in 1981, Maj. Gen. Willard Scott, Goodpaster's successor as superintendent, ordered the development of a plan for academic majors. After much debate, the Academic Board recommended a program of sixteen optional majors split evenly between the two tracks. The mathematics, science, and engineering track would consist of majors in chemistry, civil engineering, computer science, electrical engineering, engineering management, engineering physics, mathematical science, and mechanical engineering. The humanities and public affairs track would have majors in behavioral science, economics, foreign language, geography, history, literature, management, and political science. Cadets who did not wish to declare a major could take a less specialized field of study in one of twenty-nine disciplines. The curriculum proposal would add a new core course — terrain analysis — and keep the number of area and elective courses constant at twelve; hence, the total number of courses required for graduation would increase to forty-four. The majority of Academic Board members voted to approve the new curriculum in October 1982. Scott endorsed the plan, forwarded it to the army, and received approval in time for implementation in academic year 1983–1984 (table 4.9).[159]

The implementation of academic majors culminated a period of far-reaching curricular change at West Point. In less than twenty-five years, the Academy went from a completely prescribed curriculum to one that allowed cadets the same degree of specialization offered on most college campuses. Much of the change was the result of external forces, but as we have seen, the Academic Board was capable of making significant changes on its own.[160] There would be many more changes in subsequent years, but the model of a curriculum with a three-quarters study-in-breadth component coupled with a one-quarter study-in-depth component would endure to the present.[161]

The arrival of Lt. Gen. Dave Palmer as the superintendent in 1986 brought another round of reform to the curriculum. Palmer placed great emphasis on strategic planning as the engine for change, and he had a keen understanding of how the various developmental programs at West Point fit together. In the area of academics, his strategic review coincided with the Academy's decennial accreditation by the Middle States Commission on Higher Education. The momentum of the accreditation process abetted his agenda for academic reform and the results were therefore significant.

Palmer concluded that cadets were once again overscheduled. He noted that the minimum number of courses for graduation had decreased from forty-eight just prior to the 1976 cheating incident to forty just after; since then, the minimum number of courses had crept back to forty-four. The heavy academic load, Palmer believed, prevented most cadets from devoting sufficient time to their studies. Consequently, he ordered a return to the forty-course curriculum starting in academic year 1990–1991 (table 4.9). Thirty-one of the forty courses were mandatory — fifteen in mathematics, science, and engineering and sixteen in the humanities and social sciences — and nine were electives. The decision was unpopular with the Academic Board, but Palmer considered it essential to ease the congested cadet schedule and promote excellence in academics. The reduction in courses, Palmer noted, gave cadets "a pretty heavy load for the base line, and if they want to do more, they can." In fact, about two-thirds of the cadets during Palmer's tenure chose to declare a major, which required a minimum of twelve electives and thus boosted the total number of courses to forty-three. In subsequent years, the number of cadets opting for a major rose steadily, with about 86 percent choosing to do so in 2006 (the last year before academic majors became mandatory).[162]

At the same time he reduced the number of courses for graduation, Palmer increased engineering instruction for cadets concentrating in the nonquantitative disciplines. Palmer agreed with members of the Academic Board that all cadets, regardless of specialization, should understand the engineering thought process. He therefore approved a curriculum committee recommendation for a five-course engineering sequence in one of six disciplines — civil, mechanical, environmental, nuclear, systems, or computer engineering. The five engineering courses, part of the core curriculum, reflected the Academy's commitment to helping cadets apply their mathematical and scientific knowledge to solving practical problems.[163]

The most important of Palmer's academic reforms was easy to overlook because it was procedural rather than tangible. Specifically, he implemented a strategic planning process that guided Academy leaders in answering two fundamental questions about the curriculum. First, what were the desired outcomes for cadet education? Second, how well was the Academy achieving those outcomes? The first question led to the development of academic goals in nine areas — mathematical and scientific competency, engineering and technology, cultural awareness, historical perspective, understanding human behavior, creative thinking, moral reasoning, clear expression, and commitment to lifelong learning. The goals focused the Academic Board's attention on matching the curriculum to the challenges cadets would face after graduation. The second question resulted in procedures for measuring the effectiveness of the curriculum and thus guiding the process of change. For each academic goal, the dean appointed a faculty team to develop a learning model and assess the effectiveness of the curriculum in that area. Over the next few years, the processes for goal setting and goal assessment matured considerably. In 1997, the dean described these processes in a seminal publication, "Educating Army Leaders for the 21st Century," that provided a blueprint for curricular design and assessment.[164] West Point was at the cutting edge of assessment theory and practice, and it provided the model for many other colleges and universities.[165]

The last significant curriculum change came a decade after Palmer had retired. Lt. Gen. Daniel Christman, superintendent from 1996 to 2001, had

TABLE 4.9 Comparison of Curricula, Academic Years 1983–1984, 1990–1991, and 2006–2007

	Academic Year 1983–1984		Academic Year 1990–1991		Academic Year 2006–2007	
Class	1st Semester	2nd Semester	1st Semester	2nd Semester	1st Semester	2nd Semester
Fourth (1st year)	Mathematics	Mathematics	Mathematics	Mathematics	Mathematics	Mathematics
	English	English	English	English	English	English
	Chemistry	Chemistry	Chemistry	Chemistry	Chemistry	Chemistry
	History	History	History	History	History	History
	Psychology	Computer Science	Psychology	Computer Science	Psychology	Information Technology
Third (2nd year)	Mathematics	Mathematics	Mathematics	Mathematics	Mathematics	Mathematics
	Physics	Physics	Physics	Physics	Physics	Physics
	Foreign Language	Foreign Language	Foreign Language	Foreign Language	Foreign Language	Foreign Language
	Political Science	Economics	Political Science	Economics	Economics	Political Science
	Philosophy	Terrain Analysis	Philosophy	Terrain Analysis	Philosophy	Physical Geography
	—	Elective	—	—	—	—
Second (3rd year)	Area Course 1	Area Course 2	Engineering Course 1	Engineering Course 2	Engineering Course 1	Engineering Course 2
	International Relations	Electrical Engineering	Engineering Course 3	International Relations	Information Systems	Advanced Composition
	Literature	Leadership	Literature	Leadership	International Relations	Military Leadership
	Military History	Military History	Military History	Military History	Elective	Elective
	Engineering Mechanics	Thermo-fluid Dynamics	Elective	Elective	Elective	Elective
	—	Elective	—	—	—	—
First (4th year)	Area Course 3	Area Course 4	Engineering Course 4	Engineering Course 5	Engineering Course 3	Constitutional and Military Law
	Engineering	Engineering	Law	Elective	Military History	Military History
	Law	Law	Elective	Elective	Elective	Elective
	Elective	Elective	Elective	Elective	Elective	Elective
	Elective	Elective	Elective	Elective	Elective	Elective
	Elective	Elective	—	—	—	—
Total	44 courses (32 core, 12 area or elective)		40 courses (31 core, 9 elective)		40 courses (30 core, 10 elective)	

Notes: Adapted from 1983–84 Catalog, 35; 1990–91 Catalog, 33; and 2006–07 Catalog. The forty courses in the academic year 1990–1991 curriculum were the minimum for cadets taking a field of study; cadets declaring majors took at least three additional courses.

served in senior staff positions that heightened his awareness of the new challenges cadets would face upon graduation.[166] He believed that the cadets would
need, in addition to the basic competencies provided by the West Point education, equal measures of cultural awareness and familiarity with information
technology. Following a curriculum review and another decennial accreditation, Christman reduced the engineering sequence from five courses to three.
With the time thus saved, he added a course in information technology and
another in a foreign culture (selected from a list approved by each academic
department). Additionally, the new curriculum required first classmen to undergo an "integrative experience"—a capstone exercise demanding an interdisciplinary approach to problem solving. The specific design of the integrative
experience varied depending on each cadet's major, but all integrative experiences required analysis of the social, technological, economic, and political
considerations bearing on a problem.[167]

VI.   RECENT TRENDS

Before closing the chapter on academics at West Point, five trends since the
cheating incident of 1976 deserve mention. Collectively, they demonstrate
the distance West Point has traveled in challenging the paternal and attritional
assumptions that undergirded the curriculum in the nineteenth century and
much of the twentieth. Some things have not changed: the academic program
at the beginning of the twenty-first century still puts heavy demands on cadets
to build their character and intellect; moreover, the Academy still discharges
cadets each year for academic failure. Despite these continuities, however, the
paternal and attritional aspects of the academic program have waned considerably. In their place, diversity of experience and a more forgiving attitude toward
academic failure now characterize the West Point experience. In this regard, the
academic program mirrored the changes in other developmental programs,
particularly leader development and character building.

The first trend was the huge expansion of academic enrichment activities
available to cadets. Millions of dollars in contributions from individuals, alumni
classes, corporations, and foundations helped to pay for "margin-of-excellence"
programs that allowed cadets to apply and contextualize their academic studies.
Many of the experiences came during the academic year, but the most significant ones occurred during the spring and summer breaks, when cadets had extended periods for travel and discretionary activities. Cadets had many options,
including internships with executive agencies, Congress, the Supreme Court,
nongovernmental organizations, research laboratories, and think tanks. They
could travel to most of the countries in the world on staff rides, educational

tours, local development projects, military academy exchanges, and cultural immersions. They could spend time at research archives, lead community service projects, and visit the grim sites of the Holocaust.[168]

The semester-abroad program, begun in the mid-1990s and managed by the Department of Foreign Languages, was particularly important as an academic enrichment activity. For the first few years, the Academy limited the program to only two cadets per year, and always to the French military academy at St. Cyr. (The French reciprocated by sending two St. Cyr cadets to West Point.) After the terror attacks of 11 September 2001, however, a new emphasis on cultural education — and generous funding from Congress — led to rapid expansion of the program.[169] Eleven cadets studied abroad in 2005; eighty-six did so in 2007. By 2009, the number had jumped to 140, with cadets studying in military and civilian institutions in virtually every corner of the world.[170] Cadets derived enormous benefit from their overseas experiences. Besides mastering the host language, they gained confidence in themselves, empathy for other peoples and cultures, and mature perspectives on the issues they would face as officers.

The second trend — creation of academic "centers of excellence"—likewise enriched the intellectual environment at West Point. Superintendent Palmer started the trend by establishing the Performance Enhancement Center in 1989.[171] Although focused initially on improving the competitiveness of athletes through applied sports psychology, the center soon expanded its offerings to other areas of development. Renamed the Center for Enhanced Performance in 1992, it absorbed the remedial reading and study skills programs that had existed since the late 1950s. It created a new course, Student Success, which applied the principles of sports psychology — goal setting, cognitive control, and stress management — to academic study skills. It hired academic counselors to help individual cadets; two of the counselors worked in direct support of the football team. Within a few years, the center expanded its reach to leader training, thus becoming a valuable resource for cadets seeking to improve in any of the three principal developmental programs — academic, military, or physical.[172]

Another of Palmer's creations was the Operations Research Center, founded in 1990 in the Department of Systems Engineering. The new center enabled cadet engineering majors to work on academic projects having direct relevance to the army. One team of cadets, for example, designed systems to identify and destroy the improvised mines used by insurgents against US military forces in Iraq and Afghanistan. Other projects focused on improving battlefield command and control, strengthening tactical body armor, countering cyber attacks, and reducing traffic congestion around army bases. As army agencies became aware of the reservoir of intellectual talent within the Corps of Cadets, the Operations Research Center's activities and funding expanded proportionally.[173]

The success of the Center for Enhanced Performance and the Operations Research Center led to the creation of other academic centers. The Center for Teaching Excellence, established in 1994, provided consultation to the departments on teaching methods; its signature offering was a two-year "master-teacher" program for developing the instructional skills of faculty members.[174] In the Department of Social Sciences, the Combating Terrorism Center opened in 2003. It conducted research, published reports, sponsored cadet trips and internships, and offered courses leading to an academic minor in terrorism studies.[175] In the Department of History, the Center for Oral History opened in 2007 as a means of recording the first-person narratives of soldier experiences. The resulting interview records, in both audio and video formats, provided a rich archive of primary sources for cadet education and inspiration. Also in 2007, the Department of Foreign Languages established the Center for Languages, Cultures, and Regional Studies to advance cadet education in foreign cultures. Finally, the Department of Law established the Center for the Rule of Law in 2009 to promote the US military's advancement of international justice and human rights.[176]

The third trend since 1976 was the gradual shift in cadet majors from mathematics, science, and engineering to the humanities and public affairs. For two decades after the advent of majors in 1983, the majority of cadets chose to focus their studies in the former disciplines, but starting in 2002, the reverse was true. By 2007, the number of cadets in the humanities and public affairs had grown considerably, to more than 60 percent of the graduating class.[177] It is difficult to know for sure what motivated cadets in their selection of majors, but the timing of the shift — shortly after the 2001 terror attacks — was probably not coincidental. The likelihood of facing combat soon after graduation may have influenced cadets to study disciplines that offered context for the wars they would fight. Whatever the reasons, the trend away from the quantitative disciplines worried army leaders. West Point had long been the largest provider of new officers with science and engineering backgrounds, and the wars in Afghanistan and Iraq increased the demand for them. The situation revived the debate between those who favored greater specialization at West Point versus those who preferred the option of graduate schooling to produced qualified scientists and engineers.[178]

The fourth trend was the change in faculty composition. Congress required West Point to begin hiring civilian instructors starting in 1993; within a few years, civilians comprised 25 percent of the faculty.[179] There had been civilians at West Point for a long time — mostly foreign language instructors and, starting in 1971, visiting professors — but their numbers were too small to influence the military culture at the Academy. Once the legislation took effect, however, civilians quickly put their stamp on the institution. They added intellectual depth to every discipline, provided new approaches to curriculum design and pedagogy, and mentored the junior faculty. Their long-term employment lent stability to academic policies and procedures, particularly as they rose to leadership positions within the departments, on the dean's staff, and in the superintendent's faculty council.

The fifth trend was the dramatic decline in separations for academic failure and, conversely, the corresponding rise in graduation rates. During the 1970s, cadet classes graduated at an average rate of about 63 percent; during the 1980s, the average rose to about 68 percent. The graduation rate peaked at slightly over 81 percent in 1995, and remained very close to that level afterward.[180] There were many reasons for the rise in graduation rates, such as advances in pedagogy, curriculum design, and assessment. Additionally, the Center for Enhanced Performance helped many academically weak cadets complete the rigorous curriculum. Also lessening cadet attrition was the reduction in the number of courses required for graduation, as well as the privilege of majoring in a discipline of choice.

The biggest reason for the improved graduation rates, however, was the rejection of attritional assumptions that had characterized the West Point developmental experience since the time of Thayer. Through the 1960s, Academy leaders ruthlessly discharged deficient cadets, thus allowing more time to teach the cadets who remained.[181] Maj. Gen. William D. Connor, superintendent from 1932 to 1938, epitomized the attritional attitude. He believed that the Academy best served the national interest by eliminating the poorest students as soon as possible. "The real truth," he asserted, "is that most young men who are found deficient are usually well below the average in their classes and in only a few exceptional cases is there any special reason to believe that the men so separated are any great loss to the government."[182]

In the aftermath of the 1976 cheating incident, Academy leaders gradually tempered the attritional impulse in academics. The attitudinal change was reflected in adjustments to policies that had hampered intellectual development. For example, academic departments stopped posting weekly grades to encourage cadets to focus more on learning than on their class standing. They allowed free discussion of classroom work, including tests, as soon as class was over and collaboration on some homework assignments, provided cadets documented the assistance they received.[183]

Other policy changes reflected more directly the erosion of attritional attitudes. In particular, the Academic Board became increasingly tolerant of academic deficiency, but the change was slow at first. Through the 1960s, cadets who failed an academic course normally faced separation. The Academic Board offered reexamination to many of the separated cadets, but a passing grade meant turn-back to the next class, not reinstatement with the original class. In borderline cases of deficiency, particularly those involving cadets with strong leader potential, the Academic Board might retain the cadets on "conditioned" (i.e., probationary) status. A conditioned cadet would continue with his normal classes and have the chance of demonstrating his proficiency at some point during the next semester. If all went well, the Academic Board would remove the condition and the cadet would graduate with his class; if not, the cadet faced separation. Although reexaminations and conditioning saved some cadets from separation through the 1960s, the academic system was still highly attritional. Any cadet who failed more than one course could count on dismissal.[184]

The Academic Board began to moderate its hard line in the 1970s. A new "summer academic remediation program" allowed conditioned cadets to resolve their deficiencies during a three-week session in June. In 1977, the remediation program expanded into a four-week summer academic term during which a deficient cadet could retake a failed course in its entirety; if successful, the cadet would rejoin his or her class without losing ground.[185] For cadets who failed multiple courses but showed leader potential in other areas, turn-back became an increasingly popular option for the Academic Board.[186] The net effect of the summer term and turn-back initiatives was to allow cadets many more chances to succeed and, therefore, to gradually lower the academic attrition rate.[187]

In the first decade of the twenty-first century, the Academic Board went even further in retaining academically marginal cadets. It expanded the number of summer terms from one to three, thus allowing academically weak cadets more flexibility in remediating their failures. It used the turn-back option liberally and retained cadets who failed multiple courses in the same year or who failed the same courses more than once. In short, the Academic Board turned attritionalism on its head — rather than winnowing out the cadets who were "well below the average," it made every effort to help those same cadets graduate. Provided an academically marginal cadet showed a positive attitude and avoided serious disciplinary problems, he or she had a good chance of eventually graduating and receiving an officer's commission.

The clearest expression of the Academic Board's new leniency was an experiment in 2008 to allow academic underloading for some cadets. The experiment was a reprise of an initiative in 1980 to help cadet-athletes manage the competing pressures of academics and athletics. Under the earlier system, cadet-athletes would voluntarily take a summer course to lighten the load during the academic year, when athletic practices took up much of their free time. There were many objections to the 1980 underloading experiment, which lasted only briefly. The 2008 experiment was virtually identical to the earlier program, and its long-term prospects are not yet clear. The three-decade decline of attritional attitudes, however, suggests that there will be fewer obstacles to its acceptance now than before.[188]

Part of the reason behind the decline in attritionalism was the changing composition of the Corps of Cadets. Starting in the 1970s, Academy leaders committed themselves to affirmative action policies that brought to West Point an increasing number of students with weak academic credentials. Meanwhile, the heightened priority given to intercollegiate athletics led to the admission of more recruited athletes, the most academically at-risk cadet population. This trend accelerated in the early twenty-first century. In 2003, the admissions office classified about 6 percent of the incoming class as being academically at risk; by 2009, the number of at-risk cadets had grown to 12 percent, with roughly two-thirds of them being recruited athletes. Since Academy leaders had fashioned the policies that allowed this situation to develop, they felt obligated to devote resources to help the weaker students succeed.[189]

Another reason for the decline of attritionalism was the onset of war in Iraq and Afghanistan after the domestic terror attacks of 2001. The stress of repeated military deployments induced many army officers to leave the service before reaching retirement, thus exacerbating a trend that had been under way for several decades.[190] Compounding the problem was a steady drop in the number of college students enrolled in the Reserve Officer Training Corps. Under these circumstances, Academy leaders sought to increase the number of graduates by reducing attrition to the lowest possible level.[191]

The combination of factors, internal and external to West Point, pushed Academy leaders to great lengths to lower cadet attrition. We have surveyed some of the new policies, procedures, and organizations that advanced this cause; less obvious was the added effort on the part of every faculty member to assist cadets who needed help. The increased workload was difficult to measure, as it came in the form of extra time spent in grading tests, providing additional instruction, and counseling.[192] These efforts seemed to be effective: despite the growing numbers of weak students in the Corps of Cadets, the high graduation rates first achieved in the 1990s have endured. Moreover, minorities and recruited athletes have graduated at rates that are equal to, or only slightly below, the rate of the Corps as a whole. To be sure, many cadets failed many courses during those years, but the academic safety net that had gradually developed since 1976 enabled a high percentage of the weakest cadets to eventually graduate.

★   ★   ★

In 2009, *Forbes* magazine proclaimed West Point to be the number one college in the nation.[193] *Forbes* found much to like at the Academy since its methodology weighted educational outcomes (e.g., graduation rates) more heavily than the academic credentials of the student body. Academy leaders were understandably proud of the recognition, which seemed to validate the quality of the education and the effectiveness of the academic support system for weaker students.

Still, many Academy leaders recognized that high graduation rates represented a double-edged sword. On the one hand, West Point was producing more graduates for the army; on the other, a growing number of them were academically marginal. The situation raised troubling questions. Was West Point admitting candidates of the highest possible quality? Was it producing the best possible officers for the army? Was the traditional focus on intellectual development still the defining feature (along with character building) of the West Point experience? The answers to these questions would take a generation to answer, as the Long Gray Line absorbed the newest graduates into its ranks.

CHAPTER FIVE

Sabers and Goalposts

THE PHYSICAL PROGRAM

WITH THE APPOINTMENT of Herman J. Koehler as Master of the Sword in 1885, West Point soon had a high-quality physical education program to match its already impressive academic program.[1] Koehler imposed on fourth-class cadets a daily regimen of exercise that brought dramatic improvements in their strength and endurance. His success convinced the Academic Board to make physical education mandatory for all cadets starting in 1905.

An important, but voluntary, component of Koehler's physical program was competitive athletics. Varsity sports appealed to the most gifted athletes, while intramural sports were available to all others. Koehler believed strongly in the value of competitive sports and encouraged as many cadets as possible to participate. His efforts were rewarded when Douglas MacArthur became the superintendent after World War I and made intramural athletics mandatory for all cadets.

Academy leaders were scrupulous in harnessing athletics to the needs of cadet development. They put strict limits on the time available for practice and competition to ensure that other developmental goals took precedence over sports. With few exceptions, they assigned officers as coaches to ensure that athletic endeavors complemented leader development and character building, rather than instilling a win-at-all-cost mentality. They discouraged overt recruitment of outside players, relying instead on the native athletic talent of the Corps of Cadets.[2] They disqualified cadets who were deficient in any academic subject from participating in varsity sports. They limited the privileges granted to athletes to safeguard the tradition of equal treatment within the Corps of Cadets.

Between 1920 and 1940, the Academy's physical program, as designed by Koehler, was more effective in achieving the Academy's leader development goals than at any time before or since. Academy leaders worked hard to ensure that the mandatory and voluntary components of the program complemented the intellectual and character-building priorities of cadet development.

Since 1940, the mandatory elements of the physical program have evolved and strengthened. Academy leaders instituted new methods of instruction and testing and recruited higher-quality faculty members, many of whom had advanced academic degrees. A new physical aptitude examination disqualified cadet candidates who were physically weak. Cognitive courses in physical education and, later, an academic major in kinesiology complemented the traditional physical-activity courses. Advances in physiology, psychology, and sports medicine enhanced the performance and safety of cadets in the program. Despite these and other improvements, however, the broad outlines of Koehler's program of physical education remained unchanged.

In one important area, however, the physical program departed from the principles and procedures that Koehler had established. Starting in 1941, intercollegiate athletics assumed an increasing level of importance, particularly with the astounding success of the head football coach, Earl Blaik. National collegiate football championships in 1944 and 1945 coincided with the greatest victories for American armies overseas during World War II. The result was to mythologize football at West Point and ultimately to transform intercollegiate athletics — football in particular — from a component of the physical program to an institutional goal unto itself.

In the early 1980s, following several years of lackluster performances by varsity teams, the Academy's institutional priorities shifted in favor of athletics. Within a few years, intercollegiate athletics became as commercialized and professionalized at West Point as they had been at many other major colleges and universities. The resulting emphasis on winning conflicted with the principles Koehler had established for competitive sports.

Those who favored the heightened priority on intercollegiate athletics claimed that fielding winning teams would attract higher-quality cadet candidates and produce better officers for the army. Although the evidence of many years refutes both claims, senior Academy leaders have continued to emphasize intercollegiate athletics as an integral part of the West Point experience.

I.   EVERY CADET PHYSICALLY FIT

Herman Koehler, the indomitable master of the sword from 1885 to 1923, seemed like a force of nature at West Point. At the time of the centennial cel-

Capt. Herman Koehler, Master of the
Sword from 1885 to 1924.

ebration, he had been on the Academy staff for seventeen years. He was then
forty-two years old — twice the age of the average cadet, yet more fit than any
of them. He was five feet, nine inches tall and weighed about one hundred and
ninety pounds. His enormous biceps measured nineteen and one-half inches
around when flexed. As a former national champion in gymnastics, he had
a perfectly sculpted and conditioned body and ramrod straight posture. Although gentlemanly and affable, his black mustache enhanced his image as a
fierce and demanding taskmaster.[3]

Koehler was a magnificent instructor.[4] He taught all of the physical education subjects and could outperform the cadets in virtually any physical endeavor.
He had a deep, booming voice that enabled him to lead large formations in
physical training or to correct an unsuspecting cadet from afar.[5] At every opportunity, he turned his physical education classes into leadership seminars. He
talked earnestly to cadets about professional military values — self-discipline,
perseverance, courage, commitment. An associate of Koehler's recalled that,

during these soliloquies on the moral dimensions of officership, "You could hear a pin drop."[6]

Koehler was the originator of the "setting-up exercises," calisthenics designed for the "harmonious development of the entire body."[7] Cadets performed the exercises in mass formation in response to commands from the instructor. Koehler was uncompromising in requiring precise movements and vigorous execution. He also demanded proper posture: shoulders back and square, stomach in, chest out, head straight, and chin pressed rearward to straighten the neck and spine. Over the years, thousands of cadets learned to stand straight and tall under Koehler's healthy influence.[8]

First-year cadets started the physical program immediately upon their arrival during the summer. Under Koehler's supervision, they conducted setting-up exercises to condition their muscles and practice discipline; on some days, they also took dancing lessons.[9] Once the academic year began, they took gymnastics, fencing (foil, saber, and bayonet), and swimming.[10] Physical education took place every morning, except on Sunday, and lasted forty-five minutes.

In addition to his instructional duties, Koehler was an expert in applying the scientific method to physical education. He had studied experimental methodologies at the Milwaukee Normal School of Physical Training, one of the nation's premier schools for aspiring physical education professionals. From the start of his employment as the master of the sword, Koehler conducted size and strength measurements for every plebe twice a year. The first measurements were in October, the latter measurements in May. Without fail, the plebes improved dramatically from undergoing several months of Koehler's physical regimen.[11] Still, Koehler was not satisfied. The physical program, he wrote, "has not yet reached the limit of its usefulness" and would not do so until "every member of the Corps of Cadets is permitted to enjoy its benefits during the entire time of his stay at the Academy."[12] At every opportunity Koehler argued that all cadets, not just the plebes, should undergo mandatory physical training.

Koehler's views were consistent with the army's growing emphasis on preventive medicine. Army doctors in the late nineteenth century reflected the increasing professionalism of medical practitioners and their holistic approach to wellness. They viewed Koehler's work as a model for promoting health and thus reducing the onset of preventable diseases and injuries. In the case of West Point cadets, physical conditioning helped to balance the mental and emotional pressures of the academic program.[13]

The emphasis on preventive medicine, coupled with Koehler's constant prodding, convinced the Academic Board to require physical education for all cadets starting in 1905.[14] Congress already had granted Koehler an officer's commission (first lieutenant) in 1901; four years later, it authorized a promo-

Cadets in Central Area undergoing mass physical training. In addition to building strength and endurance, the exercises promoted self-discipline and unit cohesion.

tion to the rank of captain, which accorded with Koehler's expanded responsibilities as the physical education instructor for the entire Corps of Cadets.[15] Another sign of favor was the money appropriated to build a modern and spacious gymnasium. Completed in 1910, the new building was one of the finest physical education facilities on any college campus in the nation.[16]

Under the new physical education program, cadets engaged in a series of increasingly difficult activities during their four years at West Point. The plebes continued with their usual course of instruction in gymnastics, fencing, and swimming; additionally, they took introductory lessons in boxing and wrestling. The third and second classes took advanced lessons in gymnastics, fencing, boxing, and wrestling to develop "as high a standard of proficiency as time and conditions will admit." First classmen received instruction in the "theories of physical training, with a view to their practical application to the needs of our service." The upper three classes took riding, with the first classmen receiving the bulk of the instruction.[17]

To accommodate the expanded program of physical education, Superintendent Albert Mills convinced the Academic Board to change the daily schedule.

TABLE 5.1   Mandatory Physical Training Program, 1905

Class	Activity	Attendance	Hours
Fourth (1st year)	Gymnastics, Swimming, Fencing, Boxing, Wrestling	Morning or afternoon, daily except Saturday	169 periods at 45 minutes each
Third (2nd year)	Gymnastics, Fencing, Boxing, Wrestling	After last class, weekdays except Wednesday	35 periods at 40 minutes each
	Riding	Afternoon	42 periods at 60 minutes each
Second (3rd year)	Gymnastics, Fencing, Boxing, Wrestling	After last class, weekdays except Wednesday	35 periods at 45 minutes each
	Riding	After last class, weekdays except Wednesday	35 periods at 60 minutes each
First (4th year)	Theory of Physical Training	Afternoon	33 periods at 45 minutes each
	Riding	Morning	104 periods at 60 minutes each

Notes: Information adapted from Annual Report of the Superintendent, 1905, 33–35, and Regulations for the United States Military Academy, 1916 (Washington, DC: Government Printing Office, 1916), 34–36. The former source contains a detailed listing of the exercises and activities within each subject of physical education.

The principal change was to distribute the hours of the day more evenly between breakfast and lunch and between lunch and supper. By the old schedule, breakfast was at 6:30 a.m., lunch at 1:00 p.m., and supper at various times between 5:30 and 7:00 p.m.[18] Under the new schedule, breakfast was at 6:30 a.m., lunch at 12:15 p.m., and supper always at 6:00 p.m. All classes ceased at 3:30 p.m. The new schedule provided the time necessary for physical education to occur throughout the academic year and for voluntary sports after school. Mills was proud of the accomplishment: "No more important step than this, in securing and maintaining a proper physical condition in the corps of cadets, has been taken for a long time."[19]

In contrast to the mandatory nature of physical education, West Point offered a voluntary program of competitive sports. Cadets played football and baseball at the intercollegiate level as early as 1890; fencing started in 1902, basketball in 1903, hockey in 1904, and lacrosse in 1907.[20] Each of these sports, and many others, also were available at the intramural level.

The need to support and administer the competitive sports program led to the formation of a private booster organization, the Army Officers Athletic Association, in 1892. The AOAA collected donations to hire civilian coaches, purchase uniforms, and build athletic facilities. It controlled the scheduling of competitions and paid the cost of travel to Annapolis and the guarantees to the collegiate teams that came to West Point.[21] From the standpoint of the AOAA, the superintendent's only involvement was to approve the trips to the Naval Academy.[22] Lt. Col. Wright P. Edgerton, professor of mathematics, was the AOAA president in 1902 and a firm believer in the need to support competitive sports at West Point. Prior to 1890, he noted, life for cadets was "stern, harsh, almost prison-like. . . . The only amusements accorded them were the dubious ones of drill and study." With the help of the AOAA, cadets enjoyed the "recreations natural and most wholesome for their time of life. . . . They bear the burdens of the curriculum with lighter hearts, while their *esprit de corps* is greatly increased."[23]

In 1903, the AOAA was renamed the Army Athletic Association. As stated in its constitution, the purpose of the new organization was "to encourage and assist" the sports permitted by the superintendent and "to encourage athletic sports throughout the army." The organization's leadership consisted of a president, vice-president, secretary, and treasurer; they sat on a council that included representatives from each intercollegiate sport. Curiously, there were no ex-officio positions reserved for the superintendent or the commandant. At the time, this arrangement seemed appropriate for an organization supported by private funds, but it would become a source of friction later on.[24]

The Army-Navy football rivalry was the highlight of the intercollegiate sports program. Academy leaders took the contest seriously, and they made accommodations for the football team to improve the chances of winning. In the dining hall, for example, the players could arrive late for the dinner meal and eat at training tables to ensure they consumed enough calories. They had excess laundry privileges and could wear their hair longer than other cadets as a natural defense against concussions. On game days, members of the first and second teams (a total of twenty-four cadets) were allowed to stand inspection in the area of the barracks rather than in normal formation. On practice days, they alone could bathe with hot water after 4:00 p.m. When feasible, they could arrange their schedules to have the last academic hour free.

Notwithstanding these concessions, Academy leaders kept a tight rein on football and the other sports to ensure they did not compete with more important priorities for cadet development.[25] The principle that football came second to academic study and military duties, noted Mills, "has been rigidly maintained since football was established at the Military Academy."[26] He elaborated:

> Members of athletic teams should give as much time to their studies and their military duties as other cadets. In other words, West Point believes that satisfactory athletic teams can be developed by devoting to practice no more time than is allowed to all cadets at the Academy for recreational purposes. If the

most efficient team cannot be developed under this principle, then success in
athletics must be sacrificed to more important work.[27]

The cadets apparently had sufficient time to field competitive teams in several varsity sports. Between 1902 and 1912, for example, they won seven national fencing championships.[28] They were also competitive in football, which,
by the turn of the century, had become a national pastime rivaling baseball in
popularity. During the sixteen football seasons from 1890 through 1905, the
cadets won seventy, lost thirty-five, and tied eleven games.[29] The cadets loved
football, and over a third of the Corps played it.[30] Each class fielded a team,
with an officer-coach in charge. The teams played each other on an intramural
basis, and the best players migrated to the varsity team.

Although popular, college football in the early twentieth century was dangerous, even deadly. In 1905, eighteen young men died playing the game, and
President Theodore Roosevelt threatened to ban the sport if college presidents
did not act to make it safer. As one of the premier football schools, West Point
agreed to help establish rules to mitigate the brutality and foul play that characterized the sport. Participating schools convened a conference in December
1905 and formed a football governance body known as the Intercollegiate
Athletic Association of the United States. The conferees elected the West Point
representative, Capt. Palmer Pierce, as the first president of the new organization. He and the executive committee established the mission of imposing
"wise control of student athletics and sports in order to save what is salutary
and overcome the evils that have grown up."[31] The organization took its present name, the National Collegiate Athletic Association, in 1910.[32]

In 1908, Col. Hugh Scott, the superintendent from 1906 to 1910, confronted "a dangerous mess" involving intercollegiate athletics at West Point.
The situation involved about thirty officers, all members of the Army Athletic
Association, who were "obsessed with a wrong idea" about sports at the Academy.[33] Specifically, they assumed that the Association's charter as a privately
funded organization allowed them to operate independently of the superintendent and commandant. While Scott had been away on an extended absence
in 1908, these officers threatened to cancel the Army-Navy football game that
year because of a dispute with the Naval Academy over player eligibility. These
actions suggested that intercollegiate sports, because they were voluntary and
privately funded, were not under the superintendent's purview.

Scott disagreed. Even if the Army Athletic Association paid all the bills, the
superintendent was in command of West Point and the Corps of Cadets. He
was not about to let the obsession with intercollegiate athletics infringe on his
command responsibilities. He handled the situation, he recalled, by "abolish-
ing the entire Athletic Association root and branch, and making a new one of
my own creation."[34]

Under the new Army Athletic Association charter, the president (a member of the Academic Board) received direction from an Athletic Council consisting of the commandant, various officers on the superintendent's staff, master of the sword, and an officer for each major sport. This arrangement gave the superintendent plenty of leverage over the conduct of the athletics program. The official orders that announced the new organization put the matter bluntly: "It has been thought best by the Military Authorities of the Academy to take entire charge of the direction of all athletic contests and games."[35] Although it continued to be a privately funded organization, the Army Athletic Association was now firmly under the superintendent's control.

The new Athletic Council, wishing to make a clean break with the old organization, directed the master of the sword to propose a set of principles under which the Academy's physical program would operate. In response, Koehler wrote a seminal paper, *The Theory and Practice of Athletics at the Military Academy*, which has served as the blueprint of West Point's physical program ever since.[36] Koehler argued that the role of athletics at any institution should be the "development of the very highest possible standard of general excellence of the mass of its students, rather than that of a few." It was therefore no wonder that intercollegiate athletics developed more slowly at West Point than at other schools, where "winning is made their chief object."[37] Koehler believed that Academy leaders could overcome these problems because they had the power to "set athletics a hard and fast limit" and prevent "all danger of undue license on the one hand and over-indulgence on the other." Under careful supervision, athletics at West Point

> [C]an be made the pastime of the many rather than the serious business of the few, while the evils, the prostitution of the ethics of athletics, the spirit to win at all hazards, that was rapidly becoming the dominant object of college athletics, and that served only to defeat their purpose from an educational point of view, could be made impossible.[38]

Koehler's main points — that competitive athletics were a complement to the overall physical program and that winning was not the principal goal — went unchallenged for many years. As evidence, the experience of varsity athletes differed little from that of their classmates, except for the time spent on the practice field. Even then, practice was limited to three days a week during the period normally allotted to intramurals and free time. The coaching staff consisted mostly of army officers, whose first priority was to meet the developmental goals of the Academy.[39] There was no formal system of athletic recruiting, which meant that athletes had no advantages over their prospective classmates in the application process.[40] These attributes of the Academy's intercollegiate sports program may seem archaic to a twenty-first century observer, but they conformed to the principles that Koehler had brought to the Academy in 1885 and articulated formally in 1909.

There was plenty of supervision for cadets in the physical program. Koehler and his small cadre of assistants personally instructed the cadets in the mandatory subjects. Other officials included army surgeons, officer-coaches, and the athletics trainer. Scott characterized the athletics trainer position as "indispensable" and succeeded in obtaining funding from the government, rather than the Army Athletic Association, to make it permanent.[41] Despite these safeguards, however, some high-risk activities, such as riding and gymnastics, caused occasional cadet injuries, and no activity was as dangerous as football. In 1912, of the sixty-one injuries requiring hospitalization and bed rest, 75 percent were football related. Worse, according to Col. Clarence Townsley, superintendent from 1910 to 1914, football was "likely to produce more lasting injuries than riding or gymnastics."[42]

The entry of the United States into the First World War caused major disruptions to the physical program at West Point. Most significant was the loss of Herman Koehler from May 1917 to September 1918. The War Department sent him to training bases around the nation to teach military leaders how to design and lead physical training programs for their soldiers. While his work drew high praise everywhere he went, his prolonged absence denied cadets the benefits of his instruction.[43]

When the War Department condensed the curriculum from four years to three in 1917, intercollegiate athletics were suspended so that the time could be devoted to other pursuits. In early 1918, cadets asked for reinstatement of athletic privileges during the spring season. The request coincided with the German offensives on the Western Front and brought a harsh response from the Superintendent, Col. Samuel Tillman. "Whatever views as to the value of voluntary athletics may prevail at other places," he scolded, "*they should be permitted and promoted only as* aids *to the duties here imposed and not as* substitutes *for them.*" Tillman believed that athletics, although fun and developmental, were no substitute for military training or the "more important and higher preparation for which the Military Academy was established."[44]

Tillman had spent many years as the professor of chemistry, mineralogy, and geology before his recall from retirement to be the superintendent in 1917. Being an academic at heart, he chafed at the War Department's decision to condense the curriculum. Like many of his colleagues, he was wary of sports because they competed for academic time; his attitude presaged the three-way tensions between the proponents of academics, military training, and athletics that would grow in subsequent years. As it happened, the man who replaced Tillman as superintendent could not have viewed competitive athletics more differently.

II. Every Cadet an Athlete—The Interwar Era

Brig. Gen. Douglas MacArthur replaced Tillman in June 1919. Having just returned from wartime duty in France, he knew firsthand that "troops in poor physical condition are worthless."[45] As the new superintendent, he was determined that cadets would be in top physical condition upon their commissioning as officers. He would achieve this goal through competitive athletics, which had several benefits. First, they honed "the qualities of leadership, quickness of decision, promptness of action, mental and muscular coordination, aggressiveness, and courage." Additionally, they strengthened "that indefinable spirit of group interest and pride which we know as morale."[46] Finally, sports afforded cadets opportunities to mingle with civilians and thus counterbalanced the paternalistic leanings of the Academic Board.[47] MacArthur's devotion to athletics led him to compose an adage that he had chiseled above the door of the gymnasium: "Upon the fields of friendly strife are sown the seeds that, upon other fields, on other days, will bear the fruits of victory."[48]

MacArthur moved quickly to establish a mandatory program of intramural athletics (table 5.2). It required MacArthur only to decide to do so; the athletics themselves already existed, and it was Koehler who got the job of implementing the superintendent's order. The program was an instant success, with cadets competing aggressively on the fields of friendly strife. The program soon was dubbed "intramurder" because of its ferocity.[49] A further encouragement to athletics was the commandant's decision to incorporate athletics into the cadet rating scheme; henceforth, a cadet's athletic prowess would count for 15 percent of his leadership rating (a component of his overall order of merit). Additionally, he curtailed drill to provide more time for athletics.[50]

With mandatory athletics in place, Academy leaders no longer saw the need for upper-class cadets to take physical education classes during academic time. They considered after-school athletics—combined with riding, military drill, and parade—sufficient to maintain individual fitness.[51] The plebes, however, were not so lucky. Every weekday morning, they endured a grueling regimen of setting-up exercises, body building, and elementary gymnastics. Twice a week, after class, they participated in athletics with the rest of the Corps of Cadets.[52] Under MacArthur, "every man an athlete" became the rallying cry.[53] All cadets, regardless of athletic ability, would participate in intramurals, and they would play the sports that were most popular—that is, the sports that their soldiers were likely to play. Additionally, they would learn to play "carry over" sports— soccer, lacrosse, track and field, golf, tennis—that they could enjoy well into their adult lives.[54] Between 70 and 75 percent of cadets participated in intramural sports; the remainder played on the varsity teams.[55]

MacArthur was fascinated by intercollegiate athletics. According to his ad-

TABLE 5.2   First Program of Intramural Athletics, 1920–1921

Season	Sports	Remarks
Summer	Baseball Golf Gymnastics Polo Soccer Swimming Tennis Track and Field	July–August (six weeks), five days per week, one hour per day One sport per week (Not every cadet participated in every sport.) Fourth class only
Fall	Basketball Corrective Exercises Cross Country Fencing Football Golf Gymnastics Lacrosse Polo Swimming Tennis	1 September–3 November All cadets, except those playing intercollegiate sports
Spring	Baseball Golf Gymnastics Polo Soccer Swimming Tennis Track and Field	15 April–2 June All cadets, except those playing intercollegiate sports

Notes: Adapted from Degen, *The Evolution of Physical Education at the United States Military Academy*, 55.

jutant, William Ganoe, the young superintendent attended team practices frequently and "vicariously played every position of every game he saw."[56] His love of sports and conviction of their value to cadet development led him to expand the number of varsity teams. At the time of his arrival as the superintendent, the only intercollegiate squads were baseball, football, basketball, and hockey. MacArthur continued all those sports and added lacrosse, rifle, tennis, boxing, polo, soccer, swimming, wrestling, outdoor track, golf, and cross country (table 5.3).

Although MacArthur had lettered in baseball as a cadet, his greatest love was football. The sport seemed to resemble most closely the chaos, violence, and bodily contact characteristic of war. He therefore resolved to promote football by actively recruiting the most talented players to West Point. Some members of the Academic Board resented the superintendent's emphasis on athletics, but MacArthur was unapologetic: "I will be bold and frank in seeking candidates with athletic reputation and background. We have nothing to hide."[57] True to his word, he announced to alumni, boosters, and coaches that the Academy wanted good football players. He authorized officers to conduct recruiting trips to all corners of the country. In so doing, he formalized a prac-

TABLE 5.3   Varsity Sports at West Point

Men			Women		
Varsity Sport	*Started*	*Note*	*Varsity Sport*	*Started*	*Note*
Baseball	1890		Basketball	1977	
Football	1890		Cross Country	1978	
Fencing	1902	1	Gymnastics	1978	10
Basketball	1903		Swimming	1978	
Hockey	1904		Track (indoor)	1978	
Lacrosse	1907	2	Volleyball	1978	
Rifle	1919		Softball	1979	
Tennis	1920		Tennis	1979	
Boxing	1921	3	Track (outdoor)	1979	
Polo	1921	4	Soccer	1986	
Soccer	1921				
Swimming	1921				
Wrestling	1921				
Track (outdoor)	1921				
Golf	1922				
Cross Country	1922	5			
Pistol	1923	6			
Gymnastics	1926				
Track (indoor)	1942				
Squash	1948	7			
150-pound Football	1957				
Water Polo	1975	8			
Volleyball	1975	9			

Notes:
1. No matches from 1913–1922 and 1955–1966; discontinued in 1979
2. No games in 1908 and from 1911–1920
3. Discontinued in 1955
4. Discontinued in 1943
5. No meets from 1923–1927
6. Discontinued in 1993
7. Discontinued in 1988
8. Discontinued in 1993
9. Discontinued in 1979
10. Discontinued in 1978 (varsity sport for only one year)

Notes: Information provided to author by the Army Sports Information Office. See also Dineen, *Illustrated History of Sports at the U.S. Military Academy*, 272. Some sports, such as rifle, pistol, water polo, boxing, and men's volleyball, have migrated between varsity and club status.

tice that had been going on covertly for many years, but had been frowned upon by the Academic Board.[58]

West Point had big advantages in recruiting athletes. Most significant was the Academy's refusal to observe the NCAA's three-year varsity eligibility rule, to which most colleges adhered. As a result, a three-year letterman at a civilian college could have a second playing career by entering West Point prior to his twenty-second birthday — the maximum permissible age of entry.[59] In contrast, the maximum entry age at Annapolis was only twenty years, which made West Point the destination of choice for athletes wishing to extend their collegiate playing careers by attending a service academy.[60] Edgar Garbisch was one such athlete. After playing football for four years at Washington and Jefferson College, he entered the Academy in 1921 and played for another four years as a cadet. Garbisch twice earned All America honors at West Point as an offensive lineman; additionally, his place-kicking skills provided the margin of victory in two Army-Navy games.[61] There were many other such players, and they contributed to the success of West Point's football program during the 1920s and 1930s.[62]

Academy leaders would not observe the three-year eligibility rule because of their commitment to treating every cadet equally. All cadets had the same opportunities and privileges, and they lived under the same rules and restrictions.[63] In defense of this democratic principle, Academy officials refused to discriminate against a cadet athlete on account of his previous playing experience. Additionally, they justified the practice of recruiting accomplished athletes by reminding their critics of the physical demands of military service. Even if these arguments were sincere, however, they gave West Point a heavy advantage over its athletic rivals and a bad image when it came to sportsmanship. The issue came to a head in 1927, when the Naval Academy adopted the three-year eligibility rule and insisted that the teams it played do the same.[64] West Point officials refused to yield, which resulted in the cancellation of the Army-Navy football games in 1928 and 1929.[65]

The Academy's focus on physical education and competitive sports made the Corps of Cadets the nation's fittest student body. The evidence of this distinction came from the results of standardized physical fitness testing. In 1923, the National Amateur Athletic Federation established collegiate fitness standards, and the War Department immediately directed the Academy to evaluate the cadets. Cadets were tested in all four of the prescribed events: 100-yard dash, running broad jump, running high jump, and bar vault. West Point took first place among eighty-eight competing colleges with an overall score of 326.84 points out of a possible 400 points (81.7 percent). In the freshman category, West Point also scored first with 319 points (79.7 percent). West Point earned the "excellent college" rating, which was just below the varsity athletic rating. This outcome confirmed that the cadets were, as a group, exceptionally fit compared to their civilian peers.[66]

The master of the sword could not have been happier. Now in the twilight of his career, Herman Koehler's vision for a robust physical development program for all cadets had become a reality. Moreover, the principles upon which the physical program rested were precisely those that he had established years before. Koehler therefore could retire in 1923 with a sense of pride in his grand accomplishments.[67]

MacArthur's successor, Brig. Gen. Fred Sladen, was also a staunch supporter of the physical program. Competitive sports, he noted, "form a community of interest about which Corps spirit and Corps camaraderie center. Through them class distinctions of all kinds are eliminated."[68] The second point was particularly important. Once mandatory sports were in place, upper-class cadets had less reason to torment the plebes. The Board of Visitors, which had often criticized the Academy for its inability to eliminate hazing, commented favorably on the trend: "It is difficult to haze the same lad that one also fosters as a team mate."[69] Sladen cautioned, however, that athletics had to be pursued without "permitting them to encroach upon those sterner military or academic duties upon which the successful mastery of the curriculum depends."[70]

In 1929, the War Department ordered the Academy to cease recruiting athletes.[71] Regardless, the directive did not require West Point to observe the three-year eligibility rule; neither did it alter the Academy's advantage of having a higher maximum entry age than the Naval Academy. West Point therefore continued to enjoy an influx of experienced players, even though it could no longer overtly extend the helping hand of coaches and recruiters. Enough collegiate athletes matriculated to allow the West Point football team to continue its unbroken string of winning seasons through 1938.[72] In that year, the Academy finally adopted the three-year eligibility rule and thus lost its recruiting advantage. Not coincidentally, West Point suffered two consecutive losing seasons in 1939 and 1940.[73] It was quite a shock, as the last time the football team had experienced a losing season was in 1906.

New athletic facilities built during the 1920s and 1930s reflected the emerging priority on athletics. In 1924, construction began on a 16,000-seat football stadium immediately west of Lusk Reservoir; completed in November, it became one of the most picturesque college football venues in the nation.[74] A new indoor hockey rink, opened in January 1931, stood immediately south of the reservoir; this facility ensured that the Academy could field an intercollegiate hockey team every year regardless of the weather. Additions to the gymnasium went up in 1935 and 1938 to provide more space for physical education, intramurals, and intercollegiate athletics.[75]

Construction of the new athletic facilities would have been impossible without the largesse of the Army Athletic Association. Annual membership dues helped to fill the coffers, but the greatest revenue came from the sale of football tickets. From the beginning, Academy leaders boasted that the Army Athletic Association supported more than just intercollegiate athletics. It "has furnished many recreational facilities for the cadets and has assisted greatly in providing facilities for the intramural athletics."[76] Moreover, it paid for the travel of varsity teams to distant competitions and, occasionally, for the travel of the Corps of Cadets as spectators. The financial solvency of the Association was vital because Academy officials scrupulously avoided asking for government funds to support intercollegiate athletics. They noted the voluntary nature of varsity sports and the fact that only a minority of cadets directly benefited from them. Using congressionally appropriated funds, even in the unlikely event they were made available, would therefore be inappropriate in the eyes of West Point leaders.

The years between the two world wars were the physical program's golden era at West Point. All cadets participated in physical education and intramurals, and many competed in varsity sports. Both the mandatory and voluntary components of the program elevated professional development over the quest for victory. Nonetheless, West Point teams won many more contests than they lost. During the 1920s and 1930s, for example, Academy teams won over 66 percent of their varsity competitions (table 5.4). There is little doubt that the Academy's eligibility and recruitment policies during those years had much to do with the strong performance of Academy teams. Just as important, however, were the above-average physical fitness of the Corps of Cadets and the dedicated coaching and mentorship provided by officers on the faculty.

The experience of Garrison Davidson, class of 1927, provides an example of the conditions under which the cadets played and the faculty supervised competitive sports during the interwar period. As a cadet, Davidson played end on his company football team, which won the Corps championship in November 1923. The following November, he was a starter at the same position during the Army-Navy game. By his own admission, he was neither big—five feet, ten inches tall and 169 pounds—nor fast, but he was "a good blocker and tackler, had reasonably fast reactions and loved the game."[77]

On the train home from the 1926 Army-Navy game, the head coach invited Davidson to stay at West Point following graduation to coach the ends on the plebe team. Since "service in the Army was not too appealing in those peaceful times," Davidson accepted the offer.[78] He spent three years coaching the plebes at his old position; following that, he coached the junior varsity for two years and was the head coach of the plebe football team for one year.

In the summer of 1932, Davidson unexpectedly received an offer to be the head football coach following the upcoming season. The choice had come down to either him or Earl Blaik, a 1920 graduate of West Point who lettered

TABLE 5.4 Win-Loss-Tie Record of All Varsity Sports by Decade

Academic Year	No. of Contests	No. Won	No. Lost	No. Tied	Win Percentage	Nonloss Percentage
1890–1900	124	60	57	7	48.39	54.03
1900–1910	388	254	116	18	65.46	70.10
1910–1920	449	301	139	9	67.04	69.04
1920–1930	1,398	928	421	49	66.38	69.89
1930–1940	1,476	1,006	429	41	68.16	70.93
1940–1950	1,689	1,118	523	48	66.19	69.03
1950–1960	1,903	1,188	664	51	62.43	65.11
1960–1970	2,253	1,596	627	30	70.84	72.17
1970–1980	3,077	1,834	1,210	33	59.60	60.68
1980–1990	4,515	2,711	1,754	50	60.04	61.15
1990–2000	4,246	2,215	1,983	48	52.17	53.30
2000–2010	4,135	2,110	1,940	85	51.03	53.08
Totals	25,653	15,321	9,863	469	59.72	61.55

Notes: Each decade starts with academic year XX00–XX01 and ends with academic year XX99–XX00. The lone exception is the first decade in the table, which includes the results of the spring 1890 baseball season (i.e., academic year 1889–1890). The author wishes to acknowledge Madeline Salvani, a senior public affairs specialist in the Army Sports Information Office, who helped compile the win-loss records for each intercollegiate varsity team since 1890. This task was surprisingly difficult, as it required gathering data from various sources, but primarily from the media guide for each sport (available at www.goarmysports.com). The task also required interpreting the sometimes contradictory, biased, or vague record-keeping of generations past.

in three sports as a cadet. Blaik resigned his commission in 1922 and soon became a football coach at the University of Wisconsin before joining the Academy's coaching staff in 1927. Although Blaik had more experience as a coach, Davidson got the job because Academy leaders thought it "desirable to have a graduate still on active duty as head coach."[79]

Davidson assumed his new duties in January 1933. At twenty-eight years old — still a second lieutenant — he was the youngest head football coach in West Point's history. He recalled with amusement that he was making only $125 per month, a far cry from the "five figure annual salaries paid the coaches of our major opponents."[80]

Despite the paltry salary, Davidson had the job that other officers could only dream about. College football had become a hugely popular sport in the United States by the mid-1930s. Professional sports at the time were still in their infancy, so the big college football games attracted enormous public attention. The game against Notre Dame, always in New York City during the 1930s, was one of those spectacles; the Army-Navy game was another. The latter contest was the object of fanatical interest in the small interwar army, which consisted of only two active divisions and a smattering of smaller units in far-flung locations. (A similar situation prevailed in the navy.) Under these circumstances, the head coach of the West Point football team, according to Davidson, "rivaled the Chief of Staff in prominence and prestige, perhaps exceeding him in these regards as far as the general public was concerned."[81]

The chief of staff at the time was none other than Douglas MacArthur, whose fanaticism for West Point football had no equal. Following Davidson's first season as head coach, during which the team went undefeated except for a heartbreaking 13–12 loss to Notre Dame, MacArthur called Davidson to Washington. One of the chief's trusted aides, Maj. Dwight D. Eisenhower, ushered Davidson into MacArthur's office for the meeting. MacArthur greeted Davidson warmly, sat him down, and then "paced . . . back and forth behind his desk reviewing the past season and analyzing the outlook for the next essentially in monologue."[82] MacArthur promised to assign to West Point any officer Davidson needed for the coaching staff. Additionally, he required Davidson, during future seasons, to prepare an after-action report on each game

Army football officer-coaches in 1934 (*left to right*): First Lieutenants Maurice F. Daly (Bataan Death March survivor; died on a Japanese prisoner ship), Russell P. (Red) Reeder (disabled from wounds suffered in World War II), Blackshear M. Bryan (future superintendent), Garrison Davidson (head coach, future superintendent), William H. Wood (Bronze Star Medal in World War II), LaVerne G. Saunders (recipient of the Distinguished Service Medal and Navy Cross during World War II), Edward J. Doyle (killed in combat in North Africa during World War II).

for MacArthur; if time did not permit a written report, Davidson was to render it telephonically to Eisenhower.[83]

In the five football seasons from 1933 to 1937, Davidson compiled a superior record of thirty-five wins, eleven losses, and one tie. The young coach never suffered a losing season, and he is still one of the most successful football coaches in the Academy's history. Years later, after a distinguished army career that included extensive combat action in World War II and the Korean War and four years as the superintendent of West Point, Davidson expounded on the reasons for his success. The coaching staff in his day consisted of men who were "professional army officers first and amateur coaches second." As colleagues in the profession of arms, they "enjoyed the characteristics of a close knit family, mutual respect and affection, a genuine interest in the common success and welfare" of each other. In that regard, they were of a "similar breed" to the cadets and understood how best to motivate them in the context of the higher mission of producing officers for the army. He concluded,

> The significance of whatever we achieved as football coaches was not the win/ loss record per se but the fact that it was achieved without recruiting, with players who found their own ways to West Point and were taught by a dedicated group of professional army officers.[84]

Davidson was not sugar-coating his recollections of athletics at West Point during the interwar period. He was, in fact, precisely in line with the thinking of senior Academy leaders on the philosophy of physical education. As we saw earlier, intellectual development and character building were the two most important priorities at West Point, and the rise of intercollegiate athletics did nothing to change them prior to World War II. Lt. Col. Robert C. Richardson, the commandant from 1929 to 1933, emphasized this point during a keynote address at the annual convention of the National Collegiate Athletic Association. In words reminiscent of Koehler's *Theory and Practice of Athletics at the Military Academy*, Richardson explained to the conferees the philosophy guiding athletics at West Point.

> When we use the term athletics, we have in mind primarily the physical development of the cadet. . . . Athletics do not mean the development of athletes primarily for participation in intercollegiate sports with emphasis placed entirely on a small group of students who happen to possess native athletic ability. . . . The athletes whom we develop are the by-product of our system rather than the object for which the system is planned or for which it exists. This conception of an athletic program is the only one which is consistent

with the general aims and philosophy of the school. Any other would tend to defeat the purpose for which West Point exists.[85]

Academy policies governing the participation of cadets in varsity athletics reflected the philosophy that Davidson and Richardson described. To be eligible to play, cadets had to be proficient in all academic and military subjects. Once a cadet became deficient, he was immediately dropped from the team roster and ineligible to compete until his grades had recovered. These strict standards forced coaches to spend as much time counseling and mentoring cadets as working with them on the playing fields. For this reason, only West Point graduates were allowed to coach football, the sport with the largest cadet participation. As Richardson explained, the graduates were more likely than civilian coaches to "understand the conditions under which the coaching must be done" and were "better able to get results out of the men."[86]

III.   NO SUBSTITUTE FOR VICTORY

World War II brought major changes to the physical program at West Point. Those changes responded to the guidance from senior army commanders "to insure that our troops are toughened in mind as well as body. . . . The weak in spirit and in physique must be eliminated." [87] Accordingly, Academy leaders put great emphasis on the physical program even as the overall curriculum shortened to three years for the duration of the war.[88] They added new courses, emphasized instructor training, transitioned from indoor gymnastics to "fit-to-fight" activities, and introduced periodic testing to monitor cadet progress (table 5.5). The commandant made time for the added instruction by reducing leaves and holidays and lengthening the training day during the summers. Plebes continued to take physical education classes most mornings, and all cadets participated in physical training at least two afternoons per week.[89]

Although cadets had undergone physical testing since 1885, West Point had no definitive policy on what constituted adequate fitness. Consequently, even the weakest cadets never faced separation for physical deficiency. This situation became a focus of concern starting in the 1930s. Capt. William A. Holbrook, master of the sword from 1934 to 1938, noted that other colleges had begun making physical education a graduation requirement and recommended that West Point do the same. A committee of professors disagreed, however. They noted that graduation credit was awarded for "achievement that is capable of careful and accurate measurement. It has not been shown that the attainment of physical proficiency is capable of such measurement."[90]

Determined to overcome the professors' objections, Holbrook encouraged his civilian instructors to attend graduate school to study assessment techniques. One of those instructors, Lloyd O. Appleton, enrolled at Columbia University during the summer of 1937.[91] He surveyed the evaluation methods used at other institutions and developed a ten-event test that would be suitable for use at West Point.[92] In academic year 1941–1942, the new master of the sword, Maj. John Harmony, administered the test to all fourth classmen as part of the gymnastics course.[93] Confident in the reliability of the testing data, Harmony made two recommendations: first, proficiency in physical education should be a requirement for graduation; second, applicants to West Point should be required to pass a physical aptitude test.

In June 1942, Harmony recommended the separation of six first classmen who, in his opinion, had failed to achieve the minimum level of physical fitness required of an officer. The superintendent, Maj. Gen. Francis Wilby, was not pleased with the cadets, but he allowed them to graduate because the Academy had yet to establish an official policy for dealing with physical deficiency. Once the cadets graduated, however, Wilby ordered Harmony to conduct a study on physical standards and to recommend a policy for deficient cadets.[94] Harmony gave the mission to Appleton, who recommended the adoption of his ten-event test as a measure of cadet fitness. Wilby approved the recommendation in early 1943 and, for the first time in West Point's history, physical fitness became a graduation requirement.[95]

Henceforth, the plebes took the test twice — immediately upon entry in the summer and one month prior to the end of the academic year. Upperclassmen took the test annually, about three months prior to the end of classes. Any cadet who failed the test (i.e., scored in the bottom seven percentiles) underwent remedial training before being retested. Subsequent failures resulted in the cadet being declared deficient by the Academic Board.[96] The first time a cadet was separated for such deficiency was in 1944.[97]

Once they had succeeded in making physical fitness a graduation requirement, instructors in the Office of Physical Education experimented with different forms of testing. They modified Appleton's ten-event test from time to time, and they added tests to measure different aspects of physical ability. In 1944, for example, they instituted a five-minute swim test and an indoor obstacle course — a grueling test of total-body fitness that has changed only slightly in the decades since its adoption.[98] Cadets were tested annually, as shown in table 5.5.

In 1947, West Point implemented Harmony's second recommendation — that is, physical testing for applicants to West Point. Known as the Physical Aptitude Examination, the test consisted of events designed to measure strength, coordination, endurance, speed, flexibility, and cardiovascular fitness; applicants who scored in the bottom three percentiles were disqualified. Implemen-

TABLE 5.5   Three-year Physical Training Curriculum (number
of instructional periods), Academic Year 1945–1946

Class	Summer	Academic Year Morning	Academic Year Afternoon
Fourth (1st year)	Physical Training (conditioning exercises, group games, and athletics) (20) Physical Testing (2)	Physical Training (120) Gymnastics (20) Boxing (20) Wrestling (20) Swimming (20) Individual Sports (20) Physical Testing (4)	Military Calisthenics (28) Intramural Sports (44)
Third (2nd year)	Intramural Sports (12)		Coaching Techniques (12) Advanced Swimming (7) Unarmed Combat (7) Individual Sports (7) Physical Testing (4) Intramural Sports (44)
First (3rd year)	Instructor Training (12)		Advanced Swimming (7) Unarmed Combat (7) Advanced Gymnastics (7) Individual Sports (7) Advanced Boxing (7) Riding (32) Military Calisthenics (28) Physical Testing (3) Intramural Sports (44)

Notes: Annual Report of the Superintendent, 1946, Appendix A. The war-shortened curriculum eliminated the
second-class year; hence, cadets became first classmen immediately after their third-class year. Although World
War II ended in 1945, the three-year wartime curriculum continued through June 1946. Academic year
1945–1946 therefore saw the most refined version of the wartime program for physical education. Fencing,
which had been a part of fourth-class physical education through academic year 1944–1945, was discontinued.
Intramural sports were basketball, crew, cross country, football, lacrosse, tennis, track (fall); basketball, boxing,
handball, squash, swimming, volleyball, wrestling (winter); and crew, soccer, softball, tennis, water polo
(spring). Physical testing consisted of a ten-event physical efficiency test, five-minute swim test, and an indoor
obstacle course. The advanced swimming program for first classmen included certification by the American
Red Cross as swim instructors. Physically deficient cadets attended special exercise sessions twice a week in lieu
of other physical activities. Deficient swimmers met four times a week for remedial instruction.

tation of the test reflected the growing body of research on the correlation
between physical fitness and leadership ability. A wartime study conducted by
the new master of the sword, Maj. Francis M. Greene, for example, showed
that a disproportionate number of cadets selected for leadership positions were
high achievers physically.[99] The Physical Aptitude Examination (now called the
Cadet Fitness Assessment) has become a permanent fixture of the Academy's
admissions process.[100]

The work of Appleton, Holbrook, Harmony, and Greene reflected the rise
of specialization and professionalism within the field of physical education.

Early in the twentieth century, Koehler was the only physical education professional at West Point. His staff consisted of professional athletes, with plenty of experience but no theoretical training, and military officers selected on the basis of their records as cadets and officers. By the mid-1930s, however, most of the civilian instructors were professional physical educators with at least a bachelor's degree; as we have seen, some went on to graduate school.

The credentials of the military officers assigned as physical education instructors likewise improved. Immediately following World War II, the army began sending these officers to graduate school before their arrival at West Point.[101] Outside observers hailed these improvements in the physical program. In 1948, for example, a board of consultants predicted that if the present policies continued, "in ten years the Academy should have the best teaching staff of any institution of a similar type in the country."[102]

From the standpoint of intercollegiate athletics, World War II was a boon to West Point. In 1942, Congress expanded the size of the Corps by over 25 percent to help meet wartime officer requirements. The unintended consequence of the expansion was to enhance the Academy's athletic competitiveness relative to civilian colleges, where enrollments were plummeting.[103] Meanwhile, federal rules deferred service academy applicants from conscription, which encouraged talented athletes to seek admission to West Point as a means of extending their playing days. Even President Franklin Roosevelt abetted the Academy's competitiveness by ordering the continuation of varsity sports during the war. His intent was to relieve the stress on cadets and to preserve a popular national pastime, but the effect was to give sports at West Point the priority of a military mission.[104]

With so many advantages, West Point teams excelled during and immediately after the war. In academic year 1943–1944, for example, the basketball, lacrosse, and boxing teams won national championships. A year later, the football, baseball, gymnastics, wrestling, swimming, and tennis teams went undefeated; the football and track teams won national championships, and the golf team won the regional championship.[105] In academic year 1945–1946, football repeated as the national champion, and the cross-country and boxing teams won national or regional titles.[106] In the fall of 1946, the football team had its third straight undefeated season; by 1950, it had compiled an amazing record of fifty-seven wins and only three losses during the previous seven seasons.[107] The success of the athletics program encouraged its continued growth; by academic year 1947–1948, it consisted of seventeen intercollegiate sports, all funded by the Army Athletic Association. That year, the overall win percentage was an enviable 67.5 percent.[108]

No one was more influential in the Academy's meteoric rise in athletics than the football coach, Earl Blaik, hired in 1941. The superintendent at that time was Maj. Gen. Robert Eichelberger, an ardent supporter of the football team who had known Blaik since the two of them had served together at West Point in early 1930s.[109] Troubled by the losing seasons of 1939 and 1940, Eichelberger gave Blaik the mission of building a winning team. Blaik accepted the job on the condition that he could actively recruit quality athletes; this was an important point now that the Academy had to abide by the three-year eligibility rule. Then, unexpectedly, the NCAA suspended that rule as a means of helping colleges field varsity teams as their enrollments declined during the war. The rule change, along with Blaik's license to recruit athletes, added to the advantages the Academy already enjoyed because of the war. For a few years at least, the fields of friendly strife were tilted steeply in favor of West Point.[110]

Blaik was as serious about winning at football as American generals were about winning at war. His skill as a recruiter and coach, along with the competitive advantages of the Academy during the war, allowed him to rebuild the football team quickly. He achieved success during the three seasons from 1941 through 1943, but nothing like that of the following three seasons, from 1944 through 1946. Among sports fans, Blaik was as famous as the generals directing American armies overseas.

The coincident fortunes of the West Point football team and the United States Army were hard to miss. Blaik's first national championship season occurred in the fall of 1944, as Eisenhower's armies pursued German forces in Northwest Europe and MacArthur's landed in the Philippines. The pride and enthusiasm that Americans felt for their fighting men carried over to the army's football team at West Point. The fusion of heroic images — military and athletic — was an easy mental leap for millions of Americans. Henceforth, the football team would be the most visible face of West Point, which, in turn, was the most visible face of the army.

With the stakes seemingly so high, winning at football took on the seriousness of a military mission. Blaik therefore pushed his players hard on the field and scorned any approach to the game that would not lead to victory. The successful coach, he explained, secured

> [A] willing acceptance from his men that victory or success demands a special price. The play-for-fun approach will lead the player to revolt against the coach and, eventually, even against the game itself, because play-for-fun never can lead to victory. This does not mean that the Spartan dictates of work, courage, sacrifice, and selflessness turn football into something that is no longer a game. But the essence of the game, the only "fun" of the game, if you will, is the soul-satisfying awareness that comes not only with victory but also with the concurrent realization that victory more than justifies all the communal work and sacrifice that went into it.[111]

Coach Earl Blaik (USMA 1920) with the 1942 football team. Hugely
successful as West Point's head football coach for eighteen years, his emphasis
on winning undermined key developmental goals of the Academy.

Blaik's focus on winning was in stark contrast to the philosophy of competitive athletics that had prevailed at the Academy up to that point. Koehler had
warned against the "prostitution of the ethos of athletics, the spirit to win at all
hazards, that is the dominant object of college athletics, and that serves only to
defeat their purpose from an educational point of view." [112] With the arrival of
Blaik, however, winning at sports became an institutional goal whose importance would grow to dangerous proportions in subsequent years.

The consequences of this dramatic shift were as unfortunate as they were
inevitable. In 1951, the Academy experienced a major cheating incident centered on the vaunted football team. The singular focus on winning had nurtured an environment in which many football players and others close to the
team engaged in systematic, long-term, and widespread cheating. This incident, covered in detail in chapter 8, had many causes, but at root was the win-
at-all-cost mentality that Blaik advocated as a coach and advanced through his
relentless pursuit of victories. Koehler would have been heartbroken by the way
the physical program had been contorted to achieve athletic "success."

The superintendents kept close watch over the athletics program for the
next few years, but they made no substantive changes in how it operated. Blaik

was therefore able to rebuild the football team quickly after losing most of his players to the cheating incident. He suffered the first and only losing season of his career in 1951, but his purgatory was short lived. In 1952, his team won as many games as it lost (and tied one), and the following year it won seven games and ended the season ranked fourteenth in the nation. The highlight of that campaign was a stunning upset of seventh-ranked Duke University, following a goal-line stand in the final seconds of play.[113] Regardless of his shortcomings, Blaik had proven once again that he was a peerless football coach.

Garrison Davidson made the physical program a high priority upon becoming the superintendent in 1956. He had three main areas of concern. First, he was troubled by his assessment of the physical conditioning of cadets — their performance as junior lieutenants at the army's airborne and ranger schools (mandatory for West Point graduates starting in 1954) convinced him that "our standards were still too low."[114] Second, he wanted to expand the participation of cadets in intercollegiate athletics and to increase their success in all sports; concurrently, he wanted to avoid the abuses — particularly the obsession with winning — that had caused turmoil at the Academy in recent years. Finally, he sought better management of intercollegiate sports to facilitate his agenda for improving the physical program overall.[115]

Davidson moved aggressively to improve the physical conditioning of the Corps. The quickest way was to admit more cadet candidates who already had achieved a high level of fitness. Accordingly, in 1957 he raised the disqualification threshold on the Physical Aptitude Examination from the lowest 3 percent to the lowest 10 percent of the test-takers; three years later, he raised it to the lowest 15 percent. For those already admitted as cadets, Davidson increased the frequency of physical testing from once a year to once each semester.[116] Additionally, he encouraged the Academic Board to take a hard line against cadets who failed to maintain an acceptable level of fitness. While separations for academic failure stayed about the same during the Davidson years, separations for physical failure rose sharply. The class of 1960, for example, experienced a 2.2 percent attrition rate for failures in the physical program; that was the highest in West Point's history so far and more than seven times higher than the separation rate of a decade earlier. Davidson believed that separations for physical deficiency would hover between 2 and 3 percent for a few years until "our present entrance standards and recruiting efforts begin to bear fruit."[117]

Davidson believed strongly in the value of competitive sports in developing military leaders. He therefore sought to increase the number of participating cadets and to help them be as successful as possible. Toward this end, he established the principle of equality of opportunity in intercollegiate athletics to ensure that all cadet-athletes, not just football players, had the support and resources to represent the Academy with distinction. He doubled the quota of recruited athletes so that coaches in all sports could bring in talented players.

Previously, the football team had a near monopoly on recruited athletes; henceforth, they had fewer than half of the total.[118]

Coach Blaik was not happy. Although the actual number of football recruits was slightly higher than before, the few extra athletes, he argued, would not be enough to keep the team competitive in the long run. As the director of athletics (as well as the football coach), Blaik had coordinated a multiyear schedule of football games with many tough opponents. He therefore insisted that more recruited players were necessary to meet the competitive challenge. Additionally, he pointed out that the football team underwrote the Academy's entire intercollegiate athletics program; on that basis alone, he argued, it was deserving of preferential treatment.[119]

Davidson would have none of it. He worried that the effort necessary to succeed at such a high level of competitiveness would eventually "reintroduce into the Corps of Cadets pressures and tensions inimical to its unity and to the proper accomplishment of the mission of the Military Academy." He was referring, of course, to the focus on winning that had led to the 1951 cheating incident, yet Blaik seemed oblivious to it. According to Davidson, Blaik "was so intent on football and the success of the team that he was blinded to the possible side effects of his intensity of purpose."[120] To insulate the Academy from the worst aspects of competitive athletics, Davidson mandated scheduling changes to ensure that the team would face as many "breathers" as "powerhouses," and he insisted that the director of athletics implement his equality-for-all-sports policy. These directives frustrated Blaik, who had previously enjoyed autonomy in managing the athletics program. They ranked high among the reasons he chose to retire shortly after the 1958 football season.[121]

One might assume that the Academy's varsity teams had performed poorly, given Davidson's determination to expand athletic recruiting to all sports. On the contrary, they were quite competitive — just not enough for the demanding superintendent. During academic year 1957–1958, West Point teams won 64 percent of their varsity competitions, with about 47 percent of cadets — the large majority of whom were unrecruited — participating in at least one intercollegiate sport.[122] Despite the success, Davidson complained that the overall performance of varsity teams was "somewhat below the high quality of performance the Academy seeks to achieve." He blamed the situation on the failure to attract enough well-rounded student-athletes who could meet the high standards "appropriate to a manly institution" like West Point.[123]

How could Davidson believe that raising the number of athletic recruits would not lower the academic and military standards of the Corps of Cadets? The answer was that he had great faith in the ability of West Point to attract an abundance of talented young men who could excel in all developmental areas. Given the academic performance of the cadet-athletes of the era, his optimism was justified. In 1956, for example, the standardized test scores of the entering class (i.e., the class of 1960) showed little difference between the future varsity athletes and the rest of the class (table 5.6a). Moreover, the academic performance of the varsity athletes in the class remained strong throughout their four years, despite the added pressures of playing competitive sports (tables 5.6b and 5.6c). From the perspective of academic performance, one could not distinguish between a varsity athlete and his nonvarsity classmates. The most renowned student-athlete of the era, Peter Dawkins, validated the idea that West Point could attract a surfeit of intellectually and athletically talented young men.[124]

Davidson's final reform was to provide the director of physical education the same rank and tenure as the professors who headed the academic departments.[125] Once Congress passed the necessary legislation in 1958, the Academic Board appointed Lt. Col. Frank J. Kobes as the first permanent director of physical education since Herman Koehler.[126] He served in the position until 1974 and retired as a brigadier general, just like the retiring heads of the academic departments. His longevity enabled him to provide stable and consistent leadership of the physical education program.[127]

In early 1959, the Middle States Association of Colleges and Secondary Schools published its accreditation report on West Point. It lauded the Academy for its robust physical program of mandatory and voluntary activities (table 5.7). Additionally, it made pointed comments about the Academy's success in putting restraints on intercollegiate athletics, particularly football. The accreditors were convinced that Davidson had quashed the impulse to allow "big-time football" to get out of hand.[128] Perhaps they were impressed by Davidson's refusal to allow the undefeated 1958 football team to accept an invitation to play in the Cotton Bowl in December. In explaining the decision, Davidson noted that cadets needed the time to study for their examinations. Besides, "the regular nine-game schedule," he explained, "produces all the benefits which can reasonably be sought from the playing of intercollegiate football."[129]

During the 1960s, West Point reaped the fruits of Davidson's athletic reforms. About one half of the Corps of Cadets participated in varsity sports and, on the whole, they were highly successful.[130] Nineteen hundred sixty-five was the best year ever. Army won 76 percent of its varsity contests and twelve of seventeen contests against Navy (one tie). The lightweight football team won the Eastern Intercollegiate Championship for the fifth time in eight years. Both the pistol and rifle teams were ranked number one in the nation. The soccer team reached the NCAA semifinals, and the basketball team finished third in the prestigious National Invitational Tournament. West Point athletes earned All America distinction in football, lightweight football, basketball, wrestling, swimming, lacrosse, rifle, and pistol.[131] Never before or since the 1960s has West Point experienced such a successful decade of sports.[132]

TABLE 5.6A   Comparison of Standardized Test Scores between
Varsity Athletes and All Other Cadets, Class of 1960

Cadet Category	SAT Verbal	SAT- Math	Achievement Test in Intermediate Mathematics	Achievement Test in English Composition
Varsity Athletes	547	627	647	554
All Others	555	626	626	546

Notes: SAT stands for Scholastic Aptitude Test. It was a common measure of aptitude for academic work at the college level. The achievement tests, in contrast, measured acquired knowledge in the subject areas. The Educational Testing Service prepared both types of tests. Middle States Association of Colleges and Secondary Schools, *Evaluation Report, 15–18 February 1959*, 36.

TABLE 5.6B   Comparison of Grade Point Average (3.0 scale)
between Varsity Athletes and All Other Cadets

Cadet Category	Class of 1958	Class of 1959	Class of 1960
Varsity Athletes	2.407	2.412	2.427
All others	2.418	2.402	2.421

Notes: Middle States Association of Colleges and Secondary Schools, *Evaluation Report, 15–18 February 1959*, 36.

TABLE 5.6C   Percentage (number) of Varsity Athletes in Each
Academic Quartile

Academic Rank	Class of 1958 (573 cadets)	Class of 1959 (507 cadets)	Class of 1960 (600 cadets)
First Quartile	21.7 (35)	26.5 (52)	27.7 (78)
Second Quartile	24.2 (39)	27.0 (53)	22.7 (64)
Third Quartile	31.7 (51)	20.9 (41)	24.5 (69)
Fourth Quartile	22.4 (36)	25.5 (50)	25.2 (71)

Notes: See table 5.6b notes. The percentages in the second and third columns do not add up to 100 percent because of rounding.

IV.   A FORK IN THE ROAD

At this point in the story — around 1970 — we will depart from the protocol of considering intercollegiate athletics as a component of the Academy's overall physical program. Instead, we will treat it as a separate program, which is, in fact, what Academy leaders had allowed it to become. The split started during World War II as West Point basked in the glow of athletic success, especially

TABLE 5.7   Physical Training Curriculum (number of
instructional periods), Academic Year 1958–1959

Class	Summer	Academic Year
Fourth (1st year)	Conditioning Exercises (8) Mass Athletics (20) Corps Squad Screening (26) Swim Test (1) Posture Lecture (1)	Basic Physical Education (gymnastics, boxing, wrestling, swimming) (60) Recreation Skills (golf and tennis) (90)
Third (2nd year)	Conditioning Exercises and Running (12) Physical Testing (2)	Athletic Skills (basketball, handball, squash, badminton, volleyball, unarmed combat) (28) Physical Testing (3)
Second (3rd year)		Coaching Techniques Instruction (8) Conduct of Conditioning Exercises (9) Physical Testing (3)
First (4th year)		Administration of Physical Training and Athletic Programs (7) Physical Testing (4)
All		Fall Intramurals (25) Winter Intramurals (voluntary) (20) Spring Intramurals (20)

Notes: Adapted from *Report Prepared for the Commission on Institutions of Higher Education of the Middle States Association of Colleges and Secondary Schools*, November 1958, General Headquarters File 080, Middle States Association of Colleges and Secondary Schools, Record Group 404, West Point Archives, 107.

in football. Even after the 1951 cheating scandal, the excitement, prestige, and profits associated with a top-tier intercollegiate athletics program were intoxicating. The superintendents of the 1950s and 1960s did their best to mitigate the worst aspects of intercollegiate sports. Reflecting their unease about the potential pitfalls, they closely supervised the athletics program and frequently reassured the alumni that West Point athletes were "outstanding representatives of the Corps of Cadets and the United States Army."[133]

The conditions that brought success to the intercollegiate athletics program in the 1960s did not last long. Seismic shifts were underway, both at West Point and in American society. Internally, the expansion of the Corps of Cadets starting in 1964 reduced the percentage of recruited athletes in the student body as the number of varsity teams remained constant; recruited athletes were increasingly a group apart, at least in relative numbers. Meanwhile, the expansion put the athletic infrastructure under great strain as intramural and club teams competed with varsity squads for practice fields and playing time. These problems were irksome, but manageable. More serious were external forces over which the Academy had no control.

As we have seen in previous chapters, the Vietnam War had a powerfully negative influence on West Point. The accelerating antiwar movement discouraged many potential candidates from considering West Point as a college option. There were barely enough qualified applicants to fill the classes of the early 1970s, and athletic recruiting suffered correspondingly.

Another negative influence was the rapid evolution of intercollegiate athletics in America. Collegiate sports had been commercialized and professionalized for a long time, but they became especially so in the 1960s with new and effective methods of marketing. Starting in 1961, for example, millions of Americans tuned their televisions to *ABC's Wide World of Sports* and experienced vicariously the "thrill of victory and the agony of defeat."[134] In 1967, the Green Bay Packers and Kansas City Chiefs played in the first "Superbowl" to determine the champions of professional football. This television spectacle, more popular every year, was emblematic of Americans' fascination with sports and the enormous payouts that went to the best players, teams, coaches, and associated business interests. College sports increasingly took on the attributes of their professional counterparts in the sports-entertainment industry. Like elsewhere in the business world, the measures of success in sports entertainment were tangible and quantifiable — in particular, win-loss records and monetary profits. Under such conditions, it was easy to lose sight of the intangible, qualitative outcomes that had been the original goals of athletics, at least at West Point.

The internal and external forces impacting West Point created a challenging environment for Academy sports during the 1970s. The most obvious consequence was the decline in the competitiveness of varsity teams, as shown in table 5.4. The lofty 70.8 percent win rate of the 1960s dropped to 59.6 percent over the next ten years. Typifying the malaise was the horrid 1973 football season — 0 wins and 10 losses — the worst in West Point history to that point. The Academy still produced many fine athletes and teams, but the relative decline from the 1960s was troubling to those who had grown accustomed to a higher standard of excellence.

A less obvious challenge for Academy sports, but equally serious, was the tenuous financial situation of the Army Athletic Association. Throughout most of its history, the Association had underwritten the Academy's sports program through private donations and football revenues. Additionally, it had invested large sums in athletic infrastructure and club and intramural sports. The rising competitiveness of intercollegiate athletics, however, made everything more expensive. Recruiting was especially costly, as colleges and universities competed fiercely for the best talent. They raised coaches' salaries, improved their athletic facilities, and expanded their public-relations and advertising budgets.

The Army Athletic Association did its best to cut costs, but the only viable solution was to generate new income. The chairman of the Athletic Board,

Col. Gilbert W. Kirby, favored a donor-incentive program that gave preferential treatment to those who contributed the most money. Additionally, he wanted to elevate the problem to army leaders: "Our position should be that if the Department of the Army wants the intercollegiate program to continue at the same level then they are going to have to pay for a substantial part of it."[135] Neither the alumni nor the army was ready for these departures from tradition.[136]

Some of the army's most senior leaders were deeply troubled by the underperformance of the football team during the 1970s (thirty-six wins, sixty-eight losses, and three ties during the decade). Commissioned in the 1940s and 1950s, they had embraced the notion that the fortunes of West Point and the football team were inextricably linked. Americans, they believed, expected West Point to win at football, just as they expected the Army to win at war. The authorities therefore resolved to resuscitate the football team without retreating from the NCAA's top level of competition.[137] Toward that end, Maj. Gen. Sidney Berry, superintendent from 1974 to 1977, established the ambitious goal of winning "at least 75 percent of the contests in every sport and beating the other service academy teams more often than they beat us."[138]

The concerns of senior army leaders were reflected in the report of the West Point Study Group, published shortly after the 1976 cheating incident. The study group examined every aspect of the Academy and offered recommendations for improvement. Concerning competitive athletics, it concluded that intramural and club sports were sound, but "the intercollegiate athletic program needs revitalization." Of particular concern was football, on which "the perception of success of the intercollegiate athletic program hinges." Without a winning team, "there is a resultant negative impact on the esprit de corps of the community, the national image of the Academy, and the financial posture of the [Army Athletic Association]." The study group cited several contributing factors to the poor performance of the team, but chief among them was the lack of institutional commitment to sports. "Excellence in athletics," it concluded, "is as inherent to the mission of the Military Academy as excellence in studies and military training."[139] With the imprimatur of the army chief of staff, the report of the West Point Study Group set in motion a cascade of changes that would fundamentally alter the priority of intercollegiate athletics at West Point.

One major change — the revitalization of the Academy's athletic facilities — was long overdue. Existing athletic venues were old and cramped, especially since the expansion of the Corps of Cadets and the creation of women's competitive teams. Consequently, Congress appropriated money for a new athletic complex housing a 5,000-seat basketball arena and a 2,500-seat hockey rink that provided vastly improved facilities for those sports.[140] Another notable improvement was the installation of artificial turf in the football stadium.[141]

Changes to admissions policies were less visible, but no less influential for intercollegiate athletics. In 1978, Gen. Andrew Goodpaster, superintendent from 1977 to 1981, approved a class-composition goal for recruited athletes, thus transferring to the athletic director control over a sizable portion of each entering class.[142] The new arrangement freed the athletic director from having to fight with the Academic Board over each recruit whose whole-person credentials were weak. Provided a recruited athlete could meet minimum entry standards, he or she could not be displaced by a higher-quality candidate in a different class-composition category. For athletes who did not meet minimum standards, new policies streamlined the process for seeking an exception from the Academic Board. There were sure to be such cases, as the superintendent authorized the annual admission of twenty-five "high-potential" players — a euphemism for blue-chip recruits who otherwise would be academically ineligible.[143]

In addition to the changes in admissions policies, Goodpaster formed a series of study groups to recommend ways of strengthening intercollegiate athletics, with a focus on football. One of their reports made amply clear that Koehler's theory of athletics at West Point was obsolete: "Everyone associated with the institution must support the philosophy that the intercollegiate athletic program is the top of the hierarchy of competitive athletics and must receive first priority in that area of cadet development."[144] Another report, even more specific, cited the "judgment of the Chief of Staff of the U.S. Army and the Superintendent, USMA, concerning the utmost importance of a successful Army Football Program." Because of its popularity and prestige, football should receive "a dominant position relative to other sports" at the Academy.[145] From these basic premises flowed many seemingly logical recommendations for assisting varsity athletes — for example, no classes during the last academic hour; underloading of courses during the academic year; make-up classes for athletes who missed the regularly scheduled ones; deferral of term-end examinations; excusal from morning formations and guard duties; and constructive credit for certain physical education requirements. Senior Academy leaders — especially the commandant, Brig. Gen. Joseph Franklin — moved aggressively to experiment with these and other measures.[146]

These accommodations did not go far enough for some sports advocates. According to one of the study groups, the greatest obstacle to success was the Academy's inability to offer varsity athletes "the opportunity to compete for a place in professional athletics." The potential to play professionally would supposedly attract cadet candidates "who have exceptionally high potential for leadership and service"; their contributions to institutional goals were likely "to be far greater than the contributions that can be made as a junior officer."[147] The professional-sports option was not implemented at the time, but it gained traction a few years later as the football team continued its long decline.

Goodpaster made key personnel changes in hopes of resuscitating the football program. In 1979, he hired Lou Saban, a gifted coach who had been successful in the professional football leagues. Saban became quickly frustrated by the constraints under which he had to work; after one unsuccessful season, he tendered his resignation.[148] His replacement, Ed Cavanaugh, lasted a little longer, but with no better luck on the football field.[149] A far more successful hire was the new athletics director, Carl Ullrich, a talented administrator who had served five years as the assistant athletic director at the Naval Academy. He had much experience supervising athletic recruiting, admissions procedures, finances, advertising, and compliance with NCAA bylaws; moreover, he was respectful of the service academies' mission and tolerant of constraints under which they competed. His hiring satisfied a recommendation of the West Point Study Group to improve the business operations of the Army Athletic Association.[150]

In seeking to improve the intercollegiate athletics program, Goodpaster approved many of the recommendations of his review bodies. Regardless, he understood the need for putting limits on athletics, which he believed could "become a fetish" in the hands of misguided enthusiasts.[151] While he defended the accommodations he had made for athletes, he was nervous about where the intercollegiate program was headed. "My concern was that we not attempt to get that top level of competition — national level of competition — because of what that implies, because of the burdens that would put on the cadets. . . . I don't think that fits within the preparation of our people as officers."[152] Goodpaster's relative restraint may have frustrated those who sought to restore the winning tradition to football; by the end of his tenure, he "sensed some impatience and disappointment" on the part of army senior leaders.[153] His retirement in 1981 allowed those leaders to intervene once again in the "problem" of football at West Point.

In late 1983, then-Col. Wesley Clark was a trusted aide to the new army chief of staff, Gen. John A. Wickham. Both were graduates of West Point, and both were troubled by the mediocrity of their alma mater's football team over the previous decade.[154] According to Clark, the Academy's poor performance in intercollegiate athletics suggested that West Point had "lost its winning spirit." He therefore urged Wickham to pursue the matter during an upcoming meeting with the superintendent, Lt. Gen. Willard Scott, and the new football coach, Jim Young.[155] Wickham accepted Clark's advice and prepared unequivocal guidance: "All of us," he told Scott, must give "the necessary support to prove that [Young] and his team can be winners. . . . There is no doubt in my mind that the performance of cadets on the athletic field reflects on their thirst for victory and influences their attitude toward being winners."[156]

The guidance of the army's highest-ranking officer was crystal clear, but even before receiving it Scott had made intercollegiate athletics one of his top priorities as superintendent.[157] He encouraged the recruitment of high numbers of athletes and approved an increase in the class-composition goal for that group.[158] He expanded a program to allow graduating cadets to stay at West Point to serve as assistant coaches.[159] Athletes received more tutoring and additional instruction for academics, and football players underwent new strength-development and nutritional programs.[160] Regulations concerning class absences were relaxed to allow more practice and travel time.[161] At Commandant Franklin's urging, Scott exempted in-season varsity athletes from the physical education testing required of other cadets.[162] He allowed the athletic director to attend Academic Board meetings as a nonvoting member and to comment on admissions and deficiency cases dealing with recruited athletes.[163] The effect of these and many other measures gave intercollegiate athletics — football in particular — an institutional priority not seen since the heady days of Earl Blaik's championship teams of the mid-1940s.

The efforts to revive the football program seemed to pay off starting in 1984. The team achieved a record of eight wins, three losses, and one tie — the first winning season since 1977. Coaches' polls placed it among the top twenty-five teams in the nation. It played (and won) its first postseason bowl game; moreover, it was awarded the Commander-in-Chief Trophy for defeating the football teams of the two other service academies. Even the basketball team, under Coach Les Wothke, did well (sixteen wins, thirteen losses), achieving the first winning season in eight years.[164] The lacrosse team, under first-year Coach Jack Emmer, ended the season ranked fifth in the nation. Hockey, wrestling, and men's and women's swimming also had highly successful seasons.[165]

The success of Jim Young's football squads seemed to validate the institutional efforts to resurrect the football program. During his eight years as the head coach, the team had six winning seasons, played in three bowl games (two of them victories), and amassed an overall record of fifty-one wins, thirty-nine losses, and one tie. As subsequent seasons were to prove, however, the outcome was due mostly to Young's coaching brilliance rather than the changes of the previous few years.[166] In the two decades following Young's departure after the 1990 campaign, the football team experienced only two winning seasons. Additionally, the cumulative win rate of all intercollegiate teams hovered just above 50 percent. Despite the investment of much time, energy, and money in supporting the sports program, West Point never came close to matching the athletic record of the decades prior to 1970.

Lt. Gen. Dave Palmer, superintendent from 1986 to 1991, was a beneficiary of the goodwill generated from Young's winning football teams.[167] Regardless, he was deeply troubled by the trends in college sports. "One of the major problems facing West Point in both the near future and in the distant future," he believed, "was intercollegiate athletics and where it was going. And it appeared to be going in directions antithetical to our values."[168]

To determine the scope of the problem at West Point, he formed a special panel "to consider all aspects of competitive sports."[169] In anticipation of serving on the panel, the director of physical education, Col. James Anderson, co-wrote a paper that reprised Koehler's philosophy of athletics. His basic premise was that competitive sports could contribute to building character, but only when they functioned "under good educational leadership, in the context of a sound educational philosophy and [when] properly directed and controlled." The byproducts of sports under these conditions were a sense of fair play, sportsmanship, and principles of justice. While the desire to win was not antithetical to these values, it sometimes could "become of paramount importance to the exclusion of other values."[170]

Palmer approved measures to strengthen the athletics program while providing close supervision over it. He eliminated mandatory supper to give teams more practice time without intruding on the evening study period.[171] He established the Performance Enhancement Center, staffed with experts in sports psychology, to help cadets master the mental techniques of higher-level competition.[172] He assigned to Anderson the task of supervising all club sports, in addition to the intramural sports he already controlled.[173] He encouraged the formation of the Patriot League — a conference of schools devoted to academic excellence — and enrolled West Point as a full member.[174] Finally, he rejected the recommendation to subordinate the athletic director to the commandant and to give him control over club athletics as well as intercollegiate athletics. Wary of the expansive scope of the athletic director's duties, Palmer resolved to keep him under the superintendent's direct supervision.[175]

Palmer recognized that his success in overseeing athletics depended in large part on the policies of the NCAA. He therefore accepted an invitation to serve on the NCAA Presidents' Commission, a governance body established in 1984 to help college administrators reassert their authority over intercollegiate athletics.[176] Palmer worked closely with likeminded colleagues who pushed hard for reform. In 1989, they convinced the NCAA's executive director, Richard D. Schultz, to test a concept for athletics certification — a process analogous to academic accreditation. After a two-year pilot program involving thirty-four Division 1 schools (including West Point), NCAA members voted to establish the certification program in 1993.[177]

During the 1990s, the football team returned to its former mediocrity under the new head coach, Bob Sutton. The noteworthy exception came in 1996, when the team went 10–2 and nearly upset Auburn University in the Independence Bowl. In the afterglow of that season, the superintendent, Lt. Gen. Daniel Christman, opted to join Conference USA in football starting in 1998.

The decision ended West Point's independent status in hopes of reaping greater rewards in the increasingly commercialized and professionalized world of college sports. Sutton supported the move. "Today, in intercollegiate athletics," he explained, "television revenue and the opportunity to play in bowl games" were the driving forces in Division 1 football. Joining a conference would allow West Point to harness both of those forces.[178]

As it turned out, Conference USA was a disaster for West Point. The football team's conference record during its seven years of membership was nine wins and forty-one losses; included in that unhappy stretch was a winless season (thirteen losses) that was the worst in Division 1 college football history. After leaving the conference in 2004 and returning to independent status, the disappointments continued. The overall record during the thirteen years from 1997 through 2009 was 37 wins and 115 losses — that is, a win percentage of 24 percent. Against the other service academies, the record was even worse — 3 wins and 26 losses (an 11.5 percent win rate). Even the men's basketball team, which had not had a winning season since 1984–1985, boasted a better record than football.

Christman and his two successors, Lt. Gen. William Lennox and Lt. Gen. Franklin Hagenbeck, were devotees of intercollegiate sports and therefore deeply troubled by the football team's dismal record. They believed strongly in the developmental value of the sport, as well as its ability to advance institutional goals in the areas of fund-raising, admissions, and strategic communication. Football was the linchpin of the intercollegiate athletics program since it involved more cadets than any other sport by far, had the greatest visibility, and generated the most income. Consequently, Lennox formed a football study group in 2003 that included Nebraska football coach Tom Osborne and Dallas Cowboys coach Bill Parcells. Hagenbeck assembled another study group in 2008, this time with former West Point athletes and coaches.[179]

There was no mistaking the priority that football had assumed at West Point. In a widely distributed letter to the Academy's football fans, Hagenbeck declared that he was "absolutely determined to restore the tradition of winning football," which he characterized as a "critical mission."[180] He and his predecessors took bold steps to accomplish this mission, although none of them seriously considered dropping to a lower competitive level in some sports.[181]

The emphasis on athletics manifested itself in many ways. In the first decade of the twenty-first century, for example, about $92 million were invested in the athletics infrastructure as a means of attracting better athletes to West Point.[182] Donors were solicited to finance the construction of on-post housing for the athletics director and coaches; with few exceptions, these new homes were the largest and most sumptuous quarters at West Point.[183] Greater numbers of academically at-risk candidates — the large majority being recruited athletes — were admitted to the Academy.[184] Policies governing the frequency and timing of varsity competitions were relaxed, resulting in a dramatic rise in class absences for athletes.[185] Training regulations were changed to permit grouping of recruited athletes into the same basic training companies; during the last two weeks of the summer, they were physically removed from the field and transported to athletic dormitories to begin training.[186] An "alternate-service option" gave cadet athletes the opportunity to enter professional sports immediately upon graduation.[187] The US Military Academy Preparatory School was moved to West Point to allow greater coordination between the two coaching staffs.[188] For the first time, one of West Point's strategic goals specifically mentioned the need to have a winning sports program.[189] The athletics director became a permanent, voting member of the Academic Board and was granted status equivalent to a brigadier general in matters of governance and protocol.[190]

Most indicative of the new emphasis on intercollegiate athletics was the distribution of government funds. Heretofore, the Army Athletic Association had borne all, or the large majority of, the cost of running West Point's intercollegiate program. The budgetary dollars appropriated by Congress were limited to paying the salaries of the relatively few federal employees and military officers in the athletic director's office, as well as other related expenses.[191] As noted previously, however, the days of surpluses in the Army Athletic Association coffers had long passed, and the athletics program routinely ran deficits.[192] In 2003, Lennox convinced army leaders to provide about $5 million dollars of additional funds to support intercollegiate athletics. The money went to hiring the full complement of coaches allowed by the NCAA and to bolstering athletic recruiting.[193] In subsequent years, the army did not earmark the additional funds specifically for athletics; rather, it provided all of West Point's operating funds in a lump sum and allowed the superintendent to distribute the money in accordance with his priorities.

The superintendents' emphasis on varsity sports, coupled with the heightened influence of the athletic director in Academy governance, ensured that the intercollegiate sports program received a progressively larger serving of the budget pie. As shown in table 5.8, the percentage of government funding for varsity sports nearly doubled from 1999 through 2010. At the same time, the percentage of funding for the military and physical programs (i.e., the commandant's areas of responsibility) declined sharply; similarly, the admissions program took heavy cuts. The percentage of funds for the academic program increased modestly, but that was due to the need for hiring additional faculty to accommodate the 10 percent expansion of the Corps of Cadets around the middle of the decade.[194]

The foregoing pages make clear two divergent trends relating to the Academy's intercollegiate athletics program between 1970 and 2010. First, the

TABLE 5.8   Percentage of Appropriated Funds Distributed to West Point Programs, with Total Budget (in $ millions) on Bottom Row

Fiscal Year	1999	2000	2001	2002	2003	2004	2005	2006	2007	2008	2009	2010
Headquarters	20.9	20.8	21.3	28.2	23.2	21.3	17.7	17.4	17.3	15.8	19.6	19.8
Commandant	27.5	25.8	23.2	20.2	20.5	25.2	20.6	20.8	21.7	20.8	21.0	19.9
Dean	39.9	41.6	41.4	41.3	41.2	38.6	47.4	45.6	45.7	48.5	45.8	45.5
Admissions	5.4	4.8	4.7	4.5	3.7	3.9	4.0	3.9	3 .6	3.7	3.2	3.4
Intercollegiate Athletics	6.3	7.0	9.4	5.8	11.4	11.0	10.3	12.3	11.7	11.2	10.4	11.4
Total Budget (in $ millions)	51.1	58.2	63.1	68.9	78.2	83.3	86.5	92.1	92.1	95.5	102.1	99.3

Notes: Data from the Plans and Resources Division, Office of the Dean, 12 May 2010. Not included in the table is the cost of operating the cadet dining facility, which ranged from $8.9 million to $12.8 million during the years in question. Also not included are appropriations earmarked for activities mandated by higher authorities (e.g., Department of Defense language initiative).

competitiveness of the Academy's varsity teams declined markedly. Second, the investment of time, effort, and money to fix this perceived problem increased significantly. On the surface, these trends indicated that Academy leaders, even after forty years, had failed to find the right combination of policies, coaches, players, resources, and other ingredients for winning. The real problem, however, went much deeper. Specifically, the mission of producing leaders of character—the sole reason for the Academy's existence—was at odds with the efforts needed to excel in the commercialized and professionalized world of Division 1 sports.

In his farewell address to Congress in 1951, Douglas MacArthur uttered the now-famous dictum, "In war, there is no substitute for victory." [195] Fortunately for West Point and the nation, the same is not true for sports.

V.   PHYSICAL EDUCATION— NEW DIRECTIONS, SAME PHILOSOPHY

Whereas intercollegiate athletics became a separate program in the years after 1970, the physical program retained the form and spirit pioneered by Herman Koehler. All cadets continued to take physical education during the academic year, play competitive sports at the intramural or club levels (unless they were members of intercollegiate teams), and undergo periodic physical testing. The changes that occurred after 1970—there were many—refined and strength-ened the physical program in ways that Koehler would have applauded.

Many of the changes were the doing of Col. James Anderson, master of the sword from 1974 to 1997.[196] One of Anderson's top priorities was to bring "a more solid, intellectual background" to the physical program since he con-sidered much of the instruction to be "army training as opposed to physical education." He informed his civilian instructors that their long-term advance-ment depended on earning a doctoral degree; he wanted "a faculty that was more capable, that had more intellectual experiences themselves."[197] The focus on education proved important as the Academy soon experienced a dramatic demographic shift—the admission of women in 1976—that required careful study grounded in scientific methods.

Nowhere were the challenges of integration greater than in the physical program. Many of those who objected to women in the Corps of Cadets ar-gued that the Academy's physical standards should apply equally to all, male or female. Anderson knew that such expectations were unrealistic because of the studies his PhD faculty had completed prior to the women's matriculation. The most important study, "Project 60," had tested young women between the ages of sixteen and eighteen on a variety of physical training activities. There were two principal findings. First, women were more physically capable than the experimenters had expected; second, even above-average women "performed at a level below that achieved by the average male cadet." Several follow-up studies, conducted after women had been admitted as cadets, confirmed and refined the initial findings.[198]

These studies led Anderson to design an exercise program that accounted for the physiological differences of women. His goal was "to challenge the women at the same level we are challenging the men—a comparable effort, not necessarily equal performance."[199] He established separate grading scales—one male, one female—for the majority of physical education events that were com-mon for both sexes. Once grading norms were refined over several years, men and women passed and failed these events at roughly the same rates.

Besides the dual grading scale, the presence of women required minor changes to the structure of the physical program. Anderson found, for ex-ample, that most women could not easily handle the heavy M-14 rifle during basic training exercise sessions; he therefore substituted resistance exercises for all cadets. Another change was to establish separate running formations based on ability rather than having all cadets run together. During the academic year, women took self-defense courses in lieu of boxing and wrestling. The indoor obstacle course was modified slightly to accommodate the physiology of women.[200] Despite these and other changes, however, the physical program was notable more for what remained than what changed. Anderson stayed true to the congressional mandate of making only the "minimum essential adjustments . . . required because of physiological differences between male and female individuals."[201]

Symbolic of the advances of women at the Academy was the appointment of Col. Maureen LeBoeuf to replace Anderson in 1997. LeBoeuf had served as an instructor in the Department of Physical Education in the late 1980s and returned for a second tour of duty in the mid-1990s as the director of instruction. Upon her selection as master of the sword, she became the first woman to serve as a department head and to sit on the Academic Board.[202] The unprecedented appointment brought mixed reviews. Those familiar with LeBoeuf's personal and professional qualifications applauded the decision. Many others, however, accused Superintendent Christman of undermining the "warrior ethos" at West Point. He received irate calls from high-ranking graduates, even a former army chief of staff, who recoiled at the thought of a female master of the sword. LeBoeuf's subsequent performance silenced most of the critics, but Christman recalled the episode as "one of the lowest points that I've experienced as Superintendent."[203]

One of LeBoeuf's first tasks was to end a tense employment situation relating to the department's civilian instructors. During the early 1990s, the precarious financial situation of the Army Athletic Association jeopardized the ability to pay the salaries of coaches. The superintendent, Lt. Gen. Howard Graves, had addressed the problem by establishing seventeen "instructor-coach" positions in the Department of Physical Education. The coaches would transition to the government payroll and perform duties as physical education instructors during the off seasons; not surprisingly, neither the master of the sword nor the athletics director was happy with the arrangement.[204] Concurrently, Col. Anderson was pressing his civilian instructors (including the instructor-coaches) to earn doctoral degrees as a requirement for advancement. These stresses caused anger and frustration within the department. "It was a mess," recalled then-Lt. Col. LeBoeuf, who, as director of instruction, was the person responsible for managing these personnel issues. Immediately upon becoming the department head, she rescinded the PhD requirement; a few years later, she was successful in relieving her staff of varsity coaching duties.[205] From then on, the split between physical education and intercollegiate athletics was complete.

Although earning a doctorate was no longer required, the several instructors who had earned the degree made substantial contributions to the physical education program. In particular, they took the lead in designing a series of cognitive courses that schooled cadets in the theories of physical conditioning. The first such course, offered to plebes starting in 1979, was "Fundamentals of Personal Fitness." Over the next few years, this course—and another entitled "Army Fitness Development"—were tailored to satisfy the requirements of the

army's "master fitness trainer" program. Cadets certified as master fitness trainers were qualified to design conditioning programs for their army units after
graduation.[206] Other cognitive courses were added to the curriculum, including some with academic course credit. Eventually, these curricular initiatives
resulted in the creation of an academic major in kinesiology, the science of
human physical performance.[207]

Concurrent with the creation of cognitive courses, the Department of
Physical Education expanded the menu of elective courses focusing on various forms of physical activity. The courses were offered primarily to third-class
cadets as a means of developing self-confidence and aptitude in a broad range
of "lifetime physical activities." The electives included professionally oriented
skills, such as close-quarters combat, advanced combatives, water safety, scuba,
and group-exercise leadership. Also included were sports-oriented courses,
such as alpine skiing, aerobic fitness, and strength development.

Recent changes to the physical education program more evenly distributed the requirements formerly concentrated in the plebe year. Swimming,
for example, moved from the fourth-class to the second-class year, and a new
first-class course in "combat applications" replaced wrestling (formerly in the
fourth-class year). The overall effect of these and other changes was to ensure a
progressive, rigorous, and professionally oriented physical education program
that prepared cadets to succeed in the intensely physical profession of arms
(table 5.9).

Competitive sports continued to be an important part of the physical program. While intercollegiate athletics were the most competitive, club sports—
under the direction of the master of the sword starting in 1988—also played
at a high level. Cadets who played on club teams did not enter West Point as
recruited athletes; instead, they tried out for their teams of choice once they arrived as cadets. Team coaches, the vast majority of whom were volunteer faculty
and staff members, developed the players' natural talents to field competitive
teams.[208] Because the master of the sword, not the athletics director, supervised
the administation of club sports, the focus was on character and leader development primarily and winning secondarily. Although the level of competition
usually was a notch below that of the varsity teams, the developmental benefits
of the club sports were at least as great as those of the varsity sports. Moreover,
club athletes had more flexibility in their schedules to attend to other priorities,
such as academics and military training.

In contrast to the declining fortunes of the intercollegiate athletics program,
the Academy's twenty-seven club sports showed that cadets were highly competitive when they played at an appropriate level of competition. During the
first decade of the twenty-first century, the Academy's club teams won thirty-
two national championships—an amazing record of achievement (table 5.10).

TABLE 5.9 Physical Education Program, Academic Year 2009–2010

Class	Objective	Summer Training	Academic Year
Fourth (1st year)	Develop foundation of physical fitness and motor skills.	Combatives	PE115: Fundamentals of Combatives (women) PE116: Boxing (men) PE117: Military Movement (gymnastics) PE150: Fundamentals of Personal Fitness Physical Test (fall and spring) Competitive Sports
Third (2nd year)	Enhance physical fitness, self-confidence, and personal wellness.	Combatives	Lifetime Physical Activity (various courses) Physical Test (fall and spring) Competitive Sports
Second (3rd year)	Achieve optimal physical fitness; understand principles and theories leading to a healthy, active lifestyle.	Fitness cadre	PE320: Survival Swimming PE350: Army Fitness Development Physical Test (fall and spring) Indoor Obstacle Course Competitive Sports
First (4th year)	Broaden physical capabilities; develop leadership skills in physical education.	Fitness cadre	PE460: Combat Applications Physical Test (fall and spring) Competitive Sports

Notes: Adapted from *Physical Program* (West Point: Office of the Commandant, Academic Year 2009–2010), Table 1–2, 13.

In some cases, the championship teams played against varsity competition during the season. Some club teams that did not win championships were still highly competitive at the national level; the rugby team, for example, routinely ranked among the best in the country, even though its principal opponents operated on the varsity model.

In recent years, the Department of Physical Education has redoubled its efforts to stay true to the spirit of Herman Koehler. It has kept its focus on individual cadet development through physical education and competitive athletics. The byproduct of these focus areas was character development, a core mission of the Academy. In 2007, the Institute for International Sport recognized the department as "one of the 15 most influential sports 'teams' in America," out of about 1,500 nominees. The Institute was impressed by the department's work in designing programs "to teach character and instill leadership principles." In accepting the award, the director of physical education, Col. Gregory Daniels, explained that sports do not "inherently teach character, but

TABLE 5.10 National Championships
Won by Academy Club Sports Teams,
2000–2010

Academic Year	Championship Team
2000–2001	Team Handball (men's)
	Team Handball (women's)
2001–2002	Team Handball (women's)
2002–2003	Team Handball (women's)
2003–2004	
2004–2005	Fencing (women's)
	Fencing (men's)
	Men's Varsity Four (crew)
	Team Handball (women's)
2005–2006	Fencing (men's)
	Pistol (men's)
	Sport Parachute
	Team Handball (men's)
	Team Handball (women's)
2006–2007	Cycling
	Fencing (women's)
	Team Handball (men's)
	Team Handball (women's)
2007–2008	Boxing
	Pistol (women's)
	Team Handball (men's)
2008–2009	Boxing
	Judo
	Men's Novice Four
	Pistol (men's)
	Team Handball (men's)
	Triathlon
	Women's Varsity Four (crew)
2009–2010	Boxing
	Judo
	Pistol (men's)
	Team Handball (men's)
	Triathlon

Notes: Information provided to author by Col. James C.
Flowers, director of cadet activities (DCA), 28 January 2011.
The DCA is responsible for providing funding for club
sports.

in the hands of a skilled coach and caring mentor, sports can be a superb way to imbue some of life's best lessons."[209] One of those lessons, as true today as it was in Koehler's era, is that, in sports, if not in war, there are indeed acceptable alternatives to winning.

★ ★ ★

The physical program at West Point has few, if any, equals in higher education. From the beginning, Academy leaders ensured that an integrated curriculum of physical education, testing, and competitive sports built strong cadet bodies and character. The principles that underlay the physical program, established by Herman Koehler early in the twentieth century, remain central to the program today.

Intercollegiate athletics began as part of the physical program, and for many years Academy leaders successfully harnessed them to the needs of cadet development. Over time, however, the forces of commercialism and professionalism cleaved varsity sports from the physical program. To be sure, cadets who played on varsity teams still derived some of the developmental benefits of competitive sports, but other, less wholesome influences undermined the original purpose of participation in those sports. The negative effects of intercollegiate athletics have been especially noticeable since 1970, as Academy leaders have struggled to succeed in an athletic environment governed by business principles. The overall failure of this endeavor has yet to inspire a rethinking of the assumptions and goals that govern intercollegiate sports at West Point. Until that happens, the Academy will continue to fritter its resources in areas tangential to the institution's core mission.

CHAPTER SIX

The Spartan Academy

MILITARY TRAINING

MILITARY TRAINING for cadets improved dramatically over the course
of the twentieth century. Its progress reflected the growth of military
professionalism as the army expanded and modernized to meet the global commitments of the nation. Despite these improvements, however, Academy leaders succeeded in keeping military training general in nature and preventing it
from intruding too heavily on other development programs.

The greatest improvements in military training resulted from the nation's
involvement in war. Following the Spanish-American War, Academy leaders
realized the need to prepare cadets for the practical challenges that awaited
them as officers at home and abroad. World War I further dramatized the need
for tactically proficient junior officers who could assume their duties quickly
and competently upon reaching their first units. Moreover, it exposed the inad-
equacy of West Point's facilities for conducting high-quality military training.

Of all the wars since 1898, none had as great an impact on military training
at West Point as World War II. In the years leading up to that conflict, Academy leaders acquired large tracts of contiguous land to expand maneuver areas
and build modern training facilities; these additions dramatically improved the
quality and efficiency of cadet training. For the most part, the patterns of training that developed for each class during World War II have continued to the
present.

Since World War II, successive commandants have enhanced the training
received by cadets. They increased rigor and realism and sought to incorporate
scenarios relevant to the warfare that cadets were likely to experience after graduation. Additionally, they expanded the range of training activities available

209

to cadets, both at West Point and in distant venues. By the early twenty-first century, cadets received some of the finest training available in the army.

I. MILITARY TRAINING THROUGH
THE FIRST WORLD WAR

As discussed previously, the Academic Board unveiled a new curriculum in 1902, the centennial year. At first glance, little had changed. The curriculum remained heavily oriented on mathematics, science, and engineering, which used "the rational faculties to the best advantage."[1] Development of a cadet's intellect and character remained the highest priority for cadet education; in contrast, acquiring the practical knowledge of the military profession could wait until after graduation.

While Academy leaders gave primacy to theoretical knowledge, they could not ignore the hands-on military training that would equip graduates with the practical knowledge to succeed as junior officers. The Spanish-American War and ongoing operations in the Philippines underscored the importance of such instruction, as West Point officers would bear heavy professional responsibilities very soon after graduation. Accordingly, the new curriculum reflected Academic Board members' "full appreciation . . . of the immense advantage of practical knowledge." In making the curricular changes, they professed a commitment to helping cadets "secure as wide familiarity as possible with the technical and practical bearing of all subjects studied."[2]

The quality of military training already had improved considerably under the supervision of Otto T. Hein, the commandant during the first years of Albert Mills's tenure as superintendent (1898–1906).[3] Hein was an 1870 graduate of the Academy who had spent seven years on the western frontier and five as the military attaché in Vienna before returning to the West Point. Familiar with Prussian advances in the art of war, he was dismayed by the Academy's antiquated training methods. In the latter nineteenth century, the cadets' military training centered on parade-field drill, lectures, and demonstrations; there was relatively little hands-on training of the sort that would prepare cadets for the practical skills they would need as officers in the twentieth-century army. Hein moved aggressively to improve the situation by adding rigor, realism, and variety wherever possible. To begin, he issued cadets a field service uniform and standard army field equipment for summer training. The cadets, now properly outfitted, underwent hands-on training in each of the principal branches of the service, starting with basic soldier skills and advancing to small-unit missions. During the academic year, Hein rotated cadets through a variety of leadership positions in the Corps to prepare them for comparable duties as officers. His tactical officers gave lectures on army administrative procedures to familiarize cadets with the complexities of leading and managing units; he even published the lectures in a pamphlet that cadets could take with them into the army. By the time of his departure in 1901, Hein had begun a process of modernization in the area of military training that would continue through the next century.[4]

Under the new curriculum of 1902, several departments devoted themselves all or in part to the delivery of military training. Most conspicuous was the Department of Tactics, headed by the new commandant, Lt. Col. Charles G. Treat. Under Treat were about a dozen officers responsible for military instruction and physical education.[5] The Department of Tactics controlled about 28 percent of programmed cadet time, the majority of which came during the summer months. The rest came during the academic year, mostly between the hours of 4:00 and 6:00 p.m. on weekdays. The instruction covered the principal combat branches—infantry, cavalry, field artillery, and coast artillery.[6] With minor variation and gradual improvement, the training program in place in 1902 continued through World War I.

Cadets in all four classes underwent infantry training. During the academic year, they practiced the manual of arms, parade-field drills, tent pitching, entrenching, tactical guard duty, bayonet exercises, and rifle marksmanship techniques. During the summer, the cadets (minus the rising second class on furlough) reviewed these subjects and added rifle qualification and collective training tasks through battalion level. Starting in 1905, the summer culminated in late August with a "practice march" beyond the borders of the military reservation that lasted up to two weeks.[7] During the march, cadets organized as a battalion, practiced field craft, and conducted a variety of small-unit tactical missions. First classmen acted as officers during the exercise and thus received an intensive dose of leader training at the start of their final year at the Academy.

An important addition to infantry training in the early twentieth century was rifle marksmanship. Commandant Treat was the catalyst; he procured the new model 1903 Springfield rifle for the cadets and began a progressive program of training through the four cadet years. Plebes started with the basics—disassembly and assembly, aiming techniques, and dry-fire exercises—while upperclassmen conducted advanced training in the gymnasium shooting gallery and on the firing range. The first classmen fired for qualification during the summer and could wear the appropriate rifle qualification badge on their uniforms for the remainder of the year. Within a few years the marksmanship program would yield impressive results. More than one-quarter of the class of 1916, for example, fired "expert"—the most ever up to that point.[8]

Even in so basic a skill as marksmanship, Academy leaders were careful to limit its scope. There was limited time for military training, and the goal in each area was familiarization, not specialization. For this reason Superintendent Mills stopped sending cadets to the summer marksmanship competitions sponsored by the army. He had allowed a small contingent of cadets to make the trip in August 1905 at the urging of the secretary of war. Unfortunately, the time and effort needed to prepare the cadets "seriously interfered with the general instruction of other cadets in target practice, and the team missed the valuable experience of the practice march which the remainder of the battalion participated in."[9] Mills concluded that the generalized training common to the entire Corps of Cadets was more important than the specialty training afforded a few. In this regard he reflected the consensus view of the Academic Board about the goals of a West Point education. Mills's successor, Hugh Scott, affirmed the consensus by continuing the ban on sending cadets to the army's marksmanship competitions.[10]

The upper three classes received cavalry instruction at various times during the year. Third- and second-class cadets learned basic riding techniques and how to care for the horses. First classmen practiced elementary cavalry drills on the parade field during the academic year and in the early summer.[11] Successive commandants encouraged recreational riding to reinforce the training; Treat even obtained polo ponies to promote the equestrian sport and thus add "zest and interest" to the riding program.[12] During the August practice march, selected first classmen would operate as a cavalry troop and conduct standard tactical missions — reconnaissance, interdiction, exploitation, deception.

Throughout the year, enlisted troopers from the West Point cavalry detachment supported the cadets' equestrian training. They were under the command of the senior instructor of cavalry tactics, a member of the commandant's staff. In 1907, the quality of cavalry instruction improved when a detachment from the all-black 9th Cavalry Regiment arrived for duty. Replacing the all-white detachment that had suffered from morale and discipline problems, the "Buffalo Soldiers" quickly established an enviable record of achievement.[13] Superintendent Hugh Scott noted that the new troopers were well motivated and disciplined and kept the horses and equipment in better condition than before their arrival.[14] They continued serving until 1947, when the army disbanded the last of its horse cavalry units.[15]

Artillery training was reserved primarily for the upper three classes. The various forms of artillery — coast, light, siege, and mountain — each had its peculiarities and therefore required separate training sessions. Light artillery, for example, depended on horses for transport, whereas the coast artillery battery operated from a fixed carriage. In all cases, cadets learned how to operate and maintain the pieces and to understand the nature and effect of the different types of ammunition. Live ammunition was scarce, so much of the training was simulated — a real drawback for any serious artilleryman. When live ammuni-

Coast artillery training at Trophy Point.

tion was available, cadets fired the weapons at targets on Storm King Mountain, immediately north of the cadet area.[16] Supporting the instruction was the enlisted artillery detachment, commanded by the senior instructor of artillery tactics.

Coast artillery, by virtue of its large size, posed special challenges for cadet training. The War Department was hard pressed to provide modern guns and ammunition to an army base unlikely ever to be attacked by enemy battleships. Consequently, the cadets had long used mismatched, obsolete guns that defied efforts to train effectively. In 1907, however, the situation improved when Congress appropriated money to build a coast artillery emplacement at Trophy Point. About the same time, the chief of ordnance provided two modern six-inch guns with disappearing carriages and subcaliber devices that allowed realistic firing without the bulky ammunition.[17] The installation of a sixty-inch searchlight near the gun emplacement in 1909 completed the package and allowed high-quality training. When first-class cadets traveled that summer to Fort Hancock, New Jersey, for coast artillery gunnery, 80 percent of their rounds from the six-inch guns scored direct hits.[18]

Artillery training, like infantry marksmanship training, had the potential of getting out of hand. In 1910, for example, the commandant, Frederick Sibley,

Cadets learn bridge-building techniques.

noted the "urgent need" for submarine mine equipment as a complement to the coast artillery emplacement.[19] The War Department was unconvinced that cadets needed such specialized training, and nothing came of the request.

Overall, the summer training program executed by the Department of Tactics in the early century was head and shoulders above what had existed before. Cadets stayed busy with challenging hands-on training that gave them reasonable familiarity with the basic branches of the army. At least one "old grad" was impressed. David C. Shanks, a staff officer from the Army Inspector General's office, visited West Point for ten days in July 1915 and rendered a highly positive report. After complimenting the cadets' appearance and discipline, he put into context the improvements he had seen in tactical training. "Possibly nothing more strongly impresses an older graduate than the practical and diversified nature of the instruction now given to cadets."[20]

While the Department of Tactics controlled the lion's share of cadet military training, other departments also had responsibilities in that area. The Department of Practical Military Engineering, for example, covered many of the hands-on skills needed to erect tactical bridges, employ siege materials, dig entrenchments, conduct topographical surveys, operate signaling equipment, and invent field expedients of every type. Most of the training occurred during the summer to leverage the favorable weather. The instructor of practical military engineering, a captain in the Corps of Engineers, commanded the detachment of engineer soldiers that supported engineer training for the cadets. By virtue of his role in cadet education, he occupied a seat on the Academic Board.[21]

Added to the military training program in 1902 was a series of lectures on military hygiene for second-class cadets. The change was the result of the army's experience in the war with Spain, in which far more Americans died from disease and poor sanitation than from combat. The West Point surgeon and his staff of army doctors delivered the lectures coincident with the cadets' study of chemistry; by then the cadets were "admirably grounded in the mathematical, chemical, and general physical knowledge necessary to readily become good sanitary engineers."[22] In recognition of his new role in cadet training, the surgeon received the title of Professor of Military Hygiene and a seat on the Academic Board.[23]

Other departments straddled the divide between academics and military training, particularly as cadets reached the senior year. The Department of Ordnance and Gunnery, for example, taught first classmen how to maintain motor vehicles, use machine tools, perform basic carpentry skills, and handle ammunition—all in addition to teaching the underlying engineering principles. As the army acquired modern equipment—trucks, tanks, airplanes, mobile artillery—these theoretical and practical skills would prove useful to the cadets, especially once they became officers.

First classmen also took instruction from the Department of Civil and Military Engineering, a hybrid organization with seemingly incongruent missions. One of the department's responsibilities was to teach the engineering techniques for building bridges, fortifications, and other militarily useful structures, thus providing the theoretical complement to the training given by the Department of Practical Military Engineering. The department's other mission was to teach an academic course in military history—the same course begun by Dennis Hart Mahan and refined consistently since the mid-1800s.[24] This course, long a cadet favorite, had achieved exalted status at West Point. There was no other course like it anywhere, and Academy leaders considered it an ideal capstone for cadets about to become officers. In the early years of the twentieth century, the course focused primarily on the campaigns of Napoleon, the American Civil War, and the wars of German unification. After each of the world wars, the scope of the course expanded to cover those campaigns as well.

In April 1902, the head of the Department of Civil and Military Engineering, Gustav J. Fiebeger, took the entire first class to the Gettysburg battlefield for an educational experience known as a "staff ride." Copied from the German

General Staff's *Führerreise*, the staff ride required participants to assume the roles of the historical commanders and talk through the strategy and tactics that determined the outcome of the battle. The discussions thus generated were effective in applying theory to practice, and many observers attributed the conspicuous successes of the Prussian (later German) General Staff in the Franco-Prussian War largely to those staff rides. The cadet experience at Gettysburg was similarly beneficial, as Fiebeger's after-action report made clear.

> The visit to this field was found even more valuable to the cadets of the first class than was at first thought probable. The anticipation of the visit greatly stimulated their interest in all their military studies; this interest was evinced on the field by their numerous and intelligent questions. The time and space problems in tactics, as well as the effects of local topography, were impressed upon them in a manner impossible in simple description or even by the aid of the best maps.[25]

While Fiebeger's history course resided in the domain of education, not training, its applicability to the practical side of the profession was obvious. Superintendent Mills considered the staff rides to be of "incalculable benefit in the training of our young officers."[26] The Academic Board was sufficiently impressed to make the Gettysburg trip an annual event, at least until the early graduations during World War I made them untenable. After the war, the Corps of Cadets had expanded to the point that the trips were no longer deemed feasible for the entire first class.[27]

The success of the staff rides led to many other class trips for practical military training. Starting in 1903, the Department of Ordnance and Gunnery took first classmen on trips to the army gun factory at Watervliet Arsenal, New York, and to the ordnance proving ground at Sandy Hook, New Jersey. The visits were timed so that the practical experience followed closely the theoretical instruction in the classroom. In the summer of 1904, first classmen trekked to nearby coast artillery stations for gunnery practice and submarine defense training; the number and scope of these trips expanded in subsequent years.[28]

On other occasions the entire Corps of Cadets attended special events that allowed them to train while showcasing themselves to the public. In March 1905, for example, cadets traveled to Washington to march in the inaugural parade for Theodore Roosevelt; they organized as a battalion of infantry, troop of cavalry, battery of artillery, and platoon of mountain (pack-mule) artillery. In June 1907, they attended the Tercentennial Exposition at Jamestown for a week of training; they sailed to the Chesapeake on a naval transport and had the opportunity of boarding other navy ships while they were there.[29] Everyone agreed with the instructor of ordnance and gunnery that the benefits of these trips "cannot be overestimated." The cadets gained experiences that made "an indelible impression on their minds. . . . Their horizon has been broadened."[30]

The growth in the number of cadet trips, for both military and academic pursuits, continued through the century, abating only during time of war. Each new trip chipped away at the assumptions that had justified the cloistering of cadets on the West Point reservation. It turned out that cadets flourished when given added responsibilities and new opportunities and they craved connection with the outside world. The new experiences broadened their horizons and enhanced their ability to cope with the multiplicity of challenges they would encounter as officers.

One of the oldest traditions of military training at West Point was the summer encampment on the Plain.[31] Immediately following the June graduation, the Corps of Cadets (minus the second class on furlough) would set up their tents in perfect alignment on the field adjacent to the ruins of Fort Clinton. The encampment had the feel of a well-ordered military city. There were company streets, formal guard posts, a regular schedule of bugle calls and ceremonies, and a vibrant social life. During the morning hours the cadets would train at various locations around the installation, but after lunch they normally had the rest of the day off. They could engage in sports, play cards, bathe in the river, and escort visitors; at night there were concerts and hops. The assemblage of so many cadets in one place and with plenty of free time was a magnet for young ladies of the Mid-Hudson Valley and far beyond. Without question, the encampment was the epicenter of the summer social scene, and it was that way by design. The leisurely pace gave cadets the time to bond with their classmates and recover from the mental exertions of the academic year.

The plebes, of course, found the summer encampment less inviting than the upperclassmen. Upon reporting to West Point in June, they underwent a difficult three-week indoctrination known as Beast Barracks. During this period, they lived in the barracks under the watchful eyes of a cadre of officers and specially selected cadets. Once the greenhorns learned the rudiments of military discipline, basic military skills, and customs and traditions of the Corps, they joined the upperclassmen in the encampment, where they pulled guard duty and performed other mundane tasks when not in scheduled training. There were strict rules — and in 1902 even a law — prohibiting hazing, but some upperclassmen could not resist the temptation. Yearlings in particular made a sport of tormenting the newcomers in many invidious ways. Most of the hazing remained below the threshold of illegality, but there were ample reports of disciplinary action against upperclassmen who went too far.[32]

The program of year-round military training just described remained relatively unchanged until the United States declared war on Germany on 2 April

A cadet first sergeant inspects the guard during the summer encampment.
The guards consist of first-class cadets (chevrons on upper sleeve), third-class
cadets (chevrons on lower sleeve), and fourth-class cadets (no chevrons).

1917. With a sudden need for more officers, the War Department ordered
the class of 1917 to graduate immediately (20 April) and the class of 1918 to
graduate on 30 August, ten months ahead of schedule. The newly designated
"Class of August 1917" took a mix of academic classes and military training until 7 July; afterward they focused solely on military training. It was the normal
summer curriculum, albeit more intense. An added twist was the presence of
language professors sent by Harvard president Abbott L. Lowell to teach the
first classmen basic French as time permitted.[33]

With the new senior class preparing feverishly for its August graduation,
the rising second class[34] took on the responsibility of training the incoming
plebes. Superintendent Samuel Tillman reduced the second-class furlough to
one month instead of the normal three; he then staggered the absences to ensure that there would be enough second classmen on hand throughout the
summer to serve as cadre members. To discourage hazing during this frenetic
period, Tillman billeted the new cadets in the barracks (as opposed to tents on
the Plain) for the entire summer.[35]

The practice march that summer lasted twelve days instead of the usual six.
The added training prompted the commandant, Guy V. Henry, to report that
the first classmen were "as well prepared as other graduated classes; this is due

to changes which have been made in the methods and scope of instruction." Henry was referring to advances in the quality of training over the past two decades and the initiatives to give first classmen more responsibility for training the under-classes. The collective effect of these improvements developed in cadets "self-confidence, the art of instructing and ability to command."[36]

While this may have been true, it was also true that cadets had been given little exposure to the changes in warfare evident on the European battlefields. Instead of learning how to operate in a high-intensity combat environment, cadets were conducting foot marches with mule packs, horse cavalry, and primitive forms of communication. Cadet training may have been more rigorous than before, but Academy leaders — and army leaders in general — had done little to adapt military training to the realities of modern combat.[37] For the moment, army leaders would console themselves that they had built a great expeditionary army and led it to victory against the Germans — indisputably true. The more perceptive among them, however, recognized that they had entered a new era of warfare, one that rendered obsolete the relaxed summer training environment at West Point.[38]

II. MILITARY TRAINING THROUGH THE SECOND WORLD WAR

Few army officers understood the dynamics of modern war better than Douglas MacArthur, who reported to West Point as the superintendent in June 1919. MacArthur had been the chief of staff of the 42nd Infantry Division, composed of National Guard units from twenty-six states, as it organized and deployed to France for the war. Later he commanded the division's 84th Infantry Brigade in combat during the Meuse-Argonne offensive in late 1918. He was a lead-from-the-front commander with intimate knowledge of the motivations and abilities of soldiers. In selecting MacArthur as the new superintendent, Army Chief of Staff Peyton March intended to shake up the status quo at West Point by breaking the hold of the nineteenth-century assumptions that heavily influenced the curriculum, including military training.

For someone just returning from war, watching the summer encampment of 1919 must have been disorienting. The West Point environment — highly structured, meticulously manicured, and insulated from the untidy normality of civilian life — was far removed from the conditions that cadets would encounter as officers. The real world was in fact unstructured, messy, and chaotic, and war exaggerated those qualities to the extreme. How could Academy leaders hope to prepare cadets for officership when the training facilities were limited to what could be squeezed onto the postage stamp of a reservation that was then West Point? Why did they spend so much time on irrelevant tasks like parade-field drill and so little time with the soldiers and noncommissioned officers they would lead in war? The traditional encampment, with its schedule of training in the morning and leisure activities in the afternoon, seemed an obsolete model for preparing cadets for war.

MacArthur's solution was as simple as it was radical. Starting in 1920, first- and third-class cadets would spend the summer at Camp Dix, New Jersey, a major army training base.[39] Cadets would receive training on the weapons, equipment, and tactics used in the late war and interact with noncommissioned officers and enlisted soldiers in the field. Even better, according to MacArthur, they would "learn more of human nature, acquire understanding, sympathy, and tact. The entire experience both broadens and deepens their character." He considered this initiative "the most important single feature" of the new military training program.[40]

The cadets did in fact receive better training at Camp Dix, and many of them enjoyed the opportunity to escape the confines of West Point.[41] But the traditionalists at the Academy, including some of the officers' spouses, cried foul. The superintendent was altering traditional training methods and disrupting the social order at the staid little army post. They would miss the gaiety of relaxed summers and the active social life that centered on the Corps of Cadets.[42] But that wasn't all.

Sending the upperclassmen away for the summer required the Department of Tactics to assume sole responsibility for training the incoming plebes.[43] Commandant Robert Danford accepted the mission enthusiastically, as it would allow his tactical officers to create a positive leader environment that would gradually permeate the entire Corps of Cadets. These changes, however, harvested a bounty of ill will from graduates and cadets who believed that West Point already had reached perfection in its time-tested methods and that any tampering would be harmful. MacArthur's adjutant, William Ganoe, paraphrased the critics' argument:

> Beast Barracks made a man of me. A soldier should early learn to take hard knocks. Besides, the Supe was producing a soft, spineless discipline which would yield graduates incapable of meeting the rigors of a soldier. Altogether the Supe was allowing the cadet to become a flabby caricature of those stalwarts of former times.[44]

The forces of discontent eventually gained the upper hand. After two years, the War Department ended the Fort Dix experiment and reinstated the summer encampment at West Point. MacArthur's patron in the War Department, Chief of Staff Peyton March, had retired by then, and MacArthur was on orders

to the Philippines. The new superintendent, Frederick Sladen, touted the traditional virtues of the encampment: training at West Point was more efficient;
cadets needed a break from academic pressures; the presence of the cadets encouraged family, friends, and the public to visit West Point. Taking a swipe at
his predecessor, Sladen concluded that the success of the reestablished encampment in 1922 proved "conclusively that the practice, prevailing for more than
a century before 1920, . . . was based on sound principles."[45] Regardless of
Sladen's opinion, MacArthur had set a precedent for training that was more
rigorous and relevant to the challenges cadets would face as junior officers.
Future superintendents would build on his foundation.

The debate over summer training was part of a larger question that emerged
(and still emerges) periodically at West Point. Specifically, which developmental
domain — academic or military — should receive priority given the finite time
in the cadet schedule? This "Athens-Sparta" dichotomy was a source of controversy in the earliest years of the Academy's history, as when Alden Partridge
infuriated the faculty by paying more attention to drill than to academic subjects. Sylvanus Thayer resolved the issue, at least for the nineteenth century, by
making the four-year undergraduate experience the cornerstone of cadet development and subordinating tactical proficiency to mental discipline. The question reemerged in the twentieth century, however, as trends in warfare and the
growth of America's imperial commitments challenged old assumptions about
military training. It was increasingly likely that cadets would face challenging
professional assignments immediately upon graduation, and this possibility
militated for more robust training at West Point.[46] The early graduations of
World War I represented the most recent reprise of the idea that the Academy
should be more narrowly focused on practical military skills. Proponents of this
view lamented the return to the four-year curriculum soon after the war.[47]

The War Department reopened the debate in 1922 by convening a board
of officers to evaluate the army school system. The board arrived at a decidedly
Spartan conclusion — that the Academy should "bring its graduates into the
corps of officers properly equipped to enter upon the duties of the lowest grade
in the arm in which they may be commissioned."[48] It criticized the Academy
for devoting too much time to academics and athletics at the expense of tactical
training, a shortcoming that left cadets unable to perform at an acceptable level
upon graduation. In short, the board's opinion was that West Pointers needed
to be better platoon leaders when they reported to their first units.

The debate represented a collision of two distinct views of the Academy's
mission. In 1920, the Academic Board had conducted a thorough curriculum
review leading to the reestablishment of the four-year course of study following World War I. The Academic Board concluded that military training should
be "elementary, fundamental, and general. The tactical work is not intended to

produce glorified drill sergeants, or to qualify the cadet to be a subaltern officer in one particular branch of the service."[49] Two years later, this position was completely at odds with the thinking of the leaders in the War Department.

Sladen, himself a "Spartan," implemented some of the recommendations of the board of officers.[50] He abolished the Department of Practical Military Engineering and transferred its training functions to the Department of Tactics. Also transferred to Tactics was the military history course, from the Department of Civil and Military Engineering. According to the board of officers, the course "obviously should be handled entirely by the Tactical Department," whose officers were all graduates of the Army Service Schools.[51] Both changes were designed to consolidate military training under a strengthened commandant. The latter change proved to be ill advised, however, as military history was patently an academic course; a few years later, the course returned to Civil and Military Engineering.

Sladen's immediate successors tended to be more "Athenian" in their attitudes toward cadet development. On many occasions they reaffirmed the primacy of academics over military training and rejected the notion that West Point should graduate polished lieutenants. Superintendent Jay Benedict typified this view: "It is manifestly impossible, under modern conditions, to produce graduates proficient in all the technical duties of all the arms to which they may be assigned. The attainable objective cannot go far beyond a broad and basic military education."[52] This attitude, coupled with the advances in the academic program during the 1920s and 1930s, has led some historians to conclude that Athenian values trumped Spartan values.[53] More accurately, both academic instruction and military training advanced during this period, with the time allotted to each remaining about the same as before World War I.

Although the summer encampment was reinstated, there were a few new twists. Most significant was the introduction of air-service training in the early 1920s. Airplanes had proven their value in World War I and were fast becoming a vital part of the army structure; consequently, the War Department required cadets to receive familiarization training during the summers. First classmen henceforth spent a week at an army airfield, usually Mitchell Field on Long Island or Langley Field in Virginia. They received ground instruction on aircraft types, training methods, navigation, communication, reconnaissance, aerial photography, and tactics. The highlight of the week for the cadets was the four hours of training aloft; few of them had ever flown before.[54] By the mid-1930s, the training had expanded to a total of twenty hours.

Another change to the encampment was the increased amount of time cadets spent away from West Point to compensate for the Academy's inadequate training facilities. As MacArthur had well understood, West Point was simply too small to accommodate much of the training now required to prepare cadets for officership. For example, a new highway connecting West Point to communities to the north passed underneath the arc of artillery fire aimed at Storm King Mountain. For several years after the highway's completion in 1922, state and military officials clashed over the need to close the road when firing was in progress.[55] Another problem, emergent after World War I, concerned training for armored warfare. To properly train with track-laying vehicles, cadets needed expansive maneuver areas that were unavailable at West Point. During the 1920s, Academy leaders solved these problems by sending first classmen to other military installations for part of the summer. Typical stops included Fort Monroe (coast artillery), Fort Eustis (field artillery), and Langley Field (air service), all in Virginia, and Fort Meade (armor) in Maryland.[56] Starting in 1934, cadets also traveled to Fort Benning, Georgia, for combined-arms training. Commandant Simon B. Buckner Jr. reported enthusiastically that the cadets "lived in barracks and messed with a very superior type of enlisted man, thus giving them better appreciation of a soldier's viewpoint, a proper degree of respect for his capabilities, and an idea of the high standard to which he can be trained."[57] Ironically, these were precisely the effects MacArthur had intended to achieve fifteen years before.

Much of the training cadets received at other army bases could be done just as well at West Point and with greater efficiency if the requisite land were available. The War Department already had acquired a few small parcels, primarily to secure pure water sources for the Academy, but training considerations prompted the superintendents to request more extensive purchases. There was a burning need for an airfield, both for cadet training and to allow air-service officers on the faculty to maintain their flight certifications.[58] Weapons ranges and maneuver areas, as noted before, also were a priority. In 1930, these mounting requirements led Superintendent William R. Smith to submit to the War Department a request to purchase about 15,000 of land west and south of the Academy.[59]

Smith was delighted when Congress authorized the purchases in 1931.[60] Unfortunately no money was appropriated until 1936, and then the purchases languished as landowners refused to sell. When the Second World War began in Europe, however, army officials leveraged the federal government's power of eminent domain to force the land sales, and the process accelerated once the United States entered the war. A breakthrough came in mid-1942, when the government closed on 10,300 acres around Lake Popolopen.[61] Soon thereafter, construction began on a training camp at the lake that featured semipermanent barracks, full utilities, efficient drainage, and paved roads. Also under construction was a modern training complex including weapons ranges, assault courses, amphibious training sites, maneuver areas, and even a mock village to enable urban combat exercises. At the center of the complex was an impact area that could accommodate any size ordnance up to a 105-millimeter howitzer shell.[62] Construction was far enough along to allow third classmen to spend two weeks at Camp Popolopen in the summer of 1942; starting in 1943, they would stay the entire summer.

The new training complex put the final nail in the coffin of the summer encampment. Yearlings had always been the largest contingent in the encampment, and now they were staying at Camp Popolopen with its modern ranges, convenient facilities, and ample maneuver space. The incoming plebes who arrived in 1943 lived in the cadet barracks all summer and therefore had no reason to set up tents on the Plain. First classmen either stayed in the barracks (to train the plebes) or traveled to various other military bases to complete their training. It had taken over twenty years and another world war, but Douglas MacArthur's vision for cadet training away from the West Point garrison finally had been realized.

The training that evolved during the war was more effective than anything cadets had experienced before. Plebes no longer endured the traditional Beast Barracks but underwent an experience that closely approximated infantry basic training. The new regimen, noted Superintendent Francis B. Wilby, provided a "broader, more complete course of recruit training than has been given new cadets in the past."[63] Yearlings at Camp Popolopen fired modern weapons, conducted branch-orientation training, practiced small-unit tactics, and learned to operate wheeled and tracked vehicles.[64] First classmen had particularly busy summers. In 1944, for example, they spent most of June at Fort Benning and other bases for combined-arms field training. They returned to West Point at the end of the month for a week of instructor training, preparatory to receiving the new plebe class. For the next six weeks they divided their time between army training centers and cadet basic training; in both cases they served as cadre members responsible for training new soldiers or cadets. The summer culminated with training exercises at Pine Camp, New York, for all cadets.[65] They progressed through small-unit and combined-arms training and finished with a force-on-force exercise. The cadets organized into two opposing battalions, with the first classmen assuming leadership positions. For the last three days the cadets were integrated into units of the 5th Armored Division, which was conducting maneuvers at the time.[66]

World War II influenced West Point in other important ways. The most obvious was the curtailment of the curriculum from four years to three.[67] The fact that Congress, not the War Department, ordered the change provided reasonable assurance that there would be no further curtailments, as had happened during World War I. The legislation, enacted 1 October 1942, went into effect immediately even though the academic year was under way. Having anticipated the change, however, the Academic Board had little problem transitioning to the new schedule. It graduated the current senior class in January 1943 (after three-and-a-half years) and the current second class in June 1943 (after three years). For the remainder of the war, there would be no second class. Cadets advanced directly from being third classmen to first classmen, and the military training that formerly had been conducted during the second-class academic year was added to a busy summer schedule. The elimination of the second class put an end — permanently, as it turned out — to the three-month summer furlough, a tradition that stretched back well over one hundred years.

Another major change caused by the war was the introduction of pilot certification for cadets. The War Department authorized up to 60 percent of each class to take the training and join the Army Air Forces upon commissioning; in practice, about 40 percent actually completed the program.[68] Pilot certification was a major departure from the Academy's traditional emphasis on general military training. Moreover, it forced the Academic Board to modify the academic curriculum for the "air cadets" since much of the training would have to take place during the regular school year. The creation of two separate tracks leading to graduation troubled Academy leaders, but Army Chief of Staff George Marshall was unmoved. He asserted that the change would allow the new Army Air Forces to have "as soon as possible a larger number of commissioned flyers imbued with the traditions and standards of West Point."[69] The class of January 1943 was the first to graduate with the option of earning pilot wings; the class of 1946 was the last. A total of 1,033 cadets in five separate classes successfully completed the training.[70]

Pilot training took over a year to complete. In April of the third-class year, air cadets left West Point for primary flying schools around the country — Lakeland, Florida; Tuskegee, Alabama; Brady, Texas; Uvalde, Texas; and Chickasha, Oklahoma. Upon returning in early July (as rising first classmen), they took basic flying training at Stewart Airfield in nearby Newburgh, New York, until the end of August.[71] They flew about once a week in the fall and winter to maintain their flying proficiency and then, in March, moved into the barracks at Stewart to begin advanced training — 225 hours in the air and 255 hours of ground instruction. If all went well, they would complete their certification in time for graduation and move on to an assignment as a pilot. It was not a sure thing, however. Of the 245 air cadets in the class of January 1943, thirty-nine failed to earn their wings and four died trying.[72]

III. MILITARY TRAINING AFTER THE SECOND WORLD WAR

In 1943, Superintendent Francis B. Wilby directed the Academic Board to begin work on a new four-year curriculum for implementation after the war. Board members used the opportunity to reaffirm old assumptions about military training. First, tactical instruction should be "broad and general, preparing for all branches and with no specialization until after graduation." This point of emphasis was to justify the elimination of pilot training, which had caused class distinctions, branch jealousies, and claims of discrimination among the cadets. Rather than certifying pilots, West Point would provide familiarization training sufficient to teach cadets "the fundamentals of aviation and its part in the combat team." A second assumption was that future wars, like the last one, would be fought with forces from all services. Cadets therefore needed an "understanding and appreciation of the problems pertaining to all forces — Army, Navy and Air."[73]

With the War Department's approval of the new curriculum in September 1945, the Academic Board got its way. Pilot training ceased, and the class of 1946 was the last to graduate with wings. Additionally, the new military training program was far more oriented on combined arms and joint operations than ever before, especially for the upper two classes.

Military training for the senior class reflected these assumptions, as shown in table 6.1. First classmen started the summer in June with a two-and-a-half-week combat-arms trip to several army bases. Upon their return, the class split into two groups. Group 1 underwent a week of instructor training before serving for three-and-a-half weeks as the cadre for the plebe and yearling training. Next came two weeks of orientation at air force bases followed by a week's leave. Meanwhile, Group 2 conducted the same training in reverse. During the final two weeks of training, in late August, the entire first class conducted field maneuvers in the wooded hills of the Hudson Valley with the third and fourth classes. This was the successor to the "practice march" of the prewar era, during which cadets organized as combined-arms units and first classmen assumed the leadership roles.

Second classmen also received heavy doses of combined-arms and joint-service training during the summers. They spent the first two weeks at Camp Buckner (formerly Camp Popolopen) to hone basic tactical skills, and then they split into two groups.[74] Group 1 took four weeks of leave while Group 2 conducted air training at various army airfields; the two groups switched places for the following four weeks. In early August, the entire class reassembled at West Point in preparation for two weeks of joint amphibious training at Little Creek, Virginia, with army, navy, and marine units. Thomas J. Murphy, class of 1952, vividly remembered this experience. He and his classmates left West Point aboard the USS Okanogan, a navy transport, and disembarked at Quantico, Virginia. After preliminary training at the army's Fort Belvoir (combat engineering) and Fort Eustis (wheeled vehicle transport), the cadets conducted amphibious training at Little Creek and participated in Operation CAMID ("cadet-midshipman"). The operation culminated with a full-scale amphibious

TABLE 6.1 Postwar Military Curriculum (approved September 1945)

Class	1	2	3	4	5	6	7	8	9	10	11	12	13
						Week							
First (4th year)	(2½) Combined-arms trip		(1) Instr trng	(3½) Training cadre for 3rd and 4th classes				(2) Air training		(1) Furlough	(2) Maneuvers		(1) for academics
			(2) Air training		(1) Furlough	(1½) Instr trng	(3) Training cadre for 3rd and 4th classes						
Second (3rd year)	(2) Practical training at West Point		(4) Furlough				(4) Air training				(2) Joint amphib training with 2nd Class, USNA		(1) preparation
			(4) Air training				(4) Furlough						
Third (2nd year)	(4) Furlough				(6) Weapons and tactical training at Popolopen						(2) Maneuvers		(1)
Fourth (1st year)	(6½) Processing and basic training at West Point										(2) Maneuvers		(1)

1st Tue in June   1st weekday in July   1st Tue after Labor Day

Notes: 1. Figures in parentheses denote weeks. 2. Normally a 13-week summer will be available. Periods shown are approximate only, due to the necessity for detailed scheduling (by days) for any particular calendar year.

Source: Adapted from *Post War Curriculum*, 18.

assault on nearby Pendleton Beach under simulated combat conditions. Joining the cadets were the midshipmen and navy ROTC cadets. Murphy found his second-class summer to be the most pleasant of the four he spent as a cadet. He enjoyed the travel, training, and social life associated with that summer away from the Academy.[75]

Third-class training took place at Camp Buckner in early July, after a month's leave. Cadets received familiarization training on the basic branches of the army, including infantry, armor, artillery, engineer, and signal. Additionally, they spent time in the field practicing small-unit missions and marched to the new complex of ranges where they fired small-arms and crew-served weapons, mortars, light artillery, and antitank rockets. While the training schedule was full, cadets had time to enjoy the extensive recreational facilities and social events that became a pleasant part of the Camp Buckner experience. For the final two weeks of the summer, the third classmen joined the first and fourth classmen on a field training exercise off the military reservation.

Summer training for new cadets consisted of eight weeks of indoctrination and basic soldier skills. Army basic training replaced Beast Barracks and the summer encampment as the model for receiving and training the new cadets.

The newcomers therefore experienced less of the hazing and other indignities their predecessors had endured; regardless, the environment was still severe, designed to transform civilians quickly into soldiers. Throughout the summer they were schooled on the unique aspects of life as a cadet, including the importance of abiding by the honor code and system. The new cadets received a basic load of uniforms and equipment, endured early morning exercise, learned customs and traditions of the service, practiced combat survival skills and field craft, and toughened their feet by marching to most training sites. Training culminated with a field exercise that included the first and third classes. As a plebe, Tom Murphy experienced this exercise in August 1948. It took place on the east side of the Hudson River and included a total of seventy miles of marching, always in the morning. Occasionally they had training or guard duty in the afternoons and evenings, but usually they enjoyed movies, music, and swimming once they had established the bivouac site. The field exercise was primarily for the benefit of the upper classes, particularly the seniors. With no leadership responsibilities to burden him, new cadet Murphy's salient memories of the exercise were of the intense heat and the "pretty fair beaches" that lined the lakes where they bivouacked.[76]

While most of the military training occurred during the summer, there was plenty during the academic year as well. It took place during two different periods: for an hour during afternoon classes, between 1:00 and 3:00 p.m., and after school from 3:15 to 4:30 p.m., excluding Wednesdays.[77] Military training in the earlier period alternated with academic classes and included topics such as infantry and armor tactics, employment of artillery, troop-leading procedures, military psychology, air force orientation, and customs and traditions of the service. The training during the later period consisted primarily of dismounted drill, intramural athletics, and physical education.[78]

Not surprising, the postwar military training program just described evolved considerably from year to year. The sequence of events, and sometimes the events themselves, changed often to accommodate changing conditions. As an example, the field exercise for first, third, and fourth classmen at summer's end soon faded away. By the late 1940s it had become increasingly difficult to coordinate march routes on the patchwork of private properties in the Hudson Valley; besides, adequate maneuver space surrounding Camp Buckner was now available. The first- and second-class trips to navy and air force bases also were problematic because they relied on coordination with organizations not under West Point's control. Recognizing the many variations in the training schedule from one summer to the next, it is still accurate to say that the military program retained a strong focus on combined-arms and joint-service training through the late-1950s.

We have already seen how interservice training became a focus of the military program immediately after World War II. The topic received added emphasis following publication of the Service Academy Board report in 1950. Secretary of Defense James V. Forrestal had convened the board to find ways of strengthening the education and training of future armed forces officers at the service academies. One method was to promote joint training; hence, board members recommended that summer training programs "be arranged so that every student shall spend a minimum of six weeks in joint training . . . particularly in practice maneuvers employing the strategies, tactics and weapons of all three services."[79] West Point responded by sending fifty second-class cadets to join navy midshipmen for a three-week cruise aboard the *USS Missouri* in late summer. Shorter cruises aboard navy combat vessels took place in 1951 and 1952, but enthusiasm for the trips waned thereafter.[80]

Another way to enhance interservice cooperation was to encourage personal interaction between cadets and midshipmen throughout the year. In academic year 1945–1946, the two service academies began a program of exchange visits for senior cadets and midshipmen to foster "mutual understanding and appreciation."[81] Groups of cadets and midshipmen made the exchange visits on weekends from February through May. They stayed in each other's barracks, attended classes, dined in the mess hall, and danced at the hops. The program gradually expanded during the 1950s to include cadets from ROTC, the new Air Force Academy, and the Coast Guard Academy.[82] In 1959, the academies shifted the exchange program to the underclass years so its benefits could be felt earlier in the cadet experience.[83] By 1975, the Military, Naval, and Air Force Academies took the next logical step of establishing semester-long exchanges, normally in the fall of the junior year. Six West Point cadets went to Annapolis and another six to Colorado Springs; in return, West Point hosted a like number of air force cadets and navy midshipmen.[84] The semester exchanges, now including the Coast Guard Academy, have continued to the present.

A major innovation in the military program during the 1950s was the opportunity for cadets to act as junior officers in active-duty units. The precedent had been set during World War II, as cadets traveled to army training and maneuver centers during the summers. Starting in 1951, the Academy resumed the practice by sending small contingents of first classmen to Fort Dix, New Jersey, and Sampson Air Force Base, New York, to help train army and air force recruits.[85]

Superintendent Garrison Davidson saw great value in these leadership opportunities and expanded them significantly in 1958. In so doing, he effected the first major revision of the military training program that had been in place since the end of World War II. Davidson had become increasingly dissatisfied with the summer schedule for the second class, particularly the navy and air force training that by then had expanded to seven weeks. He complained that the training provided by the sister services gave cadets little opportunity "to implement the leadership principles taught . . . during the long period from yearling summer camp to the beginning of First Class Summer." As a corrective measure, Davidson curtailed the second-class trips by five weeks and sent the cadets to army field units to serve as assistant platoon leaders instead. Davidson was confident that the cadets would benefit from practicing leadership, interacting with soldiers and noncommissioned officers, and seeing the army "under fairly realistic conditions."[86] The program was dubbed "army orientation training"—"AOT" in Academy parlance—and was an immediate success. It henceforth became a permanent fixture of the military training program for second classmen.[87]

Davidson's AOT signaled a shift away from the interservice training that had dominated the summers of first and second classmen since World War II. Even the training during the academic year had a similar shift in emphasis. By the time Davidson left the Academy in 1960, the focus of military training for all classes reverted to the army. The joint training that remained was for second classmen; it consisted of short trips to nearby navy and air force installations in June and generic "armed forces orientation" classes during the academic year.[88] Joint training had been a good idea in principle, but in practice the challenges of coordination across service boundaries had been a drag on training effectiveness. Moreover, the benefit of emphasizing joint training so early in the cadet's military career was questionable. Without first having operational experience in the army, most cadets were too inexperienced to appreciate how the components of joint forces fit together. Finally, the new Air Force Academy was operational by then and was producing officers for that service in healthy numbers. There was no longer a need for commissioning West Pointers into the air force and therefore less urgency to conduct orientation trips to air bases.

There was another, more important, reason for the shift in emphasis. By the early 1960s, the army had sent thousands of "advisors" to South Vietnam to help that country in its fight against the communist North, and the likelihood of further involvement was high. Consequently, the new superintendent, William C. Westmoreland, formed a counterinsurgency committee within the Department of Tactics to develop a program of instruction that "will reflect the national interest in the subject."[89] The result was the adoption of a fifty-four hour curriculum in counterinsurgency over four years, including seminar-style courses for first and second classmen. By 1969, the first-class counterinsurgency course alone had expanded to twenty-four hours, with classes devoted to stability operations and infantry counterinsurgency tactics.[90] The Camp Buckner experience also reflected the growing concern with counterinsurgency, as the third classmen underwent "RECONDO" training starting in 1960 and practiced tactical missions in a mock-Vietnamese village constructed in 1965.[91]

One cadet who trained at Camp Buckner in 1967 remembered that the "whole focus of Buckner changed from what [it] had been before to preparing us to go to War In Vietnam. There was quick-reaction marksmanship, small-unit tactics, patrolling, ambushing, and calls for fire and many other things that were being done by the units in Vietnam."[92]

Another enhancement to the military program in the 1950s resulted from the army's decision to send active-duty units to help with summer training. For many years the commandant had relied on the Academy's enlisted detachments — engineer, cavalry, field artillery, and infantry — to provide the necessary support for training.[93] After World War II, however, the army concluded that the detachments represented an inefficient use of manpower and thus began reducing their size; in 1953 alone, West Point took an enlisted manpower cut of 19 percent.[94] To compensate, the army dispatched active-duty units in ever-increasing numbers to form the nucleus of the summer training cadre. By the mid-1950s, the troop package had become substantial: a reinforced infantry company, a field artillery battery, two transportation companies, and smaller detachments of armor, engineer, signal, quartermaster, medical, and military police units — a total of about 850 officers and enlisted soldiers.[95] In addition to bringing the latest tactics and techniques from the field, the support units provided cadets more opportunities to interact with noncommissioned officers and soldiers.

By the early 1960s, the military program had settled into a new routine that would endure for about a decade (table 6.2). Cadet basic training (fourth classmen) and cadet field training (third classmen) stayed essentially the same.[96] The first- and second-class experiences, however, were now quite different from those of a few years earlier. Second classmen began the summer at West Point in a June "encampment" (not to be confused with the pre-World War II encampment on the Plain). They stayed in the barracks by night and moved to local training sites by day; the training included land navigation, methods of military instruction, and weapons firing. Also scheduled during the encampment were short orientation trips to nearby army bases and sometimes to navy and air force installations.[97] For the remainder of the summer, second classmen either participated in AOT or served as squad leaders for basic training. First classmen spent June on a combat-arms orientation trip to army branch centers.[98] Once back at West Point, they provided the cadre for cadet basic training and cadet field training; those first classmen who had not yet participated in AOT did so in lieu of cadre work. Both first and second classmen took about a month's leave at some point during the summer.[99]

The military program evolved further in the early 1970s, and the biggest change was for the second class. During the 1960s, second classmen took a military instructor course as part of the June encampment in anticipation of serv-

TABLE 6.2   Military Training Program, Early 1960s
(following Davidson reforms)

Class	Academic Year (September–May)	Summer (June–August)
Fourth (1st year)	Organizational Concepts and Tactics (platoon) Map Reading Army Heritage	Cadet Basic Training Cadet Orientation
Third (2nd year)	Basic Tactics (company) Army Heritage Missions and Structure of Armed Forces Psychology	Cadet Field Training (Camp Buckner) • Small-unit Tactics • Combat-arms Orientation • Squad Leader Training
Second (3rd year)	Combined-arms Tactics (battalion) Introduction to Career Planning Ethics, Conduct, Responsibility of Leaders	June Encampment • Land Navigation • Military Instructor Training • Weapons Training • Interservice Orientation Army Orientation Training (platoon leader) or Cadre for Cadet Basic Training (squad leader)
First (4th year)	US Army in the Cold War Career Planning Branch Instruction Military Leadership Officer Code of Ethics	Combat-arms Orientation Trip Cadre for Cadet Basic Training or Cadre for Cadet Field Training or Army Orientation Training (platoon leader) Military Instructor Training

Source: Adapted from *Annual Report of the Superintendent*, 1962, 40–43; 1963, 33–34; 1964, 44; and 1965, 32–33.

ing as squad leaders for basic training. Starting in 1971, however, the course became part of the third-class military program, and the time saved allowed second classmen to attend the army's airborne (parachute) school at Fort Benning. Airborne training had several benefits for cadets — it taught military skills, boosted self-confidence, and improved motivation for an army career.[100] The last-mentioned benefit was particularly relevant given the antimilitary sentiment prevalent in American society around that time and the corresponding increase in cadet attrition. Within a few years, the menu of specialty schools available to cadets increased considerably; besides airborne school, cadets could opt for ranger, flight, jungle, and northern warfare training.[101] The expansion of the Cadet Military Skills Program, as it was officially known, put an end to the encampment for second classmen, who now had no reason to stay at West Point during June. While it reduced the number of second classmen available for cadre duty during summer training, first classmen were able to pick up the slack in this area. Following their training at the specialty schools, most second classmen participated in cadet troop leader training (CTLT), the new name for AOT.

Another major change of the early 1970s affected the first class. In 1973, Superintendent William Knowlton ended the combat-arms orientation program. Ensuring the quality of training at distant training sites was difficult, and the time and expense of transporting cadets to those locations drained resources. Moreover, the robust branch training that cadets received at Camp Buckner made some of the stops on the first-class trip redundant. Finally, Knowlton may have been swayed by the grievances of first classmen who had been on the trip the year before; virtually every cadet who wrote comments on the after-action survey form considered the trip a waste of time.[102] Elimination of the combat-arms trip gave first classmen more time to focus on their principal summer duty—filling cadre leader positions for cadet basic training, cadet field training, and special skills training.[103]

Once the changes just noted were in place, the military training program for the four classes remained basically unchanged for the rest of the century (table 6.3). Fourth classmen went through basic training while third classmen conducted field training at Camp Buckner. Second classmen underwent army specialty training, participated in CTLT, and filled summer cadre positions. First classmen served primarily as summer training cadre at West Point; additionally, they either underwent specialty training (while providing the cadet

TABLE 6.3   Military Training Program, Mid-1970s

Class	Academic Year (September–May)	Summer (June–August)
Fourth (1st year)	Small Unit Tactics (platoon) Map Reading Army Heritage	Cadet Basic Training
Third (2nd year)	Small Unit Tactics (company)	Cadet Field Training (Camp Buckner) Military Instructor Training
Second (3rd year)	Combined-arms Operations (battalion)	Army Specialty Training Cadet Troop Leader Training (platoon leader) or Basic Training Cadre (squad leader)
First (4th year)	Small Unit Training Techniques	Cadre for Cadet Basic Training or Cadre for Cadet Field Training Cadet Troop Leader Training (platoon leader) or Army Specialty Training

Source: Adapted from *Annual Report of the Superintendent*, 1975, 20–21, and 1976, 15.

leadership) or went on CTLT if they had not previously done so. During the academic year, all cadets took classroom instruction in "military science," which exposed cadets to professional topics of increasing complexity.

Although the basic structure of the 1970s training program varied little for the next few decades, three developments deserve note. First, Gen. Andrew Goodpaster, the superintendent from 1977 to 1981, shortened cadet basic training by two weeks starting in 1980. The change was in response to a recommendation by the West Point Study Group to finish the fall semester prior to Christmas rather than in mid-January.[104] Making this change was relatively simple — it required starting the fall semester two weeks early, in mid-August rather than early September. Unfortunately, it was not possible to push back the start date for cadet basic training by a like amount of time. Many northern high schools did not graduate until late June, so the reporting date for new cadets had to remain fixed in early July. The curtailment of basic training from eight weeks to six did not please the commandant, but he made the best of it by finding efficiencies rather than eliminating major training events.[105]

The second development was the result of an initiative by Superintendent Dave Palmer. Upon his arrival in 1986, he became increasingly concerned about the overscheduling of cadets during the academic year. The problem had grown acute with the establishment of academic majors and the corresponding increase in academic rigor.[106] With so much to do and so little available time, cadets often neglected to study for their military science subjects, which were taught during school hours but carried less weight than academic courses. "What's the cadet going to do," Palmer asked, "study history or study armored tactics? He's going to study history because you're going to grade him. . . . It doesn't matter what is going on in military science class."[107] This situation was frustrating for cadets and faculty alike; moreover, it suggested to cadets that military training was unimportant, a bothersome attitude that Palmer wanted to quash.

Palmer's solution was to establish a two-week "intersession" in January, just prior to the start of the second semester.[108] His intent was to underscore the importance of military training by halting academics to conduct it. He directed all the energies of the institution toward this task; accordingly, many faculty members joined the commandant's instructors in teaching the classes. This arrangement had several benefits. First and foremost, it improved military instruction since everyone — cadets, staff, and faculty — could focus solely on the task at hand. Second, cadets had more time to prepare for class during intersession; not coincidentally, the same was now true for the academic year. Third, the intersession promoted cooperation between the dean and commandant, whose organizations did not always get along amicably. Fourth, cadets had the opportunity to see their academic instructors showcasing their credentials as military professionals; the "soldier-scholar" ideal was thus on display for cadets during those two weeks in January. Finally, the commandant gained the ability to sponsor a "military art and science" field of study — that is, an academic discipline — during the academic year because military science had moved to the intersession. The last point was an important consideration for Palmer. "You could have a field of study in Elizabethan literature . . . for crying out loud, but not military studies. Well, now a cadet can have military studies."[109]

The intercessions continued for over a decade. When William Lennox became superintendent in 2001, however, he soon restored military science to the academic year. Lennox believed that cadets lacked confidence in their leadership abilities, in part because they spent too little time during the school year preparing for the leadership challenges they would face during the summers. He concluded that West Point "had become very academic" to the point of crowding out professional dialogue between cadets and instructors during the academic year.[110] Starting in 2003, he reintroduced military science into the academic year as a means of prolonging cadets' exposure to professional topics and better preparing them for their summer assignments.

Whereas the benefits of ending intersession were hard to measure, there was no denying the effect on the academic year. Cadets took a standard load of five academic courses per semester, not including physical education.[111] Reintroducing military science increased their burden and lessened the time available for academics. To compensate, the dean insisted that the military science courses should be structured to require no more than twenty minutes of preparation for each class (compared to the two hours of preparation expected for each academic class meeting).[112] Within a few years, however, the commandant succeeded in expanding the required preparation time to about an hour.[113] In 2008, a capstone military science course — MX400: Officership — became another requirement for cadets; it was nearly equivalent in rigor to most academic courses (table 6.4).[114]

The tension between military and academic priorities caused by the termination of intersession was the latest manifestation of the Athens-Sparta debate at West Point. As in the past, the tension was largely the result of the nation's involvement in war — in this case, the conflicts in Iraq and Afghanistan. The Spartans believed that academics should yield to more military training so that West Point graduates would report to their first units better prepared to assume their duties. Brig. Gen. Robert Caslen, commandant from 2006 to 2008, typified this view. He pushed hard for the establishment of MX400, designed so that "upon graduation, each new 2LT will be fully prepared for the immediate challenges of junior officership."[115] Additionally, he sought a two-week expansion of summer training, which could come only by compressing the academic year by the same amount. Despite strong opposition from the dean

TABLE 6.4   Military Training Program, 2008

Class	Academic Year (September–May)	Summer (June–August)
Fourth (1st year)	MS100: Introduction to War Fighting	Cadet Basic Training
Third (2nd year)	MS200: Fundamentals of Army Operations	Cadet Field Training (Camp Buckner)
Second (3rd year)	MS300: Platoon Operation	Army Specialty Schools Cadet Troop Leader Training (platoon leader) or Cadet Basic Training Cadre (squad leader) or Cadet Field Training Cadre (squad leader)
First (4th year)	MX400: Officership	Cadet Leader Development Training Cadre for Cadet Basic and Field Training or Cadet Troop Leader Training (platoon leader) or Army Specialty Training

Source: Adapted from *Annual Command History,* 1 July 2008–30 June 2009 (West Point, 2009), 173–84.

and professors on the Academic Board, he convinced the superintendent, Lt. Gen. Franklin Hagenbeck, to make the change in 2008.[116] The decision required the scheduling of classes on some former holidays and the shortening of spring break and the reorganizational week preceding each semester. When the arrangement proved unworkable, Hagenbeck returned one of the weeks to the dean a year later.

The Athenians opposed the expansion of military training at the expense of academics. They argued that, in the long run, focusing on intellectual development was the surest way to improve the quality of the officer corps.[117] In making their case, the Athenians clung to the notion that intellect and character were the most important developmental priorities at the Academy. This time, however, the Spartans held the upper hand, at least for the time being. Wartime requirements and the weakness of the Academic Board relative to the superintendent allowed military training to rise in priority.

With an extra week for training, the commandant instituted the last major change to the summer schedule that had been in place since the 1970s. In 2008, he established a new training requirement for the first class—a three-week exercise known as Cadet Leader Development Training (CLDT). Loosely modeled after the army's ranger school, CLDT put cadets through the most intense and realistic summer training ever conducted at West Point. Cadets rotated through leadership positions while undertaking tactical missions at the squad and platoon levels. They worked under the calculated pressures of sleep deprivation, short rations, environmental discomforts, and the stress of continuous operations. Once they established simulated combat outposts, the cadets ventured into the countryside to conduct patrols, raids, and ambushes; concurrently, they interacted with role-playing villagers who spoke indigenous languages and responded in prescribed ways to the actions of the cadets.[118]

Rather than displaying rote application of tactical doctrine, cadets in CLDT were expected to devise innovative, context-driven solutions to problems.[119] The director of military training, Col. Casey Haskins, designed the scenarios to simulate the complicated civil-military interactions of counterinsurgency operations. He expected the cadets to use the liberal education they had received in the classroom to solve the tactical challenges confronting them in the field. "We need to produce thinking leaders," he told the cadre. "We want them to use the things they've learned in training, the things they've learned in the classroom. . . . The better they get, the harder we'll make the problems. If we do it right, combat will be no more complex than West Point training."[120] Haskins's fusion of education and training suggested that the Athenian and Spartan mind-sets could exist in concert rather than in conflict.

First-class cadets participating in the rigors of Cadet Leader Development Training. For most cadets, CLDT was the best tactical training they received prior to reporting to their first units as second lieutenants.

The resources that went into CLDT came at the expense of Camp Buckner, which went from six weeks to four and no longer included time for field exercises. Haskins worried little about the trade-off; he believed that first classmen had far more to gain from tactical field training than third classmen, who were still three years from graduation. The senior cadets seemed to agree. Although most of them found CLDT difficult and exhausting, they had no trouble understanding the benefits of the training so close to graduation. One graduate recalled that CLDT was "far better" than any other training at West Point or at the army's basic course for infantry officers. It was "the most effective training that I went through to prepare me for ranger school and for being a platoon leader in Afghanistan."[121] Once again the quality of training had improved to meet the exigencies of war, just as it had done in response to every other American conflict since the Spanish-American War.

★   ★   ★

Since the beginning of the twentieth century, cadets experienced training that grew more rigorous and effective over time. The greatest gains came during and immediately after the nation's wars, when the dictates of combat lent urgency to the training mission. Cadets learned basic soldier skills, small-unit tactics, and capabilities of the army's combat branches; to a limited extent, they became familiar with the air and naval services. Additionally, they benefited from progressively better uniforms, weapons, equipment, facilities, training methods, and enlisted support.

The relationship between intellectual development and military training has long been a source of tension at West Point. Particularly during armed conflict, the proponents of military training have argued that cadets should be proficient, immediately upon graduation, in the skills required of junior officers. The proponents of intellectual development have countered that the specialization required for a particular branch or duty assignment should come through military schooling after graduation. For most of its history, the Academy has favored the latter approach, although wartime exigencies have caused frequent exceptions to the rule.

CHAPTER SEVEN

Toward a "Four-Class System"

LEADER DEVELOPMENT AT WEST POINT

WITH ITS TRADITIONAL focus on character and intellect, West Point was slow to establish a discrete program for leader development. The Academy's paternal guardians believed that leadership ability was a by-product of successfully completing the requirements for graduation; those cadets who could not keep up were therefore separated for failing to demonstrate the qualities required of an officer. The scant leadership training the cadets received during the nineteenth century came from observing the example of the officers around them and leveraging the occasional opportunities to serve in leadership roles during summer training and the academic year.

In the early decades of the twentieth century, the Academy began treating leader development more seriously. Reform-minded superintendents and commandants expanded opportunities for cadets to lead military training and to serve in chain-of-command positions. With few exceptions, however, these opportunities continued to be experiential rather than theoretical. Some superintendents — notably Douglas MacArthur — tried to strengthen leader development by loosening the Academy's paternal strictures and adding psychology to the curriculum. These reforms, limited in scope and sometimes reversed, were harbingers of the far greater changes that would come later in the century.

The Second World War began a period of rapid change in the Academy's leader development program. A variety of initiatives — organizational changes, courses in psychology and military leadership, behavioral science research, improved leadership assessment methods, expanded counseling services, and graduate education for tactical officers — complemented the practical leader training that already existed. By midcentury a formal program of leader development was in place, and by century's end it had brought major positive changes to the culture of leadership at West Point.

I.   LEADERSHIP THROUGH OSMOSIS

The mission of West Point has always been to produce leaders of character for the army. In pursuit of this mission, the Academy designed a highly structured four-year experience intended to develop cadets in manifold ways. The honor code built character; the academic curriculum broadened intellect; physical education strengthened bodies; and military training provided a basis for professional competence. Under the paternal assumptions of the nineteenth century, the moral, mental, physical, and military exertions of the West Point experience provided all that was necessary to produce effective leaders. Under attritional assumptions, cadets who failed in any of those areas showed their deficiency in the raw materials of leadership and were therefore deemed unfit for commissioning as officers.[1]

Neither the paternal nor attritional aspects of the Academy's leader development model would survive the twentieth century. Paternalism would be the first to go, as Academy leaders discovered the benefits of expanding cadet horizons through travel, added responsibilities and privileges, and exposure to new ideas. Insulating cadets from the world no longer seemed the best way to prepare them to lead in it. The American role on the world stage was becoming vastly more complex, requiring army leaders who were broadminded, mature, and self-confident. As we saw in previous chapters, cadets of the twentieth century had increasingly more opportunities to travel away from West Point than their nineteenth-century forebears, and they were becoming as cosmopolitan as any of their civilian peers.[2]

The culture of attrition would take longer to fade. Well into the twentieth century, West Point continued to be an unforgiving crucible in which to prove one's moral, mental, and physical fiber. Believing that it was better to weed out the weak cadets sooner than later, Academy officials normally separated cadets who failed even a single course or who violated the honor code no matter how slight the offense or remorseful the offender.[3] Tactical officers were stern taskmasters and enforcers of discipline whose opinions weighed heavily in decisions affecting the fate of cadets. Cadets, too, embraced the attritional mind-set when they resorted to hazing in the guise of testing the mettle of plebes and running out those too feeble to withstand the pressure. This baleful pastime flourished in the late nineteenth and early twentieth centuries despite concerted efforts of every superintendent to eradicate it.[4] Even as the worst aspects of hazing subsided, however, attritional attitudes promoted a harshly negative leadership culture that taught cadets the wrong lessons about how to motivate soldiers.

Whatever the shortcomings of its paternal and attritional environment, West Point consistently produced officers who were of high character and competence. These qualities, however, did not necessarily make them good leaders, at least at the outset. West Pointers had a reputation for being arrogant and peremptory in their dealings with soldiers. This was especially true among the civilian volunteers who swelled the ranks of the army in time of war and had no desire to be treated like plebes. Most West Pointers adjusted their leadership style in due time, but perhaps there was a better way to prepare them for leadership in the first place.[5]

Academy leaders of the early twentieth century were increasingly aware of the need to improve leader training. Brig. Gen. Albert Mills, the young superintendent who had been wounded in the Spanish-American War, was one of them. During his long tenure from 1898 to 1906, he had plenty of time to press for reform. He worked closely with like-minded commandants to broaden the cadet experience, improve military and physical training, and add balance to the heavily technical curriculum. Although the results were mixed, these efforts were harbingers of improved methods of training leaders.[6]

Much of the practical experience of leadership, particularly for first classmen, came during summer training. The encampment brought together the first, third, and fourth classes for several weeks on the Plain and nearby training sites. (The second class was on furlough for the entire summer.) Whereas the fourth classmen had no leadership role, the upper two classes helped to receive and train the new arrivals. The commandant supervised the training, which he administered through his cadre of tactical officers and instructors of artillery, cavalry, and infantry. Once cadets had mastered their individual training tasks, the officer cadre allowed them to teach those tasks to other cadets. Lt. Col. Samuel M. Mills, Jr., commandant from 1892 to 1897, explained the process that continued well into the twentieth century:

> Each Cadet has . . . the opportunity of exercising command in all the grades of noncommissioned and commissioned officer up to and including that of captain of a company. The method is progressive and follows the logical principle of assigning to a Cadet supervision and command in any drill or exercise as soon as practicable after he has himself become proficient in it. To illustrate: the third class furnishes the drillmasters for the fourth-class squads, school of the soldier. These in their work are supervised by Cadet officers of the first class, and these latter receive their instructions from a commissioned officer,

who has general charge of the drill. Thus does the Cadet have combined, almost from the beginning of his course, the practice of command and the exercise of authority in drills in which he has become proficient.[7]

Unfortunately, the cadet trainers sometimes used their authority as an excuse for hazing the plebes, and the third classmen tended to be the worst offenders. In 1906, Commandant Robert L. Howze mitigated the problem by assigning the plebe training mission solely to the first class. He was immediately pleased with the results. "The method of handling new cadets, adopted this year," he boasted, "was the best which has ever been followed." The training was distinguished by "an absence of the objectionable features heretofore existing," by which he meant the abuses heaped upon plebes by third classmen.[8]

The summer provided many valuable leadership opportunities, but none as important as the "practice march." Initiated by Howze in 1905, the exercise required cadets to train in a field environment for a week or more at the end of the summer.[9] Cadets were organized into companies that formed a provisional infantry battalion. Once on the march, they established bivouacs, learned field sanitation techniques, conducted reconnaissance, sketched maps, practiced offensive and defensive maneuvers, and performed many other related missions. The marches were valuable experiences for first classmen, who otherwise had few opportunities to practice small-unit leadership in the field. "The value of this field work cannot be overestimated," observed Howze.[10] His successors agreed, and the practice march became a standard feature of the summer training program.

Once summer training ended, the academic year provided additional, if limited, opportunities to develop leader skills. Within each company and battalion staff, upperclassmen served in officer and noncommissioned officer positions.[11] The superintendent, with the advice of the commandant, would designate one first classman per company as the cadet commander. The cadets so designated wore the rank of captain; they were then enumerated within that rank so that one of them became the "first captain"—the highest ranking cadet in the Corps. Other first classmen served as cadet lieutenants, one step down from the rank of captain but still an honor for those selected. Second classmen were cadet sergeants, and third classmen were cadet corporals.[12] Cadet captains normally retained their rank for the entire academic year, but the other positions often changed after the fall semester.

As valuable as these leadership opportunities were, they benefited only the lucky few who received them. The chosen cadets were, according to the commandant, the "most studious, soldier-like . . . , and exemplary in their general deportment."[13] During academic year 1904–1905—a typical year—only twenty-five of 114 first classmen had the opportunity to fill chain-of-command positions. The other eighty-nine — presumably the cadets most in need of leadership training — could learn only by watching their more proficient classmates.[14]

In 1914, the commandant, Lt. Col. Morton F. Smith, addressed this problem by selecting only first classmen for the captain, lieutenant, and sergeant positions. Smith's aim was to give senior cadets every possible leadership opportunity during their last year at the Academy.[15] More to the point, he wished to impress upon them the need for positive leadership. According to an inspecting officer who praised Smith's changes, first classmen would learn to use "dignified and officer-like methods. In this way the graduated cadet will join his regiment with a much better idea of the proper way of handling enlisted men, and may forego the necessity of unlearning the 'Yearling Corporal' idea imbibed at his alma mater."[16]

Another contributor to leader development during the academic year was the course in military history. Taught by the Department of Civil and Military Engineering, the course was the only one in the curriculum to provide a systematic study of leadership. Cadets focused their studies on the Napoleonic Wars, the American Civil War, and, later, the First World War, all of which provided ample material for analyzing the strengths and weaknesses of military leaders. The staff rides to Gettysburg further reinforced leader lessons by requiring cadets to assume the roles of the key commanders and staff officers during the battle. The military history course was popular among cadets because it gave authentic examples of leadership in action. In the absence of a military psychology course, it came closest to helping cadets understand the theoretical underpinnings of leadership.

During the first two decades of the twentieth century, the Academy took small steps to improve leader development and the climate of leadership in Corps of Cadets. The experience of the First World War, however, made it clear that an incremental approach would not suffice. Bold changes were needed, along with a superintendent willing and able to make them.

II.   BOLD CHANGES IN LEADER DEVELOPMENT

Brig. Gen. Douglas MacArthur, the superintendent from 1919 to 1922, had a major impact on the Academy's approach to leader development. He had been a cadet during one of the worst periods of hazing and had even testified before Congress about his shoddy treatment.[17] More recently, he had served during World War I in the 42nd Infantry ("Rainbow") Division, comprised of National Guard units from several states. As a brigade commander in combat, he became intimately familiar with the civilian-soldiers that West Pointers were likely to lead in the future. As the superintendent, he was fearful that cadets were learning the wrong lessons about how to lead those soldiers.

In the century prior to the First World War, European nations had relied on relatively small professional armies consisting mostly of conscripts from the lower echelons of society. Officers developed rigid training methods and imposed severe discipline to maintain control over this "more or less recalcitrant element" and to mold them into effective soldiers.[18] While these leader techniques may have been appropriate in the nineteenth century, they were obsolete in the twentieth. Modern war pitted nations-at-arms, with every citizen mobilized in the effort. Mass armies consisted of higher-quality soldiers that reflected a cross section of the society, and these new conditions required new leadership techniques. MacArthur, through practical experience and depth of intellect, understood these changes and their implications for officer development. "Discipline," he explained,

> [N]o longer required extreme methods. Men generally needed only to be told what to do, rather than to be forced by the fear of consequence of failure. The great numbers involved made it impossible to apply the old rigid methods which had been so successful when battle lines were not so extensive. The rule of this war can but apply to that of the future. Improvisation will be the watchword. Such changed conditions will require a modification in type of the officer, a type possessing all of the cardinal military virtues as of yore, but possessing an intimate understanding of the mechanics of human feelings, a comprehensive grasp of world and national affairs, and a liberalization of conception which amounts to a change in his psychology of command.[19]

The Corps of Cadets was in upheaval when MacArthur assumed his duties as superintendent. Early wartime graduations had skimmed off the upper classes and undermined the orderly transfer of cadet leadership and traditions from one class to the next. Morale was low from the whipsaw of changing policies about how long cadets would stay at West Point prior to graduation. These turbulent conditions contributed to a nasty outbreak of hazing that was linked to a plebe suicide on New Year's Day of 1919. As bad as the situation was, however, it provided a rare opportunity for reinvigorating an institution that had failed to keep up with the times. In surveying the situation, MacArthur resolved to make a "new West Point in the spirit of Old West Point," particularly in the methods of leader development.[20]

MacArthur directed his initial efforts at reforming the fourth-class system. The recent suicide had reinforced the popular notion that the institution encouraged sadistic behavior toward fourth classmen. In truth, many cadets and graduates condoned the practice provided it stayed within "reasonable limits,"

Brig. Gen. Douglas MacArthur,
superintendent from 1919 to 1922.

but such limits were hard to define when tradition was the only guide.[21] MacArthur therefore decided to codify the limits. In June 1919, he convened a committee of first classmen to write down the customs and procedures that governed the fourth-class system. He then gathered the entire first class to explain the purpose of the committee and to enlist their support. The finished product, forwarded to MacArthur for his approval in early August, was a fair-minded code that put an emphasis on positive leadership by upperclassmen.[22] MacArthur praised the cadets for lifting the "haze of uncertainty which has befogged the relationship of the classes" and for accepting "the responsibility for rectifying this condition."[23] Codifying the fourth-class system, he believed, was a first step in changing the "psychology of command" within the Corps of Cadets.[24]

A second step was to teach cadets the dynamics of positive leadership through formal instruction in psychology. MacArthur advocated such instruction to the Academic Board, which was in the process of designing a new four-year curriculum that would replace the three-year wartime version.[25] Although the Academic Board refused to make psychology a core course, MacArthur worked through the commandant, Lt. Col. Robert M. Danford, to teach the subject as part of military training. Danford enlisted the help of Lincoln C. Andrews, a retired cavalry officer and a respected authority on military psychology, to write a textbook for this purpose. In his preface, Andrews reminded cadets that the human element in War Is decisive: "It is the fiber of our manpower that counts. And this fiber is the peculiar care of the psychological part of soldiering — of leadership."[26] Andrews' main argument — that commanders secured the best results by developing loyalty and intelligent initiative in their soldiers and then trusting them to execute — closely paralleled MacArthur's philosophy of leadership.[27]

In pursuit of his goal to develop strong, self-confident leaders, MacArthur directed a rewrite of cadet regulations. He gave first classmen a six-hour pass on weekends, riding privileges on the east side of the Hudson River (as opposed to only the west side), expanded hours at the First Class Club, and social status commensurate with junior officers. He expanded the official responsibilities of cadet noncommissioned officers to make them more akin to the duties of noncommissioned officers in the field army. He permitted cadets of all classes to carry cash and thus "exercise within a limited scope economy and responsibility."[28] Traditionalists viewed these changes as an assault on the conventions of paternal control; MacArthur saw them as opportunities for cadets to practice responsible decision making. He understood that giving up control could be messy — surely some cadets would abuse the privileges or get into trouble — but the alternative was to stunt their social development and sense of responsibility.

MacArthur's successor, Brig. Gen. Fred W. Sladen, reversed or modified some of MacArthur's policies. For example, he revoked the cadet privilege of carrying cash, citing the need for absolute equality within the Corps. Additionally, he ended the six-hour weekend pass for first classmen, replacing it with a merit-based overnight pass once a month.[29] In the big scheme of things, however, these reversals and modifications did little to slow the process of reform that MacArthur had set in motion.[30] Over the long term, Academy leaders increasingly rejected the paternal and attritional attitudes that had shaped Academy culture and embraced the idea that cadets deserved to be treated less like children and more like developing leaders.

III. LEADERSHIP IN THEORY AND PRACTICE

The next major advance in the area of leader development occurred after World War II. Once again, the catalyst was a bright young superintendent with a distinguished combat record and an agenda for change. Maj. Gen. Maxwell Taylor, like MacArthur before him, believed that leader development at West Point was behind the times. The Academy had the mission of producing leaders, "yet nowhere in the curriculum is there a course which has the announced intention of teaching leadership."[31] While Taylor believed that the "best training for leadership is to lead," he was "convinced that there is a school approach to the acquirement of the qualities of leadership."[32]

In November 1945, Taylor directed the dean to create a course that would "give formal recognition to the instruction in Military Leadership now taking place in various departments of the Military Academy."[33] One part of the course consisted of the nineteen hours of instruction on small-unit leadership given by the commandant's staff. Another consisted of the lectures on the great commanders of history delivered by instructors from the Department of Military Art and Engineering.[34] The final component was the guest lecture program run by the Lecture Committee of the Academic Board; under Taylor's plan, the lecturers would be chosen for their accomplishments in the late war and would discuss the principles of leadership "through the recital of their own experiences."[35] Because Taylor's leadership course entailed no new work and no alteration of the existing curriculum, the Academic Board did not object. The same was not true, however, when the Army chief of staff, Dwight Eisenhower, wanted to put his stamp on leadership instruction at West Point.

During the war, Eisenhower had been introduced to the work of social scientists on the Army staff who had conducted attitudinal surveys of soldiers. Some of the studies suggested that American soldiers did not respect their officers because of the latter's poor leadership skills.[36] Believing that the behavioral sciences could improve leadership instruction at West Point, he gave Taylor clear guidance: "I should like very much to see included in the curriculum . . . a course in practical or applied psychology." Such a course would "awaken the majority of Cadets to the necessity for handling human problems on a human basis."[37]

The idea of adding psychology to the curriculum was not new. MacArthur tried to do it but had to settle with a less formal (and less permanent) arrangement under the commandant. After MacArthur's departure, the Army inspector general, Eli A. Helmick, took up the cause. Helmick had inspected Army training bases during World War I and saw firsthand the leadership shortcomings of the officer corps.[38] One of the solutions, he believed, was to teach a theoretical course in psychology at West Point as a complement to the practical

Maj. Gen. Maxwell Taylor, superintendent from 1945 to 1949.

leadership instruction given by the commandant. He made this recommendation repeatedly to the Department of War, which forwarded it to West Point for staffing. Each time the response was predictable. The Academic Board had no tolerance for a course like psychology, which, it claimed, "abounds in abstractions and abstruse theories, and seldom dwells in such phases of practical application as would tend to make officers more efficient and inspiring leaders of men."[39] With no support from the Academic Board, the War Department dropped the matter.

The Academic Board's curricular conservatism in general and dislike of psychology in particular posed big obstacles for Taylor. He had just one vote — like every other board member — and he was in the minority. Superintendents faced with similar circumstances in the past usually conceded defeat and turned to other issues that had better chances of gaining the board's approval. In this case, however, Eisenhower's clear guidance mandated action.

Taylor's solution was to establish a new organization — the Office of Military Psychology and Leadership (OMPL) — to teach the desired course. He put OMPL under the supervision of the commandant, which meant treating the psychology course as military training rather than academic instruction. Taylor had thus found a way to provide theoretical instruction in leadership without encroaching on the carefully constructed academic curriculum. More important, in creating OMPL he initiated a thirty-year process that ultimately redefined the organizational structure, content, and methodology of the leader development program at West Point. The effort culminated in 1977 with the creation of a new academic department — Behavioral Sciences and Leadership — that represented an emerging consensus about the importance of an approach to leader development that coupled theory with practical application.[40]

The OMPL had two principal functions. First, it would teach courses on the psychology of military leadership to the upper three classes. Instructors would balance between theory and practical application as they focused the cadets on "immediate post-Academy leadership responsibilities." Second, it would administer the Aptitude for the Military Service Program, a new method to assess cadets' potential as officers. The system relied in part on formal peer-evaluations that OMPL instructors administered as part of their courses.[41] To accomplish these tasks, the army assigned to OMPL seven officers — all lieutenant colonels — prior to the start of the 1946–1947 academic year, when the leadership courses would first be taught.[42]

The leadership instruction focused on the three upper classes. First-class cadets underwent forty-two hours of instruction; second- and third-class cadets took an abbreviated version. The initial feedback from those who experienced the instruction — officers, cadets, and even a few midshipmen — was generally positive. With the new courses in place, Taylor could report to the War Department that leadership development at West Point now had "both an academic and a practical side."[43]

In academic year 1947–1948, OMPL refined and expanded the content of the leadership courses, which now included all four classes. First classmen received a total of eighty-seven hours of instruction, about half of which covered basic and intermediate psychology. During the remaining time they studied leadership methods for use in the Corps of Cadets (five hours), in the field army (twenty-two hours), and in special situations (seventeen hours). Second-class cadets took fifteen hours of leadership classes that focused on their upcoming duties as cadre leaders for summer training. Third classmen took a one-hour class on adjusting to military life and nine hours of leadership methods for the Corps of Cadets. Fourth classmen received four hours on adjusting to military life and three on study habits.[44]

With the passing of another year, the framework of the leadership curriculum that would endure for the rest of the century was in place. The key change for academic year 1948–1949 was to move the course in basic psychology from the first-class to the third-class year, thus giving yearlings the benefit of this instruction prior to their service as cadre members during their second-class summer.[45] First classmen would study a variety of more advanced topics that eventually comprised one of the most comprehensive military leadership courses anywhere in the army or in academia. The instruction in basic psychology and military leadership, although resident in the Department of Tactics, evolved to the point that it was as rigorous as any of the dean's academic courses.[46] With its close ties to both the academic and military domains, OMPL straddled the divide between intellectual and professional development more than any other organization at West Point.

The OMPL's other key mission was to administer the Aptitude for the Military Service Program,[47] the new leader assessment tool begun in 1946. There were several components of assessment, but the defining feature was a system of cadet-on-cadet ratings within each company.[48] These ratings contributed to a cadet's military order of merit and allowed tactical officers to identify the top 10 percent and the bottom 10 percent of cadets in their companies. Cadets in the former group filled key leadership positions as first classmen. Cadets in the latter group received special counseling and additional ratings by cadet leaders and tactical officers; if necessary, these cadets could be referred to the professional civilian psychologist who served as the associate director of OMPL.[49] Those who continued to receive low ratings faced aptitude boards at the regimental and brigade levels and possible expulsion. Taylor defended the cadet-on-cadet ratings against those who viewed them as a popularity contest. "It is surprisingly simple to answer a question: 'Out of the twenty members of your class in A Company, whom would you want most to have at your side in battle? Whom the least'"[50]

The interest in aptitude ratings increased once researchers found a positive correlation between the ratings and officer performance in the Korean War.[51] This discovery led Superintendent Garrison Davidson to rely heavily on aptitude ratings to weed out marginal performers. During his four-year tenure (1956–1960), overall attrition trended downward but separations for leader aptitude (including physical fitness) went up sharply.[52] He did not apologize; on the contrary, Davidson liked the results and reported to the army chief of staff that the system was "accomplishing its purpose." He had long believed that the Academy allowed too many marginal performers to be commissioned, and the aptitude ratings provided an efficient way of identifying and separating them before they became officers. Given the apparent reliability of aptitude ratings in evaluating leader potential, they became a standard tool of leader assessment — but not leader development — at West Point. In one form or another, they have continued to the present.

A by-product of the Aptitude for the Military Service Program was a rapid increase in the number of cadets referred to OMPL for counseling. In academic year 1950–1951, the civilian psychologist had over one hundred counseling sessions with eighty-eight cadets referred by the tactical officers because of low scores on the aptitude assessments. He saw about one hundred more who sought counseling on their own, as well as every cadet who expressed a desire to resign (fifty-six total). The heavy workload forced OMPL to hire additional psychologists — army officers with doctoral degrees in psychology — and, in 1968, to establish the Cadet Counseling Center. By 1970 the psychologists had 660 contact hours with cadets in a variety of categories — resignations, low aptitude evaluations, self-referrals, and personal problems.

Despite the growing workload, the counseling center had a hard time winning acceptance because of lingering attritional attitudes. Traditionalists on the staff and faculty viewed the center as a means of coddling cadets too weak to endure the rigors of the Academy and therefore not fit for commissioning. Compounding the problem was the fact that the staff psychologists by the early 1970s were all Medical Service Corps officers with little practical leadership experience and correspondingly little credibility. Recognizing the problem, the director of OMPL, Col. Harry Buckley, searched for an officer who could fill both roles — psychologist and respected leader. In 1974 he selected Maj. Howard Prince, a decorated combat veteran with a doctorate in clinical psychology, to lead the center.[53]

Prince was deeply critical of the attritional mind-set that shaped the developmental programs at West Point. He resolved to use his influence in the counseling center to change "the culture, the climate, and the leadership style of the cadre and the officers."[54] In pursuit of this goal he and his staff spent much time training the officer and cadet cadres that would take charge of plebes during summer training. They presented classes in communication, counseling, and stress management that relied on proven principles of behavioral science. There were plenty of naysayers. Prince recalled the typical remark: "This is BS. Why are we doing this? Our job is to weed them out, not give them cookies and milk!"[55]

Despite the skepticism, West Point had come a long way in transforming its leadership culture. The creation of OMPL and advances in leader education, counseling, and assessment were having a positive effect, and many superintendents paid homage to these trends in their annual reports. But the process of change was frustratingly slow. In a 1969 study initiated by Commandant Bernard Rogers, for example, the fourth-class system was described as an "initiation process designed to place the Fourth Classmen in a subservient and dependent position to all upper classes."[56] A follow-up study in 1971 was more specific: "The concept of attempting to influence or develop a plebe through 'positive leadership' . . . has not yet been sold to the Corps. Good leadership . . . is present within the Fourth Class System, but it is not the norm."[57] These concerns were periodically validated by reports of "sadistic" behavior toward new cadets.[58]

Prince found a strong ally in Brig. Gen. Walter Ulmer, who arrived at West Point as the new commandant in mid-1975. Ulmer had been hand-picked for the job by the army chief of staff, Gen. Creighton Abrams, who was committed to reforming the post-Vietnam officer corps. One of Ulmer's principal missions was to transform the fourth-class system to be more in line with the tenets of army leadership doctrine. The results of Prince's interviews with cadets who quit basic training gave Ulmer reason to be concerned. When Prince asked them the reasons for leaving, most gave answers that betrayed a lack of maturity and motivation to succeed at West Point. Many others, however, seemed to have all the right qualities but were repelled by the negative leadership environment and decided "I don't want to be part of this." Prince recalled that the responses of the latter group "really got General Ulmer's attention."[59]

Lending urgency to Ulmer's task was the imminent arrival of women in 1976. He had long considered the fourth-class system to have the greatest potential for "future public embarrassment of the Military Academy."[60] Now with the presence of women — anathema to aggrieved traditionalists — the possibility of abuses increased. Academy officials would have to exercise extraordinary vigilance while building a more positive leadership culture than ever before.

The EE304 cheating incident, about the same time as the admission of women in 1976, was another catalyst for change. In its aftermath, the Academy underwent the most searching scrutiny in its long history, with the West Point Study Group providing the most probing analysis.[61] No fewer than thirty of the 156 total recommendations were in the category of leader development, and the new superintendent, Gen. Andrew Goodpaster, approved the implementation of virtually all of them. The most relevant changes were in four subcategories: fourth-class system, leadership assessment, organization of the Department of Tactics, and role of tactical officers.

The governing regulation for the fourth-class system changed immediately, in time for implementation in academic year 1978–1979. The new rules reduced by one third the amount of "fourth-class knowledge" plebes had to memorize over the course of the year.[62] They also reduced the frequency of inspections and made disciplinary standards across the Corps more consistent.

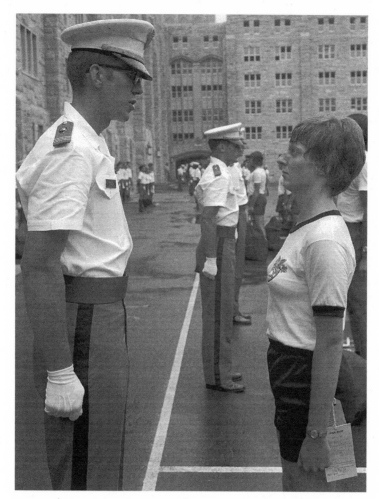

The arrival of women as cadets in 1976 gave urgency to the efforts of Academy leaders to temper the abuses of the fourth-class system.

There were many other changes in the regulation, but the most striking was the new introductory chapter — an extended essay on professionalism directed squarely at upperclassmen. The essay reinforced the ideas of positive leadership — respect, fair treatment, personal example, and acting professionally at all times. It reminded upperclassmen that leadership abuses "spark instant resentment from those in the disadvantaged position."[63] The regulation underwent further refinement in 1979 when Superintendent Goodpaster formed the Fourth Class Working Group consisting of officers and cadets. The group rewrote the regulation to bring senior-subordinate relationships at West Point more in line with those in the Army. Additionally, the group discouraged up-perclassmen from using the fourth-class system as a crutch for weak leader-ship.[64]

The new focus on positive leadership seemed to have an effect, judging from the decline in attrition during basic training. The summer attrition rates had hovered around 10.5 percent from 1971 through 1976 but dropped to 7.5 percent from 1977 through 1983. The commandant cited the "continu-ing emphasis on instilling an appropriate command climate" as a reason for the decline.[65] The after-action report on cadet basic training in 1980 was more specific.

> Strong emphasis was placed on establishing a firm, businesslike leadership atmosphere while concentrating on leading by example, teaching, demon-strating and assisting. . . . Corrections were made in a conversational tone at a comfortable distance from the individual being corrected. New cadets were not to be treated in a demeaning or humiliating manner, and increased emphasis was placed on eliminating profanity.[66]

The commanding officer of cadet basic training acknowledged that "some cadre members did not live up to these expectations."[67] Most did, however, and collectively they were shaping a leadership culture quite different than before. Basic training was still physically and emotionally stressful, but the source of the stress was shifting. Previously it had come mostly from the calculated pres-sure imposed by a snarling cadre; now it came principally from the difficulty of the training itself, with cadre members acting as facilitators in the learning process.

Leader evaluation was the second area of change arising from the report of the West Point Study Group. The earliest formal evaluation program came immediately after World War I, as Superintendent MacArthur implemented a system that incorporated all aspects of leader development and contributed to a cadet's overall order of merit.[68] His successors found the system useful and con-tinued it through World War II, after which it morphed into the Aptitude for the Military Service Program. In 1971, a new Leadership Evaluation System combined the cadet-on-cadet ratings and performance assessments from the officer chain of command; the composite score contributed to a cadet's general order of merit.[69] The West Point Study Group concluded that these assessment programs, while efficient, showed the Academy's "increasing preoccupation with the evaluation of cadet performance" rather than development of cadets as leaders. Additionally, there was "clear evidence of a strain of unreliability" in the system as cadets adapted to the increased pressure of evaluation by manipu-lating the peer ratings to the advantage of one group or another.[70]

In response to these concerns, Goodpaster established the Military Development System (MDS) in 1980 to replace all existing leadership evaluation programs.[71] As the name implied, MDS represented a philosophical shift away from the methods of the past; instead, it emphasized a developmental approach based on the principles of behavioral science.[72] Leadership assessments would continue to be a key part of MDS, but under the new procedures cadets were measured against prescribed standards, not each other. Those cadets deficient in military development went on probationary status while undergoing individually tailored programs of remediation and counseling. Continued deficiency was cause for separation, but the large majority of cadets on probation improved enough to graduate.[73]

The adoption of MDS reflected the weakening grip of attritional methods of leader development at West Point. Conversely, the notion that leadership, like intellect, could be developed through theoretical study and practical application gained strength. Provided admissions standards remained high and cadets came to West Point with the proper raw materials, the commandant could expect them to become capable leaders through the Academy's progressively developmental curriculum and positive command climate.[74]

A third area of change was the Academy's organizational structure for leader development. In 1977, the Department of Tactics was redesignated as the Office of the Commandant, equivalent in stature to the Office of the Dean. Similarly, the Office of Military Instruction and the Office of Physical Education were elevated to the status of departments, each with a seat on the Academic Board. The Office of Military Leadership (formerly the Office of Military Psychology and Leadership) became the Department of Behavioral Sciences and Leadership and moved under the control of the dean. The commandant retained control of the Cadet Counseling Center, which had been part of OML before the move. The organizational changes came with a more robust staff for the commandant, who had labored shorthanded for many decades.

The net effect of these changes was to separate theoretical instruction in leadership, now under the dean, from the practical application of leadership, still under the commandant. The separation allowed both sides to focus more narrowly on their strengths while ensuring that theory and practice remained complementary elements of cadet development. The Department of Behavioral Sciences and Leadership was critical in this regard, given its provenance in the old Department of Tactics and its continued work in educating officers and cadets in the principles of leadership. The organizational changes had another benefit—they underscored the point that the entire staff and faculty, not just the Office of the Commandant, had a part in developing cadets as leaders.[75]

A critical component of leader development was the tactical officer, and here the West Point Study Group found many problems. By law, tactical officers commanded their companies, yet the administrative burdens of the job often prevented them from devoting sufficient time to cadet development. A highly respected tactical officer of the era, Maj. Herbert Lloyd, recalled being nearly overwhelmed by the voluminous paperwork.

> It's there staring him in the face and it is just against everything he has been trained to do to get up and walk away from it. . . . So he ends up staying in the office wrestling with piddly things while major things are going on out there. . . . Simply stated, something damn well needs to be done about it.[76]

According to the West Point Study Group, the administrative burdens left tactical officers little time to interact with their cadets, other than in the role of "diligent enforcer of standards." This relationship, coupled with the "near obsession with evaluation," made it virtually impossible to be viewed, from the cadet perspective, as supportive and developmental. Furthermore, although tactical officers came to the job with impressive professional credentials, those experiences did "not guarantee correspondingly outstanding service" at West Point. They worked without "a clear, coherent and operational philosophy of leadership" from the commandants, who spent an average of only two years in the job.[77]

These problems created cleavage between tactical officers and their cadets that became painfully apparent in the wake of the EE304 cheating incident. As director of the Cadet Counseling Center, Howard Prince interviewed each of the 152 cadets about to be separated. He discovered that virtually all of the cheaters were assigned to twenty-seven of the thirty-six companies in the Corps of Cadets; conversely, there were nine companies that had come through the episode virtually unscathed. Prince had worked closely with the tactical officers all along and therefore knew them well. In his estimation,

> [T]he nine companies that had no cheaters had TAC officers that were seen by cadets and other officers as approachable and developmental. The ones that had large numbers of cheaters had TACs who were authoritarian and distant. . . . It was amazing to me to see nine companies with no cheaters. Why? Something is going on there that's different from these other companies. If it were one or two, you'd say it's random. But twenty-five percent is not random. There's something systematic there.[78]

Prince was not the only one to make the connection. Tactical Officer Lloyd believed that many of his peers who had major cheating in their companies relied too much on regulations to manage their relations with cadets. They were out of touch, focused on the wrong things, and preoccupied "with that damn paperwork."[79]

Academy leaders tried hard to improve the cadet-tactical officer relationship. Many of the changes just noted, such as adoption of the Military Development System, addressed that relationship, and no doubt there were improvements. But progress was slow and subject to backsliding if a new commandant were less sensitive than his predecessor about the issues raised by the West Point Study Group. The Academy needed a better solution to the problem of preparing tactical officers for the unique challenges of developing cadets.

IV. HOLISTIC APPROACH TO LEADERSHIP

The leader development initiatives stemming from the West Point Study Group report had been far reaching. The most profound changes, however, came a few years later during Superintendent Palmer's tenure, from 1986 to 1991. Palmer, in addition to his military credentials, was an accomplished scholar who had published well-regarded books on West Point and military strategy.[80] He understood the pressing issues at the Academy in their historical context and felt confident moving swiftly to address them. His two most important reforms were a sort of double envelopment of the objective of leader development. On one axis he employed a program for better developing cadets; on the other was a program for educating tactical officers.

During academic year 1989–1990, Palmer directed a thorough review of the fourth-class system. He had long been concerned that the system did not adequately meet the Academy's leader development goals, and the just-completed institutional self-study for academic accreditation confirmed that view. The self-study report concluded that many upperclassmen continued to violate the letter and intent of the fourth-class system or countenanced others who did so. The violations constituted various forms of negative leadership and contradicted the stated objectives of the fourth-class system to the point that "the system's hypocrisy may outweigh its benefits."[81] In response, Palmer appointed three separate committees to study the fourth-class system and recommend improvements. One committee consisted of cadets, another of staff and faculty members, and a third of alumni. While all three reports provided thoughtful comments, the staff and faculty report was by far the most critical.

> Years of custom and tradition have resulted in a system that continues to violate fundamental principles of leadership. The reason can be succinctly stated: the total subordination of one class of cadets to three upper classes of

cadets. Domination of plebes is further exacerbated by the tendency of many upperclass cadets to make operational their own purpose statements for the system (to weed out the weak; to see how they function under stress, etc.). Volumes of scientific research make clear the *fact* that social systems based on the authoritarian subordination of one group to another invariably result in serious abuse. The point is this: regardless of how well intended or written, and our emotional attachment to it notwithstanding, the current system is fundamentally flawed.[82]

The systemic nature of the problem led the staff and faculty committee to recommend abolition of the fourth-class system. In its place, the committee proposed a new Cadet Leader Development System that would combine the developmental goals for all classes into one integrated program. Palmer ordered the idea developed more fully and then approved its implementation in July 1990. The new system, known as CLDS (pronounced "kleds"), provided "the highest level framework for integrating and organizing cadet leader development experiences" across the intellectual, military, and physical domains.[83] It required the active participation of the faculty, staff, coaches, and anyone else who came in contact with cadets. The system included a plebe experience that retained many of the traditional elements of the old fourth-class system and thus insured a challenging first year. For third, second, and first classmen, however, the expectations were higher. The new system described leadership responsibilities and developmental goals that grew more demanding each year and focused on proper leader-subordinate relationships. Palmer explained that the new system was "a constantly progressive process that adds as you go along; holds you more responsible; holds you more accountable; expects you to know more; expects you to be more mature. . . . When you start looking at things that way, you start creating a system for all four classes.[84]

If CLDS was one axis of Palmer's double envelopment, tactical officer education was the other. The idea had originated in the late 1960s, when Commandant Rogers first arranged for incoming tactical officers to attend graduate school for advanced degrees in counseling and related fields. Subsequent commandants, however, made it less of a priority and sent fewer officers to school. The issue resurfaced in the recommendations of the Borman Commission and the West Point Study Group, and that led to a resurgence in graduate schooling. Unfortunately, the available programs at civilian universities were ill suited to the unique conditions at the Academy; moreover, the distance between those schools and West Point made the task of applying theory to practice difficult for the student-officers.[85]

Palmer overcame these problems by creating a graduate program of his own. He directed Prince — now the head of the Department of Behavioral Sci-

Lt. Gen. Dave Palmer, superintendent from 1986 to 1991.

ences and Leadership—to develop a master's program tailored to the needs of tactical officers. In cooperation with the commandant, Prince surveyed the tactical officers to determine the full range of their responsibilities and then designed a two-year course of study. In the first year, the student-officers would take a heavy load of graduate-level courses from West Point faculty members; in the second year, they would apply the leadership theory in a supervised practicum while serving as tactical officers. Prince did a trial run of the program in academic year 1988–1989. Palmer was pleased with the results and therefore ordered full implementation the following year. Meanwhile, the program earned accreditation and Congress granted West Point the authority to award master's degrees to the graduates. Palmer named the program after Dwight Eisenhower, the person most influential in making leadership a subject of academic study at West Point.[86]

In 1992, Congress withdrew the authority to grant master's degrees because of some lawmakers' objections to West Point being anything but an undergraduate institution.[87] Academy leaders scrambled to find an alternate arrangement that would yield the same results but stay within congressional intent. The following year they negotiated an agreement with Long Island University to administer the program remotely at West Point and to serve as the degree-granting institution. The new Tactical Officer Education Program, begun in 1993, looked much like its predecessor. Tactical officers still did all their coursework at West Point; the program director continued to be a senior faculty member in Behavioral Sciences and Leadership; and most of the instructors were on the Academy's faculty. The only real differences were that the student-officers now had civilian instructors for some of their courses (in some ways an advantage) and Long Island University issued the diplomas. This arrangement continued until 2005, when West Point concluded an agreement with the Teachers College at Columbia University to run the tactical officer curriculum, now renamed the Eisenhower Leader Development Program. Because Columbia is an easy drive (about fifty miles) from West Point, the student-officers were able to divide their time between the two locations.

Tactical officer education was not a requirement for the tactical department's most senior leaders — particularly the commandant and the brigade and regimental tactical officers. Consequently, many of them were unconvinced of the program's utility and sometimes hostile toward the healthy skepticism that graduate-level education imparted to the tactical officers. According to Prince, "They're suspicious of the program. The commandant is uneasy because these people are learning things that he isn't aware of."[88] One company tactical officer confessed to being "miserable the whole time" working for a superior who relied on attritional methods of leadership. The superior said in effect, "Forget that behavioral science BS and command your company."[89] In the two decades since the start of the Eisenhower Program, there has yet to be a graduate assigned as the commandant or a brigade tactical officer; until that happens routinely, misunderstanding and friction are likely to continue.

The graduate leadership programs produced tactical officers who approached their duties differently than most of their predecessors. In lieu of attritional leadership — whereby the tactical officer set the standard and punished those who failed to meet it — the new style of leadership was "transformational."[90] The new approach cast tactical officers as leader developers who empowered the cadets to set and enforce their own standards. Capt. Denis Fajardo, a 2008 graduate of the Eisenhower program, noted, "Typical army fashion is you tell a soldier what's wrong and how to fix it, and then they move out and do what you told them to do." Under the new style of leadership, the tactical officer would counsel cadets to identify performance problems on their own. The result was to teach cadets "how to deal with the issue. Or they make some more mistakes, and you guide them to develop another course of action — on their own." CPT Andrew Caine, a 2007 graduate, explained that his role was "to provide the vision and values by which the organization functions but leave it to the subordinate leaders to take the initiative on how to accomplish the mission."[91]

In practical terms, the new leader development environment led to looser standards of conduct, appearance, uniformity, and orderliness in all aspects of cadet life. With the cadets responsible for setting many of the standards formerly dictated by the commandant, there was wide variance in those standards from one company to the next. Some companies, for example, kept their rooms in a high state of order, while others allowed them to be in habitual disarray. The multiplicity of authorized cadet uniforms was bewildering, and it discouraged those in authority from making corrections because of their uncertainty about the correct standard. These and other manifestations of disorder disturbed many older graduates, who feared that cadets were missing an important opportunity to develop proper habits of discipline. One of those graduates noted, "In the fifties and sixties cadets left a highly disciplined military academy and entered a less disciplined Army." Since 2001, however, cadets would "enter an Army more disciplined than the Academy, and at war, and have to adjust to that."[92]

Col. Mark McKearn, the brigade tactical officer from 2007 to 2011, embraced the transformational approach to leader development, despite not having gone through the Eisenhower program.[93] He recalled that during his time as a cadet from 1977 to 1981, the tactical officers commanded the cadet companies in the traditional sense. They "made command decisions for their cadets, used their time to fuss over the right font and format for a training brief." In such an environment, cadets appeared highly disciplined, but the degree to which they internalized the disciplinary standards imposed by higher authority was questionable. Today's tactical officers, he noted, "teach, mentor, and coach a Corps that really is cadet-led. They empower the cadets and support them in their efforts."[94] In contrast to the attritional leader development methods of an earlier era, his tactical officers refrained from imposing their own solutions. With McKearn's blessing, they accepted a lower level of discipline in exchange for the developmental benefits of having the cadets set and enforce their own standards. At issue now is the proper balance between the developmental benefits of cadets setting and enforcing their own standards, on the one hand, and learning to submit to established authority and standards, on the other.

Once Palmer established the Eisenhower Program, the idea of graduate schooling for company tactical officers evolved quickly from novel to normal. Each of them received a powerful education in the theoretical foundations of leadership at the very place they were to put those theories into practice. Perhaps more noteworthy was the fact that an academic department—not the commandant—was the responsible agent for the education. Nothing else so vividly demonstrated the shift in leader culture at West Point. For the traditionalists who debunked theoretical approaches to leadership—and there were still many of them—the new arrangement was a bitter pill. For most others, the new system represented a promising direction in the process of molding leaders of character.

★ ★ ★

While the Academy's paternalism toward cadets waned in the early twentieth century, attritional attitudes remained strong for many years thereafter. The unrelenting strictness of the West Point environment culled the weak from the strong. Partly as a consequence of the attritional culture, a negative style of leadership, founded on the one-sided relationship between plebes and upperclassmen, became the norm at West Point. Many cadets learned leader techniques that were inappropriate for use in the field army, whose wartime ranks were more likely to consist of citizen-soldiers than disciplined regulars. This incongruity had to be resolved if the Academy aspired to be the nation's foremost leader development institution, as it was fond of claiming.

Some superintendents—particularly MacArthur, Taylor, Davidson, Goodpaster, and Palmer—paid close attention to these issues. They took aggressive measures to temper the worst aspects of the fourth-class system and transform the leader culture. They addressed the issues holistically since the processes of leader development were complex and interrelated. Their efforts built momentum during the century and culminated with the Cadet Leader Development System and programs for tactical officer education. While these initiatives were neither perfect nor a panacea, they allowed West Point to become a true leader *development* institution, as opposed to an unforgiving crucible in which to prove oneself fit for leadership.

CHAPTER EIGHT

A "Corps" Mission

BUILDING CHARACTER

SINCE THE TIME of Sylvanus Thayer, building character in cadets has been the most important developmental goal of the Military Academy. Thayer's conception of character had two components, the first being the personal discipline required of army officers. He nurtured cadet discipline through a rigorous academic curriculum and the imposition of a highly regimented environment insulated from the impurities of civilian society.

The second component, moral rectitude, was a quality that could be refined but not instilled. Nineteenth-century Academy leaders considered a young man's basic character to be formed by the time he became a cadet, and the disciplined West Point environment provided daily opportunities to demonstrate the quality of that character. Cadets were the guardians of their honor, individually and collectively, and were expected to report all violations committed by themselves and others. Those deemed unworthy in this area had no chance for remediation. With few exceptions, a single instance of lying or other violation of morals sullied one's honor and was grounds for court martial and dismissal.[1] Cadets who completed the four-year curriculum without compromising their honor were graduated with the greatest confidence that they were ready for officership.

The character-building process of the nineteenth century endured through the first three quarters of the twentieth. Cadets developed self-discipline by negotiating the fourth-class system, the academic curriculum, and the military and physical training programs. Meanwhile, they lived by an honor code that was the principal means of strengthening the moral component of character.[2] Informal vigilance committees and, later, an officially sanctioned honor committee monitored standards of honor and reported violations to the proper authorities; the fate of a cadet found guilty was virtually always resignation or expulsion.[3] Few questioned the moral certainty represented by the extremity of the punishment, and there was little instruction on how to apply standards of honor to the murky situations in which humans often found themselves. For most cadets, the unbending standards of character nurtured a lifelong commitment to honorable living. For others, they served merely as a disincentive to behaving badly.

Two major cheating incidents, one each in 1951 and 1976, forced Academy leaders to reconsider the single sanction of expulsion. Could a cadet who committed an honor violation learn from his mistake and become a more honorable person without being separated? The outcome of the first crisis — expulsion of every cadet found guilty of cheating — indicated that the answer was no. The outcome of the second crisis — reinstatement of the "found" cadets — reflected the growing belief that a person's character could not be adequately assessed by a single act of commission or omission.

In the years following the 1976 incident, the Academy adopted an increasingly developmental approach to the moral component of character building. Superintendents were empowered to exercise discretion in meting out punishments that ranged from strictly punitive (i.e., dismissal) to remedial. A formal program of honor education encouraged cadets to think deeply about moral and ethical issues in situations where there were no clear answers. Other programs — in leader development, gender and race relations, respect for others, and equal opportunity — complemented the new approach to character building.

Cadets of the twenty-first century, like those of the nineteenth and twentieth, were still required to uphold high standards of personal honor. In allowing remediation for some honor violations, however, the Academy rejected the absolute standards that had long justified the single sanction of expulsion. In so doing, it embraced a model for character building that corresponded to its claim of being a leader development institution.

I. AN HONOR CODE AND SYSTEM

Charles Larned, the professor of drawing from 1876 to 1911, had long been the most vocal defender of West Point's educational system. His many publications on this topic included a 1906 article that focused on the process of building character in cadets. The key to West Point's success, he argued, was the paternalism of the educational system. Rather than granting cadets the freedoms that were becoming popular at civilian schools, the Academy immersed them in a values-laden incubator insulated from the impurities of the outside world.

> Keep the adolescent soul clean and free from temptation as long as possible and build up character, mind, and body in an atmosphere as exempt from poison as it can be made. The full grown man then faces life with all three vitalities as vigorous and healthy as human conditions can ensure — with right habits acquired, and individuality crystallized. For every character that can achieve moral strength in the face of social temptations . . . there are ten who are weakened, demoralized, or destroyed.[4]

Because of the Academy's paternalism, the micro-society at West Point was a sterile caricature of the larger society outside the gates. Cadets lived in an orderly and disciplined environment. The rules governing this environment were exacting, and each person was held strictly accountable for compliance. Every detail of a cadet's life was modulated in accordance with a master plan articulated in official regulations and enforced by unbending tactical officers. Over the course of four years, cadets who negotiated the obstacles of the West Point curriculum and disciplinary system were considered, at least in theory, to have honed the intellect and refined the character essential for officership. "The diploma of West Point," Larned boasted, was a "comprehensive guaranty of character . . . having but few parallels on earth."[5]

West Point was not only paternal, but also attritional. Punishment for every transgression was swift, sure, and severe. Cadets who failed to complete the curriculum demonstrated weaknesses of character, intellect, or both, that disqualified them from commissioning. They were viewed as a drag on the faculty's time and their classmates' development, and Academy leaders felt obligated to separate them as soon as possible.

In the paternal and attritional culture that characterized West Point, there was little moral ambiguity on questions of honor. Cadets were expected to know right from wrong, and Academy overseers created a stressful environment in which to test the cadets' character on a daily basis. Chaplain Clayton Wheat emphasized the centrality of honor in the lives of cadets when he composed Cadet Prayer in 1919. Wheat's purpose was to help cadets "set forth in their own lives the ideals and principles which have long been fostered in the Corps."[6] His prayer, recited every Sunday by every cadet, asked for divine help in molding human character.

> Strengthen and increase our admiration for honest dealing and clean thinking, and suffer not our hatred of hypocrisy and pretence ever to diminish. Encourage us in our endeavor to live above the common level of life. Make us to

choose the harder right instead of the easier wrong, and never to be content with a half truth when the whole can be won. Endow us with courage that is born of loyalty to all that is noble and worthy, that scorns to compromise with vice and injustice and knows no fear when truth and right are in jeopardy. . . . Help us to maintain the honor of the Corps untarnished and unsullied and to show forth in our lives the ideals of West Point in doing our duty to Thee and our Country.[7]

World War I confirmed the importance of character to the military professional. In the crucible of combat, West Pointers outperformed their peers in leading American soldiers against the enemy. The same was true even for the cadets who had graduated early and therefore did not have the same academic preparation as other graduates.[8] In the face of postwar criticism of the military, Secretary of War Newton Baker defended West Point's defining emphasis on character. West Point, he explained, imparted a set of virtues that were essential for the soldier.

> Men may be inexact, or even untruthful, in ordinary matters and suffer as a consequence only the disesteem of their associates, or the inconveniences of unfavorable litigation, but the inexact or untruthful soldier trifles with the lives of his fellow-men and the honor of his government, and it is, therefore, no matter of idle pride, but rather of stern disciplinary necessity that makes West Point require of her students a character for trustworthiness which knows no evasions.[9]

The first postwar superintendent, Douglas MacArthur, could not have agreed more. "In the final analysis of the West Point product," he observed, "character is the most precious component."[10] Still, he was deeply critical of the paternal assumptions that undergirded the Academy's approach to developing character. Cadets were cloistered in a dreary, monotonous, and ascetic environment with slight exposure to the world around them. They lived in the grip of an oppressive and unrelenting disciplinary system with few outlets for their youthful energies and curiosity. The alleged purpose of these environmental constraints, as Larned had explained in 1906, was to nurture strong character by insulating cadets from the impurities of the outside world at an impressionable time in their lives. The actual effect, MacArthur believed, was to stunt their social and moral growth. They were naïve about human nature and more vulnerable than most to the schemes of dishonest people. The unrelenting restraints of the environment pushed cadets to take risks in conduct, including behavior that was flagrantly deceptive, despite the consequences of being caught.[11] The irony embedded in the system was obvious to MacArthur. "We boast about a cadet's truth and honesty," MacArthur noted, yet "we don't trust him to go out the gates of this medieval keep. I have been unable to discover the need for this combination of cloistered monastery and walled penitentiary."[12]

MacArthur seized the opportunity to revitalize the honor system as the Corps of Cadets expanded to its normal size of four classes by the summer of 1920. He knew, however, that he could not force it on cadets. The honor system had "developed spontaneously from the experience of generations of cadets"; it came from the "better discipline emanating from within the student body itself."[13] MacArthur therefore formed an "honor committee" of first-class cadets to articulate the standards of honorable behavior and help codify the procedures that governed the unwritten honor code.

As noted in the previous chapter, MacArthur had taken a similar approach in reconstituting the fourth-class system. The first classmen responded admirably to both tasks, and MacArthur published the results of their collective work in a pamphlet entitled *Traditions and Customs of the Corps*. The pamphlet described the quest for honor as the "most cherished sentiment in the life of the Corps." Cadets were proscribed from lying and "quibbling"—that is, using "evasive statements or taking advantage of technicalities in order to shield guilt or to defeat the ends of justice." Furthermore, cadets were honor bound not to receive "unauthorized assistance" on individual graded assignments. Finally, the Corps of Cadets, "individually and collectively," would be the "guardian of its own honor"; cadets had to report the transgressions of their peers when the offense was a breach of honor.[14]

By the time of MacArthur's departure in mid-1922, the honor committee had become an official and permanent body. It consisted of first classmen as honor representatives, one elected from each cadet company, with the class president serving as the chairman.[15] Of the committee's five essential duties, the first three were preemptive and thus exceeded the scope of the old vigilance committees: (1) educate cadets about the standards of honor under which they would live; (2) prevent the spread of practices inconsistent with the honor code; and (3) seek guidance from higher authority on honor issues needing interpretation. The last two duties were reactive and thus approximated the role of the old vigilance committees: (4) investigate alleged violations of the honor code and (5) report to the superintendent the cases that could not be dismissed.

The honor committee's duties reflected the deep involvement of the Corps in all aspects of the honor system. West Point officials encouraged that involvement because it encouraged cadets to embrace the honor code and system as their own. The cadets may not have had legal authority over the honor system, but the MacArthur reforms gave them extraordinary influence in administering it. Every subsequent superintendent respected the role of the honor committee and worked closely with it.

The MacArthur reforms created a two-level system for enforcing the honor code and gave the new honor committee an integral part in it. Under the previous single-level system, officers were in charge of investigating potential honor violations and conducting the resultant courts-martial. Under the new system, the first level of honor enforcement was the honor committee, which assumed the investigatory role and, if necessary, conducted an honor board to determine guilt or innocence. Since the honor board had no legal standing, it could only "ask" a cadet found guilty to resign; in the large majority of cases, however, nothing further was needed to convince the offender to go quietly.

If a cadet found guilty by an honor board chose to appeal the verdict, he entered the honor system's second level — trial by an officer-run court-martial. A guilty verdict in this instance almost certainly resulted in expulsion, with a discharge that could range from honorable to dishonorable depending on the severity of the offense. In the event of an acquittal, the cadet was reinstated in the Corps, but that did not exonerate him in the eyes of his peers. The cadet was likely to face a severe form of social ostracism known as the "silence," whereby all other cadets would shun him except in the performance of official duties. The silence was the Corps' most powerful tool in convincing "found" cadets to leave the Academy voluntarily rather than appeal the decision to an officer board.

As indicated by the extreme nature of the silence, cadets observed little middle ground in their conception of honor. A single sanction — dismissal (or forced resignation) — was the only acceptable punishment for a cadet found guilty of an honor violation, even if that cadet were subsequently acquitted by court-martial. For many cadets, the absolute standards and moral clarity of the honor system made life simpler and more certain. It relieved them of the inconvenience of thinking deeply about the morally ambiguous situations they were sure to confront as officers and that defied absolute standards of right and wrong. The differences between innocence or guilt, honor or dishonor, and retention or dismissal seemed deceptively simple to adjudge and understand.

In its execution, the honor system reflected an assumption about human nature held by many cadets and graduates. Specifically, a person's basic character was formed early in one's life and was therefore impervious to major change thereafter. A good character could be refined, deepened, and strengthened, but a weak one probably could not survive the demanding standards of the honor code for four years. Cadets in the latter category were best separated as soon as possible, and the single sanction was the tool for doing so. Accordingly, cadets received a stern warning: "A second chance to one who has intentionally broken the honor code will not be given and no partiality will be shown, no distinction whatever being made to class or rank."[16] The persistence of this assumption, particularly after World War II, allowed the honor system in some cases to be applied inconsistently, inflexibly, and, worst of all, unjustly.

Despite the official pronouncements about no second chances, there was an effective, if obscure, form of discretion built into the honor system. The discretion was cadet initiated and came during honor committee investigations of alleged honor offenses. The chairman of the 1924 honor committee, John Hill, recalled that "if a case was determined to be of a minor nature and was admitted by the cadet himself, it was disposed of by disciplinary means." Similarly, the 1930 chairman, William Whipple Jr., recalled that the honor committee would not find a cadet guilty in cases where it considered the violation a "small matter." The 1935 chairman, David H. Gregg, noted that a cadet with a strong record of "truth and veracity . . . should not be dismissed for a minor slip." The only "unforgiveable offense," according to Gregg, was "the premeditated crime or a series of crimes showing a dishonest frame of mind."[17] These comments confirmed the existence of a second-chance philosophy for at least some honor violations. After World War II, however, the honor committee became stricter in its judgments, and the second-chance philosophy faded into disuse.[18]

The uncompromising standards of the honor system were underscored by a debate over honorable behavior in academic settings. In 1905, Superintendent Albert Mills clarified that cadets were honor bound "to receive no information concerning their recitations or lessons from any unauthorized source."[19] The prohibition applied to all graded requirements, written or oral, and inside or outside the section room. Mills noted that this policy had been in effect previously, but in the absence of a written honor code he deemed it "wise to enunciate it in unequivocal terms."[20] The issue came up again in 1926, when Superintendent Merch Stewart ordered a review of the applicability of the honor code to academic matters. Once again the result was unequivocal. The review committee concluded that the honor code "has applied traditionally in the conduct of academic work" and should continue to do so. The fundamental rule was that "no cadet shall impart or receive any unauthorized assistance . . . which would tend to give any cadet an unfair advantage."[21]

Stewart was uncomfortable with this interpretation, as it would require courts-martial for cadets accused of academic misbehavior, albeit in the category of an honor violation.[22] He therefore imposed a policy that "cadets suspected of dishonest methods in their academic work must be given one warning before being brought to trial."[23] Over the next decade, Stewart's policy was the subject of much criticism, since it effectively allowed a cadet one free honor violation before being punished. Lt. Col. Simon B. Buckner Jr., the commandant in 1935, argued that the policy was "inconsistent with the views of both cadets and graduates" and failed "to upbuild and uphold the honor code of the Corps of Cadets."[24] Stewart's policy was abandoned soon thereafter as academic honor violations came to be treated equally with other acts of dishonor.

Recurring questions over the definition of honorable behavior pushed the Academy toward reducing the honor code to writing. The principal medium was *Bugle Notes*, the annual reference book edited by upperclassmen for each incoming class.[25] The first edition, published in 1907, included an essay by Professor Larned on the importance of honor to cadets and military professionals. Larned emphasized the absolute nature of the honor code and the single sanction for those who violated it. He urged cadets to love "Truth for Truth's sake" and to avoid the cadet who "sees neither white as white, nor black as black, but both always as gray." For cadets who could not live by the code, there were no second chances; it was "no part of the function of West Point to become a reformatory of morals."[26] Subsequent editions of *Bugle Notes* elaborated on the honor code in similar terms and, starting in 1923, included "guiding principles" to define honorable behavior in the everyday circumstances of cadet life. The first guiding principle reemphasized the uncompromising nature of the code: "No intentional breach of honor is excusable." The second did the same for nontoleration: "Everyone, offender or not, is honor bound to report any breach of honor which comes to his attention."[27]

Another attempt at documentation came in 1931, when Superintendent William Smith drafted a concise statement of the honor code: "Honor . . . is a fundamental principle of character—a virtue which implies loyalty and courage, truthfulness and self-respect, justice and generosity."[28] A few years later, Superintendent Francis Wilby issued a document that discussed the history and importance of the honor code and its relationship to cadets. It reemphasized the principle of nontoleration, which stemmed from the belief that the honor code "is mightier than any individual, friend, or stranger. In keeping with the impartial outlook any cadet will report any other cadet, or even himself, for a violation of honor."[29]

These and other attempts to document the honor code were preliminary to the efforts of Maj. Gen. Maxwell Taylor, superintendent from 1945 to 1949. Taylor's deep interest in honor prompted him to write an eight-page essay on the subject that he published in a 1948 pamphlet entitled "West Point Honor System: Its Objectives and Procedures." The essay described the nature of the honor code, its importance to military professionals, and its enforcement through the honor system. The essence of the honor code, he told cadets, could be stated concisely in a single sentence that has since become familiar to every cadet and graduate of West Point: "A cadet will neither lie, cheat nor steal."[30] In another passage, Taylor addressed the principle of nontoleration: "A cadet may be reported by one of his closest friends . . . because the men of the Corps feel that the Honor Code is bigger than any individual or any personal friendship." Not until 1970 would the nontoleration clause be added to the single-sentence statement of honor; regardless, there could be no doubt among cadets that it was part of the honor code.[31]

Taylor devoted much of his essay to the administration of the honor system. In particular, he addressed an issue that had concerned the army chief of staff, Gen. Dwight Eisenhower. Because Eisenhower considered the honor code to be "the most treasured possession of the Point," he urged Taylor not to allow its use "at the expense of the Cadets in the detection of violations of regulations."[32] Using honor in this way was a long-standing complaint of cadets, who believed that in some situations they were forced either to incriminate themselves or to commit an honor violation. Taylor clarified: "Only if a cadet indicates by a statement that he has complied or he will comply with a particular regulation does the Honor System enter into consideration." The "statement" could be given orally or in writing (e.g., a signature).[33] Taylor's explanation notwithstanding, the tension between honor and regulations continued to bedevil Academy officials and cadets long into the future.

Taylor personally addressed each incoming class on the importance of honor. His remarks to the class of 1952 distilled his views on the subject and reflected the paternal and attritional aspects of the West Point culture with respect to honor:

> Elsewhere the word "honor" is often used loosely and with little meaning. But here at West Point, honor means a definite code of living, a code imposed by the Corps of Cadets itself. There is nothing complicated about cadet ethics; it calls only for "honest dealing and clean thinking." Think true, speak true, be true, and there can be no question of your meeting the standards of honor of the Corps. But the honor code is strict and permits of no violations. The Corps itself will reject those of its members who violate the code. In this emphasis on honor, the authorities are solidly behind the cadets and join with them in the determination to protect the high reputation of the Corps of Cadets.[34]

As Taylor made clear, the single sanction for an honor violation was dismissal from the Academy. There had been occasional exceptions to this rule, but not enough to allow any cadet to think that he would be spared expulsion if he crossed the line from honorable to dishonorable behavior. Cadets knew the expectations, as well as the consequences if they failed.

II. SCANDAL

Despite Taylor's emphasis on honor, West Point was soon to endure the worst honor crisis in its history so far. Every year a handful of cadets either resigned or, if court-martialed, were dismissed for committing honor violations; in the latter case, depending on the severity of the charges, a cadet might receive less than an honorable discharge. While the numbers of cadets dismissed for honor waxed and waned over the years, they never amounted to more than a small fraction of the Corps of Cadets, and they rarely involved collusion among cadets.

That changed in 1951. In April, Academy leaders uncovered a cheating ring that was passing information pertinent to graded tests and classroom recitations. The cheating centered on the football team, although other athletes and cadet tutors also were involved. They passed the information in a variety of venues — barracks, library, hallways of academic buildings, athletic locker rooms, mess hall — always careful to avoid arousing the suspicion of their instructors and fellow cadets.[35] To obscure their misconduct, the ringleaders recruited their accomplices carefully, bypassing cadets who were unambiguous in their support for the honor code. Additionally, they succeeded in getting a few of their members elected as company honor representatives; in so doing, they undermined the integrity of the 1951 honor committee and ensured — at least until April 1951 — that none of the members of the ring would be found guilty of an honor violation. The list of cadets implicated in the cheating included the captain-elect of the football team, two All-American selections, and the top two quarterbacks, including the son of the head coach, Earl Blaik. Evidence indicated that the cheating had gone on undetected for several years; indeed, several former gridiron heroes, now serving as officers, allegedly were members of the ring.[36]

On 3 August, following several months of investigations, Secretary of the Army Frank Pace announced to a shocked nation that ninety cadets would be discharged for their complicity in the cheating ring. "The great value of West Point to the Army and to the nation," he said, "rests on the unwavering integrity of its graduates. I feel that there can be no compromise in the maintenance of the high standards of conduct on which West Point was founded."[37] West Point was a revered institution, especially in the years after the Second World War, and its football players were the darlings of the sports media. The team was ranked second in the nation at the end of the 1950 season and the prospects for 1951 were even better. The cheating incident became the top news story, pushing aside the Korean War as the focus of television, radio, and newspaper coverage.[38] Cadet Tom Murphy was at Camp Buckner on the day of the press release and immediately called home to let his family know he was not involved. His mom, in the little town of Antigo, Wisconsin, already had heard the news![39] Of course, she was relieved that her son was not involved.

Academy officials first discovered the crisis when two cadets reported the cheating ring to authorities after having been invited to join it. The commandant, Col. Paul D. Harkins, pressured the reluctant cadets to gather evidence by pretending to join the ring.[40] By late May, the undercover work had yielded enough evidence to begin formal investigative proceedings. Given the scope of the cheating and the evidence that some members of the honor committee were involved, Harkins bypassed the honor committee and formed an officer board to do the investigations instead. The board consisted of three lieutenant colonels from the Department of Tactics, all highly regarded veterans of World War II. Arthur S. Collins Jr., the First Regiment tactical officer, was the chairman.[41] Blaik pleaded with the superintendent, Maj. Gen. Frederick Irving, to elevate the investigation to the Academic Board. The honor crisis "may be a catastrophe," Blaik argued, "and it demands the most mature judgment."[42] Irving, having already approved the undercover work of the cadets and the composition of the investigative board, made no changes to the plan of action.

Ironically, it was Blaik who broke the investigation wide open. On the first day of testimony — 29 May — sixteen of nineteen cadets questioned by the Collins board denied involvement in or knowledge of the cheating ring. That afternoon, two of the cadets who had told the truth were threatened by the others in the ring and told to recant their stories. That night, a group of football players met with their coach; they admitted their complicity in the ring and asked for his advice. Blaik was shocked and saddened, but he was direct with the players: "You know how we do business in the squad and at the Military Academy. Each of you should state the facts to the board without equivocation."[43] That advice led to a breakthrough for the board, as cadets recanted their lies or told the truth from the outset of their testimony.

The officer board amassed solid cases against cheaters in the classes of 1952 and 1953, but it could not do so for the class of 1951, whose graduation was only days away. There was plenty of circumstantial evidence, but none of the twenty-eight seniors questioned by the board admitted to having given or received unauthorized help in academics. Board members had reason to believe that sixteen of the twenty-eight had cheated, but the structured core curriculum that neatly segregated one class from another reduced the chance that underclassmen could provide evidence against the seniors. Consequently, none of the eighty-three cadets discharged for cheating included members of the class of 1951.[44]

While Blaik did not condone the cheating, he argued that the institution was most to blame for it. He was particularly critical of the temptations caused by certain academic policies, particularly the Academy's habit of giving the same test to cadets in different sections over a two-day period.[45] Cadets who took a test on the first day were on their honor not to discuss it with anyone until all other cadets had taken the same test on the second day. Given the pressures to succeed academically, Blaik argued, this policy was like putting money on a table and walking away with the expectation that it would not be stolen. He believed that "every reasonable means should be taken to remove inordinate temptation." Even then, human nature dictated that there would be honor violations, but that did not mean that all violators were inherently dishonorable. Blaik favored rehabilitation for worthy cadets and railed against the uncompromising attitude of the "black-or-white advocates" of the expulsion policy. The honor system, he concluded, placed "far too much emphasis on the consequences of breaking the code and too little on an abiding commitment to the moral principle involved."[46]

The last point was key. Blaik argued that the severe consequences of violating the honor code served as "the important restraining barrier" to cadet conduct. The fear of dismissal, ostracism, and a less than honorable discharge were, for many cadets, the driving force behind their adherence to the honor code. Leniency was possible only when a cadet reported himself for a violation that otherwise would have gone undetected; in such cases, the cadet would receive an honorable discharge, rather than a lesser discharge, upon his expulsion. Blaik scoffed at the inflexibility of an honor system that bred fear rather than understanding. And he mocked the "artificial saintliness" that "redeems the offender who reports himself by giving him an honorable discharge."[47]

Another major problem with the honor system, according to Blaik, was the expectation of nontoleration among cadets. He claimed no quarrel with the proscriptions against lying, cheating, and stealing, but expecting friends to turn in one another for honor violations was "the weakness of the code." Such an expectation was "ritualistic and unreal," especially in cases where the "system is to blame." Nontoleration constituted "a stress on the honor code."[48]

Blaik saved his most biting criticism for the officers responsible for the honor code and system as it existed in 1951. He berated the "elite group of sanctimonious graduates, traditionalists narrow in their thinking who lack both compassion and understanding of young men." Too many West Point graduates, scolded Blaik, "have fixed opinions, are unimaginative, and believe they have never been wrong. . . . Regrettably, as a group they regard their views as above and apart from the mainstream of the services, as well as from that of the American society."[49] Blaik agreed with an old friend, John J. McEwan, that the cheating incident had been handled "by men of false pride and colossal egotism." McEwan was a 1917 graduate of West Point and head coach of the football team from 1923 to 1925. Like Blaik, McEwan faulted the Academy and its leaders for putting the football players under excessive pressure.

"Those who play football are under a difficult strain at West Point. . . . With the alumni demanding that we produce a winning team at any cost, are they not also guilty?"[50]

When Blaik counseled his players to tell the truth, he did so confident that the scope of the crisis would validate his criticisms of the honor system and spare the players from expulsion. He acknowledged their mistakes but argued that most of them were honorable young men who deserved a second chance. When he could not convince Irving, he wrote letters to Maxwell Taylor, now the chief of army operations, and to Gen. Lawton Collins, the chief of staff. Taylor and Collins, like most other senior leaders, were appalled by the cheating incident and had little sympathy for the guilty cadets.[51] The expulsions embittered Blaik for the rest of his life. In his memoir, he called the expelled players the "90 scapegoats" and denigrated the officers responsible for their dismissal.[52]

The board of officers appointed in August to study the causes of the honor incident came to far different conclusions than Blaik. Boyd W. Bartlett, head of the Department of Electricity, chaired the board; the other members were Col. Francis M. Greene, director of the Office of Physical Education (i.e., master of the sword), and Col. Charles H. Miles Jr., the Academy comptroller.[53] Bartlett and his colleagues conducted interviews with a large sampling of the Academy population—267 cadets, 104 officers, and ten civilians.[54] Some of the interviews were done individually, while others (cadets, in particular) were in small groups.

The board's final report, rendered in early September, was careful in its analysis and moderate in tone. Still, it drew unequivocal conclusions about the fundamental cause of the cheating incident. Academy officials responsible for intercollegiate athletics "allowed their sense of values to get out of balance. . . . Specifically the misalignment of values took the form of an over-emphasis on football." Realizing how controversial their conclusions would be, they emphasized,

> We do not want to be misunderstood. . . . The over-emphasis in question differed from that which prevails generally in modern big-time football. . . . It was created by honest and sincere people who were earnestly and vigorously working for what they believed to be the best interests of West Point and the Army as a whole. However, because of the peculiar character of the Military Academy, the impact of this over-emphasis upon the institution was greater than that in the majority of other colleges and universities.[55]

The overemphasis stemmed from a variety of pressures. Externally, a fanatical fan base, including many of "the older and more influential alumni," enjoyed the thrill of victory and the pride of association with a national football powerhouse. National media outlets played up the gridiron successes and manufactured sports heroes for an adoring public.

Internally, the pressures were equally great. A principal one resulted from the nature of the man "directing the destinies of West Point football." Coach Blaik, according to the board members, was a "person of unusual abilities, tremendous driving power, absolute singleness of purpose, and very strong personal convictions [who] carried out his mission with the utmost vigor." Superintendent Robert Eichelberger, troubled by two consecutive losing seasons in football, had hired Blaik in 1941 and made it clear that West Point "would have winning football teams."[56] For good or bad, Eichelberger could not have chosen a better man to accomplish that mission.

Over time, Blaik's extraordinary success convinced many people that fielding a nationally ranked football team was of paramount importance at the Academy. "The impression developed, in a subtle way, that many of those in authority considered this goal to transcend other aspects of the mission." The impression developed through "various acts and attitudes on the part of many people responsible for leadership."[57]

The Bartlett board devoted much attention to the consequences of the emphasis on football. Varsity players developed "strong group and personal loyalties" that transcended their loyalty to the institution. They came to view themselves as a "group apart and of such importance that they were not subject to the ordinary rules of cadet life." This attitude led to "spiritual segregation" from the Corps of Cadets that prevented them from absorbing the values and ideals of the institution.[58]

Contributing to the football subculture were the many privileges given only to football players. The special attention started even before the players became cadets. Football recruits received help in securing congressional nominations; they were invited on orientation visits to West Point at no expense to them; and they benefited from the free "cram schools" operated by the athletic department to help them pass the entrance examination. Once admitted as cadets, they received special privileges during the summers. Plebes were excused from some training to attend football practice; in the mess hall, they ate their meals at tables with varsity players rather than their cadre leaders; they received priority in selecting a foreign language for study during the academic year; and they attended parties with the football team rather than with their training companies. Third classmen could miss training at Camp Buckner to attend practice; second classmen were excused from the two-week "CAMID" (cadet-midshipmen) training exercise; and first classmen received priority in scheduling their cadre duties to accommodate the summer practice schedule. During the school year, football players received special tutoring by volunteer

officers at nonstandard times. In cases of indiscipline and poor military aptitude ratings, they sometimes benefited from the intercession of their coaches.
These privileges were in addition to those provided all intercollegiate athletes,
such as late supper, excusal from duties, and early release from classes.[59]

The success and prestige of Blaik's football program encouraged many of
his players to believe they were privileged as cadets. One of them verbalized the
sentiment in his testimony to the Collins board; the football team, he boasted,
"is the rock on which the Corps was built." From this idea emerged an easy cor-
ollary in the minds of some players — that Academy officials wanted them "to
stay proficient in academics at all costs."[60] These attitudes and practices, noted
board members, diverged from the Academy's historic commitment to equal
treatment for all cadets. "All measures to correct the situation," they argued,
"should be based on this premise."[61]

The Bartlett board was thorough in exposing the problems with football,
but less so in addressing other contributing causes of the honor crisis. There
was little doubt that football had been overemphasized and needed to be re-
aligned with institutional goals, but other problems, deeper and more systemic
than football, had set the conditions for the mass cheating. When board members concluded, for example, that academic procedures and admissions policies
were "essentially sound and healthy," they overlooked serious deficiencies that
had taken root since World War II. Similarly, they considered the honor system to be "basically sound," even though it had not prevented a large number
of cadets from cheating or tolerating those who did. To be fair, the Bartlett
board labored under time constraints and restrictive guidance and therefore
had little choice but to focus their efforts on the football team.[62] Additionally,
they recognized the need for follow-on studies in a variety of specified areas and
convinced Irving to initiate them.[63]

One of the follow-on studies focused on the non-football issues that led to
the honor crisis. Col. Greene, a veteran of the Bartlett board, headed a board of
officers to study Academy's regulations, policies, and procedures that impinged
on the honor system. They were to determine the extent to which West Point
authorities used the honor system to enforce regulations. Additionally, they
would assess the effectiveness of honor education for cadets, staff, and faculty.
In the end, Greene and his colleagues uncovered "many serious deficiencies"
that contradicted the Bartlett board's rosy assessment of Academy programs
other than football.[64]

The Greene board found that the regulations, policies, and procedures affecting cadets came from four authorities — the dean (academic departments),
commandant (Department of Tactics), cadet chain of command, and the honor
committee. In the dean's area, policies governing study procedures, test taking,
additional instruction, take-home requirements, and laboratory experiments

were inconsistent from department to department; in some cases, the inconsistencies appeared even in the same department. Definitions and interpretations of plagiarism were likewise inconsistent. In the commandant's area, the annually updated "Blue Book" provided a compendium of regulations that governed every facet of a cadet's personal and professional life. Mastering the contents of the Blue Book could be as difficult as abiding by them, as many of the regulations were detailed, confusing, and subject to interpretation.[65] Adding to the regulatory morass were the cadet chain of command and honor committee, each with its own orders, policies, and interpretations. The Greene board found the corpus of directives bewildering — "not clear, not explicit, not systematized and not compiled in a form to be readily available for either cadets or authorities."[66]

Board members concluded that Academy officials, both officer and cadet, used the honor system "to enforce every manner of orders and administrative procedures."[67] Conflating duty and honor was appropriate in many situations, but in the extreme it created subtle but serious problems that undermined the character-building goals of the Academy. In particular, the multiplicity of written regulations created gray areas where cadets could abide by the letter, but not the spirit, of the law. With honor as a mechanism to enforce regulations, the gray areas invited honor violations. Conscientious cadets might find themselves in those areas accidentally, while the less conscientious would purposely seek them out. The situation bred cynicism and, for some, encouraged attempts to "beat the system"—hardly the outcomes desired by Academy leaders.

Honor education was another area of concern. Board members noted that from 1818 to 1896 the Academy had required cadets to take a course in practical ethics taught by the chaplain. The existence of the course indicated a "past recognition of the need of planned character development" that was currently lacking. Cadets received instruction on the honor code and system during the first summer and periodically afterward, but it was "deficient" in content, presentation, timing, and frequency. The Greene board thus called for a review of honor education to strengthen the program. More important, it recommended a thorough review of the Academy's overall character-building program to determine if it is "adequately guided and coordinated and attains the overall desired coverage and results."[68]

There were fifty-five recommendations in the Greene board report that addressed the issues noted previously, as well as faculty and staff indoctrination, institutional support for the honor committee, and the processing of honor violations. Board members sensed that traditionalists would view many of their recommendations as a "mere relaxation of regulations," but they emphasized that it was not the case. The recommendations were "essential measures to correct existing situations which are adjudged unhealthy in their honor implications." For the most part, Academy leaders agreed. Forty-four of the recommendations were approved all or in part.[69]

Despite the worthy efforts of the Bartlett and Greene boards in addressing the issues that led to the honor crisis, there was still a serious omission. Neither study directly confronted the most pressing honor issue to emerge from the incident — that is, the concept of nontoleration. A troubling number of cadets, including many who were not football players, had tolerated their classmates' cheating over an extended period. Their choice of loyalty to friends over loyalty to institutional values was a painful indicator of the need for better honor education in this delicate area. The Greene board's call for a review of "overall character and moral training" was a step in the right direction.[70] Without specifically mentioning nontoleration, however, there was no assurance that this important component of the honor code would be adequately addressed. Had the concept of nontoleration taken deeper root in the Corps in the years leading up to 1951, a cheating ring could not have gone undetected for very long.

Another problem, although not the fault of Bartlett or Greene, was the failure to create a useful historical record of the crisis. Army leaders were eager to put the cheating incident behind them and to quell the negative publicity it generated. Accordingly, they labeled Bartlett and Greene reports "restricted," thus making them inaccessible except to the most dedicated and persistent researchers. Worse, the reports and associated materials were neither assembled in one place nor catalogued; rather, they ended up in scattered files at West Point and in the National Archives.[71] The lacuna in the official records complicated efforts to monitor and assess the forty-four changes resulting from the Greene report. It would be especially unfortunate twenty-five years later, when another honor crisis, even worse than the one in 1951, shook the Academy to its foundations.

In 1952, West Point paused to celebrate its sesquicentennial. It was a welcome diversion from the troubles that recently had beset the Academy and an opportunity to reaffirm the institution's relevance to the army and nation.[72] Toward this end, the Academy published an official sesquicentennial booklet that described each of its developmental programs. One of the passages discussed the importance of the difficult first summer in building character in the new cadets. The stressful environment was not meant to break a plebe's will or destroy his individuality. Rather, it was intended to initiate a "process of education" that would shape his attitude and teach him the "correct and ethical way" of doing his duty. Furthermore, it "teaches honesty, loyalty, and obedience"; virtues that were essential elements of "character building."[73]

The idea of "teaching" values may have sounded reassuring to a civilian audience, but it was contrary to what actually went on in portions of the character-building program. The recent cheating incident had shown the Academy to be unforgiving when it came to violations of the honor code. A cadet could be insubordinate, disobedient, lazy, vile, malcontented, and inconsiderate and still graduate. His classmate might harbor none of those vices but, in a momentary lapse of judgment, tell a lie. Under the protocols of the honor system, the latter cadet would be expelled, even if he were genuinely remorseful and had a solid record; moreover, there was a good chance he would leave with a less than honorable discharge. Rather than being developmental, such treatment exhibited the attritional attitudes that continued to prevail at West Point in the mid-twentieth century. Superintendent Irving, in the forward to the 1954 edition of *Bugle Notes*, verbalized the attitude when he reminded cadets, "Remember that this is a test; a test to weed out the weak and strengthen the strong; a test so gauged that only the most determined succeed."[74]

If there was a positive aspect to the 1951 honor incident, it was to shine a harsh light on the single sanction of expulsion for honor violations. Academy leaders felt compelled, out of principle and tradition, to enforce the system strictly against those who had cheated. But thoughtful observers increasingly questioned the wisdom of such an unforgiving policy at an institution that touted itself as developmental. The incongruity grew as American societal norms evolved in the postwar era, and the next quarter century would bring the issue to a head.[75]

III.   FROM ONE SCANDAL TO THE NEXT

When Garrison Davidson became the superintendent in 1956, he brought with him the conviction that character building was the most important aspect of the cadets' experience at West Point. He gave honor issues his personal attention, rather than delegating the responsibility to the commandant, as was the custom. One of his first actions was to appoint a board of senior officers to review all aspects of the honor system. The board completed its work in early 1957; although it detected "no important deficiencies," Davidson decided to conduct them annually.[76] These reviews helped Davidson stay focused on honor issues throughout his four-year tenure; moreover, they set a precedent for institutional supervision and assessment that would serve future superintendents seeking to keep a finger on the pulse of honor in the Corps of Cadets.[77]

Davidson's administration overlapped with the tenure of Maxwell Taylor as the army's chief of staff. The two men were friends, but a fascinating exchange of correspondence in 1957 revealed a sharp difference of opinion on the single sanction of expulsion for honor violations.[78] On the surface, Taylor hewed to the attritional assumptions he had espoused as superintendent. "The overriding purpose of the honor system," he told Davidson, "is to eliminate cadets

who by their conduct have created . . . doubt as to their integrity and honor."
His elaboration, however, reflected a surprising shift in his thinking. The honor
system should not be used to dismiss cadets "guilty merely of thoughtless or
perhaps inconsequential acts" that do not accurately reflect their basic character. "As we both know," he lectured Davidson,

> [R]ight and wrong outside the Military Academy is not pure white and black.
> It is one of the requirements of military leadership to establish standards of
> justice and correct behavior among officers and men. It is a defective prepara-
> tion for the exercise of this kind of leadership to allow our cadets to believe
> that justice can be administered by formula and without deep reflection upon
> circumstances and motivation. They should learn early in life to inject tolera-
> tion, judgment of human factors, and appreciation of sincere repentance into
> their decisions affecting the careers of their fellow cadets.[79]

Davidson, a traditionalist in matters of character building, resisted Taylor's
proposal for what he considered a "fundamental change in our Honor Code."[80]
He recognized that in expelling every violator of the code "we will lose a few
good risks." Taking those losses was necessary, however, to safeguard "the good
of the many and of our country rather than dilute the Honor Code by accepting 'the little lie.'"[81] Davidson told his boss, "I understand your point of view
and have tried to bring myself around to it. I find I cannot do so voluntarily. I
hope you will not insist that I try to convert the Corps to a philosophy on such
an important matter in which I do not believe."[82]

Davidson's appeal apparently had effect, as Taylor did not pursue the issue.
Still, the single sanction continued to be the subject of debate at West Point.
An officer review board convened in 1957, for example, considered the merits
of establishing a probationary period during which plebes might receive punishments short of dismissal for some honor violations. The cadet honor committee rejected the idea and, in the end, so did the officer board.[83] Within two
years, however, the Academy had taken a step in the direction of discretionary
punishment. Davidson reported that plebes still in basic training might receive
a second chance, but only in cases of "self-reported violations of a relatively
minor nature." The new policy provided a means of "easing the new cadet into
the rigid demands of the System"; moreover, it allowed the retention of cadets
who, by the act of self-reporting, proved themselves to be "acceptable risks."[84]
It was a small step, but it reflected the gradual shift away from the attritional
assumptions that underlay the character-building program at West Point.

In addition to the honor code, religion was an important means of strengthening character. Mandatory Sunday chapel had been part of cadet life since the
time of Thayer. While some cadets may have appreciated the opportunity to

nurture their spirituality, others were indifferent; in either case, they marched to the chapel, took their assigned seats, and participated in (or endured) the service.[85] There were many religiously oriented activities in addition to Sunday services. Hundreds of cadets attended voluntary morning services during the week and served as Sunday school teachers for the children of the community. During the evenings, many cadets attended Bible study, sang in the Protestant or Catholic choir, and served on acolyte squads.[86] In the mess hall before meals, Superintendent Davidson instituted a moment of silence "to make the cadet somewhat more aware of the bounties that are his."[87] In subsequent years, the silent prayer evolved into a short nondenominational prayer delivered by the adjutant before the cadets took their seats.

Mandatory chapel had come under increased scrutiny since the end of World War II. In 1946, for example, the secretary of war received a letter from an atheist whose son was interested in applying to West Point. "Will you please inform me," he asked the secretary, "under what authority this violation of our secular Constitution is being committed?" He already had been told by West Point officials that religious beliefs would have no bearing on his son's chances for admission. Maybe so, he acknowledged, but would it not be a "violation of my son's Constitutional rights and protections if he were forced . . . to attend religious services?" The secretary's response went unrecorded, but two outcomes were certain: Sunday religious services continued to be a duty for West Point cadets, and the atheist's son did not become a cadet.[88]

Another objection to mandatory chapel concerned the practice of making all cadets attend the same nondenominational Protestant service. The only exceptions were for Catholic and Jewish cadets, who attended segregated services concurrently with the Protestants. The inflexibility of this arrangement brought numerous complaints on behalf of the cadets. One was from a Christian Scientist who sought separate services for cadet coreligionists. As he explained to Secretary of War Kenneth C. Royall, Christian Scientists had a religious philosophy "diametrically opposite to the regular orthodox teaching."[89] Other letters in favor of religious choice came from senators, congressmen, and even members of the Academy's Board of Visitors.[90]

The army usually referred such correspondence to the superintendent, whose comments were the basis for preparing official responses to the complainants. The response letter of Secretary of the Army Wilbur M. Brucker to a member of Congress bore the imprint of Garrison Davidson and was typical of the Academy position on Protestant services. The Academy's policy, wrote Brucker, was "in the best interests of the individual, the Corps of Cadets and the Army." The policy had been in effect for over a century with "no indication that the religious welfare of any cadet has been impaired"; on the contrary, the common religious experience "fostered unity in the Corps of Cadets."[91]

Another response letter noted the existence at West Point of over thirty Protestant denominations, in addition to the Catholic and Jewish faiths. "All are in agreement," wrote the official, "that any further fractioning of the Corps along religious lines is undesirable."[92]

West Point continued to resist calls for change despite important Supreme Court cases that reinforced the principle of freedom of religion. In *Everson v. Board of Education* (1947), the court ruled as unconstitutional any law that would "aid one religion, aid all religions, or prefer one religion over another." Furthermore, the government could not "influence a person to go to or to remain away from church against his will."[93] Despite the clarity of this ruling and a series of related rulings in subsequent years, Academy leaders continued to require attendance at Sunday services.[94] By the 1960s, however, they had adjusted the rationale for the policy in hopes of warding off legal challenges. They now insisted that mandatory chapel was an essential component of professional development — that is, a "vehicle for the presentation of training" that made cadets more aware and appreciative of the religious beliefs of the soldiers they would lead following graduation.[95]

In January 1970, the American Civil Liberties Union filed a class-action lawsuit against Secretary of Defense Melvin Laird to challenge the policy of mandatory chapel at West Point and its sister academies. The ACLU had secured the cooperation of Cadet Michael Anderson and six Annapolis midshipmen to act as the plaintiffs in the case.[96] As the case wended its way through federal court, the army made two adjustments to the mandatory chapel policy. First, a cadet might be excused from chapel provided his request was in writing and his conviction deemed sincere. In lieu of attending services, excused cadets would take classes on the role of religion in the lives of soldiers. Second, the army allowed upperclassmen to attend segregated denominational services if accredited ministers were available on post.[97] Cadets soon had a variety of services from which to choose, including Baptist, Episcopalian, Lutheran, Orthodox, Mormon, and Christian Scientist. These policy adjustments became moot in December 1972, when an appellate court ruled mandatory chapel unconstitutional. Academy leaders were unhappy but took solace in the fact that cadets attended voluntary religious services at rates higher than expected.[98]

Another civil-liberties controversy at West Point was the practice of silencing cadets found guilty of honor violations but retained in the Corps. Two such cases sparked much criticism and negative publicity for the Academy. The first, in 1970, involved a plebe, William Puckett, who lied to an upperclassman about when he had last shined his shoes. Nagged with guilt, he soon reported the honor violation to his squad leader, who forwarded the case to the honor committee. A few days later, the honor committee found Puckett guilty of lying and asked him to resign. The deputy commandant had meanwhile counseled

Maj. Gen. William Knowlton (class of January
1943), superintendent from 1970 to 1974.
During Knowlton's tenure, West Point was the
subject of multiple civil-liberties lawsuits.

the plebe on his right to a hearing before a board of officers.[99] Puckett chose
resignation, aware that an acquittal by officers would not spare him the silence
of cadets. Puckett's congressman was enraged, press coverage was negative,
and the Academy was unrepentant. "Integrity is paramount, an absolute," explained an Academy spokesman to reporters. "If your son were drafted or under a leader whose integrity was in question, I'm sure you'd not be happy."[100]

The second case, in 1972, involved Cadet James Pelosi, a second classman
found guilty of continuing to write on a test after the instructor had told the
class to cease work. Pelosi claimed innocence and opted for an officer board,
which eventually dismissed the case on a technicality. The silence he endured
after his reinstatement made him the "Quasimodo of the Point."[101] He ate his
meals alone at a table meant for ten; anonymous tormentors opened his mail
illegally, dragged his clothes through the latrine, and subjected him to other
indignities. His determination to graduate, however, won him the grudging

respect of many cadets, and some of his old friends reestablished social contact during his senior year. By then the silence was becoming unenforceable anyway, as the Corps had grown to over four thousand cadets, many of whom were not supportive of the sanction.[102]

Following Pelosi's graduation in 1973, the honor committee decided to end the "ancient custom" of the silence. It had concluded, with much justification, that the practice brought "continuing, unattractive and frequently incorrect publicity" to the Academy. Moreover, the underlying reasons for the silence "were neither understood nor supported by many citizens, members of Congress, Army officers on active duty, and even a great many cadets."[103]

Ending the silence brought an unintended consequence. No longer intimidated by the threat of ostracism, cadets found guilty by the honor committee more frequently appealed the decisions. The officer boards that heard these cases had to observe strict rules of evidence; as a result, they overturned many of the honor committee's verdicts. The reversals embittered cadets, who resented the apparent double standard in adjudicating honor cases. Moreover, they sensed that their "ownership" of the honor system was in question as the officer boards made the honor committee increasingly irrelevant.[104]

Since the 1951 cheating incident, the trappings of legalism in the honor system had grown noticeably. This was due in large part to the Academy's efforts to purge the academic environment of unnecessary temptations to cheat; these efforts, in turn, led to a proliferation of detailed written policies governing academic procedures. The result, according to an honor review committee, was "to codify the morally obvious" and thus introduce a tendency of "strict legal interpretation" within the Corps. Cadets interpreted the policies as meaning "that which is not proscribed is permissible."[105] By the early 1970s, the societal emphasis on due process and equal protection had greatly encouraged this interpretation. According to Brig. Gen. Philip Feir, commandant from 1972 to 1975, the cadets were more "legally sophisticated" than ever before.[106]

The controversies over mandatory chapel and the silence were local manifestations of the seismic cultural changes sweeping the nation. In previous chapters we have seen how several powerful forces — the Vietnam War, civil rights movement, feminism, New Left, and counterculture — embittered Americans toward their government, nurtured a heightened sense of individualism and moral relativism, and weakened the deference once paid to traditional institutions of authority. The young men who entered West Point in the late 1960s and early 1970s reflected the mood of their society. They were more likely to challenge authority and less likely to accept traditions they did not like or understand. The rapid expansion of the Corps from 2,500 to 4,417 cadets during this period magnified these effects, as a larger student body weakened the paternal control that had lent a feeling of intimacy to the institution.[107] Similarly,

the expansion of the curriculum, while improving the quality of cadet education, diluted its effectiveness as a unifying agent.[108]

As Superintendent William Knowlton was nearing the end of his tenure in
1974, he had "great misgivings" about the honor system. A survey administered by his honor review committee had revealed three troubling indicators:
70 percent of cadets did not believe that the Corps uniformly embraced the
honor code, 60 percent believed that adherence to the spirit of the code was de-
teriorating, and 73 percent said they would not turn in a good friend for a possible honor violation.[109] He warned his successor, Sidney Berry, "Something
was rotten there."[110] The controversies over the single sanction, nontoleration,
mandatory religious services, and the silence suggested that cadets were less
inclined than before to embrace character-building traditions that clashed with
societal values. When it came to cadets embracing the honor code and system,
Knowlton acknowledged, "It takes them longer to internalize." With these
warnings in mind, Berry ordered a thorough review of the honor code and
system shortly after his arrival.[111] Still, he could not imagine the magnitude of
the honor crisis that would befall the Academy during his administration.

IV.   EE304 Cheating Incident

In March 1976, instructors in the electrical engineering core course, EE304,
uncovered widespread cheating on a graded homework project for which no
collaboration had been authorized.[112] The cheating was confined to the junior
class (class of 1977), but it was widespread—117 suspect papers were forwarded to the honor committee for investigation. The honor committee recommended full honor boards for 102 cadets; of these, fifty were found guilty.
Two of the guilty cadets resigned, but the other forty-eight chose to appeal the
verdict to a board of officers. Meanwhile, the department conducted a second,
more thorough review of the test papers; this time they compared the papers
of cadets on the same athletic teams and involved in the same extracurricular
activities. The second review, completed in late May, resulted in another 122
papers referred to the honor committee.

The magnitude of the cheating and the timing of its discovery put the honor
system under great stress. With the senior class about to graduate, the most experienced honor representatives would be unavailable to lead the investigative
effort. That left the less-experienced honor committee from the class of 1977
to assume the burden for an overwhelming number of cases. Given these challenges, Superintendent Berry dispensed with the traditional two-level honor
system. Instead, he formed review panels, composed of officers and cadets, to
investigate all subsequent EE304 honor cases.[113] The panels—not the honor

DEPARTMENT OF ELECTRICAL ENGINEERING
UNITED STATES MILITARY ACADEMY
WEST POINT, NEW YORK

MADN-D   3 March 1976

HOMEWORK COVER SHEET
EE304
COMPUTER PROBLEM
PART I

1. General:

This computer problem is divided into two parts.

(a) Part I (attached), an analytical examination of the problem has a 3.0 grade weight. Student solutions will be turned in at the beginning of Lesson E-21 (17 Mar 76 for F/H hours; 18 Mar 76 for A/C hours).

(b) Part II (to be passed out at Lesson E-21), a computer aided design requirement, has a 3.0 grade weight. Student solutions will be turned in at the beginning of Lesson E-28 (15 Apr 76 for F/H hours; 16 Apr 76 for A/C hours).

2. References:

Authorized references for this problem are:

(a) The attached problem statement.
(b) Any library reference.
(c) Any student text.
(d) Solution to this year's, (AY 75-76), EE301 Computer Problem 1 and 2.
(e) USMA Computer Center Manuals.
(f) The individual student's personal notes from this year's EE301 and EE304 courses, or a core or elective computer course.

3. Collaboration:

There will be no collaboration on Part I of this problem (Part II will be done as a team project and appropriate collaboration instructions will be issued with Part II). Upon issuance of this problem there will be no discussion of the problem with anyone except Department of Electrical Engineering Instructors. This restriction includes the prohibition of discussion of the use of the computer facilities. ISISD Computer Center personnel (Gold Coats) may not provide any form of assistance.

Cover sheet of the EE304 homework assignment that led to a major cheating incident involving the class of 1977. Cadets were required to work individually on Part I of the assignment, as stated clearly — and underscored — in paragraph 3. *Note:* personal copy of the cover sheet and entire EE304 homework assignment in author files.

committee — considered the evidence against the accused cadets and recommended whether to dismiss the cases or to forward them directly to officer boards.[114] Berry took criticism for bypassing the cadet-run honor boards, but the urgency of the situation left him with little choice.[115]

News of the cheating crisis brought intense external scrutiny of the Academy. The press provided extensive coverage, especially when, in July, cadets and their lawyers held a news conference to decry the review panels, the single sanction of expulsion, and alleged deprivations of civil rights.[116] Many members of Congress whose constituents were involved in the cheating became personally interested in the crisis. Representative Thomas J. Downey of New York, for example, visited West Point in May and June to conduct an investigation; in early August, he led an "informal public forum" in Washington that heightened congressional interest in the cheating incident.[117] The Senate Armed Services Committee conducted hearings in late June. Even the courts were involved, as several cadets initiated lawsuits to stop the honor proceedings. Although none of the lawsuits succeeded, they added to the pressures on Berry.

On 9 August, Secretary of the Army Martin Hoffmann received a letter signed by 173 congressmen asking for his personal intervention in resolving the honor crisis. The congressmen stated their belief that the punishments for the guilty cadets "should be something short of expulsion."[118] Hoffmann intended to abide by the will of Congress, but that put him at odds with Berry, who favored dismissals. "In the final analysis," argued Berry, "what we were teaching at the Military Academy was individual responsibility"; hence, the high number of honor cases "should not have made a bit of difference."[119] After heated debate, Hoffman and Berry reached a compromise: the guilty cadets would be discharged, according to tradition; subsequently, they could apply for possible readmission with the class of 1978. Of the 152 cadets who left the Academy because of the EE304 cheating incident, 148 were found eligible for readmission. In the end, ninety-eight of them reentered the Academy, with the large majority joining the class of 1978.[120]

The EE304 cheating incident subjected the Academy to the most searching scrutiny in its history. Already at work was the Academic Board, which reviewed the curriculum and revised academic procedures to ward off recurrences of mass cheating. Eclipsing the Academic Board, however, was an external review commission formed by Secretary Hoffman to investigate the cheating incident and its underlying causes. Hoffman selected Frank Borman, a 1950 graduate of West Point, to lead the commission, which conducted its work from September through mid-December 1976.[121]

In their assessment of the causes of the cheating incident, Borman and his colleagues placed much of the blame on the institution. Academy leaders had allowed unrestrained growth of a "cool-on-honor" subculture that led to wide-

Lt. Gen. Sidney Berry (class of 1948),
superintendent from 1974 to 1977. Berry's
tenure coincided with the entry of women to
West Point and the EE304 cheating incident.

spread violations of the code.[122] Honor education was "inadequate" and the administration of the honor system was "inconsistent."[123] Worse, there was irrefutable evidence of corruption within the honor committee, as numerous cases of "board fixing" were documented during the commission's investigation.[124] These problems were not confined to the class of 1977; evidence compiled by the Borman commission, honor committees, and internal Academy review boards indicated that the disaffection had been building for several years. The commissioners concluded that the problems besetting the honor system were too deep to be solved by simply expelling the cheaters. Accordingly, they recommended "sanctions other than dismissal" to provide the superintendent flexibility in dealing with the near-term crisis. Allowing lesser punishments also had long-term benefits. The commissioners believed it would strengthen the nontoleration clause by making cadets less reluctant to report a friend who committed an honor offense.[125]

Upon receiving the Borman report, Secretary Hoffmann moved swiftly to make a fundamental change to the honor system. Previously, Academy regulations had stipulated that a cadet found guilty of an honor violation "shall be separated from the Military Academy"; as of 20 January 1977, however, Hoffmann changed the wording to read: "shall *normally* be separated."[126] The revision opened the door for discretionary punishment in exceptional cases where the offense did not warrant expulsion. After 175 years and two major cheating crises, the Academy's single sanction for honor violations had been supplanted by a policy that reflected a developmental approach to character building. As we saw in chapter 7, a similar trend was under way in the Academy's program for leader development. Together, the new policies on character building and leader development represented a substantial retreat of the attritional assumptions that had characterized the West Point experience since the time of Thayer.

V.   New Directions in Character Building

Shortly after completion of the Borman study, the army chief of staff, Bernard Rogers, undertook another external review of West Point. Its purpose was to examine thoroughly all aspects of the Military Academy, not just the honor code and system. Rogers formed three committees, known collectively as the West Point Study Group (WPSG), to do the review work. The WPSG worked in cooperation with the Academy staff and faculty and had the strong backing of army leaders. Consequently, it was unusually productive in effecting reforms, many of them implemented before the WPSG submitted its final report in July 1977.[127] The reforms included the creation of new staff position — the special assistant to the commandant for honor matters — to provide full-time supervision of, and a source of counsel to, the honor committee. Also created was the Superintendent's Honor Review Committee, a permanent body to apprise the superintendent of emerging honor trends and issues. Other reforms extended honor instruction to faculty and staff members; altered the composition of honor boards to include cadets from the Corps at large rather than from only the honor committee; and changed voting procedures to allow guilty verdicts to be reached with less than a unanimous vote.[128]

Another change eliminated the two-level system of honor adjudication that had been in place, with few exceptions, since 1922.[129] As noted earlier, the system came under stress after the silence was abolished in 1973, as cadets found guilty of honor violations frequently took their cases to officer boards on appeal.[130] In October 1977, the Corps approved a proposal to replace the two-level system with a single due-process hearing that would obviate the need for an appellate officer board. Under the new procedures, three lawyers — one for the defense, one for the prosecution, and one as an at-large advisor — participated in every honor hearing. With so many lawyers present, however, the administrative proceedings became adversarial and bogged down in legalistic minutiae.[131] The Corps therefore modified the procedures again in March 1979 to allow only one lawyer who would act as an impartial, nonvoting counselor at the hearing.[132] There were subsequent adjustments, but the principle of conducting a due-process hearing at the cadet level has remained the salient feature of the honor system to the present.

Collectively, the most important contribution of the Borman and WPSG reviews was to reinforce the idea that living honorably entailed more than not lying, cheating, stealing, or tolerating those who do. "The Honor Code must be viewed as a goal toward which every honorable person aspires," noted the Borman commission, "and not as a minimum standard of behavior."[133] Similarly, the WPSG recommended that the Academy instill in cadets a comprehensive honor ethic that "subsumes the Honor Code in a broader concept." The ethic would help cadets develop a personal standard of honorable behavior and appreciate the professional obligation that "transcends individuals and individual loyalties." Academy leaders were encouraged to make the quest for honorable living "the central experience" for the cadet at West Point.[134] To help cadets internalize the honor ethic, both review bodies emphasized the need for formal ethics instruction as a basis for character development. The instruction, they insisted, *must be part of the core curriculum*." Furthermore, "ethics should be stressed throughout the entire curriculum and by all constituencies at West Point: Academic, Tactical, Athletic, and Administrative."[135]

In the years ahead, the greatest advances in character building were in educating cadets to move beyond the proscriptions of the honor code as a definition of honorable living. The core curriculum provided the most obvious examples of the new emphasis. A new course in philosophy, begun in 1978, introduced third classmen to the principles of ethical decision making; it was the first such course to be offered in nearly a century. The military history course they took as second classmen allowed them to assess how military leaders applied those principles during war and peace. The plebe course in general psychology and the senior course in military leadership likewise exercised the cadets in making ethical choices.[136] Other educational initiatives went beyond the core curriculum. Gen. Andrew Goodpaster, superintendent from 1977 to 1981, formed an ethics and professionalism committee to consider ways of enhancing the moral and ethical aspects of the cadet experience. The committee's pamphlet, "Ethics and the Military Profession," invited dialogue and research on ethical issues from the perspective of the American military.[137]

In 1981, the commandant formed a working group of officers and cadets to design a four-year program of honor education. The program went into effect that summer and represented the most comprehensive honor education effort to date (table 8.1). It emphasized the nature and importance of the honor code and its application at West Point and in the army. More important, it nurtured "an honor ethic, a set of personal beliefs and commitments that guides one's total behavior, holding honesty, fairness, and the higher moral and ethical good for all, as dominant values."[138] The program combined all honor education under the honor committee's vice chairman for education and included the participation of officers from the faculty and staff. There were training seminars for company honor representatives and information briefings for academic departments given by the honor committee chairman and the commandant's special assistant for honor.[139] Starting in 1986, West Point began hosting a yearly national honor conference for military and civilian colleges with honor codes of their own; the conference provided a forum for exchanging ideas on how "institutions develop ethical values in their students."[140]

The efforts to improve honor education and nurture an honor ethos in cadets represented a big improvement over what had existed before the 1976 cheating incident. Howard Prince, who entered West Point as a cadet in 1958, characterized his honor education as "woefully inadequate." The honor committee members in charge of the training, he recalled, were "sort of like . . . priests. 'You better do this, or else,' was the tone."[141] Anthony Hartle entered West Point two years later and remembered "talking very, very few times about the honor system." The little training he received emphasized the absolute standard of the code and uncompromising consequences of committing a violation. As a result, "there was a largely unspoken agreement that knowing less about potential violations by individuals that one knew was a good thing. Hear no evil, see no evil."[142] Kip Nygren's experience was better, but not by much. He entered the Academy in 1965 and received periodic honor training during the summer and academic year. As an upperclassman, he attended company meetings during which the honor representative discussed recently decided cases. Beyond that, however, there was little to nurture the concept of a comprehensive honor ethic. "There was only one value at that time," Nygren recalled. "It was honor. . . . There wasn't really any other value that we thought about that was important."[143] Prince, Hartle, and Nygren all found ways of developing

TABLE 8.1   Honor Education Program, 1981

Class	Summer	1st Semester	2nd Semester
Fourth (1st year)	Purpose, brief history, and basic tenets of honor code. Overview of honor system. Basic applications of honor code. Identity, truth, fairness, respect for others End-of-summer review.	Applications of honor to academics and regulations. Applications of the honor code. Honor board procedures. Spirit of the code. Honor away from West Point.	Toleration and discretion. Relationship between duty and honor. History and evolution of the code. Preparation for summer training.
Third (2nd year)	Positive aspects of living honorably. Teamwork and conflict resolution. Honor in the army. Individual responsibility as an upperclassman. End-of-summer review.	Corporate responsibility to the fourth class. Individual responsibility to the honor system. Honor above loyalty and friendship.	Duties of honor representatives. The honor ethic and other religious-philosophical systems. Handling ethical problems during summer training.
Second (3rd year)	Review of summer training experiences.	Review applications of honor to academics and regulations. Responsibility of leaders to the honor code. Comparison of other institutional honor codes and systems.	Understanding due process in the honor system. Internalization of the honor ethic. Preparation for summer training.
First (4th year)	Responsibilities of first class in setting tone.	Prepare for discussions with underclassmen. Importance of integrity to an officer. Relationship between honor and loyalty in the army.	Facilitate discussions with underclassmen. Honor ethic in wartime. Your career and the honor ethic.

Note: Adapted from *Annual Report of the Superintendent*, 1981, 38.

a strong honor ethic in their military careers, including many years of service as professors at West Point. They were quick to point out, however, that the honor education program they helped to oversee as faculty members was "far superior" to what they experienced as cadets.[144]

The integration of character building into all other developmental programs advanced significantly during the tenure of Superintendent Dave Palmer. As noted in chapter 7, Palmer's Cadet Leader Development System provided an overarching framework for developing leaders of character. He envisioned the academic, military, and physical programs operating continuously in a positive moral-ethical environment actively supported by the institution. In such a model, every department and organization at West Point had responsibility for contributing to the moral and ethical development of cadets.

In 1988, Palmer asked the army chief of staff, Gen. Carl E. Vuono, to form an external board to review the honor system at West Point. Palmer believed that the Academy was overdue for an external review since the last one to focus exclusively on the honor system had been more than a decade earlier. Additionally, he sought an independent assessment of the recommendations from two internal committees that had recently studied the honor code and system. Finally, Palmer wanted to verify that the Academy's character-building program was fully integrated into all other developmental programs — a key objective of the Cadet Leader Development Program.[145]

Vuono appointed Wesley Posvar, president of the University of Pittsburgh and a 1946 graduate of West Point, to chair the commission. After eight months of study, Posvar delivered a report that was supportive of the honor code's substance and intent. The commissioners concluded that the honor code was "a commanding ethical force" at the Academy and a "useful example for all American public service."[146] On the topic of nontoleration, the commission endorsed the view that it "is integral to the spirit of the Code and essential to its viability."[147]

Still, the commission noted several "persisting concerns." In particular, honor board members sometimes rendered not-guilty verdicts to protect the accused from potential expulsion. Additionally, Academy officials too often used the honor code as an enforcement tool for regulations. To address the first issue, the commission recommended an expansion of the discretionary punishments available to the superintendent. For the second, it admonished Academy leaders to protect the code against "irresponsible, trivial misuse by superiors"; this recommendation led to the elimination of the absence card, which cadets had long perceived as "an excessive use of the Honor Code to enforce regulations."[148] The Academy implemented, either all or in part, twenty-three of the twenty-five recommendations of the Posvar commission.[149] This record underscored the wisdom of conducting external honor reviews on a periodic basis. Since completion of the Posvar report, however, there have been no further external reviews of the honor code and system.

Palmer's immediate successors took additional steps to strengthen the character-building program. Superintendent Howard Graves (1991–1996) declared in 1992 that honor was a "bedrock value"—an "irreducible, inviolate, and unchanging" standard of character. A year later, he declared a second bedrock value — respect for others — to emphasize the principle that all people should be treated with dignity and respect.[150] The designation of these bedrock values brought corresponding resources — full-time staff officers to oversee the honor and respect programs, and many hours of programmed time for education and training. By 1995, the honor education program had expanded to fifty hours of instruction; the respect for others program consisted of sixty-three hours of instruction.[151]

The degree to which cadets embraced the bedrock values was tested in a widely reported incident in October 1994. In anticipation of an upcoming football game, several hundred cadets conducted a "spirit run" that ended with a pass through a cordon of team members. As the formation transited the narrow opening, several players groped the breasts of passing female cadets. The women reported the abuse confident that the chain of command would uphold its pledge to defend their right to be treated with respect. In the ensuing investigation, three of the players tried to explain that their gropes had been unintentional, that their hands had inadvertently brushed against the women at breast level. Their teammates, however, were disgusted by the incident and rejected the lame excuses. The gropers were isolated by their peers, renounced by the Corps, and disciplined by their superiors.

A few days later, during an unrelated interview with the *New York Times* editorial staff, Graves voluntarily divulged what had happened during the spirit run to demonstrate the Academy's commitment to its bedrock values. Although a few cadets had behaved poorly, he explained that the vast majority demonstrated a commitment to honor and respect. The result was an uncharacteristically positive article, "Wisdom at West Point," in which the newspaper lauded Graves for acting "rapidly, intelligently, and with an openness that should constitute a watershed in the armed forces' treatment of . . . sexism."[152]

Another step forward in character building came in 1998 with the creation of the Center for the Professional Military Ethic.[153] The center was responsible for designing and supervising an integrated program of ethics training that included instruction in honor and respect.[154] As it evolved through the years, the staff composition of the center reflected its integrative function. Besides the director (an army colonel), there were permanent professorships for character development, leader development, and officership. A visiting professor — a retired four-star general — provided a deep well of leadership and experience for the center. The special assistants to the commandant for honor and respect rounded out the staff.[155]

As the character-building program became more established following the 1976 cheating incident, superintendents used discretionary punishment with increasing frequency. Goodpaster adhered closely to Secretary Hoffmann's guidance that cadets found guilty of honor violations should normally be separated; accordingly, he granted discretion only 11.5 percent of the time, as shown in table 8.2. In subsequent years, however, the incidence of discretion

TABLE 8.2   Discretionary Punishment in Honor Cases, 1977–2010

Superintendent	Years	No. of Cadets Found for Honor	No. of Times Discretion Granted	% of Times Discretion Granted
Andrew Goodpaster	1977–1981	61	7	11.5
Willard Scott	1981–1986	102	26	25.5
Dave Palmer	1986–1991	140	57	40.7
Howard Graves	1991–1996	118	52	44.1
Daniel Christman	1996–2001	196	107	54.6
William Lennox	2001–2006	182	94	51.6
Franklin Hagenbeck	2006–2010	157	105	66.9
Totals	33	956	448	46.9
Average		29.0/year	13.6/year	

Notes: Information provided by the Center for the Professional Military Ethic, 14 December 2010, copy in author files. The second column of the table ("Years") is measured in academic years; hence, Lt. Gen. Goodpaster's tenure was from the start of Academic Year 1977–1978 to the end of Academic Year 1980–1981 (a total of four years). The third column ("No. of Cadets Found for Honor") includes both contested cases and cases of self-admission.

increased dramatically. It peaked under Lt. Gen. Franklin Hagenbeck, who granted discretion in over two-thirds of the cases he reviewed.

The increase in discretionary punishment owed to several factors. First, superintendents used discretion as a means of encouraging cadet acceptance of the nontoleration clause. This consideration strongly influenced Superintendent Daniel Christman, who believed that of the honor code's four proscriptions — lying, cheating, stealing, and nontolerating — the last one was the "toughest to internalize." Discretion offered cadets a way out of the "moral dilemma" of whether to turn in a friend for an honor violation.[156] A second reason for the increase in discretion was the availability of new rehabilitative tools, particularly the Honor Mentorship Program and the Army Mentorship Program. The former program, conducted at West Point, required a guilty cadet to undergo a six-month period of self-examination and reflection under the supervision of a faculty or staff member.[157] The latter program, reserved for honor code violators who were separated from the Academy, offered possible redemption through service in the army as an enlisted soldier. If the ex-cadet demonstrated that he had learned from his mistakes and was willing to recommit himself to the ideals of West Point, he could apply to the Academic Board for readmission.[158]

The third, and most important, reason for the trend toward discretionary punishment was the cultural shift that had taken place at the Academy following the 1976 cheating incident. Gone was the notion that the purpose of the honor system — and all other developmental programs — was to cull the weak from the strong. As the attritional model for producing leaders waned, it yielded to a developmental model founded on the assumption that the young men and women admitted as cadets already had the raw materials to be officers. It was up to the Academy to help them reach their potential through the various developmental programs and frequent interactions with faculty and staff mentors. If all went well, cadets would formulate a rigorous honor ethic and embrace throughout their lives beyond the Academy.[159]

Despite these positive trends in character building, a lingering issue undermined the intent and effectiveness of the honor system. By the early twenty-first century, the due-process legal protections and the lawyers who championed them had increasingly become obstacles to the goal of character building. The honor code had always demanded unequivocal integrity in word and deed; accordingly, when confronted by an accuser, a cadet was expected to be completely truthful, even when it led to self-incrimination. Due process challenged that expectation by giving cadets a chance to get "lawyered up" — that is, to seek legal counsel and thus have the time to weigh the advantages and disadvantages of confessing guilt. Defense lawyers used every legal means to have cases dismissed on technicalities, even when the evidence against a cadet was strong.[160] For the accused in such cases, the temptation to avoid punishment often overwhelmed the impulse to tell the truth; in effect, the legal system was at war with the honor system. Cadets let off the hook through the maneuvers of lawyers learned more about how to manipulate the legal system than to live honorably.[161]

The problem of legalism in the honor system defied easy resolution. Lawyers who served as defense counsels applied the law as they knew it; cadets who sought them out understandably desired the best possible legal protection. Weakening the safeguards risked returning the honor system to the tribal justice epitomized by the "silence." Unfortunately, those same protections came with problems of their own. Perhaps the future will bring a better balance between the honor and legal systems, but the tension between them is likely never to be resolved completely.[162]

Many older West Pointers who graduated under the attritional model of character building staunchly defended the system as they remembered it. Despite the supposed weaknesses, they argued, it produced officers of high intellect and character who defended the nation with courage and honor. Many fine officers did indeed graduate from West Point under the attritional model, but that does not establish a causal relationship; more likely, the strong character of West Point officers was in spite of, not because of, that model. Thoughtful observers had long understood the liabilities of absolute standards of honor that permitted no lapses of conduct. One of them, Col. Harry Buckley, was the chairman of the honor-review committee established by Superintendent Berry in 1974. He noted the "paradox" caused by the honor code mandating "an unattainable level of human behavior." Absolute compliance with the code was "unrealistic," he asserted, yet the honor system was "keyed to righteously imposing the ultimate sanction" for every violation. Buckley acknowledged that eliminating the single sanction would require judgments that "lack the simplistic purity" of the past. "But this is the nature of human affairs and cadets should not be encouraged to believe otherwise; men are not simply honorable or dishonorable, but fall all along the continuum between those two positions."[163]

The character-building program of the early twenty-first century, while still evolving, challenged cadets to do more than obey a proscriptive code of honor. It encouraged them to develop a personal honor ethic encompassing all aspects of thought and action. It challenged them to think deeply about questions of morality and ethics and, frequently, to decide what was the most right or the least wrong. Gray areas are unsettling for moral absolutists who prefer precise standards and uncompromising punishments, but gray is the shade of much of the human experience. Since cadets must live and lead in that world, the Academy adjusted its character-building methods to it.

★ ★ ★

From the start of the twentieth century, paternal and attritional assumptions strongly influenced West Point's character-building program. Academy leaders viewed character in two dimensions — personal discipline and moral rectitude. To develop the former, they immersed cadets in a strictly regulated environment and monitored them continuously. To strengthen the latter, they required cadets to live under a prescriptive honor code. Cadets who completed the curriculum and maintained their honor bright were considered to have the character worthy of army officers. Those who failed in either category demonstrated a lack of character and were separated.

Formal establishment of the honor system gave cadets a central role in enforcing the honor code. Cadets took the responsibility seriously, embracing the prohibitions against lying, cheating, stealing, and tolerating violations of the code. Although there was some subjectivity in applying these standards, particularly before the Second World War, for the most part the system was inflexible and unforgiving in its application. Those found guilty of an honor violation either resigned under pressure from the Corps or were discharged as a result of courts-martial.

Two major cheating incidents led officers and cadets to reconsider the wisdom of the nontoleration clause and the single sanction of expulsion. While nontoleration remained an integral part of the honor code, superintendents received authority to levy punishments other than separation for cadets guilty of honor violations. Meanwhile, the Academy took steps to help cadets develop an honor ethic that far exceeded the proscriptions of the honor code. These developments reflected a healthy acknowledgment that human character is imperfect but improvable and that many of the ethical problems facing army officers have no clear solutions. With the new character-building program in place, most cadets graduated from West Point better prepared for the world as it is, rather than the world as we might wish it to be.

CHAPTER NINE

Conclusion

CHARACTER AND INTELLECT

SINCE ITS FOUNDING in 1802, the Military Academy's purpose has remained fixed: to produce leaders of character for the army. Since its centennial in 1902, the Academy's methods of achieving that purpose have undergone dramatic change. Most of those changes were positive. The academic, military, and physical programs, for example, evolved steadily to a high level of excellence. A culture of positive leadership, buoyed by the theoretical concepts of the behavioral sciences, complemented experiential methods of leader development. A comprehensive program of instruction in honor, respect, and professional ethics replaced hard-edged assumptions about human character and its supposed inability to improve. Reforms in the admissions process succeeded for the most part in raising the overall quality of the Corps of Cadets.

These positive changes were compromised, however, by systemic problems that grew increasingly worse in the aftermath of the 1976 cheating incident. The problems, most evident in the areas of governance, admissions, and intercollegiate athletics, blurred the Academy's focus on character and intellect as the key developmental goals. West Point was and is an impressive institution, but until these problems are remedied, it will operate below its potential as a leader development institution for the army and nation.

I. THE LODESTARS—CHARACTER AND INTELLECT

At his fifty-year reunion at West Point in 1965, former President Dwight D. Eisenhower was overheard telling his classmate, Gen. Omar N. Bradley, "You

know, Brad, this goddamn place hasn't changed a friggin' bit since we graduated in 1915."[1] While it is difficult to know what prompted Eisenhower's ill-
tempered comment, there can be no doubt that it was far off the mark. During
the five decades following his graduation, the Academy had in fact changed
dramatically, and the pace of change only accelerated in the subsequent five
decades.

Much of the change resulted from the decline of paternalism at West Point.
Academy leaders originally had designed a structured, controlling environment to insulate cadets from the corrupting influences of life outside the gates.
The extent to which they achieved that goal during the nineteenth century
was uncertain; by the start of the twentieth century, however, they had little
doubt that the disadvantages of the paternal environment outweighed the advantages. Paternalism stifled cadets' learning, stunted their social development,
and denied them leadership opportunities. It was hardly the tool for preparing
young leaders for the challenges they would face as army officers in a turbulent
world. Once Academy leaders recognized these problems, they gradually lifted
one restriction after another. The pace of change accelerated as they observed
the benefits of treating cadets more like adults than children.

The academic and military programs were the greatest beneficiaries of the
decline in paternalism. At the start of the twentieth century, cadets took a rigid
academic curriculum based heavily on mathematics, science, and engineering.
A century later, they enjoyed a rich academic program that imparted intellectual breadth through a diversified core curriculum and intellectual depth
through the implementation of an academic majors program. Similarly, military training expanded in scope and improved in quality, thus giving West
Point graduates a solid base of professional knowledge as they began their
military careers. Cadets still complained about the strictures of Academy life,
but they could not deny the excellence of the developmental opportunities
available to them. The diversity and scope of these opportunities had a positive effect on the quality of West Point graduates and on the stature of institution. By the early twenty-first century, the Academy had achieved a reputation
as an elite undergraduate institution and one of the premier leader development institutions in the world.

The changes at West Point resulted also from a decline in attritional attitudes, although the trend took longer to manifest itself than the waning of
paternalism. By the late twentieth century, a culture of positive leadership dras-
tically reduced the attrition caused by hazing and offered cadets a model for
developing effective leadership styles. Separations for academic failure declined
as deficient cadets took remedial courses during the summers and benefited
from academic-support services; provided they were motivated to succeed,

cadets received ample opportunities to pass their courses even if they arrived at West Point poorly prepared for college work. Tactical officers increasingly assumed the role of coach and mentor in place of the stern, unforgiving task-master of old. Even honor cases resulted in far fewer separations, primarily because superintendents relied heavily on discretionary punishment designed to allow cadets to learn from their mistakes. The totality of these changes led to dramatically higher graduation rates in the late twentieth and early twenty-first centuries.

The decline of paternal and attritional attitudes did not change the focus on character and intellect as the two most important developmental goals at West Point. Still, that focus blurred from time to time. In the area of character de-velopment, for example, two major cheating incidents — one each in 1951 and 1976 — dramatized the weaknesses of the honor system. Out of these troubles came substantial reforms that strengthened character development overall. In the area of intellectual development, the rise of several competing interests — especially extracurricular activities, physical education, military training, and varsity sports — placed greater demands on cadet time. Nonetheless, improve-ments in the quality of the curriculum and faculty (military and civilian) earned West Point a reputation for academic excellence.

Just as the focus on character and intellect secured the Academy's past suc-cesses, it remains the key for future success. Character and intellect take a long time to develop, but they are the most important attributes in determining the quality of West Point graduates and providing enlightened leadership for the army and nation. This is not to say that military and physical training are unim-portant. Junior officers, in particular, rely heavily on tactical competence and physical vigor to accomplish their missions. As one's military career progresses, however, moral courage and depth of intellect are the more probable sources of success, especially for those who rise to senior levels of leadership. Sylvanus Thayer recognized the importance of character and intellect to military officers and therefore designed the Academy to nurture those qualities. Ever since then, the dominance and success of West Point officers in the highest reaches of rank and power have affirmed his wisdom in this regard.[2]

Three systemic problems emerged in the last quarter of the twentieth cen-tury that weakened the focus on character and intellect. The first, governance, was the most serious because of its role in shaping the environment for all other Academy functions, programs, and priorities. A second problem resided in the admissions system, which allowed a large number of lower-quality ap-plicants to enter West Point and thus displace more-qualified applicants. The third problem, closely related to the second, was the effect of intercollegiate athletics on the overall quality of the Corps of Cadets.

II. GOVERNANCE

As noted in chapter 2, the aggregation of power by the superintendent occurred gradually after World War II as West Point expanded in size and scope. Following the 1976 cheating incident, however, the governing authority tilted quickly and decisively in favor of the superintendent. Most outside observers applauded the trend since they viewed the Academic Board as a relic of a simpler time and an obstacle to effective governance. More than anything else, they blamed it for not discerning the problems that led to the EE304 cheating incident. The Academic Board was an easy target, partly because it was indeed in need of reform, but more so because few outsiders understood its true value as the defender of institutional values and priorities.

The rebalancing of the governing equilibrium brought a new set of problems. The Academic Board lost jurisdiction to the newly formed policy board, even in areas that belonged logically to the former body. As a result, the Academic Board gradually became moribund; by the first decade of the twenty-first century, it met infrequently and only to conduct routine business — usually to determine the fate of cadets who had failed one course or another during the semester. No longer did it engage in the substantive policy debates that had formerly characterized its proceedings. In 1959, for example, the intensity of the Academic Board's debate over curriculum reform was so intense that Garrison Davidson later quipped, "Blood was drawn but the wounded lived."[3] Those debates resulted in far-reaching reform that represented Academy governance at its finest. A half-century later, Academic Board members conducted their business docilely, providing polite recommendations to the superintendent on a narrow range of issues. To remind the Academic Board members that their role was advisory only, Superintendent Daniel Christman initiated the practice of closing each meeting with a pointed statement, "I accept the votes of the Academic Board," excepting whatever he vetoed.[4]

There is little chance of going back to the time when the Academic Board was regulatory rather than advisory. No superintendent would advocate such a thing, and army leaders therefore would have no reason to turn back the clock. For better or worse, West Point has migrated to a system of governance better suited to a military organization than an academic institution. Modern superintendents have the freedom to impose their will on the Academy much as they had done in their previous military commands. That they could do so made them less sensitive than they might have been to the issues associated with leading an academic institution. To their collective credit, the superintendents usually acted wisely and thus benefited the institution. There were many exceptions, however, and the continuation of the centralized form of governance leaves open the possibility of many more.

The biggest drawback of centralized governance is the tendency of superintendents to marginalize the very body that has the most to offer them. Members of the Academic Board are long-term professionals who attain their positions through a rigorous selection process that favors intellect, character, professional excellence, and commitment to the institution. Virtually all of them have had many years' experience both as army officers in the field and as scholars and teachers in academia. These attributes give the board members great value as advisors, but that value is wasted unless the superintendent interacts with them regularly. Engaging the Academic Board is the surest way of receiving well-considered advice on all matters relating to cadets, faculty, and the integrated (academic, military, physical, ethical) curriculum. Likewise, it is the surest defense against policies that divert the Academy's focus from the developmental goals of character and intellect.

The focus on character and intellect has blurred on several occasions since the centennial. The first was during World War I, as short-sighted army leaders nearly destroyed West Point by turning it into a training base for a short course in officership. The gains to be had from such a policy were miniscule, yet the potential for long-term damage to the military establishment was great. Fortunately the end of the war came soon enough to forestall the wholesale transformation of the Academy. Even more fortunate was the arrival of Douglas MacArthur to repair the institution's foundation and build anew.

The second blurring was after World War II, as Academy officials allowed enthusiasm for intercollegiate athletics — football in particular — to undermine both academics and honor. The 1951 cheating incident underscored the fragility of institutional values in the face of such outside pressures. In their haste to get the crisis behind them, however, Academy leaders failed to make the necessary changes and establish safeguards to prevent similar problems in the future.

A quarter-century later, a combination of internal and external forces caused the focus on intellect and character to blur yet again. The result, in 1976, was the worst cheating incident in Academy history. Unlike the previous incident, however, this one resulted in a comprehensive examination of all aspects of the Academy. The most comprehensive review, conducted by the West Point Study Group, recommended changes to make governance more efficient (but not necessarily more effective) and to refocus the Academy on the developmental goals of character and intellect. Andrew Goodpaster was a catalyst for the changes, and Dave Palmer brought them to their most refined state.

As the twentieth century drew to a close, the institution's focus blurred anew, and once again the culprit was intercollegiate athletics. Willard Scott used athletics as a means of rebuilding morale and, with the support of army leaders, began the process of elevating sport beyond its ancillary role in cadet development. Subsequent superintendents, with the exception of Palmer and Howard Graves, lent ever-increasing emphasis to intercollegiate athletics at the expense of more important institutional priorities.[5] By the end of the twentieth century, and even more so in the early twenty-first, intercollegiate athletics had assumed a stature on par with the other developmental programs, despite involving only a quarter of the Corps of Cadets. If history is a guide, this misplaced emphasis will eventually bring much grief to the Academy before varsity sports are returned to their important but secondary role in cadet development.

How might the Academy's governance structure be improved? There are many ways to do it, but three points stand out.

Given the centralized command structure now in place, the most effective way to strengthen governance is to select the right officers as superintendents. Ideally, candidates for the position would have broad professional experiences, including instructor duty and leadership of an academic institution, such as the Army War College or the Command and General Staff College. Additionally, they would embody the soldier-scholar ideal and embrace a collaborative style of governance. These credentials are far more important than an officer's branch specialty or record of combat, as Dave Palmer, one of West Point's most successful superintendents, noted shortly before his retirement in 1991. In correspondence to the army chief of staff about the search for the next superintendent, Palmer opined,

> The branch of the officer is not as important as it might be in many other jobs. The "warrior" image is borne mostly by the Commandant; the "scholar" image principally by the Dean. (Which is not to say that the Commandant need not be intelligent nor that the Dean need not be a soldier — both must be exemplars as military leaders.) The Superintendent should be a person of wisdom and balance with a record as a general officer in the field, the school house, and high staff.[6]

A superintendent armed with such attributes would likely have an easier time understanding the difference between commanding a military organization and leading an academic institution. Additionally, the officer probably would have greater empathy for the work of the faculty and staff and thus nurture an environment of mutual trust and cooperation. Finally, such a superintendent would be less likely to pursue short-term policies inimical to the institution's commitment to character and intellect.

Another way to improve governance would be to reinvigorate the Academic Board to provide counsel on all matters related to cadets, faculty, and the integrated curriculum. The Academic Board performed this task to a fault prior to 1976, but its purview narrowed sharply in subsequent years when it became an advisory body only. In the absence of a strong Academic Board, some superintendents relied more on the policy board for counsel, but that body's indistinct charter and short-term membership gave it less stability and therefore less utility.[7] Given the weakness of the Academic Board and the impermanence of the policy board, it is no wonder that the most serious problems now facing the Academy date from the time of the 1976 cheating incident, when the current governance structure took shape.

Reenergizing the Academic Board implies bringing all issues relevant to the Academy's mission under its purview. Examples of those issues include curricular reform, scheduling of cadet time, program integration, program assessment, the honor code and system, admissions, and intercollegiate athletics (as they impact the aforementioned issues). Standing committees composed of representatives from across the Academy could be organized in each area and report to the Academic Board as necessary to conduct business. The superintendent could then benefit from the detailed work of the standing committees and the mature debate of the Academic Board prior to making a final decision. Such a system would be a major improvement over the centralized governance methods that have prevailed at West Point in recent decades.[8]

Finally, greater faculty involvement at all levels would make governance more effective. West Point is blessed with many talented and committed faculty members, but the vast majority of them do not sit on the Academic Board. The ability to tap the wisdom of this group would benefit the institution's most senior leaders. Civilian faculty members — who arrived in force in the mid-1990s and now represent 25 percent of the teaching cadre — are a particularly underused resource. Many of them have achieved high academic rank, but their talents have yet to be fully used at an institution still new to the idea of a strong civilian presence.[9]

III. ADMISSIONS

Nothing is more important to graduating outstanding officers than admitting outstanding young men and women as cadets. The admissions motto, "The Corps Starts Here," is apt justification for wise policies and robust resources in this area. It is therefore surprising to discover how poorly the admissions program has fared since the start of the twenty-first century; not as surprising is the growing number of poorly qualified candidates who have entered West Point during those years. The former trend has much to do with the latter.

For most of the twentieth century, Academy leaders steadily raised the quality of the Corps of Cadets. There were big gains shortly after World War II, when physical fitness became an entrance requirement. Additional improvements occurred during the superintendency of Garrison Davidson, who established the whole-person criteria that are still used as the basis for selecting the most qualified candidates. Another period of reform came during the long tenure of Director of Admissions Manley Rogers, who oversaw the rapid expansion in the number of minorities and the arrival of women in the Corps of Cadets.

In recent years, countervailing forces have weakened the gains in the admissions system. Most serious has been the steep decline in human and financial resources applied to admissions in the 2000s. While the number of applicants to West Point remained high overall, the ability of the admissions office to seek out the best candidates, particularly among hard-to-reach minority populations, suffered. The changes at USMAPS were additional blows to the admissions program. Rather than favoring enlisted soldiers who exhibited officer potential — the original mandate of the preparatory school — USMAPS instead became an entryway for underqualified minorities and recruited athletes who otherwise would have been unlikely to gain admission to West Point. Being accepted at USMAPS was tantamount to receiving an appointment to the Academy; provided a student did not flunk out, drop out, or get kicked out, he or she was virtually certain to become a cadet the following year.[10]

There was nothing inherently wrong with reserving spaces for minorities and recruited athletes; in fact, the Academy and the army potentially benefited by having cadets of diverse race, background, and talent. Reaping those benefits, however, depended on admitting minorities and athletes who at least could meet the Academy's minimum qualifications, and preferably much more. As noted in chapter 3, policy changes in the mid-1990s ensured that the USMAPS graduates, as a whole, would be the weakest segment of the Corps of Cadets. The fact that they comprised 15 percent of each entering class represented a blow to the long-term strength of the officer corps.[11] Whether or not they liked this state of affairs, admissions officials had no choice in the matter because they lacked the resources to find more qualified minorities and athletes.

The dilution of the quality of the Corps of Cadets coincided with historically high attrition rates for West Point officers.[12] Since the 1980s, Academy graduates have resigned their commissions in great numbers; many of the most talented officers were among them.[13] The reasons for the high attrition are hard to pin down, but the fact remains that the pool of top-quality officers drains quickly after graduation from the Academy. It therefore makes sense to make the pool as deep as possible before graduation. The best way to do that is to admit the highest-caliber candidates from the populations most likely to give long-term service to the army — that is, scholars and leaders, not recruited athletes. Unfortunately the policy changes at USMAPS have had much the opposite effect.

The defenders of the status quo argue that cadets who enter West Point through USMAPS graduate at a rate that is only slightly below the rest of the Corps of Cadets. They are correct. The reasons for the high graduation rates reflect the waning of attritional attitudes at the Academy. A multilayered safety net — academic underloading, a strong tutoring program, dedicated academic counselors for athletes, summer school for deficient cadets, liberal use of "turn-back," creation of the Center for Enhanced Performance, and so forth — give even the weakest cadets a good chance of passing their courses.[14] Moreover, the faculty and staff are exceedingly committed as teachers and mentors; consequently, they devote much time and effort to pulling the weak cadets through the eye of the needle to graduation.

Graduating hundreds of such cadets each year speaks well of the academic support system in place at the Academy, but it likely does not produce the best officers for the army. The candidates who enter West Point via USMAPS displace an equal number of candidates who, on average, have far greater potential for officership. To argue otherwise is to dismiss over half a century's experience with the whole-person criteria that define what the Academy considers optimal for success. The army needs the best possible officer talent, and that is what inspired generations of Academy leaders to seek reforms in the admissions system that would yield higher-quality candidates. The current USMAPS admissions policy undermines their effort.

To reverse the negative trends in the admissions program, more human and financial resources are needed. Army budget managers might oppose such a solution, given West Point's success in attracting high numbers of applicants every year; they would claim that the Academy does not need more resources for something it already does well. In response, Academy officials must be forceful and persistent in arguing that the goal is to raise quality, not quantity, and that meeting that goal would improve the character and intellect of the officer corps in the long term.

In the short term, the Academy might draw on the generosity of donors to help fund the admissions program. The money would be most effective in areas where there are big potential gains, such as in minority recruiting. Once the Academy succeeds in admitting higher-caliber candidates, the army would likely be more willing to provide the resources necessary to sustain the effort. In 2010, West Point was far behind the other service academies in the area of minority recruitment. Unless it redresses the problem, it will have no choice but to continue admitting high numbers of underqualified candidates in pursuit of its class-composition goals for minorities.

A second essential corrective to the problems in admissions is to return USMAPS to its original mandate of preparing enlisted soldiers — real enlisted soldiers, not "invitational reservists"—to enter West Point.[15] The army is filled with high-quality soldiers, virtually all of whom are high school graduates with tested leader skills. Since many soldiers are women and minorities, returning USMAPS to its original purpose would not hurt, and would probably help, the Academy's minority recruiting effort. As the quality of the USMAPS student body increases, the quality of the Corps of Cadets would do likewise. The biggest challenge in effecting this change would be to recruit enough enlisted soldiers each year, but a modest increase in resources could yield big results in this area. Enlisted soldiers form a well-defined target population and, in general, they already demonstrate leader skills and a propensity to serve in the military. Under these conditions, the Academy's recruiting dollars would go much farther in the army than in the civilian society.

A third corrective would be to restore the recruiting field force consisting of reserve officers (Military Academy Liaison Officers — MALO) and civilian volunteers (district representatives). [16] They are vital in identifying promising candidates, motivating them to apply, and guiding them through the labyrinthine admissions process. They are particularly useful in supporting the minority recruitment process and in covering areas of the country that are underrepresented in the Corps of Cadets. In the early 1990s, the admissions office had about 350 MALOs in the field; by 2011, the number had dwindled to 67. Similarly, funding for the MALO program declined precipitously from over $200,000 per year in the late 1990s to about $25,000 in 2010.[17] The declines in personnel and money devoted to the field-force mission reflected the fortunes of the West Point admissions program in general.

IV.   INTERCOLLEGIATE ATHLETICS

Of the three most pressing problems facing the Academy today, the heightened emphasis on intercollegiate athletics may be most dangerous of all and the most difficult to solve. Varsity sports have a long and glorious history at West Point, and the fervor of Academy sports fans is legendary. Arguing for a deemphasis on intercollegiate athletics inevitably invites spirited responses from those who see only the positive side of sports. Their vociferous support of intercollegiate athletics would give pause to any reform-minded superintendent; consequently, significant changes may be possible only after the next sports-induced crisis at the Academy.

Economic pressures offer increasing justification for lowering the profile of intercollegiate athletics. Across the nation, only the most successful athletics programs run annual surpluses, thus requiring most institutions to support varsity sports out of their operating funds.[18] West Point has been in the latter group since the 1970s, when the Army Athletic Association no longer had the means to pay the entire athletics bill. Superintendents therefore resorted to siphoning funds from other programs to pay the high cost of sports. As noted in chapter 5, varsity sports consumed over 11 percent of the Academy's budget in 2010, an increase of almost 100 percent from a dozen years earlier. It did not matter that varsity sports were neither a graduation requirement nor an activity common to most cadets. In the competition for scarce resources, intercollegiate athletics trumped every other program at the Academy.

The priority given to intercollegiate athletics might be justified if it advanced the Academy's purpose of producing leaders of character for the army. Unfortunately, the overall effect has been negative, as recruited athletes have displaced higher-quality applicants to West Point for several decades. Varsity sports at West Point began a long decline starting in the 1970s, and Academy leaders worked hard to reverse the trend. Rather than allowing Academy teams to compete at a lower level, however, they chose to seek better athletes, often at the expense of whole-person qualifications. The creation of class-composition goals exacerbated the situation, as the athletics director gained control over nearly one-quarter of each entering class. Whereas the Academy did not always meet its class-composition goals for minorities, the athletics director virtually always got as many recruits as he desired. This arrangement freed the athletics director from having to seek the Academic Board's approval every time he wanted to admit a relatively weak candidate. Instead, he could recruit within his protected class-composition goal — a quota, really — even though the large majority of the candidates he brought in had weaker whole-person credentials than the rest of the class.

Some recruited athletes had high whole-person scores and earned their admission to West Point on that basis alone. In general, however, recruited athletes performed poorly overall. Many of those athletes were among the 15 percent of each entering class that came from USMAPS; many others were athletes whose whole-person credentials were barely high enough to allow direct admission. Whatever their origin, they represented a drain on the overall quality of the Corps of Cadets and underperformed in every area except athletics. Once commissioned, they had less longevity and professional success than their nonathlete classmates.[19]

Ideally, West Point teams should compete at a level that would preclude the need to admit athletes with whole-person credentials that are far below average. Were that to happen, the Academy's varsity teams would be less competitive nationally and donor dollars directed at improving intercollegiate athletics would decline. These are the only significant drawbacks, however — if indeed they are drawbacks — and the advantages would far outweigh them. Among the many benefits, none is more important than allowing the Academy to admit candidates with better overall credentials and thus to graduate cadets with greater potential for officership. Given the Academy's purpose, this should be an overriding argument even for the most ardent supporters of West Point's intercollegiate teams.

Such changes cannot be implemented until the Academy jettisons the class-composition goal for recruited athletes. This goal represents the institution's commitment to an activity that is overly expensive, lowers the quality of the Corps of Cadets, and yields a poor return following graduation. Whereas class-composition goals for racial minorities are appropriate for aligning the demographics of the Corps of Cadets with that of the army and society, there is no comparable justification for recruiting athletes.

From 1996 through 2009, the Academy's football team did not have a single winning season.[20] It did not matter at all in terms of mission accomplishment. There was no discernable drop in the quality of the officers graduated from West Point during that period. The unprecedented thirteen-year drought debunked once and for all the misguided notion that the fortunes of the army and the Academy's football team were inextricably linked. Yet the superintendents during those years went to great lengths to promote the success of the team; in some cases, they made short-sighted decisions that undermined the institution's values and the quality of the Corps of Cadets.

If army and West Point leaders are worried that a poor athletic record adversely affects admissions, then their fears are misplaced. Every shred of evidence indicates that deemphasizing intercollegiate athletics would raise the quality of the Corps of Cadets and keep West Point graduates in the army longer and at higher rank. Moreover, deemphasizing athletics unilaterally (i.e., without the other service academies) would work to West Point's benefit in attracting more of the candidates it purportedly seeks — well-rounded men and women who are mentally bright, physically fit, and of high character. Taking a stand against the commercialized and professionalized world of intercollegiate sports would underscore the Academy's commitment to character and intellect as the top developmental goals. West Point's own studies show that cadet candidates — other than those recruited for athletics — are attracted to the Academy for precisely those reasons.

Douglas MacArthur popularized the idea that the fields of friendly strife help to mold cadets into officers who will achieve victories on "other fields, on other days." Few would disagree with this notion. But MacArthur's dictum does not justify emphasizing intercollegiate athletics to the point of undermining more important Academy priorities. Competitive sports can live in harmony with other developmental goals once Academy leaders set a level of competition that obviates the need to recruit athletic specialists. West Point still would get plenty of talented athletes, and they would fill the rosters of the club teams that win so many championships from year to year and the intramural teams that compete fiercely within the Corps of Cadets. Club and intramural athletes play for the love of the sport under the watchful eyes of the faculty and staff; as a result, they accrue the benefits of competitive athletics that Herman Koehler envisioned over a century ago. Club and intramural sports may never enjoy the spectator appeal and competitiveness of their varsity counterparts, but they are better suited to the developmental mission of the Academy.

V. CODA

Jason Amerine graduated from West Point in 1993. In most ways, he had been an average cadet. He played intramural sports, marched with his cadet company (H-3) during parades, and volunteered as an usher during chapel services. He studied hard to pass his core courses, including an even balance of mathematics, science, and engineering on the one hand and humanities and social sciences on the other. He chose Arabic as his academic major and served as the president of the Arabic language club during his senior year.

In one important way, Amerine was not average. Unlike most of his classmates who were ambivalent about long-term military service, he had little doubt that he would stay in the army for an extended career. He chose the infantry as his initial branch of service, but his long-term goal was to serve as a Special Forces officer. Following six years in the infantry, including assignments in Panama and Korea, Amerine achieved that goal and earned the right to wear the Green Beret.

On 11 September 2001 — the day of the terror strikes against the World Trade Center and the Pentagon — Amerine was in command of Operational Detachment Alpha ("ODA" or "A-team") 574, part of 5th Special Forces Group out of Fort Campbell, Kentucky. The A-team, consisting of Amerine and eleven other Special Forces soldiers, was then in Kazakhstan training with indigenous forces, but it immediately redeployed to Fort Campbell to begin training for a new mission in Afghanistan. ODA 574 was to infiltrate into Oruzgan province, link up with Hamid Karzai and his Pashtun rebel force, and help them overthrow the Taliban regime in the province. The Taliban had begun its rise to power in Oruzgan province, and it was a safe haven for Al Qaeda, the organization responsible for the terror attacks. Successful military operations there would help to destabilize the Taliban's hold throughout the country and deny Al Qaeda refuge.[21]

In early October, Amerine's A-team secretly entered Oruzgan province and made the linkup.[22] Amerine recalled having very little time to "get to know [Karzai], build trust, then go to war."[23] He did so nonetheless, and much more. Over the next two months, ODA 574 helped train Karzai's men while providing the weapons, ammunition, training, food, and money necessary to turn them into an effective fighting force. Amerine led this force on an incredible odyssey that broke the back of the Taliban in Oruzgan province and resulted in the fall of the Taliban regime.

Amerine and his men became Karzai's most valued asset during that time. They organized forces, led attacks and defenses, and called in enormous quantities of precision-guided munitions to disrupt and defeat the enemy. Amerine supervised all these activities; concurrently, he served for the time being as the senior American liaison to Afghanistan's most important political leader. He served Karzai as a military planner, political advisor, and personal confidant. Just as important, he was a key source of intelligence for higher US commanders in the theater of war.

The capital of Oruzgan province is the small town of Tarin Kowt, about fifty miles north of Kandahar and the place where the Taliban began. Fed up with the excesses of Taliban rule, the townspeople killed their mayor in mid-November and drove off his henchmen. Karzai moved in with his small force of two hundred rebels to protect the town and begin the process of fomenting uprisings in areas still under Taliban control. Upon learning of the mayor's demise and the presence of the rebels in Tarin Kowt, the Taliban commander in Kandahar sent a force of about five hundred fighters north to retake the town and defeat the rebels. He did not know that ODA 574 was there with Karzai, but he became painfully aware as events unfolded.

Upon receiving word of the enemy's advance, Amerine positioned part of his A-team on high ground overlooking the wide valley leading to Tarin Kowt. As the enemy column approached, he and his men targeted the vehicles with a lethal rain of precision-guided munitions launched from US aircraft circling overhead. Later, other A-team members directed the defense of Tarin Kowt against Taliban ground forces. After four hours of fighting, the outnumbered rebels had achieved a dramatic victory, sending the remnants of the Taliban force fleeing toward Kandahar. A jubilant Karzai declared a great victory, and local mullahs expressed their satisfaction at the outcome. According to Amerine, it was "psychologically a crushing victory for us."[24]

For the remainder of November, Amerine's men pummeled enemy forces wherever they appeared. They called in continuous airstrikes on Taliban convoys in the area around Tarin Kowt; meanwhile, they organized an increasingly large and effective rebel force for Karzai, who was succeeding in winning the support of tribal leaders. With most of Oruzgan province under his control, and with his military strength growing daily, he resolved to seize Kandahar, the last major Taliban stronghold in Afghanistan. The attack began in early December, with Amerine leading from the front and personally directing the fighting of his team members and the rebel force. The presence of the Americans emboldened the rebels and disheartened the Taliban, who were on the verge of collapse.

On 3 December, as Karzai's force was nearing Kandahar, an American lieutenant colonel and a headquarters element arrived to assume control of combat operations. ODA 574 was pulled off the front line and given a much-deserved break on a hilltop to the rear. As Amerine and his men read the mail that the headquarters element had brought forward, an errant bomb struck their position. Three A-team members and several Afghan fighters were killed and scores were wounded, including Amerine. Despite the tragedy, Kandahar fell to the rebels two days later and the Taliban dispersed into the mountains. In recognition of their heroic service, ODA 574 earned three Silver Stars, seven Bronze Star Medals (three for valor), and eleven Purple Hearts. The A-team's extraordinary performance brought outsized success in a highly uncertain, complex, and lethal environment.

Amerine's success in Afghanistan relied in large part on the superb military training he had received in the US Army. He had attended the basic and advanced infantry courses, as well as the army's airborne and free-fall schools. He had been a top graduate at ranger school, renowned for producing tough, resilient, and confident leaders. He had undergone various Special Forces training courses, which imparted military skills possessed by only the most elite soldiers. In short, he and his teammates in ODA 574 were among the best trained fighters in the world.

He also benefited from a high level of physical fitness. As an infantry and Special Forces officer, he exercised regularly and led a healthy lifestyle. He sharpened his physical skills to ensure success at the many army schools he attended. He had always been in good shape overall, but as an officer he focused principally on those activities he expected to undertake during operational missions. Hence, much of his conditioning in the army consisted of marching long distances, carrying heavy loads, and enduring fatigue and hardship.

Amerine's most important preparation, however, came long before he set foot in Afghanistan or even before he became an officer. It consisted of the long-term development of character and intellect that enabled him to give form and direction to the military skills he would acquire in the army. West Point was certainly not the only place where he developed character and intellect, but just as certainly it was the most important place.[25] For four years he lived in a developmental environment that required absolute integrity and adherence to the noble values of the professional military ethic. At the same time, he completed a rigorous course of study whose overarching goal was to produce leaders who can "anticipate and respond effectively to the uncertainties of a changing technological, social, political, and economic world."[26] Amerine was unusually serious about his studies, as he majored in a discipline — Arabic — that he believed would have direct application to his military career. Even if he had chosen a different major, however, he would have benefited equally from the intellectual broadening of a high-quality liberal-arts education. Looking back on the leadership challenges he faced in Afghanistan, he noted, "You aren't going to have every answer. It's going to be a lot more art than science."[27] That is precisely the environment in which leaders of character and intellect thrive most.

If West Point is to continue its past success, if it is to produce even better officers in the future, there is no surer way than to focus intensely on character and intellect. The Academy's greatest leaders have understood this imperative and focused their strategic vision on it. Its future leaders would do well to do the same.

Appendix A

SUPERINTENDENTS

Name	Class	Tenure	Remarks
Williams, Jonathan	—	1801–1803	Resigned 20 June 1803
Williams, Jonathan	—	1805–1812	Reappointed 19 April 1805
Swift, Joseph Gardner	1802	1812–1814	First West Point graduate
Partridge, Alden	1806	1814–1817	
Thayer, Sylvanus	1808	1817–1833	
DeRussy, Rene Edward	1812	1833–1838	
Delafield, Richard	1818	1838–1845	
Brewerton, Henry	1819	1845–1852	
Lee, Robert Edward	1829	1852–1855	
Barnard, Jon Gross	1833	1855–1856	
Delafield, Richard	1818	1856–1861	
Beauregard, Pierre Gustave T.	1838	1861–1861	23–28 January 1861
Delafield, Richard	1818	1861–1861	28 January– 1 March 1861
Bowman, Alexander Hamilton	1825	1861–1864	
Tower, Zealous Bates	1841	1864–1864	8 July– 8 September 1864
Cullum, George Washington	1833	1864–1866	
Pitcher, Thomas Gamble	1845	1866–1871	
Ruger, Thomas Howard	1854	1871–1876	
Schofield, John McAllister	1853	1876–1881	
Howard, Oliver Otis	1854	1881–1882	
Merritt, Wesley	1860	1882–1887	
Parke, John Grubb	1849	1887–1889	
Wilson, John M.	1860	1889–1893	
Ernst, Oswald H.	1864	1893–1898	
Mills, Albert Leopold	1879	1898–1906	
Scott, Hugh Lenox	1876	1906–1910	
Barry, Thomas Henry	1877	1910–1912	

Name	Class	Tenure	Remarks
Townsley, Clarence Page	1881	1912–1916	
Biddle, John	1881	1916–1917	
Tillman, Samuel Escue	1869	1917–1919	
MacArthur, Douglas	1903	1919–1922	
Sladen, Fred Winchester	1890	1922–1926	Commandant, 1911–1914
Stewart, Merch Brandt	1896	1926–1927	Commandant, 1923–1926
Winans, Edwin Baruch	1891	1927–1928	
Smith, William Ruthven	1892	1928–1932	
Connor, William D.	1897	1932–1938	
Benedict, Jay Leland	1904	1938–1940	
Eichelberger, Robert Lawrence	1909	1940–1942	
Wilby, Francis Bowditch	1905	1942–1945	
Taylor, Maxwell Davenport	1922	1945–1949	
Moore, Bryant Edward	August 1917	1949–1951	
Irving, Frederick Augustus	April 1917	1951–1954	Commandant, 1941–1942
Bryan, Blackshear Morrison	14 June 1922	1954–1956	
Davidson, Garrison Holt	1927	1956–1960	
Westmoreland, William Childs	1936	1960–1963	
Lampert, James Benjamin	1936	1963–1966	
Bennett, Donald V.	1940	1966–1968	
Koster, Samuel William	1942	1968–1970	
Knowlton, William Allen	January 1943	1970–1974	
Berry, Sidney Bryan	1948	1974–1977	
Goodpaster, Andrew Jackson	1939	1977–1981	
Scott, Willard Warren, Jr.	1948	1981–1986	
Palmer, Dave Richard	1956	1986–1991	
Graves, Howard Dwayne	1961	1991–1996	
Christman, Daniel William	1965	1996–2001	
Lennox, William James, Jr.	1971	2001–2006	
Hagenbeck, Franklin Lee	1971	2006–2010	
Huntoon, David Holmes, Jr.	1973	2010–	

Appendix B

COMMANDANTS

Name	Class	Tenure	Remarks
Gardiner, George W.	1814	1817–1818	
Bliss, John	—	1818–1819	
Bell, John R.	1812	1819–1820	
Worth, William J.	—	1820–1828	
Hitchcock, Ethan Allen	1817	1829–1833	
Fowle, John	—	1833–1838	
Smith, Charles Ferguson	1825	1838–1842	
Thomas, John Addison	1833	1842–1845	
Alden, Bradford Ripley	1831	1845–1852	
Garnett, Robert Selden	1841	1852–1854	
Walker, William Henry Talbot	1837	1854–1856	
Hardee, William Joseph	1838	1856–1860	
Reynolds, John Fulton	1841	1860–1861	
Augur, Christopher Columbus	1843	1861–1861	August–December 1861
Garrard, Kenner	1851	1861–1862	
Clitz, Henry Boynton	1845	1862–1864	
Tidball, John Caldwell	1848	1864–1864	July–September 1864
Black, Henry M.	1847	1864–1870	
Upton, Emory	1861	1870–1875	
Neill, Thomas H.	1847	1875–1879	
Lazelle, Henry M.	1855	1879–1882	
Hasbrouck, Henry Cornelius	May 1861	1882–1888	
Hawkins, Hamilton S.	—	1888–1892	
Mills, Samuel Meyers, Jr.	1865	1892–1897	
Hein, Otto Louis	1882	1897–1901	
Treat, Charles Gould	1882	1901–1905	
Howze, Robert Lee	1888	1905–1909	
Sibley, Frederick William	1874	1909–1911	
Sladen, Fred Winchester	1890	1911–1914	Superintendent, 1922–1926

Name	Class	Tenure	Remarks
Smith, Morton F.	1895	1914–1916	
Henry, Guy V.	1898	1916–1918	
Bugge, Jens	1895	1918–1919	
Danford, Robert Melville	1904	1919–1923	
Stewart, Merch Brandt	1896	1923–1926	Superintendent, 1926–1927
Hodges, Campbell Blackshear	1903	1926–1929	
Richardson, Robert Charlwood, Jr.	1904	1929–1933	
Buckner, Simon Bolivar, Jr.	1908	1933–1936	
McCunniff, Dennis Edward	1913	1936–1937	
Ryder, Charles Wolcott	1915	1937–1941	
Irving, Frederick Augustus	April 1917	1941–1942	Superintendent, 1951–1954
Gallagher, Philip Edward	June 1918	1942–1943	
Honnen, George	1920	1943–1946	
Higgins, Gerald Joseph	1934	1946–1948	
Harkins, Paul D.	1929	1948–1951	
Waters, John Knight	1931	1951–1952	
Michaelis, John Hersey	1936	1952–1954	
Messinger, Edwin John	1931	1954–1956	
Throckmorton, John Lathrop	1935	1956–1959	
Rich, Charles Wythe Gleaves	1935	1956–1961	
Stilwell, Richard Giles	1938	1961–1963	
Davidson, Michael Shannon	1939	1963–1965	
Scott, Richard Pressly	1941	1965–1967	
Rogers, Bernard William	June 1943	1967–1969	
Walker, Sam Sims	1946	1969–1972	
Feir, Philip Robert	1949	1972–1975	
Ulmer, Walter Francis, Jr.	1952	1975–1977	
Bard, John Chapman	1954	1977–1979	
Franklin, Joseph Powel	1955	1979–1982	
Moellering, John Henry	1959	1982–1984	
Boylan, Peter James, Jr.	1961	1984–1987	
Gorden, Fred Augustus	1962	1987–1989	
Bramlett, David Anthony	1964	1989–1992	
Foley, Robert Franklin	1963	1992–1994	
McFarren, Freddy E.	1966	1994–1995	
St. Onge, Robert Joseph	1969	1995–1997	
Abizaid, John P.	1973	1997–1999	
Olson, Eric Thorne	1972	1999–2002	
Brooks, Leo A., Jr.	1979	2002–2004	

Name	Class	Tenure	Remarks
Scaparrotti, Curtis M.	1978	2004–2006	
Caslen, Robert L., Jr.	1975	2006–2008	
Linnington, Michael S.	1980	2008–2009	
Rapp, William E.	1984	2009–2011	
Martin, Theodore D.	1983	2011–	

Appendix C

DEANS OF THE ACADEMIC BOARD

Name	Class	Tenure	Remarks
Alexander, Roger Gordon	1907	1945–1947	Acting Dean, 1945–1946
Jones, Harris	April 1917	1947–1956	Acting Dean, 1947
Stamps, Thomas Dodson	August 1917	1956–1957	
Counts, Gerald Alford	August 1917	1957–1959	
Bessell, William Weston, Jr.	1920	1959–1965	
Jannarone, John Robert	1938	1965–1973	
Smith, Frederick Adair, Jr.	1944	1974–1985	
Flint, Roy K.	—	1985–1990	
Galloway, Gerald Edward, Jr.	1957	1990–1995	
Lamkin, Fletcher McCarthy	1964	1995–2000	
Kaufman, Daniel Joseph	1968	2000–2005	
Finnegan, Patrick	1971	2005–2010	
Trainor, Timothy E.	1983	2010–	

Appendix D

MASTERS OF THE SWORD

Name	Class	Tenure	Remarks
Thomas, Pierre	—	1814–1825	Civilian
Tranque, Pierre	—	1825–1827	Civilian
Simon, Louis S.	—	1827–1832	Civilian
Jumel, N. Albert	—	1832–1837	Civilian
Dupare, Ferdinand	—	1837–1840	Civilian
Boulet, H. G.	—	1840–1843	Civilian
Wayne, Henry C.	1838	1843–1846	
De Janon, Patrice	—	1846–1857	Civilian
Lorentz, Antone	—	1858–1882	Civilian
Farrow, Edward S.	1876	1882–1884	
Koehler, Herman J.	—	1885–1923	Commissioned in 1901
Hoge, Benjamin F.	1914	1924–1924	January–July
Stearns, Cuthbert P.	1909	1924–1927	
Kelly, Edward L.	1909	1927–1930	
Byers, Clovis Ethelbert	1920	1930–1930	March–June
Rayner, Harold M.	1912	1930–1934	
Miley, William M.	June 1918	1934–1934	April–June
Holbrook, Willard A., Jr.	November 1918	1934–1938	
Smythe, George W.	1924	1938–1940	
Harmony, John W.	1923	1940–1943	
Fritzsche, Carl F.	1928	1943–1944	
Greene, Francis M.	1922	1944–1952	
Machen, Edwin A., Jr.	1938	1952–1953	
Kobes, Frank J., Jr.	1939	1953–1974	Permanent position, 1959
Anderson, James L.	1956	1974–1997	
LeBoeuf, Maureen	—	1997–2004	
Daniels, Gregory	—	2004–	

Appendix E

GRADUATE MANAGERS OF ATHLETICS

Name	Class	Tenure	Remarks
Ridgway, Matthew B.	April 1917	1922–1924	
Copthorne, William A.	1913	1924–1927	
Fleming, Philip B.	1911	1927–1933	
Worsham, Ludson D.	1916	1933–1936	
Devers, Jacob L.	1909	1936–1938	
Hibbs, Louis E.	1916	1938–1942	
Jones, Lawrence McC.	August 1917	1942–1948	
Broshous, Charles R.	1933	1948–1948	June–July
Krueger, Orrin C.	1931	1948–1951	
Draper, Philip H., Jr.	1929	1951–1953	
Schwenk, James T. L.	1939	1953–1956	
Roberts, Francis J.	1942	1956–1959	

DIRECTORS OF INTERCOLLEGIATE ATHLETICS

Name	Class	Tenure	Remarks
Blaik, Earl H.	1920	1948–1959	Civilian (commissioned during World War II)
Roberts, Francis J.	1942	1959–1959	Acting, February–July
Adams Emory S., Jr.	1940	1959–1963	
Murphy, Raymond P.	1942	1963–1966	
Capka, Jerry G.	1944	1966–1968	
Dielens, August J., Jr.	1950	1969–1971	
Schuder, William J.	1947	1971–1976	
Call, William T., Jr.	—	1976–1977	Acting
Murphy, Raymond P.	1942	1977–1980	Major General (retired)
Johnson, Charles R.	1955	1980–1980	Acting, May–September

Name	Class	Tenure	Remarks
Ullrich, Carl F.	—	1980–1990	Civilian
Vanderbush, Albert, III	1961	1990–1999	Colonel (retired)
Greenspan, Richard I.	—	1999–2004	Civilian
Knowlton, James A.	1982	2004–2005	Acting
Anderson, Kevin B.	—	2005–2010	Civilian
Johnson, Samuel H.	1982	2010–2011	Acting
Corrigan, Eugene F.	—	2011–	Civilian

Notes

CHAPTER ONE

1. US Military Academy, *The Centennial of the United States Military Academy 1802–1902*, vol. 1, 20. A media account of the day's events is in "Day of Glory for West Point," *New York Times*, 12 June 1902, 1.

2. There are several competent surveys of the history of the Military Academy. The best one is also the most recent: Crackel, *West Point: A Bicentennial History*. See also Ambrose, *Duty, Honor, Country: A History of West Point*; Forman, *West Point: A History of the United States Military Academy*; and Fleming, *West Point: The Men and Times of the United States Military Academy*.

3. George Washington, "Sentiments on a Peace Establishment," 2 May 1783, in *The Writings of George Washington from the Original Manuscript Sources, 1745–1799*, John C. Fitzpatrick, ed., 39 vols. (Washington, D.C.: Government Printing Office, 1931–44), vol. 26, 374–76.

4. George Washington to Alexander Hamilton, 12 December 1799, quoted in Forman, *West Point*, 16.

5. *An Act providing for raising and organizing a Corps of Artillerists and Engineers*, 9 May 1794, *Statutes at Large*, 3rd Cong., 1st Sess., 1: 366–67. To clarify, the Corps of Artillerists and Engineers was a single command that included a mix of artillery batteries and engineer companies.

6. *An Act to augment the Army of the United States, and for other purposes*, 16 July 1798, *Statutes at Large*, 5th Cong., 2nd Sess., 1: 605; *An Act for the better organizing of the Troops of the United States; and for other purposes*, 3 March 1799, Statutes at Large, 5th Cong., 3rd Sess., 1: 749–55.

7. The most detailed plan, drafted by Alexander Hamilton, envisioned a network of five schools. Other proposals were drafted by Gen. Benjamin Lincoln, Baron von Steuben, Gen. Jedediah Huntington, Secretary of War Timothy Pickering, and others. Several suggested West Point as a favorable location. Forman, *West Point*, 16.

8. Part of the problem in hiring the teachers was Adams's "invincible aversion to the appointment of foreigners." Unfortunately, there was a dearth of qualified Americans for the teaching positions. Adams to Secretary of War Samuel Dexter, 25 July 1800, quoted in Crackel, *West Point*, 42. Adams began appointing cadets in May 1800, but no more than a dozen were at West Point by March 1802. US Military Academy, *Centennial*, vol. 2, 49.

9. *An Act Fixing the Military Peace Establishment of the United States*, 16 March 1802, *Statutes at Large*, 7th Cong., 1st Sess., 2: 137.

10. In the short term, Jefferson favored the sons of Republicans to counterbalance the Federalist influence in the officer corps.

11. The irony of Jefferson — the prototypical Republican and staunch opponent of standing armies — supporting the creation of a military academy generated much historical debate. Stephen Ambrose advanced the view that Jefferson, acting on Enlightenment principles, searched for a "rational, revolutionary defense policy, one that would defend the state at the least possible cost and the smallest conceivable risk." The key to such a policy was an officer corps whose members came from the society at large, could expand the army and command citizen-soldiers in time of war, and would stay aloof from politics. Equally important was to create an officer corps trained in the sciences and willing to "use their knowledge for the benefit of society." *Duty, Honor, Country*, 6, 18. Theodore Crackel found Ambrose's explanation incomplete. Instead, he ascribed the creation of the Academy to Jefferson's "effort to break the Federalists' hold on the strings of government. . . .The President's new school would prepare loyal young Republicans for commissioned service in his reformed army." *West Point*, 50.

12. The Royal Military Academy was founded in 1741. The École de Génie was founded in 1748; in 1794, it became the École Polytechnique.

13. John Keegan, *The Mask of Command* (New York: Viking Press, 1987), 177–80.

14. Williams quoted in Moten, *The Delafield Commission and the American Military Profession*, 28.

15. Theodore Crackel cautions against exaggerating the extent of the scientific education at West Point in the earliest years. "While other institutions were offering higher mathematics, astronomy, natural philosophy, and chemistry as a matter of course, the Military Academy offered only the rudiments of mathematics and military fortification. . . . In many ways the curriculum was more like that of a secondary or even an elementary school than a college." *West Point*, 48.

16. For a detailed account of the United States Military Philosophical Society, see Forman, *West Point*, 20–35. Indicative of the Society's prominence was its impressive list of members, including Thomas Jefferson, James Madison, John Quincy Adams, James Monroe, John Marshall, DeWitt Clinton, Robert Fulton, Eli Whitney, Joel Barlow, and Bushrod Washington. The Society ceased to exist in 1813, following Williams' resignation as superintendent and the start of hostilities with England, both in 1812.

17. In the years leading up to the War of 1812, Williams designed and supervised the construction of the defensive fortifications in New York Harbor. One of the fortifications (Castle Williams) bears his name.

18. The prohibition against engineer officers commanding nonengineer units originated during the Revolutionary War, when most of the engineers were foreigners. Given the establishment of the Military Academy, Williams viewed the prohibition as obsolete and insulting. Jefferson's refusal to lift the prohibition induced Williams to resign his post in June 1803, although he returned in April 1805 upon receiving a new commission as a lieutenant colonel. Forman, *West Point*, 26.

19. Moten, *The Delafield Commission*, 29; Crackel, *West Point*, 70–71.

20. The legislation is confusing on the authorized size of the student body. It states an upper limit of 250 cadets, but this number is for "artillery, cavalry, riflemen or infantry"

cadets only. The number does not include the ten engineer cadets allowed under previous legislation, which would bring the total to 260.

21. Congress did not bestow the title of "professor" on the teacher of drawing or the teacher of French until 1846.

22. *An Act Making Further Provision for the Corps of Engineers*, 29 April 1812, *Statutes at Large*, 12th Cong., 1st Sess., 2: 720–21. While the frustrations just described influenced Williams' decision to resign, more decisive was the administration's refusal to give him the wartime command of the fortifications he had built in New York Harbor.

23. Swift appointed Adam Empie, an Episcopal minister, to serve concurrently as the West Point chaplain and the teacher of geography, history, and ethics. He appointed Pierre Thomas as the swordmaster. Swift, *The Memoirs of Gen. Joseph Gardner Swift, LL. D., U.S.A.*, 111, 123; Crackel, *West Point*, 73.

24. Ambrose, *Duty, Honor, Country*, 55–56.

25. Morrison, *"The Best School in the World," West Point, the Pre-Civil War Years, 1833–1866*, 3; Crackel, *West Point*, 72–73.

26. Crackel, *West Point*, 76–80. Partridge was found guilty of disobedience to orders and mutiny. The charges stemmed from his refusal to yield command of West Point to Sylvanus Thayer.

27. Despite the poor showing overall, West Pointers distinguished themselves in the fighting. There were eighty-nine Academy graduates at the start of the War of 1812. Of the sixty-five graduates in active service, one-sixth were killed in action and several more were wounded. One-fifth of the survivors received one or more brevet promotions for meritorious service as engineer officers. Forman, *West Point*, 34–35.

28. Swift, *Memoirs*, 138.

29. Ambrose, *Duty, Honor, Country*, 65–66; Moten, *The Delafield Commission*, 30–31.

30. My understanding of the Thayer years at West Point draws heavily on Moten, *The Delafield Commission*, 30–38, and Crackel, *West Point*, 81–105.

31. Col. John E. Wool, the army's inspector general, objected to the imposition of an engineering curriculum for all cadets. In 1819, he reminded Secretary of War John C. Calhoun that "the great victories which had called forth the admiration of every age were not achieved by 'the rule and compass' or 'the measurement of angles.'" Quoted in Morrison, *"The Best School in the World,"* 24.

32. Ibid., 24; Ambrose, *Duty, Honor, Country*, 75.

33. *An Act to procure the necessary surveys, plans, and estimates upon the subject of roads and canals*, 30 April 1824, *Statues at Large*, 18th Cong., 1st Sess., 4:22–23.

34. Thayer to Chief of Engineers Alexander Macomb, 14 December 1825, quoted in Crackel, *West Point*, 53. In passing the 1824 legislation, Congress unwittingly opened the Academy to criticism that it was a bastion of privilege and elitism. Many West Point graduates, lured by the promise of high pay, resigned their commissions to take lucrative civilian jobs in engineering. The fact that they had received their education at government expense embittered the Academy's critics. In light of these and other criticisms, Congress repealed the act in 1838. For more on this topic, see Robert P. Wetteman Jr., "West Point, the Jacksonians, and the Army's Controversial Role in National Improvements," in Lance Betros, ed., *West Point: Two Centuries and Beyond*, 144–66.

35. Ambrose, *Duty, Honor, Country*, 147.

36. US War Department, *General Regulations for the Army*, 342. The only authorized absence from West Point was the summer-long furlough at the conclusion of the second year. All other absences required the special approval of Academy leaders.

37. The "eggnog riot," on Christmas Eve of 1826, reflected the disciplinary problems of the Corps. Cadet Jefferson Davis and other southerners invited classmates to drink with them. The cadets were soon inebriated and caused significant damage to the barracks. Thayer eventually expelled nineteen of the cadets. Davis was awarded a lesser punishment and remained a cadet. Crackel, *West Point*, 88.

38. Woodbridge to Gen. George Cullum, 25 October 1872, quoted in Forman, *West Point*, 49.

39. Although the student body at West Point was commonly called the Corps of Cadets, in the 1820s there were at most four companies, or roughly a battalion.

40. The summer encampment, another of Thayer's innovations, met the requirement of the 1812 legislation that required cadets to be "encamped at least three months of each year" for military training. A description of the encampment is in chapter 6.

41. *Annual Report of the Superintendent*, 1896, 124–25.

42. Thayer to the academic staff, August 1817, in Adams, *The West Point Thayer Papers, 1808–1872*.

43. US War Department, *General Regulations for the Army*, 327.

44. An excellent analysis of the composition, responsibilities, and influence of the Academic Board is in Crackel, *West Point*, 94–96.

45. *General Regulations for the Army*, 327–28. The Board of Visitors under Thayer included many prominent Americans, such as DeWitt Clinton (governor of New York), Oliver Wolcott (governor of Connecticut), Sam Houston (congressman from Tennessee).

46. *An Act making appropriations for the support of the army and of the military academy . . .* , 1 March 1843, *Statutes at Large*, 27th Cong., 3rd sess., 5: 606.

47. Detailed admission information by year appears in Reed, *Cadet Life at West Point*, appendix, xv. The Academic Board administered the entrance examinations orally through 1870; thereafter all examinations were written. US Military Academy, *Centennial*, 1:229.

48. Reed, *Cadet Life at West Point*, appendix, xiv–xv. Compounding the attrition problem was the fact that some of the young men nominated for cadetships never reported to West Point. The no-show rate for the years from 1840 through 1859 was just under 7 percent.

49. *The Centennial of the United States Military Academy 1802–1902*, vol. 2, 120.

50. Croffut, *Fifty Years in Camp and Field*, 67. In addition to Jackson's hostility, Thayer was stung by vocal critics of the Academy in Congress, as well as publication of Alden Partridge's vitriolic attack on West Point, *The Military Academy, at West Point, Unmasked: or, Corruption and Military Despotism Exposed* (Washington, DC: J. Elliot, 1830). Upon his resignation as superintendent, Thayer was reassigned and eventually retired in 1863 with the rank of brigadier general. Jackson died in 1845 and was buried at his Tennessee estate, known as the Hermitage. Ironically, a few years after Jackson's death, the governor of Tennessee proffered to the federal government a five hundred acre parcel of the Hermitage—including Jackson's mansion and tomb—provided the government would use the site as "a

branch of the Military Academy at West Point." Although Congress declined the offer, one must assume that Jackson turned over in his grave while Thayer had a good laugh. Senate Committee on Military Affairs, *Act of the Legislature of Tennessee, Respecting the Purchase of the Hermitage*, report accompanying bill S587, prepared by Senator James C. Jones, 12 February 1857, 34th Cong., 3rd sess., 1.

51. Although Thayer had resigned by the time Bartlett and Church received their appointments to professor, he had known them very well as cadets and junior officers and groomed them for future service on the faculty. Bartlett, for example, graduated first in his class and served as an assistant mathematics instructor during his last two years as a cadet. Shortly after graduation, he served for two years as an assistant instructor of engineering. Church likewise graduated first in his class. Upon graduation, he immediately joined the faculty and served his entire career at West Point.

52. The 1812 legislation, previously discussed, gave legal authority to the "academical staff," interpreted to mean the Academic Board. Starting in 1821, the War Department's regulations for the Military Academy formalized the structure of the Academic Board and specified its powers and responsibilities.

53. Forman, *West Point*, 72.

54. Winfield Scott, report to Congress, 25 July 1860, quoted in Forman, *West Point*, 61.

55. *Report of the Board of Visitors*, 1838, 7.

56. Crackel, *West Point*, 127.

57. The most thorough account of the five-year curriculum is Morrison, "*The Best School in the World*," 114–25.

58. Because of the five-year curriculum, there were five classes at West Point at the outbreak of the Civil War. On 6 May 1861, the War Department graduated the senior class, and the following month it graduated the next senior class. The removal of the top two classes meant that there would be only four classes at West Point once the new plebe class entered in July. This situation allowed the Academic Board to return to the four-year curriculum for the duration of the war, and the five-year experiment was never repeated.

59. Of the 278 cadets assigned at the start of the war, eighty-six were southerners; of these, sixty-five resigned. Superintendent Bowman ordered all remaining cadets to take an oath of allegiance. All of them did so eventually and fought for the Union. Ambrose, *Duty, Honor, Country*, 172.

60. Williams, "The Attack upon West Point during the Civil War," 491–504. Cameron accused West Point graduates of "extraordinary treachery" and suggested that the mass defections represented a "radical defect in the system of education" at West Point (493). Senator James H. Lane commented mordantly that if the Confederacy should win the war, an appropriate epitaph for the United States would be "Died of West Point pro-slaveryism" (503).

61. Academy leaders painstakingly quantified the contributions of West Pointers during the Civil War. According to Charles Larned, at the conclusion of the war "all the armies in the field on both sides were commanded by graduates; nearly all the corps; a large majority of the divisions; the staff corps of organization, of supply, and of science of both forces; and many of the brigades. Every important battle of the war was commanded on one or both sides by a graduate—generally both. Out of sixty on the list given below, containing

all the very important battles and campaigns, all but five were commanded on both sides by graduates. Of the five exceptions the Army on one side was commanded by a graduate, and in four of these was victorious." Larned, "The Genius of West Point," in *Centennial*, 1: 489.

62. Thayer advocated a division of the curriculum after the second year. Cadets strong in mathematics would continue with the current course of study, while the others would take studies more helpful for the combat branches of the army. Ambrose, *Duty, Honor, Country*, 208–09.

63. Curriculum reform was an issue raised frequently by the Board of Visitors, senior army leaders, civilian academics, and superintendents. In 1891, for example, the adjutant general of the army, John C. Kelton, recommended a division of the curriculum into two tracks — one for engineers, artillery, and ordnance and one for infantry and cavalry. Letter from Kelton to the Board of Visitors, 9 June 1891, in *Annual Report of the Board of Visitors*, 1891, 20.

64. Horace Porter, "Address by the Orator of the Day," in *Centennial*, vol. 1, 37.

65. Ellis and Moore, *School for Soldiers: West Point and the Profession of Arms*, 40–41. Most educators had rejected the theory of transference by the 1920s. *School for Soldiers*, 41, note 24.

66. Charles Larned, "The Genius of West Point," in *Centennial*, vol. 1, 480.

67. The most prominent advocate of the elective principle in higher education was Charles W. Eliot, president of Harvard from 1869 to 1909. Frederick Rudolph discusses Eliot's legacy in *The American College and University: A History*, 290–95.

68. Quoted in Crackel, *West Point*, 160.

69. US Military Academy, *Annual Report of the Superintendent*, 1896, 23.

70. Simons, *Liberal Education in the Service Academies*, 56. The new training emphasis was evident in Congress' 1866 decision to allow the superintendent to be an officer of any branch of the army, rather than, as formerly, restricting the position to officers of the Corps of Engineers.

71. Crackel, *West Point*, 141. Crackel also argues that the first postwar superintendent, Thomas Gamble Pitcher, proved "ineffectual" in maintaining an adequate level of discipline. Pitcher was the first nonengineer officer to be appointed superintendent following the 1866 law that allowed officers of any branch of service to hold the position. Pitcher's tenure, observed Crackel, "was so undistinguished that it is tempting to suggest that he was appointed to demonstrate the imprudence of this departure from tradition" (141–42).

72. Ambrose, *Duty, Honor, Country*, 225.

73. Comments of Samuel E. Tillman (class of 1869), professor of chemistry, mineralogy, and geology from 1880 to 1911 and superintendent from 1917 to 1919. *Annual Report of the Superintendent*, 1918, 6.

74. *Centennial*, vol. 2, 118–23. These pages list a chronology of events pertaining to hazing and the efforts of authorities to stop it. The measures included a War Department requirement that cadets sign a pledge that they would not engage in hazing plebes.

75. Hein, *Memories of Long Ago*, 263–64.

76. "Victim of Hazing at West Point Dies in Agony," *New York Journal*, December 4, 1900.

77. *Military Academy Appropriations Act of 1901*, 2 March 1901, *Statutes at Large*, 56th

Cong., 2nd sess. A detailed account of hazing in general and the Booz hazing incident in particular is Philip W. Leon, *Bullies and Cowards: The West Point Hazing Scandal, 1898–1901* (Westport, CT: Greenwood Press, 2000).

78. Lewis Sorley relates the case of Cadet Orsemus Boyd, who in 1865 was forced by upper classmen to leave the Academy for allegedly committing a theft. Boyd was innocent and very lucky. Superintendent George Cullum happened to see him in civilian clothes heading toward the dock. After hearing Boyd's story, Cullum initiated an investigation that exonerated the cadet. He described the actions of the upper classmen as a "flagrant outrage" and "highly subversive of good order and military discipline;" still, he defended the motives of the upper classmen, who "acted upon a high sense of honor." Sorley, *Honor Bright*, 27.

79. My understanding of the physical development program at West Point during the nineteenth century relies heavily on Forman, *West Point*, 175–85, and Robert Degen, "The Evolution of Physical Education at the United States Military Academy" (West Point: Office of Physical Education, 1967), 17–31.

80. US Military Academy, *Report of the Board of Visitors*, 1826, 13.

81. Ibid., 1881, 7.

82. The title of "Sword Master" was changed to "Master of the Sword" in 1881. Forman, *West Point*, 176.

83. *Annual Report of the Superintendent*, 1892, 7. The greatest weakness of the physical education program—one that Koehler was the first to admit—was its exclusive focus on the fourth class. Only plebes had mandatory physical training, whereas upper classmen were expected to maintain voluntarily the fitness they had developed as plebes. Koehler recommended that cadets of all classes undergo daily physical training, but nothing came of the recommendation until after World War I.

84. Special Orders No. 120, 2 November 1847, in US Military Academy, "Post Orders."

85. Forman, *West Point*, 176, 182.

86. The Naval Academy had fielded a football team since 1879; between 1886 and 1890, they played a total of twenty-one games, winning twelve of them. At West Point, only Leonard Prince, Butler Ames, and Dennis Michie had ever played the game. Michie was the team captain and coach in 1890 and 1891. As an officer, he was killed in action during the Spanish-American War. The football stadium at West Point is named in his honor. Schoor, *100 Years of Army-Navy Football*, 2–3.

87. The AOAA sponsored all intercollegiate and intramural athletics, not just football. Intercollegiate football and baseball started in 1890; basketball was added in 1893 and fencing in 1902. Intramural sports included bowling, gymnastics, and general athletics (track and field events). The menu of competitive sports, both intercollegiate and intramural, expanded rapidly in the twentieth century. Degen, "The Evolution of Physical Education at the United States Military Academy," 50.

88. *Annual Report of the Superintendent*, 1894, 27.

89. There was no Army-Navy football game from 1894 through 1898 or in 1909, 1917, 1918, 1928, and 1929.

90. Charles Larned, "West Point and Our Military Future," 151–52.

91. The preferred solution was to raise admission standards, as noted in chapter 3.

92. Charles Larned, "West Point and Higher Education," 20.

93. Of the fifty-four cadets who graduated in the class of 1902, the Academic Board recommended only seven for service in the Corps of Engineers.

CHAPTER TWO

1. The elderly Wheeler had been a Confederate general during the Civil War. Afterward, as a long-serving Congressman from Alabama, he worked assiduously to heal the sectional wounds of the nation. Upon the outbreak of the war with Spain, President William McKinley commissioned him as a major general in the United States Army, thus giving Wheeler the rare distinction of serving as a general officer in both the Confederate and United States armies.

2. *National Cyclopaedia of American Biography*, 555.

3. Virgil Carrington Jones, *Roosevelt's Rough Riders* (Garden City, NJ: Doubleday, 1971), 178, 184.

4. Hein had been assigned to West Point as the commandant of cadets. He became the acting superintendent when the permanent superintendent, Col. Oswald H. Ernst, departed to assume a wartime command. Hein's permanent rank was captain, but as the commandant he received the temporary rank of lieutenant colonel. US Military Academy, *Annual Report of the Superintendent*, 1899, 15.

5. Theodore Roosevelt remained a friend and patron of Mills following the Spanish-American War. It is likely that Roosevelt, the assistant secretary of the navy and a prominent Republican, had a hand in Mills's appointment as superintendent, although I found no definitive evidence of this connection. Gen. Wheeler also may have been influential in the appointment. In a dispatch to the secretary of war, Wheeler noted Mills's "good and brave conduct" in Cuba that "enlisted my highest admiration." "Wheeler Praises Mills: Thanks Secretary of War for the Latter's Appointment," *New York Times*, 24 August 1898, 3.

6. If Lt. Col. Hein was chagrined at Mills' appointment, he was gracious enough not to show it. The two men worked together for the next three years, with Hein recalling that their personal and professional relationships "were always pleasant." The young superintendent "sustained and supported me, in all of the measures which I undertook, for the advancement and improvement of my department." Hein, *Memories of Long Ago*, 270.

7. Edgar W. Bass (USMA 1868) had been the professor of mathematics since 1878. He retired on 7 October 1898, just three weeks after Mills assumed his post as superintendent; consequently, I did not consider him in this analysis.

8. Mills hired the prominent landscape architects, Frederick Law Olmsted and John Charles Olmsted, to develop "a general plan for landscape improvement at West Point. . . . This plan, combined with the forestry and building plans, constitutes a complete plan for improvements." *Annual Report of the Superintendent*, 1904, 14.

9. A discussion of the specific projects authorized by the 1902 legislation is in *Annual Report of the Superintendent*, 1903, 57. In 1905, Congress appropriated additional money that brought the total to $7.5 million. *Annual Report of the Superintendent*, 1906, 17.

10. The advisory board consisted of the professors of drawing (Charles W. Larned), chemistry, mineralogy, and geology (Samuel E. Tillman), civil and military engineering (Gustav J. Fieberger), mathematics (Wright P. Edgerton), modern languages (Edward E.

Wood); also on the board was the instructor of ordnance and gunnery (Frank E. Hobbs). Theodore Crackel speculates that the professors' opposed the Trophy Point construction because it did not include new homes for them. Crackel, *West Point*, 174. Perhaps this is true, but I could find no objective evidence of this thinking.

11. "The New West Point," *Army and Navy Journal*, 30 July 1904.

12. The advisory board's letter is dated 6 July 1904; Mills's letter (which included the advisory board letter as an attachment) is dated 19 August 1904. Box 1, "Correspondence 1903–1904 ref. new buildings at West Point," Samuel E. Tillman papers, Records Group 404, West Point Archives. Further evidence of the acrimony between Mills and the professors is in the 1904 *Annual Report of the Superintendent*. While acknowledging that his plan "evoked some criticism," Mills claimed that it stemmed from the professors' "misconception" of his proposal and their "extremely conservative views" (14).

13. See chapter 4, table 4.1, Curriculum for Academic Year 1903–1904.

14. Crackel, *West Point*, 181.

15. *Army and Navy Journal*, 24 September 1904, quoted in Crackel, *West Point*, 181.

16. Mills's comments, made in 1905, appeared in an army staff study completed in 1927, when the War Department was considering changes to the governance structure at West Point. Col. G. A. Lynch to Assistant Chief of Staff, G3, "Relations of Academic Board to the Superintendent," 23 August 1927, file packet on "Powers of the Academic Board," AGO Central Files 1926–1939, Records Group 407, National Archives, College Park, MD. The staff study was classified "secret" until its declassification in January 1947.

17. Letter to editor, *Army and Navy Journal*, undated (probably April 1905), box 1, folder "Papers concerning the Academy," Tillman Papers, West Point Archives.

18. *Annual Report of the Superintendent*, 1911, 10.

19. Scott, *Some Memories of a Soldier*, 420.

20. Ibid., 421.

21. *Annual Report of the Superintendent*, 1910, 20.

22. The superintendent's home, Quarters 100, was built in 1820 adjacent to the cadet barracks. It has housed every superintendent since Sylvanus Thayer. Its proximity to the cadet area reflected the paternal attitudes characteristic of the Academy's first century.

23. *Annual Report of the Superintendent*, 1910, 20.

24. As a result of the controversy surrounding the case of Cadet Oscar Booz (chapter 1), Congress passed strict antihazing legislation in 1902. The law required dismissal of cadets found guilty of hazing and disallowed them from readmission.

25. Scott, *Some Memories of a Soldier*, 442–44.

26. Ibid., 423.

27. Ambrose, *Duty, Honor, Country*, 246–47.

28. Scott, *Some Memories of a Soldier*, 425.

29. Ibid., 421.

30. *Annual Report of the Superintendent*, 1912, 37.

31. *Annual Report of the Superintendent*, 1911, 39.

32. *Annual Report of the Superintendent*, 1916, 57.

33. The three superintendents from 1919 to 1927 were brigadier generals. For the next fifty years, the superintendents were major generals with a few exceptions. Both Jay L.

Benedict (1938–1940) and Robert Eichelberger (1940–1942) were brigadier generals upon entering the job; Eichelberger was promoted to major general before he left. Black-shear M. Bryan (1954–1956) was a lieutenant general. Garrison Davidson (1956–1960) entered the job as a major general but was promoted to lieutenant general about a year later. Since 1977, all superintendents have been lieutenant generals.

34. Tillman Papers, unpublished memoir, box 2, IV.18, West Point Archives. Hinden-burg was the chief of the German General Staff, but in practice he commanded all German forces. In early 1917, he was still greatly admired by American officers who viewed the Ger-man military establishment as the most professional and competent in the world.

35. *Annual Report of the Superintendent*, 1919, 63.

36. Army leaders recognized Tillman's contributions by promoting him to brigadier general and awarding him the Distinguished Service Cross, the highest award for service. General Orders No. 28, US Military Academy, 24 June 1942, West Point Archives.

37. The first captain is the highest ranking cadet in the Corps. The commandant selects the cadet for this position based on his (now his or her) overall excellence.

38. MacArthur received the temporary rank of brigadier general during World War I to go with his assignment as a brigade commander in the 42nd Infantry (Rainbow) Division and, later, as the division commander. Whereas most officers lost their temporary rank after the war, MacArthur retained his in anticipation of his next assignment as West Point superintendent. His regular army (i.e., permanent) promotion to brigadier general came in January 1920. MacArthur, *Reminiscences*, 83. MacArthur's wartime heroics earned him two Distinguished Service Crosses, seven Silver Stars, and several foreign awards for gallantry, including the Legion of Honor and the Croix de Guerre. Col. Fitzugh Lee Minnigerode, "The Spirit of West Point," *New York Times*, 19 December 1920, BR2.

39. March had been a trusted senior aide to Lt. Gen. Arthur MacArthur, Douglas's father, during combat in the Philippines in 1899. Afterward, March took a personal interest in the young MacArthur and watched with great satisfaction as Douglas built a distin-guished combat record in France. For the relationship between March and MacArthur, see Danford, "USMA's 31st Superintendent," 12–13.

40. Ibid., 77.

41. My characterization of MacArthur's tenure as superintendent relies primarily on two sources: Ganoe, *MacArthur Close-Up*, and Ambrose, *Duty, Honor, Country*. Both accounts are thorough and very positive; Ganoe's is hagiographic. When used with care, however, they offer insights about MacArthur's personality, character, and leadership style that are unmatched in any other source.

42. MacArthur, *Reminiscences*, 77.

43. According to MacArthur's adjutant, William A. Ganoe, the senior professors on the Academic Board constituted an "Old Guard" of conservatism and complacency. The younger members tended to be more progressive and therefore more supportive of MacAr-thur's views. In particular, Commandant Robert Danford was a likeminded reformer who enthusiastically endorsed MacArthur's efforts to improve the leader development system at the Academy. Ganoe, *MacArthur Close-Up*, 35.

44. Ambrose, *Duty, Honor, Country*, 265–70.

45. Ganoe, *MacArthur Close-Up*, 141–42.

46. Ibid. Ganoe worked simultaneously as MacArthur's adjutant and the Academic Board's secretary and therefore personally witnessed the interactions between the superintendent and the "old guard" professors. His account of those interactions, although biased heavily in MacArthur's favor, provides valuable insights about the substance of the differences.

47. *Annual Report of the Superintendent*, 1921, 6.

48. "New West Point," *New York Times*, 10 October 1920, 87.

49. William Ganoe noted the opposition of senior faculty members to moving summer training to Fort Dix.

50. Memorandum from Conner to the chief of staff, 2 November 1926, and letter from chief of staff to Stewart, 23 November 1926, file packet on "Curriculum," AGO Central Files, 1926–1939, "West Point," Records Groups 407, National Archives, College Park, MD.

51. The main recommendations were: (1) establish a program for new instructor training prior to the start of the academic year; (2) introduce a short course on contemporary issues for fourth-classmen; (3) reduce daily grading; (4) reform entry requirements; (5) move descriptive geometry from the Department of Mathematics to the Department of Drawing. The last point was the only one to address the mathematics curriculum directly, and it merely redistributed the load rather than lightened it.

52. The ensuing report, entitled "Relations of Academic Board to the Superintendent, United States Military Academy," 23 August 1927, was written by one of Parker's senior subordinates, Col. G. A. Lynch. It was classified "secret" until its declassification in 1947. See file packet labeled "Powers of the Academic Board," AGO Central Files 1926–1939, Records Group 407, National Archives, College Park, MD.

53. At the Naval Academy, the superintendent had three votes on that institution's Academic Board, and department heads served for only three years before being reassigned to other navy billets. At the army's service schools, the commandants received counsel from faculty leaders but could make independent decisions.

54. The extended quote appears in a draft memorandum dated 24 August 1927 that is filed with the larger report. Although unsigned and missing a signature block, other correspondence in the file packet suggests that it was meant for Parker's signature. The unnamed superintendent's description of the professor leaves little doubt about the two men's identities. Fieberger served from 1896 (three years before MacArthur entered West Point) to 1922 (the end of MacArthur's tenure as superintendent); as the professor of civil and military engineering, he was responsible for the military history course at West Point.

55. Memorandum from Parker to the chief of staff, 25 August 1927, file packet on "Powers of the Academic Board," AGO Central Files 1926–1939, Records Group 407, National Archives, College Park, MD.

56. Memorandum from adjutant general to Smith, 3 March 1928, file packet on "Curriculum, USMA," AGO Central Files 1920–1939, Records Group 407, National Archives, College Park, MD.

57. Letter from Benedict to adjutant general, 16 November 1940, file 351, Army-AG Project Decimal Files 1940–1945, Military Posts and Reservations, Records Group 407, National Archives, College Park, MD.

58. Crackel, *West Point*, 190.

59. Letter from Stimson to Wilby, 18 September 1942, file 334, Army-AG Project Decimal Files 1940–1945, Military Posts and Reservations, Records Group 407, National Archives, College Park, MD.

60. Chapter 6 discusses the creation of pilot training for selected cadets during World War II.

61. Commandants were highly regarded officers who usually spent no more than three years at West Point to keep them competitive for promotion and future command opportunities. They came from the line army and would return there; hence, their perspective was short term and action oriented. They were often frustrated by the temperament of the professors, whose permanency gave them a collective perspective that was long term and deliberative.

62. Letter from Wilby to chief of staff, 27 August 1942, and response letter from assistant chief of staff for personnel to Wilby, 14 September 1942, file 351.01, Army-AG Project Decimal Files 1940–1945, Military Posts and Reservations, Records Group 407, National Archives, College Park, MD. The two exceptions were Col. Paul D. Harkins (1948–1951) and Col. John K. Waters (1951–1952); both officers later became four-star generals.

63. US Military Academy, *Post War Curriculum*, 21.

64. *Annual Report of the Superintendent*, 1902, 19.

65. By 1913, West Point had enlisted detachments for engineers, ordnance, cavalry, field artillery, quartermaster, and army service (general logistical support). Another enlisted element, although not classified as a detachment, was the band. The total enlisted population in that year was 686. The largest enlisted organization was the army service detachment, which numbered about two hundred and was commanded by the post quartermaster officer, usually a major. *Annual Report of the Superintendent*, 1913, 43–45.

66. *Annual Report of the Superintendent*, 1938, 1; *Official Register of the Officers and Cadets of the U.S. Military Academy*, 1938, 8. The surgeon doubled as the professor of military hygiene; as such, he occupied a seat on the Academic Board.

67. *Annual Report of the Superintendent*, 1938, 1.

68. Ibid., 1939, 1; *Official Register of the Officers and Cadets of the U.S. Military Academy*, 1939, 8; 1945, 7.

69. *Annual Report of the Superintendent*, 1938, 2; *Official Register of the Officers and Cadets of the U.S. Military Academy*, 1945, 32.

70. The peak of personnel strength came in 1974, with 825 officers, 777 enlisted soldiers, and 2,655 full-time civilian employees. *Annual Report of the Superintendent*, 1974, 84.

71. *Annual Report of the Superintendent*, 1946, 1. Taylor's staff featured the same numerical designations used in a tactical division: G-1 (personnel), G-2 (intelligence), G-3 (operations), and G-4 (logistics). The G-1 and G-4 staff sections were established in 1945; a combined G-2/G-3 staff section followed a year later.

72. Robert J. Meyer, "The 1802nd Special Regiment, U.S.M.A.," *Assembly* 14, no. 4 (January 1956): 1. The 1802nd was redesignated as the 1st Regimental Combat Team in 1956 and as the First Battle Group, First Infantry, in 1958.

73. The preparatory school was commonly known by its acronym, USMAPS. Taylor

had overall command of both the school, for which there was a commandant, and Stewart Airfield, for which there was a colonel in command. Chapter 3 provides fuller coverage of USMAPS.

74. West Point's organizational structure evolved considerably during the mid-1950s. By 1955, Superintendent Blackshear Bryan had replaced Taylor's numbered G-staff with three principal staff agencies — personnel and administration, logistics, and comptroller. *Annual Report of the Superintendent*, 1955, 51.

75. *Annual Report of the Superintendent*, 1947, 15.

76. The Office of Military Psychology and Leadership began under the commandant but eventually became an academic department (Behavioral Sciences and Leadership) under the dean. Chapter 7 discusses the origin and significance of these two organizations.

77. Dr. Karl Compton headed the review board. He praised the Academy for its commitment to providing a broad education rather than allowing cadets to specialize (that is, to choose academic majors).

78. An excellent analysis of Taylor's tenure as superintendent is in Crackel, *West Point*, 211–15.

79. Memorandum from Irving to chief of staff, 8 January 1954, file 351 USMA, Army-AG Project Decimal File 1951–1952, Military Posts and Reservations, Records Group 407, National Archives, College Park, MD. Irving was especially sensitive to the plight of those professors who had served during World War II as general officers but agreed to serve at West Point as colonels afterward.

80. US Congress, *Statutes at Large*, 70A, chap. 369, sec. 3962, 230 (1956).

81. Robert D. McFadden, "Lieut. Gen. G. H. Davidson, 88, Strategist in Wars," *New York Times* (online edition), 27 December 1992.

82. Davidson, "Grandpa Gar," 163.

83. *Annual Report of the Superintendent*, 1957, 7.

84. Gruenther, a former Supreme Commander, Allied Powers, Europe, was the brother of Davidson's wife, Verone.

85. *Annual Report of the Superintendent*, 1959, 11.

86. Davidson, "Grandpa Gar," 163–64.

87. Ibid., 164.

88. Ibid., 165. The Academic Board rejected Davidson's reform agenda in one notable area; specifically, military training did not diminish, and in some ways increased, during the academic year. See chapter 6.

89. US Military Academy, *An Institutional Self-Evaluation of the United States Military Academy*, i.

90. The academic accreditation report of 1959 noted that the "members of the non-permanent faculty have little opportunity to exert material influence on over-all policy" relating to the curriculum. Middle States Association of Colleges and Secondary Schools, *Evaluation Report*, 71. The problem was understandable, given the short tenures (usually three years) of the junior military faculty. With the arrival of permanent associate professors, however, the situation was more noticeable and troublesome. In the aftermath of the 1976 mass-cheating incident (discussed later), investigators would cite the marginalization of the PAPs and junior faculty as contributory to the conditions that led to the cheating.

91. *Annual Report of the Superintendent*, 1943, 1–2.

92. Chapter 3 provides fuller detail on the recruiting crisis of the late 1960s.

93. Seymour M. Hersh, "33 Teachers at West Point Leave Army in 18 Months," *New York Times*, 25 June 1972, 1. The Medal of Honor recipient was Capt. Paul Bucha, an instructor in the Department of Social Sciences and a veteran of the Vietnam War.

94. A highly negative portrayal of West Point was Bruce Galloway and Robert Bowie Johnson, *West Point: America's Power Fraternity* (New York: Simon and Schuster, 1973). Johnson was a 1965 graduate of the Academy. Other negative publications included Ward Just, *Military Men* (New York: Knopf, 1970); Josiah Bunting (a former history instructor), *The Lionheads: A Novel* (New York: G. Braziller, 1972); Edward L. King, *The Death of the Army: A Pre-Mortem* (New York: Saturday Review Press, 1972); Anthony Herbert, *Soldier* (New York: Holt, Rinehart and Winston, 1973). A balanced analysis of West Point, but still with sharp edges and a generally negative conclusion, was Joseph Ellis and Robert Moore, *School for Soldiers*. Neither Ellis nor Moore is a West Point graduate, but both served on the faculty as military officers in the departments of history and English, respectively.

95. The General Accounting Office study focused on cost, cadet attrition, and financial management. The Department of Defense Committee on Excellence in Education, chaired by Deputy Secretary William Clements, considered all levels of officer education, including the programs of the three service academies. US Military Academy, *The United States Military Academy in Perspective, 1969–1979*, 4.

96. The 1976 cheating incident is covered in greater detail in chapter 8.

97. Frank Borman, *Report to the Secretary of the Army*, 10.

98. Ibid., 17.

99. Quoted in Ibid., 79.

100. Ibid.

101. Ibid., 21.

102. Charles H. Schilling to Borman, 19 December 1976, quoted in Crackel, *West Point*, 249.

103. Letter from Col. Walter J. Renfroe Jr., to Rogers, 15 February 1977, unmarked file, box 25, Bernard Rogers papers, National Defense University, Washington, DC. Renfroe's colleague, Col. Jack M. Pollin, head of the Department of Mathematics, wrote a letter to the secretary of the army criticizing the Borman commission's proposal to retire professors at thirty years. He called the proposal "baseless and insulting to a group of officers whose dedication to WestPoint and the United States Army is as great as I have witnessed in over 32 years of commissioned service." Letter from Pollin to Martin R. Hoffmann, 16 December 1976, file labeled "Correspondence w/Staff/Faculty/Alumni," box 25, Rogers papers.

104. Superintendent Sidney Berry characterized the committee members as "very active, intelligent, aggressive, eager officers." Their experience on the faculty and staff probably made them more receptive to the complaints recorded in the Borman report concerning the professoriate. There was not a single committee member who had formerly been a professor at West Point. Sidney B. Berry Jr., interview by Robert F. Broyles, 1983, transcript, 2: 1016.

105. The thoroughness of the WPSG report merits special note. In my extensive re-

search of the Military Academy, I have come across no other external committee report that so ably balances breadth, analysis, clarity, and cogency. The quality of the report had much to do with Gen. Rogers's deep personal interest in the work of the WPSG. He received periodic reviews from the three investigative committee chairmen and provided guidance that influenced the WPSG's final recommendations. Memorandum for record, "USMA Continuing Study Groups, IPR w/Chief of Staff, Army," 16 June 1977, file on "Immediate Action Group," box 25, Bernard Rogers papers, National Defense University, Washington, DC.

106. The last four recommendations in the WPSG report addressed the United States Military Academy Preparatory School; hence, the number dealing solely with the Military Academy was 152.

107. West Point Study Group, *Final Report of the West Point Study Group*, 9.

108. In practice, only two department heads sat on the policy board. I have chosen not to capitalize "policy board" because this body proved transitory.

109. *Final Report of the West Point Study Group*, 9.

110. All quotes are from Crackel, *West Point*, 252. Crackel provides excellent coverage of the key governance issues in the wake of the 1976 cheating incident. In contrast to my interpretation, he believes that the Academic Board was justifiably conservative and that the diminution of its power relative to the superintendent was a blow to the Academy's stability as an educational institution.

111. Rogers contacted Goodpaster in December 1976 for advice about the qualities to look for in the next superintendent. Goodpaster recommended hiring a senior officer "on his final tour, or in the circumstances, bringing back a retired officer who had long command in complex assignments. He [Rogers] spoke of the importance of getting somebody who had had a fair amount of academic work and would have academic credentials and I concurred in that." At that point, Rogers asked Goodpaster to take the job, and the latter agreed. Andrew J. Goodpaster, interview by Dr. Stephen Grove, 12 May 1981, transcript, 1.

112. Howard Prince, interview by author, 16 July 2007, transcript, 34.

113. Goodpaster acknowledged his contacts with the three committees of the WPSG prior to his appointment as the superintendent. He recalled, "Their reports had no surprises for me." Goodpaster interview by Dr. Stephen Grove, 12 May 1981, transcript, 4.

114. *Annual Report of the Superintendent*, 1978, 35.

115. *Annual Report of the Superintendent*, 1979, 54.

116. Bagnal supervised activities relating to personnel, security, operations, logistics, audiovisual systems, engineering and housing, finance, inspections, public affairs, legal matters, admissions, and chaplain activities. Charles W. Bagnal, interview by Dr. Stephen Grove, 21 May 1980, 4. Bagnal served from 1977 to 1980. His successor was Arthur E. Brown Jr. from 1980 to 1981. Bagnal and Brown were the only two officers to serve as deputy superintendents. Upon Goodpaster's retirement in 1981, the army eliminated the deputy position.

117. *Final Report of the West Point Study Group*, 1.

118. The Academy's 1999 self-study report for academic accreditation cited weaknesses in strategic planning. US Military Academy, *Institutional Self-Study: Report of the United*

States Military Academy, 45–51. The shortcoming also was evident to perceptive observers within the Academy. Col. Patrick Toffler, the first director of the Office of Policy, Planning, and Analysis (1993 to 1998) admitted that "we've just never done a very good job of it. . . . We haven't devoted time and people to it." Patrick Toffler, interview by Dr. Stephen Grove, transcript, 14 July 1998, 55. The conspicuous exception to the neglect of strategic planning was the tenure of Lt. Gen. Dave Palmer, discussed later.

119. "Regulations for the United States Military Academy," 5 January 1979, described the new governance structure. Army Regulation 210-26, "United States Military Academy," 26 August 2002, incorporated the Academy regulation and twenty-three interim changes into a new army regulation.

120. *Annual Report of the Superintendent*, 1985, 6–7.

121. The policy applied only to "Professors USMA" (PUSMA), officers whose appointments were ratified by the Senate. By law, PUSMAs may serve on active duty until they are sixty-four years old. The dean and all academic department heads were PUSMAs, as well as a few deputy department heads. The PUSMAs were senior to permanent associate professors (PAP), who did not need Senate confirmation and whose commissioned service was limited to thirty years for colonels (less for lower ranking PAPs). The PUSMAs and PAPs were considered "tenured" professors insofar as they were assured of a set number of years on the faculty, barring removal for inefficiency or misconduct. West Point has never had an official tenure system, although the criteria and procedures for removal of PUSMAs and PAPs were akin to those found in most civilian colleges and universities with tenure systems.

122. Wickham approved the tenure-review policy in 1984, during Willard Scott's tenure as superintendent; however, the reviews did not begin until Scott's successor, Dave R. Palmer, developed the assessment criteria. Dave R. Palmer, interview by author, 17 July 2007, transcript, 5. The tenure-review procedures appear in Dean's Policy and Operating Memorandum 3–12, "Performance Review of Permanent Professors," 10 March 1995, Office of the Dean, 1–2.

123. Two of the three professors who left early were forced out. Superintendent Berry asked Col. Frederick C. Lough (Law) and Col. Elliott C. Cutler (Electrical Engineering) to retire based on their association with the cheating incident of 1976. According to Berry, Lough demonstrated "negative leadership" of the legal staff during the crisis. Cutler was retired for designing an electrical engineering requirement that "placed temptation in front of the cadets. . . . It just was not very smart." Despite these issues, Berry praised both professors' overall professional record and prevailed on the army to have both of them advanced to brigadier general upon their retirements. Berry interview transcript, 2: 1025–26.

124. Crackel, *West Point*, 260. See in particular Appendix B, "Rate of Departure and the Tenure of Members of the Academic Board, 1801–2000," 292–96.

125. Lt. Gen. David H. Huntoon Jr. became the fifty-eighth superintendent in July 2010. As of this writing, he has shown more willingness than his predecessors to interact with the Academic Board, but it is still too early to characterize his leadership style.

126. Daniel Christman (1996–2001) used the policy board only for the program reviews of the major activity directors rather than to deliberate on broad policy issues. William Lennox (2001–2006) considered it unwieldy and therefore did not use it. His succes-

sor, Franklin Hagenbeck, initially relied on a small circle of advisors known as the "board of directors," but reconstituted the policy board in early 2009. Lt. Gen. David Huntoon disbanded the policy board in early 2011, citing as reasons its indistinct charter and overlap with the Academic Board. Daniel W. Christman, interview by Dr. Stephen Grove, 23 April 2001, transcript, 113. William Lennox, interview by Dr. Stephen Grove, 22 September 2005, transcript, 90.

127. Palmer was a student of West Point history and authored a well-regarded book on West Point during the Revolutionary War: *The River and the Rock: The History of Fortress West Point, 1775–1783* (New York: Greenwood Publishing Corp., 1969).

128. Dave R. Palmer, interview by Dr. Stephen Grove, 13 June 1991, transcript, 6.

129. Ibid., 2.

130. Donnithorne, *Preparing for West Point's Third Century*, 2.

131. US Military Academy, *2002 — and Beyond: A Roadmap to Our Third Century*, 3–4. In 1998, Superintendent Daniel Christman revised the mission statement to emphasize the desire for West Point graduates to serve the nation as career army officers. The most recent revision came in 2005, but the changes were stylistic only. The current mission statement reads: "To educate, train, and inspire the Corps of Cadets so that each graduate is a commissioned leader of character committed to the values of Duty, Honor, Country and prepared for a career of professional excellence and service to the Nation as an officer in the United States Army."

132. The thoroughness of the strategic assessment was reflected in the Academy's self-study report for academic accreditation. See US Military Academy, *Institutional Self-Study 1988–1989*.

133. Palmer interview transcript, 13 June 1991, 3.

134. Prince interview transcript, 25; Donnithorne, *Preparing for West Point's Third Century*, 68.

135. The OLDI was a new staff agency; it did not replace the special assistant for policy and planning, which Palmer renamed as the special assistant for strategic planning.

136. The Academy Schedule is the subject of USMA Regulation 1-1, updated annually. Palmer used the term "poachers" to denote the well-intentioned instructors, coaches, tactical officers, and others who put excessive demands on cadet time. He recalled that he did not have to reprimand too many poachers before others got the message. "It didn't take long. You must be firm with a new policy or it quickly becomes so riddled with exceptions that it has no effect. I held very firmly to the schedule, and after a handful of individuals had been chastised for 'poaching,' it became accepted and followed." Dave R. Palmer, interview by author, 17 July 2007, transcript, 42.

137. Palmer's decision to do away with Saturday classes ended a tradition that was nearly 170 years old. Sylvanus Thayer first established Saturday classes early in his tenure (1817–1833) as superintendent.

138. See chapter 6.

139. The Cadet Leader Development System is the subject of USMA Circular 1-101, updated periodically. See chapter 7 for fuller coverage of CLDS.

140. For a detailed explanation of the accomplishments of the Palmer years, see Donnithorne, *Preparing for West Point's Third Century*.

141. Prince interview transcript, 40.

142. Anthony Hartle, interview by author, 13 July 2007, 10.

143. Much of the discontent stemmed from Palmer's curricular reforms, particularly the decisions to reduce the number of required courses for graduation to forty and the elimination of Saturday classes. The changes were in response to a long-standing concern that cadets were overburdened with academic requirements and therefore could acquire only a superficial knowledge of the material. Regardless, some members of the Academic Board resented Palmer's intrusion in an area that was traditionally the reserve of the professors. For a contemporary perspective of the resistance of some Academic Board members to Palmer's changes, see Prince interview transcript, 42.

144. Palmer interview transcript, 3 July 1991, 49. Palmer was not the only reform-minded superintendent to face resistance from members of the staff and faculty. Gen. Goodpaster recalled similar problems as he led the Academy through the difficult years following the 1976 cheating scandal. "You can question the methods — the wisdom of the methods — and they should be questioned," he noted. "But on the military side, once a decision is made and it is within the prerogative of the Superintendent or other person in authority, then because it is a military institution, it's incumbent on people to accept that and to try to make the thing work." Andrew J. Goodpaster, interview by James Johnson, 10 March 1988, transcript, 62.

145. Palmer interview transcript, 17 July 2007, 5.

146. Senator John Glenn, a member of the Senate Armed Services Committee, initiated the proposal to increase the active-duty service obligation for graduates of all service academies. Palmer expended much effort in helping to defeat the measure in the Senate. Palmer interview transcript, 17 July 2007, 63–64.

147. Palmer interview transcript, 13 June 1991, 6–7.

148. West Point was the consensus choice of selectors for the title of national football champion in 1944 and 1945. In 1946, the Academy shared the title with Notre Dame.

149. Chapter 3 provides fuller coverage of the relationship between athletic recruiting and cadet performance.

150. Willard Scott commented on the fanaticism of some alumni concerning football. In 1981, as he prepared to assume command at West Point, a graduate who had played on the undefeated 1958 team demanded that he revive the football program. Scott suspected that the graduate's emotion was the result of hurt pride rather than a rational concern about the winning spirit of the Corps of Cadets. Still, Scott became a convert: "I've changed my mind about that subject, and did very early on. Athletics is indeed considered by a significant population to be a manifestation of whether or not you have courage, winning attitude, pride, and all those sort of things." Willard W. Scott, interview by Dr. Stephen Grove, 4.

151. Chapter 5 provides fuller coverage of the role of intercollegiate athletics at West Point.

152. Memorandum from Secretary of the Army Francis J. Harvey to chief of staff, subject: "Release from Active Duty to Participate in Activities with Recruiting or Public Affairs Benefit to the United States Army," 2 April 2005, copy in author's files. As evidence that the alternate service option was targeted at athletes, no other cadets benefited from the

policy during the three years it was in effect. In designing the policy, Lennox coordinated with the army's chief personnel officer, Franklin Hagenbeck, Lennox's West Point classmate and successor as superintendent.

153. David Robinson, a two-time All-American basketball player in college, graduated in 1987 from the Naval Academy. Following two years of active duty, he played professional basketball with the San Antonio Spurs from 1989 to 2003. Roger Staubach graduated from the Naval Academy in 1965. He was the starting quarterback for three years and won the Heisman Trophy, given to the nation's best collegiate football player, in 1963. After four years in the navy, including a one-year tour in Vietnam, he played professional football with the Dallas Cowboys from 1969 to 1979.

154. Rick Gosselin, "Duty Calls: Army Says Cadets Can Turn Pro Now," *The Dallas Morning News*, 30 March 2008.

155. See, for example, Brian Lewis, "Army's Caleb Campbell Marches into NFL," *New York Post*, 29 April 2008.

156. Tillman died in combat on 22 April 2004. The cause of death was friendly fire.

157. Reid Cherner, "Enlisting Controversy," *USA Today,* 29 April 2008, 3C.

158. Thomas Hauser, "Hypocrisy at West Point," SecondsOut.com, 7 April 2008 (sports newspaper online); available from http://secondsout.com/Columns/index.cfm? ccs = 208&cs = 24285, accessed 7 April 2008.

159. Chris Freind, "The Army Sells Out to the NFL," *The (Philadelphia) Bulletin*, 30 April 2008.

160. Memorandum from Undersecretary of Defense David Chu to service secretaries, subject: "Policy for Academy and ROTC Graduates Seeking to Participate in Professional Sports before Completion of the Active Duty Service Obligation," 30 April 2008, copy in author's files.

161. See, for example, Kevin Hench, "Army Earns Black Eye for Campbell Situation," *Fox Sports.com*, 26 July 2008. Campbell was not the only West Point athlete in 2008 who attempted to enter professional sports. Three other football players, including one who had commanded a cadet regiment, had tryouts with NFL teams. None made the cut.

162. "Restoring the winning tradition" was the mantra of Superintendents Lennox and Hagenbeck in the first decade of the twenty-first century. In pursuit of this goal, the Association of Graduates established the Restoring the Winning Tradition Fund in 2004 to support the football program. "President's Letter," *Assembly* 63, no. 2 (November/ December 2004), 6.

163. Col. Kelly Kruger, background interview by author, 19 May 2009. Kruger was the director of the Office of Policy, Plans, and Analysis from 2005 to 2009.

CHAPTER THREE

1. Representatives were elected from the states, whereas delegates represented the US territories and the District of Columbia. Although Article I of the US Constitution precludes delegates from voting in the House of Representatives, the 1843 law included their numbers in establishing the size of the Corps of Cadets.

2. US Military Academy, *Centennial*, 226–27.

3. Congress made the first change in 1900 and the second in 1902. The 1900 legislation increased the United States-at-large nominations (i.e., those reserved for the president) to thirty; two years later, Congress increased the allocation to forty.

4. The average authorized strength of the Corps during the 1890s was about 364 cadets. The actual strength was always lower, for reasons discussed later.

5. Prior to the 1910 legislation, a congressional district could have only one cadet at West Point at a time. Henceforth there could be a one-year overlap of an outgoing cadet with an incoming cadet from the same district. The effect was to expand the Corps by 25 percent. The law had a sunset clause, but subsequent legislation in 1916 made the expansion permanent.

6. US Military Academy, *Information Relative to the Appointment and Admission of Cadets to the United States Military Academy*, 1925 edition (Washington, DC: Government Printing Office, 1924), 1.

7. Congress subsequently added two United States-at-large appointments for the vice president and forty more for the president, thus raising the United States-at-large allocation to 122 and the authorized strength of the Corps of Cadets to 1,378 by 1927. In that year, twenty of the president's at-large nominees continued to be selected from among graduates of honor military schools. The four Filipino cadets could be commissioned only into the Philippine Scouts. Not included are foreign cadets, whose attendance at West Point required Congressional approval; prior to World War I, the number of foreign cadets never exceeded five. US Military Academy, *Information Relative to the Appointment and Admission of Cadets to the United States Military Academy, West Point, N. Y.*, 1927 edition (Washington, DC: Government Printing Office, 1926), 1.

8. In 1898, immediately prior to the Spanish-American War, West Pointers comprised 61 percent of the officer corps. Subsequent percentages were: 39.5 (1902), 38.0 (1917), 33.0 (1920), 22.1 (1922), 32.0 (1930), 38.6 (1934). Congressional testimony, Brig. Gen. Andrew Moses to House Military Affairs Committee, 22 April 1935, file packet on "Legislation re: increase number of Cadets West Point," AGO Central Files 1926–1939, Records Group 407, National Archives, College Park, MD.

9. The percentage is calculated using the authorized strength figures from 1927 (1,374 cadets) and 1935 (1,964 cadets).

10. When Congress first authorized cadetships for honor schools in 1916, the school principals were allowed to certify the academic qualifications of their top graduates and thus have them exempted from the written entrance examination. This privilege lasted through World War II; afterward, the top students from each honor school took the same entrance examination as all other competitive candidates. The top scorers, regardless of school, were awarded the appointments. US Military Academy, *Catalog of Information 1949–50*, 15.

11. Certain practical limits obviously applied. For example, there was a finite number of sons of deceased veterans. Similarly, the Regular Army and National Guard had a finite number of soldiers. That said, any physically qualified young man within each category could seek a competitive appointment.

12. The number of alternates designated by appointing officials increased over time. For most of the nineteenth century, members of Congress named a principal and only one

alternate. In the mid-twentieth century the number of alternates had risen to three and by the end of the century the number was ten.

13. *Annual Report of the Superintendent*, 1902, 10.

14. Superintendent Thomas H. Barry, for example, devoted several pages of his 1911 annual report to lamenting the poor academic performance of nominees on the West Point entrance examination. The Academy, noted Barry, "is not a primary school. The courses of instruction given here presuppose a foundation in the rudimentary branches. When such a foundation does not exist no encouragement should be given to try the examinations." *Annual Report of the Superintendent*, 1911, 46.

15. In April 1913, for example, only 198 of the 387 nominees (51 percent) passed the entrance examination. This was better than usual. *Annual Report of the Superintendent*, 1913, 14.

16. The 50 percent graduation rate applies to the ten years from 1892 to 1902. From 1902 to 1912, the graduation rate was about 70 percent—a big improvement, but still not as high as Academy officials would have liked. *Annual Report of the Superintendent*, 1913, 14.

17. *Centennial*, 1, 228.

18. Ibid., 229.

19. The focus of the West Point entrance exam was on mastery of the subjects required by law. The exam therefore put a premium on computational abilities (mathematics) and memorization of facts (non-quantitative subjects) rather than on cognitive abilities. Students preparing for the exam spent long hours cramming their heads with information that they were sure to forget soon afterward. It is very likely that the entrance exam disqualified many capable nominees who had not committed the required information to memory.

20. A provision of the 1942 law that expanded the Corps to 2,496 cadets allowed Academy officials to create a "qualified alternate" list that would alleviate this problem.

21. In May 1940, Representative George H. Bender from Ohio informed the War Department, "It is my desire that the existing vacancy to the United States Military Academy be carried over until 1941 as I do not wish to nominate a candidate at this time." Not wanting to be hounded by potential candidates in his district, Bender added, "I should like to request that no further information be given out concerning this vacancy." Such letters were not uncommon in the annual correspondence between the War Department and members of Congress. Letter from Bender to the Adjutant General, 24 May 1940, file on "West Point," AGO Central Files 1926–1939, Records Group 407, National Archives, College Park, MD.

22. *Annual Report of the Superintendent*, 1913, 13; letter from Robert Eichelberger (superintendent) to Adjutant General, 11 March 1941, AGO Central Files 1926–1939, file on "R.O.T.C.," Records Group 407, National Archives, College Park, MD.

23. Comments of Hugh L. Scott, *Annual Report of the Superintendent*, 1908, 5.

24. Mallory, *Compiled Statutes of the United States, 1913*, 935.

25. *Centennial*, 1, 228.

26. More accurately, the Academic Board convinced a reluctant secretary of war to allow the use of certificates. Root warned, "I am . . . very doubtful as to the wisdom of applying the system of admission by certificate to the Military Academy." Aware that some

institutions granted their certificates liberally, Root feared that weak students would use the certificates to gain entry to West Point and then flunk out. As it turned out, Root's concerns were valid. Quoted in Nye, "The United States Military Academy in an Era of Educational Reform, 1900–1925," 82, note 24.

27. Rudolph, *The American College and University*, 282–86.

28. *Annual Report of the Superintendent*, 1902, 8. The Academic Board recognized that not all certificates were equal and therefore put strict conditions on their acceptance—first, the "properly attested examination paper" from a public competitive written examination (e.g., Civil Service test); second, a certificate from an accredited high school; third, a certificate from an accredited college. In the first two cases, the certificates had to reflect mastery of the subjects covered on the West Point admissions test. *Centennial*, 1, 228–29.

29. *Annual Report of the Superintendent*, 1907, 20.

30. To have their certificates accepted at West Point, students had to show proficiency in subjects that totaled at least fourteen units of work as defined by the College Entry Examination Board. A total of seven-and-a-half credits in mathematics, English, and history were mandatory. War Department General Orders no. 3, 23 January 1914; no. 38, 22 May 1914; no 19, 7 April 1915. In addition to the course requirements, West Point required certificate holders to have grades "well above the passing mark," including no failing grades. *Annual Report of the Superintendent*, 1920, 14.

31. *Annual Report of the Superintendent*, 1924, 9–10. From 1919 to 1923, 73.7 percent of cadets entered with certificates; of these, 27.2 percent were lost in the first six months. In comparison, of the 26.3 percent who gained entry by passing the written exam, only 10.9 percent flunked out in the first six months.

32. Superintendent Clarence P. Townsley made this recommendation in his 1914 *Annual Report*, 10–11.

33. Superintendent Thomas H. Barry made this recommendation in his 1911 *Annual Report*, 42.

34. Superintendent Fred W. Sladen made this recommendation in his 1924 *Annual Report*, 9.

35. File packet on "Rates of Academic Deficiency at West Point," 18 August 1934, AGO Central Files 1926–1939, Records Group 407, National Archives, College Park, MD.

36. *Annual Report of the Superintendent*, 1944, 1–2.

37. By the Second World War, entrance exams of all types were much shorter than the three-day testing marathons of the early century. In 1944, for example, the standard West Point entrance exam consisted of two three-hour exams administered on a single day—mathematics in the morning and English test in the afternoon; additionally, candidates without official credit for US history took a special three-hour exam on a second day. Candidates with secondary school certificates took a validating exam consisting of two sections—one in mathematics (morning) and one in English (afternoon); alternatively, they could take the College Entrance Examination Board's Scholastic Aptitude Test in their home districts and report the scores to West Point. College certificate holders took the one-hour West Point Aptitude Test.

38. The maximum permissible age of entry to West Point was normally twenty-two years old, but Congress raised the age to twenty-four years old for veterans of World War II.

Despite the popularity of GI Bill benefits, there were enough young veterans interested in Academy education to fill 50 percent of the four classes that entered from 1945 to 1948. Murphy, *West Point Cadet, 1948–1952*, 57.

39. An analysis of the factors hindering recruitment at the service academies is in the letter from Secretary of the Army Kenneth C. Royall to Representative Albert L. Reeves Jr., 10 November 1947, file on "Military Posts and Reservations," Army-AG Project Decimal Files 1946–1948, Records Group 407, National Archives, College Park, MD.

40. Ibid. Royall's letter provides data showing elevated rates of resignation immediately following the two world wars.

41. Included in this figure are the qualified alternates who gained their appointments as cadets following the normal date of admission. The admission of qualified alternates is discussed later.

42. *Annual Report of the Superintendent*, 1950, 4. This change made high school certificates irrelevant since anyone without a college certificate now had to take the achievement tests.

43. Department of the Army Circular No. 350-5, 10 August 1955, file 351.12 USMA, General Correspondence 1955–56, Records of the AGO, 1917– , Records Group 407, National Archives, College Park, MD. See also letter from Superintendent Frederick A. Irving to Frank H. Bowles, Director of College Entrance Examination Board, 2 July 1954, file 334, "Admissions Committee 1954–55: Adoption of CEEB Tests (Registrar's Files)," Records Group 404, West Point Archives.

44. US Military Academy, *Information Relative to the Appointment and Admission of Cadets to the United States Military Academy, West Point, N. Y.*, 1944 edition (Washington, DC: Government Printing Office, 1943), 4.

45. *Annual Report of the Superintendent*, 1943, 2. The class that entered in July 1943 was larger than usual because of the expansion legislation of the previous year. The total class strength once the qualified alternates arrived was 1065.

46. Taylor, *West Point: Its Objectives and Methods*, 13. Several of Taylor's predecessors also made this recommendation. MG Francis B. Wilby, for example, proposed a similar plan four years earlier in his "Report of the Superintendent on the Three Year Course of Instruction" (30 January 1943). He was not optimistic of effecting the change through legislation, although a few congressmen had voluntarily allowed the Academic Board to vet their nominees "for some time now" (5).

47. Maxwell D. Taylor, interview by Richard A. Manion, 19 October 1972, transcript, Senior Officers Debriefing Program, Military History Institute, Carlisle Barracks, PA, 14.

48. *Annual Report of the Superintendent*, 1959, 3.

49. The Civil Service Commission and the College Entrance Examination Board both offered tests that could be used to prequalify potential nominees within each congressional district.

50. Of the 15 percent not using the congressional competitive method of nomination, 10 percent designated a primary nominee and unnumbered alternates. Five percent designated a principal nominee and numbered alternates; this was the most restrictive method of appointment. "Admissions Process" briefing slides, undated, USMA Directorate of Admissions, obtained July 2008.

51. Letters from Wilby to the Adjutant General, 16 December 1943 and 4 November 1944, and memorandum from Director of Military Personnel Division to the G1, 30 November 1944, file AG 351.11, "Military Posts and Reservations," Army-AG Project Decimal Files 1940–1945, Records Group 407, National Archives, College Park, MD. Wilby pointed out in the 4 November letter that most of the cadets discharged in 1944 for academics would not have qualified for entry under his proposed system. In contrast, an applicant who failed to gain entry because of a marginal grade on the entrance exam was a staff sergeant with combat experience in the Pacific who came highly recommended by his superiors and the Academic Board members who interviewed him.

52. *Annual Report of the Superintendent*, 1946, 4.

53. Of the 562 nominees screened in 1914, for example, 142 (25 percent) had disqualifying medical problems. The most common disqualifiers were deficiency in height, weight, or chest measurement; general appearance; defective vision (poorer than 20/40 unaided); and heart trouble. *Annual Report of the Superintendent*, 1914, 9.

54. Douglas MacArthur, superintendent from 1919 to 1922, is most widely credited with addressing the physical fitness shortcomings of the Corps of Cadets in the early twentieth century. The credit is well deserved, but other superintendents also made physical fitness a priority for cadets. See chapter 5 for more detail.

55. *Annual Report of the Superintendent*, 1942, 9.

56. *Annual Report of the Superintendent*, 1947, 3.

57. The PAE became the Candidate Fitness Assessment (CFA) in 2006, when the Military, Naval, and Air Force Academies agreed to use a common test. The CFA was a slightly modified version of the PAE that focused more on health-related fitness rather than physical skills. The change in focus was due in part to the declining level of physical fitness in the nation's youth. Whereas the PAE consisted of about 70 percent skill-related events and 30 percent health-related events, the Candidate Fitness Assessment reversed those percentages.

58. Letter from Taylor to Adjutant General, 21 March 1946, file 351.11, "Military Posts and Reservations," Army-AGO Project Decimal Files 1946–1948, Records Group 407, National Archives, College Park, MD.

59. The Personnel Research Section (PRS) of the Adjutant General's Office conducted most of the studies requested by Taylor and his successors. Examples of pertinent studies include "West Point Selection Examination for Predicting of First Term Academic Performance of 1943 Fourth Classmen" (PRS #522); "Follow-up Study of Officer Performance of West Point Graduates" (PRS #767); "Prediction of Aptitude for Service from a Battery of Physical Efficiency Tests" (PRS #780); and "An Exploratory Study of the Relationship of West Point Class Standing and Achievement of the Rank of General Officer" (PRS #843). A full list of reports is in file 351.11 USMA, "Military Posts and Reservations," Army-AG Project Decimal Files 1951–1952, Records Group 407, National Archives, College Park, MD.

60. The two most import research centers, both established shortly after World War II, were the Office of Military Psychology and Leadership and the Office of Institutional Research.

61. Letter from Davidson to Deputy Chief of Staff for Military Operations, 31 May

1957, p. 3, file USMA 351.11, General Correspondence 1957–1958, Records of the AGO 1917– , Records Group 407, National Archives, College Park, MD.

62. The goal was set by the Department of Defense Service Academy Board, whose 1950 report recommended that the service academies provide, in times of peace, "not less than one-half the Regular officers" for the armed forces. Stearns, *A Report and Recommendation to the Secretary of Defense*, 6. West Point needed to graduate about 600 cadets annually to achieve the 50 percent goal, about one hundred more than its output in the late 1950s.

63. Letter from Davidson to Deputy Chief of Staff for Military Operations, 31 May 1957, p. 3, file USMA 351.11, General Correspondence 1957–1958, Records of the AGO 1917– , Records Group 407, National Archives, College Park, MD.

64. Ibid. Davidson originally proposed percentage weights of 55 (mental), 10 (physical), and 35 (leadership), but the approved program slightly increased the mental weight to 60 percent at the expense of leadership, which dropped to 30 percent. The leadership potential category has expanded over the years to include a growing list of extracurricular activities in which students develop their leadership skills.

65. Preparatory schools already existed to help civilian candidates gain entry to West Point. Academy officials generally looked down on these schools for "deadening the reasoning faculties" of students with elementary work designed solely to pass the entrance exam. Comments of Albert Mills, *Annual Report of the Superintendent*, 1902, 8.

66. Ignoffo, "A Brief History of USMAPS," 26. Recent West Point graduates served as the instructors and used old entrance exams as a guide.

67. *Annual Report of the Superintendent*, 1944, 1. Collectively, the enlisted soldiers vying for competitive appointments in 1943 did poorly on the West Point entrance exam in the spring of 1943. The reason was that the corps preparatory schools had shut down because of the war. Once civilian colleges took over the preparatory program, the success rate of enlisted candidates returned to normal levels.

68. Edson L. Garrabrants quoted in Ignoffo, "A Brief History of USMAPS," 12. The Lafayette and Amherst programs lasted from 1943 to 1946. The Cornell program lasted from 1943 to 1945.

69. Frequent changes in USMAPS admissions policy led to the piecemeal assignment of soldier-students throughout the year. The faculty therefore resorted to "semi-tutorial instruction with classes being initiated on an almost monthly basis." By 1954 this inefficient system gave way to a ten-month, two-semester program modeled after a normal academic year. USMAPS Study Group staff paper, 4 April 1979, file 703-01, "USMA Admissions Files, Prep School, Part II (1979)," Records Group 404, West Point Archives.

70. The early years at Fort Belvoir were not easy. At first USMAPS occupied an abandoned hospital with converted classrooms stuffed with old medical equipment. In 1966 the school moved to reconditioned barracks that proved more commodious and efficient. Ignoffo, "A Brief History of USMAPS," 12–13. In 1975, the school moved to Fort Monmouth, New Jersey.

71. According to the USMAPS website, "Since 1951, West Point Prep graduates have comprised 11% of the Corps of Cadets, yet they have held 25% of the senior leadership positions of the Corps." "A History of Success," USMAPS, http://www.usma.edu/USMAPS/pages/history/history_home.htm, accessed 28 December 2010.

72. The outgoing adjutant in 1912, Robert C. Davis, described the workings of his office in the 1912 *Annual Report of the Superintendent* (38–39). He had a staff of nine civilian
and six enlisted clerks working in five divisions: records and mailing, discipline, military,
academics, and printing and binding. The academic division "has charge of all work connected with the examination of candidates." The work of admissions touched most of the
divisions in one way or another.

73. *Annual Report of the Superintendent*, 1947, 2.

74. Congress initially established the position as "Registrar" in 1959. Soon thereafter
the position was renamed "Registrar and Director of Admissions" and, eventually, "Director of Admissions." The new position was similar to a professorship in that it would be
filled by a colonel who could remain on active duty until turning sixty-four years old. Unlike a permanent professor, the Director of Admissions could not be elevated to brigadier
general upon retirement. After an exhaustive search, Robert S. Day was selected as the first
Director of Admissions.

75. Army Regulation 350-56, "Education and Training: U.S. Military Academy Admissions Program," approved 29 July 1960, established the West Point admissions program
as an official Army program. Previously, superintendents relied on the voluntary cooperation of the six continental army commanders to recruit enlisted soldiers interested in
competing for an Academy appointment. The new regulation required these commands to
appoint liaison officers and candidate advisory officers who would cooperate with the West
Point admissions office. *Annual Report of the Superintendent*, 1961, 2.

76. The Cadet Public Relations Council was an extracurricular activity under the
control of the commandant until 1975, when it became an official arm of the Directorate of
Admissions.

77. As an example of the growing reach of the admissions office, the staff contacted
18,000 young men in one way or another during academic year 1962–1963. Thirty-
nine percent of the class of 1966 acknowledged having received counsel through the admissions office. *Annual Report of the Superintendent*, 1963, 50.

78. *Annual Report of the Superintendent*, 1924, 20.

79. *Annual Report of the Superintendent*, 1948, 46–47. Not all the publicity was positive. A mass-cheating incident in 1951 resulted in the expulsion of most of the varsity
football team and a huge amount of negative press coverage.

80. *Annual Report of the Superintendent*, 1957, 106.

81. *West Point Plebe*, *West Point Yearling*, *West Point Second Classman*, and *West Point
First Classman*. All published by Duell, Sloan, and Pearce in 1955, 1956, 1957, and 1958,
respectively.

82. Garrison H. Davidson, "I Have 2,500 Sons," *Saturday Evening Post*, 1 February
1958; Verone G. Davidson, "My Two Families," *American Weekly*, 11 August 1957.

83. *Annual Report of the Superintendent*, 1957, 106.

84. Ibid., 1962, 22–26. Further evidence of the rising quality of incoming classes appears in a series of charts and tables in the 1963 *Annual Report of the Superintendent*, pages
48–50.

85. Westmoreland, *A Soldier Reports*, 36–37.

86. William C. Westmoreland, interview by Martin L. Ganderson, 1982, transcript,

Senior Officer Oral History Program, US Army Military History Institute, Carlisle, PA, 5. The plan for annual increases in the size of the Corps leading to the authorized strength of 4,417 appears on page 66 of the 1964 *Annual Report of the Superintendent*.

87. In the years just prior to the legislation, West Point provided about 25 percent of the Army's new officers. *Annual Report of the Superintendent*, 1963, 52.

88. Prior to 1962, members of Congress could nominate a total of four candidates. From 1962 to 1969, they could nominate six. The law changed again in 1969 to allow ten nominees. *Annual Report of the Superintendent*, 1969, 7. As of this writing, there have been no further increases.

89. Prior to 1969, congressmen used only the first and third options. Since then, they used all three methods. US Military Academy, *Catalogue 1969/1970*, 89.

90. *Annual Report of the Superintendent*, 1963, 48.

91. *Annual Report of the Superintendent*, 1968, 12.

92. "Comparison of Admissions Data: Classes of 1961 thru 1980," *Assembly* 35, no. 4 (March 1977): 44. The SAT mean scores were converted according to the "SAT I Mean Score Equivalents" chart on the College Board website. College Board, http://professionals .collegeboard.com/data-reports-research/sat/equivalence-tables/sat-mean, accessed 10 March 2009. Despite the drop in the number of qualified applicants, West Point refused to lower academic standards; hence the mean SAT test scores of the class that entered in 1968 were virtually unchanged from the three previous years.

93. Nye, "The Inadvertent Demise of the Traditional Academy, 1945–1995," 5–6. The disincentives not only affected potential candidates but also cadets. While cadet attrition hovered around 30 percent from 1958 to 1968, losses due to motivation increased sharply (from 8 to 18 percent) as those due to academics declined (from 14 to 4 percent). US Military Academy, *An Institutional Self-Evaluation of the United States Military Academy*, 25.

94. *Annual Report of the Superintendent*, 1968, 13.

95. Ibid., 10.

96. "Director of Admissions Assesses the USMA Admissions Program," *Assembly* 44, no. 1 (June 1985): 12; "Comparison of Admissions Data: Classes of 1961 thru 1980," *Assembly* 35, no. 4 (March 1977): 44.

97. "USMA Admissions Liaison Officers," *Assembly* 29, no. 4 (Winter 1971): 28.

98. "Director of Admissions Assesses the USMA Admissions Program," *Assembly* 44, no. 1 (June 1985): 12. E-mail correspondence from Col. Deborah McDonald, director of admissions, to author, 7 February 2011, copy in author files. As a captain, McDonald served in the Directorate of Admissions from 1985 to 1988 and worked closely with the MALOs.

99. Research had shown that the College Board achievement tests were poor predictors of academic success at West Point. In contrast, the Scholastic Aptitude Test, which measured cognitive ability rather than acquired knowledge, was far more useful as a predictive tool. *Annual Report of the Superintendent*, 1973, 6–7.

100. "Staff and Faculty Support of USMA Admissions," *Assembly* 51, no. 5 (May 1993): 30. The initiatives discussed here have continued to the present in one form or another.

101. Harry S. Truman, Executive Order 9981, "Desegregation of the Armed Forces," July 26, 1948.

102. Project Outreach fact sheet, 12 March 1979, file 703-01, "USMA Admissions Files, Admissions Program, 1979," Records Group 404, West Point Archives. Project Outreach officers focused their efforts on eighth- and ninth-grade students since older students had already begun building the scholastic record that would determine their competitiveness for college. Additionally, they worked with grass-roots community organizations, such as the Urban League, National Association for the Advancement of Colored People, and the League of United Latin American Citizens.

103. *Board of Visitors Report*, 28 December 1979, 7.

104. *Institutional Self-Study: Report of the United States Military Academy* (West Point: Office of the Dean, June 1999), 37. The ideas of this paragraph were influenced by Crackel, *West Point*, 237–38.

105. In contrast to the relative calm that characterized the admissions office, the rest of the Academy worked frenetically to prepare. One of Superintendent Sidney Berry's many concerns, for example, was how the tails of the full-dress coat worn by cadets during parades accentuated a woman's derrière in an unflattering way. Berry was less delicate: "When you put those tails on that dress coat over the woman's bottom, it looks like hell." Sidney B. Berry Jr., interview by Robert F. Broyles, 1983, transcript, Senior Officer Oral History Program, US Army Military History Institute, Carlisle, PA, 936.

106. *Annual Report of the Superintendent*, 1976, 22.

107. Ibid., 20.

108. "Director of Admissions Assesses the USMA Admissions Program," *Assembly* 44, no. 1 (June 1985): 13.

109. Of particular interest was the reverse-discrimination case of *Regents of The University of California v. Bakke*, 438 US 265 (1978), under consideration by the Supreme Court at the same time Rogers and Pollin were formulating their policy proposal. In June 1978, the court ruled (5–4) that college admissions boards could not use fixed racial quotas in meeting their affirmative-action goals for student body diversity.

110. "Director of Admissions Assesses the USMA Admissions Program," *Assembly* 44, no. 1 (June 1985): 13.

111. "Academic Board Directive on the Qualification of Candidates," 7 December 1977, file 703-01, USMA admissions files, Prep School, Part II (1979), Records Group 404, West Point Archives.

112. "Report of the Admissions Study Group," 17 February 1981, file 703-01, "USMA Admissions Files, Admissions Study Group Report (1981)," Records Group 404, West Point Archives.

113. From 1988 to 2002, an average of 12,414 applicants per year opened files with the admissions office. The highest number was 14,664 in 1988; the lowest was 9,895 in 2001. "Fiscal Year 2002 Assessment Report" (West Point: Office of Policy, Plans, and Analysis, 27 December 2002), 8.

114. US General Accounting Office, "Service Academies — Historical Proportion of New Officers during Benchmark Periods," 1. High officer attrition and a decline in the number of officers provided by the R.O.T.C. program added to the urgency of restoring the Corps of Cadets to its former size.

115. The reduction in the size of the admissions staff was partly the result of lever-

aging information technology to economize on resources. The director of admissions, Col. Michael Jones, believed that computers could make his staff smaller and more efficient. "Admissions," he boasted, "has been the only [directorate] at West Point that has voluntarily decreased its size. I have never gone to the Superintendent for an increase in my basic budget." Michael Jones, interview by author, 5 January 2008, transcript, 44. Jones's enthusiasm for economy does not explain the severe (37 percent) reduction in the admissions budget between 1999 and 2010.

116. At the end of 2010, the number of minority outreach staff members in the admissions office had dwindled to six. The corresponding numbers at the Naval Academy and Air Force Academy were seventeen and twenty-seven, respectively. The personnel shortage and other problems led the director of admissions, Col. Deborah McDonald, to initiate an external study of the West Point admissions program. The study group confirmed the existence of severe problems, especially in the area of minority recruitment: "The unfocused and under-resourced approach to diversity management at the United States Military Academy precludes the consistent production of classes of cadets that meet the Academy's class composition goals, and falls short of meeting the needs of the Army for diverse leadership in accordance with its composition." Signal Mountain Associates, "Briefing to West Point Admissions: Diversity and In-service Recruiting," 14–16 December 2010, Office of the Director of Admissions, West Point.

117. The decline in the number of MALOs was the result of budget pressures on the US Army Reserve Command (USARC) as it helped fight wars in Iraq and Afghanistan. During the 1990s, USARC budgeted nearly $200,000 a year to pay MALOs; by 2011, the amount was $25,000. E-mail correspondence from Col. Deborah McDonald, director of admissions, to author, 7 February 2011, copy in author files. According to an external review of the Directorate of Admissions in 2010, the MALO force had degraded "to the point of relative ineffectiveness across the United States." Signal Mountain Associates, "Briefing to West Point Admissions: Diversity and In-service Recruiting," 14–16 December 2010, Office of the Director of Admissions, West Point.

118. The admissions budget went from $5.4 million in 1999 to $3.4 million in 2010. Data provided to author by Plans and Resources Division, Office of the Dean, 12 May 2010. For a comparison of the Academy's budget priorities from 1999 to 2010, see table 5.8, "Percentage of Appropriated Funds Distributed to West Point Programs," in chapter 5.

119. The Signal Mountain Associates study, noted earlier, concluded that West Point's admissions marketing efforts "appear under resourced and insufficiently targeted toward in-service and minority recruiting to effect any positive result." "Briefing to West Point Admissions: Diversity and In-service Recruiting," 14–16 December 2010, Office of the Director of Admissions, West Point.

120. Army leaders had removed USMAPS from the superintendent's command authority in 1957, when the school moved from Stewart Air Force Base (Newburgh, New York) to Fort Belvoir, Virginia. Nonetheless, successive superintendents remained deeply interested in USMAPS because of its influence on the composition of the Corps of Cadets. Following the publication of a US General Accounting Office report questioning the effectiveness of USMAPS, Superintendent Howard Graves formed a review committee to study the issues. One of the committee's recommendations — to place USMAPS under the

command of the superintendent — was implemented in 1995. US Government Account-ability Office, *DoD Service Academies: Academy Preparatory Schools Need a Clearer Mission and Better Oversight*, GAO/NSIAD-92-57 (Washington, DC, March 1992); memorandum from Deputy Chief of Staff for Personnel to Deputy Chief of Staff for Operations, "Con-cept Plan — Transfer of Command and Staff Responsibility for the United States Military Academy Preparatory School," 21 June 1995, copy in author's files; US Military Academy, *Years of Continuity and Progress*, 29.

121. Memorandum from Deputy Chief of Staff for Personnel to Deputy Chief of Staff for Operations, "Concept Plan — Transfer of Command and Staff Responsibility for the United States Military Academy Preparatory School," 21 June 1995, 2, copy in author's files. Beginning in 1965, USMAPS expanded its enrollment to include a limited number of minorities and recruited athletes who enlisted in the Army Reserve or National Guard with the sole intent of eventually going to West Point. Provided they passed all their courses, students in these two categories usually were assured of getting an appointment. The num-ber of minorities and athletes so enrolled remained below 25 percent of USMAPS student body until the early 2000s; at that point, recruited athletes were allowed to fill 40 percent of the seats at USMAPS. A large portion of minority candidates were admitted to West Point via this route. "A History of Success," United States Military Academy Preparatory School website, http://www.usma.edu/USMAPS/pages/history/history_home.htm, ac-cessed 31 May 10. USMAPS moved from Fort Monmouth, New Jersey, to West Point in 2011.

122. Telephone interview with Col. Tyge Rugenstein, USMAPS commandant, 27 May 2010.

123. Memorandum from Deputy Chief of Staff for Personnel to Deputy Chief of Staff for Operations, "Concept Plan — Transfer of Command and Staff Responsibility for the United States Military Academy Preparatory School," 21 June 1995, 4, copy in author's files. The USMAPS admissions criteria also appear in the Academic Board Directive for the Admissions Committee. The 2010–2011 version of this document (dated 4 Novem-ber 2010) states, "Candidates who are not academically qualified to attend USMA will be considered for USMAPS" (11).

124. See, for example, Butler and Houston, *Attrition and Admission Scores, Class of 1975*. The report notes positive correlation between the whole-man score and graduation rates. In particular, the academic component of the whole-man score, known as the CEER (college entrance examination rank), was the best predictor of success. Michael Jones, direc-tor of admissions from 1995 to 2008, summarized the findings of decades of research: "If you had to throw everything else away and disband the admissions committee and the Academic Board and use just one indicator for success here at the Academy and out in the Army, it would be the CEER score." Michael Jones, interview by author, 5 January 2008, transcript, 25.

125. Some graduates favored a heavier concentration of practical military training in an effort to graduate more polished junior officers. Their arguments were usually loudest during and immediately after major wars. Still, the majority of graduates understood the importance of producing officers with the intellectual basis for long-term contributions at high levels of command. See chapter 6 for a discussion of the debate between the propo-nents of academic and military development.

126. In 2010, the decline in the class-composition goal for recruited athletes and the increase of the goals for scholars and leaders culminated a multiyear effort on the part of key members of the Academic Board. In particular, Col. David Allbee, chairman of the Admissions Committee (and head of the Department of Chemistry and Life Sciences), pressed his colleagues to approve the changes as a means of lessening the emphasis on intercollegiate athletics. Although a moral victory for Allbee and his allies on the Academic Board, the changes did nothing to alter the number of recruited athletes actually admitted to West Point. Recruited athletes had comprised about 20 percent of the incoming classes from 2004 through 2008 — in other words, the athletic director could man all of his intercollegiate teams with a 20 percent share of the Corps of Cadets. Reducing the class-composition goal for athletes from 20–25 percent to 18–23 therefore had no negative impact on his recruiting. Vincent Lan and Gene Lesinski, "2014 Class Composition Goals," 25 June 2009, Institutional Research and Assessment Branch, Office of the G5, West Point.

127. It should be noted that a considerable number of admitted candidates fall into more than one category. For example, a Hispanic female who graduated as valedictorian of her high school class, served as class president, and earned all-state honors in basketball would meet five class-composition goals — minority, female, scholar, leader, and athlete. While such cases complicate the task of comparing the qualifications of cadets across the class-composition categories, the general trends noted before remain valid.

128. Letter from Rogers to Lt. Gen. Lloyd R. Leavitt Jr., 9 July 1984, file 703-01, "USMA Admissions Files, Admissions Program (1984)," Records Group 404, West Point Archives.

129. See endnote 13.

130. The minimum qualification scores for the SAT math and verbal tests were both set at 560. A nominee who achieved those scores was "qualified" for entry even though the combined 1,120 score was about 180 points below the average for his class. (The maximum score possible on each component was 800; the maximum possible combined score was 1,600.)

131. Until 1980, the director of athletics always had been an active-duty, retired, or former Army officer. The switch to a civilian director was a response to a recommendation of the West Point Study Group to install someone with expertise in business management as well as athletics. Virtually the entire coaching staff is now civilian.

132. Studies have shown the SAT to be a dependable predictor of graduation rates. See, for example, Peter D. Salins, "The Test Passes, Colleges Fail," *New York Times* (online edition), 17 November 2008, http://www.nytimes.com/2008/11/18/opinion/18salins .html?th&emc=th (accessed 18 November 2008). From 1997 to 2006, Salins was provost of the State University of New York (SUNY), one of the largest university systems in the country. Following a careful study of SAT scores at several SUNY campuses, he concluded, "Only those campuses whose incoming students' SAT scores improved substantially saw gains in graduation rates."

133. Justification for each of the class-composition goals is in "Fiscal Year 1996 Assessment Report" (West Point: Office of Policy, Planning, and Analysis, September 1997), B-2. The justification for reserving 20–25 percent of each class for recruited athletes is to "field high quality intercollegiate teams."

134. The National Collegiate Athletic Association's highest level of competition is Di-

vision I, followed in descending order by Division II and Division III. The Military, Naval, and Air Force Academies all compete at the Division I level.

135. Fried, "Punting our Future: College Athletics and Admissions," available from the Carnegie Foundation for the Advancement of Teaching, http://www.carnegiefoundation .org, accessed 27 May 2007. Two of the more influential studies discussed in Fried's article are Shulman and Bowen, *The Game of Life*, and Bowen and Levin, *Reclaiming the Game*.

136. Ganoe, *MacArthur Close-Up*, 78.

137. Blaik, *The Red Blaik Story*, 394.

138. Stanley Woodward, "With the College Athletes in their Diversified Affairs," *New York Herald Tribune*, 28 January 1934, 17. Army had not lost to Navy since 1921. During that period there were two ties and two years in which the academies did not play each other. The exodus of so many plebe football players in 1934 may explain why Army lost two of the next three games against Navy. Another example of high academic failure among athletes is reported in "West Point Athletes among 70 Flunking," *New York Times*, 22 January 1928, 13. In that instance, twenty-two of the seventy cadets separated for academics were football players.

139. Perhaps the most influential congressional liaison was Col. Lawrence McCeney "Biff" Jones, class of August 1917 and a star football player at Army. Jones subsequently coached at Louisiana State University, and was a coach and athletic director at Army, Oklahoma, and Nebraska. He was responsible for recruiting Blaik as an Army coach in 1927. During Blaik's tenure as head coach in the 1940s and 1950s, Jones lobbied representatives and senators to nominate Blaik's football recruits. McWilliams, *A Return to Glory*, 431.

140. Ibid., 237.

141. Other sports also recruited, but football had the most recruited athletes by far. In addition to being the head football coach, Blaik served as the athletics director for most of his tenure at West Point. He openly favored football over all other sports because of its prestige and ability to raise enough money to pay for the entire athletics program.

142. Blaik, *The Red Blaik Story*, 395.

143. Ibid., 397. The friction between Blaik and Davidson went back to the time when the two of them were Army football coaches together during the late-1920s and 1930s.

144. Memorandum from Col. Edwin V. Sutherland (chairman of the Admissions Committee) to the Academic Board, "Additional Allocation for Athletes—Class of 1979," 7 May 1975, *Proceedings of the Academic Board* 88 (9 May 1975), Tab L, West Point Archives.

145. Under the system of class-composition goals, the athletic director had virtual ownership of up to 25 percent of each incoming class. The only condition was that a recruited athlete had to meet West Point's minimum entry standards. If a highly recruited athlete fell short of meeting the minimum standards, the athletic director could seek an exception from the Academic Board. The board members rarely turned down the athletic director because, even if they did so, the appointment would go to another recruited athlete rather than a higher-quality candidate on the national waiting list.

146. Survey results showing first-priority reasons for candidates selecting West Point (classes of 2002 through 2006) appear in "Fiscal Year 2002 Assessment Report" (West Point: Office of Policy, Plans, and Analysis, 27 December 2002), 8. The top reasons were self-development, West Point's reputation, the desire to be an Army officer, the academic

program, and leadership training. A 2008 study by a private public-relations firm had virtually the same findings. Artemis Strategy Group, "Brand and Communications Assessment," briefing slides presented at West Point, 15 July 2008.

147. Michael Jones, interview by author, 5 January 2008, transcript, 38.

148. See, for example, the tabulated information on "GPA and Test Scores by Sport Group" (p. 47) and "Special Admissions Information" (p. 48) in US Military Academy, *2007–2008 Division 1 Athletics Certification Self-Study Report.*

149. Institutional Research and Analysis Branch, "USMA Retention," briefing slides, 21 August 2008 (West Point: Office of Policy, Planning, and Assessment), copy in author files. Football players, as a group, were particularly prone to high attrition as officers.

150. On 3 June 1950, the Personnel Research Section of the Adjutant General's Office completed a report entitled "An Exploratory Study of the Relationship of West Point Class Standing and Achievement of the Rank of General Officer." Although tentative in its conclusions, the report showed that general officers who had graduated from West Point typically exceeded their classmates by a wide margin in academic performance. A copy of the report is on file at the Military History Institute, Carlisle, PA. Another report, conducted a few months after the 1951 cheating incident involving the football team, focused on the general officers from the West Point classes of 1903 through 1937 (the most recent class with a general officer). The total population of graduates from those years numbered 6,695, of whom 828 (12.4 percent) became general officers. Included in the total population were 1,227 varsity letter winners, of whom 121 (9.8 percent) became generals. Also included in the total population were 203 graduates designated as "distinguished cadets" by virtue of their academic performance; of this group, 52 (25.6 percent) achieved general officer rank. The results of the report are in a memorandum from the Adjutant General of the Army to the superintendent, Maj. Gen. Frederick A. Irving, 22 August 1951, file 351.01-351.1 USMA, Military Posts and Reservations, Army-AG Project Decimal File 1951–1952, Records Group 407, National Archives, College Park, MD.

151. Attainment of the rank of colonel represents a commonly used threshold of high success in a military career. Promotion to that rank is highly competitive and thus reflective of an officer's significant accomplishments and potential. Colonels may serve up to thirty years on active duty; general officers may serve longer. This definition of success is not meant to imply that officers of lower rank are incapable of making significant professional contributions during their careers.

152. In this context, "recruited athlete" refers to a cadet candidate who was individually contacted and recruited by representatives of the director of intercollegiate athletics in accordance with the bylaws of the National Collegiate Athletic Association. It should be noted that many nonrecruited cadets also played and lettered in varsity sports.

153. The differences shown in table 3.11 compare the promotion experience of recruited athletes with that of the Corps of Cadets as a whole. The differences would be more striking if the comparison were between recruited athletes, on the one hand, and their nonathlete classmates, on the other.

154. MacArthur composed the inspirational words that were chiseled above the main doors of the West Point gymnasium: "Upon the fields of friendly strife are sown the seeds that, upon other fields, on other days, will bear the fruits of victory."

155. See Taylor Branch, "The Shame of College Sports," *The Atlantic* [online edition], October 2011, for a critique of the distribution of benefits in intercollegiate athletics.

CHAPTER FOUR

1. Ambrose, *Duty, Honor, Country*, 192; Andrew Delbanco, "Colleges: An Endangered Species?" *The New York Review of Books* 52, no. 4 (10 March 2005), 4.

2. *Annual Report of the Superintendent*, 1902, 10.

3. Ibid. Because Academy leaders were sensitive to the criticism that the West Point curriculum was too theoretical, they took pains to tout the practical aspects of the new curriculum. Superintendent Albert Mills pointed out that "practical professional knowledge, both scientific and strictly military, [has] not been ignored. . . . This idea of making the knowledge itself practical permeates all the departments and is second only to the aim of securing the best training and development." Mills cited as evidence the professional subjects taught in the departments of Civil and Military Engineering, Tactics, Practical Military Engineering, and Law. *Annual Report of the Superintendent*, 1902, 11. While there was no denying the practical utility of these disciplines, the critics focused on the heavy doses of mathematics and science that greatly reduced the time available for other subjects important to the aspiring army officer.

4. Ibid., 7; US Military Academy, *Official Register of the Officers and Cadets of the U.S. Military Academy*, 1903, 31–32.

5. *Annual Report of the Superintendent*, 1905, 9.

6. The three-month expansion of the curriculum is covered in fuller detail in chapter 2.

7. John C. Adams, a Yale professor, was the first head of the Department of English and History. Unfortunately, the legislation authorizing the position provided only for a civilian "instructor," not a military "professor"; hence, Adams did not have legal authority over the members of his department and could not sit on the Academic Board. These frustrations induced him to leave the Academy after only two years. His replacement, Lucius H. Holt, also from Yale, was more fortunate. Congress commissioned him as an officer with the "rank, pay, allowances, title, and status of the other professors," which made him a full member of the Academic Board. Mallory, *Compiled Statutes of the United States, 1913*, 928. Holt headed the Department of English and History from 1910 to 1921 and the Department of Economics, Government, and History from 1921 to 1930.

8. "Regulations for Recitation Rooms," *Annual Report of the Superintendent*, 1896, 75–76.

9. Depending on the difficulty of the advance work, instructors would occasionally dispense with graded exercises and teach the assigned material during the class period. This was a rare reprieve from the self-study that characterized the West Point educational system. A detailed account of the educational methods at the Academy in the early twentieth century is Samuel E. Tillman, "Academic History of the Military Academy, 1802–1902," in US Military Academy, *Centennial*, 223–374. Included in these pages are comprehensive histories of each of the academic departments existing in 1902.

10. *Annual Report of the Superintendent*, 1906, 16.

11. Ibid., 13.

12. *Annual Report of the Superintendent*, 1907, 19.

13. Ibid., 36.

14. *Annual Report of the Superintendent*, 1914, 38.

15. Ibid., 23.

16. Daily grading in plebe mathematics continued at least through the 1970s. Author recollection.

17. The secretary of war, Elihu Root, conceived the trip as a means of providing more effective instruction in the military art. *Annual Report of the Superintendent*, 1902, 7. A fuller discussion of the annual trips to Gettysburg is in chapter 6.

18. *Annual Report of the Superintendent*, 1903, 8.

19. *Annual Report of the Superintendent*, 1915, 34.

20. *Annual Report of the Superintendent*, 1913, 14.

21. *Annual Report of the Superintendent*, 1911, 11.

22. *Annual Report of the Superintendent*, 1907, 19.

23. Between 1802 and 1890, a total of 3,741 cadets graduated from West Point. Of these, 615 (16.4 percent) took five or more years to do so. Reed, *Cadet Life at West Point*, appendix, xvi.

24. *Annual Report of the Superintendent*, 1916, 29.

25. Chapter 2 discusses the details surrounding Tillman's appointment as superintendent.

26. Tillman Papers, unpublished memoir, box 2, IV.19, West Point Archives.

27. Ibid.

28. *Annual Report of the Superintendent*, 1919, 27. The professor of mathematics, Col. Charles P. Echols, complained that wartime conditions forced his remaining instructors to teach three eighty-five minute classes per day, six days per week — an exhausting teaching load.

29. Tillman Papers, unpublished memoir, box 2, IV.19, West Point Archives.

30. *Annual Report of the Superintendent*, 1919, 28.

31. Crackel, *West Point*, 188; Nye, "The United States Military Academy in an Era of Educational Reform, 1900–1925," 294.

32. *Annual Report of the Superintendent*, 1919, 5, 12.

33. Chapter 2 examines the relationship between MacArthur and the Academic Board in more detail.

34. MacArthur quoted in Beukema, *The United States Military Academy*, 38.

35. Telegram from Pershing to Morin, 5 February 1920, reprinted in "Report of the Superintendent on the Course of Instruction of the United States Military Academy," 29 June 1942, file 351.051, Military Posts and Reservations, AGO Project Decimal Files 1940–1945, Records Group 407, National Archives, College Park, MD.

36. An Act making appropriation for the support of the Military Academy for the fiscal year ending June 30, 1921, and for other purposes, P.L. 66-166, chap. 112; 41 Stat. 538; Forman, *West Point*, 195.

37. Although nominally a four-year class, cadets in the class of 1922 entered West Point in November and December of 1918 and therefore experienced slightly less than the full four-year curriculum.

38. *Annual Report of the Superintendent*, 1920, 5.

39. The Department of Modern Languages stopped teaching Spanish during World War I and confined its instruction to French. During academic year 1919–1920, instruction in both languages resumed, with half of the class taking Spanish, the other half French. The following year, the Academic Board required cadets to take both languages. With the reinstatement of the four-year curriculum starting in the fall of 1921, cadets took two semesters of French and one of Spanish. Beukema, *The United States Military Academy*, 46.

40. A "full course" met daily throughout the academic year; a "half-course" met on alternating days. The Academic Board determined that a reasonable academic load for cadets would be a total of three full courses (six half-courses) a year, or twelve full courses (twenty-four half-courses) over four years. Some subjects, like plebe mathematics and natural and experimental philosophy, were full courses; most, however, were half-courses. For simplicity in table 4.3a, all course entries are measured in half-courses.

41. *Annual Report of the Superintendent*, 1920, 21.

42. Ganoe, *MacArthur Close-Up*, 97.

43. Ibid., 93.

44. The MacArthur initiatives in education are discussed in various sources: *Annual Report of the Superintendent*, 1920, 36–40; *Annual Report of the Superintendent*, 1921, 18; Ganoe, *MacArthur Close-Up*, 101, 117; Ambrose, *Duty, Honor, County*, 268–69.

45. Lovell, *Neither Athens Nor Sparta?*

46. Letter from Callan to the Adjutant General, 25 January 1926, and letter from Hagood to the Adjutant General, 27 January 1926, both in file packet on "Graduates USMA" dated 8 January 1926, AGO Central Files 1926–1939, Records Group 407, National Archives, College Park, MD. Emphasis in original document. In contrast to Callan's and Hagood's comments, Brig. Gen. Merch Stewart believed that the Academy placed too much emphasis on the "purely educational factor" and too little on "general training." Stewart had spent nearly eleven years at West Point in various capacities — cadet, tactical officer, commandant, and superintendent. He was serving in the last position in 1927 when he made the comment quoted above. Stewart to the Adjutant General, 14 April 1927, file packet on "Curriculum USMA," AGO Central Files 1926–1939, West Point, Records Group 407, National Archives, College Park, MD.

47. In early 1923, the army imposed severe cuts in faculty strength that caused class size to increase to about eighteen cadets per section, 50 percent larger than normal. Superintendent Sladen immediately recommended a return to previous manning levels that had kept class size no larger than twelve cadets per section. In August 1924, the army restored most of the lost faculty positions, which allowed classroom size to stabilize at 12.5 fourth classmen, 13.5 third classmen, 14.5 second classmen, and 15.5 first classmen per section. *Annual Report of the Superintendent*, 1923, 5–6, 9; Ibid., 4. Since then, class size has remained fairly constant at about sixteen cadets per section.

48. Ibid., 1925, 19. In 1902, Cecil Rhodes established the trust that would fund the eponymous scholarship; two years later the first scholarship winners were announced. Although the Academy did not start competing until 1925, it now ranks fourth among American colleges and universities in the number of scholarships received by its graduates.

49. Ibid., 1926, 1.

50. The Army Reorganization Act of 1920 authorized the War Department to pay tuition expenses for officers going to graduate school, but no money was made available to officers until 1927. 66 P.L. 242; 66 Cong., Ch. 227; 41 Stat. 786; Forman, *West Point*, 199. In 1939, Brig. Gen. Jay L. Benedict, superintendent from 1938 to 1940, noted the advantages of sending officers to graduate school. The education translated into a "marked improvement in instruction" at the Academy and helped to keep faculty credentials roughly equivalent with those of other undergraduate institutions. Additionally, the funds spent on education "benefit the government in the broadening of officers and better fitting them for future command and staff duty." *Annual Report of the Superintendent*, 1939, 4.

51. Forman, *West Point*, 198

52. When the Association of American Universities discontinued its listing of accredited institutions in 1949, the Academy initiated a relationship with the Middle States Association of Colleges and Secondary Schools for accreditation of its academic program. The first MSACSS accreditation was in 1949, with subsequent ones conducted regularly every ten years. US Military Academy, *An Institutional Self-Evaluation of the United States Military Academy*, 1969, 5.

53. US Military Academy, General Orders 45, 28 September 1926, West Point Archives.

54. Memorandum from army G-3 to chief of staff, 1 February 1933, and letter from Douglas MacArthur to chairman of the House Committee on Military Affairs, John J. McSwain, 4 February 1933, file packet on "Granting of Degrees to Graduates of West Point," AGO Central Files 1926–1939, Records Group 407, National Archives, College Park, MD. MacArthur was the army chief of staff from 21 November 1930 to 1 October 1935 and, as a former superintendent, continued to be keenly interested in Academy affairs.

55. *Annual Report of the Superintendent*, 1931, 3. The Department of Physics operated provisionally from 1931 to 1934, when Congress passed legislation making the reorganization official. War Department Bulletin No. 5, 13 June 1934, copy in AGO Central files 1926–1939, West Point, Records Group 407, National Archives, College Park, MD.

56. As a result of these changes, the department was renamed the Department of Mechanics in 1942.

57. The Department of Civil and Military Engineering had been responsible for teaching mechanical, civil, and military engineering as well as the course in military art. Once it lost responsibility for mechanical engineering, its coursework was divided evenly between civil and military engineering and military art; accordingly, in 1942 the department was renamed Military Art and Engineering.

58. Crackel, *West Point*, 202–03.

59. Forman, *West Point*, 197.

60. *Annual Report of the Superintendent*, 1940, 1.

61. Overseas travel was popular with cadets during the two-month summer furlough between their third-class and second-class years. In 1941, for example, 133 members of the class of 1943 planned to travel abroad. One of the more adventurous cadets was William Knowlton, a future superintendent and four-star general, whose six-week itinerary took him to Panama, Ecuador, Peru, Chile, Argentina, Uruguay, Brazil, Trinidad, Guatemala, and Mexico. Academy leaders encouraged such travel as a means of allowing cadets to

improve their language skills and broaden their cultural education. The trips were generally well received by the host nations. The Venezuelan Minister of War and Navy, Isaias Medina, told Secretary of War Henry Stimson that the visits of West Point cadets were valuable in "the forming of close ties of good fellowship between those who will be the future officers of the Armies of our two countries." Memorandum from commandant to superintendent, 28 May 1941, and letter from Medina to Stimson, 23 August 1940, both in file 210.68, Military Posts and Reservations (West Point), Army-AG Project Decimal Files 1940–1945, Records Group 407, National Archives, College Park, MD.

62. *Annual Report of the Superintendent*, 1942, 5.

63. *Annual Report of the Superintendent*, 1944, 25. The head of the Department of Modern Languages noted the presence of highly talented temporary officers, some of whom had been full professors at civilian universities. These officers "have brought new ideas and have in general provided that desirable contact with college methods and procedures that was obtainable formerly only by the visits to the colleges made from time to time by the head of the Department," 5. One of the temporary officers was Sumner Willard, later the head of the Department of Foreign Languages. Crackel, *West Point*, 210.

64. Memorandum from Brig. Gen. C. R. Huebner to Commander of Services of Supply, Lt. Gen. Brehon Somervell, 11 July 1942, file 351.051, Military Posts and Reservations (West Point), Army-AG Project Decimal Files 1940–1945, Records Group 407, National Archives, College Park, MD.

65. An Act to authorize a reduction in the course of instruction at the United States Military Academy, 77 Cong. Ch. 573; 77 P.L. 724; 56 Stat. 763. West Point was not alone in shortening its curriculum to three years during the war. Of the 550 US colleges then in existence, about 85 percent did the same. Rather than lose course content, most of the colleges cut vacation time and found other efficiencies. Forman, *West Point*, 203.

66. Letter from adjutant general to Wilby, 13 October 1942, letter from Secretary of War Henry Stimson to Wilby, 18 September 1942, and memorandum from G-3 to deputy chief of staff, file 334 ("Plan for Initiating 3-Year Course"), Military Posts and Reservations (West Point), Army-AG Project Decimal Files 1940–1945, Records Group 407, National Archives, College Park, MD. The members of the external review board were Dr. Karl T. Compton (President of the Massachusetts Institute of Technology), Dr. James B. Conant (President of Harvard University), Maj. Gen. H. R. Bull (Army Ground Forces), Col. L. S. Smith (Army Air Forces), Brig. Gen. C. R. Huebner (Services of Supply), and Brig. Gen. I. H. Edwards (War Department General Staff).

67. "Report of the Superintendent on the Three Year Course of Instruction at the United States Military Academy," 30 January 1943, file 351, Military Posts and Reservations (West Point), Army-AG Project Decimal Files 1940–1945, Records Group 407, National Archives, College Park, MD.

68. German was added to the curriculum in 1941, Portuguese in 1942, and Russian in 1945. Concurrent with these changes, the Department of Modern Languages shifted the focus of instruction from reading and writing to speaking the languages. Patricia B. Genung, "Teaching Foreign Languages at West Point," in Betros, ed., *West Point: Two Centuries and Beyond*, 521–22. Although not opposed to the change, Superintendent Wilby

noted that it "will violate the long established practice of giving the same course of studies to all cadets." *Annual Report of the Superintendent*, 1941, 4.

69. *Annual Report of the Superintendent*, 1942, 8.

70. The changes noted in the paragraph are discussed in the opening pages of the *Annual Report of the Superintendent*, 1941 through 1944. In recognition of these curricular changes, the War Department renamed four departments in 1942: Civil and Military Engineering to Military Art and Engineering; Natural and Experimental Philosophy to Mechanics; Drawing to Military Topography and Graphics; and Ordnance and Science of Gunnery to Ordnance.

71. See chapter 6 for a fuller discussion of pilot training.

72. The adjustments made by each academic department on account of pilot training are discussed in the *Annual Report of the Superintendent*, 1943, 3–11.

73. Wilby first asked to reinstate the four-year curriculum in January 1944. The War Department disapproved the request and directed Wilby to try again in November. The correspondence continued until the War Department gave its approval in May 1945. Letter from Wilby to Lt. Gen. Brehon Sommervell, 11 January 1944, and 1st endorsement from adjutant general to Wilby, 29 January 1944, file 351.051, Military Posts and Reservations (West Point) Army-AG Project Decimal Files 1940–1945, Records Group 407, National Archives, College Park, MD.

74. *Annual Report of the Superintendent*, 1946, 18. One of the members of the newly designated class of 1948 was Sidney Berry, superintendent from 1974 to 1977. Berry would have liked to graduate in 1947 and regretted having to stay the extra year since some of the added courses were poorly conceived and executed. One such course was in animal management, during which Berry and his classmates learned how to clean a horse's dock—the circular area directly beneath its tail. He recalled good naturedly, "In the center of the bulls eye is where the excreta emerges and we learned how to clean that horse's dock with practical, hands-on application." Sidney B. Berry Jr., interview by Robert F. Broyles, 1983, transcript, 2 vols. (Senior Officer Oral History Program, US Army Military History Institute, Carlisle, PA), 1: 26.

75. US Military Academy, *Post War Curriculum at the U. S. Military Academy*, 8.

76. Ibid., 21–22.

77. Alexander's appointment was provisional. Once Congress passed legislation making the position permanent in 1947, Brig. Gen. Harris Jones, formerly the professor of mathematics, filled the job on a permanent basis.

78. Three of the new professors were particularly noteworthy. Col. Vincent J. Esposito (Military Art and Engineering) published several important works of military history, including the *West Point Atlas of American Wars*, 2 vols. (New York: Praeger, 1959), a masterpiece of history and cartography. Col. William W. Bessell Jr. (Mathematics) eventually became the dean. Col. George A. Lincoln (Social Sciences) was a prominent scholar in national security affairs and, later, a member of the National Security Council.

79. With the war over, many of the temporary instructors requested release from active duty to return to their civilian pursuits. The War Department refused those requests until their replacements had finished graduate school. Despite the disappointment, the tempo-

rary officers continued their work in a way that Academy officials described as "entirely satisfactory." *Annual Report of the Superintendent*, 1945. 5.

80. Maxwell D. Taylor, interview by Col. Richard A. Manion, 19 October 1972, transcript, 6.

81. Maxwell D. Taylor, *West Point Looks Ahead* (West Point: USMA, March 1946), 3. By academic year 1945–1946, the military history course had expanded to 101 class periods, one half of all the instruction given by the Department of Military Art and Engineering. The classes were eighty minutes in length, which gave them the same high priority as mathematics, science, and engineering classes. The subcourses included the great campaigns before Napoleon, campaigns of Napoleon, American Civil War, World War I, and World War II. *Annual Report of the Superintendent*, 1946, 14.

82. Taylor, *West Point Looks Ahead*, 2–3.

83. Other members of the board included Dr. James P. Baxter (President of Williams College), Lt. Gen. Troy H. Middleton (Comptroller, Louisiana State University), and several active-duty major generals and brigadier generals representing various components of the army. *Annual Report of the Superintendent*, 1946, 1–2.

84. Taylor, *West Point Looks Ahead*, "Foreword."

85. The establishment of the Office of Military Psychology and Leadership (OMPL) and the courses it offered are covered in fuller detail in chapter 7. Besides teaching applied psychology and leadership, OMPL administered the commandant's new Aptitude for the Military Service program for assessing the leadership potential of cadets.

86. Taylor, *West Point*, 6.

87. Robert L. Stearns, "A Report and Recommendation to the Secretary of Defense," 1.

88. Ibid., 3.

89. Ibid., 1949, 8, 12, 22–23.

90. Ibid., 21–22.

91. During the 1950s, the academic departments increasingly allowed their incoming instructors two years at graduate school. In contrast, the Department of Military Art and Engineering required its military history instructors to be graduates of the army's Command and General Staff College and therefore did not send them to civilian graduate school. This policy began to change in 1965, when the department experimented by sending three of its officers to Duke University, which had a strong graduate program in military history. The experiment worked well, thus prompting the department to continue and expand the program in subsequent years. Recollection of Lt. Gen. Dave Palmer (a military history instructor in the late-1960s) to author, July 2007.

92. Faculty members in every department published books and articles, but the Department of Social Sciences was the most productive. Within a three-year period, several important books appeared in print: George A. Lincoln, *International Relations* (West Point, 1949); Department of Social Sciences, *Contemporary Foreign Governments* (New York: Rinehart & Co., 1949); Department of Social Sciences, *Economies of National Security* (West Point, 1950); Department of Social Sciences, *Principles of Insurance* (Harrisburg, PA: Military Services Publishing Co., 1950); J. S. Harnett, *Principles of Finance for Junior Officers* (West Point, 1951). All of these books were used in Department of Social Sciences courses.

93. Berry's awards during the Korean War Included two Silver Stars, a Bronze Star for

Valor, a Purple Heart, and the Combat Infantryman's Badge. Association of Graduates, *Register of Graduates and Former Cadets of the United States Military Academy* (West Point: USMA, annual), Cullum number 16631–1948.

94. Berry interview transcript, 1: 351–53.

95. *Annual Report of the Superintendent*, 1951, 34.

96. *Annual Report of the Superintendent*, 1950, 27. The SCUSA continues to be conducted annually by the Department of Social Sciences and is the premier student conference of its type in the nation.

97. Berry interview transcript, 1: 368.

98. *Annual Report of the Superintendent*, 1948, 5.

99. Ibid., 1958, 19.

100. Davidson received a promotion to lieutenant general in 1957.

101. Garrison Holt Davidson, "Plain Talk," *Assembly* 15, no. 4 (January 1957): 1.

102. In 1958, only 2 percent of the West Point faculty held a doctoral degree, 65 percent held a master's degree, 32 percent held a bachelor's degree, and 1 percent had no college degree. Of the twenty-one permanent professors, only four held a doctoral degree. Davidson ordered all but the most senior nondoctoral professors to work toward completion of the degree. Moreover, he established a policy limiting the selection of future professors to officers who already had a doctorate or who were likely to complete the degree very soon. The sabbatical leave policy Davidson established in 1957 enabled those professors lacking a doctorate to complete the degree. Col. Charles H. Schilling (Military Art and Engineering) and Col. Elliott C. Cutler (Electrical Engineering) earned their doctorates this way. *Annual Report of the Superintendent*, 1959, 12; US Military Academy, *Report Prepared for the Commission on Institutions of Higher Education of the Middle States Association of Colleges and Secondary Schools*, November 1958, General Headquarters File 080, Middle States Association of Colleges and Secondary Schools, West Point Archives, iii, 64.

103. Davidson, "Grandpa Gar," 155, 161, 163.

104. *Annual Report of the Superintendent*, 1960, 27.

105. Davidson, "Grandpa Gar," 156, 161.

106. *Annual Report of the Superintendent*, 1957, 7.

107. As an example of the thoroughness of the curricular review, see John R. Jannarone, et al., "Superintendent's Curriculum Study.": Report of the Working Committee on the Present Curriculum and Future Trends," 31 August 1958, West Point Archives.

108. Davidson, "Grandpa Gar," 163, 165.

109. *Annual Report of the Superintendent*, 1960, 9.

110. Ibid., 42. By 1974, when Davidson penned his memoirs, the number of elective offerings had ballooned to 164. Ironically, he came to believe in later years that the elective program had expanded too far. He argued in his memoirs against further expansion of electives "to avoid unduly diluting the Academy's efforts toward its main goal." He sharpened the argument as a member of the Academy's board of visitors in the early 1980s. Davidson, "Grandpa Gar," 166.

111. As a result of the curricular changes of 1959, the departments of Mathematics, Military Art and Engineering, Military Topography and Graphics, Physics and Chemistry, and Social Sciences immediately began offering advanced courses. The Department of For-

eign Languages had been offering them for several years in French, German, and Spanish. *Annual Report of the Superintendent*, 1960, 53, 61–62, 64, 68, 70.

112. *Annual Report of the Superintendent*, 1959, 11.

113. Quoted in ibid., 2. The accrediting board noted one area of concern: "The methods of instruction cause one to wonder whether there is undue emphasis on 'grades' and whether there is as much opportunity for expressing individual viewpoints and for extended project work as might be desirable." Middle States Association of Colleges and Secondary Schools, *Evaluation Report*, 15–18 February 1959, 3.

114. The number of cadet validations increased dramatically during the decade. In academic year 1960–1961, forty-seven cadets validated one or more core courses; in academic year 1970–1971, the number swelled to 1,209, an increase of almost 2,500 percent. During the same period, the size of the Corps of Cadets expanded from 2,496 to 4,417, an increase of about 77 percent. *Annual Report of the Superintendent*, 1972, Appendix E.

115. Daniel W. Christman, interview by Stephen Grove, 29 September 1998, transcript, 6.

116. *Annual Report of the Superintendent*, 1965, iv.

117. Ibid., 1963, 9. Research on cadet attitudes toward academics reflected great satisfaction with the expansion of elective courses. Surveys administered to first classmen in 1969, 1970, and 1971 showed that electives were "academic motivators" for cadets, most of whom "consistently aspire to graduate degrees." Morgovsky, *Trends in Responses to First Class Questionnaire 1969, 1970, 1971*.

118. *Annual Report of the Superintendent*, 1963, 3.

119. *Annual Report of the Superintendent*, 1970, 9.

120. *Annual Report of the Superintendent*, 1968, 4–5. The authority to take eight electives started in academic year 1968–1969 for cadets concentrating their electives in national security and public affairs. Within two years, the Academic Board extended the authority to cadets concentrating in the humanities. US Military Academy, *1970/1971 Catalog*, 18–19.

121. Although the new core curriculum contained an equal number of quantitative and nonquantitative courses, many of the former courses had greater weight than the latter. For example, plebe mathematics courses were worth 7.5 credit hours because they met six times a week; in contrast, most nonquantitative courses were worth 4.0 or 2.5 credit hours and met on alternating days. The imbalance of credit hours meant that cadets still spent more time in the quantitative half of the core curriculum, despite the parity in the number of courses. For a complete listing of courses and credit hours, consult "Academic Program" in the *1971/1972 Catalog*. Cadets did not have to declare an elective concentration if they preferred to take courses in multiple disciplinary areas.

122. US Military Academy, *1971/1972 Catalog*, 37. Within a few years, the number of academic departments residing in Thayer Hall had dropped to four: History, Mathematics, Behavioral Sciences and Leadership, and Electrical Engineering and Computer Science. In 1989, the museum moved to Olmstead Hall at the Pershing Center immediately south of West Point in Highland Falls, New York; the move put the museum over a mile away from the main academic area and therefore complicated its efforts to support cadet education.

123. When first established in December 1962, the Academic Computing Center consisted of three GE-225 computers in Thayer Hall. During its first semester of operation,

approximately seven hundred fourth classmen and seventy-five faculty members learned to write computer programs. An improved facility, also in Thayer Hall, opened in May 1965; later that year, a new time-sharing system allowed cadets to use the computers from remote locations, such as laboratories and other classrooms. *Annual Report of the Superintendent*, 1964, 22–23; *Annual Report of the Superintendent*, 1965, vi.

124. *Annual Report of the Superintendent*, 1962, 5.

125. Ibid., 7.

126. *Annual Report of the Superintendent*, 1965, ix. Academy leaders advised cadets to postpone their graduate schooling until after they had served for two or more years in the field army. Otherwise, the student-officers would report to their first tactical units with plenty of education but little experience in dealing with soldiers. Raymond Winkel, who graduated in the top 5 percent of the class of 1967, would have gone to graduate school immediately had not a respected mentor advised him against it. He went to Vietnam instead, where he was seriously wounded by an enemy mine. After a long recovery, Winkel studied physics at the University of California at Berkeley and taught in the Department of Physics at West Point. He served as the head of the department from 1987 until his retirement in 2009. Raymond Winkel, interview by author, 18 June 2009, transcript, 6–7. In 1974, the army withdrew the option of immediate graduate schooling; henceforth, distinguished graduates would matriculate between their fourth and tenth year of service, provided their record of service merited the privilege of graduate schooling. This change was partly in response to the case of a cadet who had graduated in 1968, immediately began graduate study at Harvard, and, while there, applied for classification as a conscientious objector. *Annual Report of the Superintendent*, 1971, 13.

127. *Annual Report of the Superintendent*, 1963, 25.

128. *Annual Report of the Superintendent*, 1970, 9; 1971, 11–12; 1977, 8. Brig. Gen. John Jannarone, the dean from 1965 to 1973, was the driving force behind the creation of the faculty research program and the Science Research Laboratory. After graduating first in his West Point class (1938), he spent the rest of his life in science. He worked on the Manhattan Project during World War II and achieved national recognition as a physicist. He became the head of the Department of Physics in 1964 and, a year later, the dean. In the latter capacity, he advanced scientific research at West Point to the point of worrying some Academic Board members that cadets would opt to leave the military for careers in science and technology. E-mail correspondence with William B. Streett, first director of the Science Research Laboratory, 11 August 2007, author files.

129. Between 1969 and 1974, West Point received a total of $198,200 in research funds; by 1980, the amount was $309,500. *Annual Report of the Superintendent*, 1980, 12. In 2008, the total was over $18 million. Information paper, "FY09 West Point Funding from Other Sources," 24 August 2009, Office of Policy, Plans, and Analysis, West Point.

130. A 1969 study of cadet perceptions concluded: "The majority of cadets feels that the introduction of more electives enhances the academic climate at USMA; moreover, 70% do not believe that USMA has gone far enough in this area. The feeling of the Class of 1969 was clearly positive towards the further development of a majors-type program." Morgovsky, *Educational Aspirations and Academic Environment*, 2.

131. The continued improvement of the academic program was evident in the strong

performance of first classmen on the GRE Aptitude Test, another standardized test taken by college seniors. Just as they had done in the 1950s, graduating cadets scored well above their civilian peers. For example, the average score of the class of 1964 was in the seventy-sixth percentile in verbal skills and in the ninety-third percentile in quantitative skills; these scores were representative of the performance of other West Point classes during the 1960s. The high scores suggested that West Point was succeeding in its mission of providing a first-rate education to cadets. *Annual Report of the Superintendent*, 1965, 25.

132. Hecox, *The Performance of USMA Graduates*. Hecox used the results of the GRE Aptitude Test to compare officers from various commissioning sources. West Point graduates far exceeded their peers in every category of measurement.

133. Dr. John J. Meng, executive vice president of Fordham University and head of the Middle States Association of Colleges and Secondary Schools evaluation team, quoted in Hecox, *The Performance of USMA Graduates*, 3.

134. Cutler, Schilling, and Dick, "Minority Report, Curriculum Revision, Academic Board Actions 17–18 April, 1968," Charles Schilling Papers, West Point Library, quoted in Crackel, *West Point*, 262.

135. US Military Academy, *Institutional Self-Evaluation of the United States Military Academy: A Report Prepared for the Commission on Institutions of Higher Education of the Middle States Association of Colleges and Secondary Schools*, January 1969, 7–8.

136. *Annual Report of the Superintendent*, 1969, 5–6.

137. *Annual Report of the Superintendent*, 1973, 10–11. The members of the review board were Mr. Frederick Kappel, former chairman of the board of American Telephone and Telegraph Corporation; Dr. Roy H. Lamson, Department of Humanities, Massachusetts Institute of Technology; Dr. Frank A. Rose, former president of the University of Alabama; and Gen. C. H. Bonesteel, US Army, retired. The continued existence of Saturday classes at West Point may have inspired the review panel's concern about cadet time. Few other colleges and universities still required their students to attend weekend classes.

138. *Annual Report of the Superintendent*, 1974, 11; Crackel, *West Point*, 262–63. The only two exceptions to the lesson drop plan were third-class mathematics and fourth-class foreign languages. In addition to the 10 percent cuts, the Academic Board required cadets concentrating in the humanities or in national security and public affairs to take an additional mathematics course. This change equalized the number of mathematics courses that every cadet had to take and reduced the number of allowable electives in the two concentrations from eight to seven.

139. *Annual Report of the Superintendent*, 1977, 5; Crackel, *West Point*, 263; Berry interview transcript, 2: 959–61.

140. Borman graduated from West Point in 1950 and achieved fame as an astronaut. He was the commander of Apollo 8, the first mission to orbit the moon. Following his retirement from the military, he had a successful business career that culminated as chief executive officer of Eastern Airlines from 1975 to 1986.

141. Cadet performance on the Graduate Record Exam suggested the trend toward academic mediocrity. For example, the scores for the class of 1978 on the three components of the test were 505 verbal, 637 quantitative, and 561 analytical. In comparison, the national means were 503 verbal, 525 quantitative, and 513 analytical. Although the

cadets still outscored their civilian peers in all measures, the difference between their scores had narrowed considerably over the previous decade. *Annual Report of the Superintendent*, 1978, 6.

142. Frank Borman, *Report to the Secretary of the Army*, 11.

143. West Point Study Group, *Final Report of the West Point Study Group*, 4.

144. Gen. Goodpaster, although the most senior officer in the army, voluntarily gave up one star during the time he served as the superintendent (1977 to 1981). See chapter 2.

145. *Annual Report of the Superintendent*, 1978, 18–21, 42. The reduction of the core curriculum brought painful cuts for some departments. For example, the Department of Chemistry's core course went from two semesters to one; the same happened to the military history course in the Department of History. (Both of the lost semesters returned a few years later.) The Department of Mathematics eliminated much material on multivariable calculus. Fluid mechanics (Department of Mechanics) was removed from the core curriculum.

146. Ibid., 68–69. Other perceived weaknesses included the inability to write well or to relate well to enlisted soldiers.

147. *Final Report of the West Point Study Group*, 14. Also commenting on the need for the academic program to encourage greater mental agility among cadets were visiting professors, accreditation officials from the Middle States Association of Colleges and Secondary Schools, and internal review committees. Col. Patrick Hoy, chairman of the West Point curriculum committee in 1982, summarized their collective opinions to the Academic Board. Academic courses at West Point, he noted, "emphasize correct solutions and teach cadets how to solve specific types of problems at the expense of developing their capacity to analyze critically, to wrestle with questions of broader intellectual scope, and to assimilate, integrate, and synthesize knowledge from disparate scholarly areas into a coherent whole. In short, we tend to inhibit initiative, innovation, and creative thinking." Memorandum from Hoy to the Academic Board, 11 May 1982, "Proceedings of the Academic Board," 27 September 1982, Tab E, 27.

148. Brig. Gen. Fletcher M. Lamkin, West Point class of 1964 and dean from 1995 to 2000, recalled the mechanistic approach to learning that characterized much of the West Point academic experience in the early 1960s. Lamkin described academics as rigorous, but only because of the volume of material and the frequency of evaluation. "It was sheer volume and regurgitation. There were very few . . . opportunities to really do any deep, reflective thinking about a subject." Lamkin's remarks underscored the emphasis on finding the "approved solution"—that is, the precise answer to a problem that would earn a passing grade—rather than best solution in the context of political, social, and economic considerations. Fletcher Lamkin, interview by Stephen Grove, 12 May 2000, transcript, 1.

149. Ironically, the West Point Study Group claimed not to favor majors; instead, it preferred "interdisciplinary areas of concentration [to] ensure a desired degree of specialization without the high costs involved in accredited majors." One senses that the study group was simply paying lip service to the conservatism of the Academic Board, since there was no mistaking the direction in which the curriculum was headed. *Final Report of the West Point Study Group*, 15.

150. Ibid., 16.

151. The disciplinary field was in "psychology/sociology," and it came under the "national security and public affairs" area of concentration. Ibid., 9–10.

152. *Annual Report of the Superintendent*, 1977, 4. The Department of Defense study, "Review of Faculty Mix at the U.S. Service Academies and Senior Intermediate Colleges" (16 March 1977), recommended an increase in the number of civilians on the service academy faculties. The first year-long visiting professor at West Point was Dr. Jay Luvaas, a distinguished military historian from Allegheny College. The author's experience with the many visiting professors who have served in the Department of History has been nothing but positive.

153. *Annual Report of the Superintendent*, 1978, 3, 44. Exceptions to the policy on sixty-minute classes were the periodic laboratory periods in the sciences and one ninety-minute mathematics class per week. Ibid., 18.

154. Andrew J. Goodpaster, interview by James Johnson, 10 March 1988, transcript, 46. See chapter 3 for coverage of admissions policies relating to minorities and athletes.

155. Although deleted as core courses, American Institutions and the third semester of foreign language became "area courses" for cadets enrolled in the humanities and public affairs track. *1981–82 Catalog*, 39.

156. *Annual Report of the Superintendent*, 1981, 9–10.

157. The representation of the core curriculum as a "professional major" became popular among Academy leaders who opposed academic majors. The term appears in several curriculum committee memoranda in the fall of 1982, when the proposal for academic majors was under review by the Academic Board. See, for example, Col. Patrick Hoy's "The Notion of Education: Majors at West Point" in "Proceedings of the Academic Board," 13 September 1982, Tab DD, West Point Archives.

158. Ibid., 9. The programs in civil, mechanical, and electrical engineering received ABET accreditation in 1985. Accreditation for other engineering programs followed over the next few years.

159. Willard Scott, "Letter to Graduates," *Assembly* 42, no. 1 (June 1983); Crackel, *West Point*, 265. For an extended discussion of the advantages and disadvantages of academic majors, see the reports of the curriculum committee chair, Col. Patrick Hoy, to the Academic Board. "Proceedings of the Academic Board," 11 May 1982 (Tab EE) and 13 September 1982 (Tab DD), West Point Archives.

160. See chapter 2.

161. Although the Academy had developed a solid reputation for academic excellence, there were still many critics. Mitchell Zais (USMA 1969), a former instructor who later became the president of Newberry College and the superintendent of education in South Carolina, argued in 1990 that the curriculum "remains an anachronism, despite recent revisions. While mandating academic work in tangential fields, West Point has failed to require an adequate study of war." Zais, "West Point: Sword Making or Swordsmanship?," 57. Roger Nye offers a variation of the same idea in "The Inadvertent Demise of the Traditional Academy, 1945–1995."

162. Lt. Gen. Dave Palmer, interview by Stephen Grove, 24 June 1991, transcript, 22. Under a program known as "Project Enrichment," Palmer took several measures, in addition to reducing the course load, to give cadets more time and to enhance the quality of the

developmental experience. For example, he reduced the number of graded physical education requirements and made the evening meal optional. Most significant, he moved all of
the military training normally given during the academic year to a two-week "intercession"
in January, just prior to the start of the second semester. See chapter 6 for a fuller discussion
of the intercession. Information on the percentage of cadets choosing to declare majors is
from the Operations and Registrar Division, Office of the Dean.

163. Donnithorne, *Preparing for West Point's Third Century*. Palmer's curricular
changes led to a restructuring of the academic departments. In 1989, the Department of
Geography and Computer Science gave up the latter discipline to Electrical Engineering, which became the Department of Electrical Engineering and Computer Science. The
new Department of Systems Engineering evolved from the engineering management
courses resident in the Department of Engineering, now dissolved, and the Department
of Mechanics. The latter department reorganized to become the Department of Civil and
Mechanical Engineering. In 1990, the Department of Geography evolved into the Department of Geography and Environmental Engineering. Theodore Crackel provides an excellent genealogy of the academic departments at West Point from 1802 to 2002. Crackel,
West Point, Appendix A.

164. Office of the Dean, *Educating Army Leaders for the 21st Century* (West Point,
1997). The second edition, released in 2002, was renamed *Educating Future Army Officers
for a Changing World*. A third edition (same name) appeared in 2007.

165. Elizabeth Redden, "Mapping Student Learning with Precision," *Inside Higher
Education*, 18 July 2008, http://www.insidehighered.com/news/2008/07/18/westpoint,
accessed 7 September 2009.

166. Immediately prior to his assignment as superintendent, Christman served for
twenty-one months as a senior assistant to the chairman of the Joint Chiefs of Staff, Gen.
John M. Shalikashvili. Concurrently, he worked with Secretary of State Warren Christo-
pher as a member of the Middle East Peace Negotiating Team and in arms control negotia-
tions with the Russian Federation.

167. George B. Forsythe and Bruce Keith, "The Evolving USMA Academic Curriculum, 1952–2002," in Lance Betros, ed., *West Point*, 383–84.

168. Most of the money available for cadet enrichment activities came through the
fund-raising arm of the Association of Graduates, a nonprofit organization that supports
Academy priorities. The Association was founded in 1869 to reconcile the divisions in the
alumni community caused by the Civil War. After World War II, it gradually broadened
its scope to include supporting the initiatives of the superintendent. "West Point Association of Graduates," http://www.westpointaog.org/NetCommunity/Page.aspx?pid=409,
accessed 18 October 2009.

169. In February 2004, the Department of Defense implemented the Language
Transformation Initiative to make substantial improvements in the quality and quantity of
language training for members of the armed forces. The Defense effort was part of a larger
program to improve foreign language proficiency nationally. As part of the initiative, West
Point received generous funding to hire twenty-three extra foreign language instructors
and to expand the semester-abroad program for cadets. Gerry J. Gilmore, "Bush Kicks
Off National Foreign Language Initiative," *Department of Defense News*, 5 January 2006,

http://www.defenselink.mil/news/newsarticle.aspx?id=14684, accessed 20 September 2009.

170. Data on the semester-abroad program appears on the website of the Center for Languages, Cultures, and Regional Studies (part of the Department of Foreign Languages), http://www.dean.usma.edu/centers/clcrs/, accessed 11 October 2009.

171. The oldest center of excellence at West Point — the Office of Economic and Manpower Analysis (OEMA) — was founded in 1983. The OEMA was the brainchild of then-Lt. Gen. Maxwell Thurman, the army's deputy chief of staff for personnel, who sought to apply econometric analysis to the problem of attracting high-quality recruits for the army. Housed in the Department of Social Sciences, OEMA continues to provide army-level support on a variety of personnel-related issues. Although its military staff teaches economics to cadets, OEMA's primary focus is not on West Point. For this reason, I chose not to include it as an "academic" center of excellence.

172. Carl Ohlson (director of the Center for Enhanced Performance), "History of CEP," unpublished brief history provided to author, 5 May 2008. West Point's first program for enhancing reading and study skills started in the Department of English in 1959. In 1964, the West Point library opened an Academic Skills Center and began offering a comprehensive reading improvement program. Pleased with the results, the dean hired a civilian director to lead the new Reading and Study Skills Center. The purpose of the center was to diagnose and remediate academic weaknesses through formal courses during the academic year and summer school. Although the courses did not satisfy graduation requirements, they helped weaker cadets in the required courses. The courses now offered by the Center for Enhanced Performance are derivatives of the earlier offerings of the Reading and Study Skills Center.

173. Operations Research Center website, http://usmasvdfcase6se:19387/Pages/AboutSE.aspx, accessed 18 September 2009.

174. In 2011, the center's name changed to the Center for Faculty Excellence.

175. Mr. Vincent Viola, a 1977 graduate of West Point, was chairman of the New York Mercantile Exchange at the time of the 11 September 2001 terror attacks. He lost many friends and business associates when the twin towers of the World Trade Center collapsed. Those losses inspired him to make the lead donation for establishing the Combating Terrorism Center. "Combating Terrorism Center at West Point," http://ctc.usma.edu/about.asp, accessed 18 September 2009.

176. Center for Teaching Excellence, http://www.dean.usma.edu/centers/cte/Master.cfm; Center for Oral History, http://www.westpointcoh.org/; "West Point Center for the Rule of Law Dedicated," *Pointer View*, 23 April 2009, http://www.westpoint.edu/Dcomm/PV/yr2009/09APR23.pdf; Center for Cultures, Languages, and Regional Studies, http://www.dean.usma.edu/centers/clcrs/contact.htm. All websites accessed 20 September 2009. Another center of excellence — the Center for Holocaust and Genocide Studies — was about to open in the Department of History.

177. Data provided by the Operations and Registrar Division, Office of the Dean, West Point, 8 September 2009.

178. As of this writing, the army was considering policies for increasing the number of

cadets entering the Corps of Engineers. Additionally, Academy leaders made special appeals to cadets to encourage them to major in science and engineering.

179. An Act to authorize appropriations for fiscal year 1993 for military activities of the Department of Defense, 23 October 1992, P.L. 102-484, 106 Stat. 2410. The law authorized the secretary of the army to employ "as many civilians as professors, instructors, and lecturers at the Academy as the Secretary considers necessary." Successive secretaries set a goal of making the faculty 25 percent civilian. The law applied equally to the Air Force Academy.

180. Graduation data obtained from two sources: Office of Institutional Research, West Point, and US General Accounting Office, *Service Academies*, GAO/NSIAD-92-90, 9.

181. The exception was during World War II, when the Academic Board conditioned or turned back most of the cadets who failed courses. See the *Official Register of the Officers and Cadets of the U.S. Military Academy* for the disposition of deficiency cases during the war years.

182. Letter from Connor to the Adjutant General, 15 November 1934, file packet on rates of academic deficiency (18 August 1934), AGO Central Files 1926–39, Records Group 407, National Archives, College Park, MD.

183. *Annual Report of the Superintendent*, 1977, 7. In making the academic policy changes noted here, the Academic Board accepted the recommendations of the curriculum study group formed by Superintendent Berry immediately after the 1976 cheating incident. "Report of the Special Study Group on Academic Procedures," 21 July 1976, in *Proceedings of the Academic Board*, vol. 89, 24 July 1976, Tab GG, West Point Archives.

184. The overall academic failure rate during the 1960s was between 3 and 4 percent per year. *Annual Report of the Superintendent*, 1968, 14. The rate for fourth classmen was considerably higher, and that of first classmen considerably lower, than the overall rate of attrition.

185. The four-week term was known officially as the "summer term academic program," or "STAP." A cadet enrolled in STAP could take only one course; hence, a cadet who failed more than one course would likely face separation. A cadet who successfully completed STAP would receive the appropriate passing grade, which would appear on the transcript and contribute to his or her grade point average.

186. Starting in 1979, West Point received authority to graduate turn-backs in December — that is, after the first semester of the fifth year — if they could make up the failed courses by then. On 22 December, five cadets who had been turned back to the class of 1980 graduated after meeting all academic requirements. It was the first time since 1942 that the Academy had graduated cadets at mid-year. *Annual Report of the Superintendent*, 1980, 9. The minutes of Academic Board meetings since 1976 are replete with examples of cadets being retained at West Point despite failing multiple courses. See, for example, the disposition of cases from the third and fourth classes in *Proceedings of the Academic Board*, vol. 95, 28 May 1982, Tab P, West Point Archives.

187. My interpretation of the Academic Board's handling of cadet deficiency in academics comes from a review of the *Proceedings of the Academic Board* for the decades since the 1960s, as well as personal experience as a Board member. The *Proceedings* include the

disposition of every case of cadet failure and, in general, demonstrate the commitment of the Academic Board to treat cadets with fairness and consistency. Three times a year — once each after the fall, spring, and summer terms — the Academic Board convenes to consider the fate of every cadet who has failed an academic course, military training, or physical development. The meetings can be long and contentious, but in the end, the Academic Board virtually always leans toward compassion when considering how to deal with cadet failure. The author doubts that any other college in America is as scrupulous as West Point in reviewing every case of failure and offering chances for remediation.

188. *Annual Report of the Superintendent*, 1980, 10. While some nonathletes (e.g., those with onerous leadership duties) were also eligible for academic underloading, the principal aim of the program was to help athletes, who made up 88 percent of the first summer-school class in June 1980. The underloading policy was troubling for some Academic Board members, who believed that it reflected an unhealthy elevation of intercollegiate athletics by privileging a select minority and coddling cadets who otherwise might not be able to complete the academic program. The 1981 edition of the *Annual Report of the Superintendent* noted that the underloading policy showed "mixed results" and was under review (10). The program apparently ended that year, as there is no further mention of it in subsequent annual reports. The 2008 reprise of academic underloading was part of a larger program to assist at-risk cadets — primarily recruited athletes — in passing their courses. Col. Curtis Carver (Vice-Dean for Education), slide packet on "Superintendent's Examination of First Year and Beyond Program," 8 September 2009, Office of the Dean.

189. The admissions office used the college entry examination rank, or "CEER," as the principal tool to evaluate the academic credentials of cadet candidates. The CEER was derived by combining the candidate's high school rank and standardized test scores, and it had a proven record in predicting a cadet's academic performance. Cadets who were academically at risk were those whose CEER was below the Academy's established minimum; they needed the approval of the Academic Board to gain entry as cadets. At-risk percentages for 2003 and 2009 are in a slide packet prepared by Col. Curtis Carver, Vice-Dean for Education, "Superintendent's Examination of First Year and Beyond Program," 8 September 2009, Office of the Dean. The percentage of recruited athletes comprising the at-risk population for the entering classes in 2007 through 2009 is reported in US Military Academy, *2007–2008 Division 1 Athletics Certification Self-Study*, 8 May 2008, 48, West Point Archives.

190. Slide packet on "USMA Retention," 21 August 2008, Institutional Research and Analysis Branch, Office of Policy, Planning, and Assessment, West Point.

191. Greg Bruno, "West Point Wants to Expand Number of Students," *Times Herald-Record Online*, 1 February 2007, http://www.recordonline.com/apps/pbcs.dll/article?AID=/20070201/NEWS/702010337, accessed 18 October 2007.

192. A discussion of the increased faculty burden associated with policies to lower attrition is in *Institutional Self-Study: Report of the United States Military Academy, September 2009* (West Point: Office of the Dean), 27–28.

193. David M. Ewalt and Hana R. Alberts, "America's Best Colleges," *Forbes*, 5 August

2009. Several other rankings around the same time also placed West Point among the nation's top colleges. For example, on 20 August 2009, *US News & World Report* named West Point the best public liberal arts college in the nation. "2010 America's Best Colleges Rankings," http://colleges.usnews.rankingsandreviews.com/best-colleges/liberal-arts-rankings, accessed 4 October 2009.

CHAPTER FIVE

1. See chapter 1 for a discussion of Koehler's work prior to 1902.

2. The exception was during the 1920s. Douglas MacArthur openly encouraged the recruitment of athletes by coaches and interested graduates. The practice continued until 1929, when the War Department ordered it stopped.

3. My description of Herman Koehler relies heavily on Maher (with Reeder and Reeder Campion), *Bringing Up the Brass*, 60–68.

4. During a 1915 visit to West Point, Lt. Col. D. C. Shanks watched in amazement as Koehler led the Corps of Cadets in an unrehearsed session of physical drill and exercise. Shanks, a staff officer for the army's inspector general, was no stranger to army training techniques. He described Koehler as "one of the very best instructors I have ever seen." In his report to the War Department, Shanks recommended Koehler's style of physical training for the entire army. *Annual Report of the Superintendent*, 1915, 11–12.

5. Koehler's stentorian voice was an asset when he led physical exercise at training camps during World War I.

6. The quoted words are those of Maher, *Bringing Up the Brass*, 64.

7. Koehler, *Koehler's West Point Manual of Disciplinary Physical Training*, 13.

8. Baumer, "Every Man an Alert, Thinking Athlete," 45.

9. Cadets had taken dancing since the earliest days of the Academy. The activity had the dual benefit of helping cadets become gentlemen and providing them physical exercise. US Military Academy, *Centennial*, 1: 908.

10. Ibid., 902–07. To be proficient in swimming, cadets had to stay afloat for ten minutes using the breast stroke. In Koehler's estimation, at least 70 percent of the new cadets could not swim well enough to pass the diagnostic test.

11. There were twenty-six measurements for body size, including those for height, weight, chest (normal), chest (expanded), right upper arm (flexed), and left upper arm (flexed). Additionally, there were seven measures of strength, including the pull up, dip, and exercises for the arms, back, and legs. The average increase in the girth of the cadet chest (normal) was 1.32 inches; the average girth of the right upper arm (flexed) grew by 1.02 inches. Cadets who could do, on average, 7.11 pull ups in October increased to 10.40 in May; similarly, cadets increased their dips from 4.95 to 10.44. *Centennial*, 1: 901.

12. Ibid., 1: 899.

13. In addition to promoting exercise, army doctors advocated design improvements for service uniforms, which were often too hot and restrictive. Cadet uniforms were particularly uncomfortable. The high collars and close-fitting tunics interfered with physical development, restricted circulation and breathing, and sometimes caused nausea, head-

aches, and faintness. The vain cadets exacerbated the problems by keeping the uniforms closely tailored to accentuate their slim waists and rigid posture. Gillett, *The Army Medical Department 1865–1917*, 48.

14. Koehler reported in the 1913 edition of the *Annual Report of the Superintendent* (19) that the decision to require all cadets to take physical education came from President Theodore Roosevelt in 1905. I have been unable to corroborate this assertion, although Roosevelt's interest in physical fitness and the affairs of the Military Academy are well known. Even if the order did not emanate from the White House, however, Koehler had other powerful supporters. Brig. Gen. Albert Mills, the superintendent from 1898 to 1906, favored physical education for all cadets, as did Lt. Col. Charles G. Treat, the commandant from 1901 to 1905. Treat noted the "splendid physical condition" of cadets at the end of their first year. Keeping them in shape, he argued, would be wise "even at the sacrifice of some of the time devoted to their mental training." Treat's comments suggest why the prospect of mandatory physical training was not universally popular among Academic Board members, most of whom were professors. *Annual Report of the Superintendent*, 1902, 27.

15. In granting Koehler an officer's commission, Congress responded to the repeated requests of Academy superintendents. The implementing legislation, in effect, militarized the position of master of the sword. Upon Koehler's retirement from the military, the master of the sword's duties would thereafter be performed by "an officer of the line of the Army to be selected for that purpose by the Secretary of War." Mallory, *Compiled Statutes of the United States, 1913*, 941–42.

16. The building was later named in honor of Capt. Thomas J. Hayes IV, class of 1966, who died in Vietnam in 1968. Although renovated in 2003–2004, it has retained its original features and ambiance and is the central facility within the larger Arvin Cadet Physical Development Center, completed in 2004.

17. *Annual Report of the Superintendent*, 1905, 35. Koehler had taught all of the plebe courses in physical education until 1900, when he received one officer assistant. When the physical education program expanded to all classes in 1905, the Academy hired Francis Dohs to teach gymnastics and Louis Vauthier to teach fencing. Additionally, Thomas Jenkins, a former world heavyweight champion in wrestling, was hired to teach that sport, as well as boxing and swimming. Riding practice took place outdoors during good weather and inside the new riding hall during bad weather. Degen, *The Evolution of Physical Education at the United States Military Academy*, 42–43.

18. See chapter 1, table 1.1, for the daily schedule at West Point during the nineteenth century.

19. *Annual Report of the Superintendent*, 1906, 9. The daily schedule for cadets continued to experience minor adjustments; see, for example, the 1916 and 1920 editions of *Regulations for the United States Military Academy* (Washington, DC: Government Printing Office). Still, the principle of providing sufficient time for physical training has prevailed to the present.

20. The cadets did not field an intercollegiate lacrosse team in 1908 and from 1911 through 1920. Fencing was discontinued as a varsity sport from 1913 through 1922 and from 1955 through 1966; it became a club sport starting in 1979. Dineen, *The Illustrated History of Sports at the U.S. Military Academy*, 272–73, 280.

21. At the time, cadet teams played all of their games at West Point, with the exception of the competitions against the Naval Academy. Other collegiate teams therefore required a guarantee that they would not lose money by traveling to West Point to compete against the cadets.

22. The AOAA was similar to the athletics booster organizations at many other colleges. Alumni groups took control over intercollegiate athletics, especially football, because the faculty and administrators wanted nothing to do with managing sports, which they viewed as a distraction from intellectual development. Ambrose, *Duty, Honor, Country*, 307.

23. "President's Report," *Annual Report of the Army Officers Athletic Association*, 1902, 4.

24. "Constitution and By-Laws of the Army Athletic Association," 21 December 1903, in *Annual Report of the Army Athletic Association*, 1903, 49.

25. *Annual Report of the Superintendent*, 1904, 10–11.

26. Ibid., 11.

27. *Annual Report of the Superintendent*, 1906, 10.

28. The Racquet and Tennis Club of New York City awarded an annual fencing trophy to the best intercollegiate team. West Point won the trophy in 1902, 1903, 1904, 1906, 1908, 1909, and 1912. *Semi-annual Report of the Army Athletic Council*, Winter and Spring, 1918–1919, West Point Archives.

29. Herman Koehler was the head coach of the varsity football team for four seasons, from 1897 to 1900. He compiled an impressive record of nineteen wins, eleven defeats, and three ties.

30. *Annual Report of the Army Athletic Association*, 1906, 11.

31. Ibid., 6. Sadly, Cadet Eugene Byrne died in 1909 while playing in a football game against Harvard. Army canceled the rest of its games for that season, and Academy leaders seriously considered eliminating the sport. That winter, however, the IAAUS agreed to make significant changes to the rules; most important, players were prohibited from interlocking their arms to block opponents; teams had to have seven of their eleven men on the line of scrimmage at the time of the snap; and coaches could substitute players more freely than before, thus allowing fatigued players to be rested. With these and other changes in place, West Point continued to play the sport. Ambrose, *Duty, Honor, Country*, 312–13; *Annual Report of the Superintendent*, 1910, 10.

32. A brief but useful history of the National Collegiate Athletic Association is at http://www.ncaa.org/wps/portal/ncaahome?WCM_GLOBAL_CONTEXT = /ncaa/ncaa/ about + the + ncaa/overview/history.html. The organization is commonly referred to by its acronym, NCAA.

33. Scott, *Some Memories of a Soldier*, 436.

34. Ibid., 436–37.

35. USMA Special Orders, No. 110, 12 June 1908, West Point Archives.

36. Koehler, *The Theory and Practice of Athletics at the Military Academy*.

37. Ibid., 2.

38. Ibid., 3–4.

39. In the 1914 *Annual Report of the Superintendent*, Koehler acknowledged that the Academy could not belittle the desire to win if it desired to remain competitive in sports. Still, the cadets must learn that "no matter how much prominence is given to winning there

are other more lasting benefits to be derived from competitive athletics." To dramatize this point, Academy officials switched "from professional to Army coaching"; only the baseball team still had a civilian coach. According to Koehler, the switch had no impact on the quality of the teams and encouraged greater participation by cadets (20).

40. Although there was no formal recruiting system, West Point had advantages that ensured a steady stream of talented athletes, as will be seen later.

41. *Annual Report of the Superintendent*, 1909, 12.

42. *Annual Report of the Superintendent*, 1913, 6. As an example of the hazards of football, Cadet Dwight D. Eisenhower, class of 1915, injured his knee while playing on the 1912 football team. The injury forced him to give up the sport and caused him pain for the rest of his life.

43. *Annual Report of the Superintendent*, 1919, 16–17. One of Koehler's trips was to the Plattsburgh, New York, training camp for two weeks in the summer of 1917. He conducted classes and mass drills in physical training and bayonet fighting, sometimes leading formations consisting of thousands of soldiers at a time. According to a contemporary newspaper account of the training, Koehler "put more ginger into the camp than anything else. The men march with more snap, [and] candidates in charge of companies give their commands with more precision." "Major Koehler Goes West," *New York Times*, 8 July 1917.

44. Memorandum No. 27, Headquarters USMA, 4 April 1918, West Point Archives. Emphasis in original document.

45. MacArthur, *Reminiscences*, 81.

46. *Annual Report of the Superintendent*, 1922, 11.

47. MacArthur used athletics as a means of giving cadets more exposure to the public. He allowed the football team to play against Yale in New Haven, Harvard in Boston, and Notre Dame in New York City, and he arranged for the Corps of Cadets to attend the games. Previously, football trips had been limited to the Army-Navy game in New York City. Blaik, "A Cadet under MacArthur," 11.

48. The quote appears prominently over an archway in the main hallway of the Arvin Cadet Physical Development Center.

49. Maher, *Bringing Up the Brass*, 66.

50. Ganoe, *MacArthur Close-Up*, 86. The commandant was Robert M. Danford, who strongly supported MacArthur's efforts to raise the level of physical fitness among cadets.

51. In the early 1920s, riding was gradually phased out for second- and third-class cadets. By academic year 1923–1924, only first classmen took the subject, on alternating days (including some Saturdays). Change No. 17, dated 13 December 1923, posted to *Regulations for the United States Military Academy, 1902*, 28–29.

52. *Annual Report of the Superintendent*, 1920, 40. As part of the athletics program, fourth-class cadets were required to take dancing instruction once a week. The instruction started in December and lasted until early April or until individual cadets were proficient, whichever came first. Dancing classes, held indoors, provided exercise during a time of the year when outdoor activities were limited due to the weather.

53. *Bugle Notes*, 1921–1922, 82.

54. Ganoe, *MacArthur Close-Up*, 85–87.

55. Degen, *The Evolution of Physical Education at the United States Military Academy*, 55.

56. Ganoe, *MacArthur Close-Up*, 74.

57. Quote attributed to MacArthur in Ganoe, *MacArthur Close-Up*, 76. Concerning the resistance of the Academic Board to MacArthur's athletic recruiting policy, Earl Blaik recalled, "Then, as now, there was far from complete acceptance of his policy by the Corps and graduates." Blaik, "A Cadet under MacArthur," 11.

58. Ganoe, *MacArthur Close-Up*, 76–77.

59. At the Naval Academy, the minimum entry age was sixteen years, and the maximum age was twenty. At the Military Academy, the minimum entry age was seventeen, the maximum twenty-two. Following World War I, Congress raised the maximum entry age at West Point to twenty-four years for soldiers who had served in the military during the First World War; this law further advantaged Academy recruiting efforts. See chapter 3.

60. This was a sore point between the two academies, and twice during the first decade of the century it put the rivalry in jeopardy. In 1903, the Navy Athletic Association nearly canceled the Army-Navy football game to protest West Point's advantage in recruiting experienced players from other colleges. Navy officials noted that West Point's maximum entry age of twenty-two years would have permitted the entrance to West Point of all but three members of the 1902 varsity teams of Yale and Harvard; in contrast, only one member of those teams could have entered the Naval Academy. The 1902 Army-Navy game illustrated the practical effect of the disparity. In that game, the midshipmen averaged twenty years old and 158 pounds, compared to twenty-two years and 175 pounds for the cadets. Despite their obvious advantage, West Point officials were unmoved. To adopt rules, they argued, that "would prevent some of our cadets from enjoying the privileges granted to others, is so contrary to the spirit of our institution that we cannot entertain it." With the booster clubs of the two academies at loggerheads, the superintendents met to resolve the issue, but they agreed only to hold the 1903 football game as usual and to convene a joint committee to set the conditions under which future games would be played. "President's Report," 21 December 1903, *Annual Report of the Army Athletic Association*, 1903, 3–8. The agreement they reached expired in a few years, and by 1908 the dispute emerged once again. This was the incident, discussed earlier, that prompted Superintendent Hugh Scott to reorganize the Army Athletic Association to ensure proper oversight. The change ensured the continuance of the Army-Navy football game, but it did nothing to change the recruiting advantage enjoyed by West Point.

61. Garbisch graduated seventeenth out of 245 cadets in the class of 1925. He was commissioned in the Corps of Engineers and saw combat duty in the European Theater during World War II, retiring as a colonel after twenty years. National Football Foundation, "College Football Hall of Fame," http://www.collegefootball.org/famersearch.php?id=20109, accessed 16 March 2010.

62. The *New York Times* reported that West Point football teams "have constantly been replenished with players who have already been broken in at other colleges." The players included Daly, Torney, Graves, Bunker, Doe, Pullen, Hyatt, Oliphant, and McQuarrie. The same article noted that the Naval Academy rarely got experienced players "chiefly on account of its low age limit." "Not to Enter Navy," 4 January 1920, S3. Despite West Point's advantage in maximum age of entry, the two service academies competed fairly evenly in football during the 1920s.

63. The implementation of a mandatory program of intramural sports appealed to MacArthur in part because it treated all cadets equally — that is, it made them all athletes. Ganoe, *MacArthur Close-Up*, 85.

64. The ongoing conflict between the Military Academy and the Naval Academy over varsity eligibility reached the halls of Congress. Representative Fred A. Britten, member of the House Naval Affairs Committee, argued that West Point should abide by the three-year rule, just as Annapolis did. Representative John M. Morin, chairman of the House Military Affairs Committee, disagreed. Limiting a cadet's varsity career to three years, he believed, "would be in direct violation of that democratic spirit in the cadet corps which for years has been one of the outstanding characteristics of West Point. Every West Point cadet has exactly the same rights, privileges, opportunities, prohibitions, and restrictions that his classmates have. . . . No handicap is placed on him because of his brilliant athletic record, and no advantage given except that which he himself earns." "Morin, in Congress, Backs Army Stand," *New York Times*, 21 December 1927, 20. The Naval Academy was not the only school to criticize West Point for not observing the three-year eligibility rule. See "Yale Daily News Criticizes Army," *New York Times*, 8 November 1932, 30.

65. The conflict over player eligibility remained unresolved until 1930, when the two academies agreed to play a postseason charity football game to provide financial relief for unemployed workers during the Great Depression. Another charity game followed in 1931. The huge proceeds of the two games — nearly a million dollars total — made clear that there was much to gain by a resumption of the rivalry, which came officially in 1932. "Army-Navy Renew Move to End Break," *New York Times*, 3 January 1932, S1.

66. *Annual Report of the Superintendent*, 1923, 18–19.

67. Upon his retirement in December 1923, Koehler was hired as the executive officer of the Army Athletic Association. By virtue of this position, he was a member of the USMA Athletic Board. *Annual Report of the Superintendent*, 1924, 11.

68. *Annual Report of the Superintendent*, 1923, 17.

69. *Report of the Board of Visitors*, 1921, 30. This report is appended to the 1922 *Annual Report of the Superintendent* and starts on page 25; hence, the quoted passage would appear on page 6 of the stand-alone Board of Visitors report. The author could not find the stand-alone Board of Visitors report in the West Point Archives.

70. *Annual Report of the Superintendent*, 1923, 18.

71. Davidson, "Grandpa Gar," 50.

72. Despite the ban on formal recruiting, informal contacts with talented collegiate players continued, sometimes to the embarrassment of the Academy. One such incident prompted Congressman Hamilton Fish to demand a War Department investigation into the "proselytizing of football players" by Academy officials. Over a three-year period, Fish repeatedly uncovered evidence that "star college players are encouraged and solicited to enter West Point." The army chief of staff, Douglas MacArthur, referred the investigation to the superintendent. "Fish Asks War Department to Investigate Football Conditions at West Point," *New York Times*, 30 January 1931, 24.

73. Earl Blaik, "Varsity Sports at West Point," *Assembly* 13, no. 3 (October 1954): 4.

74. According to one New York City newspaper account, the new stadium was the "loveliest in the East." It was shaped like a horseshoe with the open end facing eastward.

Spectators in the west stands therefore could gaze at the reservoir in the foreground and the rugged hills of the Hudson Highlands in the background.

75. Forman, *West Point*, 188.

76. *Annual Report of the Superintendent*, 1931, 9.

77. Davidson, "Grandpa Gar," 12.

78. Ibid., 15.

79. Ibid., 23.

80. Ibid., 26. Davidson continues to hold the distinction of being the youngest head coach in the history of West Point football.

81. Ibid., 25.

82. Ibid., 38.

83. Thomas Davidson, the superintendent's son, graciously provided the author copies of the reports Davidson sent MacArthur.

84. Ibid., 50, 51, 60.

85. Richardson, "An Intimate Picture of Athletics at West Point," 95–96.

86. Ibid., 100. Richardson's explanation of the Academy's eligibility rules in 1932 differed only slightly from an official rendering of the rules in 1937. See letter from Maj. Gen. William Connor (superintendent) to Maj. Gen. Malin Craig (chief of staff), 12 December 1937, "Eligibility Rules for Athletics at the United States Military Academy," Adjutant General's Office Central Files 1926–39, box 2020, Records Group 407, National Archives, College Park, MD.

87. Letter from Lt. Gen. Brehon B. Somervell, commander of Army Service Forces, to various army commanders, 2 May 1942, reprinted in Appleton, "The Relationship between Physical Ability and Success at the United States Military Academy," 3.

88. West Point was not alone in shortening its curriculum during the war. About 85 percent of the nation's colleges did the same, primarily by cutting vacations. Forman, *West Point*, 203.

89. *Annual Report of the Superintendent*, 1944, 12.

90. Quoted in Degen, "The Evolution of Physical Education at the United States Military Academy," 62.

91. Although his first graduate school experience was at Columbia University, Appleton eventually earned a doctorate in physical education from New York University. The research leading to his dissertation, "The Relationship between Physical Ability and Success at the United States Military Academy," provided the theoretical basis for the testing and evaluation procedures used by the Office (later the Department) of Physical Education.

92. The ten events were a 300-yard run, dodge run, standing broad jump, vertical jump, vault, rope climb, sit up, chin up, dip, and softball throw. The events measured a cadet's upper-body strength, motor coordination, leg strength, speed, and endurance. Degen, "The Evolution of Physical Education at the United States Military Academy," 68–69.

93. *Annual Report of the Superintendent*, 1942, paragraph 8 (no page number).

94. Degen, "The Evolution of Physical Education at the United States Military Academy," 65.

95. Appleton's undated study, "Military Physical Efficiency," was completed in the spring of 1942. It compiled the testing data he had developed over the previous few years.

A complete copy of the study is appended to a memorandum from Col. A. G. Whipple (Adjutant) to the General Committee, 25 March 1943, file 351.051, "Physical Training Course 1937–1945," West Point Archives. Wilby's approval of Appleton's work is documented in General Orders No. 13, 21 April 1943, West Point Archives.

96. General Orders No. 13, 21 April 1943, West Point Archives. The standards for determining deficiency changed in early 1946. Rather than use a percentage standard (i.e., failure for the lowest 7 percent), cadets would be held to performance-based standards. General Orders No. 7, 20 February 1946, West Point Archives.

97. Degen, "The Evolution of Physical Education at the United States Military Academy," 67. Examples of Academic Board actions against cadets deficient in military physical efficiency are found in file 351.051, "Physical Training Course 1937–1945," West Point Archives.

98. The indoor obstacle course has become a rite of passage for generations of West Point cadets. The agony of running the course is matched only by the relief in successfully completing it. In 2010, the events of the indoor obstacle course were: low crawl (twenty feet), tire run, two-hand vault, shelf mount, high-bar walk, through-the-tire jump, balance beam (forty feet), forward roll, wall scale (seven feet), horizontal ladder, rope climb to upper-level running track, and run (one lap with ten-pound medicine ball, one lap with baton, one lap empty-handed). A passing score for men is three minutes, thirty seconds, or less; for women, a passing score is five minutes, twenty-nine seconds, or less. "IOCT Information," Department of Physical Education website, http://www.usma.edu/dpe/default .htm, accessed 24 November 2010.

99. Greene offered ample data to demonstrate the effectiveness of physical testing as a predictor of success as a cadet and officer. He discovered strong correlations between a cadet's physical aptitude and military rating. For example, cadets in the classes of 1945 and 1946 who were high in physical aptitude held a disproportionate share of the cadet officer positions. Those who were low in physical aptitude had more psychological problems and higher resignation rates. *Procedure for Examination of Cadets in Physical Aptitude* (West Point: Office of Physical Education, 1946), 2. Lloyd Appleton did much of the research for the Greene study, which formed the basis of his doctoral dissertation. He noted that the correlations described earlier were most noticeable at the high and low extremes of physical ability. Appleton, "The Relationship between Physical Ability and Success at the United States Military Academy."

100. Chapter 3 discusses the Physical Aptitude Examination in greater detail. For many years, the staff of the Office of Physical Education and officers detailed by the Department of the Army would administer the examination at various locations around the country. This arrangement was effective but increasingly burdensome; eventually (by the mid-1990s), administration of the examination was decentralized so that any military officer or qualified physical education instructor could test a cadet candidate. Unfortunately, the change lessened the reliability of the test in assessing the physical aptitude of cadet candidates. James Anderson, interview by Stephen Grove, 12 May 1997, transcript, 24–25.

101. *Annual Report of the Superintendent*, 1946, 23. The decision to send inbound military instructors to graduate school applied not just to the Office of Physical Education, but also to the academic departments. See chapter 4 on this point.

102. Degen, "The Evolution of Physical Education at the United States Military Academy," 77. Superintendent Maxwell Taylor formed the board in 1946; the board's report was completed the following year. The board included two of the nation's leading physical education professionals — Dr. Charles H. McCloy (University of Iowa) and Dr. Clifford Lee Brownell (Columbia University). Taylor, *West Point*, 7.

103. *Annual Report of the Superintendent*, 1943, 1–2. See chapter 3 for a discussion of the 1942 expansion of the Corps of Cadets.

104. Roosevelt personally gave his guidance on athletics to Superintendent Wilby in January 1942, during Wilby's trip to Washington. Crackel, *West Point*, 207. Wilby's counterpart at the Naval Academy received similar guidance.

105. *Annual Report of the Superintendent*, 1945, 20.

106. *Annual Report of the Superintendent*, 1946, 25.

107. *Annual Report of the Superintendent*, 1947, 36. Although the 1946 football team had a 9–0–1 record, it ranked second to Notre Dame (8–0–1) in most national polls. The two teams had played each other to a scoreless tie that season. The seven-season record included four tied games.

108. *Annual Report of the Superintendent*, 1948, 44. In addition to intercollegiate sports, the Army Athletic Association supported numerous club sports. The latter group included handball, sailing, skeet shooting, skiing, water polo, weight lifting, and squash. *Annual Report of the Superintendent*, 1946, 24.

109. Eichelberger was the West Point adjutant from August 1932 to April 1935. Blaik was an assistant coach at West Point from 1927 to the end of the 1933 season.

110. The suspension of the NCAA's three-year varsity eligibility rule advantaged both service academies, but West Point gained more because of its higher maximum entry age. Barney Poole took advantage of the situation. After lettering in football at the University of Mississippi and the University of North Carolina, he entered West Point in 1943. He played on the cadet team for three years, earning All American honors in 1944. Instead of graduating and serving his military commitment, however, he purposely flunked out so that he could enroll once again at the University of Mississippi and continue playing football. Poole played varsity football for a total of seven years. Although he achieved fame as both a collegiate and professional football player, he did so by deliberately manipulating military deferment policies and NCAA eligibility rules. Letter, Maj. Gen. William Connor (superintendent) to Maj. Gen. Malin Craig (chief of staff), 12 December 1937, "Eligibility Rules for Athletics at the United States Military Academy," Adjutant General's Office Central Files 1926–39, box 2020, Records Group 407, National Archives, College Park, MD; Franklin Berkey, "Freshmen Eligibility: Age-Old Dilemma Still Debated," *The Daily Collegian*, online edition, 24 April 1992, http://www.collegian.psu.edu/archive/1992/04/04-24-92cm/04-24-92cm-2.asp, accessed 3 April 2010; National Football Foundation, "Hall of Famer Barney Poole Dies," College Football Hall of Fame, 13 April 2005, http://www.collegefootball.org/news.php?id=589, accessed 3 April 2010.

111. Blaik, *The Red Blaik Story*, 127.

112. *Annual Report of the Superintendent*, 1914, 19–20.

113. Allison Danzig, "Cadets Stop Drive: Army Halts Duke on One Inch Line in Last Minute to Save Victory," *New York Times*, 18 October 1953, S1.

114. *Annual Report of the Superintendent*, 1957, 10.

115. Davidson's concerns are reflected in his thorough memoir, "Grandpa Gar," especially pages 169–70. On the rift between varsity athletes and the rest of the Corps of Cadets, see *Annual Report of the Superintendent*, 1957, 10.

116. Davidson, "Grandpa Gar," 169.

117. *Annual Report of the Superintendent*, 1960, 19 (statistic), 7 (quote). The class of 1960 started with 765 cadets; seventeen (2.2 percent) were separated for physical deficiency.

118. *Annual Report of the Superintendent*, 1957, 11. According to Davidson, "there was no question that sports other than football were being neglected" by the current recruiting policies. Consequently, most cadets were denied equal opportunity to "achieve according to his individual ability." Davidson, "Grandpa Gar," 171. See chapter 3 for more detail on Davidson's athletic recruiting policies.

119. Blaik believed that the financial viability of the intercollegiate athletics program depended on "establishing a continuingly realistic football program. Once we had done this, and had somehow arranged for more appointments, we could also improve the other sports." Blaik, *The Red Blaik Story*, 397.

120. Davidson, "Grandpa Gar," 170.

121. Blaik chose to retire for a number of reasons, not the least of which was his desire to leave in the glow of an undefeated season in 1958 and a ranking of third in the nation. Also, he had received an offer to become a vice president of the AVCO Corporation, a research firm in the field of missiles and space exploration. His tense relationship with the superintendent, however, was also a factor in the decision. In his memoirs, Blaik betrayed his feeling that Davidson had meddled inappropriately in his affairs: "When General Davidson became superintendent I had been head football coach for fifteen years, director of athletics for ten years and chairman of the Athletic Board for seven years. However, the Supe was an old coach, and old coaches never die; they just write directives." Blaik, *The Red Blaik Story*, 393. Davidson described Blaik as a "fine football coach but a lousy director of athletics." He was about to relieve Blaik of the latter duty when Blaik submitted his resignation. Davidson, "Grandpa Gar," 171, 174.

122. The win percentage would have been higher had it included the results of competitions in the military sports of rifle and pistol. The rifle team went undefeated in twelve matches, and the pistol team won eight of nine matches. *Annual Report of the Superintendent*, 1958, 11. The percentage of cadets participating in intercollegiate athletics included the players on junior varsity and plebe teams. A detailed accounting of the cadet participation in sports is in "Superintendent's Curriculum Study: Report of the Working Committee on the Present Curriculum and Future Trends," 31 August 1958, West Point Archives, IX–14.

123. *Annual Report of the Superintendent*, 1958, 12.

124. The accomplishments of Peter Dawkins (class of 1959) at West Point are legendary. He was captain of the 1958 football team, which went undefeated and was ranked number three in the nation. He was a unanimous All American selection at halfback and won both the Heisman and Maxwell trophies as the best college football player in the

nation. Dawkins was the president of his West Point class and, in his senior year, the First Captain of the Corps of Cadets. Also that year, he won a Rhodes Scholarship. After twenty-four years of commissioned service, he retired as a brigadier general and entered private business.

125. Davidson, "Grandpa Gar," 169.

126. Kobes's appointment came officially on 12 June 1959, when the Senate confirmed his nomination. *Annual Report of the Superintendent*, 1959, 18. Kobes first became the director of physical education in 1953. He was a 1939 graduate of West Point and a varsity football player when Davidson was the head coach. Kobes was wounded during World War II and took a disability retirement in 1946. He returned to active duty as a lieutenant colonel in 1951 to serve as a tactical officer; two years later he became the director of physical education. Following the 1958 legislation that made his position permanent, Kobes was promoted to colonel and served for an additional sixteen years. He retired in 1974 as a brigadier general. Association of Graduates, *Register of Graduates and Former Cadets of the United States Military Academy*, 4–198.

127. One of Kobes' predecessors, Col. Francis M. Greene, served almost a decade — from 1944 to 1952 — as the master of the sword and, later, director of physical education. (The title of "master of the sword" changed officially to "director of physical education" in 1947.) Greene's contributions to physical education (noted earlier) demonstrated the benefits of longevity in the position and facilitated Davidson's move to make the position permanent.

128. "Evaluation Report for the Middle States Association of Colleges and Secondary Schools (MSACSS) Commission on Higher Education," 15–18 February 1959, West Point Archives.

129. "Army Reaffirms Policy by Rejecting Bids to Play in Cotton, Orange Bowls," *New York Times*, 13 November 1958, 47. Davidson's successors would be less resistant to playing in postseason bowl games. Maj. Gen. Samuel Koster, for example, approved a policy that would allow postseason play only "in the most prestigious bowls, i.e., Sugar Bowl, Orange Bowl, Cotton Bowl or Gator Bowl." Participation would permit the football team to "be representative of the Academy's ideals." USMA memorandum, 10 April 1968, "The Intercollegiate Athletic Policy of the United States Military Academy," *Proceedings of the Athletic Board* (October–December 1968), 5 November 1968. The cadets' first bowl appearance came in 1984 (Cherry Bowl, in Pontiac, Michigan).

130. *Annual Report of the Superintendent*, 1963, 40. In addition to the varsity teams, West Point fielded four junior varsity and seventeen plebe teams that competed on an inter-collegiate basis. Additionally, there were many club sports — that is, teams that competed against other colleges but were not governed by the National Collegiate Athletic Association and were not allowed to recruit athletes.

131. *Annual Report of the Superintendent*, 1965, ix.

132. Collectively, the classes of the 1960s were the most talented ever to enter the Academy. The admissions reforms of the late 1950s ensured a steady flow of high-quality applicants who excelled in the classrooms, on the athletic fields, and as officers in the army. See chapter 3.

133. Comments of Maj. Gen. James B. Lampert, superintendent from 1963 to 1966, *Annual Report of the Superintendent*, 1963, vi. Similar comments appear in many other official and unofficial documents of the era, especially following the 1951 cheating incident.

134. The quoted words were part of the melodramatic opening of each show.

135. Memorandum from Kirby to the Athletic Board, 16 June 1975, "Analysis of Admissions Support, Army Athletic Association," box labeled "Athletic Committee Meeting," West Point Archives. Other recommended cost-cutting measures included elimination of certain varsity sports and replacement of civilian coaches by instructors in the Office of Physical Education. Both measures were implemented to varying degrees. Memorandum from Col. William J. Schuder to Athletic Board, 9 January 1976, "FY 1977 Budget for Army Athletic Association," in box "Athletic Committee Meetings," West Point Archives.

136. The Army Athletic Association had always favored the West Point alumni in distributing tickets and seating at football games. As a class rose in seniority, for example, it sat ever closer to the fifty-yard line. Financial pressures eventually undermined this tradition, but not until the first decade of the twenty-first century. Concerning funding from the Department of the Army, the Army Athletic Association had long boasted of running the athletic program purely through private funds. Appropriated funds were used solely to pay military salaries and provide for equipment and services enjoyed by the entire Corps of Cadets. That tradition, too, began to yield under the financial pressures of the 1970s.

137. The chairman of the Athletic Committee, Col. Gilbert Kirby, noted that the hockey team had done well playing in Division II, the next step down from the highest level (Division I) of NCAA competition. The football team played in Division I, but was struggling. Kirby concluded, "If we cannot do well in Division I, then we should go to Division II." I have found no evidence indicating that Kirby's suggestion was taken seriously by superintendents or higher army authorities. Memorandum from Kirby to director of intercollegiate athletics, "Performance of Army Intercollegiate Athletic Teams," 24 February 1976, box labeled "Athletic Committee Meetings," West Point Archives.

138. Letter from Berry to Gen. Bernard Rogers (army chief of staff), 30 November 1976, file "Athletic Director," box 26, Bernard Rogers Papers, National Defense University, Washington DC. The second part of Berry's goal reflected dissatisfaction with West Point's poor athletic performance against the Naval Academy. During the ten academic years from 1970 to 1980, West Point won only 37 percent of its interservice competitions. Memorandum from Lt. Col. Samuel M. Burney (assistant director of alumni affairs) to Athletic Committee, 6 May 1983, Athletic Committee minutes, 24 May 1983, in box "Athletic Committee Meetings 1983," West Point Archives.

139. *Final Report of the West Point Study Group*, 125. The West Point Study Group consisted of three subordinate committees, each headed by a general officer. Chapter 2 describes the composition and functions of the West Point Study Group in more detail.

140. *Annual Report of the Superintendent*, 1986, 100. The new athletic center, completed in 1985, relieved pressure on the field house, which had served as a multipurpose sports venue since the late 1930s. The new facility was named for Maj. Don Holleder, class of 1956, who was killed in Vietnam in 1967. Holleder earned All American honors in football as an end following the 1954 season (his junior year). During his senior year, he played quarterback and led the team to a 6–3–0 record and a victory over the Naval Academy.

141. The artificial turf was first installed in 1977. It has been replaced and upgraded on several occasions since then.

142. Chapter 3 examines the athletic recruiting process in detail.

143. Goodpaster discussed these and other measures to improve the fortunes of the football team in a letter to Gen. Edward C. Meyer (army chief of staff), 7 January 1980, file 201-01, "Instruction Files, Regulations for USMA," box S.161 (1980) 201-01 Instruction Files, Regulations for USMA Including Statutes, West Point Archives.

144. "Report of the Physical Development Working Group," chap. 5, 2, in Athletic Committee Minutes, 21 August 1979, file "Athletic Committee Minutes, July–September 1979," box Athletic Committee Meetings, West Point Archives.

145. "Report of the Excellence in Army Football Working Group," 14 April 1980, 4, copy in author files.

146. Brig. Gen. Joseph Franklin, the commandant from 1979 to 1982, was a staunch advocate of measures to revitalize the football program. Success in that endeavor, he insisted, required the cooperation of everyone at West Point. "Where there are people who are saying that football isn't important to us, then we're going to have trouble with the program. And that more than anything else is what we need to correct now. By brute force we have wrenched the admission system into responsiveness. We have done things in the academic programs for counseling, for study halls, for monitoring the athletes, for giving them the second [afternoon] hour free, making some compensations in their physical education program to recognize their contributions and the sacrifices. . . . I'm not unhappy with anything we've done." Joseph P. Franklin, interview by Maj. Charles A. Morris, 14 June 1982, transcript, 16. Others were less enthused. Col. James Anderson, the director of physical education, recalled that Franklin's "focus was so much on football, getting a winning football team was the most important thing that could happen here. I love football . . . but it's not the most important thing." Anderson interview, 44.

147. "Report of the Physical Development Working Group," chap. 5, 16, in Athletic Committee Minutes, 21 August 1979, file "Athletic Committee Minutes, July–September 1979," box Athletic Committee Meetings, West Point Archives. Another recommendation for the "pro-option" is in the "Report of the Excellence in Army Football Working Group," 14 April 1980, Annex C, 19, copy in author files. Army leaders eventually would implement a policy allowing cadets to enter professional sports immediately after graduation. See chapter 2.

148. In retrospect, Goodpaster rued the decision to hire Saban, but at the time he needed to move quickly to find a replacement for the outgoing coach, Homer Smith, following the 1978 season. "We were up against the wall, we needed to replace the coach and we were concerned over the fact that Coach Saban was a traveler. . . . I had no doubt . . . of his sincere intent at the moment to stay. But his sincere intents can change, and it did when he saw some of the restraints and some of the conditions in which it's necessary to operate there at the Military Academy." Saban's one-year record at West Point was 2–8–1. Andrew Goodpaster, interview by LTC James Johnson, 7 March 1988, transcript, 55.

149. Cavanaugh's three-year record was 10–21–2.

150. *Annual Report of the Superintendent*, 1980, 88. Despite his advocacy of the intercollegiate athletics program, Ullrich opposed the proposal for allowing cadets to play

professional sports immediately following graduation. "The service academies," he wrote, "are special. I think, as coaches and administrators, we might wish to grant service academy graduates the opportunity. . . . However, being aware of and living with the real reason for our existence, we oppose such a ruling." Memorandum for record, "Pro Football Option," 18 August 1986, file "Athletic Committee Meeting 1986," box Athletic committee Meetings 1986, 1987, West Point Archives.

151. Andrew Goodpaster, interview by Dr. Stephen Grove, 12 May 1981, transcript, 55.

152. Andrew Goodpaster, interview by LTC James Johnson, 7 March 1988, transcript, 57.

153. Andrew Goodpaster, interview by Dr. Stephen Grove, 12 May 1981, transcript, 11.

154. Wesley Clark graduated from West Point in 1966 and rose to the rank of general. His culminating assignment was as commander of NATO forces from 1997 to 2000. In September 2003, he entered the race for the Democratic nomination for president of the United States; he withdrew in February 2004.

155. Clark conveyed his comments to Wickham in a memorandum, "The Winning Spirit at West Point," 17 December 1983, John A. Wickham Papers, National Defense University Archives, Washington, DC. Upon reading the memorandum, Wickham appended a handwritten note: "Excellent piece. Give copies to SA, DAS, VCSA." The acronyms stand for Secretary of the Army, Director of the Army Staff, and Vice Chief of Staff of the Army, respectively.

156. Wickham's guidance is taken from a follow-up letter to Scott, 30 December 1983, file "West Point," Special Subject Files P thru W, box 54, John A. Wickham Papers, National Defense University Archives, Washington DC.

157. Upon his retirement, Scott listed his top three priorities as (1) integration of women, (2) varsity sports, and (3) honor. *Annual Report of the Superintendent*, 1986, 105.

158. Scott reported to the Board of Visitors that the class of 1986 included 337 recruited athletes, far exceeding the 260 scholars and 310 leaders that were also part of the class (as categorized by class-composition goals). According to Scott, 337 was a "good number; that is what we are after." *Annual Report of the Board of Visitors*, 31 December 1982, 70. On 24 November 1982, the Academic Board approved Ullrich's request to increase the class-composition goal for recruited athletes from 15 to 20 percent to 20 to 25 percent. *Proceedings of the Academic Board* 95 (24 November 1982), Tab I.

159. The army authorized the graduate assistant-coach program near the end of Goodpaster's tenure as superintendent. Under the program, newly commissioned West Point officers remained at the Academy for up to a year to coach the teams on which they recently had played. The Department of the Army approved the program for implementation in 1981. There were fourteen graduate-assistant coaches initially, but Scott increased the number to twenty-two in 1982 and twenty-five in 1985. Office of the Director of Intercollegiate Athletics Policy No. 29, "Graduate Assistant Coach Program," 6 February 1987, Dean's Reading File, Athletic Committee, September 1982–July 1987, box Athletic Committee Meeting 1986, 1987, West Point Archives.

160. *Annual Report of the Board of Visitors*, 31 December 1984, 26.

161. During the 1970s, USMA Regulation 28-12, "Athletic Regulations," had

included an annex for each sport that specified the maximum number of "academic half days" team members could miss during the playing season. Revisions to the regulation in the early 1980s removed these limits. Henceforth, the loss of academic time would be "reviewed each year by the [director of athletics] and the Dean. . . . Disagreements, if any, will be discussed by the Athletic Committee, which will submit a recommendation to the Superintendent." The new arrangement led to a gradual increase in the amount of lost academic time for athletes, as each exception granted by the Superintendent established a new benchmark for the amount of time devoted to athletics. USMA Regulation 28-12, paragraph 5.a., 20 June 1986, file "Dean's Reading File, Athletic Committee, July–December 1987," box Athletic Committee Meetings, 1986 and 1987, West Point Archives.

162. The director of physical education, Col. James Anderson, fumed about the policy, which allowed some varsity athletes to receive grades based on their athletic performance rather than on physical education testing. The issue was one of fairness. He questioned why athletes should receive this grading privilege "when other members of their class are graded solely on their performances on three fitness tests." *Annual Report of the Superintendent*, 1983, 48.

163. Howard Prince, interview by author, 16 July 2007, transcript, 46. Prince was the head of the Department of Behavioral Science and Leadership from 1978 to 1990 and thus a member of the Academic Board. He recalled that Ullrich's appeals on behalf of recruited athletes put pressure on board members to grant waivers to poorly qualified candidates and to treat their deficiencies as cadets leniently. Prince characterized Ullrich's presence at Academic Board meetings as a "creeping influence" that raised the priority given to intercollegiate athletics.

164. The 1984–1985 season was the last time (through 2009–2010) that the basketball team had more wins than losses. *2009–10 Army Basketball Information Guide* (West Point: Office of Athletic Communications), 95–101.

165. *Annual Report of the Superintendent*, 1985, 78.

166. Much of Young's success owed to his decision to schedule many second-tier (i.e., NCAA Division 1AA) opponents. His record against those teams was twenty-three wins and six losses; against top-tier (i.e., Division 1A) opponents, his record was twenty-eight wins, thirty-three losses, and one tie.

167. West Point won the Army-Navy football game four of five times during Palmer's tenure. These wins muted the criticism that previous superintendents had endured from Academy graduates about the football program.

168. Dave R. Palmer, interview by Stephen Grove, 24 June 1991, transcript, 35.

169. Letter from Palmer to select panel on competitive sports, 3 December 1987, file "Athletic Committee Meeting, February–August 1988," box Athletic Committee Meetings 1988, 1989, West Point Archives.

170. James Anderson and Edward Shea, "The Role of Competitive Sports in Support of the Purpose and Mission of the Academy," fourth draft, 23 November 1987, file "Dean's Reading File, Athletic Committee July–December 1987," box Athletic Committee Meetings 1986, 1987, West Point Archives.

171. Eliminating mandatory supper answered the concerns not just of the athletic

director. Club sports and extracurricular clubs also benefited from having more time for their respective activities.

172. The Performance Enhancement Center is currently known as the Center for Enhanced Performance. See chapter 7 for a fuller discussion.

173. Palmer put the Department of Physical Education in charge of the club sports program in 1988. Anderson welcomed the move, as it gave him control over two of the Academy's three competitive athletics programs. In both club and intramural sports, he could now pursue the "educational model" of sport as opposed to the "win, money, prestige model, where you play to win so you can make money, so you gain prestige for the institution or the people who are involved in the sport." James Anderson, interview by Stephen Grove, 14 May 1997, transcript, 35.

174. The Patriot League started in 1986 as the Colonial League; the name change came in 1990. In 1989, Carl Ullrich became the league's first full-time executive director while still filling the athletic director position at West Point. The founding members of the Colonial League were Bucknell University, Colgate University, Fordham University, College of the Holy Cross, Lafayette College, and Lehigh University. Upon becoming the Patriot League, West Point joined. Subsequent entrants were the Naval Academy (1991) and American University (2001). Most of West Point's varsity teams competed in the Patriot League, the principal exception being football. "Patriot League History," official website of the Patriot League, http://www.patriotleague.org/school-bio/patr-school-bio-history .html, accessed 18 July 2010.

175. Donnithorne, *Preparing for West Point's Third Century*, 42.

176. Palmer explained his decision to join the Presidents' Commission despite his heavy responsibilities as the superintendent: "I thought this was a way, maybe, to have an influence on college athletics. And my aim was to try to bring college athletics back to our mold if we could. . . . I think it had gotten too far away from what we believed." Palmer interview transcript, 35. Thorough coverage of the formation and work of the Presidents' Commission is in Crowley, *In the Arena*, 65–67.

177. Athletic certifications were required on a decennial basis. In addition to participating in the pilot program in 1991–1992, West Point so far has undergone two certifications — in 1997–1999 and 2007–2009 — both of which were successful. The self-study reports for all three certifications are in the West Point Archives. The Board of Visitors praised the Academy's leadership for advancing the idea of athletics certification. Board members noted that West Point "is uniquely positioned to be a national leader and role model in the administration and operation of intercollegiate athletics." *Annual Report of the Board of Visitors*, 1992, 12.

178. Tarik El-Bshir, "Army Joins Its First Conference (USA)," *New York Times*, 11 March 1997. According to Christman, another benefit of joining Conference USA was the national exposure it would give to the Academy.

179. The 2008 study group included former football coaches Jim Young and Bob Sutton, Duke University basketball coach Mike Krzyzewski, and several former cadet football players: Gen. (retired) Thomas Schwartz, Gen. (retired) David Bramlett, Brig. Gen. (retired) Pete Dawkins, Rollie Stichweh, Rob Healy, and Harry Walters. Irene Brown, "Supe Announces New Study Group," *Pointer View*, 22 June 2007, 1.

180. Letter from Hagenbeck to Army Football Fans, 24 January 2008, Office of the Superintendent. See also Justin Rodriguez, "Panel's Mission: Reverse Army Football's Losing Ways," *Times Herald-Record*, 23 June 2007.

181. According to Christman, playing at the highest competitive level in football "was important, not because it had always been that way, but because it was one of the very, very best windows for the rest of the country to see the Academy." After briefly exploring the idea of dropping down one level, he concluded, "There was no way we could get national exposure through television at the time that I became Superintendent. . . . I was really worried at the time . . . about how few families in America understood that we had a Military Academy and that it was an opportunity for a great undergraduate education." Daniel Christman, interview by author, 8 June 2007, transcript, 4.

182. The construction projects were made possible through the largesse of donors who contributed to the West Point Association of Graduates during the bicentennial capital campaign. The total amount raised during the campaign was $220 million, of which 37 percent went to athletics facilities. The most expensive projects were the Kimsey Athletic Center (athletics offices, strength center, sports museum — $31.0 million), Randall Hall (athletics offices — $10.7 million), Hoffman Press Box (football stadium press facility — $10.3 million), Anderson Rugby Center ($7.1 million), Caufield Crew and Sailing Center ($5.2 million), Lichtenberg Tennis Center ($5.0 million), Gross Sports Center (gymnastics — $3.0 million), Tronsrue Marksmanship Center ($2.4 million), and Shea Stadium (track and field — $2.4 million). Shortly after completion of the capital campaign, another major gift allowed construction of the Foley Athletic Facility (indoor football field — $10.2 million). The total amount of spending on athletic facilities in the first decade of the twenty-first century was $91.9 million. Information provided to author by the West Point Association of Graduates.

183. William J. Lennox, interview by Stephen Grove, Part III, 20 March 2006, transcript, 41–42. Most of the new homes were in a small neighborhood at the north end of the main post, across the street from the hospital.

184. In 2003, about 6 percent of the incoming class was considered "at risk" by the admissions office; by 2009, the percentage had doubled. About two-thirds of the at-risk population consisted of recruited athletes.

185. In academic year 2000–2001, varsity team members missed a total of 7,334 class periods — the highest amount recorded in any category except "cadet-in-charge of quarters" (a daylong duty required every day in every cadet company). That number grew steadily over the next few years, peaking at 15,221 in academic year 2007–2008. After an institutional effort to reduce absences during academic year 2009–2010, the number of class absences for athletes dropped moderately to 12,298 — still well above the number at the beginning of the decade. Class-absence data provided to author by the Institutional Research and Analysis Branch, G-5, West Point, 14 May 2010. Copy in author files.

186. Lennox interview, 40.

187. See chapter 2. Although the Department of Defense ordered the army to terminate the alternate-service option, army assignment policies continued to accommodate the professional aspirations of West Point athletes. For example, a graduating cadet who was drafted by a professional team might be assigned as a graduate assistant coach at West

Point for nine months and then shipped to a military school for basic officer training. These activities would consume most of the required two years of service before the officer-athlete could request to leave active duty; all other graduates had to serve five years before they could request to leave active duty.

188. Superintendent Lennox was instrumental in convincing army leaders to move USMAPS to West Point. His argument drew strength from the Department of Defense's 2005 decision to close Fort Monmouth, where USMAPS had resided since 1975. According to Lennox, the move would be "an immense advantage in recruiting . . . because you'll be able to have the experts see those cadet candidates more frequently than they do now." In advocating the move of USMAPS, Lennox acted on the recommendation of the football study group, which he had convened in 2003. Lennox interview, 41.

189. In 2009, Lt. Gen. Franklin Hagenbeck approved the first-ever strategic goal specifically for intercollegiate athletics: "Our Athletic program will provide an unparalleled athletic experience that contributes to West Point's mission by coaching, developing and inspiring cadets to compete at the highest level in broad-based Intercollegiate and Division I Athletic programs that emphasize scholarly excellence, leadership development, growth in character, ethical conduct, winning and sportsmanship, while creating a lifetime commitment to service as a professional officer in the United States Army." None of the traditional cadet developmental programs (academic, military, and physical) received its own strategic goal. "Strategic Guidance for the United States Military Academy," July 2009, Office of Policy, Planning, and Assessment.

190. Memorandum from Lt. Gen. William J. Lennox to Academic Board, "Academic Board Composition," 30 June 2004, Office of the Dean.

191. As an example, in 1979, the athletic director's total budget was $2,333,300, of which only $219,000 (9.4 percent) came from appropriated money. Minutes of the Athletic Committee, 3 July 1979, Tab G, file "Athletic Committee Minutes, June 1979," box Athletic Committee Meetings, West Point Archives.

192. West Point was hardly alone in the problem of funding for intercollegiate athletics. According to a 2004 study, fewer than a dozen schools, regardless of the level of competition, earned a profit from their sports programs. Amy Merrick, "Another Money-Losing Season," *Wall Street Journal*, online edition, 20 September 2004.

193. Lennox interview, 42.

194. Another reason for the modest rise in the Dean's budget was the increasing seniority of the civilian faculty, who (unlike the military faculty) were paid from the West Point budget, rather than the larger army budget.

195. Farewell speech to Congress, 19 April 1951. Unfortunately, the quote is often shortened, and thus distorted, by dropping the first two words.

196. For a concise history of the changes in the physical education program during this period, see Remley, "Physical Education at the United States Military Academy 1966–1992," 5–18.

197. Anderson interview, 19–20.

198. Peterson et al., *Project 60*, 111. Selected comments of the cadets who assisted as trainers for the study are found on pages 102–10; several of the comments provide examples of the view that women should be held to the same standards as men. Other studies,

all published by the Office (or Department) of Physical Education, include: Stauffer, *Project Summertime*; Stauffer, *Project Body Composition, Part I: The Prediction of Selected Body Composition Measures of United States Military Academy Men and Women* (August 1977); Stauffer, *Project Body Composition, Part II: Comparison of U.S. Military Academy Men and Women on Selected Anthropometric and Body Composition Measures* (December 1977); Stauffer, *Project Body Composition, Part III: Anthropometrical Assessment of USMA Men and Women* (March 1978); Stauffer and Hayford, *Comparison of U.S. Military Academy Men and Women*; and Stauffer and T. Hoffman, *Sex Difference in Strength* (May 1979). All studies in West Point Archives.

199. Anderson interview, 31.

200. Changes to the physical program on account of gender are discussed in the Anderson interview, 21–30. Concerning the indoor obstacle course, Anderson replaced the parallel bars (which required cadets to traverse lengthwise by "walking" with their straight arms) with the balance beam. Because women generally had narrower shoulders than men, they had to reach farther out to reach the parallel bars, which put greater strain on their shoulders. The balance beam, in contrast, challenged both genders equally and exercised a physical skill that had previously gone untested. Another change was to relax the standard for women in negotiating the vault obstacle — whereas the men were allowed to use only their hands in getting over the obstacle, the women could negotiate it any way they liked.

201. Public Law 94-106.

202. Assuming command of an organization dominated by men was not easy for LeBoeuf: In her opinion, "It was not . . . a very welcoming culture in the department. . . . I could smell the testosterone." Maureen LeBoeuf, interview by Stephen Grove, 13 January 2004, transcript, 37.

203. Daniel W. Christman, interview by Stephen Grove, 29 August 2000, transcript, 62.

204. The possibility of using physical education instructors to coach varsity teams had been discussed at least since the late 1970s. An illuminating discussion of this issue, including the consequences for the individuals who would fill the instructor-coach positions, appears in the minutes of the Athletic Committee meetings from March through June 1979.

205. LeBoeuf interview, 39–40, 47.

206. *Annual Report of the Superintendent*, 1980, 39–40. For the first few years, the course was known as "Foundations of Physical Performance." Insertion of the course into the physical education curriculum pushed wrestling (men) and one of the two self-defense courses (women) into the third-class year. In academic year 1985–1986, the course moved to the third-class year, thus displacing wrestling and self-defense back to the plebe year. *Annual Report of the Superintendent*, 1985, 56. Another reversal — back to the arrangement of academic year 1979–1980 — came two years later to accommodate the requirements of the master fitness trainer program. *Annual Report of the Superintendent*, 1988, 69.

207. Created in 2006, the kinesiology major is the scientific study of muscular and cardiovascular physiology, energy balance, exercise adherence, physical skill acquisition, and motor control. The Department of Chemistry and Life Sciences officially sponsors the major, but the Department of Physical Education designs, teaches, and administers it. *Physical Program* (West Point: Office of the Commandant, academic year 2009–2010), chapter 11. The kinesiology major was first conceived in 1982 by Dr. Roger Wiley, the visiting profes-

sor in the Department of Physical Education at the time. The eventual establishment of the major owed in part to the need for senior army leaders who were sensitive to the challenges of recruiting and training soldiers from an increasingly unfit population. Telephone interview between author and Col. Gregory Daniels, master of the sword, 24 November 2010, West Point.

208. The only club sport to have a paid coach was rugby, starting in 2006. This exception was the result of the generosity of donors who were patrons of the sport and fans of West Point. E-mail correspondence with Col. James C. Flowers, director of cadet activities, 28 January 2011, copy in author files.

209. Eric Bartelt, "USMA Named One of 15 Top Sports Education Teams," *Pointer View*, 2 November 2007, 4.

CHAPTER SIX

1. *Annual Report of the Superintendent*, 1902, 10.

2. Ibid., 11.

3. Mills and Hein overlapped at West Point from 1898–1901. They had much in common: cavalrymen assigned to the 1st Cavalry Regiment; experience in the Indian campaigns; well connected politically to Theodore Roosevelt and his circle of associates. The two men got along well despite the fact that Mills, before becoming superintendent, had been Hein's junior. See chapter 2.

4. Hein, *Memories of Long Ago*, 267–81; Ambrose, *Duty, Honor, Country*, 244–45.

5. Physical education, although under the purview of the commandant, is the focus of chapter 6.

6. "Programme of Practical Military Instruction in the Department of Tactics," *Annual Report of the Superintendent*, 1902, 28–30.

7. Lt. Col. Robert L. Howze, commandant from 1905 to 1909, initiated the practice marches, believing that "great practical benefit will result." *Annual Report of the Superintendent*, 1905, 32. His successors agreed, as the practice march became a standard feature of the summer encampment until the Second World War.

8. *Annual Report of the Superintendent*, 1916, 18.

9. *Annual Report of the Superintendent*, 1905, 7.

10. *Annual Report of the Superintendent*, 1909, 9–10.

11. With completion of the new cavalry barracks and stables at the south end of the reservation in 1909, cadets moved to that location for their cavalry training. The distance from the stables to the barracks, about a mile, complicated efforts to conduct the training during the academic year.

12. *Annual Report of the Superintendent*, 1904, 32.

13. Kabel-Ballard, "The Lives of West Point's Buffalo Soldiers," in Betros, *West Point*, 323–28.

14. *Annual Report of the Superintendent*, 1907, 11.

15. The troopers were reassigned to the cadet mess detachment, effective 1 September 1948. *Annual Report of the Superintendent*, 1948, 48.

16. Firing at Storm King Mountain came with liabilities. In 1898, Henry Metcalf, a retired army officer living in the village of Cold Spring (directly across the river from the mountain), wrote a letter of complaint to the secretary of war. He noted that shells fired from the big guns sometimes ricocheted off the mountain and sent shards of metal, rocks, and other debris flying in all directions. While no one had been killed or injured so far, "local life insurance men had threatened to increase their premiums if something was not done quickly." The letter had the desired effect, as the acting superintendent (Otto Hein) took steps to make the firing safer. "Villagers Out of Danger," *New York Times*, 26 July 1898, 7.

17. A subcaliber device fits snugly inside the barrel of the weapon and fires a small projectile that goes a relatively short distance but otherwise has flight characteristics similar to a full-size projectile. It provides an efficient and effective way to conduct artillery training without the cost and safety concerns of live ammunition.

18. *Annual Report of the Superintendent*, 1907, 9; *Annual Report of the Superintendent*, 1909, 9.

19. *Annual Report of the Superintendent*, 1910, 45.

20. *Annual Report of the Superintendent*, 1915, 11. Shanks graduated from the Academy in 1884.

21. Ibid., 31. The instructor of practical engineering doubled as the West Point engineer officer. Since he worked directly for the superintendent in both capacities, he merited a seat on the Academic Board. In contrast, the senior instructors of infantry, cavalry, and artillery, all of whom worked for the commandant in the Department of Tactics, did not have a seat on the board.

22. Ibid., 15.

23. The USMA surgeon lost his academic title shortly after World War II and his seat on the Academic Board in 2004. Memorandum from William J. Lennox (superintendent) to Academic Board, "Academic Board Composition," 30 June 2004, Office of the Dean, West Point.

24. The Department of History continues to teach this core course, now called *History of the Military Art*, to first classmen. It consists of a total of eighty lessons spread over two semesters.

25. *Annual Report of the Superintendent*, 1902, 56.

26. Ibid., 7.

27. Staff rides would regain prominence later in the century following the creation of the Department of History in 1969.

28. The coast artillery stations most often visited by the cadets were Fort Hancock (Sandy Hook, NJ), Fort H. G. Wright (Fisher's Island, NY), and Fort Totten (Long Island, NY).

29. *Annual Report of the Superintendent*, 1907, 51.

30. *Annual Report of the Superintendent*, 1903, 8.

31. The Plain is the plateau overlooking the Hudson River on which reside the cadet barracks, academic buildings, parade field, Trophy Point, and the summer encampment site.

32. Academy leaders could not purge hazing completely, despite their best efforts. During the period covered by the 1909 *Annual Report*, for example, Superintendent Hugh

Scott dismissed one first classman and six third classmen for this offense. He noted with exasperation that there "are a few in almost every class who deliberately violate the act of Congress" forbidding hazing (8).

33. The French instructors endeared themselves to the cadets by sharing all the hardships of cadet life. They camped with the cadets on the Plain, ate the same food, and accompanied them to training sites, including the practice march at summer's end. *Annual Report of the Superintendent*, 1918, 3–4.

34. This was the original class of 1919, which now was scheduled to graduate a year early — in June 1918. The members of this class would be second classmen for only about four months — that is, until the graduation of the class of August 1917. Afterward they would be the new first class.

35. *Annual Report of the Superintendent*, 1918, 15.

36. Ibid., 18. Another three-year class graduated in June 1918, followed by rapid-fire graduations of two more classes on 1 November. The carefully laid plans for academic and military instruction were thrown into upheaval until the War Department authorized the reestablishment of the four-year curriculum shortly after World War I. See chapter 4.

37. Ambrose, *Duty, Honor, Country*, 251. In contrast to cadet training, civilian volunteers at the Plattsburgh military camp in northern New York and other similar camps were undergoing training adapted to trench warfare, machine guns, and high-explosive artillery. The young men at these "preparedness camps," many of whom would receive officer commissions as the army expanded for war, were getting at least a taste of what was in store for them in France. The preparedness movement and associated training camps are discussed in John Garry Clifford, *The Citizen Soldiers: The Plattsburgh Training Camp Movement, 1913–1920* (Lexington, KY: University of Kentucky Press, 1972). A good description of the training received at the camps is in the Olin O. Ellis and Enoch B. Garey, *The Plattsburg Manual: A Handbook for Military Training* (New York: The Century Co., 1917).

38. The early graduation of several West Point classes lightened the teaching load for the academic departments. Some professors used the opportunity to travel to France to observe Allied training and operations and bring back insights that could add relevancy to their academic classes. For example, Gustav J. Fiebeger, Professor of Civil and Military Engineering, brought back War Department technical manuals to serve as textbooks in the military engineering course. This was one of the few ways during World War I that Academy leaders adapted the cadets' education and training to the grim realities of modern war. The lecture series in military hygiene was another. Besides Fiebeger, Professors Charles P. Echols (Mathematics), Clifton C. Carter (Natural and Experimental Philosophy), Cornelius D. Willcox (Modern Languages), and Edwin R. Stuart (Drawing) traveled to France at various times in 1917 and 1918. *Annual Report of the Superintendent*, 1918, 20. For a discussion of the lack of preparedness of US forces in World War I, see Rod Paschall, *The Defeat of Imperial Germany* (Algonquin Books of Chapel Hill, 1989), 167–69.

39. MacArthur did not change the tradition of summer furlough for the second class; hence, only two classes (first and third) made the trip to Fort Dix.

40. MacArthur, *Reminiscences*, 81; *Annual Report of the Superintendent*, 1922, 8. Lt. Col. Morton F. Smith, the highly respected commandant who died in office in 1916, also was an advocate of conducting summer training away from West Point, "where numerous

social and other attractions tend to interfere with the work." Smith was confident that he could get better results if cadets spent the summer at training areas "some distance from the post" and "under service conditions." While it is unclear whether or not MacArthur was influenced by Smith's thinking, the two men clearly were of one mind on the issue of cadet training. His untimely death denied West Point an advocate of rigorous military training at a time when it was badly needed. *Annual Report of the Superintendent*, 1916, 17–18.

41. For brief accounts of the cadet training experience at Camp Dix, see "Cadets Leave Camp Dix," *New York Times*, 19 August 1920, 9, and "900 Cadets End Hikes," *New York Times*, 28 August 1921, 25.

42. Blaik, "A Cadet under MacArthur," 11.

43. "Record Class Enters West Point," *New York Times*, 2 July 1920, 13.

44. Ganoe, *MacArthur Close Up*, 107.

45. *Annual Report of the Superintendent*, 1923, 7.

46. Many historians have examined the "Athens-Sparta" dichotomy at the Military Academy. The most comprehensive treatment is Lovell's *Neither Athens Nor Sparta?*, which has been most helpful in my understanding of the subject.

47. Ambrose, *Duty, Honor, Country*, 256.

48. War Department Special Orders 29-0, 4 February 1922.

49. *Annual Report of the Superintendent*, 1920, 7.

50. Sladen, now the superintendent, had been the commandant from 1911 to 1914.

51. *Annual Report of the Superintendent*, 1923, 5.

52. *Annual Report of the Superintendent*, 1939, 4. Even the chief of the army's field artillery branch understood the value of keeping military training general. In response to Benedict's query about the quality of artillery training at the Academy, he noted that the technical knowledge of the West Point graduate who reports to the field artillery basic course was "greatly inferior" to that of honor graduates of the ROTC program. Regardless, he believed West Point "should be kept a cultural and character building institution" and therefore characterized the field artillery instruction there as "satisfactory." Second endorsement, 16 April 1940, letter from Benedict to the Adjutant General, 1 April 1940, file 351.02-351.04, "Military Posts and Reservations," Army-AG Project Decimal Files 1940–1945, Records Group 407, National Archives, College Park, MD.

53. See, for example, Forman, *The Educational Objectives of the U.S. Military Academy*, 2nd ed., 12.

54. *Annual Report of the Superintendent*, 1925, 1.

55. The road at issue was New York Route 218, an iconic highway gouged out of the side of Storm King Mountain and offering majestic views of the Hudson Valley. Opened in 1922, the highway immediately became the main thoroughfare for motor traffic between West Point and all points north. On the days when cadets were conducting artillery training, Academy officials would block the road for hours on end and thus incur the wrath of neighboring communities. "Solution Near on West Point Road," *New York Times*, 2 August 1927, 36.

56. *Annual Report of the Superintendent*, 1929, 1.

57. Letter from Buckner to Maj. Gen. William Connor (superintendent), 10 January 1935, file packet on "Summer Training for Cadets, 1st Class, US Military Academy–1935,"

Adjutant General's Office Central Files 1926–1939, Record Group 407, National Archives, College Park, MD.

58. An assignment to West Point was a hardship tour for army aviators because of the difficulty in maintaining flight certification. Lt. E. E. Partridge, an aviator assigned to the Department of Mathematics, attempted to keep his certification current by driving to Mitchell Field, Long Island, two weekends per month to fly. After fifteen such trips, however, he concluded that the time and energy associated with the trips were not worth the benefit; hence, he requested "most urgently that I be relieved from duty here." Although Superintendent Smith and the Chief of the Air Corps disapproved the request, both strongly recommended the construction of an airfield at or near West Point. Letter from Partridge to the Adjutant General, 27 March 1930, file packet on "Request for relief from USMA assignment—ref. 1LT E. E. Partridge," Adjutant General's Office Central Files 1926–1939, Records Group 407, National Archives, College Park, MD.

59. *Annual Report of the Superintendent*, 1930, 2.

60. Public Law 71-795, 3 March 1931, *US Statutes at Large*, vol. 41, 1491.

61. Within two years, the total area of the new land increased to 15,085 acres. Thirty-four of the new acres were recovered from the shallows east of the West Shore Railroad line at the level of the Hudson River. By straightening the tracks and filling in the marshy area between tracks and "Target Hill" above, the Academy gained valuable new fields for training and athletics. *Annual Report of the Superintendent*, 1944, 26.

62. Crackel, *West Point*, 208. The progress of acquiring land and building training facilities around Lake Popolopen is described in detail in the 1942, 1943, and 1944 Annual Reports.

63. *Annual Report of the Superintendent*, 1942, 8. Although "Beast Barracks" ceased to exist by 1942, the name has continued to be used informally to denote the entire summer experience of fourth classmen.

64. The West Point cavalry detachment received four scout cars in time for summer training in 1941, and a few light tanks arrived shortly thereafter. *Annual Report of the Superintendent*, 1941, 5.

65. Pine Camp later became Fort Drum, a major army base near Watertown, New York. The only cadets who did not participate in the Pine Camp exercise were those in pilot training, discussed later.

66. *Annual Report of the Superintendent*, 1944, 13. This was not the first time cadets had joined maneuver units for training. In 1941, Superintendent Robert Eichelberger sent first classmen to Camp Dix to observe the operation of a reception station for new recruits. While there, the cadets were posted for two days to various units of the 44th Division and served as junior officers while the division maneuvered in the field. Eichelberger noted that the training, "even for so brief a period, was a distinct innovation in training methods at West Point." *Annual Report of the Superintendent*, 1941, 5.

67. *Annual Report of the Superintendent*, 1943, 1.

68. The Army Air Corps became the Army Air Forces in June 1941. The new organization would have the command hierarchy necessary for the vast expansion of air units necessary to fight the war.

69. Marshall to class of 1941, 29 May 1941, as reported in "Editorial," *Washington*

Herald, 9 June 1941, file 353, "Military Posts and Reservations," Army-AG Project Decimal Files 1940–1945, Record Group 407, National Archives, College Park, MD.

70. Crackel, *West Point*, 208–09.

71. Stewart Airfield opened in August 1942. It started out small but expanded quickly to become a major airfield and, eventually, a US Air Force base.

72. *Annual Report of the Superintendent*, 1943, 23; *Annual Report of the Superintendent*, 1945, 16–17, 27.

73. United States Military Academy, *Post War Curriculum at the U. S. Military Academy, West Point, New York, September 1945*, 56.

74. Camp Popolopen was renamed Camp Buckner in honor of Simon Bolivar Buckner Jr., commandant from 1933 to 1936. Buckner was killed by enemy artillery while commanding the Tenth Army during the invasion of Okinawa in June 1945. He was the last American general killed during World War II.

75. Murphy, *West Point Cadet, 1948–1952*, 147.

76. Ibid., 69.

77. There were two exceptions to the afternoon-only training. Second classmen took twenty hours of tactics instruction in the mornings when they did not have to meet for electricity class. Also, fourth classmen took physical training at least three mornings per week during academic hours. Wednesdays after school were left free for cadet discretionary use.

78. The latter two activities are covered more fully in chapter 6.

79. Stearns, *A Report and Recommendation to the Secretary of Defense*, 15. Board members included Dwight Eisenhower, then president of Columbia University, and the superintendents of the Military, Naval, and Air Force academies.

80. *Annual Report of the Superintendent*, 1953, 46.

81. *Annual Report of the Superintendent*, 1946, 22.

82. *Annual Report of the Superintendent*, 1953, 46.

83. *Annual Report of the Superintendent*, 1959, 52.

84. *Annual Report of the Superintendent*, 1975, 5.

85. *Annual Report of the Superintendent*, 1952, 48.

86. *Annual Report of the Superintendent*, 1957, 9; Davidson, "Grandpa Gar," 168.

87. West Point's current Cadet Troop Leader Training (CTLT) program is the successor to AOT and the progeny of Davidson's 1958 initiative. CTLT is primarily for second classmen, but first classmen also may participate if they were unable to do so the previous year.

88. The second-class training scheduled for June 1961 demonstrates the point. During their two weeks of training at West Point, second classmen visited a few signal corps and air defense (i.e., army) installations, as well as the navy's submarine school in New London, Connecticut, and Stewart Air Force Base in Newburgh, New York. Both the navy and air force trips were local and brief; they were scheduled around other training conducted at the Academy.

89. *Annual Report of the Superintendent*, 1962, 14.

90. *Annual Report of the Superintendent*, 1970, 41.

91. RECONDO, an acronym combining "reconnaissance" and "commando," was a three-day "Ranger-type" experience emphasizing patrolling, small-unit leadership. The training strengthened infantry skills in general, but was particularly well suited to counter-

insurgency missions. *Annual Report of the Superintendent*, 1961, 11; *Annual Report of the Superintendent*, 1966, 16–17.

92. Michael Jones, interview by author, 5 January 2008, transcript, 4.

93. The infantry detachment was relatively new (1941), but the others had been around for decades. The coast artillery detachment was disbanded in 1947; its soldiers were absorbed into the artillery detachment.

94. *Annual Report of the Superintendent*, 1953, 77. The enlisted detachments may not have been needed year round for cadet training, but they performed other useful functions at West Point that otherwise would have required the hiring of civilian workers. For this reason, superintendents were generally not enthusiastic about the troop cuts.

95. Letter from the Adjutant General to various addressees, subject: "Additional Troop Requirement, Summer Training 1955, USMA," 13 April 1955, file 250.53-351.1, "USMA," Army-AG Decimal File 1953–1954, Projects—Military Schools, Record Group 407, National Archives, College Park, MD.

96. Starting in 1965, third classmen spent a week at Fort Knox for tank training. *Annual Report of the Superintendent*, 1965, 32. With few exceptions, the Fort Knox training continued annually through 2009; at that point, budgetary constraints and the move of the Armor School to the infantry center at Fort Benning, Georgia, ended it, at least temporarily.

97. In 1963, for example, second classmen visited naval installations at Newport and Quonset Point, Rhode Island, and New London, Connecticut, to learn about the navy's surface, air, and submarine forces. They also visited Cape Kennedy and Eglin Air Force Base, Florida, to become familiar with the missions of the Tactical Air Command (TAC), Strategic Air Command (SAC), and Air Defense Command. *Annual Report of the Superintendent*, 1964, 40. As was the case in the 1950s, enthusiasm for the interservice trips waned quickly, and within a year or two they were removed entirely from the second-class summer schedule. By the late 1960s, the only interservice training that remained was accomplished during the academic year in a classroom setting.

98. The usual stops were Fort Benning, Georgia (infantry), Fort Knox, Kentucky (armor), Fort Sill, Oklahoma (artillery and guided missile), Fort Bliss, Texas (air defense artillery), and Fort Belvoir, Virginia (engineer).

99. *Annual Report of the Superintendent*, 1963, 33–34.

100. *Annual Report of the Superintendent*, 1970, 37. Many second-class cadets who resigned prior to the start of the academic year mentioned the June encampment as a reason for leaving. A large part of the reason for adding airborne training was thus motivational: "to help cadets make an informed, careful choice about the Army at that juncture, to develop self-confidence and leadership, to acquire additional military skills, and to increase the cadet's exposure to the military environment away from West Point." *Board of Visitors Report*, 29 November 1977, 18.

101. *Annual Report of the Superintendent*, 1973, 1–2. The menu of available schools varied from year to year. Ranger training, for example, ceased to be offered after 1980. Added to the menu by the early 1980s were the army's Air Assault School, the air force's Survival, Evasion, Resistance, and Escape School, and the navy's Special Naval Warfare Orientation Course.

102. One cadet wrote, "The 1st Class Trip (bummer) is a real waste of time (mine) and money (yours)." Another griped, "The trip was so rotten I'd probably get in trouble if I wrote the words which describe it." Even the one relatively positive comment had a negative flip side: "The First Class trip was enjoyable and educational. . . . First classmen should be treated as intelligent, mature people and not pampered like blundering idiots." Liveoak, *Summary of Responses, Reorganization Week Questionnaire*, 23. Upper-class cadets, particularly first classmen, are notoriously cynical about West Point, so these comments must be viewed with a grain of salt. Even after correcting for the cynicism, however, these and the other survey comments in the Liveoak study stand out for their vitriol.

103. Relatively few first classmen attended specialty schools, but those who did were assigned leadership positions. For example, they filled the cadet commander and cadet first sergeant positions for the contingent of second-class cadets who went to Airborne School. Recollection of author, who attended Airborne School in 1976 as a first classman and who served as the first sergeant for the company of cadets, most of whom were second classmen.

104. For many decades prior to 1980, cadets took their term-end examinations in January, almost immediately after returning from the holiday break. It was an apt beginning to what West Pointers have affectionately called the "gloom period."

105. The commandant at the time was Brig. Gen. Joseph Franklin. While he dutifully executed the condensed summer training program, he stressed to the superintendent in his end-of-tour report, "We definitely need more time in CBT" [cadet basic training]. Memorandum from Franklin to Lt. Gen. Willard Scott, "After Action Report," 28 June 1982, copy in author's files.

106. Academic majors program went into effect in 1983. See chapter 3.

107. Dave R. Palmer, interview by author, 17 July 2007, transcript, 33.

108. The first intercession was in January 1990. A good discussion of this topic in the context of the many other reforms of the Palmer era is in Donnithorne, *Preparing for West Point's Third Century*, especially chapter 3, "Military Program."

109. Dave R. Palmer, interview by Stephen Grove, 24 June 1991, transcript, 28. The military art and science field of study eventually became an academic major of the same name. Although the Department of History provided oversight of the major, the Department of Military Instruction developed the curriculum and provided the instructors. In the early years of its existence, the field of study (later the major) had a reputation for academic laxity. The problem was addressed through the appointment of a tenured military professor to direct the program starting in 2007. Almost immediately the program's structure and rigor improved; the following year the program's name changed to "defense and strategic studies." The revised course of study "combines military science, history, economics, political science, geography, leadership, information technology, and law to understand the nature of war and the role of the military as an instrument of national power. Using a foundation in historical case studies, cadets examine the relationship between contemporary defense policy, operations, strategy, and generalship by focusing on the strategic, operational, and tactical levels of war." "2012 Defense and Strategic Studies Major Curriculum," *Academic Program: Curriculum and Course Descriptions* (West Point: Office of the Dean, 13 May 2010).

110. Lennox was influenced by reading Ed Ruggero's *Duty First: A Year in the Life*

of West Point and the Making of American Leaders (Harper Paperbacks, 2002). The book's assertion that cadets were unsure leaders troubled Lennox: "I had never heard of West Pointers not feeling confident about leadership and I saw that in the book and that really disturbed me. So what I wanted to do was to get their level of confidence and their level of competence up in the tasks that they were going to be working that summer." William J. Lennox, interview by Stephen Grove, 27 March 2006, transcript, 32.

111. Many cadets took more than five academic courses per semester. For example, cadets majoring in engineering had to take up to eighteen disciplinary courses, which required overloading during several semesters. Many other cadets voluntarily took extra courses as a means of rounding out their studies.

112. Brig. Gen. Daniel Kaufman, dean from 2001 to 2006, lamented the reintroduction of military science into the academic year. He believed that military intercession, while not perfect, had largely achieved the goals Palmer had sought. "We had . . . sort of figured it out," he noted, "and, I think, it was actually pretty good." Kaufman succeeded in limiting military science courses to only .5 credits — the equivalent of twenty minutes of outside preparation for class — when those courses were reintroduced into the academic year in 2003. Daniel Kaufman, interview by Stephen Grove, 10 May 2005, transcript, 27.

113. Prior to 2006, cadets took military science courses every semester; each course was worth .5 credit hours. Starting in 2006, cadets began taking only one military science course per academic year, but each course was worth 1.5 credit hours — a net increase of .5 credit hours per year. "Military Art and Science Curriculum," *Academic Program: Curriculum and Course Descriptions* (West Point: Office of the Dean, 7 September 2010), online edition.

114. The weight of the capstone course, *MX400: Officership*, was 2.0 credits.

115. Scope statement, "MX400: Officership," *Academic Program: Curriculum and Course Descriptions* (West Point: Office of the Dean, 29 June 2010), online edition.

116. Hagenbeck acknowledged, "This decision is contentious. Nonetheless, I believe that the tradeoff of academic year changes for a 12-week summer term may increase our ability to develop leaders of character." E-mail message from Hagenbeck to the Academic Board, "Academy Schedule," 15 February 2008, author's files.

117. Brig. Gen. Daniel Kaufman reflected the Athenian view. Asked what he would do to strengthen the West Point experience for cadets, he replied, "I would eliminate the requirement for military development school" (e.g., airborne or air assault) during the summer. In place of those experiences, Kaufman favored summer-long cultural immersion opportunities for large numbers of cadets. "The benefits, I think, would be significant in terms of not just language skill, but cultural understanding, maturity, social development, all the things we want our cadets to do." Kaufman interview, 59–60.

118. John Ryan, "West Point rolling out more real-life curriculum," *Army Times*, 8 November 2010, 32.

119. Department of Military Instruction, "Outcomes-Based Training at West Point," briefing packet, 20 September 2009, copy in author files.

120. Transcript of comments from Col. Haskins to CLDT cadre, 21 May 2010, copy in author's files. Two of Haskins's other initiatives were to make the cadet cadre primarily responsible for summer training and to hold them accountable for training outcomes rather

than the processes used to achieve them. Accordingly, he required first and second classmen to be the principal instructors for cadet basic training and cadet field training. (This mission had traditionally gone to the army units that deployed to West Point during the summer months specifically to assist with the training.) Haskins recognized that cadets "will give worse classes than sergeants would," but that did not matter. "If we hold them accountable for the results and don't worry too much about how ugly the process is by which they get those results, they'll surprise us. Their dedication and their ingenuity will be better than a polished performance—and they'll learn more about leadership."

121. E-mail correspondence from 2nd Lt. Benjamin Field (West Point class of 2009) to Col. Casey Haskins, 5 September 2010, copy in author's files.

CHAPTER SEVEN

1. The professor of drawing, Charles Larned, was the most eloquent spokesman for the Academy's paternal approach to developing leaders. West Point, he noted, "is responsible to the Nation and not to the individual, both in its methods and in its results." Consequently, "it can not leave to the student an independent initiative in any matter bearing upon his development as a professional soldier. It is a machine in which a heterogeneous mass of raw material is transformed in the short space of four years into a finished product, molded, tested, and stamped with the sterling mark which has come to be recognized the world over." Military leadership was thus the product of the developmental environment he and his colleagues designed. Charles Larned, "The Genius of West Point," in *Centennial*, I: 471.

2. There were many indicators of the growing sophistication of cadets relative to their counterparts in civilian schools. They included consistently higher scores on the Graduate Record Examination (particularly in social sciences), unusual success in Rhodes Scholarship competitions, and frequent foreign travel during the summers.

3. Academics and honor both had relatively objective standards that simplified the task of eliminating the weak. The same was not true of military potential, for which the standards were more subjective and therefore more forgiving.

4. Superintendent John M. Schofield was so appalled by the culture of hazing that he penned a "Definition of Discipline" for cadets. His compelling words became part of the knowledge required to be memorized by fourth classmen. "The discipline which makes the soldiers of a free country reliable in battle is not to be gained by harsh or tyrannical treatment. On the contrary, such treatment is far more likely to destroy than to make an army. It is possible to impart instruction and to give commands in such manner and such a tone of voice to inspire in the soldier no feeling but an intense desire to obey, while the opposite manner and tone of voice cannot fail to excite strong resentment and a desire to disobey." Schofield address to cadets, 11 August 1879, West Point, NY.

5. William A. Ganoe, MacArthur's adjutant at West Point, recalled being admonished by a senior sergeant for being overzealous in making a verbal correction: "I should tell you *that* isn't done in the Service." Robert Danford, the commandant during MacArthur's tenure as superintendent, had a similar incident. As a young lieutenant at Fort Riley, Kansas, he spoke to soldiers in a harsh and demeaning way in earshot of his commander, who promptly counseled him. "Mr. Danford, we do not handle the American soldier the way a

Yearling handles a Plebe at West Point." Both incidents are recounted in Ganoe, *MacArthur Close Up*, 103–04.

6. Mills's efforts to reform academics, physical education, and military training are covered in chapters 4, 5, and 6, respectively.

7. "Historical Sketch of the Tactical Department," *Centennial*, I: 392.

8. *Annual Report of the Superintendent*, 1906, 37.

9. Ibid. Cadets had gone on short practice marches prior to 1906 that usually lasted less than twenty-four hours. Howze lengthened the exercise to about a week and required all cadets in the summer encampment to participate. This initiative created many more leadership opportunities for the upper classes.

10. Ibid., 36.

11. Cadet rank was for training and administrative purposes only. The legal commander of each cadet company was the tactical officer; similarly, the commandant was the legal commander of the battalion (later, the regiment or brigade) of cadets.

12. An example of cadet organization and leadership positions is "Battalion Organization," *Howitzer*, 1905, 36–37. Annual listings of the cadet chain of command during the early decades of the twentieth century are in the *Official Register of the Officers and Cadets of the U.S. Military Academy*.

13. *Official Register of the Officers and Cadets of the U.S. Military Academy*, 1905, 8.

14. Ibid.

15. *Official Register of the Officers and Cadets of the U.S. Military Academy*, 1914, 45. The change allowed sixty-two of the 162 members of the class of 1915 (about 37 percent) to fill a leader position during their senior year.

16. The quote is from the report of Lt. D. C. Shanks, office of the army inspector general. Shanks visited West Point from 15 through 25 July 1914 and rendered a positive assessment of the advances in training and leader development. An extract of the report is in *Annual Report of the Superintendent*, 1915, 11–13.

17. During the testimony, MacArthur was asked to admit that he had been hazed cruelly and to name the guilty cadets. Responding obliquely in a way that foreshadowed his political acumen (and no doubt exasperated his interlocutor), MacArthur acknowledged that the treatment was cruel but would name only those cadets who already had admitted guilt or resigned from the Academy. Manchester, *American Caesar*, 52. Recalling his testimony years later, MacArthur said that hazing "was practiced with a worthy goal" but sometimes its methods could be "violent and uncontrolled." MacArthur, *Reminiscences*, 25.

18. MacArthur quoted in *Annual Report of the Superintendent*, 1920, 3.

19. Ibid., 4. MacArthur's views accorded with those of progressive military thinkers in other developed countries. The Polish military theorist, Jean de Bloch, for example, had written extensively on the growing destructiveness of modern war and the consequent need for military commanders to change their tactical methods. "Formerly," he noted, "there was every reason for making the soldier first of all an automaton" who marched into battle under strict control and in tidy, compact formations. Unfortunately, the tactical doctrine that governed these formations had "not progressed commensurately with the technical improvements in arms." De Bloch's warnings went unheeded by most military professionals until the carnage of the First World War. Jean de Bloch, "The Transvaal War: Its Lessons

in Regard to Militarism and Army Re-organization," *The Journal of the Royal United Service Institution* 45, no. 286 (December 1901): 1419.

20. Ibid.

21. Samuel Tillman, MacArthur's predecessor as superintendent, also dealt with hazing issues. While unequivocal in his condemnation of abusive hazing, he was traditional in his views toward the practice. Hazing, he believed, trained cadets in "alertness and military bearing. . . . Each class knows that its predecessors have practiced it, the authorities and alumni all acknowledge its beneficial effects within reason." Tillman memoirs (unpublished), box 2, folder: "Typescript of Memoirs," Tillman Papers, USMA Archives. A detailed history of hazing from its beginnings in the mid-nineteenth century to World War I appears in Tillman's 1918 *Annual Report of the Superintendent*, 4–12.

22. "Resolutions of the Class of 1920 to the Commandant," 4 August 1919, West Point Archives, copy in author's files. MacArthur published the document in modified form as *Traditions and Customs of the Corps of Cadets* (West Point: US Military Academy, 1920).

23. MacArthur to acting commandant, 2nd endorsement, 6 August 1919, to "Resolutions of the Class of 1920 to the Commandant," 4 August 1919, copy in author's files. The committee of first classmen was headed by Earl H. Blaik, the future head football coach. Blaik noted in his memoirs that "most of our classmates supported the new order. But there were still some among our 300-plus who stubbornly resisted anything that eased the burden of the plebes, since it had not been eased in their own plebedom." Blaik, *The Red Blaik Story*, 32–33.

24. *Annual Report of the Superintendent*, 1920, 4.

25. Ambrose, *Duty, Honor, Country*, 269.

26. Andrews, *Military Manpower*, v.

27. The Academic Board authorized Danford's instructors to teach leadership classes to cadets on Saturday mornings. Ganoe, *MacArthur Close Up*, 106. I have found no evidence that Danford's theory-base instruction in leadership endured beyond his tenure as commandant.

28. *Annual Report of the Superintendent*, 1921, 11–12. Cadets had never been allowed to carry money; rather, they purchased items through debit accounts maintained by the USMA Treasurer. The point of this policy was to maintain absolute equality among cadets. Rich or poor, cadets were on equal financial footing at West Point.

29. First classmen taking overnight passes had to be under 50 percent of their demerit allowance for the month. Sladen provided statistics in his annual reports showing that cadets were motivated to avoid demerits in exchange for pass privileges.

30. By 1940, for example, first classmen once again could carry cash and had expanded pass and escorting privileges. The superintendent made the changes with the intent of "easing the transition from cadet to officer," which would have sounded familiar to MacArthur. *Annual Report of the Superintendent*, 1940, 5.

31. Memorandum from Taylor to dean and commandant, 26 September 1945, file 351.051, "Military Psychology and Leadership Course 1946–1948," USMA Archives.

32. Memorandum from Taylor to the Department of Tactics, 17 October 1945, file 351.051, "Military Psychology and Leadership Course 1946–1948," USMA Archives.

33. Taylor to the dean, 1 November 1945, file 351.051, "Military Psychology and Leadership Course 1946–1948," USMA Archives.

34. In 1942, the Department of Civil and Military Engineering was redesignated the Department of Military Art and Engineering to better describe the courses it taught.

35. Taylor delivered one of the lectures himself. He gave cadets an eloquent discourse on three qualities of successful leadership — devotion to soldiers, human understanding, and professional competence. Like MacArthur, Taylor tried to impress upon the cadets that citizen-soldiers of a democracy resent harsh and disrespectful treatment. "Leading the American Soldier," 27 May 1945, USMA Archives.

36. See, for example, the studies that were published in Samuel A. Stouffer, et al., *The American Soldier* (New York: John Wiley and Sons, 1949).

37. Letter from Eisenhower to Taylor, 2 January 1946, in Chandler and Galambos, eds., *The Papers of Dwight David Eisenhower*, 7: 709–11.

38. "Picks Helmick for Inspector General," *New York Times*, 6 November 1921.

39. Memorandum from Helmick to Army Chief of Staff, 29 July 1927, file packet on "Instruction in Psychology and Leadership at the U.S. Military Academy," Adjutant General's Office Central Files 1926–1939, Records Group 407, National Archives, College Park, MD.

40. Much of the time required for psychology came from the hours already allotted to other military training. In particular, cavalry instruction was easy to give up since World War II had rendered horses in battle obsolete.

41. *Annual Report of the Superintendent*, 1946, 20–23. Taylor discusses the purpose of the aptitude ratings in his memoir, *Swords and Plowshares*, 121.

42. *Official Register of the Officers and Cadets of the U.S. Military Academy*, 1947, 22. The OMPL staff included a director, associate director, aptitude officer, and four instructors.

43. Taylor to War Department, 16 July 1946, reprinted in *Assembly* 5 (October 1946), 3.

44. *Annual Report of the Superintendent*, 1948, 29–30.

45. Ibid., 36–37.

46. In academic year 1962–1963, the Academic Board expanded the basic psychology course to forty-five hours — that is, a full semester — and moved it from the fall to the spring semester of the third-class year. Concurrently, it moved the first-class course in military leadership from the spring to the fall semester. The purpose of these moves was to bring the two courses closer together in the curriculum (one year separation rather than two). *Annual Report of the Superintendent*, 1963, 35.

47. Depending on the source, this program goes by different names: Aptitude for the Military Service, Aptitude for the Service, or Aptitude for Service System.

48. The cadet-on-cadet ratings included, at various times, ratings of lowerclassmen by upperclassmen, peer ratings, and self-evaluations. Of the three, peer ratings were most problematic because classmates within a company sometimes conspired to manipulate the ratings to the advantage or disadvantage of particular cadets. For this reason, some commandants decided to remove peer ratings from the aptitude system. In 1956, for example, only the evaluations from upper-class cadets (2/3 weight) and tactical officers (1/3 weight) factored into a cadet's aptitude rank. Department of Tactics, *Aptitude for the Service*, 2.

49. The initial staffing of the Office of Military Psychology and Leadership included a

director, associate director, aptitude officer, and four instructors. All were military officers except the associate director, a civilian psychologist who provided cadets counseling services as needed. *Annual Report of the Superintendent*, 1946, 23.

50. Taylor, *Swords and Plowshares*, 121.

51. A study of the records of recent graduates in the Korean conflict showed that their performance "related favorably to Aptitude for the Service ratings given while cadets." *Annual Report of the Superintendent*, 1953, 53. Several agencies collaborated on research projects relevant to cadets. OMPL, the Office of Institutional Research, the Department of Physical Education, and the USMA medical detachment were the principal contributors at West Point. Additionally, the personnel research branch of the Army Adjutant General's Office frequently worked with West Point researchers. The Office of Institutional Research has hundreds of these reports on file.

52. *Annual Report of the Superintendent*, 1960, 7–8. The table, "Percentage of Class Strength Separated for the Classes 1950–1963," on page 19 shows a spike in separations starting in 1956, the year Davidson became superintendent. Davidson predicted that aptitude losses would fluctuate between 2 and 3 percent per year "until our present entrance standards and recruiting efforts begin to bear fruit." See chapter 3 for coverage of Davidson's effort to raise admission standards.

53. Howard Prince, interview by author, 16 July 2007, transcript, 9.

54. Howard Prince, interview by Stephen Grove, 6 September 1990, transcript, 34.

55. Ibid., 35.

56. Quoted in Crackel, *West Point*, 270.

57. William B. Seely, Robert C. Carroll, and Neal Schmitt, "Evaluation of the Fourth Class System," Research Report No. 71-2, OMPL, April 1971, 8, copy in author files.

58. "Called Sadistic: West Point Hit on Hazing," *Chicago Tribune*, 16 October 1973, 2. A plebe who left the Academy shortly after basic training reported that upperclassmen would not let him sleep some nights or eat any more food "than could be held in the palm of one hand." Worse, he did not feel that he had been singled out; rather, the treatment was characteristic of "a few egocentrics who place their own sadistic pleasures ahead of the academy's high principles."

59. Ibid., 36.

60. Quoted in *Final Report of the West Point Study Group*, 115.

61. The West Point Study Group and related reviews are discussed more fully in chapter 4.

62. US Military Academy, *The Fourth Class System 1978–1979*. The previous version of the regulation devoted an entire annex to fourth-class knowledge. Each month plebes had to master a new body of knowledge while retaining what they had learned to date. The knowledge included current events, Army heritage, military customs, West Point history and traditions, basic branch information, weapons and equipment characteristics, and many other topics of professional interest. The knowledge also included frivolous information, such as "The Days," a recitation of upcoming events with the number of days to each. "Fourth Class Knowledge Annex" to US Military Academy, *The Fourth Class System 1977–1978*.

63. *The Fourth Class System 1978–1979*, 2.

64. *Annual Report of the Superintendent*, 1980, 31.

65. Another reason for the decline was a "lock-in" system whereby new cadets were not allowed to leave the Academy for three (later increased to four) weeks. *Annual Report of the Superintendent*, 1983, 38.

66. Office of the Commandant, "After Action Report and Commander's Evaluation: Cadet Basic Training 1980," West Point, 17 September 1981, USMA Archives.

67. Ibid.

68. The rating scheme was the idea of Commandant Robert Danford, who strongly supported MacArthur's reform agenda at West Point. Danford, "USMA's 31st Superintendent," 14. Curiously, Danford's military rating scheme gave the most weight—30 percent—to "scholarship." Leadership, athletics, and instructor ability each received 15 percent, followed by demerit record (10 percent), military bearing and orderliness (9 percent), and extracurricular activities (6 percent). *Annual Report of the Superintendent*, 1920, 10.

69. *Annual Report of the Superintendent*, 1971, 35.

70. *Final Report of the West Point Study Group*, 111.

71. The Leadership Evaluation System evolved into the Cadet Leader Assessment System (CLAS) in 1978. Under CLAS, the company tactical officer had "primary responsibility for the cadet's leadership development." The CLAS existed for two years before being replaced by the Military Development System, which was the culmination of the process of subordinating assessment to the more important goal of development. *Annual Report of the Superintendent*, 1978, 24.

72. *Annual Report of the Superintendent*, 1982, 25.

73. In academic years 1980–1981 and 1981–1982, a total of 211 cadets were placed on MDS probation. Of these, thirty-two were separated. *Annual Report of the Superintendent*, 1981, 34; *Annual Report of the* Superintendent, 1982, 25.

74. Design of the Military Development System was the work of many hands, but the deputy commandant, Col. Jarold Hutchinson, played a prominent role. Just prior to his assignment at the Academy, he served as a member of the West Point Study Group. He therefore had a thorough understanding of the leader development issues at West Point and could harness the energies of the commandant's staff to address them. Hutchinson's other important credentials were academic. He had a master's degree in counseling which, at the time, was a rarity in the Department of Tactics.

75. The West Point Study Group commented pointedly on the conscious withdrawal of some officers from the process of leader development. One faculty member explained, "The TAC and I are two separate parts of the total system. He teaches the military stuff and hands out quill. I teach the academics and pass out grades. I don't do his job and he doesn't do mine." *Final Report of the West Point Study Group*, 99.

76. Herbert Lloyd, interview by Stephen Grove, June 1978, transcript, 28.

77. *Final Report of the West Point Study Group*, 98–105.

78. Prince interview transcript, 16 July 2007, 17. In making these comments, Prince emphasized more than once that his impressions were subjective rather than scientific. Still, he was very confident in his characterization of the leader styles of tactical officers.

79. Lloyd interview transcript, 51. Lloyd commanded Company B-2, one of the nine companies untouched by the cheating incident. In addition to Lloyd and Prince, some of

the more perceptive cadets could see the connection between the frequency of cheating and the leadership style of the tactical officers. Cadet Robert Mathis concluded in a paper for his advanced leadership class that the negative leadership of some tactical officers "created an atmosphere where violation of regulations was normal or the 'in thing' to do and that it created a large grey area concerning honor and regulations." Robert Mathis, telephonic interview by author, 15 February 2009.

80. See, for example, Dave R. Palmer, *The River and the Rock: The History of Fortress West Point, 1775–1783* (New York: Greenwood Publishing Corp., 1969) and *The Way of the Fox: American Strategy in the War for America, 1775–1783* (Westport, CT: Greenwood Press, 1975).

81. US Military Academy, *Institutional Self-Study 1988–1989*, 48.

82. "Report of the Staff and Faculty Fourth Class System Review Committee," 25 April 1990, copy in author's files; emphasis in original. The alumni committee, headed by Gen. Samuel Walker (commandant from 1969–1972 and, in 1990, the superintendent of the Virginia Military Institute), affirmed the goals of the fourth-class system as stated in USCC Circular 351.1. Its recommendations were conservative, focusing on procedural issues such as mess hall etiquette, plebe duties, and supervision during Reorganization Week (between the end of summer training and the start of the school year). The cadet committee, headed by Michael Thorsen (deputy brigade commander), was more critical of the fourth-class system than the alumni committee. Its principal recommendation was to "increase cadet autonomy" over the leader development system to fix the problems. Both the alumni and cadet committees agreed with the staff and faculty committee on the potential benefits of replacing the fourth-class system with an integrated four-year developmental program. "Report of the [Alumni] Leader Development–Fourth Class System Committee," May 1990; "Cadet Committee Review of the Fourth Class System," 20 April 1990. Both documents in author's files.

83. US Military Academy, "Cadet Leader Development System" (interim final draft), July 1990, 2.

84. Palmer interview transcript, 17 July 2007, 38.

85. Donnithorne, *Preparing for West Point's Third Century*, 74.

86. The full name was the "Dwight David Eisenhower Program of Graduate Studies in Leader Development." The Eisenhower program was advantageous in lessening the high cost of civilian graduate school. Tactical officers would come directly to West Point and live in government quarters during their year of study.

87. The Eisenhower Program was caught up in a web of contentious and interrelated service academy issues that the Senate Armed Services Committee was debating in 1992. The issues included active-duty service obligation for service academy graduates, composition of the faculty, number of general officers at the academies, and air force pilot retention. In the political give and take that followed, West Point lost the authority to operate a master's program. The handful of officers who went through the Eisenhower Program and received their master's degrees directly from West Point have the rare distinction of possessing a USMA diploma awarding a graduate degree. Prince interview transcript, 16 July 2007, 38.

88. Ibid., 59.

89. Ibid., 60. "BS," in this case, was "bull shit," not "bachelor of science." The author has heard similar complaints from the student-officers he has taught in the Eisenhower Leader Development Program.

90. Transformational leadership describes a process of interaction between leaders and followers that emphasizes mutual respect and understanding of each other's motives and expectations. The concept is studied in the discipline of organizational psychology and is therefore well understood by the officers in the graduate leadership program. It is developed most fully in Bernard M. Bass, *Transformational Leadership: Industrial, Military and Educational Impact* (Mahwah, NJ: Lawrence Erlbaum & Associates, 1998).

91. Both quotes appear in Ted Spiegel, "The Eisenhower Leadership Development Program," *Assembly* (October–December 2009): 17–19.

92. E-mail correspondence between retired Col. Richard Swain (USMA 1966) and author, 6 July 2006, author files. Swain was paraphrasing the comments of Gen. Frederick M. Franks Jr. (USMA 1959), who, at the time, was serving at West Point as the distinguished scholar in the Simon Center for the Professional Military Ethic. Swain served as the "professor of officership" in the Center and worked closely with Franks. He was "inclined to agree" with Franks on the latter's assessment of discipline in the Corps of Cadets.

93. Like most of his predecessors, McKearn had commanded successfully at the battalion and brigade levels. By experience and temperament, he favored the transformational approach to leader development described here.

94. Spiegel, "The Eisenhower Leadership Development Program," 17.

CHAPTER EIGHT

1. Although the modern honor code cites four categories of honor violations—lying, cheating, stealing, and tolerating those who lie, cheat, or steal—the nineteenth century honor code focused principally on lying. There is scattered evidence that Thayer considered cheating to be an honor violation, but for most of the century it was treated as a breach of discipline instead. Stealing was added to the list of honor offenses in the late-nineteenth century, although it had always been punishable by court-martial.

2. Another important method of strengthening the moral component of character was mandatory Sunday chapel, discussed later in the chapter.

3. As noted in chapter 1, the vigilance committees of the late-nineteenth century were unofficial bodies whose work was not sanctioned by the Department of Tactics. The committees achieved semiofficial status around the turn of the century as each company, with the tacit acceptance of Academy officials, began electing a first-classman to serve on the committee for the year.

4. Larned, "West Point and Higher Education," *Army and Navy Journal*, 19.

5. Larned, "West Point and Higher Education," *Army and Navy Life and the United Service*, 20.

6. US Military Academy, *Bugle Notes* 30 (1938–1939), 51.

7. Ibid., 49–50. The Cadet Prayer appears in every edition of *Bugle Notes*.

8. West Point graduates dominated the senior leadership positions in the army during World War I. The army chief of staff (Peyton March), commander of the Ameri-

can Expeditionary Force (John J. Pershing), and all three army commanders in France (Hunger Liggett, Robert L. Bullard, and Joseph T. Dickman) were graduates, as were thirty-four of the thirty-eight corps and division commanders at the end of the war. The loss rate of West Point officers was another indicator of their contributions at the epicenter of the war. For example, West Point first lieutenants assigned to battalions in the theater of operations suffered 195 losses per thousand, compared to about thirty losses per thousand for all other first lieutenants. Similar imbalances occurred at higher ranks. Forman, *West Point*, 173.

9. Letter from Baker to Julius Kahn (chairman of the House Military Affairs Committee), 17 May 1920, packet on "Curriculum USMA," AGO Central Files 1926–1939, West Point, Records Group 407, National Archives, College Park, MD.

10. MacArthur, *Reminiscences*, 80.

11. A common deceptive practice was to stuff one's bed with clothes or a blanket to fool the nighttime inspector into thinking that the cadet was present in the room when, in fact, he was beyond authorized limits. Sometimes West Point authorities considered bed stuffing to be an honor violation; at other times, they viewed it only as a breach of discipline.

12. Ganoe, *MacArthur Close-Up*, 113. Although Ganoe used quotation marks, the words ascribed to MacArthur are most likely a paraphrase.

13. *Annual Report of the Superintendent*, 1921, 8.

14. USMA, class of 1920, *Traditions and Customs of the Corps*, 5–6.

15. According to the 1921–1922 edition of *Bugle Notes*, the class president filled the role of honor committee chairman. A questionnaire sent to all of the chairmen from 1924 to 1974, however, indicated that the honor committee sometimes elected its chairman from among the company honor representatives. Harry A. Buckley, "Report of Superintendent's Special Study Group on Honor at West Point," 23 May 1975, West Point Archives, A-6.

16. *Bugle Notes* 15 (1923–1924), 49.

17. All quotations are from Buckley, "Report of Superintendent's Special Study Group on Honor at West Point," A-14. The report includes the results of a questionnaire sent to all honor committee chairmen from 1924 to 1975. Quotations ascribed to the 1924 chairman, John Hill, and the 1930 chairman, William Whipple Jr., were taken from their answers to the question, "Was there a policy of giving a 'second chance' to violators?" The quotation of the 1935 chairman, David H. Gregg, came from the "Honor Book, USCC," which contains the notes of successive honor committee chairmen.

18. According to the Buckley report, "Except for isolated aberrations, indications are that the 'second chance' philosophy on the Honor Committee level had passed away by 1940. The Honor Chairmen in the 1940s so indicate, and the 1941 *Howitzer* flatly states in reference to the Honor Committee that 'theirs is the solemn duty of administering justice to all offenders, for whom there is no sympathy, no mercy, no second chance.'" Ibid., A-15.

19. *Annual Report of the Superintendent*, 1905, 6.

20. Ibid.

21. Review committee quoted in Sorley, *Honor Bright*, 45.

22. Lewis Sorley speculates that Stewart's undistinguished cadet record in academics

and leadership may have influenced him to be sympathetic toward cadets who cheat in academic work. *Honor Bright*, 55, n.36.

23. Ibid., 45.

24. Ibid., 45–46.

25. The reference book was first published in 1907 under the name *The West-Point Hand-Book*. One year later, the name changed to *Bugle Notes* and has remained so named ever since.

26. Young Men's Christian Association (West Point chapter), *The West Point Hand-Book* (West Point: USMA, 1907), 29.

27. *Bugle Notes* 15 (1923–1924), 49.

28. Quoted in Crackel, *West Point*, 219.

29. "Honor System, U.S. Corps of Cadets," 6 December 1944, West Point Archives, quoted in Sorley, *Honor Bright*, 48.

30. Taylor, "West Point Honor System: Its Objectives and Procedures," 5. Curiously, Taylor used the term "honor system" to denote both the code and the system. As his discussion made clear, however, he well understood the difference between the two.

31. Several secondary sources assert that the nontoleration clause was added to the single-sentence honor code in 1970. See, for example, the introductory memorandum (1 June 1970) in Camp Buckner Honor Instruction Presented to the class of 1973 (West Point: US Military Academy, 1970), 1.

32. Letter from Eisenhower to Taylor, 2 January 1946, in Chandler and Galambos, *The Papers of Dwight David Eisenhower*, 7: 709–11.

33. Taylor, *West Point Honor System*, 5–6.

34. Maxwell Taylor, "Address to the Class of 1952," 1 July 1948, reprinted in Murphy, *West Point Cadet, 1948–1952*, 22.

35. Lewis Sorley offers evidence suggesting that at least one academic department suspected widespread cheating among cadets prior to discovery of the cheating ring. In May 1950, an unnamed department purposely inserted an error into the answer sheet for a test that was to be given repetitively over a two-day period. Cadets who took the test on the first day would receive the answer sheet immediately thereafter, but they were honor bound not to discuss the test or the answers until everyone had taken the test. The department's intent was to see if the error would appear in the answers of cadets who took the test on the second day. Upon learning of the entrapment scheme, the commandant protested strongly and had it stopped before any honor violations were discovered. Sorley pondered whether the department's action "was motivated by early indications of the problem that soon surfaced in such a major way." *Honor Bright*, 63.

36. McWilliams, *A Return to Glory*, 40. McWilliams's account of the 1951 cheating incident is by far the best available and is the basis for the summary provided here.

37. "Texts of Expulsion Statements," *New York Times*, 4 August 1951, 5.

38. See, for example, Austin Stevens, "West Point Ousts 90 Cadets for Cheating in Classroom; Football Players Involved," *New York Times*, 4 August 1951, 1. The front page and much of the first section were devoted to coverage of the cheating incident.

39. Murphy, *West Point Cadet*, 213.

40. The two cadets were under enormous emotional strain throughout the ordeal

and long afterward. One of them wrote to Coach Blaik years later to say that he regretted having gone undercover to expose other cadets. By then he had clearly rejected the concept of nontoleration, even though he was a currently serving officer in the Air Force. He could not accept the notion that military officers, as members of a profession, must not tolerate dishonorable acts among their peers. The letter, and Blaik's response, appear on pages 452–57 in *The Red Blaik Story*.

41. The three lieutenant colonels, by coincidence, all had graduated from West Point in 1930. In addition to Collins, they were Jefferson J. Irvin and Tracy B. Harrington.

42. Quoted in McWilliams, *A Return to Glory*, 92. Blaik and Harkins had a less than cordial relationship. Harkins was troubled by the institutional emphasis on football, while Blaik accused the commandant of being resentful of the football team's success.

43. Ibid., 91.

44. Ibid., 104.

45. In 1942, Congress increased the size of the Corps from 1,964 to 2,500 cadets, thus requiring the establishment of a second cadet regiment. Prior to then, the single regiment simplified academic scheduling by allowing the departments to teach individual lessons all on the same day. The creation of a second regiment forced the departments to teach individual lessons over a two-day period, but the democratic principle of giving every cadet exactly the same test remained in place. Cadets were on their honor not to discuss graded requirements with other cadets until everyone had completed the requirements.

46. Blaik, *The Red Blaik Story*, 449.

47. Ibid., 450.

48. Ibid., 467.

49. Ibid., 468. In his memoirs, Blaik named Taylor, Harkins, and Col. John Waters (assistant commandant) as exemplars of the unflattering description given here. His venomous attacks on their character and professionalism reflected the deep hurt and embarrassment he suffered because of the cheating incident.

50. Letter from McEwan to Blaik, reprinted in ibid., 460.

51. Blaik reported that Taylor ordered him "to desist in any attempt" to help the discharged cadets receive honorable discharges. Ibid., 466.

52. Ibid., especially chapters 15 and 24.

53. These selections represented the dean (academic departments), commandant (Department of Tactics), and the superintendent's staff.

54. "Proceedings of a Board of Officers Appointed by Letter Orders, Headquarters, USMA, 13 August 1951" (hereafter "Bartlett Board Report"), 7 September 1951, Exhibit B, file 351.1, Honor Violations (90) (Bartlett Board), Part IV 1951–52, General Correspondence; Records of the Deputy Chief of Staff, Personnel and Administration; West Point Archives.

55. Ibid., 17. Emphasis in original document.

56. Ibid., 13. Blaik's appointment represented a break with two previous Academy policies. First, no longer would the head coach have to be an active-duty army officer. Second, height and weight restrictions for cadets were modified to allow Blaik to recruit bigger men for the team.

57. Ibid., 18.

58. Ibid.

59. Ibid., Exhibit E.

60. Ibid., 19.

61. Ibid., 25.

62. Superintendent Irving directed that the board proceed with "least practicable delay." Letter Orders, 13 August 1951, Exhibit A, Bartlett Board Report. Additionally, the army chief of staff, Gen. Lawton Collins, provided guidance about the focus of the study. Collins believed that a "contributing factor" to the honor crisis had been the "separation of the athletic groups, particularly the football squad, from the environmental influences of the Corps of Cadets." With this guidance in mind, the Bartlett board's focus narrowed on the football team and its relationship to the rest of the Corps of Cadets. Letter from Lt. Gen. Maxwell Taylor to Irving, 3 August 1951, reprinted in McWilliams, *A Return to Glory*, 299.

63. For example, the Bartlett board discerned a serious problem of infighting among the competing interests at West Point. They recommended a study into the "whole area of inter-agency and inter-departmental unity in presenting Military Academy policies to the Corps of Cadets" (32). For a thorough analysis of the influences and pressures on the Bartlett board and how they shaped the board's conclusions, see McWilliams, *A Return to Glory*, 313–25.

64. "Proceedings of a Board of Officers Appointed by Orders No. 56, Headquarters USCC, 17 October 1951" (hereafter "Greene Board Report"), January 1952, file 351.1 Honor Administrative File 1951 (Greene Board), Records of the Deputy Chief of Staff, Personnel and Administration, West Point Archives, 37.

65. Two examples of Blue Book regulations that needed interpretation were the "all right" reporting protocol and the absence card, both of which were tools for checking accountability of cadets in the barracks. The "all right" was a verbal check of a cadet's activities and whereabouts. When an inspector asked a cadet, "All right?," the usual answer was, "All right," assuming the respondent was in conformance with regulations on gambling, hazing, limits, liquor, and narcotics. The absence card was a physical device in a cadet's room that indicated his whereabouts during call to quarters (i.e., when cadets were required to be in their rooms studying or sleeping). If a cadet left his room, he was obliged to mark the card and was on his honor to be where the marked card indicated.

66. Greene Board Report, 6.

67. Ibid.

68. Ibid., 30.

69. Memorandum (first endorsement) from Lt. Col. W. H. Holdridge to Col. John K. Waters (commandant), 23 December 1952, subject: "Recommendations of a Board of Officers Appointed to Study Regulations Impinging on Honor," appended to front of Greene Board Report.

70. Ibid., 316.

71. Bill McWilliams deserves much credit for his multiyear effort to discover the whereabouts of existing records of the cheating incident and incorporate them into *A Return to Glory*.

72. Besides the honor incident, West Point suffered the loss of nineteen cadets killed

in a plane crash in December 1951 and the disappearance of another cadet under mysterious circumstances in 1950. Additionally, the Korean War had claimed the lives of a former superintendent, Maj. Gen. Bryant E. Moore, and several recent graduates. Murphy, *West Point Cadet*, 227–28; *Annual Report of the Superintendent*, 1951, 1–2.

73. Essay, "To Instill Discipline," in George S. Pappas, *West Point Sesquicentennial 1802–1952*, no page number.

74. *Bugle Notes* 46 (1954–1955), 4.

75. Given the scrutiny of the honor system after the cheating incident, another mass-cheating incident at West Point seemed unthinkable. If Coach Blaik is to be believed, however, there was such an incident a few years later. He gave a vivid account in his memoirs of an incident involving 174 second-class cadets who falsified their grades on a self-scored test given by an academic department. The incident came to light when one of the cadets who had taken the test was accused of cheating and asked by the honor committee to resign. The cadet took the matter to the superintendent (left unnamed by Blaik), explained that he was one of many who had cheated, and threatened to expose the scope of the incident if he were forced out. After investigating the cadet's claim and discovering the true scope of the problem, the superintendent privately sought Blaik's advice on how to proceed. Blaik counseled him not to conduct an inquiry and to quash any further discussion of the incident. "If you dismiss 174 cadets so shortly after the 1951 scandal I dare say you might as well lock the main gate, as the fetish we have made of the word honor before the public will no longer have validity. In fact, there will be no respect for West Point in Congress or among American citizens and a Congressional investigation would make the Academy leadership appear incredibly naïve in its judgment of human nature." According to Blaik, the superintendent dropped the case and thus forestalled another honor crisis. *The Red Blaik Story*, 448. I have been unable to find evidence to corroborate Blaik's claim of another major cheating incident.

76. *Annual Report of the Superintendent*, 1957, 9.

77. The standing committee on honor became known as the Superintendent's Honor Review Committee. It served several successive superintendents until lapsing during William Lennox's tenure as superintendent.

78. I am indebted to Lewis Sorley for making me aware of the Taylor-Davidson correspondence.

79. Letter from Taylor to Davidson, 1 November 1957, no. 13, file 351.1 Honor (1957), Adjutant General's Files, West Point Archives.

80. Letter from Davidson to Taylor, 4 December 1957, no. 13, file 351.1 Honor (1957), Adjutant General's Files, West Point Archives.

81. Ibid.

82. Ibid.

83. Sorley, 71.

84. *Annual Report of the Superintendent*, 1960, 26.

85. The commandant required cadets to "conform to the rules of the [religious] service" or face disciplinary action. Commandant of Cadets, *Regulations for the Interior Discipline and Police of the United States Corps of Cadets* ("Blue Book") (West Point: US Military Academy Press, 1902), 10.

86. *Annual Report of the Superintendent*, 1965, xii.

87. *Annual Report of the Superintendent*, 1960, 26.

88. Letter from Arthur Cromwell to Secretary of War Robert P. Patterson, 16 April 1946, file AG 009-199, Military Posts and Reservations, Army-AG Project Decimal Files 1946–1948, Records Group 407, National Archives, College Park, MD. The *Official Register of the Officers and Cadets of the U.S. Military Academy* has no record of a cadet with the last name of Cromwell during the years in question.

89. Letter from W. J. Beaman to Secretary of the Army Kenneth C. Royall, 26 October 1948, file AG 351, Military Posts and Reservations, Army-AG Project Decimal Files 1946–1948, Records Group 407, National Archives, College Park, MD. Another of Beaman's arguments was that the Naval Academy already had granted segregated services for Christian Scientists.

90. See, for example, letters from Senator Arthur V. Watkins (1957), Representative Henry Aldous Dixon (1957), Representative William L. Springer (1957), and Senator Irving M. Ives (1958) in file USMA 252.53-351.01, General Correspondence 1957–1958, Records of the AGO 1917– , Records Group 407, National Archives, College Park, MD.

91. Brucker to Multer, 25 October 1957, file USMA 000-250.52, General Correspondence 1957–1958, Records of the AGO, 1917– , Records Group 407, National Archives, College Park, MD.

92. Letter from West Point adjutant general to army chief of chaplains, 22 November 1948, file AG 351, Military Posts and Reservations, Army-AG Project Decimal Files 1946–1948, Records Group 407, National Archives, College Park, MD.

93. *Everson v. Board of Education of Ewing Township*, 330 US 1 (1947), 16.

94. Other important rulings confirming freedom of religion were: *Illinois ex rel. McCollum v. Board of Education of School District No. 71, Champaign County*, 333 US 203 (1948); *Torcaso v. Watkins*, 367 US 488 (1961); *School District of Abington Township v. Schempp*, 374-US 203 (1961); and *Engel v. Vitale*, 370 US 421 (1962).

95. *Annual Report of the Superintendent*, 1971, 37.

96. *Anderson v. Laird*, 466 F.2d 283 (DC Cir. 1972). Cadet Anderson was a senior at the time of the lawsuit and graduated in 1970. Four other cadets, all in the class of 1969, had attempted to end mandatory chapel, but were unable to do so prior to their graduation; they were Lucian Truscott IV, Robert Leslie, David Vaught, and Richard Swick. The story of all five cadets appears in Gelfand, *Sea Change at Annapolis*, 79–108.

97. *Annual Report of the Superintendent*, 1971, 37.

98. *Annual Report of the Superintendent*, 1973, 37.

99. *Annual Report of the Superintendent*, 1971, 38. In discussing the Puckett affair, the commandant expressed frustration not with the separation of the cadet but with the alleged inaccuracies of the news accounts.

100. Dana Adams Schmidt, "Lie on a Shoeshine Washes Out Cadet," *New York Times*, 20 November 1970, 15.

101. "An End to Silence," *Time*, 18 June 1973, 24–25.

102. According to media reports, Pelosi had been charged with continuing to write on a quiz sheet after the instructor had told the class to cease work. This was true, but there

was more to the story. Pelosi had not merely written a few extra words after being told to stop. He allegedly filled in answers during the time he was supposed to be self-grading the quiz. A classmate saw the incident and reported it to the instructor. During the next class, the instructor gave another quiz and, afterward, personally observed Pelosi filling in answers during the self-grading. The cadet who reported the incident the first time also saw it the second time. Army officials worried that the public response to the Pelosi case might influence litigation in other federal cases relating to the honor system; hence, they advised the superintendent to avoid further public comments. Ellis and Moore, *School for Soldiers*, 171. See in particular note 31, 268–69.

103. *Annual Report of the Superintendent*, 1974, 1, 34.

104. Sorley, *Honor Bright*, 99–100.

105. Quoted in ibid., 100. The honor review committee consisted of Cols. Vincent J. Esposito (chairman), Charles R. Broshous, and Julian J. Ewell, all senior professors.

106. Ibid., 99.

107. Superintendents had long understood the potential ill effects of expanding the Corps of Cadets. As an example, it was Fred Sladen's "firm opinion" in 1923 that West Point should focus on producing "quality rather than quantity." Further expansions would risk lessening the "close contact with and close supervision of the individual cadet" that had been the hallmark of the West Point experience. *Annual Report of the Superintendent*, 1923, 15. Donald V. Bennett admitted in 1967 that his "central concern as Superintendent has been to cope with the problems of maintaining standards of intellectual and professional excellence in the face of this expanding student population." Ibid., 1967, 1. As we have seen, however, a few superintendents (e.g., Douglas MacArthur and William Westmoreland) welcomed the idea of a bigger Corps of Cadets.

108. During the mid-1960s, an external review group, headed by Lt. Gen. (retired) Charles H. Bonesteel, commented prophetically on the potential ill effects of social changes on the Academy: "The final basic finding . . . pertains to the extremely subtle problem of keeping the Academy properly in tune with the changing viewpoints of youth regarding many traditional values of our older, more stabilized society. . . . There are no tangible evidences . . . that such currents are as yet affecting the Corps of cadets. Nevertheless, there could arise future conflicts between the traditional philosophy which governs the Military Academy as an institution and some of the influences for change which may be brought to bear on young men in the future. The Group has no comments on this matter other than to caution that this incipient problem must not be lost sight of. It might even arise in regard to such basics as the Honor System, the motivational receptivity of the future cadet, or in the esteem with which the motto 'Duty, Honor, Country' is held." "Report by the Superintendent's Curriculum Review Group," 18 April 1966. Bonesteel's colleagues on the review group were John E. Vance and Brig. Gen. (retired) K. E. Fields.

109. Statistics cited in Sidney Berry, memorandum for record, "A Preliminary Analysis—Why an Honor Problem at West Point in 1976?," 14 June 1976, file labeled "Early Actions," box 25, Bernard Rogers Papers, National Defense University, Washington, DC, 10.

110. Sidney B. Berry Jr., interview by Robert F. Broyles, 1983, transcript, 2: 927.

111. Harry A. Buckley et al., "Report of Superintendent's Special Study Group on Honor at West Point," 23 May 1975, West Point Archives.

112. For a detailed account of the cheating incident and its resolution, see *Annual Report of the Superintendent*, 1977, 34–43.

113. Berry might have formed the review panels sooner and with more confidence had he been able to study the Academy's response to the honor crisis of 1951. Unfortunately, he found "none or very few records" in the West Point archives. In their haste to put the cheating incident behind them, Academy leaders had neglected to establish a solid archival record that might help future superintendents deal with another mass-cheating incident. Historians eventually gathered the scattered records and wrote an historical narrative of the events, but not until after Berry was left to reinvent solutions for an old problem. Berry did not repeat the error; he directed his staff to keep complete records that are now housed in the West Point archives. Berry interview transcript, 2: 1034.

114. Berry interview transcript, 2: 998. Berry appointed Col. Gilbert W. Kirby, head of the Department of Earth, Space and Graphic Science, to lead the internal review panels. The Department of Law provided legal advice during the reviews. Because of the heavy workload during the summer of 1976, the army temporarily assigned sixty-three lawyers to the department to augment the twenty-two permanently assigned lawyers. *Annual Report of the Superintendent*, 1977, 17.

115. Upon becoming superintendent in 1974, Berry subscribed to the notion that the honor system should be run by the cadets. He was therefore reluctant to interfere with the investigations of the honor committee and inclined to approve its recommendations. His attitude changed, however, after reviewing the case of Cadet Stephen Verr, who had entered the Academy in July 1975 and was found guilty of an honor violation about two months later. Berry did not think the evidence in the case would stand legal review, so he refused to forward it to the secretary of the army, the approval authority for all honor dismissals. News of Berry's decision embittered cadets. According to a tactical officer, there "were damn near riots" in some of the companies, and Verr had to be sequestered to protect him from physical harm. Herbert Lloyd, interview by Stephen Grove, June 1978, transcript, 41.

116. The press conference was on 23 July 1976 at the Hotel Thayer, on the grounds of West Point. James Feron, "Group of Cadets Accuses Academy," *New York Times*, 24 July 1976, 10.

117. James Feron, "West Point Cadets at House 'Hearing' Ask End of Ouster for Code Violators," *New York Times*, 5 August 1976, 49. Michael T. Rose, a lawyer representing some of the accused cadets, wrote a detailed summary of the points made during the House hearing: "Synopsis of What Was Said about the Current Honor Code Violation 'Scandal' at West Point during the *ad hoc* Public Forum on August 4, 1976, Chaired by Congressman Thomas J. Downey of New York," file labeled "Correspondence w/Michael T. Rose," box 25, Bernard W. Rogers papers, National Defense University, Washington, DC.

118. *Annual Report of the Superintendent*, 1977, 37.

119. Berry interview transcript, 2: 1018.

120. *Annual Report of the Superintendent*, 1977, 43. A total of eighty-five of the re-admitted cadets joined the class of 1978.

121. Borman, et al., *Report to the Secretary of the Army*.

122. Ibid., 65.

123. Ibid., vi.

124. There were several varieties of corruption. In some cases, company honor representatives — cadets supposedly elected by virtue of their sense of integrity — had committed honor violations. Four members of the 1977 honor committee, for example, were found guilty of cheating on the EE304 project, and another resigned while under investigation. In other cases, first-class honor representatives were reluctant to find their classmates guilty. During academic year 1975–1976, for example, only one accused first classmen out of sixteen was found guilty by an honor board, and in that case the board consisted of second-class honor representatives. The 6 percent conviction rate for first classmen during that year contrasted with the 80 percent rate for plebes. Finally, some companies purposely elected honor representatives who were "indifferent to the Honor System" or who took "a liberal view toward the interpretation of the Honor Code." This helps to explain the many honor acquittals by votes of 11 (guilty) to 1 (not guilty) in cases with strong evidence. Borman, *Report to Secretary of the Army*, 45–48.

125. Ibid., 19. The Borman commissioners endorsed the importance of nontoleration but acknowledged that it was the most difficult part of the code to internalize; hence, they favored giving cadets "options in addition to reporting an honor violation," such as counseling or warning a violator. In the end, the nontoleration clause remained a part of the honor code, and there was no change to the requirement for cadets to report honor violations.

126. *Annual Report of the Superintendent*, 1977, 42. Italics by author.

127. West Point Study Group, *Final Report of the West Point Study Group*. See chapter 2 for details on the composition and mandate of the WPSG. Other external reviews were conducted by the board of visitors, the Department of Defense Committee on Excellence in Education, and the deputy general counsel of the army. *Annual Report of the Superintendent*, 1977, 38.

128. Ibid., 137–38. In mid-1976, the Academic Board ended the practice of giving identical examinations to cadets in different class hours; hence, the WPSG did not need to address the issue. Sorley, *Honor Bright*, 116.

129. The two exceptions were the 1951 and 1976 honor incidents.

130. From 1965 to 1973 (the year the silence was ended), the cadet honor committee found a total of 305 cadets guilty of honor violations; of these, only fifteen (5 percent) appealed their cases to an officer board. From 1973 to 1975, twenty-four of forty-nine cadets (49 percent) appealed. West Point Center for the Professional Military Ethic, "Cadet Honor Code and Honor System," 10 February 2000, 8.

131. A tactical officer who observed honor boards under the new procedures complained, "The current system . . . with all the lawyers in there browbeating the junior cadets is totally ineffective." Lloyd interview transcript, 44. As a result of the legalism, the processing time for honor cases often exceeded sixty days, the standard set by the secretary of the army.

132. In the first year of the revised procedures, the average time needed to dispose of an honor case (from the date of a reported violation to the convening of an honor board) was twenty-four days, well within the sixty-day standard. *Annual Report of the Superintendent*, 1980, 33.

133. Borman, *Report to Secretary of the Army*, 19.

134. *Final Report of the West Point Study Group*, 30.

135. Quoted from the Borman report in ibid., 145. Italics in original.

136. Cadets had taken the psychology and leadership courses for many years through the Office of Military Leadership (formerly the Office of Military Psychology and Leadership), organized under the commandant. In 1977, a new academic department, Behavioral Sciences and Leadership, was formed from the instructional components of the Office of Military Leadership. Chapter 7 provides fuller coverage of this organizational change.

137. *Annual Report of the Superintendent*, 1978, 47.

138. *Annual Report of the Superintendent*, 1981, 37.

139. *Annual Report of the Superintendent*, 1984, 39.

140. *Annual Report of the Superintendent*, 1987, 49. Now called the National Conference on Ethics in America, the annual event has since been endowed by the class of 1970.

141. Howard Prince, interview by author, transcript, 16 July 2007, 4.

142. Anthony Hartle, interview by author, transcript, 13 July 2007, 6.

143. Kip Nygren, interview by author, transcript, 1 May 2007, 5.

144. The quoted words are from the Prince interview transcript (4), but all three officers expressed similar sentiments.

145. Donnithorne, *Preparing for West Point's Third Century*, 71–72.

146. Posvar et al. "Final Report of the Special Commission of the Chief of Staff," 1.

147. Ibid., 15.

148. Ibid., 17.

149. Donnithorne, *Preparing for West Point's Third Century*, 72.

150. US Military Academy, *Years of Continuity and Progress*, 11. The "respect for others" value was originally called "consideration for others." The name change was stylistic only; it had no effect on the meaning of the bedrock value.

151. Ibid., 11–15. The special assistant to the commandant for honor matters had existed since 1976; a new position, special assistant to the commandant for respect, was created shortly after the announcement that respect for others would be a bedrock value.

152. "Wisdom at West Point," *New York Times*, 2 November 1994, A22. The article contrasted West Point's appropriate response with the navy's foot dragging following the 1991 "Tailhook" scandal, in which eighty-three women and seven men were assaulted during the three-day convention for naval aviators at a Las Vegas hotel. A personal account of the incident is in the Howard Graves interview by Dr. Stephen Grove, 10 May 1996, transcript, 21–22.

153. In 2000, the center was named after philanthropist William E. Simon, who established an endowment to allow the center to operate in perpetuity.

154. The Professional Military Ethic Education program, as it is currently known, was a refinement of previous similar programs — values education training, respect for others training, company honor education training, etc.

155. As of this writing, all positions were filled by active-duty military officers except for the professor of character development and the visiting professor of officership.

156. Daniel W. Christman, interview by Stephen Grove, transcript, 7 June 2000, 114.

157. The rehabilitative effort of cadets in the Honor Mentorship Program was in addi-

tion to, not in lieu of, normally scheduled activities. Cadets in the program were demoted to cadet private, lost all privileges, and could not represent the Academy in any public forum, including athletic competition. They were required to design a personal character development plan, maintain a journal, conduct a role-model emulation interview, write an analysis of the honor violation, teach an honor class to cadets, and complete an honor development project. At the end of six months, cadets who met these requirements were restored to full membership in the Corps of Cadets. "The Honor Mentorship Program" (undated briefing slides), Simon Center for the Professional Military Ethic, U.S. Military Academy, received 13 December 2010, copy in author files.

158. The Army Mentorship Program had a transformative effect on many of the cadets who went through it. Superintendent William Lennox noted that cadets "come out of the Mentorship Program better than a cadet who's never had it. I would love to do the Mentorship Program for everybody if I could." William Lennox, interview by Stephen Grove, transcript, 27 March 2006, 66.

159. Superintendent Christman took pains to convince older graduates that the old attritional model of leader development was obsolete. Speaking at a reunion for the Class of 1951, he dismissed the notion that "by age 10, you have internalized all the precepts of ethical behavior and, therefore, when you arrive at West Point at age 18, if you make a mistake, at that point, you should be separated. . . . I patiently explained that development does *not end* at age 10. Indeed, I mentioned I'm still developing, at age 58, as the Superintendent." Daniel W. Christman, interview by Stephen Grove, transcript, 7 June 2000, 114. Emphasis in transcript.

160. A common defense gambit was to seek exclusion of incriminating evidence collected before the accused cadet had been read his legal rights under Article 31 of the Uniform Code of Military Justice (i.e., the military version of the warnings required by the Supreme Court case of *Miranda v. Arizona* (1966)). Oftentimes the incriminating evidence resulted from the accused cadet speaking truthfully and voluntarily about his actions, in the spirit of the honor code. Another defense gambit was to plea bargain — that is, to negotiate for a dismissal of one or more charges in exchange for a guilty plea in a lesser charge.

161. The ideas in this paragraph derive from the author's personal observations and his discussions with colleagues and Academy officials. The latter group includes Maj. Jason Daugherty, Special Assistant to the Commandant for Honor, 13 December 2010. In response to the frequent due-process challenges of lawyers in honor cases, Daugherty collected statistical data on the subject beginning in academic year 2010–2011. Of the twenty-five honor cases heard in the fall semester, defense lawyers filed a motion to exclude evidence or dismiss allegations in thirteen (52 percent) of them. At least five of the cases more than likely ended with not-guilty verdicts as a result of the excluded evidence. Copy of statistical information in author files.

162. Brig. Gen. William Rapp, the commandant from 2009 to 2011, was frustrated to the point of declaring, "The honor system is broken." Comments of Brig. Gen. Rapp to the General Committee, 17 November 2010, author notes. Rapp made reference to seeking a legislative solution that would disassociate the honor system from the legal system while still providing procedural safeguards against abuse. As of this writing, Academy leaders had not initiated a formal request for such legislation.

163. Buckley, "Report of Superintendent's Special Study Group on Honor at West Point," 6.

CHAPTER NINE

1. Quote appears in Nye, "The Inadvertent Demise of the Traditional Academy, 1945–1995." Nye was a faculty member in the Department of Social Sciences in 1965; later, he was the deputy head of the Department of History.

2. For understandable reasons, Academy leaders are reluctant to discuss the success of West Point officers relative to the officers produced by other commissioning sources (i.e., the Reserve Officer Training Corps and Officer Candidate School). Regardless, it is well known that West Point officers reach the highest rank and the most senior command positions in disproportionate numbers. As of 1 November 2011, for example, seven of eleven army four-star generals (64 percent) were West Point graduates. Similarly, seven of ten major generals in command of active-army divisions (70 percent) graduated from West Point. Division command is widely regarded as the most important stepping stone to becoming a four-star general, the highest rank in the military. The overrepresentation of West Pointers in these senior positions belies the fact that they accounted for less than 10 percent of the officers commissioned during the years when the current four-star generals and division commanders entered the army. US General Accounting Office, *Service Academies — Historical Proportion of New Officers during Benchmark Periods*, GAO/NSAID-92-90, 3.

3. Davidson, "Grandpa Gar," 163–64.

4. Daniel Christman, interview by Stephen Grove, 23 April 2001, transcript, 96.

5. Lt. Gen. David H. Huntoon Jr., who became the superintendent in 2010, appeared to be in the mold of Palmer and Graves concerning intercollegiate athletics.

6. Memorandum from Palmer to Chief of Staff of the Army (Gen. Carl E. Vuono), "Search for the Next Superintendent," 14 January 1991, copy in author files.

7. As an example of the policy board's indistinct charter, Superintendent Dave Palmer used the policy board to debate the proposed Cadet Leader Development System, even though CLDS dealt with Academy-level (as opposed to an installation-level) issues. The lack of clarity concerning the policy board's charter and responsibilities diminished its value in the eyes of the superintendents. Unlike the Academic Board, the policy board lacked well-defined operating procedures and a clear definition of its duties. Moreover, it had no powerful sponsor to push its agenda. Whereas the Dean was responsible for conducting the business of the Academic Board, various members of the superintendent's staff — all of whom were on short-term assignments at West Point — had the equivalent job for the policy board. These problems led Lt. Gen. William Lennox to dispense with the policy board and to rely on tight circle of advisors; in effect, governance became even more centralized than before. Lennox's successor, Lt. Gen. Franklin Hagenbeck, reestablished the policy board in response to criticism from the Middle States Commission on Higher Education (i.e., the accreditation body), but the old problems remained. The next superintendent, Lt. Gen. David Huntoon, disestablished the policy board in late 2010 with the stated intent of studying the issue of governance and devising a better system; included in his plan

was the revitalization of the Academic Board. He ultimately chose to govern without the policy board.

8. The *Final Report of the West Point Study Group*, published in 1977, included a similar scheme for standing committees. Some of the committees have survived since then, while others faded away depending on the priorities of various superintendents. At the time of this writing, there are standing committees only for curriculum and admissions. A program assessment committee was established in 2009, but its authority and jurisdiction are yet to be clarified. No committees exist for program integration, cadet scheduling, or honor. The old Superintendent's Honor Review Committee was disestablished under Lt. Gen. William Lennox; Lt. Gen. David Huntoon reestablished it in early 2012.

9. In 2011, Dr. Jean Blair, professor of computer science, was appointed the vice-dean for education. This was the first time a civilian had been given a governance position equivalent to that of an Academic Board member.

10. While at USMAPS, students had to reapply to West Point even though they already had completed an application the previous year. This was mostly a formality, however. During the 2000s, the annual attrition rate at USMAPS was about 20 percent; of the 80 percent that completed the program each year (i.e., those who did not flunk out, drop out, or get kicked out), only a tiny fraction was denied entry to West Point.

11. Each year, USMAPS graduates about two hundred students; collectively, they comprise about 15 percent of the incoming classes at West Point.

12. Officer retention at the five-year mark for West Point classes of the late 1970s and early 1980s was above 80 percent. The highest retention rate was 89.8 percent (class of 1977); the lowest was 80.4 percent (class of 1983). Over the next two decades, retention never exceeded 80 percent, and in most years it was significantly less. During those years— from 1984 through 2003—the highest retention rate was 78.1 percent (class of 1998); the lowest was 51.0 percent (class of 1988). Similar trends were apparent at the ten-, fifteen-, and twenty-year marks. Institutional Research and Analysis Branch, "USMA Retention," briefing slides, 21 August 2008 (West Point: Office of Policy, Planning, and Assessment), copy in author files.

13. Tim Kane, "Why Our Best Officers Are Leaving," *The Atlantic Magazine* [online edition], January/February 2011. Kane surveyed 250 West Point graduates from the classes of 1989, 1991, 1995, 2000, 2001, and 2004. Of these, 93 percent believed that half or more of "the best officers leave the military early rather than serving a full career."

14. See chapter 4 for a fuller discussion of the measures taken in the late twentieth century to help weak students succeed in the academic program.

15. As noted in chapter 3, USMAPS expanded its enrollment in 1965 to include a limited number of minorities and recruited athletes who enlisted in the Army Reserve or National Guard with the sole intent of eventually going to West Point. Provided they passed all their courses, students in these two categories usually were assured of getting an appointment. The number of minorities and athletes so enrolled remained below 25 percent of USMAPS student body. Today, 40 percent of the seats at USMAPS are reserved for recruited athletes.

16. Chapter 3 provides more information on the admissions field force.

17. E-mail correspondence with Col. Deborah McDonald, director of admissions, 26 January 2011, copy in author files.

18. Amy Merrick, "Another Money-Losing Season," *Wall Street Journal* [online edition], 20 September 2004. In academic year 2008–2009, the National Collegiate Athletic Association reported that only fourteen of the 120 teams in the top competitive category turned a profit. Joe Drape, "Cal-Berkeley Cuts 5 Athletic Programs," *New York Times* [online edition], 28 September 2010.

19. Institutional Research and Analysis Branch, "USMA Retention," briefing slides, 21 August 2008 (West Point: Office of Policy, Planning, and Assessment), copy in author files.

20. In 2010, the football team ended the regular season with a record of six wins and six losses and was invited to play in the Armed Forces Bowl. It defeated Southern Methodist University and thus ended the season with a winning record.

21. A useful and engaging account of Amerine's experience in Afghanistan is Carhart, *West Point Warriors*, 373–90.

22. Amerine wanted to infiltrate his team by parachute, but he was ordered to go in by helicopter instead. E-mail correspondence, Lt. Col. Jason Amerine to author, 23 February 2011, copy in author files.

23. Jason Amerine, "U.S. Army Captain Jason Amerine," interview by PBS *Frontline*, 9 July 2002, edited interview transcript. PBS online, http://www.pbs.org/wgbh/pages/frontline/shows/campaign/interviews/amerine.html,, accessed 1 January 2011.

24. Ibid.

25. E-mail correspondence, Lt. Col. Jason Amerine to author, 23 February 2011, copy in author files.

26. Office of the Dean, *Educating Future Army Officers for a Changing World*, 9.

27. Jason Amerine, "The Room Live" [online talk show], theroomlive.com, accessed 16 January 2011.

Notes on Sources

FEW INSTITUTIONS of higher learning are as well documented as the United States Military Academy. Part of the reason is West Point's status as a federal entity, which is required by law to maintain official records. For the most part, the Academy has accomplished the records-keeping task with military efficiency, much to the benefit of researchers.

With so many available sources, the scholar's greatest challenge is to identify and locate the most useful ones. Fortunately, the job is made easier by the existence of the Special Collections and Archives Division of the West Point Library. As a satellite facility of the National Archives and Records Administration, it houses Record Group 404—United States Military Academy. The records include an extensive collection of primary sources—official records, unpublished manuscripts, photographs, memoirs, maps, yearbooks, serial records, and many other valuable holdings. Additionally, it houses important secondary sources that are conveniently located at arm's length. The staff of the Special Collections and Archives Division, though overworked and undermanned, are very helpful in accessing the holdings.

Within the vast archive is a core of primary sources that is a must for any serious historian of West Point. Four primary sources head the list. First and foremost is the *Annual Report of the Superintendent*, published from 1890 through 1989. These reports provide an enormous quantity of information on every aspect of West Point; when read consecutively, they allow the reader to understand the evolution of the institution over an entire century. Second on the list is the *Official Register of the Officers and Cadets of the U.S. Military Academy*, published annually from 1818 through 1966. In addition to a comprehensive listing of the officers and cadets by year, the *Official Register* describes the curriculum, chain of command, and organizational structure of the Academy. The third core source is the *Annual Report of the Board of Visitors*, published most years since 1819. These reports highlight the issues of greatest importance to the Academy and record the opinions of powerful advocates (and a few opponents) of the institution. The West Point library has done a great service by making the aforementioned three sources—and many others—available through its website at http://www.library.usma.edu. Finally, the *Register of Graduates and Former Cadets of the United States Military Academy*, published annually by the West Point Association of Graduates, has invaluable data on every person who has ever been a cadet. Additionally, it contains much other useful information on the history of West Point.

While the Special Collections and Archives Division holds the large majority of primary sources pertinent to West Point, there are other important repositories. Several records groups at the National Archives, College Park, Maryland, contain useful information found nowhere else. The diligent researcher will uncover reports, records, official correspondence, and other materials that pertain to West Point but originated in higher headquarters and thus may never have been placed in the West Point archives. Other valuable holdings are at the Military History Institute at Carlisle, Pennsylvania, and the National War College in Washington, DC.

Another important repository is the Center for Oral History, a subelement of the Department of History at West Point. Established in 2005, it holds hundreds of interview records of prominent soldiers and statesmen. Among the many interviews are those of West Point senior leaders — superintendents, commandants, deans, department heads, and key staff officers. Most of the interviews were done by Dr. Stephen Grove, West Point's command historian from 1978 to 2008. His diligence in recording the first-person testimony of these Academy leaders resulted in the creation of a rich archive for researchers. While many of the interviews are still in their raw state, those that have been transcribed and edited constitute an invaluable resource for understanding the human side of West Point. One hopes that the Academy will find the money to complete the job that Dr. Grove started, and that his successors will continue doing interviews.

Editing interview transcripts is a long and tedious process, and the Center for Oral History had not completed the task at the time I was doing my research. It is therefore likely that some of the transcript page numbers cited in the endnotes will be incorrect. Researchers who wish to find the cited passages would have to do a word search of the transcript. This task should be easy since the Center for Oral History has all transcripts in electronic format.

The Institutional Research and Analysis Branch (IRAB) of the G5 staff section was very helpful in obtaining detailed historical data on admissions, graduation and retention rates, and many other areas of concern. The computer database of the IRAB contains retrievable information as far back as the early 1970s. For those with access to it, the database can provide an extraordinary wealth of information that is useful in discerning long-term trends. On the strength of the data provided by the IRAB, I felt confident in advancing some of the most controversial arguments in the book.

My research was aided by the existence of many excellent memoirs of West Point graduates. These personalized accounts of cadet life provided a fascinating window into the institution's history during various periods. Moreover, they put a human face on an institution that can seem imposing and impersonal from the outside.

There are many other valuable sources available to researchers, and many of them are listed in the partial bibliography. A comprehensive list of sources, particularly those available at West Point, can be obtained by seeking assistance from the staff of the Special Collections and Archives Division.

Most of the pictures appearing in this volume are from the Special Collections and Archives Division. Others are the property of the Department of Military Instruction, the West Point Museum, Thomas Davidson (son of Lt. Gen. Garrison Holt Davidson), and the author.

Finally, there are numerous endnotes that describe the location of source documents with the phrase, "in author files." As a long-term senior faculty member at West Point, I had the ability to collect many documents that might have been lost, misfiled, destroyed, or otherwise rendered difficult to locate. The West Point archives may have some or all of these documents, but I did not try to find them when I had copies (in some cases the originals) of my own. Anyone wishing to view the sources "in author files" can find them, along with my other personal papers, in the Special Collections and Archives Division.

Bibliography

PRIMARY SOURCES

Manuscript Collections

Davidson, Garrison H. Papers. West Point Archives.

Rogers, Bernard W. Papers. National Defense University, Fort McNair, Washington, DC.

Tillman, Samuel E. Papers. West Point Archives.

Westmoreland, William C. Papers. US Army Military History Institute, Carlisle Barracks, PA.

Wickham, John A., Jr. Papers. US Army Military History Institute.

Interviews

Amerine, Jason. "U.S. Army Captain Jason Amerine." Interview by PBS *Frontline*, 9 July 2002. Edited transcript. PBS online, http://www.pbs.org/wgbh/pages/frontline/shows/campaign/interviews/amerine.html.

Anderson, James, Col., US Army. Interview by Stephen Grove, 12 May 1997, West Point, NY. Transcript. West Point Center for Oral History.

Berry, Sidney B., Jr., Lt. Gen., US Army (Ret.). Interview by Robert F. Broyles, 1983. Bound transcript, 2 vols. Senior Officer Oral History Program. US Army Military History Institute, Carlisle, PA.

Christman, Daniel W., Lt. Gen., US Army. Interview by Stephen Grove, 23 April 2001, West Point, NY. Transcript. West Point Center for Oral History.

Christman, Daniel W., Lt. Gen., US Army (Ret.). Interview by author, 8 June 2007, Washington, DC Transcript. West Point Center for Oral History.

Franklin, Joseph P., Brig. Gen., US Army. Interview by Charles A. Morris, 14 June 1982, West Point, NY. Transcript. West Point Center for Oral History.

Goodpaster, Andrew J., Lt. Gen., US Army. Interview by Stephen Grove, 12 May 1981, West Point, NY. Transcript. West Point Center for Oral History.

Goodpaster, Andrew J., Gen., US Army (Ret.). Interview by James Johnson, 10 March 1988, West Point, NY. Transcript. West Point Center for Oral History.

Graves, Howard, Lt. Gen., US Army. Interview by Stephen Grove, 10 May 1996, West Point, NY. Transcript. West Point Center for Oral History.

Hartle, Anthony, Brig. Gen., US Army (Ret.). Interview by author, 13 July 2007, Round Rock, TX. Transcript. West Point Center for Oral History.

Jones, Michael, Col., US Army. Interview by author, 5 January 2008, West Point, NY. Transcript. West Point Center for Oral History.

Kaufman, Daniel, Brig. Gen., US Army. Interview by Stephen Grove, 10 May 2005, West Point. Transcript. West Point Center for Oral History.

Lamkin, Fletcher, Brig. Gen., US Army. Interview by Stephen Grove, 12 May 2000, West Point, NY. Transcript. West Point Center for Oral History.

LeBoeuf, Maureen, Col., US Army. Interview by Stephen Grove, 13 January 2004, West Point, NY. Transcript. West Point Center for Oral History.

Lennox, William J., Lt. Gen., US Army. Interview by Stephen Grove, 22 September 2005, West Point, NY. Transcript. West Point Center for Oral History.

Lennox, William J., Lt. Gen., US Army (Ret.). Interview by author, 8 June 2007, Arlington, VA. Transcript. West Point Center for Oral History.

Lloyd, Herbert, Maj., US Army. Interview by Stephen Grove, June 1978, West Point, NY. Transcript. West Point Center for Oral History.

Nygren, Kip, Col., US Army. Interview by author, 1 May 2007, West Point, NY. Transcript. West Point Center for Oral History.

Palmer, Dave R., Lt. Gen., US Army. Interview by Stephen Grove, 13 June 1991, West Point, NY. Transcript. West Point Center for Oral History.

Palmer, Dave R., Lt. Gen., US Army (Ret.). Interview by author, 16–17 July 2007, Belton, TX. Transcript. West Point Center for Oral History.

Prince, Howard, Col., US Army. Interview by Stephen Grove, 6–7 September 1990, West Point, NY. Transcript. West Point Center for Oral History.

Prince, Howard, Brig. Gen., US Army (Ret.). Interview by author, 16 July 2007, Austin, TX. Transcript. West Point Center for Oral History.

Taylor, Maxwell D., Gen., US Army (Ret.). Interview by Richard A. Manion, 19 October 1972. Transcript. Senior Officers Debriefing Program. US Army Military History Institute, Carlisle Barracks, PA.

Toffler, Patrick, Col., US Army. Interview by Stephen Grove, 14 July 1998, West Point, NY. Transcript. West Point Center for Oral History.

Westmoreland, William C., Gen., US Army (Ret.). Interview by Martin L. Ganderson, 1982. Transcript. Senior Officer Oral History Program. William C. Westmoreland Collection, Folder 5, Series IV, Oral Histories, US Army Military History Institute, Carlisle, PA.

Winkel, Raymond, Col., US Army. Interview by author, 18 June 2009, West Point, NY. Transcript. West Point Center for Oral History.

Memoirs

Blaik, Earl H. *The Red Blaik Story*. New Rochelle, NY: Arlington House, 1974.

Bradley, Omar N., and Clay Blair. *A General's Life: An Autobiography*. New York: Simon and Schuster, 1983.

Croffut, W. A., ed. *Fifty Years in Camp and Field: Diary of Major-General Ethan Allen Hitchcock, U.S.A.* New York: G. P. Putnam's Sons, 1909.

Davidson, Garrison H. "Grandpa Gar: The Saga of One Soldier as Told to His Grandchildren." Unpublished (bound) memoir, 1974, Garrison H. Davidson Papers. West Point Archives.

Hein, Otto Louis. *Memories of Long Ago*. New York: G. P. Putnam's Sons, 1925.

MacArthur, Douglas. *Reminiscences*. New York: McGraw-Hill, 1964.

Maher, Marty (with Red Reeder and Nardi Reeder Campion). *Bringing Up the Brass*. Quechee, VT: Vermont Heritage Press, 2002.

Murphy, Thomas J. *West Point Cadet, 1948–1952*. Placentia, CA: Creative Continuum, 2002.

Reed, Hugh T. *Cadet Life at West Point*. Chicago: Published by author, 1896.

Schaff, Morris. *The Spirit of Old West Point, 1858–1862*. New York: Houghton, Mifflin and Co., 1907.

Scott, Hugh L. *Some Memories of a Soldier*. New York: The Century Company, 1928.

Swift, Joseph Gardner. *The Memoirs of Gen. Joseph Gardner Swift, LL. D., U.S.A., First Graduate of the United States Military Academy, West Point, Chief Engineer U.S.A. from 1812 to 1818*. Harrison Ellery, ed. Privately printed, 1890.

Taylor, Maxwell D. *Swords and Plowshares*. New York: W. W. Norton and Co., 1972.

Westmoreland, William C. *A Soldier Reports*. Garden City, NY: Doubleday & Co., 1976.

Published and Unpublished Documents

Adams, Cindy, ed. "The West Point Thayer Papers, 1808–1872," 11 vols. West Point: Association of Graduates, 1965.

Adams, Jerome. *Report of the Admission of Women to the U.S. Military Academy: Project Athena III*. West Point: Department of Behavioral Sciences and Leadership, US Military Academy, 1979.

——. *Report of the Admission of Women to the U.S. Military Academy: Project Athena IV*. West Point: Department of Behavioral Sciences and Leadership, US Military Academy, 1980.

Annual and Semiannual Reports of the Army Athletic Association, 1903–1910, 1914–1917, 1919, and 1929–1940, 3 vols.

Artemis Strategy Group. "The United States Military Academy at West Point: Brand and Communications Assessment." Slide presentation, 15 July 2008, author's files.

Association of Graduates. *Register of Graduates and Former Cadets of the United States Military Academy*. West Point: US Military Academy, annual.

Benedict, Jay. "A Study of the Curriculum of the United States Military Academy by the Academic Board." 30 October 1940. Copy in RG407, Adjutant General's Office Project Decimal Files, Box 4479, File 351, National Archives, College Park, MD.

Beukema, Herman. *The United States Military Academy and Its Foreign Contemporaries*. West Point: US Military Academy, 1940.

Borman, Frank, et al. *Report to the Secretary of the Army by the Special Commission on the United States Military Academy*. Washington, DC: Department of the Army, 15 December 1976.

Bradley, Omar N. *Collected Writings of General Omar N. Bradley*, 6 vols. Washington, DC: Government Printing Office, 1967–1971.

Butler, Richard P. *Survey of Careerists and Non-Careerists from the USMA Classes of 1963 through 1967*. West Point: USMA Office of Institutional Research, Product Appraisal Report, 1971.

Butler, Richard P., and John W. Houston. *Attrition and Admission Scores, Class of 1975*. West Point: USMA Office of Research, 1974.

Center for the Professional Military Ethic. "Cadet Honor Code and Honor System." West Point, 10 February 2000.

Chandler, Alfred D., Jr., and Louis Galambos, eds. *The Papers of Dwight David Eisenhower*, 20 vols. Baltimore, MD: Johns Hopkins University Press, 1970–2001.

Degen, Robert. "The Evolution of Physical Education at the United States Military Academy." West Point: Office of Physical Education, 1967.

Department of Tactics. *Aptitude for the Service: A Program of Career Guidance in the Corps of Cadets*. West Point: USMA, 1956.

Donnithorne, Larry. *Preparing for West Point's Third Century: A Summary of the Years of Affirmation and Change, 1986–1991*. West Point: USMA, 1991.

Forman, Sidney. *The Educational Objectives of the U.S. Military Academy*, 2nd ed. West Point: USMA, 1951.

Goodpaster, Andrew J. "Basic Concepts for the United States Military Academy." West Point: USMA, February 1979. USMA Archives.

Greene, Francis M. "Procedure for Examination of Candidates in Physical Aptitude." West Point: Office of Physical Education, 29 July 1946, West Point Archives.

Harkins, Paul D. "A Draft of a Letter of Instruction to Incoming Tactical Officers from the Commandant." West Point: United States Corps of Cadets, 1948. UMSA Library.

Harris, Boyd M. "West Point Journal" (1975–1980). West Point Archives.

Hecox, Walter. *The Performance of USMA Graduates in the Classes of 1967, 1968 and 1969 on the Defense Officer Record Examination*. West Point: USMA Office of Research, Product Appraisal Report, 1970.

Hilliard, George S., ed. *Life, Letters, and Journals of George Ticknor*, 2 vols. Boston: James R. Osgood and Company, 1876.

Jannarone, John R. "Superintendent's Curriculum Study: Report of the Working Committee on the Present Curriculum and Future Trends." West Point, 31 August 1958, West Point Archives.

Koehler, Herman J. *The Theory and Practice of Athletics at the Military Academy*. West Point: Military Academy Printing Office, 1909.

Library of Congress. *A Century of Lawmaking for a New Nation: U.S. Congressional Documents and Debates, 1774–1875*. http://memory.loc.gov/ammem/amlaw/lawhome.html.

Liveoak, Felix L. *Summary of Responses, Reorganization Week Questionnaire (Upperclasses), Classes of 1973–1975*. West Point: USMA Office of Institutional Research, 1972.

Mallory, John Allan, compiler. *Compiled Statutes of the United States, 1913: Embracing the Statutes of the United States of a General and Permanent Nature in Force December 31, 1913*. St. Paul, MN: West Publishing Co., 1914.

Marron, Joseph E. *The Prediction of Resignations from the Military Attitude and Military Association Scales*. West Point: USMA Office of Research, 1968.

———. *The Validity of the Military Attitude and Association Scales*. West Point: USMA Office of Research, 1971.

McLaughlin, G. W. *Survey of Graduates of the United States Military Academy, Classes of 1950 to 1962 Background, Schooling and Careers*. West Point: USMA Office of Research, Product Appraisal Report, 1970.

Medsger, Gerald W. *A Survey of Ex-Cadets of the Class of 1971*. West Point: USMA Office of Research, 1971.

Middle States Association of Colleges and Secondary Schools. *Evaluation Report for the Middle States Association of Colleges and Secondary Schools Commission on Institutions of Higher Education*. 15–18 February 1959. West Point Archives.

Morgovsky, Joel. *Educational Aspirations and Academic Environment of the Graduating Class of 1969*. West Point: USMA Office of Research, 1969.

——. *Trends in Responses to First Class Questionnaire 1969, 1970, 1971: A Research Note*. West Point: USMA Office of Research, 1971.

Office of the Dean. *Academic Program: Curriculum and Course Descriptions* [online edition]. West Point: US Military Academy, 7 September 2010, http://www.dean.usma.edu/sebpublic/curriccat/static/index.htm.

——. *Educating Future Army Officers for a Changing World: Operations Concept for the Intellectual Domain of the Cadet Leader Development System*. West Point: US Military Academy, 2007.

Office of Research. *Analysis of the Characteristics of the Class of 1971*. West Point: USMA, 1968.

Pappas, George S. *West Point Sesquicentennial 1802–1952*. Buffalo, NY: Baker, Jones Hausauer, Inc., 1952.

Personnel Research Section, Personnel Research and Procedures Branch, Personnel Bureau, Adjutant General's Office. "An Exploratory Study of the Relationship of West Point Class Standing and Achievement of the Rank of General Officer." 3 June 1950. Military History Institute, Carlisle, PA.

Peterson, James A., James A. Vogel, Dennis M. Koval, and Louis F. Tomasi. *Project 60: A Comparison of Two Types of Physical Training Programs on the Performance of 16–18 Year-Old Women*. 3 May 1976. West Point: USMA, 1976.

Plummer, Michael T. "The PAE as a Measure of Total Development and Leadership" (December 1970). In *Completed Studies in Physical Education 1970–1971*, edited by R. L. Sloane and Robert W. Stauffer. West Point: Office of Physical Education, December 1971.

Posvar, Wesley. "Final Report of the Special Commission of the Chief of Staff on the Honor Code and Honor System at the United States Military Academy," 30 May 1989.

Proceedings of the Athletic Board, Series 409, West Point Archives.

Records Group 404, Records of the United States Military Academy, West Point Archives.

Records Group 407, Records of the Adjutant General's Office 1917–, National Archives, College Park, MD.

Redmund, Robert, and Robert Stauffer. "Comparison of High and Low Physical Aptitude Examination Performers in Leadership Ability and Physical Education Performance." Office of Physical Education, March 1974, West Point Archives.

Stauffer, Robert W. *Project Summertime: Comparison of USMA Men and Women on Selected Physical Performance Measures*. October 1976. West Point: USMA, 1976.

Stearns, Robert L. "A Report and Recommendation to the Secretary of Defense by the Service Academy Board." Department of Defense, 1950.

Taylor, Maxwell D. "Leading the American Soldier" (lecture). West Point, 27 May 1945, West Point Archives.

———. *West Point Honor System: Its Objectives and Procedures*. West Point: USMA, 1948, West Point Archives.

———. *West Point: Its Objectives and Methods*. West Point: USMA, November 1947.

———. *West Point Looks Ahead*. West Point: USMA, March 1946.

US Congress. *The Public Statutes at Large of the United States of America*.

US General Accounting Office. *Service Academies — Historical Data on Accessions and Attrition*. GAO/NSIAD-92-90, Washington, DC, March 1992.

US Government Accountability Office. *Academy Preparatory Schools*. GAO/NSIAD-94-56R. Washington, DC, October 5, 1993.

———. *DoD Service Academies: Academy Preparatory Schools Need a Clearer Mission and Better Oversight*. Report to the Chairman, Senate and House Committees on Armed Services. GAO/NSIAD-92-57, Washington, DC, March 1992.

———. *Military Education: DoD Needs to Enhance Performance Goals and Measures to Improve Oversight of Military Academies*. Report to the Subcommittee on Defense, Committee on Appropriations, House of Representatives. GAO-03-1000, Washington, DC, September 2003.

———. *Military Education: DoD Needs to Align Academy Preparatory Schools' Mission Statements with Overall Guidance and Establish Performance Goals*. Report to the Subcommittee on Defense, Committee on Appropriations, House of Representatives. GAO-03-1017, Washington, DC, September 2003.

———. *Military Education: Student and Faculty Perceptions of Student Life at the Military Academies*. Report to the Subcommittee on Defense, Committee on Appropriations, House of Representatives. GAO-03-1001, Washington, DC, September 2003.

USMA class of 1920. *Traditions and Customs of the Corps*. West Point: US Military Academy Printing Office, 1920.

US Military Academy. *2002 — and Beyond: A Roadmap to Our Third Century*. West Point: USMA, 1990.

———. *2007–2008 Division 1 Athletics Certification Self-Study*. 8 May 2008, West Point Archives.

———. "A Positive Approach to Physical Aptitude for Improved Selection of Cadets." March 1961, West Point Archives.

———. *Annual Report of the Board of Visitors*, 1819–2002. West Point Archives.

———. *Annual Report of the Superintendent*, 1890–1989. West Point Archives.

———. *Athletic Records, U.S. Military Academy*. West Point: US Military Academy, 1980–1947. Office of the Director of Physical Education, West Point.

———. "Basic Concepts for the United States Military Academy." February 1979.

———. *Bugle Notes*. West Point: Young Men's Christian Association, 1922–1923.

———. *Bulletin of the Association of Graduates*, No. 6–9, 1931–1941, West Point Archives.

———. *Catalog of Information 1949–50*. Washington, DC: Government Printing Office, 1949.

——. *Centennial of the United States Military Academy at West Point, New York 1802–1902*, 2 vols. Washington, DC: Government Printing Office, 1904.

——. "Fiscal Year 2002 Assessment Report." West Point: Office of Policy, Plans and Analysis, 27 December 2002.

——. *The Fourth Class System 1977–1978*. USCC Circular 600.1. West Point: USMA, 1977.

——. *The Fourth Class System 1978–1979*. USCC Circular 351.1. West Point: USMA, 1978.

——. *Information Relative to the Appointment and Admission of Cadets to the United States Military Academy, West Point, N. Y.*, 1925 edition. Washington, DC: Government Printing Office, 1924.

——. *Information Relative to the Appointment and Admission of Cadets to the United States Military Academy, West Point, N. Y.*, 1927 edition. Washington, DC: Government Printing Office, 1926.

——. *Information Relative to the Appointment and Admission of Cadets to the United States Military Academy, West Point, N. Y.*, 1944 edition. Washington, DC: Government Printing Office, 1943.

——. *Institutional Self-Evaluation of the United States Military Academy: A Report Prepared for the Commission on Institutions of Higher Education of the Middle States Association of Colleges and Secondary Schools.* West Point: US Military Academy, January 1969.

——. *Institutional Self-Study 1988–1989: Report to the Commission on Higher Education of the Middle States Association of Colleges and Schools.* West Point: US Military Academy, July 1989.

——. *Institutional Self-Study: Report of the United States Military Academy.* West Point: US Military Academy, June 1999.

——. *Institutional Self-Study: Report of the United States Military Academy.* West Point: US Military Academy, June 2009.

——. *Official Register of the Officers and Cadets of the U.S. Military Academy, West Point, New York.* West Point: US Military Academy, 1818–1966.

——. "Post Orders," vol. 3 (22 June 1846 to 14 November 1852). West Point Archives.

——. *Post War Curriculum at the U. S. Military Academy, West Point, New York.* West Point: US Military Academy, September 1945. West Point Archives.

——. "Proceedings of the Academic Board." West Point Archives.

——. *Regulations for the United States Military Academy.* Washington, DC: Government Printing Office, various years.

——. *Report Prepared for the Commission on Institutions of Higher Education of the Middle States Association of Colleges and Secondary Schools.* November 1958, General Headquarters File 080, Middle States Association of Colleges and Secondary Schools, Record Group 404, West Point Archives.

——. *Traditions and Customs of the Corps of Cadets.* West Point: USMA, 1920.

——. *The United States Military Academy in Perspective, 1969–1979: An Institutional Report Prepared for the 1980 Decennial Accreditation.* West Point: USMA, December 1979.

——. *Years of Continuity and Progress.* West Point: Office of Policy, Planning, and Analysis, June 1996.

US War Department. *General Orders and Bulletins*. Washington, DC: Government Printing Office, various years.

———. *General Regulations for the Army*. Philadelphia: M. Carey and Sons, 1821.

Vitters, Alan G., and Nora Scott Kinzer. *Report of the Admission of Women to the U. S. Military Academy: Project Athena*. West Point: Department of Behavioral Sciences and Leadership, US Military Academy, 1977.

Vitters, Alan G., and Alan George. *Report of the Admission of Women to the U.S. Military Academy: Project Athena II*. West Point: Dept. of Behavioral Sciences and Leadership, US Military Academy, 1978.

West Point Study Group. *Final Report of the West Point Study Group*. Washington, DC: Department of the Army, 27 July 1977.

Wilby, Francis B. "Report of the Superintendent on the Three Year Course of Instruction at the United States Military Academy." 30 January 1942. AGO Project Decimal Files, file 351, Records Group 407, National Archives, College Park, MD.

SECONDARY SOURCES

Books

Ambrose, Stephen E. *Duty, Honor, Country: A History of West Point*. Baltimore, MD: Johns Hopkins University Press, 1966.

Andrews, Lincoln C. *Military Manpower: Psychology as Applied to the Training of Men and the Increase of Their Effectiveness*. New York: E. P. Dutton & Company, 1920.

Baumer, William H. *Sports as Taught and Played at West Point*. Harrisburg, PA: Military Service Publishing Co, 1939.

Betros, Lance, ed. *West Point: Two Centuries and Beyond*. Abilene, TX: McWhiney Foundation Press, 2004.

Blackwell, James. *On Brave Old Army Team: The Cheating Scandal that Rocked the Nation*. Novato, CA: Presidio, 1996.

Bowen, William G., and Sarah A. Levin. *Reclaiming the Game: College Sports and Educational Values*. Princeton, NJ: Princeton University Press, 2003.

Boynton, Edward C. *History of West Point, and Its Military Importance during the American Revolution, and the Origin and Progress of the United States Military Academy*. New York: D. Van Nostrand, 1863.

Carhart, Tom. *West Point Warriors: Profiles of Duty, Honor, and Country in Battle*. New York: Warner Books, 2002.

Crackel, Theodore. *West Point: A Bicentennial History*. University of Kansas Press, 2002.

Crowley, Joseph N. *In the Arena: The NCAA's First Century*. Online publication: National Collegiate Athletic Association, 2006. Available at http://www.ncaapublications.com/p-4039-in-the-arena-the-ncaas-first-century.aspx.

Dineen, Joseph E. *The Illustrated History of Sports at the U.S. Military Academy*. Norfolk, VA: The Donning Company, 1988.

Ellis, Joseph, and Robert Moore. *School for Soldiers: West Point and the Profession of Arms*. New York: Oxford University Press, 1974.

Fleming, Bruce. *Annapolis Autumn: Life, Death, and Literature at the U.S. Naval Academy.* New York: New Press, 2005.

Fleming, Thomas J. *West Point: The Men and Times of the United States Military Academy.* New York: Morrow, 1969.

Forman, Sidney. *West Point: A History of the United States Military Academy.* New York: Columbia University Press, 1950.

Ganoe, William A. *MacArthur Close-Up.* New York: Vantage Press, 1962.

Gelfand, H. Michael. *Sea Change at Annapolis: The United States Naval Academy, 1949–2000.* Chapel Hill: The University of North Carolina Press, 2006.

Gillett, Mary. *The Army Medical Department 1865–1917.* Washington, DC: United States Army Center of Military History, 1995.

Koehler, Herman J. *Koehler's West Point Manual of Disciplinary Physical Training.* New York: E. P. Dutton & Company, 1919.

Lovell, John P. *Neither Athens Nor Sparta?: The American Service Academies in Transition.* Bloomington: Indiana University Press, 1979.

Manchester, William. *American Caesar: Douglas MacArthur, 1880–1964.* Boston: Little, Brown, 1978.

Masland, John W., and Laurence I. Radway. *Soldiers and Scholars: Military Education and National Policy.* Princeton, NJ: Princeton University Press, 1957.

McWilliams, Bill. *A Return to Glory: The Untold Story of Honor, Dishonor, and Triumph at the United States Military Academy, 1950–53.* Lynchburg, VA: Warwick House Publishers, 2000.

Morrison, James L., Jr. *"The Best School in the World": West Point, the Pre-Civil War Years, 1833–1866.* Kent, OH: Kent State University Press, 1986.

Moten, Matthew. *The Delafield Commission and the American Military Profession.* College Station: Texas A&M University Press, 2000.

The National Cyclopaedia of American Biography: Being the History of the United States as Illustrated in the Lives of the Founders, Builders, and Defenders of the Republic, and of the Men and Women who are Doing the Work and Moulding the Thought of the Present Time. New York: J. T. White Co., 1893–1901.

Rose, Michael T. *A Prayer for Relief; The Constitutional Infirmities of the Military Academies' Conduct, Honor, and Ethics Systems.* New York: New York University School of Law, 1973.

Rudolph, Frederick. *The American College and University: A History.* New York: Alfred A. Knopf, 1968.

Schoor, Gene. *100 Years of Army-Navy Football.* New York: Henry Holt and Company, 1989.

Shulman, James L., and William G. Bowen. *The Game of Life: College Sports and Educational Values.* Princeton, NJ: Princeton University Press, 2001.

Simons, William E. *Liberal Education in the Service Academies.* New York: Institute of Higher Education, 1965.

Sorley, Lewis. *Honor Bright: History and Origins of the West Point Honor Code and System.* West Point: Association of Graduates, 2009.

Summerfield, Carol J., and Mary Elizabeth Devine, eds. *International Dictionary of University Histories.* Fitzroy Dearborn Publishers, 1998.

Webb, Ernie, John D. Hart, and James E. Foley. *West Point Sketch Book*. New York: Vantage Press, 1976.

Articles and Essays

Baumer, William H. "Every Man an Alert, Thinking Athlete." *Journal of Physical Education* 36, no. 3 (January–February 1939): 44–45, 47.

Bean, Richard J. "A Brief History of Admissions to the United States Military Academy." Unpublished essay, 8 May 1967, West Point Archives.

Blaik, Earl. "A Cadet under MacArthur." *Assembly* 23 (Spring 1964): 8–11.

Danford, Robert M. "USMA's 31st Superintendent." *Assembly* 23 (Spring 1964): 12–15.

Devers, Jacob L. "The Mark of the Man on USMA." *Assembly* 23 (Spring 1964): 16–19.

Doty, Joseph. "Sports Build Character?!" *Journal of College & Character* VII, no. 3 (April 2006): 1–9.

Fried, Barbara H. "Punting our Future: College Athletics and Admissions," *Change*, May/June 2007 [journal online]. Available from Carnegie Foundation for the Advancement of Teaching, http://www.carnegiefoundation.org.

Greenleaf, Charles R. "Physical Training in the U.S. Army." Boston, MA: Proceedings of the American Association for the Advancement of Physical Education, 3–4 April 1891.

Ignoffo, Matthew. "A Brief History of USMAPS." *Assembly* 33 (March 1975): 2, and *Assembly* 34 (June 1975): 12.

Larned, Charles. "West Point and Higher Education." *Army and Navy Journal* 8, no. 12 (June 1906): 9–28.

———. "West Point and Higher Education." *Army and Navy Life* 4, no. 12 (June 1906): 9–22.

———. "West Point and Our Military Future." *Metropolitan Magazine* 22, no. 2 (May 1905): 130–54.

Nye, Roger H. "The Inadvertent Demise of the Traditional Academy, 1945–1995." Unpublished paper, November 1995. Department of History, West Point.

"Physical Education: Philosophy of the Program at West Point." *Sports International* 19, no. 2 (April 1963): 4–8.

Priest, Robert F., Jerry V. Krause, and Johnston Beach. "Four-Year Changes in College Athletes' Ethical Value Choices in Sports Situations." *Research Quarterly for Exercise and Sport* 70, no. 2 (June 1999): 170–78.

Remley, Mary L. "Physical Education at the United States Military Academy 1966–1992." Unpublished manuscript. West Point: Department of Physical Education, 30 May 1992.

Richardson, Robert C., Jr. "An Intimate Picture of Athletics at West Point." *Proceedings of the Twenty-Seventh Annual Convention of the National Collegiate Athletic Association* (30 December 1932): 94–102.

Williams, Harry. "The Attack Upon West Point during the Civil War." *Mississippi Valley Historical Review* 25, no. 4 (March 1939): 491–504.

Wood, Robert E. "An Upperclassman's View." *Assembly* 23 (Spring 1964): 4–5.

Zais, Mitchell. "West Point: Sword Making or Swordsmanship?" *Armed Forces Journal International* (March 1990): 59–62.

Dissertations

Appleton, Lloyd O. "The Relationship between Physical Ability and Success at the United States Military Academy." PhD diss., New York University, 1949.

Denton, Edgar, III. "The Formative Years of the United States Military Academy, 1775–1833." PhD diss., Syracuse University, 1964.

Dillard, Walter Scott. "The United States Military Academy, 1865–1900: The Uncertain Years." PhD diss., University of Washington, 1972.

Fielitz, Lynn Richard. "Factors Influencing the Student-Athlete's Decision to Attend the United States Military Academy." PhD diss., University of New Mexico, 2001.

Nye, Roger Hurless. "The United States Military Academy in an Era of Educational Reform, 1900–1925." PhD diss., Columbia University, 1968.

Index